CEDU 쎄듀는 A **C**omprehensive **E**nglish e**DU**cation(종합적 영어교육)의 약자입니다.

저자

김기훈 現 ㈜쎄듀 대표이사
現 메가스터디 영어영역 대표강사
前 서울특별시 교육청 외국어 교육정책자문위원회 위원

저서 천일문 / 천일문 Training Book / 천일문 GRAMMAR /
어법끝 / 어휘끝 / 첫단추 / 쎈쓰업 / 파워업 / 빈칸백서 / 오답백서
쎄듀 본영어 / 문법의 골든룰 101 / ALL씀 서술형 / 수능실감
거침없이 Writing / Grammar Q / Reading Q / Listening Q 등

쎄듀 영어교육연구센터
쎄듀 영어교육센터는 영어 콘텐츠에 대한 전문지식과 경험을 바탕으로
최고의 교육 콘텐츠를 만들고자 최선의 노력을 다하는 전문가 집단입니다.

마케팅	콘텐츠 마케팅 사업본부
영업	문병구
제작	정승호
디자인	DOTS · 윤혜영
전산 편집	김명렬
삽화	플러스툰
영문교열	Michael A. Putlack

쎄듀 빠르게
중학영어듣기
모의고사 20회

1

Structure & Features
구성 및 특징

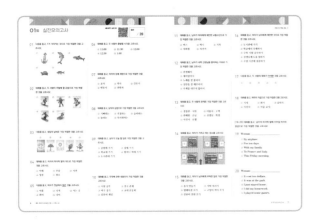

실전모의고사 20회

가장 최신의 출제 경향을 반영한 실전모의고사 20회를 수록했습니다. 1~5회는 〈시도교육청 주관 영어듣기능력평가〉에 비해 지문의 길이가 10~20% 정도 길고, 6회~20회는 20~30% 정도 긴 지문의 문제로 구성하여, 학생들이 점진적으로 문제 풀이 능력을 기를 수 있도록 구성했습니다.

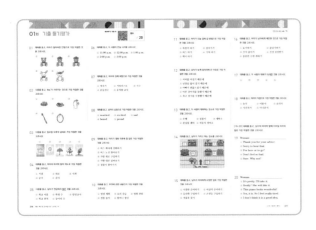

기출 듣기평가 5회

2013년부터 2015년까지 실시된 〈시도교육청 주관 영어듣기능력평가〉의 기출 문제를 총 5회분 수록했습니다. 시험 직전에 최종 점검을 하는 목적으로 문제를 풀어보시기 바랍니다.

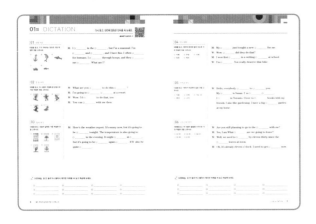

DICTATION

문제 풀이에 중요한 단서가 되는 명사, 동사, 형용사 등의 핵심 어휘와, 어휘 실력 향상에 도움이 되는 동사구, 전명구 등을 위주로 딕테이션 연습을 할 수 있도록 구성했습니다. 잘 안 들리거나 모르는 단어는 박스에 체크한 뒤 페이지 하단의 어휘복습 코너에 적어 놓고 복습하세요. 아울러, 문장과 문장 사이에 일정한 간격을 두어, 학생들이 단어를 직접 써볼 수 있도록 마련했습니다.

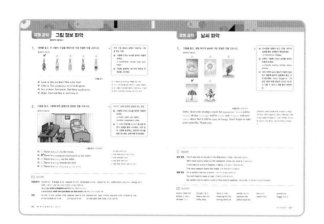

문제 유형 공략 및 필수 표현 익히기

〈시도교육청 주관 영어듣기능력평가〉 기출 문제를 면밀히 분석하여 총 16개의 유형으로 분류하고 문제 공략법을 소개했습니다. 또한 유형별 주요표현과 필수어휘 등도 함께 수록했으므로 시험을 보기 전에 꼭 확인해 보세요.

다양한 교사용 부가자료 및 학습 지원

쎄듀 홈페이지에 들어오시면 다양한 교사용 부가자료가 준비되어 있습니다.

- Q&A 게시판
- 본문 수록 어휘
- 딕테이션 음원
- 본문 스크립트
- 모의고사 음원
- 문항 단위 음원

Contents
목차

실전모의고사
20회

01회 실전모의고사

점수 / 20

01 다음을 듣고, 'I'가 가리키는 것으로 가장 적절한 것을 고르시오.

①   ②   ③

④   ⑤

02 대화를 듣고, 두 사람이 주말에 할 운동으로 가장 적절한 것을 고르시오.

①   ②   ③

④   ⑤

03 다음을 듣고, 내일의 날씨로 가장 적절한 것을 고르시오.

①   ②   ③   ④   ⑤

04 대화를 듣고, 여자의 마지막 말의 의도로 가장 적절한 것을 고르시오.

① 이해   ② 꾸중   ③ 사과
④ 칭찬   ⑤ 위로

05 다음을 듣고, 여자가 언급하지 <u>않은</u> 것을 고르시오.

① 이름   ② 국적   ③ 사는 곳
④ 취미   ⑤ 나이

06 대화를 듣고, 두 사람이 출발할 시각을 고르시오.

① 11:00   ② 11:30   ③ 12:00
④ 12:30   ⑤ 1:00

07 대화를 듣고, 여자의 장래 희망으로 가장 적절한 것을 고르시오.

① 교사   ② 의사   ③ 간호사
④ 변호사   ⑤ 과학자

08 대화를 듣고, 남자의 심정으로 가장 적절한 것을 고르시오.

① 기뻐하는   ② 걱정하는   ③ 슬퍼하는
④ 놀라는   ⑤ 부러워하는

09 대화를 듣고, 남자가 오늘 할 일로 가장 적절한 것을 고르시오.

① 공원에 가기   ② 집에 가기
③ 학교에 가기   ④ 할머니 댁에 가기
⑤ 도서관에 가기

10 대화를 듣고, 무엇에 관한 내용인지 가장 적절한 것을 고르시오.

① 시험 공부   ② 친구 관계
③ 야구 경기   ④ 교내 운동회
⑤ 컴퓨터 게임

11 대화를 듣고, 남자가 여자에게 제안한 교통수단으로 가장 적절한 것을 고르시오.

① 버스   ② 택시   ③ 기차
④ 지하철   ⑤ 자전거

12 대화를 듣고, 남자가 과학 선생님을 좋아하는 이유로 가장 적절한 것을 고르시오.

① 친절해서
② 재미있어서
③ 노래를 잘 불러서
④ 상담을 잘 해주어서
⑤ 숙제를 내주지 않아서

13 대화를 듣고, 두 사람의 관계로 가장 적절한 것을 고르시오.

① 경찰관 - 시민   ② 미용사 - 고객
③ 판매원 - 손님   ④ 선생님 - 학생
⑤ 사진사 - 모델

14 대화를 듣고, 여자가 가려고 하는 장소를 고르시오.

15 대화를 듣고, 여자가 남자에게 부탁한 일로 가장 적절한 것을 고르시오.

① 음식 만들기   ② 식탁 차리기
③ 텔레비전 끄기   ④ 고양이 먹이 주기
⑤ 컴퓨터 전원 끄기

16 대화를 듣고, 여자가 남자에게 제안한 것으로 가장 적절한 것을 고르시오.

① 도서관에 가기
② 학교에서 숙제하기
③ 수학 시험 공부하기
④ 선생님께 도움 청하기
⑤ 수업 시간에 집중하기

17 다음을 듣고, 두 사람의 대화가 <u>어색한</u> 것을 고르시오.

①   ②   ③   ④   ⑤

18 대화를 듣고, 여자의 직업으로 가장 적절한 것을 고르시오.

① 기자   ② 화가   ③ 음악가
④ 사진사   ⑤ 미술 교사

[19-20] 대화를 듣고, 남자의 마지막 말에 이어질 여자의 응답으로 가장 적절한 것을 고르시오.

19 Woman: _____

① By airplane.
② For ten days.
③ With my family.
④ To France and Italy.
⑤ This Friday morning.

20 Woman: _____

① It cost ten dollars.
② It was at the park.
③ I just stayed home.
④ I did my homework.
⑤ I played some games.

01 화제 추론

다음을 듣고, 'I'가 가리키는 것으로 가장 적절한 것을 고르시오.

① ② ③
④ ⑤

M: I ☐ _____ in the ☐ _____ , but I'm a mammal. I'm ☐ _____ and ☐ _____ , and I have fins. I often ☐ _____ for humans. I ☐ _____ through hoops, and they ☐ _____ me ☐ _____ . What am I?

02 할 일 파악

대화를 듣고, 두 사람이 주말에 할 운동으로 가장 적절한 것을 고르시오.

① ② ③
④ ⑤

W: What are you ☐ _____ to do this ☐ _____ ?
M: I'm going to ☐ _____ ☐ _____ at a resort.
W: Wow. I'd ☐ _____ to do that, too.
M: You can ☐ _____ with me then.

03 날씨 파악

다음을 듣고, 내일의 날씨로 가장 적절한 것을 고르시오.

① ② ③
④ ⑤

M: Here's the weather report. It's sunny now, but it's going to be ☐ _____ tonight. The temperature is also going to go ☐ _____ in the evening. It might ☐ _____ at ☐ _____ , but it's going to be ☐ _____ again ☐ _____ . It'll also be quite ☐ _____ .

✏️ **어휘복습** 잘 안 들리거나 몰라서 체크한 어휘를 써 놓고 복습해 보세요.

☐ _____   ☐ _____   ☐ _____   ☐ _____
☐ _____   ☐ _____   ☐ _____   ☐ _____
☐ _____   ☐ _____   ☐ _____   ☐ _____

04 의도 파악

대화를 듣고, 여자의 마지막 말의 의도로 가장 적절한 것을 고르시오.

① 이해 　② 구충 　③ 사과
④ 칭찬 　⑤ 위로

M: My □ _____ just bought a new □ _____ for me.

W: Wow. □ _____ did they do that?

M: I won first □ _____ in a writing □ _____ at school.

W: I'm □ _____. You really deserve that bike.

05 미언급 파악

다음을 듣고, 여자가 언급하지 <u>않은</u> 것을 고르시오.

① 이름 　② 국적 　③ 사는 곳
④ 취미 　⑤ 나이

W: Hello, everybody. □ _____ to □ _____ you.

My □ _____ is Susan. I'm □ _____ □ _____.

I □ _____ in Toronto. I love to □ _____ books with my

friends. I also like gardening. I have a big □ _____ garden

at my home.

06 숫자 정보 파악

대화를 듣고, 두 사람이 출발할 시각을 고르시오.

① 11:00 　② 11:30 　③ 12:00
④ 12:30 　⑤ 1:00

W: Are you still planning to go to the □ _____ with me?

M: Yes, I am. What □ _____ are we going to leave?

W: Well, we need to □ _____ by eleven thirty since the

□ _____ leaves at noon.

M: Oh, it's already eleven o'clock. I need to get □ _____ now.

✎ **어휘복습** 잘 안 들리거나 몰라서 체크한 어휘를 써 놓고 복습해 보세요.

□ _____　□ _____　□ _____　□ _____

□ _____　□ _____　□ _____　□ _____

□ _____　□ _____　□ _____　□ _____

07 장래 희망 파악

대화를 듣고, 여자의 장래 희망으로 가장 적절한 것을 고르시오.

① 교사 ② 의사 ③ 간호사
④ 변호사 ⑤ 과학자

W: What do you □ _____ to be in the □ _____?

M: I'd like to be a □ _____. I want to help sick people. What about you?

W: I want to be a □ _____ .

M: Oh, that's why you □ _____ so hard in □ _____ class.

08 심정 추론

대화를 듣고, 남자의 심정으로 가장 적절한 것을 고르시오.

① 기뻐하는 ② 걱정하는
③ 슬퍼하는 ④ 놀라는
⑤ 부러워하는

W: Hi, Jeff. □ _____ are you doing □ _____?

M: I'm going to a pizza □ _____ with my □ _____ .

W: Oh, yeah? □ _____ are you going there?

M: I got an A+ on my □ _____ . My parents and I are both □ _____ .

W: Wow, congratulations! I hope you □ _____ dinner.

09 할 일 파악

대화를 듣고, 남자가 오늘 할 일로 가장 적절한 것을 고르시오.

① 공원에 가기
② 집에 가기
③ 학교에 가기
④ 할머니 댁에 가기
⑤ 도서관에 가기

W: Why don't you □ _____ to the □ _____ with me?

M: I'd love to do that, □ _____ I □ _____ .

W: □ _____ not? Are you going □ _____?

M: No. I'm going to □ _____ my □ _____ at her home. I promised to go there.

W: It's □ _____ you're going to visit her. Have □ _____ .

✎ **어휘복습** 잘 안 들리거나 몰라서 체크한 어휘를 써 놓고 복습해 보세요.

□ _____   □ _____   □ _____   □ _____

□ _____   □ _____   □ _____   □ _____

□ _____   □ _____   □ _____   □ _____

10 화제 추론

대화를 듣고, 무엇에 관한 내용인지 가장 적절한 것을 고르시오.

① 시험 공부 ② 친구 관계
③ 야구 경기 ④ 교내 운동회
⑤ 컴퓨터 게임

M: I'm really □ _____ forward to □ _____.
W: Oh, that's right. It's □ _____ day at school.
M: Yeah. We will run some □ _____ and play sports.
W: I hope our class □ _____ the □ _____ game.
M: I'm □ _____ we will. We have the □ _____ players.

11 교통수단 찾기

대화를 듣고, 남자가 여자에게 제안한 교통수단으로 가장 적절한 것을 고르시오.

① 버스 ② 택시 ③ 기차
④ 지하철 ⑤ 자전거

W: □ _____ do you think we should □ _____ □ _____ the concert?
M: Let's □ _____ the □ _____ there.
W: But the bus will be □ _____ with passengers □ _____.
M: That's a good point. □ _____ □ _____ taking a □ _____ then?
W: All right. That will be more □ _____ for us.

12 이유 파악

대화를 듣고, 남자가 과학 선생님을 좋아하는 이유로 가장 적절한 것을 고르시오.

① 친절해서
② 재미있어서
③ 노래를 잘 불러서
④ 상담을 잘 해주어서
⑤ 숙제를 내주지 않아서

W: Our □ _____ teacher is great. He is □ _____ to everyone.
M: Do you like him? I □ _____ the □ _____ teacher.
W: Why do you like her? Is she a □ _____ teacher?
M: She's very good. And she tells many □ _____ □ _____ in class.

✎ **어휘복습** 잘 안 들리거나 몰라서 체크한 어휘를 써 놓고 복습해 보세요.

□ _____ □ _____ □ _____ □ _____
□ _____ □ _____ □ _____ □ _____
□ _____ □ _____ □ _____ □ _____

13 관계 추론

대화를 듣고, 두 사람의 관계로 가장 적절한 것을 고르시오.

① 경찰관 - 시민
② 미용사 - 고객
③ 판매원 - 손님
④ 선생님 - 학생
⑤ 사진사 - 모델

M: How □ _____ I □ _____ you, ma'am?

W: I just saw a man □ _____ a woman's □ _____.

M: Can you □ _____ the man?

W: Yes. He is □ _____ and has □ _____ hair.

M: What is he □ _____?

W: He's wearing blue □ _____ and a red □ _____.

14 위치 찾기

대화를 듣고, 여자가 가려고 하는 장소를 고르시오.

M: Pardon me. You look □ _____. Do you need any □ _____?

W: Yes, please. I'm □ _____ □ _____ the library.

M: Ah, okay. Go □ _____ to the □ _____. Then, turn □ _____.

W: Okay, what do I do □ _____?

M: □ _____ about fifty meters. It's the □ _____ building on the □ _____.

W: Is there anything else you can tell me?

M: It's □ _____ the □ _____. You can't miss it.

✎ **어휘복습** 잘 안 들리거나 몰라서 체크한 어휘를 써 놓고 복습해 보세요.

□ _____   □ _____   □ _____   □ _____

□ _____   □ _____   □ _____   □ _____

□ _____   □ _____   □ _____   □ _____

15 부탁 파악

대화를 듣고, 여자가 남자에게 부탁한 일로 가장 적절한 것을 고르시오.

① 음식 만들기
② 식탁 차리기
③ 텔레비전 끄기
④ 고양이 먹이 주기
⑤ 컴퓨터 전원 끄기

W: Tim, it's time for dinner. □ _____ playing computer □ _____.

M: Can you □ _____ a minute, Mom?

W: Sorry, but I need you now. Please □ _____ the □ _____ on the table.

M: Can't Angie do that? She's just □ _____ TV now.

W: No, she can't. She's □ _____ the cat □ _____ now.

16 제안 파악

대화를 듣고, 여자가 남자에게 제안한 것으로 가장 적절한 것을 고르시오.

① 도서관에 가기
② 학교에서 숙제하기
③ 수학 시험 공부하기
④ 선생님께 도움 청하기
⑤ 수업 시간에 집중하기

W: Jason, why are you □ _____ □ _____ your backpack?

M: I'm going to □ _____ Harold at the □ _____. We need to □ _____ our math □ _____.

W: Do you □ _____ the material?

M: No, it's too □ _____ for me. So we will try to □ _____ it □ _____.

W: Why don't you □ _____ your □ _____ for □ _____ tomorrow?

M: Okay. I'll do that. □ _____ for the □ _____.

✎ **어휘복습** 잘 안 들리거나 몰라서 체크한 어휘를 써 놓고 복습해 보세요.

□ _____   □ _____   □ _____   □ _____

□ _____   □ _____   □ _____   □ _____

□ _____   □ _____   □ _____   □ _____

17 어색한 대화 찾기

다음을 듣고, 두 사람의 대화가 <u>어색한</u> 것을 고르시오.

①   ②   ③   ④   ⑤

① W: Are you □ _____ now?

    M: □ _____ really. I just □ _____.

② W: □ _____ does Alice □ _____?

    M: She's in the same □ _____ as me.

③ W: What □ _____ is it?

    M: It's ten □ _____ seven.

④ W: Can I □ _____ a pencil?

    M: □ _____ □ _____. Take this one.

⑤ W: Do you □ _____ apples?

    M: Yes, but I □ _____ oranges.

18 직업 파악

대화를 듣고, 여자의 직업으로 가장 적절한 것을 고르시오.

① 기자   ② 화가   ③ 음악가
④ 사진사   ⑤ 미술 교사

M: This □ _____ looks □ _____.

W: Thanks for saying that. A □ _____ wants to □ _____ it.

M: How did you □ _____ it so □ _____?

W: My □ _____ teacher was really □ _____.

M: I □ _____ I could make art like that.

✎ **어휘복습** 잘 안 들리거나 몰라서 체크한 어휘를 써 놓고 복습해 보세요.

□ _____   □ _____   □ _____   □ _____

□ _____   □ _____   □ _____   □ _____

□ _____   □ _____   □ _____   □ _____

알맞은 응답 찾기

대화를 듣고, 남자의 마지막 말에 이어질 여자의 응답으로 가장 적절한 것을 고르시오.

Woman: _____
① By airplane.
② For ten days.
③ With my family.
④ To France and Italy.
⑤ This Friday morning.

M: Are you going to □ _____ a □ _____ this summer?

W: Yes. My family □ _____ □ _____ to Europe.

M: Wow. That □ _____ fun. □ _____ are you going to □ _____?

W: _____

20 알맞은 응답 찾기

대화를 듣고, 남자의 마지막 말에 이어질 여자의 응답으로 가장 적절한 것을 고르시오.

Woman: _____
① It cost ten dollars.
② It was at the park.
③ I just stayed home.
④ I did my homework.
⑤ I played some games.

M: Did you have a □ _____ time at the □ _____?

W: Yes, I did. I □ _____ a lot of □ _____.

M: Really? What □ _____ did you do there?

W: _____

✎ **어휘복습** 잘 안 들리거나 몰라서 체크한 어휘를 써 놓고 복습해 보세요.

□ _____ □ _____ □ _____ □ _____
□ _____ □ _____ □ _____ □ _____
□ _____ □ _____ □ _____ □ _____

O2회 실전모의고사

01 다음을 듣고, 'it'이 가리키는 것으로 가장 적절한 것을 고르시오.

02 대화를 듣고, 무엇에 관한 내용인지 가장 적절한 것을 고르시오.

① 숙제   ② 축구 경기
③ 반장 선거   ④ 방과 후 활동
⑤ 새로운 동아리 가입

03 다음을 듣고, 내일 부산의 날씨로 가장 적절한 것을 고르시오.

①   ②   ③   ④   ⑤

04 대화를 듣고, 남자의 마지막 말의 의도로 가장 적절한 것을 고르시오.

① 격려   ② 충고   ③ 초대
④ 실망   ⑤ 허락

05 다음을 듣고, 여자가 언급하지 <u>않은</u> 것을 고르시오.

① 베이컨   ② 토스트   ③ 샌드위치
④ 햄버거   ⑤ 감자튀김

06 대화를 듣고, 두 사람이 만나기로 한 시각을 고르시오.

① 6:00   ② 6:30   ③ 7:00
④ 7:30   ⑤ 8:00

07 대화를 듣고, 두 사람이 대화 직후에 할 일로 가장 적절한 것을 고르시오.

① 필기하기   ② 문구점 가기
③ 펜을 교환하기   ④ 학교 갈 준비하기
⑤ 온라인으로 쇼핑하기

08 대화를 듣고, 남자의 심정으로 가장 적절한 것을 고르시오.

① 외로움   ② 걱정   ③ 분노
④ 미안함   ⑤ 부러움

09 대화를 듣고, 여자가 지난 주말에 한 일로 가장 적절한 것을 고르시오.

① 해변 가기   ② 그림 그리기
③ 해산물 먹기   ④ 수영하기
⑤ 친구의 집 방문하기

10 대화를 듣고, 남자가 지불할 금액을 고르시오.

① $3   ② $4   ③ $6
④ $7   ⑤ $10

11 다음을 듣고, 두 사람의 대화가 <u>어색한</u> 것을 고르시오.

① ② ③ ④ ⑤

16 대화를 듣고, 남자가 셔츠를 사지 <u>못한</u> 이유로 가장 적절한 것을 고르시오.

① 너무 비싸서
② 지갑을 두고 와서
③ 가게 문이 닫혀서
④ 원하는 색이 없어서
⑤ 맞는 사이즈가 없어서

12 대화를 듣고, 여자가 미술 동아리에 가입한 이유로 가장 적절한 것을 고르시오.

① 화가가 되고 싶어서
② 작품을 전시하고 싶어서
③ 미술 선생님을 좋아해서
④ 친구가 가입하라고 해서
⑤ 그림 그리는 방법을 배우고 싶어서

17 대화를 듣고, 남자가 주말에 할 일로 가장 적절한 것을 고르시오.

① 집에 가기
② 이메일 보내기
③ 친구를 방문하기
④ 친구에게 전화하기
⑤ 가족과 저녁 식사하기

18 대화를 듣고, 남자가 전화를 건 목적으로 가장 적절한 것을 고르시오.

① 숙제를 물어보려고
② 시험에 대해 알아보려고
③ 늦은 것에 대해 사과하려고
④ 수업이 언제인지 물어보려고
⑤ 노트를 빌릴 수 있는지 물어보려고

13 대화를 듣고, 두 사람의 관계로 가장 적절한 것을 고르시오.

① 승무원 - 승객
② 학생 - 교사
③ 경찰 - 시민
④ 의사 - 환자
⑤ 식당 종업원 - 손님

[19-20] 대화를 듣고, 남자의 마지막 말에 이어질 여자의 응답으로 가장 적절한 것을 고르시오.

19 Woman: _____

① That's okay.
② You're welcome.
③ Sure. Here you are.
④ Yes, I bought it for you.
⑤ No, I can't see it from here.

14 대화를 듣고, 여자가 남자에게 부탁한 일로 가장 적절한 것을 고르시오.

① 빵 굽기
② 부엌 청소하기
③ 계란 요리하기
④ 식료품점에 가기
⑤ 동생과 이야기하기

20 Woman: _____

① Here's the remote control.
② I'll turn the TV down a bit.
③ It's a documentary on dolphins.
④ Yes, you can change the channel.
⑤ That's my favorite show you're watching.

15 대화를 듣고, 두 사람이 만나기로 한 장소를 고르시오.

① 학교
② 남자의 집
③ 도서관
④ 버스 정류장
⑤ 공원

다시 듣고, 빈칸에 알맞은 단어를 써 보세요.

◄)) MP3 실전 02-1

01 화제 추론

다음을 듣고, 'it'이 가리키는 것으로 가장 적절한 것을 고르시오.

① ② ③

④ ⑤

M: It is a kind of □_____. It is made of □_____, and it has very □_____ □_____. You use it when you want to □_____ something like □_____ and big □_____. You can □_____ it with one or two hands when you use it.

02 화제 추론

대화를 듣고, 무엇에 관한 내용인지 가장 적절한 것을 고르시오.

① 숙제
② 축구 경기
③ 반장 선거
④ 방과 후 활동
⑤ 새로운 동아리 가입

M: Hey, Melissa. □_____ did you do □_____ □_____ today?
W: I had a club □_____ at □_____ o'clock.
M: Really? □_____ □_____ are you in?
W: I'm a member of the □_____ club. I'm the □_____.
M: I guess you were busy. I was busy, too. I had □_____ □_____ for an hour.
W: Great. Did you enjoy it?
M: It was hard work, but I liked it a lot.

03 날씨 파악

다음을 듣고, 내일 부산의 날씨로 가장 적절한 것을 고르시오.

① ② ③

④ ⑤

M: Hi, everyone. Let's look at □_____ weather across the country. There will be □_____ skies in Seoul and Daejeon. Unfortunately, it's going to be □_____ in □_____ while Daegu is going to get lots of □_____. Gwangju is □_____ sunny weather, but it will be very □_____.

✏ **어휘복습** 잘 안 들리거나 몰라서 체크한 어휘를 써 놓고 복습해 보세요.

□ _____   □ _____   □ _____   □ _____
□ _____   □ _____   □ _____   □ _____
□ _____   □ _____   □ _____   □ _____

04 의도 파악

대화를 듣고, 남자의 마지막 말의 의도로 가장 적절한 것을 고르시오.

① 격려   ② 충고   ③ 초대
④ 실망   ⑤ 허락

M: □ _____ was your □ _____ swimming □ _____?

W: It was fun, but I was □ _____ of the □ _____.

M: Don't □ _____. You can learn quickly.

W: Do you really think so?

M: Yes, I do. I know that you □ _____ □ _____ it.

05 미언급 파악

다음을 듣고, 여자가 언급하지 <u>않은</u> 것을 고르시오.

① 베이컨   ② 토스트   ③ 샌드위치
④ 햄버거   ⑤ 감자튀김

W: This morning, I had □ _____ and □ _____ for □ _____. I also had a glass of □ _____. I was busy during □ _____, so I only ate a □ _____. For □ _____, I went to Burger Time with my friends. I ate a chicken sandwich and had some □ _____.

06 숫자 정보 파악

대화를 듣고, 두 사람이 만나기로 한 시각을 고르시오.

① 6:00   ② 6:30   ③ 7:00
④ 7:30   ⑤ 8:00

W: I'm glad we're going to the □ _____ on Friday.

M: It should be a lot of fun. □ _____ □ _____ do you want to □ _____?

W: Let's go there at □ _____ □ _____.

M: But the □ _____ doesn't start until □ _____ □ _____.

W: Oh, then let's □ _____ □ _____ at □ _____.

M: That's a good idea. Let's meet at the bus stop.

✎ **어휘복습** 잘 안 들리거나 몰라서 체크한 어휘를 써 놓고 복습해 보세요.

□ _____	□ _____	□ _____	□ _____
□ _____	□ _____	□ _____	□ _____
□ _____	□ _____	□ _____	□ _____

07 할 일 파악

대화를 듣고, 두 사람이 대화 직후에 할 일로 가장 적절한 것을 고르시오.

① 필기하기
② 문구점 가기
③ 펜을 교환하기
④ 학교 갈 준비하기
⑤ 온라인으로 쇼핑하기

W: I need to □_____ some supplies for □_____.
M: So do I. □_____ are you going to □_____?
W: I have to buy some □_____, pens, and □_____.
M: Are you going to □_____ everything on the □_____?
W: I'd rather buy the items at the stationery □_____. Shall we □_____ there together?
M: Good idea. Let's go now.

08 심정 추론

대화를 듣고, 남자의 심정으로 가장 적절한 것을 고르시오.

① 외로움   ② 걱정   ③ 분노
④ 미안함   ⑤ 부러움

W: □_____ didn't you go to the □_____ with us last night?
M: I just felt like □_____ home.
W: Are you □_____ about your dog? Is she still □_____?
M: Yes. I □_____ she gets □_____ soon.
W: I'm sure she'll be fine in a few days.

09 한 일 파악

대화를 듣고, 여자가 지난 주말에 한 일로 가장 적절한 것을 고르시오.

① 해변 가기
② 그림 그리기
③ 해산물 먹기
④ 수영하기
⑤ 친구의 집 방문하기

W: Jim, how was your □_____?
M: It was great. I went to the □_____ with my family.
W: Wow. □_____ did you do there?
M: We □_____ swimming and □_____ lots of seafood. □_____ □_____ you?
W: I □_____ a picture. It's my newest □_____.
M: I'd love to see it.

✎ **어휘복습** 잘 안 들리거나 몰라서 체크한 어휘를 써 놓고 복습해 보세요.

□ _____   □ _____   □ _____   □ _____

□ _____   □ _____   □ _____   □ _____

□ _____   □ _____   □ _____   □ _____

대화를 듣고, 남자가 지불할 금액을 고르시오.

① $3   ② $4   ③ $6
④ $7   ⑤ $10

M: I'd love to have a hamburger. □ _____ □ _____ is one?

W: Hamburgers □ _____ □ _____ dollars □ _____.
Would you like a □ _____, too?

M: Yes. How much is a soda?

W: A □ _____ soda is □ _____ dollar.

M: That sounds perfect. I'd like □ _____ hamburgers and a
□ _____ soda, please.

W: That will □ _____ □ _____ dollars.

M: Okay. Here's a ten-dollar bill.

다음을 듣고, 두 사람의 대화가 어색한 것을 고르시오.

①   ②   ③   ④   ⑤

① M: Do you know □ _____ □ _____?
   W: Yes, it's a □ _____ □ _____ one.

② M: □ _____ is your □ _____ type of movie?
   W: I really □ _____ action films.

③ M: □ _____ □ _____ do you meet your friends?
   W: I like playing sports with them.

④ M: □ _____ do you think of this □ _____?
   W: It's beautiful. I love it.

⑤ M: Did you have a good time?
   W: Not really. I was □ _____.

✎ **어휘복습** 잘 안 들리거나 몰라서 체크한 어휘를 써 놓고 복습해 보세요.

□ _____   □ _____   □ _____   □ _____

□ _____   □ _____   □ _____   □ _____

□ _____   □ _____   □ _____   □ _____

12 이유 파악

대화를 듣고, 여자가 미술 동아리에 가입한 이유로 가장 적절한 것을 고르시오.

① 화가가 되고 싶어서
② 작품을 전시하고 싶어서
③ 미술 선생님을 좋아해서
④ 친구가 가입하라고 해서
⑤ 그림 그리는 방법을 배우고 싶어서

M: Jenny, you're in the □ _____ □ _____, aren't you?

W: Yes, that's correct. I □ _____ the club last year.

M: I'd like to learn how to □ _____. Do you enjoy it?

W: Yes, it's a lot of fun. I □ _____ up so that I could □ _____ my □ _____.

M: That's interesting.

13 관계 추론

대화를 듣고, 두 사람의 관계로 가장 적절한 것을 고르시오.

① 승무원 – 승객
② 학생 – 교사
③ 경찰 – 시민
④ 의사 – 환자
⑤ 식당 종업원 – 손님

M: Good morning. How are you?

W: Good morning, sir. May I see your □ _____ □ _____, please?

M: Yes, here it is.

W: You're in □ _____ forty-four B. Just □ _____ right down that □ _____.

M: I appreciate it.

14 부탁 파악

대화를 듣고, 여자가 남자에게 부탁한 일로 가장 적절한 것을 고르시오.

① 빵 굽기
② 부엌 청소하기
③ 계란 요리하기
④ 식료품점에 가기
⑤ 동생과 이야기하기

M: Something □ _____ delicious. □ _____ are you doing?

W: I'm □ _____ a cake. It's your □ _____ birthday.

M: That's right. Can I do □ _____ for you?

W: We □ _____ □ _____. Can you □ _____ some at the □ _____ store, please?

M: Sure. I'll be right back.

✎ **어휘복습** 잘 안 들리거나 몰라서 체크한 어휘를 써 놓고 복습해 보세요.

□ _____   □ _____   □ _____   □ _____
□ _____   □ _____   □ _____   □ _____
□ _____   □ _____   □ _____   □ _____

대화를 듣고, 두 사람이 만나기로 한 장소를 고르시오.

① 학교　　　② 남자의 집
③ 도서관　　④ 버스 정류장
⑤ 공원

W: Hello.

M: Hi, Tina. It's Eric. Do you want to □ _____ with Dan and me?

W: Sure. □ _____ and □ _____ are we going to □ _____?

M: We're going to go to the □ _____ at □ _____.

W: I've □ _____ been there. Can I meet you at the □ _____ □ _____ near your □ _____ instead?

M: Sure. I'll see you there □ _____ an hour.

대화를 듣고, 남자가 셔츠를 사지 못한 이유로 가장 적절한 것을 고르시오.

① 너무 비싸서
② 지갑을 두고 와서
③ 가게 문이 닫혀서
④ 원하는 색이 없어서
⑤ 맞는 사이즈가 없어서

W: Kevin, is that the new □ _____ you wanted to buy □ _____?

M: No, it's not. I □ _____ get a shirt yesterday.

W: What happened? Was the shirt too □ _____?

M: No. I □ _____ a size □ _____, □ _____ the store □ _____ had □ _____ T-shirts.

W: That's too bad.

✎ **어휘복습** 잘 안 들리거나 몰라서 체크한 어휘를 써 놓고 복습해 보세요.

□ _____　□ _____　□ _____　□ _____

□ _____　□ _____　□ _____　□ _____

□ _____　□ _____　□ _____　□ _____

17 할 일 파악

대화를 듣고, 남자가 주말에 할 일로 가장 적절한 것을 고르시오.

① 집에 가기
② 이메일 보내기
③ 친구를 방문하기
④ 친구에게 전화하기
⑤ 가족과 저녁 식사하기

M: Mom, I just got an □_____ □_____ my friend George.

W: How is he doing? Didn't he move?

M: Yes, he □_____ to another city with his family □_____ □_____.

W: Does he enjoy his □_____ home?

M: He's having fun. Can I □_____ □_____ this weekend?

W: Sure. You can □_____ the bus when you visit him.

18 전화 목적 파악

대화를 듣고, 남자가 전화를 건 목적으로 가장 적절한 것을 고르시오.

① 숙제를 물어보려고
② 시험에 대해 알아보려고
③ 늦은 것에 대해 사과하려고
④ 수업이 언제인지 물어보려고
⑤ 노트를 빌릴 수 있는지 물어보려고

W: Hello.

M: Hello, Stephanie. It's Chris. Did you go to □_____ □_____ today?

W: Yes, I did. □_____?

M: I woke up late and □_____ that □_____. Do we have any □_____?

W: Yes, we do.

M: What is it?

W: We have to read chapter two. And we'll have a short □_____ □_____.

M: Thanks for the information.

✎ **어휘복습** 잘 안 들리거나 몰라서 체크한 어휘를 써 놓고 복습해 보세요.

□ _____   □ _____   □ _____   □ _____

□ _____   □ _____   □ _____   □ _____

□ _____   □ _____   □ _____   □ _____

대화를 듣고, 남자의 마지막 말에 이어질 여자의 응답으로 가장 적절한 것을 고르시오.

Woman: _____

① That's okay.
② You're welcome.
③ Sure. Here you are.
④ Yes, I bought it for you.
⑤ No, I can't see it from here.

M: Is that a new digital camera?

W: Yes, it is. My parents □ _____ it to □ _____ for my

　□ _____ .

M: It looks really nice. Can I see it?

W: _____

대화를 듣고, 남자의 마지막 말에 이어질 여자의 응답으로 가장 적절한 것을 고르시오.

Woman: _____

① Here's the remote control.
② I'll turn the TV down a bit.
③ It's a documentary on dolphins.
④ Yes, you can change the channel.
⑤ That's my favorite show you're watching.

W: Are you □ _____ that □ _____ now?

M: Yes, I am.

W: □ _____ is it going to □ _____ ?

M: It's going to □ _____ in □ _____ minutes.

W: Good. I need to watch something then.

M: □ _____ are you going to □ _____ ?

W: _____

✏ **어휘복습** 잘 안 들리거나 몰라서 체크한 어휘를 써 놓고 복습해 보세요.

□ _____   □ _____   □ _____   □ _____

□ _____   □ _____   □ _____   □ _____

□ _____   □ _____   □ _____   □ _____

🔊 MP3 실전 03

점수
/ **20**

01 대화를 듣고, 남자가 구매할 공책으로 가장 적절한 것을 고르시오.

①   ②   ③

④   ⑤

02 다음을 듣고, 오늘 오후의 날씨로 가장 적절한 것을 고르시오.

① ② ③ ④ ⑤

03 대화를 듣고, 남자의 마지막 말의 의도로 가장 적절한 것을 고르시오.
① 초대 ② 동의 ③ 꾸중
④ 거절 ⑤ 위로

04 다음을 듣고, 남자가 언급하지 않은 것을 고르시오.
① 이름 ② 나이 ③ 취미
④ 장래 희망 ⑤ 좋아하는 과목

05 대화를 듣고, 두 사람이 만나기로 한 시각을 고르시오.
① 6:00 ② 6:30 ③ 7:00
④ 7:30 ⑤ 8:00

06 대화를 듣고, 여자의 장래 희망으로 가장 적절한 것을 고르시오.
① 음악가 ② 교사 ③ 과학자
④ 조종사 ⑤ 역사학자

07 대화를 듣고, 남자의 심정으로 가장 적절한 것을 고르시오.
① 불안함 ② 지루함 ③ 신남
④ 우울함 ⑤ 감격

08 대화를 듣고, 여자가 대화 직후에 할 일로 가장 적절한 것을 고르시오.
① 팝콘 사기 ② 티켓 사기
③ 영화관에 가기 ④ 영화 관람하기
⑤ 영화관에 전화하기

09 대화를 듣고, 무엇에 관한 내용인지 가장 적절한 것을 고르시오.
① 동물 ② 소풍 ③ 현장 학습
④ 숙제 ⑤ 시험 일정

10 대화를 듣고, 두 사람이 이용할 교통수단으로 가장 적절한 것을 고르시오.
① 자동차 ② 택시 ③ 지하철
④ 기차 ⑤ 버스

11 대화를 듣고, 여자가 어제 학교에 결석한 이유로 가장 적절한 것을 고르시오.

① 병원에 가서
② 목이 아파서
③ 늦잠을 자서
④ 병문안을 가서
⑤ 눈병에 걸려서

12 대화를 듣고, 두 사람의 관계로 가장 적절한 것을 고르시오.

① 교사 - 학생
② 경찰관 - 도둑
③ 배우 - 영화감독
④ 의사 - 환자
⑤ 코치 - 운동선수

13 대화를 듣고, 남자가 가려고 하는 장소를 고르시오.

14 대화를 듣고, 여자가 남자에게 부탁한 일로 가장 적절한 것을 고르시오.

① 전등 끄기
② 바닥 쓸기
③ 칠판 지우기
④ 쓰레기통 비우기
⑤ 숙제 제출하기

15 대화를 듣고, 여자가 남자에게 제안한 것으로 가장 적절한 것을 고르시오.

① 휴식 취하기
② 엽서 보내기
③ 사진 찍기
④ 수영하기
⑤ 해변에 가기

16 다음을 듣고, 두 사람의 대화가 어색한 것을 고르시오.

①　　②　　③　　④　　⑤

17 대화를 듣고, 남자의 직업으로 가장 적절한 것을 고르시오.

① 교사
② 의사
③ 운전 기사
④ 약사
⑤ 판매원

18 다음을 듣고, 'this'가 가리키는 것으로 가장 적절한 것을 고르시오.

① 　② 　③

④ 　⑤

[19-20] 대화를 듣고, 여자의 마지막 말에 이어질 남자의 응답으로 가장 적절한 것을 고르시오.

19 Man: _____

① That's great news.
② I bet you had fun.
③ How was the weather?
④ Don't forget next time.
⑤ I'm going to the beach soon.

20 Man: _____

① Here's my library card.
② I already finished my paper.
③ No, the library isn't open now.
④ You can check out books there.
⑤ I can tell you how to get there.

03회 DICTATION

다시 듣고, 빈칸에 알맞은 단어를 써 보세요.

◀◎ MP3 실전 03-1

01 그림 정보 파악

대화를 듣고, 남자가 구매할 공책으로 가장 적절한 것을 고르시오.

① ② ③

④ ⑤

M: How do you like this □ _____ ?

W: It's nice. The □ _____ on the □ _____ look nice.

M: I □ _____ . I need a new notebook □ _____ □ _____ .

W: Then □ _____ should □ _____ this one.

M: □ _____ . I'll □ _____ it.

02 날씨 파악

다음을 듣고, 오늘 오후의 날씨로 가장 적절한 것을 고르시오.

① ② ③

④ ⑤

W: Good morning, everyone. Here's the □ _____ for □ _____ . Right □ _____ , it's cool and □ _____ . But it's going to be warm and □ _____ in the □ _____ . In the □ _____ , there will be lots of □ _____ in the sky. And it will start to □ _____ at □ _____ .

03 의도 파악

대화를 듣고, 남자의 마지막 말의 의도로 가장 적절한 것을 고르시오.

① 초대 ② 동의 ③ 꾸중
④ 거절 ⑤ 위로

W: Hi, Greg. □ _____ are you □ _____ ?

M: I'm □ _____ □ _____ at home right now. Why?

W: I'm □ _____ □ _____ a □ _____ with my parents □ _____ . Would you like to □ _____ □ _____ us?

M: I'd □ _____ □ _____ , □ _____ I have to finish my □ _____ . I'm really sorry.

✎ **어휘복습** 잘 안 들리거나 몰라서 체크한 어휘를 써 놓고 복습해 보세요.

□ _____ □ _____ □ _____ □ _____

□ _____ □ _____ □ _____ □ _____

□ _____ □ _____ □ _____ □ _____

04 미언급 파악

다음을 듣고, 남자가 언급하지 <u>않은</u> 것을 고르시오.

① 이름　　　② 나이
③ 취미　　　④ 장래 희망
⑤ 좋아하는 과목

M: Hello. It's a pleasure to meet you. Let me □ _____ you □ _____ □ _____. My □ _____ is Peter Jenkins. I'm □ _____ years old, and I'm □ _____ London. My □ _____ is riding my □ _____. I □ _____ to be a □ _____ in the future. I hope we can □ _____ □ _____. Thank you.

05 숫자 정보 파악

대화를 듣고, 두 사람이 만나기로 한 시각을 고르시오.

① 6:00　　② 6:30　　③ 7:00
④ 7:30　　⑤ 8:00

W: Let's □ _____ □ _____ early tomorrow □ _____.
M: Sure. □ _____ should we □ _____? I wake up at □ _____ □ _____ every day.
W: □ _____ □ _____ seven then?
M: I have to eat □ _____ first. Let's meet at □ _____ □ _____.
W: Okay. See you tomorrow.

06 장래 희망 파악

대화를 듣고, 여자의 장래 희망으로 가장 적절한 것을 고르시오.

① 음악가　　② 교사　　③ 과학자
④ 조종사　　⑤ 역사학자

M: What's your □ _____ □ _____, Cindy?
W: It's □ _____. How about you?
M: I like □ _____. I want to be a □ _____ in the future.
W: That's interesting.
M: How about you? What do you □ _____ □ _____ □ _____?
W: I want to be a history □ _____.

✎ **어휘복습** 잘 안 들리거나 몰라서 체크한 어휘를 써 놓고 복습해 보세요.

□ _____　　□ _____　　□ _____　　□ _____
□ _____　　□ _____　　□ _____　　□ _____
□ _____　　□ _____　　□ _____　　□ _____

07 심정 추론

대화를 듣고, 남자의 심정으로 가장 적절한 것을 고르시오.

① 불안함　② 지루함　③ 신남
④ 우울함　⑤ 감격

W: You're really □ _____ today, John. What's the □ _____?

M: I □ _____ in the school □ _____ this morning.

W: Really? How was it?

M: I □ _____ my □ _____, so lots of people □ _____ □ _____ me.

W: I understand how you □ _____. Try to □ _____ about it.

08 할 일 파악

대화를 듣고, 여자가 대화 직후에 할 일로 가장 적절한 것을 고르시오.

① 팝콘 사기　　② 티켓 사기
③ 영화관에 가기　④ 영화 관람하기
⑤ 영화관에 전화하기

W: That □ _____ action movie is □ _____ □ _____ tomorrow.

M: Why don't we get □ _____ for it?

W: The □ _____ is too □ _____ □ _____. I can't go there.

M: We can □ _____ the tickets □ _____. It's easy.

W: □ _____ □ _____. I'll do that now.

09 화제 추론

대화를 듣고, 무엇에 관한 내용인지 가장 적절한 것을 고르시오.

① 동물　② 소풍　③ 현장 학습
④ 숙제　⑤ 시험 일정

M: We're going on a □ _____ □ _____ tomorrow, aren't we?

W: No, we're not. The □ _____ is going to be □ _____ all week.

M: Really? Then □ _____ are we going to go □ _____?

W: We'll □ _____ it next □ _____.

M: I see.

✎ **어휘복습** 잘 안 들리거나 몰라서 체크한 어휘를 써 놓고 복습해 보세요.

□ _____　　□ _____　　□ _____　　□ _____

□ _____　　□ _____　　□ _____　　□ _____

□ _____　　□ _____　　□ _____　　□ _____

10 교통수단 찾기

대화를 듣고, 두 사람이 이용할 교통수단으로 가장 적절한 것을 고르시오.

① 자동차   ② 택시   ③ 지하철
④ 기차   ⑤ 버스

M: We need to □ _____ □ _____ tonight.

W: Okay. Do you want to □ _____ the □ _____?

M: No. □ _____ will be too □ _____ tonight.

W: Why don't we □ _____ the □ _____ then?

M: Sure. That will be □ _____ □ _____ a taxi or the bus.

11 이유 파악

대화를 듣고, 여자가 어제 학교에 결석한 이유로 가장 적절한 것을 고르시오.

① 병원에 가서
② 목이 아파서
③ 늦잠을 자서
④ 병문안을 가서
⑤ 눈병에 걸려서

M: Why were you □ _____ □ _____ □ _____ yesterday?

W: My mother had to take me to □ _____ □ _____
□ _____.

M: What happened? Did you □ _____ a □ _____?

W: Yes, and I □ _____ □ _____ bad □ _____.

M: How do you feel now? Do you □ _____ □ _____?

W: Yes. Thanks for asking.

12 관계 추론

대화를 듣고, 두 사람의 관계로 가장 적절한 것을 고르시오.

① 교사 – 학생
② 경찰관 – 도둑
③ 배우 – 영화감독
④ 의사 – 환자
⑤ 코치 – 운동선수

M: □ _____ should I □ _____ in the next □ _____?

W: You're going to □ _____ a □ _____ with the bad guy.

M: Am I going to □ _____ anything?

W: Yes. You'll have a □ _____. You're going to be in a
□ _____.

M: Okay. Let me □ _____ my □ _____ for a minute.

✎ **어휘복습** 잘 안 들리거나 몰라서 체크한 어휘를 써 놓고 복습해 보세요.

□ _____   □ _____   □ _____   □ _____

□ _____   □ _____   □ _____   □ _____

□ _____   □ _____   □ _____   □ _____

13 위치 찾기

대화를 듣고, 남자가 가려고 하는 장소를 고르시오.

M: Pardon me. Can you tell me □ _____ the □ _____ is?

W: Sure. □ _____ □ _____ until you get to the □ _____.
Then, □ _____ □ _____.

M: Okay. I will go straight and then turn left.

W: Right. Then, walk straight □ _____ □ _____ □ _____.
The bank will be □ _____ your □ _____. It's □ _____
□ _____ the □ _____.

M: Thank you very much.

14 부탁 파악

대화를 듣고, 여자가 남자에게 부탁한 일로 가장 적절한 것을 고르시오.

① 전등 끄기
② 바닥 쓸기
③ 칠판 지우기
④ 쓰레기통 비우기
⑤ 숙제 제출하기

W: Harry, are you □ _____ right now?

M: No, I'm not, Ms. Crawford. Do you want me to □ _____ the
□ _____?

W: No, Jim will do that. Could you please □ _____ the
□ _____ □ _____?

M: Yes, I can. Can I do □ _____ else?

W: That's all right. Thanks, Harry.

✎ **어휘복습** 잘 안 들리거나 몰라서 체크한 어휘를 써 놓고 복습해 보세요.

□ _____   □ _____   □ _____   □ _____

□ _____   □ _____   □ _____   □ _____

□ _____   □ _____   □ _____   □ _____

15 제안 파악

대화를 듣고, 여자가 남자에게 제안한 것으로 가장 적절한 것을 고르시오.

① 휴식 취하기　② 엽서 보내기
③ 사진 찍기　④ 수영하기
⑤ 해변에 가기

M: I'm going to □ _____ □ _____ □ _____ to Hawaii this week.

W: Have a great time. Why don't you □ _____ me a □ _____?

M: Okay. I'll send you one □ _____ a picture of a □ _____.

W: Thanks. □ _____ are you going to □ _____ there?

M: I want to go □ _____ and □ _____.

16 어색한 대화 찾기

다음을 듣고, 두 사람의 대화가 <u>어색한</u> 것을 고르시오.

①　②　③　④　⑤

① W: I'm very □ _____ about that.
　 M: You're welcome.

② W: □ _____ □ _____ does it take to get there?
　 M: About □ _____ □ _____.

③ W: Hi, Steve. How are you today?
　 M: I'm very good. Thanks.

④ W: □ _____ is that man over there?
　 M: His □ _____ is James.

⑤ W: □ _____ you for the □ _____.
　 M: It's my □ _____.

✎ **어휘복습** 잘 안 들리거나 몰라서 체크한 어휘를 써 놓고 복습해 보세요.

□ _____　□ _____　□ _____　□ _____
□ _____　□ _____　□ _____　□ _____
□ _____　□ _____　□ _____　□ _____

17 직업 파악

대화를 듣고, 남자의 직업으로 가장 적절한 것을 고르시오.

① 교사　　② 의사　　③ 운전 기사
④ 약사　　⑤ 판매원

W: Good morning, Dustin. Are you busy now?

M: Yes, I am. I have to see a □ _____.

W: I hope the patient isn't □ _____ □ _____.

M: He might need □ _____.

W: That's not good.

M: Yeah. Let's talk □ _____ today.

18 화제 추론

다음을 듣고, 'this'가 가리키는 것으로 가장 적절한 것을 고르시오.

① ② ③
④ ⑤

W: Do you like to □ _____ □ _____ the □ _____? If you want to look at them □ _____, you can use this. This makes □ _____ objects appear □ _____. You can also use this to look at the □ _____ and the □ _____. What is this?

✎ **어휘복습** 잘 안 들리거나 몰라서 체크한 어휘를 써 놓고 복습해 보세요.

□ _____　　□ _____　　□ _____　　□ _____

□ _____　　□ _____　　□ _____　　□ _____

□ _____　　□ _____　　□ _____　　□ _____

대화를 듣고, 여자의 마지막 말에 이어질 남자의 응답으로 가장 적절한 것을 고르시오.

Man:_____

① That's great news.
② I bet you had fun.
③ How was the weather?
④ Don't forget next time.
⑤ I'm going to the beach soon.

M: Your □ _____ is really □ _____ . What happened?

W: I went to the □ _____ yesterday.

M: Didn't you □ _____ any suntan lotion?

W: No, I didn't. So I got □ _____ .

M: _____

대화를 듣고, 여자의 마지막 말에 이어질 남자의 응답으로 가장 적절한 것을 고르시오.

Man:_____

① Here's my library card.
② I already finished my paper.
③ No, the library isn't open now.
④ You can check out books there.
⑤ I can tell you how to get there.

W: I have to do some □ _____ for a science □ _____ .

M: □ _____ do you have to □ _____ it?

W: I should give it to my teacher □ _____ □ _____ . I need to □ _____ to the □ _____ today.

M: The library should □ _____ the □ _____ you need.

W: But I don't know □ _____ the library is.

M: _____

✎ **어휘복습** 잘 안 들리거나 몰라서 체크한 어휘를 써 놓고 복습해 보세요.

□ _____   □ _____   □ _____   □ _____
□ _____   □ _____   □ _____   □ _____
□ _____   □ _____   □ _____   □ _____

04회 실전모의고사

점수 / 20

01 대화를 듣고, 남자가 구매할 물건으로 가장 적절한 것을 고르시오.

02 다음을 듣고, 목요일의 날씨로 가장 적절한 것을 고르시오.

03 대화를 듣고, 여자의 마지막 말의 의도로 가장 적절한 것을 고르시오.

① 동의   ② 초대   ③ 제안
④ 거절   ⑤ 사과

04 다음을 듣고, 남자가 언급하지 <u>않은</u> 것을 고르시오.

① 가족 수   ② 아버지의 직업
③ 어머니의 취미   ④ 형의 나이
⑤ 여동생의 학년

05 대화를 듣고, 두 사람이 만나기로 한 시각을 고르시오.

① 4:00   ② 4:30   ③ 5:00
④ 5:30   ⑤ 6:00

06 대화를 듣고, 남자의 장래 희망으로 가장 적절한 것을 고르시오.

① 음악가   ② 화가   ③ 사진작가
④ 배우   ⑤ 운동선수

07 대화를 듣고, 여자의 심정으로 가장 적절한 것을 고르시오.

① 화남   ② 기쁨   ③ 두려움
④ 부러움   ⑤ 걱정스러움

08 대화를 듣고, 남자가 대화 직후에 할 일로 가장 적절한 것을 고르시오.

① 식탁 치우기   ② 숙제하기
③ 후식 나르기   ④ 설거지하기
⑤ 친구들과 놀기

09 대화를 듣고, 무엇에 관한 내용인지 가장 적절한 것을 고르시오.

① 저녁 약속   ② 새로운 게임
③ 학교 행사   ④ 취미 활동
⑤ 축제에서 한 일

10 대화를 듣고, 여자가 선택할 교통수단으로 가장 적절한 것을 고르시오.

① 지하철   ② 기차   ③ 택시
④ 버스   ⑤ 비행기

11 대화를 듣고, 여자가 어제 전화를 건 이유로 가장 적절한 것을 고르시오.

① 야구 경기에 초대하려고
② 시험에 대해 물어보려고
③ 집에 언제 가는지 알아보려고
④ 친구의 전화번호를 물어보려고
⑤ 버스 정류장에서 만나자고 말하려고

12 대화를 듣고, 두 사람이 대화하고 있는 장소로 가장 적절한 곳을 고르시오.

① 우체국   ② 은행   ③ 과일가게
④ 슈퍼마켓   ⑤ 식당

13 대화를 듣고, 남자가 가려고 하는 장소를 고르시오.

14 대화를 듣고, 남자가 여자에게 부탁한 일로 가장 적절한 것을 고르시오.

① 방 청소해 주기
② 버스 시간표 알려주기
③ 버스 카드 가져다 주기
④ 책상 위에 책 정리해 놓기
⑤ 버스 정류장에 데려다 주기

15 대화를 듣고, 여자가 남자에게 제안한 것으로 가장 적절한 것을 고르시오.

① 밴드에 가입하기
② 플루트 배우기
③ 매일 트럼펫 연습하기
④ 밴드 연습에 참여하기
⑤ 콘서트 준비하기

16 다음을 듣고, 두 사람의 대화가 어색한 것을 고르시오.

①   ②   ③   ④   ⑤

17 대화를 듣고, 남자의 직업으로 가장 적절한 것을 고르시오.

① 세탁업자   ② 판매원   ③ 집배원
④ 택시 기사   ⑤ 디자이너

18 다음을 듣고, 'this'가 가리키는 것으로 가장 적절한 것을 고르시오.

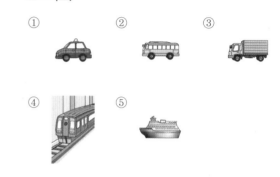

[19-20] 대화를 듣고, 남자의 마지막 말에 이어질 여자의 응답으로 가장 적절한 것을 고르시오.

19 Woman: _____

① That's good to hear.
② I think I did well on it.
③ No, you don't look tired.
④ I can solve that question.
⑤ Go to sleep earlier next time.

20 Woman: _____

① I'm playing a game now.
② I had science class this morning.
③ Yes, I'm going to the park.
④ My cousin is visiting my home.
⑤ The park is located near the school.

01 그림 정보 파악

대화를 듣고, 남자가 구매할 물건으로 가장 적절한 것을 고르시오.

① ② ③ ④ ⑤

W: Good afternoon. May I help you?

M: Hello. I'm □ _____ □ _____ a blouse for my daughter.

W: How about this one □ _____ □ _____ □ _____ it?

M: It's okay, but the one with the □ _____ looks □ _____.
I'll □ _____ □ _____.

W: Good choice. That's our □ _____ □ _____ blouse.

02 날씨 파악

다음을 듣고, 목요일의 날씨로 가장 적절한 것을 고르시오.

① ② ③ ④ ⑤

W: Hello, everyone. The weekend is almost over. □ _____, it's going to be □ _____ □ _____. On □ _____, it's going to be □ _____ □ _____ □ _____ □ _____. On □ _____, the weather will be □ _____ and □ _____. It's going to □ _____ on □ _____ and □ _____. And it will be □ _____ on □ _____.

03 의도 파악

대화를 듣고, 여자의 마지막 말의 의도로 가장 적절한 것을 고르시오.

① 동의 ② 초대 ③ 제안
④ 거절 ⑤ 사과

W: □ _____ are you □ _____, Louis?

M: I'm □ _____ a □ _____. Flying kites is my newest □ _____.

W: I see. Is it □ _____ to fly a kite?

M: Yes, it is. Would you like to □ _____ □ _____ □ _____ □ _____ in the park?

W: □ _____ □ _____ □ _____ do that.

✎ **어휘복습** 잘 안 들리거나 몰라서 체크한 어휘를 써 놓고 복습해 보세요.

□ _____ □ _____ □ _____ □ _____

□ _____ □ _____ □ _____ □ _____

□ _____ □ _____ □ _____ □ _____

04 미언급 파악

다음을 듣고, 남자가 언급하지 <u>않은</u> 것을 고르시오.

① 가족 수   ② 아버지의 직업
③ 어머니의 취미   ④ 형의 나이
⑤ 여동생의 학년

M: I'd like to □ _____ □ _____ my family right now. There are □ _____ people in my □ _____. My father is a □ _____, and my mother □ _____ □ _____ books. My older brother is in the □ _____. My younger sister is in the □ _____ □ _____ in □ _____ school. I have the best family.

05 숫자 정보 파악

대화를 듣고, 두 사람이 만나기로 한 시각을 고르시오.

① 4:00   ② 4:30   ③ 5:00
④ 5:30   ⑤ 6:00

W: Hello.
M: Hello, Wendy. It's Peter. □ _____ is your grandfather □ _____?
W: His train arrives at □ _____ □ _____ this □ _____.
M: Okay. I'll □ _____ you □ _____ at your house □ _____ □ _____.
W: Great. □ _____ □ _____ taking me to the train station.
M: You're welcome.

06 장래 희망 파악

대화를 듣고, 남자의 장래 희망으로 가장 적절한 것을 고르시오.

① 음악가   ② 화가   ③ 사진작가
④ 배우   ⑤ 운동선수

W: I love this □ _____ hanging on the wall.
M: Thanks. I □ _____ it last week.
W: Did you paint this? You're really □ _____ □ _____ painting.
M: Thanks. I would like to □ _____ an □ _____.
W: You're □ _____. I think you'll become a great artist.

✎ **어휘복습** 잘 안 들리거나 몰라서 체크한 어휘를 써 놓고 복습해 보세요.

□ _____   □ _____   □ _____   □ _____
□ _____   □ _____   □ _____   □ _____
□ _____   □ _____   □ _____   □ _____

07 심정 추론

대화를 듣고, 여자의 심정으로 가장 적절한 것을 고르시오.

① 화남   ② 기쁨   ③ 두려움
④ 부러움   ⑤ 걱정스러움

M: □ _____ are you □ _____ such □ _____ □ _____ now?

W: My son's teacher called. He □ _____ □ _____ while he was playing basketball.

M: Is it □ _____?

W: I don't know. But I'm □ _____ □ _____, so I need to go there soon.

M: I have a car. I'll □ _____ □ _____ □ _____ right now.

W: Thanks so much.

08 할 일 파악

대화를 듣고, 남자가 대화 직후에 할 일로 가장 적절한 것을 고르시오.

① 식탁 치우기   ② 숙제하기
③ 후식 나르기   ④ 설거지하기
⑤ 친구들과 놀기

M: Thanks for □ _____, Mom. It was delicious.

W: I'm □ _____ that you □ _____ it.

M: Will you □ _____ □ _____, please? I need to do my □ _____.

W: Okay, but you need to □ _____ the □ _____ first.

M: I thought it was Tina's □ _____ to do that.

W: Your sister is going to □ _____ □ _____ the □ _____ tonight.

M: Okay.

✎ **어휘복습** 잘 안 들리거나 몰라서 체크한 어휘를 써 놓고 복습해 보세요.

□ _____   □ _____   □ _____   □ _____

□ _____   □ _____   □ _____   □ _____

□ _____   □ _____   □ _____   □ _____

대화를 듣고, 무엇에 관한 내용인지 가장 적절한 것을 고르시오.

① 저녁 약속　　② 새로운 게임
③ 학교 행사　　④ 취미 활동
⑤ 축제에서 한 일

W: □ _____ did you □ _____ the □ _____ today?
M: It was a lot of □ _____. I liked playing the games.
W: So did I. Some of the □ _____ was □ _____, too.
M: I didn't □ _____ any. What did you □ _____ the
　 □ _____?
W: The Mexican food was really □ _____.

대화를 듣고, 여자가 선택할 교통수단으로 가장 적절한 것을 고르시오.

① 지하철　　② 기차　　③ 택시
④ 버스　　⑤ 비행기

W: I □ _____ four □ _____ □ _____ to Daejeon, please.
M: Sorry, but the □ _____ □ _____ just □ _____.
W: That's □ _____. What should I do?
M: The □ _____ □ _____ is □ _____ the □ _____.
　 You should go over there.
W: Thanks for the advice. I'll □ _____ there right □ _____.

대화를 듣고, 여자가 어제 전화를 건 이유로 가장 적절한 것을 고르시오.

① 야구 경기에 초대하려고
② 시험에 대해 물어보려고
③ 집에 언제 가는지 알아보려고
④ 친구의 전화번호를 물어보려고
⑤ 버스 정류장에서 만나자고 말하려고

W: I □ _____ you □ _____, but you □ _____ □ _____ the
　 □ _____.
M: I'm sorry. I was □ _____ □ _____ then, so I didn't know
　 you called me.
W: I understand. Did you □ _____ □ _____ at the baseball
　 game?
M: Yes, it was □ _____. By the way, □ _____ did you
　 □ _____ □ _____?
W: I wanted to □ _____ you □ _____ today's □ _____.
　 But I called Brad □ _____.
M: Good. I'm glad you talked to him.

✎ **어휘복습** 잘 안 들리거나 몰라서 체크한 어휘를 써 놓고 복습해 보세요.

□ _____　　□ _____　　□ _____　　□ _____

□ _____　　□ _____　　□ _____　　□ _____

□ _____　　□ _____　　□ _____　　□ _____

12 장소 추론

대화를 듣고, 두 사람이 대화하고 있는 장소로 가장 적절한 곳을 고르시오.

① 우체국　　　② 은행
③ 과일가게　　④ 슈퍼마켓
⑤ 식당

M: Hello. How may I help you?

W: Hi. I'd like to ☐ _____ this ☐ _____.

M: ☐ _____ are you ☐ _____ it?

W: It's going to England.

M: Do you want to send it ☐ _____ ☐ _____?

W: Yes. I want it to arrive ☐ _____.

M: Okay. ☐ _____ it ☐ _____ the ☐ _____ so I can ☐ _____ it, please.

13 위치 찾기

대화를 듣고, 남자가 가려고 하는 장소를 고르시오.

M: Could you help me, please? I'm trying to ☐ _____ ☐ _____ the clothes store.

W: The clothes store? Sure. ☐ _____ ☐ _____ to Denver Street and then ☐ _____ ☐ _____.

M: Okay. Then what should I do?

W: Go straight ☐ _____ ☐ _____ ☐ _____. You'll see the clothes store ☐ _____ ☐ _____ ☐ _____. It's ☐ _____ ☐ _____ the ☐ _____.

M: Thanks for your help.

✏️ **어휘복습** 잘 안 들리거나 몰라서 체크한 어휘를 써 놓고 복습해 보세요.

☐ _____　　☐ _____　　☐ _____　　☐ _____

☐ _____　　☐ _____　　☐ _____　　☐ _____

☐ _____　　☐ _____　　☐ _____　　☐ _____

14 부탁 파악

대화를 듣고, 남자가 여자에게 부탁한 일로 가장 적절한 것을 고르시오.

① 방 청소해 주기
② 버스 시간표 알려주기
③ 버스 카드 가져다 주기
④ 책상 위에 책 정리해 놓기
⑤ 버스 정류장에 데려다 주기

W: Hello.

M: Hi, Jane. I'm glad that you're home.

W: What's the □ _____?

M: I'm at the □ _____ □ _____, but I can't find my □ _____ □ _____.

W: □ _____ do you think it is?

M: Go to my room and look □ _____ my □ _____, please. I think I put it there last night.

W: Yeah, I □ _____ it. It was on your desk.

M: Oh, good! Can you □ _____ it □ _____ me?

W: Okay.

15 제안 파악

대화를 듣고, 여자가 남자에게 제안한 것으로 가장 적절한 것을 고르시오.

① 밴드에 가입하기
② 플루트 배우기
③ 매일 트럼펫 연습하기
④ 밴드 연습에 참여하기
⑤ 콘서트 준비하기

M: Mary, you □ _____ the □ _____ very □ _____ in band practice today.

W: □ _____ □ _____ □ _____ that, Tom.

M: I want to □ _____ the □ _____ well, but I'm □ _____ very □ _____ □ _____ it.

W: You should □ _____ at home □ _____ □ _____. I do that.

M: Really? Okay. I'll start doing that tonight.

✎ **어휘복습** 잘 안 들리거나 몰라서 체크한 어휘를 써 놓고 복습해 보세요.

□ _____   □ _____   □ _____   □ _____

□ _____   □ _____   □ _____   □ _____

□ _____   □ _____   □ _____   □ _____

16 어색한 대화 찾기

다음을 듣고, 두 사람의 대화가 어색한 것을 고르시오.

① ② ③ ④ ⑤

① W: □ _____ □ _____ does the movie start?
　M: □ _____ three forty-five.
② W: □ _____ □ _____ is a hamburger here?
　M: It's two □ _____ .
③ W: What's your □ _____ flavor of ice cream?
　M: I □ _____ vanilla the □ _____ .
④ W: □ _____ □ _____ studying with us?
　M: I'm at the library.
⑤ W: What's the □ _____ ? □ _____ are you □ _____ ?
　M: I got a □ _____ □ _____ on my test.

17 직업 파악

대화를 듣고, 남자의 직업으로 가장 적절한 것을 고르시오.

① 세탁업자　　② 판매원
③ 집배원　　④ 택시 기사
⑤ 디자이너

M: Good afternoon. Are you Ms. Williams?
W: Yes, I am. How may I help you?
M: I □ _____ a □ _____ here for you.
W: Great. This must be the □ _____ I □ _____ .
M: Could you □ _____ here, please?
W: Okay. Thank you very much.

18 화제 추론

다음을 듣고, 'this'가 가리키는 것으로 가장 적절한 것을 고르시오.

① ② ③
④ ⑤

M: Many people use this in large cities. □ _____ people can □ _____ on this at the □ _____ □ _____ . In most cities, this □ _____ □ _____ the □ _____ and □ _____ . So when you want to use this, you should □ _____ □ _____ the □ _____ . What is this?

✎ **어휘복습** 잘 안 들리거나 몰라서 체크한 어휘를 써 놓고 복습해 보세요.

□ _____　　□ _____　　□ _____　　□ _____
□ _____　　□ _____　　□ _____　　□ _____
□ _____　　□ _____　　□ _____　　□ _____

19 알맞은 응답 찾기

대화를 듣고, 남자의 마지막 말에 이어질 여자의 응답으로 가장 적절한 것을 고르시오.

Woman: _____

① That's good to hear.
② I think I did well on it.
③ No, you don't look tired.
④ I can solve that question.
⑤ Go to sleep earlier next time.

W: Why are you □ _____ so much? Did you □ _____

□ _____ □ _____ □ _____ last night?

M: Yes, I □ _____ □ _____ until three A.M. I had to

□ _____ □ _____ the □ _____ test.

W: How do you think you did on the test?

M: Not very well. I was □ _____ □ _____, so I □ _____

□ _____ □ _____ the questions.

W: _____

20 알맞은 응답 찾기

대화를 듣고, 남자의 마지막 말에 이어질 여자의 응답으로 가장 적절한 것을 고르시오.

Woman: _____

① I'm playing a game now.
② I had science class this morning.
③ Yes, I'm going to the park.
④ My cousin is visiting my home.
⑤ The park is located near the
   school.

M: Hey, are you free □ _____ □ _____?

W: What's up?

M: I am going to □ _____ □ _____. Do you want to

□ _____ □ _____?

W: □ _____ □ _____ □ _____, but I □ _____.

M: □ _____ □ _____?

W: _____

✏️ **어휘복습** 잘 안 들리거나 몰라서 체크한 어휘를 써 놓고 복습해 보세요.

□ _____   □ _____   □ _____   □ _____
□ _____   □ _____   □ _____   □ _____
□ _____   □ _____   □ _____   □ _____

01 대화를 듣고, 남자가 갖고 싶어 하는 필통으로 가장 적절한 것을 고르시오.

① 　② 　③

④ 　⑤

02 다음을 듣고, 'this'가 가리키는 것으로 가장 적절한 것을 고르시오.

① 　② 　③

④ 　⑤

03 다음을 듣고, 내일의 날씨로 가장 적절한 것을 고르시오.

①　②　③　④　⑤

04 대화를 듣고, 남자의 마지막 말의 의도로 가장 적절한 것을 고르시오.

① 제안　　② 사과　　③ 허락
④ 거절　　⑤ 축하

05 다음을 듣고, 여자가 언급하지 않은 것을 고르시오.

① 이름　　② 고향　　③ 사는 곳
④ 나이　　⑤ 장래 희망

06 대화를 듣고, 두 사람이 만날 시각을 고르시오.

① 3:00　　② 3:30　　③ 4:00
④ 4:30　　⑤ 5:00

07 대화를 듣고, 남자의 장래 희망으로 가장 적절한 것을 고르시오.

① 가수　　② 화가　　③ 작가
④ 건축가　⑤ 교사

08 대화를 듣고, 여자의 심정으로 가장 적절한 것을 고르시오.

① 화남　　② 지루함　　③ 행복함
④ 미안함　⑤ 걱정함

09 대화를 듣고, 여자가 대화 직후에 할 일로 가장 적절한 것을 고르시오.

① 이메일 보내기　　② 친구 만나기
③ 전화 걸기　　　　④ 숙제 끝내기
⑤ 전화번호 알려주기

10 대화를 듣고, 무엇에 관한 내용인지 가장 적절한 것을 고르시오.

① 춤 연습　　　　② 좋아하는 가수
③ 유행하는 노래　④ 악기 연주
⑤ 좋아하는 음악

11 대화를 듣고, 남자가 이용할 교통수단으로 가장 적절한 것을 고르시오.

① 자동차   ② 기차   ③ 비행기
④ 자전거   ⑤ 버스

12 대화를 듣고, 남자가 선생님을 찾아간 이유로 가장 적절한 것을 고르시오.

① 보고서를 제출하기 위해서
② 보고서 제출 기한을 묻기 위해서
③ 성적에 대해 상담하기 위해서
④ 아프다고 말하기 위해서
⑤ 보고서 제출 기한 연장을 요청하기 위해서

13 대화를 듣고, 두 사람의 관계로 가장 적절한 것을 고르시오.

① 교사 – 학생   ② 영화감독 – 배우
③ 경찰관 – 시민   ④ 의사 – 환자
⑤ 자동차 판매원 – 고객

14 대화를 듣고, 남자가 가려고 하는 장소를 고르시오.

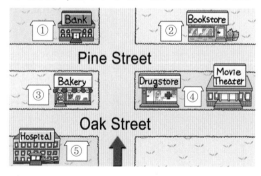

15 대화를 듣고, 여자가 남자에게 부탁한 일로 가장 적절한 것을 고르시오.

① 설거지하기   ② 꽃에 물 주기
③ 정원 꾸미기   ④ 잔디 깎기
⑤ 빨래하기

16 대화를 듣고, 여자가 남자에게 제안한 것으로 가장 적절한 것을 고르시오.

① 하이킹 같이 하기
② 숙제 도와주기
③ 시험 공부하기
④ 농구 동아리에 가입하기
⑤ 매일 농구 연습하기

17 다음을 듣고, 두 사람의 대화가 <u>어색한</u> 것을 고르시오.

①   ②   ③   ④   ⑤

18 대화를 듣고, 남자의 직업으로 가장 적절한 것을 고르시오.

① 작가   ② 도서관 사서   ③ 보육원 직원
④ 교사   ⑤ 서점 직원

[19~20] 대화를 듣고, 여자의 마지막 말에 이어질 남자의 응답으로 가장 적절한 것을 고르시오.

19 Man: _____

① Thanks a lot.
② Lunch was great.
③ Yes, I'm very hungry.
④ One hamburger, please.
⑤ No, I don't have a wallet.

20 Man: _____

① He's the same age as I am.
② He'll be here on the fifth of July.
③ Yes, I'll go home in a few minutes.
④ No, I'm not going to visit him now.
⑤ We'll visit the museum and amusement park.

01 그림 정보 파악

대화를 듣고, 남자가 갖고 싶어 하는 필통으로 가장 적절한 것을 고르시오.

① ② ③

④ ⑤

W: School is starting soon. Do you need any □ _____ □ _____?

M: Yes, I do. I have to get a new □ _____ □ _____.

W: How about this one □ _____ □ _____ a □ _____?

M: No, thanks. I □ _____ the pencil case □ _____ □ _____ a □ _____.

02 화제 추론

다음을 듣고, 'this'가 가리키는 것으로 가장 적절한 것을 고르시오.

① ② ③

④ ⑤

M: You need this when you □ _____ □ _____. You □ _____ this □ _____ your □ _____. When you wear this, you can □ _____ your □ _____ and □ _____ clearly □ _____ the □ _____. What is this?

03 날씨 파악

다음을 듣고, 내일의 날씨로 가장 적절한 것을 고르시오.

① ② ③

④ ⑤

W: Hello, everyone. This is the □ _____ □ _____ for tomorrow. We had □ _____, □ _____ weather □ _____. But the □ _____ is going to □ _____ □ _____. It will be cold and □ _____, but □ _____ □ _____ □ _____ is going to fall for a couple of days. Have a good night.

✏ **어휘복습** 잘 안 들리거나 몰라서 체크한 어휘를 써 놓고 복습해 보세요.

□ _____   □ _____   □ _____   □ _____

□ _____   □ _____   □ _____   □ _____

□ _____   □ _____   □ _____   □ _____

대화를 듣고, 남자의 마지막 말의 의도로 가장 적절한 것을 고르시오.

① 제안   ② 사과   ③ 허락
④ 거절   ⑤ 축하

W: □ _____ are you □ _____ right now, Joe?

M: I'm □ _____ □ _____ the □ _____. I'm going to □ _____ there for an hour.

W: The gym? That □ _____ like □ _____.

M: Yes, it is. You □ _____ □ _____ there □ _____ □ _____.

---

05 미언급 파악

다음을 듣고, 여자가 언급하지 <u>않은</u> 것을 고르시오.

① 이름   ② 고향   ③ 사는 곳
④ 나이   ⑤ 장래 희망

W: Good morning, everybody. I'd like to □ _____ □ _____. My □ _____ is Mina. My □ _____ is Suwon, but I □ _____ □ _____ Seoul right now. I love □ _____ my □ _____. I want to be a □ _____ and go to the Olympics one day. I need to □ _____ □ _____ every day.

---

06 숫자 정보 파악

대화를 듣고, 두 사람이 만날 시각을 고르시오.

① 3:00   ② 3:30   ③ 4:00
④ 4:30   ⑤ 5:00

M: Hi, Clara. Are you almost □ _____ □ _____ your room?

W: No, I'm □ _____ finished □ _____. So I □ _____ □ _____ □ _____ with you now.

M: Okay. Why don't you □ _____ □ _____ at the bus stop □ _____ □ _____ then?

W: I □ _____ □ _____ that □ _____. □ _____ □ _____ is fine.

M: Okay. I'll see you then.

✎ **어휘복습** 잘 안 들리거나 몰라서 체크한 어휘를 써 놓고 복습해 보세요.

□ _____   □ _____   □ _____   □ _____

□ _____   □ _____   □ _____   □ _____

□ _____   □ _____   □ _____   □ _____

07 장래 희망 파악

대화를 듣고, 남자의 장래 희망으로 가장 적절한 것을 고르시오.

① 가수 ② 화가 ③ 작가
④ 건축가 ⑤ 교사

W: This □ _____ is □ _____ . I really □ _____ it.

M: Thanks. I □ _____ it last night.

W: You did? Do you have any more stories?

M: Yes, I have many stories. I □ _____ □ _____ □ _____ a □ _____ .

08 심정 추론

대화를 듣고, 여자의 심정으로 가장 적절한 것을 고르시오.

① 화남 ② 지루함 ③ 행복함
④ 미안함 ⑤ 걱정함

M: □ _____ did you □ _____ all day, Sarah?

W: I just □ _____ here □ _____ the □ _____ , Dad.

M: It was a beautiful day. □ _____ □ _____ you go out?

W: There was □ _____ □ _____ □ _____ outside.

M: I drove by the □ _____ today. Lots of kids were playing □ _____ there.

W: Really? I'm the only person □ _____ □ _____ □ _____ .

09 할 일 파악

대화를 듣고, 여자가 대화 직후에 할 일로 가장 적절한 것을 고르시오.

① 이메일 보내기 ② 친구 만나기
③ 전화 걸기 ④ 숙제 끝내기
⑤ 전화번호 알려주기

W: Joe, do you □ _____ Sarah?

M: Sure. We are □ _____ □ _____ with each other.

W: I need to □ _____ □ _____ her, but I don't know her □ _____ □ _____ .

M: I can □ _____ you her □ _____ . It's five nine four, two oh three four.

W: Thanks. I'm going to □ _____ □ _____ □ _____ □ _____ .

✎ **어휘복습** 잘 안 들리거나 몰라서 체크한 어휘를 써 놓고 복습해 보세요.

□ _____ □ _____ □ _____ □ _____

□ _____ □ _____ □ _____ □ _____

□ _____ □ _____ □ _____ □ _____

10 화제 추론

대화를 듣고, 무엇에 관한 내용인지 가장 적절한 것을 고르시오.

① 춤 연습　　② 좋아하는 가수
③ 유행하는 노래　④ 악기 연주
⑤ 좋아하는 음악

M: What's your □ _____ type of □ _____ ?

W: I love □ _____ □ _____ .

M: Why do you like it?

W: I can □ _____ □ _____ it. And many of the songs □ _____ □ _____ , too. Do you like music?

M: Yes, I do. I like □ _____ □ _____ the most.

11 교통수단 찾기

대화를 듣고, 남자가 이용할 교통수단으로 가장 적절한 것을 고르시오.

① 자동차　② 기차　③ 비행기
④ 자전거　⑤ 버스

W: Joe, □ _____ are you □ _____ this Saturday?

M: I'm going to □ _____ a □ _____ near Daejeon.

W: □ _____ are you going to □ _____ there?

M: I'll □ _____ a □ _____ there.

W: I see. That will be □ _____ □ _____ driving a □ _____ .

12 이유 파악

대화를 듣고, 남자가 선생님을 찾아간 이유로 가장 적절한 것을 고르시오.

① 보고서를 제출하기 위해서
② 보고서 제출 기한을 묻기 위해서
③ 성적에 대해 상담하기 위해서
④ 아프다고 말하기 위해서
⑤ 보고서 제출 기한 연장을 요청하기 위해서

M: Good morning, Ms. Park. May I □ _____ □ _____ you, please?

W: Hello, Minho. Please □ _____ □ _____ . □ _____ do you □ _____ ?

M: I have a □ _____ □ _____ our □ _____ . □ _____ should we □ _____ it to you?

W: You need to finish it □ _____ this □ _____ .

M: Thank you very much.

✎ **어휘복습** 잘 안 들리거나 몰라서 체크한 어휘를 써 놓고 복습해 보세요.

□ _____　　□ _____　　□ _____　　□ _____

□ _____　　□ _____　　□ _____　　□ _____

□ _____　　□ _____　　□ _____　　□ _____

13 관계 추론

대화를 듣고, 두 사람의 관계로 가장 적절한 것을 고르시오.

① 교사 – 학생
② 영화감독 – 배우
③ 경찰관 – 시민
④ 의사 – 환자
⑤ 자동차 판매원 – 고객

M: May I see your □ _____ □ _____, please?

W: What's the □ _____?

M: You were □ _____ □ _____ □ _____. You have to □ _____ □ _____ near the school.

W: I'm sorry. I didn't know that.

M: I have to □ _____ you a □ _____.

W: I understand.

14 위치 찾기

대화를 듣고, 남자가 가려고 하는 장소를 고르시오.

M: Hello. I'm looking for a □ _____ □ _____. Is there one □ _____ □ _____?

W: Yes, there is. □ _____ □ _____ □ _____ □ _____ to Pine Street. Then, □ _____ □ _____.

M: Okay. What should I do □ _____?

W: Go □ _____ the □ _____. It will be □ _____ your □ _____. It's □ _____ the □ _____ and the movie □ _____.

M: Thank you for your help.

✏️ **어휘복습** 잘 안 들리거나 몰라서 체크한 어휘를 써 놓고 복습해 보세요.

□ _____   □ _____   □ _____   □ _____

□ _____   □ _____   □ _____   □ _____

□ _____   □ _____   □ _____   □ _____

15 부탁 파악

대화를 듣고, 여자가 남자에게 부탁한 일로 가장 적절한 것을 고르시오.

① 설거지하기　② 꽃에 물 주기
③ 정원 꾸미기　④ 잔디 깎기
⑤ 빨래하기

W: Why don't we □ _____ the □ _____ today?

M: But the □ _____ is so □ _____. How about □ _____ in the □ _____ outside?

W: That sounds nice. I will □ _____ the □ _____ first.

M: Okay. Shall we do that together?

W: No. Can you □ _____ the □ _____?

M. Sure. □ _____ □ _____.

16 제안 파악

대화를 듣고, 여자가 남자에게 제안한 것으로 가장 적절한 것을 고르시오.

① 하이킹 같이 하기
② 숙제 도와주기
③ 시험 공부하기
④ 농구 동아리에 가입하기
⑤ 매일 농구 연습하기

M: Sue, did you □ _____ a □ _____?

W: Yes, I did. I'm in the □ _____ club. What about you?

M: I'm not sure.

W: You □ _____ basketball □ _____ □ _____ □ _____. You should join the □ _____ □ _____.

M: But I'm □ _____ very □ _____ □ _____ □ _____. Other players are better.

W: That's okay. You will □ _____ □ _____ playing with them.

17 어색한 대화 찾기

다음을 듣고, 두 사람의 대화가 <u>어색한</u> 것을 고르시오.

① ② ③ ④ ⑤

① W: □ _____ for your help.

M: You're □ _____.

② W: Do you □ _____ some □ _____?

M: Yes, it's five twenty.

③ W: Are you □ _____?

M: No, I'm □ _____ □ _____.

④ W: I think I □ _____ a □ _____.

M: What □ _____?

⑤ W: What's your □ _____ □ _____?

M: I really love □ _____.

18 직업 파악

대화를 듣고, 남자의 직업으로 가장 적절한 것을 고르시오.

① 작가   ② 도서관 사서
③ 보육원 직원   ④ 교사
⑤ 서점 직원

M: Hello. This is the city □ _____.

W: Hi. I'm □ _____ □ _____ a □ _____. The □ _____ is *The Dog's Adventure*.

M: That's a □ _____ children's □ _____. We have it.

W: Is it □ _____ □ _____ now?

M: No, it's not. You can □ _____ here and □ _____ it.

✎ **어휘복습** 잘 안 들리거나 몰라서 체크한 어휘를 써 놓고 복습해 보세요.

□ _____   □ _____   □ _____   □ _____

□ _____   □ _____   □ _____   □ _____

□ _____   □ _____   □ _____   □ _____

19 알맞은 응답 찾기

대화를 듣고, 여자의 마지막 말에 이어질 남자의 응답으로 가장 적절한 것을 고르시오.

Man: _____

① Thanks a lot.
② Lunch was great.
③ Yes, I'm very hungry.
④ One hamburger, please.
⑤ No, I don't have a wallet.

M: Oh, no. I □ _____ have any □ _____.

W: □ _____ is your □ _____?

M: I left it □ _____ □ _____.

W: That's okay. I can □ _____ □ _____ your □ _____.

M: _____

20 알맞은 응답 찾기

대화를 듣고, 여자의 마지막 말에 이어질 남자의 응답으로 가장 적절한 것을 고르시오.

Man: _____

① He's the same age as I am.
② He'll be here on the fifth of July.
③ Yes, I'll go home in a few minutes.
④ No, I'm not going to visit him now.
⑤ We'll visit the museum and amusement park.

W: Karen told me your □ _____ is going to □ _____ this summer.

M: That's right. It's his □ _____ visit to □ _____.

W: □ _____ are you going to □ _____ □ _____ him?

M: We're going to □ _____ him to some □ _____ □ _____.

W: □ _____ are you going to go?

M: _____

✎ **어휘복습** 잘 안 들리거나 몰라서 체크한 어휘를 써 놓고 복습해 보세요.

□ _____   □ _____   □ _____   □ _____

□ _____   □ _____   □ _____   □ _____

□ _____   □ _____   □ _____   □ _____

점수 / 20

01 다음을 듣고, 그림을 가장 적절히 묘사한 것을 고르시오.

① ② ③ ④ ⑤

02 다음을 듣고, 'this'가 가리키는 것으로 가장 적절한 것을 고르시오.

① ② ③
④ ⑤

03 대화를 듣고, 남자의 마지막 말의 의도로 가장 적절한 것을 고르시오.

① 감사   ② 불평   ③ 축하
④ 거절   ⑤ 초대

04 대화를 듣고, 남자가 대화 직후에 할 일로 가장 적절한 것을 고르시오.

① 숙제하기   ② 요리하기   ③ 농구하기
④ 상 차리기   ⑤ 설거지하기

05 다음을 듣고, 남자의 사진에 <u>없는</u> 사람을 고르시오.

① 할머니   ② 아버지   ③ 누나
④ 어머니   ⑤ 형

06 다음을 듣고, 오늘 밤의 날씨로 가장 적절한 것을 고르시오.

①   ②   ③   ④   ⑤

07 대화를 듣고, 현재 시각을 고르시오.

① 3:00   ② 3:15   ③ 3:30
④ 3:45   ⑤ 4:00

08 대화를 듣고, 무엇에 관한 내용인지 가장 적절한 것을 고르시오.

① 여행하기   ② 그림 그리기
③ 미술관 가기   ④ 시험 공부하기
⑤ 일찍 일어나기

09 대화를 듣고, 여자의 심정으로 가장 적절한 것을 고르시오.

① 기쁨   ② 불안   ③ 당황
④ 걱정   ⑤ 슬픔

10 대화를 듣고, 남자가 이용할 교통수단으로 가장 적절한 것을 고르시오.

① 자동차   ② 자전거   ③ 버스
④ 오토바이   ⑤ 지하철

11 대화를 듣고, 여자가 지불할 금액을 고르시오.

① $20   ② $30   ③ $40
④ $50   ⑤ $80

12 대화를 듣고, 두 사람의 관계로 가장 적절한 것을 고르시오.

① 엄마 – 아들   ② 교사 – 학부모
③ 교사 – 학생   ④ 의사 – 환자
⑤ 경찰 – 시민

13 대화를 듣고, 남자가 학교에 돌아가려는 이유로 가장 적절한 것을 고르시오.

① 축구를 하려고
② 교과서를 찾으려고
③ 과학 실험을 하려고
④ 보고서를 제출하려고
⑤ 친구들과 과제를 하려고

14 대화를 듣고, 여자가 남자에게 제안한 것으로 가장 적절한 것을 고르시오.

① 운동 자주 하기
② 수업에 집중하기
③ 고급 음식점에 가기
④ 건강에 좋은 음식 먹기
⑤ 스포츠 팀에 가입하기

15 대화를 듣고, 여자가 가려고 하는 장소를 고르시오.

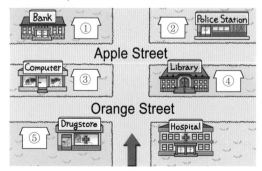

16 다음을 듣고, 박물관에 대한 내용과 일치하지 <u>않는</u> 것을 고르시오.

① 새로 생겼다.   ② 토요일에도 열린다.
③ 오후 6시에 닫는다.   ④ 입장료는 5달러이다.
⑤ 2층 건물이다.

17 다음을 듣고, 두 사람의 대화가 <u>어색한</u> 것을 고르시오.

①   ②   ③   ④   ⑤

18 다음을 듣고, 남자의 심정으로 가장 적절한 것을 고르시오.

① 당황   ② 기쁨   ③ 분노
④ 외로움   ⑤ 자랑스러움

[19-20] 대화를 듣고, 남자의 마지막 말에 이어질 여자의 응답으로 가장 적절한 것을 고르시오.

19 Woman: _____
① No, I don't like it either.
② Yes, we can go together.
③ You can ask for a discount.
④ I'm going to return the shirt.
⑤ No problem. Take your time.

20 Woman: _____
① Yes, it's really cold.
② I've got my umbrella.
③ I'm wearing my jacket.
④ Winter is coming soon.
⑤ It's warm and sunny now.

01 그림 정보 파악

다음을 듣고, 그림을 가장 적절히 묘사한 것을 고르시오.

① ② ③ ④ ⑤

① Two boys are □ _____ the □ _____.
② Two boys are □ _____ in a □ _____.
③ Two boys are □ _____ □ _____.
④ Two boys are □ _____ in a □ _____.
⑤ Two boys are □ _____ in a □ _____.

02 화제 추론

다음을 듣고, 'this'가 가리키는 것으로 가장 적절한 것을 고르시오.

① ② ③

④ ⑤

M: Most □ _____ use this. They often use this □ _____ they □ _____ a □ _____. First, they □ _____ their □ _____. Then, they use this to □ _____ their □ _____ look □ _____. They □ _____ in a □ _____ and use this to □ _____ their hair. Some people □ _____ this with them in their □ _____.

03 의도 파악

대화를 듣고, 남자의 마지막 말의 의도로 가장 적절한 것을 고르시오.

① 감사 ② 불평 ③ 축하
④ 거절 ⑤ 초대

M: I □ _____ my □ _____ on the □ _____ yesterday. Did someone □ _____ it?
W: Can you tell me □ _____ it □ _____ □ _____?
M: It's a □ _____ □ _____. My □ _____ is □ _____ it. My name is Jason Smith.
W: Yes, we have your wallet. It's □ _____ □ _____.
M: Wow, I appreciate it a lot.

✎ 어휘복습 잘 안 들리거나 몰라서 체크한 어휘를 써 놓고 복습해 보세요.

□ _____ □ _____ □ _____ □ _____
□ _____ □ _____ □ _____ □ _____
□ _____ □ _____ □ _____ □ _____

04 할 일 파악

대화를 듣고, 남자가 대화 직후에 할 일로 가장 적절한 것을 고르시오.

① 숙제하기　　② 요리하기
③ 농구하기　　④ 상 차리기
⑤ 설거지하기

M: Mom, I □ _____ my □ _____. Can I □ _____ □ _____ now?

W: I think you should □ _____ □ _____. It's almost □ _____.

M: But I want to □ _____ basketball □ _____ it gets □ _____.

W: You can do that □ _____. Why don't you □ _____ me with □ _____?

M: Okay. Do you want me to □ _____ the □ _____?

W: Yes, please. Thanks.

05 미언급 파악

다음을 듣고, 남자의 사진에 없는 사람을 고르시오.

① 할머니　② 아버지　③ 누나
④ 어머니　⑤ 형

M: Let me show you a □ _____ of my □ _____. You can see my □ _____ and □ _____ here. Both of them □ _____ with □ _____. My □ _____ is right here. He is a □ _____ □ _____. This is my □ _____ □ _____ □ _____ him. She works at a □ _____. And here is my older □ _____. He and I □ _____ □ _____ each other.

06 날씨 파악

다음을 듣고, 오늘 밤의 날씨로 가장 적절한 것을 고르시오.

① 　② 　③

④ 　⑤

M: Good afternoon. I hope you're having a great day. It's time for a short □ _____ □ _____. It's □ _____ □ _____ right □ _____. But the rain will □ _____ around five. It's going to be □ _____ □ _____ and □ _____ □ _____. But there will be □ _____ skies tomorrow □ _____ and □ _____.

✏ **어휘복습** 잘 안 들리거나 몰라서 체크한 어휘를 써 놓고 복습해 보세요.

□ _____　　□ _____　　□ _____　　□ _____
□ _____　　□ _____　　□ _____　　□ _____
□ _____　　□ _____　　□ _____　　□ _____

07 숫자 정보 파악

대화를 듣고, 현재 시각을 고르시오.

① 3:00 ② 3:15 ③ 3:30
④ 3:45 ⑤ 4:00

M: Julie, □ _____ are your □ _____ □ _____ over?

W: They're going to be □ _____ at □ _____ .

M: At four? But it's □ _____ □ _____ □ _____ . We only have □ _____ minutes to □ _____ up.

W: You're right. Let's □ _____ .

M: Okay. You □ _____ the □ _____ , and I'll clean the □ _____ □ _____ .

08 화제 추론

대화를 듣고, 무엇에 관한 내용인지 가장 적절한 것을 고르시오.

① 여행하기   ② 그림 그리기
③ 미술관 가기   ④ 시험 공부하기
⑤ 일찍 일어나기

M: Do we really have to □ _____ to the □ _____ □ _____ on Saturday?

W: Yes, we do. We have to do our art □ _____ .

M: But I don't want to □ _____ it. It's □ _____ □ _____ .

W: I know, but we have to □ _____ □ _____ the □ _____ .

M: Okay. What time shall we go? At three?

W: Let's go □ _____ . How about □ _____ in the □ _____ ?

M: Okay.

09 심정 추론

대화를 듣고, 여자의 심정으로 가장 적절한 것을 고르시오.

① 기쁨   ② 불안   ③ 당황
④ 걱정   ⑤ 슬픔

M: Lisa, why are you □ _____ ? What's □ _____ ?

W: I'm so □ _____ right now.

M: Did □ _____ □ _____ happen to you?

W: I just saw the final □ _____ of *My Life*. My favorite □ _____ □ _____ .

M: That's why you're crying? I can't believe it.

✏ **어휘복습** 잘 안 들리거나 몰라서 체크한 어휘를 써 놓고 복습해 보세요.

□ _____   □ _____   □ _____   □ _____

□ _____   □ _____   □ _____   □ _____

□ _____   □ _____   □ _____   □ _____

10 교통수단 찾기

대화를 듣고, 남자가 이용할 교통수단으로 가장 적절한 것을 고르시오.

① 자동차　　② 자전거
③ 버스　　　④ 오토바이
⑤ 지하철

W: Eric, are you □ _____ to the □ _____ tomorrow?

M: □ _____, I am. Are you going there, too?

W: Yes. I'm going to □ _____ the □ _____ there. How about you?

M: I'm going to □ _____ my □ _____.

W: Isn't that □ _____? There are lots of buses and cars on the □ _____.

M: Don't worry. I'll be □ _____.

11 숫자 정보 파악

대화를 듣고, 여자가 지불할 금액을 고르시오.

① $20　　② $30　　③ $40
④ $50　　⑤ $80

M: Good afternoon. May I help you?

W: I'd like to □ _____ this □ _____ □ _____. It's □ _____ □ _____, right?

M: It's on □ _____ today, so you can □ _____ □ _____ □ _____.

W: Wow. I only have to □ _____ □ _____ dollars for it. That's great news.

M: Would you like to buy □ _____ □ _____ then?

W: No. I □ _____ have □ _____ □ _____ to buy two games.

✎ **어휘복습** 잘 안 들리거나 몰라서 체크한 어휘를 써 놓고 복습해 보세요.

□ _____　　□ _____　　□ _____　　□ _____

□ _____　　□ _____　　□ _____　　□ _____

□ _____　　□ _____　　□ _____　　□ _____

12 관계 추론

대화를 듣고, 두 사람의 관계로 가장 적절한 것을 고르시오.

① 엄마 – 아들　　② 교사 – 학부모
③ 교사 – 학생　　④ 의사 – 환자
⑤ 경찰 – 시민

W: Hello.

M: Hello. Is this Minho's □ _____?

W: Yes, □ _____ □ _____ □ _____. Who's □ _____, please?

M: This is Jiho Kim calling from Central □ _____ □ _____. Minho is a □ _____ in my □ _____.

W: Is there a □ _____?

M: Yes, there is. Minho isn't □ _____ □ _____ today. I think he needs to □ _____ □ _____.

W: I'll □ _____ □ _____ soon. Thanks for calling.

13 이유 파악

대화를 듣고, 남자가 학교에 돌아가려는 이유로 가장 적절한 것을 고르시오.

① 축구를 하려고
② 교과서를 찾으려고
③ 과학 실험을 하려고
④ 보고서를 제출하려고
⑤ 친구들과 과제를 하려고

M: Mom, I'm □ _____ to □ _____ for a while.

W: You're going to school? But you □ _____ □ _____ from school □ _____ minutes □ _____.

M: I □ _____ □ _____ meet Sarah and Tom.

W: Why? Are you going to □ _____ □ _____ together?

M: □ _____, we're not. We're going to □ _____ □ _____ our history □ _____.

W: Okay. □ _____ be □ _____ for □ _____.

✏ **어휘복습** 잘 안 들리거나 몰라서 체크한 어휘를 써 놓고 복습해 보세요.

□ _____　　□ _____　　□ _____　　□ _____

□ _____　　□ _____　　□ _____　　□ _____

□ _____　　□ _____　　□ _____　　□ _____

14 제안 파악

대화를 듣고, 여자가 남자에게 제안한 것으로 가장 적절한 것을 고르시오.

① 운동 자주 하기
② 수업에 집중하기
③ 고급 음식점에 가기
④ 건강에 좋은 음식 먹기
⑤ 스포츠 팀에 가입하기

M: I □ _____ have any □ _____ these days.

W: What's the matter?

M: I □ _____ really □ _____ in gym class. I can □ _____ play sports □ _____ a few □ _____.

W: You should □ _____ eating □ _____ □ _____.

M: What do you mean?

W: □ _____ eating □ _____ □ _____. Eat more □ _____ and □ _____ instead.

M: Okay. I'll □ _____ that.

15 위치 찾기

대화를 듣고, 여자가 가려고 하는 장소를 고르시오.

W: Hello. Can you tell me □ _____ the □ _____ □ _____ is?

M: Sure. It's on Apple Street. Just go straight □ _____ □ _____.

W: Okay. Should I turn left or right?

M: □ _____ □ _____. It's the □ _____ building □ _____ your □ _____. It's □ _____ the □ _____ store.

W: Thanks for your help.

16 내용 일치 파악

다음을 듣고, 박물관에 대한 내용과 일치하지 않는 것을 고르시오.

① 새로 생겼다.
② 토요일에도 열린다.
③ 오후 6시에 닫는다.
④ 입장료는 5달러이다.
⑤ 2층 건물이다.

M: The □ _____ □ _____ is on the □ _____ of Lake Street and Second Avenue. It is □ _____ from □ _____ to □ _____. It opens at □ _____ A.M. and closes at □ _____ P.M. each day. It □ _____ □ _____ □ _____ to enter the museum. The museum has □ _____ □ _____. It □ _____ many □ _____ from around the world.

✏ **어휘복습** 잘 안 들리거나 몰라서 체크한 어휘를 써 놓고 복습해 보세요.

□ _____
□ _____
□ _____
□ _____
□ _____
□ _____
□ _____
□ _____
□ _____
□ _____
□ _____
□ _____

17 어색한 대화 찾기

다음을 듣고, 두 사람의 대화가 <u>어색한</u> 것을 고르시오.

①   ②   ③   ④   ⑤

① M: □ _____ do you □ _____ the new □ _____ ?

    W: Yes, she □ _____ □ _____ my friend.

② M: You □ _____ □ _____ . What's up?

    W: My parents just bought me a □ _____ .

③ M: Let's □ _____ □ _____ this winter.

    W: That's a great idea.

④ M: □ _____ □ _____ of book are you reading now?

    W: I'm reading a □ _____ □ _____ .

⑤ M: Do you have any □ _____ ?

    W: Yes, I have □ _____ and □ _____ homework.

18 심정 추론

다음을 듣고, 남자의 심정으로 가장 적절한 것을 고르시오.

① 당황   ② 기쁨
③ 분노   ④ 외로움
⑤ 자랑스러움

M: A boy □ _____ to □ _____ in the □ _____ . He sees □ _____ □ _____ studying. He asks □ _____ they are □ _____ . They say that they have a □ _____ □ _____ . He says that he □ _____ to □ _____ . Math is the boy's □ _____ class. Then, the □ _____ walks into the □ _____ and tells the students to □ _____ their □ _____ .

✎ **어휘복습** 잘 안 들리거나 몰라서 체크한 어휘를 써 놓고 복습해 보세요.

□ _____   □ _____   □ _____   □ _____

□ _____   □ _____   □ _____   □ _____

□ _____   □ _____   □ _____   □ _____

대화를 듣고, 남자의 마지막 말에 이어질 여
자의 응답으로 가장 적절한 것을 고르시오.

Woman: _____
① No, I don't like it either.
② Yes, we can go together.
③ You can ask for a discount.
④ I'm going to return the shirt.
⑤ No problem. Take your time.

W: □ _____ do you □ _____ the □ _____ you just bought?

M: I □ _____ my □ _____ . I don't like it.

W: You can return it. □ _____ □ _____ you □ _____ □ _____ to the store?

M: Okay. □ _____ □ _____ □ _____ waiting here for me?

W: _____

대화를 듣고, 남자의 마지막 말에 이어질 여
자의 응답으로 가장 적절한 것을 고르시오.

Woman: _____
① Yes, it's really cold.
② I've got my umbrella.
③ I'm wearing my jacket.
④ Winter is coming soon.
⑤ It's warm and sunny now.

W: Are you □ _____ to □ _____ □ _____ ?

M: Yes, I am. Let me □ _____ □ _____ my jacket.

W: □ _____? You don't need a jacket today.

M: Really? How's the □ _____?

W: _____

✎ **어휘복습** 잘 안 들리거나 몰라서 체크한 어휘를 써 놓고 복습해 보세요.

□ _____ □ _____ □ _____ □ _____

□ _____ □ _____ □ _____ □ _____

□ _____ □ _____ □ _____ □ _____

01 다음을 듣고, 'I'가 가리키는 것으로 가장 적절한 것을 고르시오.

①   ②   ③

④   ⑤

02 다음을 듣고, 인천의 날씨로 가장 적절한 것을 고르시오.

①   ②   ③   ④   ⑤

03 대화를 듣고, 여자가 필요로 하지 <u>않는</u> 물건을 고르시오.

① eggs ② apples
③ chicken ④ orange juice
⑤ bananas

04 대화를 듣고, 여자의 마지막 말의 의도로 가장 적절한 것을 고르시오.

① 제안 ② 꾸중 ③ 칭찬
④ 허락 ⑤ 무관심

05 대화를 듣고, 무엇에 관한 내용인지 가장 적절한 것을 고르시오.

① 교과서 ② 학교 수업 ③ 학생증
④ 학교 축제 ⑤ 도서관 카드

06 대화를 듣고, 여행사가 토요일에 문을 닫는 시각을 고르시오.

① 2:00 ② 3:00 ③ 4:00
④ 5:00 ⑤ 6:00

07 대화를 듣고, 두 사람이 바닷가에서 할 일로 가장 적절한 것을 고르시오.

①   ②   ③

④   ⑤

08 대화를 듣고, 남자의 심정으로 가장 적절한 것을 고르시오.

① 흥분 ② 놀라움 ③ 혼란
④ 실망 ⑤ 기쁨

09 대화를 듣고, 남자의 장래 희망으로 가장 적절한 것을 고르시오.

① 작가 ② 기자 ③ 의사
④ 화가 ⑤ 사진작가

10 대화를 듣고, 남자의 직업으로 가장 적절한 것을 고르시오.

① 시장 ② 조종사 ③ 택시 기사
④ 여행 가이드 ⑤ 컴퓨터 프로그래머

11 대화를 듣고, 두 사람이 대화하고 있는 장소로 가장 적절한 곳을 고르시오.

① 사진관　　② 학교　　③ 공항
④ 슈퍼마켓　　⑤ 면허 시험장

12 대화를 듣고, 남자가 기뻐하는 이유로 가장 적절한 것을 고르시오.

① 오늘이 생일이라서
② 부모님께 용돈을 받아서
③ 새 컴퓨터를 갖게 되어서
④ 컴퓨터 게임을 할 거라서
⑤ 시험에서 좋은 성적을 얻어서

13 대화를 듣고, 두 사람의 관계로 가장 적절한 것을 고르시오.

① 의사 - 환자　　② 아버지 - 딸
③ 승무원 - 승객　　④ 판매원 - 고객
⑤ 감독 - 운동선수

14 대화를 듣고, 여자가 남자에게 부탁한 일로 가장 적절한 것을 고르시오.

① 팝콘 사오기
② 리모컨 고치기
③ 함께 영화 보기
④ 다른 DVD 빌리기
⑤ DVD 플레이어 고치기

15 대화를 듣고, 남자가 지불할 금액을 고르시오.

① $10　　② $12　　③ $15
④ $16　　⑤ $18

16 대화를 듣고, 남자가 전화를 건 목적으로 가장 적절한 것을 고르시오.

① 돈을 빌리려고
② 기차 시간을 물어보려고
③ 여자의 집 주소를 물어보려고
④ 버스 정류장 위치를 물어보려고
⑤ 집까지 태워 줄 것을 요청하려고

17 다음을 듣고, 두 사람의 대화가 어색한 것을 고르시오.

①　　②　　③　　④　　⑤

18 대화를 듣고, 남자에 대한 설명으로 일치하는 것을 고르시오.

① 카메라를 교환했다.
② 수리센터에서 일한다.
③ 새 카메라를 좋아한다.
④ 카메라를 땅에 떨어뜨렸다.
⑤ 다른 카메라를 받으러 갈 것이다.

[19-20] 대화를 듣고, 여자의 마지막 말에 이어질 남자의 응답으로 가장 적절한 것을 고르시오.

19 Man: _____

① I live at 43 Main Street.
② You should arrive by 6.
③ You can visit me on Sunday.
④ About 10 people will be there.
⑤ We're going to order some pizzas.

20 Man: _____

① Yes, we have science after lunch.
② I didn't join a club last year either.
③ I'm in it. You should join me.
④ No, there isn't a club meeting today.
⑤ The cycling club should be lots of fun.

01 화제 추론

다음을 듣고, 'I'가 가리키는 것으로 가장 적절한 것을 고르시오.

① ② ③

④ ⑤

W: I am a type of □ _____. People often use me when they □ _____ on long □ _____ or when they have many things to □ _____. They □ _____ their □ _____ inside me. Then, they □ _____ me to the □ _____. They usually □ _____ carry me on the □ _____ because sometimes I am □ _____ □ _____. But they can carry me □ _____ because I have □ _____ and a □ _____.

02 날씨 파악

다음을 듣고, 인천의 날씨로 가장 적절한 것을 고르시오.

① ② ③

④ ⑤

W: It's time for the □ _____ weather □ _____. □ _____ is coming from Japan. So Gangneung will get lots of □ _____ today. Daegu and Busan will be very □ _____.
In Gwangju, it will be □ _____ and □ _____ today.
There will be □ _____, □ _____ skies in Seoul.
And Incheon will have □ _____ □ _____, too.

03 미언급 파악

대화를 듣고, 여자가 필요로 하지 <u>않는</u> 물건을 고르시오.

① eggs   ② apples
③ chicken   ④ orange juice
⑤ bananas

M: What are you doing now?
W: I'm □ _____ a shopping □ _____. I'm going to the □ _____ today.
M: Are you going to □ _____ □ _____?
W: □ _____, I □ _____ have them. But I □ _____ □ _____, □ _____, and □ _____ □ _____.
M: How about □ _____?
W: Thanks. I have to □ _____ some bananas, □ _____.

✎ **어휘복습** 잘 안 들리거나 몰라서 체크한 어휘를 써 놓고 복습해 보세요.

□ _____   □ _____   □ _____   □ _____
□ _____   □ _____   □ _____   □ _____
□ _____   □ _____   □ _____   □ _____

04 의도 파악

대화를 듣고, 여자의 마지막 말의 의도로 가장 적절한 것을 고르시오.

① 제안　　② 꾸중　　③ 칭찬
④ 허락　　⑤ 무관심

M: Mom, I'm going to □ _____ out □ _____ a □ _____.

W: □ _____ □ _____ you take Rusty with you?

M: He likes to run. I'm □ _____ □ _____ to run with him.

W: But □ _____ need □ _____. And he's your dog. You should □ _____ □ _____ of him.

M: You're right. I'll □ _____ him to the □ _____ with me.

W: That's a good boy!

05 화제 추론

대화를 듣고, 무엇에 관한 내용인지 가장 적절한 것을 고르시오.

① 교과서　　　② 학교 수업
③ 학생증　　　④ 학교 축제
⑤ 도서관 카드

M: I'd like to □ _____ □ _____ these □ _____, please.

W: Do you have a □ _____ □ _____?

M: □ _____, I don't. Can I □ _____ □ _____ here?

W: □ _____, you can. Do you have a □ _____ □ _____ card?

M: Here you are.

W: Hold on a minute. Please □ _____ □ _____ this □ _____ first.

06 숫자 정보 파악

대화를 듣고, 여행사가 토요일에 문을 닫는 시각을 고르시오.

① 2:00　　② 3:00　　③ 4:00
④ 5:00　　⑤ 6:00

W: We need to □ _____ □ _____ □ _____ for our trip. Let's go to the □ _____ □ _____.

M: It's □ _____. I think it's □ _____ today.

W: □ _____, it's open. But it □ _____ at □ _____ today.

M: We need to □ _____ □ _____ then. □ _____ already □ _____.

W: Right. Let's go now.

✎ **어휘복습** 잘 안 들리거나 몰라서 체크한 어휘를 써 놓고 복습해 보세요.

□ _____　□ _____　□ _____　□ _____

□ _____　□ _____　□ _____　□ _____

□ _____　□ _____　□ _____　□ _____

07 할 일 파악

대화를 듣고, 두 사람이 바닷가에서 할 일로 가장 적절한 것을 고르시오.

① ② ③
④ ⑤

M: I'm really □ _____ about our □ _____ to the □ _____.
W: So am I. □ _____ should we □ _____ there?
M: I don't want to go on a □ _____. I'll □ _____ □ _____.
W: That's okay. We can go □ _____ and have some □ _____.
M: Snorkeling is fine. But I don't like seafood.
W: That's too bad.

08 심정 추론

대화를 듣고, 남자의 심정으로 가장 적절한 것을 고르시오.

① 흥분　② 놀라움　③ 혼란
④ 실망　⑤ 기쁨

W: □ _____ aren't you □ _____ with your □ _____?
M: Jeremy □ _____ a □ _____ □ _____. He can't meet me today.
W: Did he say why?
M: He has to go to the □ _____ with his □ _____.
W: You must be □ _____.
M: □ _____ □ _____. We were planning to play tennis this afternoon.

09 장래 희망 파악

대화를 듣고, 남자의 장래 희망으로 가장 적절한 것을 고르시오.

① 작가　② 기자　③ 의사
④ 화가　⑤ 사진작가

M: Do you still □ _____ to be a □ _____ in the □ _____?
W: That's □ _____. I want to □ _____ □ _____ □ _____ get better. How about you?
M: I'm □ _____ in □ _____.
W: So you want to be an □ _____?
M: □ _____. I want to be a □ _____. I'd like to □ _____ □ _____ a □ _____.

✎ **어휘복습** 잘 안 들리거나 몰라서 체크한 어휘를 써 놓고 복습해 보세요.

□ _____　□ _____　□ _____　□ _____
□ _____　□ _____　□ _____　□ _____
□ _____　□ _____　□ _____　□ _____

10 직업 파악

대화를 듣고, 남자의 직업으로 가장 적절한 것을 고르시오.

① 시장　　　　② 조종사
③ 택시 기사　　④ 여행 가이드
⑤ 컴퓨터 프로그래머

M: Good morning. □ _____ are you □ _____?

W: I need to go to □ _____ □ _____.

M: City Hall? Okay. It will □ _____ about □ _____ □ _____ to get there.

W: Can you please □ _____ □ _____? I'm □ _____ for a □ _____.

M: No problem. □ _____ □ _____ is your meeting?

W: I need to □ _____ □ _____ □ _____ ten thirty.

11 장소 추론

대화를 듣고, 두 사람이 대화하고 있는 장소로 가장 적절한 곳을 고르시오.

① 사진관　　　② 학교
③ 공항　　　　④ 슈퍼마켓
⑤ 면허 시험장

W: Hello. What can I do for you?

M: I need a □ _____ for my □ _____ □ _____.

W: Okay. □ _____ in that □ _____, please.

M: Will this □ _____ □ _____? I'm in a □ _____.

W: It will only □ _____ about □ _____ minutes after I □ _____ your □ _____.

12 이유 파악

대화를 듣고, 남자가 기뻐하는 이유로 가장 적절한 것을 고르시오.

① 오늘이 생일이라서
② 부모님께 용돈을 받아서
③ 새 컴퓨터를 갖게 되어서
④ 컴퓨터 게임을 할 거라서
⑤ 시험에서 좋은 성적을 얻어서

W: You □ _____ really □ _____, Ted.

M: I can't □ _____ □ _____ today.

W: What's going on?

M: My □ _____ are going to □ _____ a new □ _____ for me. I □ _____ □ _____.

W: Wow. That sounds great. □ _____.

✎ **어휘복습** 잘 안 들리거나 몰라서 체크한 어휘를 써 놓고 복습해 보세요.

□ _____　　□ _____　　□ _____　　□ _____

□ _____　　□ _____　　□ _____　　□ _____

□ _____　　□ _____　　□ _____　　□ _____

13 관계 추론

대화를 듣고, 두 사람의 관계로 가장 적절한 것을 고르시오.

① 의사 – 환자
② 아버지 – 딸
③ 승무원 – 승객
④ 판매원 – 고객
⑤ 감독 – 운동선수

M: □ _____ do the □ _____ □ _____?

W: They are a □ _____ □ _____. Do you have them in a □ _____ □ _____?

M: Sorry. Those are the only ones we have. □ _____ □ _____ looking at □ _____ □ _____?

W: The shoes over there look pretty.

M: Great. We □ _____ them in your □ _____. Hold on a minute.

W: Okay.

14 부탁 파악

대화를 듣고, 여자가 남자에게 부탁한 일로 가장 적절한 것을 고르시오.

① 팝콘 사오기
② 리모컨 고치기
③ 함께 영화 보기
④ 다른 DVD 빌리기
⑤ DVD 플레이어 고치기

M: Why aren't you □ _____ the □ _____?

W: The DVD player isn't □ _____. I think it's □ _____.

M: Did you try to □ _____ it?

W: I □ _____ at it. But I don't know what's □ _____. Can you □ _____ to □ _____ it?

M: Sure. Let me □ _____ □ _____ □ _____ at it now.

✏ **어휘복습** 잘 안 들리거나 몰라서 체크한 어휘를 써 놓고 복습해 보세요.

□ _____ □ _____ □ _____ □ _____

□ _____ □ _____ □ _____ □ _____

□ _____ □ _____ □ _____ □ _____

15 숫자 정보 파악

대화를 듣고, 남자가 지불할 금액을 고르시오.

① $10   ② $12   ③ $15
④ $16   ⑤ $18

M: □_____ □_____ are the pizzas?

W: A □_____ pizza costs □_____ □_____, and a □_____ pizza costs □_____ dollars.

M: Okay. I'll take a □_____ pepperoni pizza.

W: You have to pay □_____ dollars □_____ for pepperoni. So your □_____ is □_____ dollars.

M: That's fine. Here's □_____ dollars.

W: Thank you. And here's your □_____.

16 전화 목적 파악

대화를 듣고, 남자가 전화를 건 목적으로 가장 적절한 것을 고르시오.

① 돈을 빌리려고
② 기차 시간을 물어보려고
③ 여자의 집 주소를 물어보려고
④ 버스 정류장 위치를 물어보려고
⑤ 집까지 태워 줄 것을 요청하려고

W: Hello.

M: Hi, Mom. It's Steve. Are you □_____?

W: □_____ □_____. Where are you?

M: I'm at the □_____ □_____, but I □_____ the bus home.

W: Do you need me to □_____ □_____ and □_____ you □_____?

M: Yes, please. I don't have □_____ □_____ for a taxi.

W: Okay. I'll be there □_____ □_____ □_____.

✎ **어휘복습** 잘 안 들리거나 몰라서 체크한 어휘를 써 놓고 복습해 보세요.

□_____   □_____   □_____   □_____

□_____   □_____   □_____   □_____

□_____   □_____   □_____   □_____

17 어색한 대화 찾기

다음을 듣고, 두 사람의 대화가 <u>어색한</u> 것을 고르시오.

①   ②   ③   ④   ⑤

① W: □ _____ would you like to □ _____?

    M: □ _____ □ _____ some pasta and a glass of iced tea.

② W: □ _____ is your hometown?

    M: I was □ _____ in Seoul.

③ W: Can you show me □ _____ to □ _____ this problem?

    M: Sure. It's really □ _____.

④ W: □ _____ □ _____ did you see yesterday?

    M: We saw it in the □ _____.

⑤ W: □ _____ □ _____ does it cost to take the bus?

    M: A bus ticket □ _____ two dollars.

18 내용 일치 파악

대화를 듣고, 남자에 대한 설명으로 일치하는 것을 고르시오.

① 카메라를 교환했다.
② 수리센터에서 일한다.
③ 새 카메라를 좋아한다.
④ 카메라를 땅에 떨어뜨렸다.
⑤ 다른 카메라를 받으러 갈 것이다.

W: Hi, Mark. □ _____ is your new □ _____?

M: It's □ _____. It □ _____ yesterday.

W: Did you □ _____ it to the □ _____ center?

M: I'm going there □ _____ □ _____. I want to □ _____ it for another one.

W: I'm □ _____ to hear that. I hope you can get a □ _____ camera.

✎ **어휘복습** 잘 안 들리거나 몰라서 체크한 어휘를 써 놓고 복습해 보세요.

□ _____   □ _____   □ _____   □ _____

□ _____   □ _____   □ _____   □ _____

□ _____   □ _____   □ _____   □ _____

대화를 듣고, 여자의 마지막 말에 이어질 남
자의 응답으로 가장 적절한 것을 고르시오.

Man: _____

① I live at 43 Main Street.
② You should arrive by 6.
③ You can visit me on Sunday.
④ About 10 people will be there.
⑤ We're going to order some
   pizzas.

M: I'm having a □ _____ at my house this □ _____ . Would
   you like to □ _____ ?
W: Sure. Do you want me to □ _____ anything?
M: That's □ _____ □ _____ . There will be lots of food.
W: Great. □ _____ should I be □ _____ ?
M: _____

대화를 듣고, 여자의 마지막 말에 이어질 남
자의 응답으로 가장 적절한 것을 고르시오.

Man: _____

① Yes, we have science after
   lunch.
② I didn't join a club last year
   either.
③ I'm in it. You should join me.
④ No, there isn't a club meeting
   today.
⑤ The cycling club should be lots
   of fun.

M: Did you □ _____ the cycling □ _____ at □ _____ ?
W: I □ _____ to, □ _____ I don't have a □ _____ .
M: So □ _____ □ _____ do you want to become a □ _____
   of?
W: I'm thinking about □ _____ ' the □ _____ club.
M: _____

✎ **어휘복습** 잘 안 들리거나 몰라서 체크한 어휘를 써 놓고 복습해 보세요.

□ _____ □ _____ □ _____ □ _____

□ _____ □ _____ □ _____ □ _____

□ _____ □ _____ □ _____ □ _____

01 대화를 듣고, 여자의 일기장이 있는 곳으로 가장 적절한 곳을 고르시오.

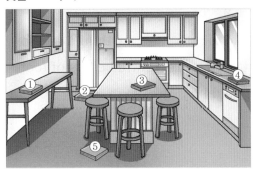

02 다음을 듣고, 무엇에 관한 내용인지 가장 적절한 것을 고르시오.

① 수업 주제　② 수업 규칙　③ 시험 범위
④ 숙제 기한　⑤ 교재 구매

03 다음을 듣고, 오늘 오전의 날씨로 가장 적절한 것을 고르시오.

　①　　②　　③　　④　　⑤

04 대화를 듣고, Tina가 유럽에서 하지 <u>않은</u> 것을 고르시오.

① 스페인 방문　② 박물관 방문
③ 친척 만나기　④ 유럽 음식 먹기
⑤ 프랑스어 배우기

05 대화를 듣고, 두 사람이 대화 직후에 할 일로 가장 적절한 것을 고르시오.

① 요리하기　　② 집에 가기
③ 식사 하기　　④ 상점에 가기
⑤ 쇼핑 목록 작성하기

06 대화를 듣고, 무엇에 관한 내용인지 가장 적절한 것을 고르시오.

① 매점 위치　　　② 티켓 구매
③ 할인 조건　　　④ 놀이기구 위치
⑤ 롤러코스터 탑승

07 대화를 듣고, 여자가 아침식사를 하는 시각을 고르시오.

① 6:30　　　② 6:45　　　③ 7:00
④ 7:15　　　⑤ 7:30

08 대화를 듣고, 남자의 마지막 말의 의도로 가장 적절한 것을 고르시오.

① 거절　　　② 동의　　　③ 초대
④ 요청　　　⑤ 조언

09 대화를 듣고, 남자의 심정으로 가장 적절한 것을 고르시오.

① 만족　　　② 질투　　　③ 좌절
④ 미안함　　⑤ 즐거움

10 대화를 듣고, 여자가 한 일로 가장 적절한 것을 고르시오.

① 건강식 먹기　　　② 병원 가기
③ 약 복용하기　　　④ 휴식 취하기
⑤ 열심히 운동하기

11 대화를 듣고, 두 사람이 이용할 교통수단으로 가장 적절한 것을 고르시오.

① 택시　　　② 버스　　　③ 기차
④ 비행기　　⑤ 지하철

12 대화를 듣고, 연극 공연 날짜로 가장 적절한 것을 고르시오.

①
②
③
④
⑤

13 대화를 듣고, 두 사람의 관계로 가장 적절한 것을 고르시오.

① 엄마 – 아들
② 승무원 – 승객
③ 조종사 – 승무원
④ 음식점 종업원 – 고객
⑤ 자동차 정비공 – 고객

14 대화를 듣고, 여자가 스웨터를 반품하려는 이유로 가장 적절한 것을 고르시오.

① 너무 커서
② 얼룩이 있어서
③ 구멍이 있어서
④ 색깔이 마음에 안 들어서
⑤ 스타일이 마음에 안 들어서

15 대화를 듣고, 남자가 여자에게 부탁한 일로 가장 적절한 것을 고르시오.

① 식물 돌보기　　② 우편물 찾아오기
③ 함께 시골에 가기　④ 개에게 먹이 주기
⑤ 조부모님께 전화하기

16 대화를 듣고, 남자가 여자에게 제안한 것으로 가장 적절한 것을 고르시오.

① 전화기 끄기　　② 전화기 고치기
③ 새 전화기 사기　④ 전화기 교환하기
⑤ 수리 센터에 연락하기

17 대화를 듣고, 여자가 가려고 하는 장소를 고르시오.

18 다음을 듣고, 두 사람의 대화가 어색한 것을 고르시오.

①　　②　　③　　④　　⑤

[19–20] 대화를 듣고, 여자의 마지막 말에 이어질 남자의 응답으로 가장 적절한 것을 고르시오.

19 Man: _____
① The concert starts at 8:00.
② No, the tickets were free.
③ Would you like to go there?
④ I think we'll have a great time.
⑤ It's going to be at Star Stadium.

20 Man: _____
① Have a happy birthday.
② No, I don't like the color.
③ I think the design looks nice.
④ Yes, that would be wonderful.
⑤ When is your birthday party?

01 그림 정보 파악

대화를 듣고, 여자의 일기장이 있는 곳으로 가장 적절한 곳을 고르시오.

W: Dad, I can't find my □ _____ . I think I □ _____ it □ _____ here. Can you help me find it?

M: Sure. Is that it on the □ _____ in □ _____ of the □ _____ ?

W: No, that's Joe's history notebook. It's □ _____ on the □ _____ □ _____ □ _____ . That's Mom's cookbook.

M: Is this it on the □ _____ ? Your □ _____ is on the front.

W: Yes, □ _____ □ _____ . Thanks for helping me, Dad.

02 화제 추론

다음을 듣고, 무엇에 관한 내용인지 가장 적절한 것을 고르시오.

① 수업 주제 ② 수업 규칙
③ 시험 범위 ④ 숙제 기한
⑤ 교재 구매

M: Good morning, everybody. □ _____ to my □ _____ . We're going to have class □ _____ □ _____ A.M. to □ _____ A.M. □ _____ □ _____ of the □ _____ . I want you to have fun in my class. But I also want you to □ _____ □ _____ . Please □ _____ □ _____ to other students or □ _____ □ _____ your □ _____ during class. Please □ _____ □ _____ if you don't understand something. All right, let's begin our first class.

✎ **어휘복습** 잘 안 들리거나 몰라서 체크한 어휘를 써 놓고 복습해 보세요.

□ _____   □ _____   □ _____   □ _____
□ _____   □ _____   □ _____   □ _____
□ _____   □ _____   □ _____   □ _____

다음을 듣고, 오늘 오전의 날씨로 가장 적절한 것을 고르시오.

① ② ③
④ ⑤

W: Good morning, everybody. □ _____ □ _____, we □ _____ □ _____ skies for this □ _____. We were □ _____. As you can see, it's □ _____ a lot right □ _____. The □ _____ weather is going to □ _____ this □ _____. It will be □ _____ for the □ _____ of the □ _____. There will be □ _____ □ _____ □ _____ morning, and the □ _____ will □ _____ □ _____ to around five degrees then.

대화를 듣고, Tina가 유럽에서 하지 않은 것을 고르시오.

① 스페인 방문
② 박물관 방문
③ 친척 만나기
④ 유럽 음식 먹기
⑤ 프랑스어 배우기

M: Hi, Tina. How was your □ _____ to □ _____?
W: It was □ _____. I □ _____ to many □ _____ in four countries.
M: Wow! Sounds like you had a wonderful time.
W: Of course. And I □ _____ my □ _____ and □ _____ in □ _____.
M: Really? Do they □ _____ □ _____?
W: Yes, they do. They □ _____ some □ _____ □ _____ for me.

대화를 듣고, 두 사람이 대화 직후에 할 일로 가장 적절한 것을 고르시오.

① 요리하기
② 집에 가기
③ 식사 하기
④ 상점에 가기
⑤ 쇼핑 목록 작성하기

M: Did you □ _____ □ _____ on your shopping □ _____?
W: Yes, I did. The □ _____ were □ _____.
M: Great. So can we □ _____ □ _____ now?
W: Oh, wait. I need to go to □ _____ □ _____ □ _____.
M: □ _____ □ _____. But please □ _____. I want to go home and have some food.

✎ **어휘복습** 잘 안 들리거나 몰라서 체크한 어휘를 써 놓고 복습해 보세요.

□ _____   □ _____   □ _____   □ _____
□ _____   □ _____   □ _____   □ _____
□ _____   □ _____   □ _____   □ _____

06 화제 추론

대화를 듣고, 무엇에 관한 내용인지 가장 적절한 것을 고르시오.

① 매점 위치
② 티켓 구매
③ 할인 조건
④ 놀이기구 위치
⑤ 롤러코스터 탑승

W: Excuse me. Can I see your □ _____? You need a ticket to □ _____ the □ _____ □ _____.

M: □ _____ can I buy a ticket? I am looking for the □ _____ □ _____.

W: Go to that □ _____ over there.

M: □ _____ □ _____ does it □ _____ to buy □ _____?

W: Tickets cost fifteen dollars for adults and ten dollars for children.

M: Thanks for your help.

07 숫자 정보 파악

대화를 듣고, 여자가 아침식사를 하는 시각을 고르시오.

① 6:30   ② 6:45   ③ 7:00
④ 7:15   ⑤ 7:30

M: □ _____ do you do in the □ _____, Kate?

W: I □ _____ □ _____ at □ _____ □ _____ every day. And then I □ _____ a □ _____.

M: Do you □ _____ □ _____?

W: Of course. I have breakfast at □ _____ □ _____. Then, I □ _____ my □ _____ at □ _____ □ _____.

M: Why do you leave at that time?

W: I don't want to □ _____ my □ _____. My bus leaves at □ _____ □ _____.

✎ **어휘복습** 잘 안 들리거나 몰라서 체크한 어휘를 써 놓고 복습해 보세요.

□ _____   □ _____   □ _____   □ _____

□ _____   □ _____   □ _____   □ _____

□ _____   □ _____   □ _____   □ _____

08 의도 파악

대화를 듣고, 남자의 마지막 말의 의도로 가장 적절한 것을 고르시오.

① 거절 　② 동의 　③ 초대
④ 요청 　⑤ 조언

W: Are you □ _____ this □ _____?
M: No, I'm not. I don't have any □ _____. Why?
W: I'm going to help □ _____ up the □ _____. Would you like to do that □ _____ □ _____?
M: What are you going to do?
W: We will □ _____ □ _____ □ _____ in the park and □ _____ it away. We'll help make the park look better.
M: What a □ _____ □ _____. I will be □ _____ to □ _____.

09 심정 추론

대화를 듣고, 남자의 심정으로 가장 적절한 것을 고르시오.

① 만족 　② 질투 　③ 좌절
④ 미안함 　⑤ 즐거움

W: □ _____ are you □ _____ about, Jim?
M: I'm trying to □ _____ this □ _____ □ _____. But I □ _____ □ _____ how to do it. It's really □ _____.
W: Did you □ _____ the □ _____ for □ _____?
M: Mr. Kim isn't in his office now. And my friends don't know how to □ _____ the □ _____ either.
W: I'm sorry I can't help you. As you know, I'm □ _____ at math.

10 한 일 파악

대화를 듣고, 여자가 한 일로 가장 적절한 것을 고르시오.

① 건강식 먹기
② 병원 가기
③ 약 복용하기
④ 휴식 취하기
⑤ 열심히 운동하기

M: Wendy, how are you □ _____? You're not □ _____ □ _____, are you?
W: I'm □ _____ □ _____ today, Mark. Thanks for asking.
M: You were really sick three days ago, but you □ _____ □ _____ now. Did you □ _____ some □ _____?
W: No, I just □ _____ in □ _____. I really □ _____ a lot of □ _____.
M: I'm □ _____ you're □ _____ again.

✏️ **어휘복습** 잘 안 들리거나 몰라서 체크한 어휘를 써 놓고 복습해 보세요.

□ _____　　□ _____　　□ _____　　□ _____
□ _____　　□ _____　　□ _____　　□ _____
□ _____　　□ _____　　□ _____　　□ _____

11 교통수단 찾기

대화를 듣고, 두 사람이 이용할 교통수단으로 가장 적절한 것을 고르시오.

① 택시   ② 버스   ③ 기차
④ 비행기   ⑤ 지하철

W: That was a long □ _____. We're finally here in Paris.
M: □ _____ do you want to □ _____ to the □ _____?
W: We could □ _____ the □ _____. What do you think about it?
M: We've got too □ _____ □ _____. Let's just □ _____ a □ _____ there.
W: □ _____ thinking. I think the taxi stand is □ _____ □ _____ near the bus stop.

12 숫자 정보 파악

대화를 듣고, 연극 공연 날짜로 가장 적절한 것을 고르시오.

① SEPTEMBER 3   ② SEPTEMBER 22   ③ SEPTEMBER 25
④ SEPTEMBER 28   ⑤ SEPTEMBER 30

W: Are you □ _____ for the □ _____?
M: I'm not sure. We're □ _____ □ _____, but we're running □ _____ □ _____ □ _____.
W: What do you mean? The play is on □ _____ □ _____, isn't it?
M: □ _____, it □ _____. We're going to perform on September □ _____ □ _____ now.
W: □ _____ is the □ _____ □ _____. So you only have □ _____ more □ _____ to practice.
M: I know. I hope we can do well.

✎ **어휘복습** 잘 안 들리거나 몰라서 체크한 어휘를 써 놓고 복습해 보세요.

□ _____   □ _____   □ _____   □ _____
□ _____   □ _____   □ _____   □ _____
□ _____   □ _____   □ _____   □ _____

13 관계 추론

대화를 듣고, 두 사람의 관계로 가장 적절한 것을 고르시오.

① 엄마 – 아들
② 승무원 – 승객
③ 조종사 – 승무원
④ 음식점 종업원 – 고객
⑤ 자동차 정비공 – 고객

W: Can I get you □ _____ to □ _____?
M: Yes, please. I'd like a glass of □ _____ □ _____.
W: No problem. Here you are.
M: Do you know □ _____ we're going to □ _____?
W: We'll □ _____ in about □ _____ □ _____. So we're right □ _____ □ _____.
M: Great. Thanks for the information.

14 이유 파악

대화를 듣고, 여자가 스웨터를 반품하려는 이유로 가장 적절한 것을 고르시오.

① 너무 커서
② 얼룩이 있어서
③ 구멍이 있어서
④ 색깔이 마음에 안 들어서
⑤ 스타일이 마음에 안 들어서

M: Good evening. Can I help you with something?
W: Yes, please. I'd like to □ _____ this □ _____.
M: □ _____? Is it too □ _____?
W: It □ _____ fine, but I □ _____ a small □ _____ in the back.
M: □ _____ □ _____ about that. I will □ _____ this for □ _____ □ _____ right now.

15 부탁 파악

대화를 듣고, 남자가 여자에게 부탁한 일로 가장 적절한 것을 고르시오.

① 식물 돌보기
② 우편물 찾아오기
③ 함께 시골에 가기
④ 개에게 먹이 주기
⑤ 조부모님께 전화하기

M: Janet, I'm going to □ _____ at my grandmother's house for a □ _____.
W: That's great. I hope you □ _____ a □ _____ □ _____.
M: Do you □ _____ □ _____ □ _____ of my □ _____ for me?
W: □ _____, I don't. □ _____ should I □ _____?
M: I'll take them to your house tomorrow. And I'll □ _____ you □ _____ to □ _____ them.
W: No problem. I'm glad I can help you.

✎ **어휘복습** 잘 안 들리거나 몰라서 체크한 어휘를 써 놓고 복습해 보세요.

□ _____   □ _____   □ _____   □ _____

□ _____   □ _____   □ _____   □ _____

□ _____   □ _____   □ _____   □ _____

16 제안 파악

대화를 듣고, 남자가 여자에게 제안한 것으로 가장 적절한 것을 고르시오.

① 전화기 끄기
② 전화기 고치기
③ 새 전화기 사기
④ 전화기 교환하기
⑤ 수리 센터에 연락하기

M: You look □ _____, Sarah. What's the □ _____?

W: There's a □ _____ with my □ _____. I can't □ _____ any □ _____ □ _____.

M: Try □ _____ it □ _____ for a few minutes. That might □ _____.

W: Are you □ _____ about □ _____?

M: My phone had the □ _____ □ _____. The person at the □ _____ □ _____ told me to do that.

W: Wow, thanks for the □ _____.

17 위치 찾기

대화를 듣고, 여자가 가려고 하는 장소를 고르시오.

M: Hello.

W: Hi, Steve. It's Carol. I can't find the □ _____.

M: Tell me □ _____ □ _____ □ _____.

W: I'm at the □ _____ of □ _____ Street and □ _____ □ _____.

M: Okay. □ _____ □ _____ one block to □ _____ Street. Then, □ _____ □ _____.

W: Turn right? All right. Then what?

M: The restaurant will be on the □ _____. It's □ _____ the □ _____ and the □ _____.

✏️ **어휘복습** 잘 안 들리거나 몰라서 체크한 어휘를 써 놓고 복습해 보세요.

□ _____   □ _____   □ _____   □ _____

□ _____   □ _____   □ _____   □ _____

□ _____   □ _____   □ _____   □ _____

18 어색한 대화 찾기

다음을 듣고, 두 사람의 대화가 <u>어색한</u> 것을 고르시오.

①   ②   ③   ④   ⑤

① M: □ _____ □ _____ is your sister?

    W: She's about one hundred fifty-five centimeters tall.

② M: □ _____ did you do last □ _____ ?

    W: I □ _____ □ _____ with my friends.

③ M: □ _____ □ _____ know Susan?

    W: □ _____ , we are good friends.

④ M: □ _____ do you □ _____ today?

    W: I'm □ _____ □ _____ . I'm having a great day.

⑤ M: May I □ _____ your □ _____ , please?

    W: Yes, I borrowed it from the □ _____ .

19 알맞은 응답 찾기

대화를 듣고, 여자의 마지막 말에 이어질 남자의 응답으로 가장 적절한 것을 고르시오.

Man: _____

① The concert starts at 8:00.

② No, the tickets were free.

③ Would you like to go there?

④ I think we'll have a great time.

⑤ It's going to be at Star Stadium.

M: I got two □ _____ for the □ _____ tonight.

W: Concert? What concert are you talking about?

M: It's a rock concert. Five □ _____ are going to □ _____ .

W: That sounds □ _____ . □ _____ is it going to be?

M: _____

20 알맞은 응답 찾기

대화를 듣고, 여자의 마지막 말에 이어질 남자의 응답으로 가장 적절한 것을 고르시오.

Man: _____

① Have a happy birthday.

② No, I don't like the color.

③ I think the design looks nice.

④ Yes, that would be wonderful.

⑤ When is your birthday party?

M: That's a really nice □ _____ you're □ _____ .

W: Thanks. My mom □ _____ it for my □ _____ .

M: That's □ _____ . I love it.

W: Would you like her to □ _____ one □ _____ □ _____ ?

M: _____

✎ **어휘복습** 잘 안 들리거나 몰라서 체크한 어휘를 써 놓고 복습해 보세요.

□ _____   □ _____   □ _____   □ _____

□ _____   □ _____   □ _____   □ _____

□ _____   □ _____   □ _____   □ _____

09회 실전모의고사

점수 / 20

01 다음을 듣고, 오늘 밤 부산의 날씨로 가장 적절한 것을 고르시오.

① ② ③ ④ ⑤

02 다음을 듣고, 'it'이 가리키는 것으로 가장 적절한 것을 고르시오.

① ② ③

④ ⑤

03 대화를 듣고, 여자의 직업으로 가장 적절한 것을 고르시오.

① 음식점 종업원　　② 여행 가이드
③ 항공기 승무원　　④ 호텔 종업원
⑤ 택시 기사

04 대화를 듣고, 여자의 마지막 말의 의도로 가장 적절한 것을 고르시오.

① 위로　　② 제안　　③ 충고
④ 동의　　⑤ 감사

05 대화를 듣고, 여자에 대한 설명으로 알맞은 것을 고르시오.

① 남자의 친구이다.
② 남자의 신임 상사이다.
③ 회사에서 1년간 일했다.
④ 컴퓨터 프로그래머이다.
⑤ 자신의 일에 대해 초조해 한다.

06 대화를 듣고, 여자가 남자에게 부탁한 일로 가장 적절한 것을 고르시오.

① 숙제 끝내기
② 거실 청소하기
③ 식료품점에 가기
④ 요리하는 것 돕기
⑤ 친구들을 식사에 초대하기

07 대화를 듣고, 여자가 부산에 도착할 시각을 고르시오.

① 3:00　　② 4:20　　③ 7:20
④ 7:40　　⑤ 8:00

08 대화를 듣고, 여자의 월요일 시간표에 없는 과목을 고르시오.

① 수학　　② 과학　　③ 음악
④ 체육　　⑤ 사회

09 대화를 듣고, 남자의 심정으로 가장 적절한 것을 고르시오.

① happy　　② angry　　③ bored
④ sad　　⑤ excited

10 대화를 듣고, 두 사람이 오늘 오후에 할 일로 가장 적절한 것을 고르시오.

① 산책하기　　　② 음식점 가기
③ 자전거 타기　　④ 음식 배달시키기
⑤ 공원으로 소풍 가기

정답 및 해설 **p. 31**

11 대화를 듣고, 무엇에 관한 내용인지 가장 적절한 것을 고르시오.

① 축구 경기　② 밴드 연습　③ 올해 목표
④ 학교 시험　⑤ 숙제

12 대화를 듣고, 남자가 여자에게 제안한 것으로 가장 적절한 것을 고르시오.

① 영어 신문 읽기
② 영어책 구매하기
③ 여러 번 적어 보기
④ 여러 번 반복해서 듣기
⑤ 여러 번 큰 소리로 읽기

13 대화를 듣고, 여자가 선택할 교통수단으로 가장 적절한 것을 고르시오.

① 비행기　② 버스　③ 지하철
④ 기차　⑤ 자동차

14 대화를 듣고, 두 사람의 관계로 가장 적절한 것을 고르시오.

① 교사 - 학생　② 교사 - 학부모
③ 기자 - 운동선수　④ 감독 - 운동선수
⑤ 운전 기사 - 승객

15 대화를 듣고, 남자가 지불할 금액을 고르시오.

① 3,000원　② 5,000원　③ 8,000원
④ 10,000원　⑤ 12,000원

16 대화를 듣고, 두 사람이 만나기로 한 장소로 가장 적절한 곳을 고르시오.

① 버스 정류장　② 남자의 집
③ 여자의 집　④ 옷 가게
⑤ 학교

17 대화를 듣고, 여자가 만화 동아리에 가입한 이유로 가장 적절한 것을 고르시오.

① 친구가 권유해서
② 재미있어 보여서
③ 친구를 사귀고 싶어서
④ 만화가가 되고 싶어서
⑤ 만화 그리는 것을 배우고 싶어서

18 다음을 듣고, 두 사람의 대화가 <u>어색한</u> 것을 고르시오.

①　②　③　④　⑤

[19-20] 대화를 듣고, 여자의 마지막 말에 이어질 남자의 응답으로 가장 적절한 것을 고르시오.

19 Man: _____

① Thanks for coming here.
② Yes, I'm listening to them.
③ I enjoy listening to music.
④ No, your friends can't visit.
⑤ Please turn the volume down.

20 Man: _____

① No news is good news.
② Another teacher told me.
③ I got an A on the science test.
④ Yes, she's such a good teacher.
⑤ She's moving to the countryside.

01 날씨 파악

다음을 듣고, 오늘 밤 부산의 날씨로 가장 적절한 것을 고르시오.

① ② ③
④ ⑤

M: Good morning, listeners. It's time for the day's weather forecast. It's a □ _____ day □ _____ in the country. The rain is going to □ _____ until tomorrow. But it will be □ _____ in □ _____ and on Jeju Island. Those two places will have □ _____ □ _____ in the □ _____ □ _____ will get □ _____ at □ _____.

02 화제 추론

다음을 듣고, 'it'이 가리키는 것으로 가장 적절한 것을 고르시오.

① ② ③
④ ⑤

W: This □ _____ in the □ _____ and on □ _____.
It □ _____ very □ _____ but can □ _____ very well.
It has a □ _____ □ _____ □ _____ its □ _____.
When animals see it, it □ _____ in its shell. So the animals cannot □ _____ it.

03 직업 파악

대화를 듣고, 여자의 직업으로 가장 적절한 것을 고르시오.

① 음식점 종업원   ② 여행 가이드
③ 항공기 승무원   ④ 호텔 종업원
⑤ 택시 기사

W: Welcome to Korea. Are you □ _____ □ _____ Los Angeles, California?
M: Yes, we are. Are you Ms. Park □ _____ Elite □ _____?
W: Yes, I am. It's very nice to meet you. Did you □ _____ a □ _____ □ _____?
M: Yes, but it was very long. We'd like to □ _____ □ _____ to our □ _____ soon.
W: I'll □ _____ □ _____ to your □ _____ right away.
After you get some rest, we can go out to a restaurant.

✎ **어휘복습** 잘 안 들리거나 몰라서 체크한 어휘를 써 놓고 복습해 보세요.

□ _____   □ _____   □ _____   □ _____
□ _____   □ _____   □ _____   □ _____
□ _____   □ _____   □ _____   □ _____

04 의도 파악

대화를 듣고, 여자의 마지막 말의 의도로 가장 적절한 것을 고르시오.

① 위로　　② 제안　　③ 충고
④ 동의　　⑤ 감사

W: Hello, Jason. Can you go to Mark's birthday party today?

M: I'd love to go there, but I can't. I have to □ _____ to the □ _____ now.

W: Why are you going there? Are you □ _____?

M: No, I'm not. But my □ _____ fell down, so she □ _____ □ _____.

W: I'm really □ _____ to hear that. But □ _____ be too □ _____. I'm sure that she will □ _____ □ _____ soon.

05 내용 일치 파악

대화를 듣고, 여자에 대한 설명으로 알맞은 것을 고르시오.

① 남자의 친구이다.
② 남자의 신임 상사이다.
③ 회사에서 1년간 일했다.
④ 컴퓨터 프로그래머이다.
⑤ 자신의 일에 대해 초조해 한다

M: Hello. Are you a new □ _____ here?

W: Yes, I am. My name is Janet, and this is my □ _____ □ _____ at □ _____ here.

M: It's nice to meet you, Janet. □ _____ □ _____ of work will you be □ _____ here?

W: I'm going to □ _____ □ _____ a □ _____ □ _____. It's nice to meet you, too.

06 부탁 파악

대화를 듣고, 여자가 남자에게 부탁한 일로 가장 적절한 것을 고르시오.

① 숙제 끝내기
② 거실 청소하기
③ 식료품점에 가기
④ 요리하는 것 돕기
⑤ 친구들을 식사에 초대하기

M: Mom, you □ _____ □ _____ you're really □ _____.

W: I am. Some guests are □ _____ for □ _____ tonight.

M: I see. That's why you're □ _____ now.

W: That's right. Can you □ _____ the □ _____ □ _____?

M: □ _____. I'll start □ _____ □ _____.

✏ **어휘복습** 잘 안 들리거나 몰라서 체크한 어휘를 써 놓고 복습해 보세요.

□ _____　　□ _____　　□ _____　　□ _____

□ _____　　□ _____　　□ _____　　□ _____

□ _____　　□ _____　　□ _____　　□ _____

07 숫자 정보 파악

대화를 듣고, 여자가 부산에 도착할 시각을 고르시오.

① 3:00 ② 4:20
③ 7:20 ④ 7:40
⑤ 8:00

W: Thanks for □ _____ me □ _____ □ _____ to the train station, Dad.

M: No problem. Please call me □ _____ □ _____ □ _____ you get to Busan.

W: I will. I will □ _____ there around □ _____ □ _____ □ _____ .

M: It's four twenty □ _____ . □ _____ □ _____ will your train □ _____ □ _____ ?

W: I'll get there at □ _____ □ _____ . And Aunt Jenny will □ _____ me □ _____ there at eight.

08 미언급 파악

대화를 듣고, 여자의 월요일 시간표에 없는 과목을 고르시오.

① 수학   ② 과학   ③ 음악
④ 체육   ⑤ 사회

M: Sue, do you □ _____ your □ _____ yet? Which □ _____ do you have □ _____ □ _____ ?

W: I've got □ _____ and □ _____ in the morning.

M: So do I. What about the □ _____ □ _____ ?

W: I've got □ _____ class, □ _____ , and □ _____ studies in the afternoon.

M: What about □ _____ or □ _____ ? Do you have □ _____ of them?

W: No, I don't have any of them on Monday

✏️ **어휘복습** 잘 안 들리거나 몰라서 체크한 어휘를 써 놓고 복습해 보세요.

□ _____   □ _____   □ _____   □ _____

□ _____   □ _____   □ _____   □ _____

□ _____   □ _____   □ _____   □ _____

09 심정 추론

대화를 듣고, 남자의 심정으로 가장 적절한 것을 고르시오.

① happy ② angry
③ bored ④ sad
⑤ excited

W: □ _____ is your dog □ _____? Is he still □ _____?

M: Yes, he is. He's very old, so it □ _____ him a □ _____
□ _____ to □ _____ □ _____.

W: I'm so □ _____ to hear that.

M: I □ _____ he can be □ _____ soon.

W: □ _____ □ _____. I'm sure he'll be okay soon.

10 할 일 파악

대화를 듣고, 두 사람이 오늘 오후에 할 일로 가장 적절한 것을 고르시오.

① 산책하기
② 음식점 가기
③ 자전거 타기
④ 음식 배달시키기
⑤ 공원으로 소풍 가기

M: It's a beautiful spring day. Why don't we □ _____ our
□ _____ at the park?

W: I'm really tired. Let's □ _____ some □ _____ and
□ _____ □ _____.

M: I just ate lunch, so I'm not hungry.

W: Okay. Then how about □ _____ □ _____ for a □ _____?

M: □ _____. Let's go.

11 화제 추론

대화를 듣고, 무엇에 관한 내용인지 가장 적절한 것을 고르시오.

① 축구 경기 ② 밴드 연습
③ 올해 목표 ④ 학교 시험
⑤ 숙제

W: Hi, Tim. □ _____ was your □ _____ game today?

M: We □ _____ again.

W: I'm sorry to hear that. □ _____ was the □ _____?

M: It was four to three. I □ _____ two □ _____, but it wasn't enough.

W: At least you did well. I'm sure you'll □ _____ □ _____ next time.

✏️ **어휘복습** 잘 안 들리거나 몰라서 체크한 어휘를 써 놓고 복습해 보세요.

□ _____ □ _____ □ _____ □ _____

□ _____ □ _____ □ _____ □ _____

□ _____ □ _____ □ _____ □ _____

12 제안 파악

대화를 듣고, 남자가 여자에게 제안한 것으로 가장 적절한 것을 고르시오.

① 영어 신문 읽기
② 영어책 구매하기
③ 여러 번 적어 보기
④ 여러 번 반복해서 듣기
⑤ 여러 번 큰 소리로 읽기

W: It's □ _____ for me to □ _____ □ _____ in □ _____ when I read them.
M: Don't try memorizing them like that. You □ _____ a □ _____ □ _____ to learn English.
W: What should I do then?
M: □ _____ each □ _____ out □ _____ many times. That will □ _____ you □ _____ them.
W: Really? Okay. I'll □ _____ them □ _____ from now on.

13 교통수단 찾기

대화를 듣고, 여자가 선택할 교통수단으로 가장 적절한 것을 고르시오.

① 비행기   ② 버스   ③ 지하철
④ 기차   ⑤ 자동차

M: Hey, Karen. Do you have □ _____ for this □ _____?
W: Yes, I do. I'm □ _____ □ _____ with my family.
M: That sounds like fun. □ _____ are you going to □ _____ there?
W: We were planning to □ _____ there. □ _____ we decided to □ _____ a □ _____ there □ _____.
M: That's a good idea. It will be more □ _____ to go that way.

14 관계 추론

대화를 듣고, 두 사람의 관계로 가장 적절한 것을 고르시오.

① 교사 – 학생
② 교사 – 학부모
③ 기자 – 운동선수
④ 감독 – 운동선수
⑤ 운전 기사 – 승객

M: Congratulations on □ _____ a □ _____ □ _____ today.
W: Thank you so much for saying that.
M: Would you like to □ _____ □ _____ to your □ _____? You're □ _____ live □ _____ right now.
W: □ _____ you all for your □ _____ and □ _____. I'm glad that I didn't let you down.
M: Congratulations once again. And □ _____ □ _____ in your next event.

✎ **어휘복습** 잘 안 들리거나 몰라서 체크한 어휘를 써 놓고 복습해 보세요.

□ _____   □ _____   □ _____   □ _____
□ _____   □ _____   □ _____   □ _____
□ _____   □ _____   □ _____   □ _____

15 숫자 정보 파악

대화를 듣고, 남자가 지불할 금액을 고르시오.

① 3,000원　　　② 5,000원
③ 8,000원　　　④ 10,000원
⑤ 12,000원

W: Good afternoon. How may I help you?

M: Hello. I'm □ _____ □ _____ a □ _____ □ _____.

W: □ _____ □ _____ this □ _____ one? Many students like this one a lot.

M: It looks great. □ _____ □ _____ does it □ _____?

W: It's □ _____ □ _____ won. But you can buy □ _____ of them for □ _____ thousand won.

M: I only □ _____ □ _____. Here's ten thousand won.

16 장소 추론

대화를 듣고, 두 사람이 만나기로 한 장소로 가장 적절한 곳을 고르시오.

① 버스 정류장　　② 남자의 집
③ 여자의 집　　　④ 옷 가게
⑤ 학교

W: Hi, Chris. Can you □ _____ □ _____ with me today?

M: Sure. I have some □ _____ □ _____ in the □ _____. □ _____ shall we □ _____?

W: Let's □ _____ at the □ _____ □ _____ at □ _____.

M: Okay. □ _____ □ _____ two o'clock?

W: Um... I need to go home to change my clothes. How about meeting at three thirty?

M: □ _____ □ _____. See you then.

17 이유 파악

대화를 듣고, 여자가 만화 동아리에 가입한 이유로 가장 적절한 것을 고르시오.

① 친구가 권유해서
② 재미있어 보여서
③ 친구를 사귀고 싶어서
④ 만화가가 되고 싶어서
⑤ 만화 그리는 것을 배우고 싶어서

M: Which □ _____ did you □ _____ □ _____ for, Tina?

W: I □ _____ the □ _____ □ _____.

M: I didn't know you like cartoons. Are you □ _____ □ _____ □ _____ them?

W: No, I □ _____ draw them □ _____ □ _____. But I □ _____ to □ _____. □ _____ □ _____ I joined the club.

M: It sounds like fun. Maybe I should sign up for it, too.

18 어색한 대화 찾기

다음을 듣고, 두 사람의 대화가 <u>어색한</u> 것을 고르시오.

①   ②   ③   ④   ⑤

① M: Can you □ _____ me some □ _____, please?
　 W: Sure. What can I do for you?

② M: Do you □ _____ a blue pencil?
　 W: Sorry, but I □ _____ □ _____ one.

③ M: I think I □ _____ my science □ _____.
　 W: That's □ _____ □ _____.

④ M: Where did you go □ _____ □ _____?
　 W: I □ _____ some □ _____ in Hawaii.

⑤ M: What's the weather like □ _____?
　 W: It was rainy □ _____ □ _____.

✎ **어휘복습** 잘 안 들리거나 몰라서 체크한 어휘를 써 놓고 복습해 보세요.

□ _____　□ _____　□ _____　□ _____

□ _____　□ _____　□ _____　□ _____

□ _____　□ _____　□ _____　□ _____

대화를 듣고, 여자의 마지막 말에 이어질 남자의 응답으로 가장 적절한 것을 고르시오.

Man: _____
① Thanks for coming here.
② Yes, I'm listening to them.
③ I enjoy listening to music.
④ No, your friends can't visit.
⑤ Please turn the volume down.

M: Jenny, □ _____ □ _____ □ _____ right now?

W: □ _____ □ _____ my □ _____ with my friends.

M: What did you say? I □ _____ □ _____ you. What's that terrible □ _____?

W: My friends and I are in my room. We're □ _____ to □ _____.

M: _____

대화를 듣고, 여자의 마지막 말에 이어질 남자의 응답으로 가장 적절한 것을 고르시오.

Man: _____
① No news is good news.
② Another teacher told me.
③ I got an A on the science test.
④ Yes, she's such a good teacher.
⑤ She's moving to the countryside.

W: Dave, what's the □ _____?

M: I just heard that □ _____ science □ _____ is going to □ _____ to □ _____ □ _____ next month.

W: No way.

M: You like her a lot, don't you?

W: Yes, she's my □ _____ □ _____. □ _____ did you □ _____ □ _____ she's moving?

M: _____

✎ **어휘복습** 잘 안 들리거나 몰라서 체크한 어휘를 써 놓고 복습해 보세요.

□ _____   □ _____   □ _____   □ _____
□ _____   □ _____   □ _____   □ _____
□ _____   □ _____   □ _____   □ _____

점수 / 20

01 대화를 듣고, David의 집으로 가장 적절한 것을 고르시오.

①   ②   ③

④   ⑤

02 대화를 듣고, 무엇에 관한 내용인지 가장 적절한 것을 고르시오.

① 생일 선물 구매　② 어머니 날 선물
③ 인기 있는 선물　④ 새로 나온 향수
⑤ 좋아하는 향수

03 다음을 듣고, 여자가 언급하지 않은 것을 고르시오.

① 태어난 곳　② 자란 곳　③ 구사하는 언어
④ 장래 희망　⑤ 애완동물의 수

04 대화를 듣고, 여자가 주말에 할 일로 가장 적절한 것을 고르시오.

① 박물관 가기　② 파마하기　③ 미술관 가기
④ 머리 자르기　⑤ 공원 가기

05 대화를 듣고, 두 사람이 볼 영화가 시작하는 시각을 고르시오.

① 7:00　② 7:30　③ 7:40
④ 7:45　⑤ 8:00

06 다음을 듣고, 내일 오전 대구의 날씨로 가장 적절한 것을 고르시오.

①   ②   ③   ④   ⑤

07 대화를 듣고, 여자가 남자에게 제안한 것으로 가장 적절한 것을 고르시오.

① 약 먹기　　　　② 침대에 눕기
③ 축구 연습하기　④ 따뜻한 물에 목욕하기
⑤ 우산을 가지고 다니기

08 대화를 듣고, 여자의 장래 희망으로 가장 적절한 것을 고르시오.

① 기자　　　　② 패션 모델
③ 건축가　　　④ 가방 디자이너
⑤ 의류 디자이너

09 다음을 듣고, 'this'가 가리키는 것으로 가장 적절한 것을 고르시오.

① 1월　　② 5월　　③ 8월
④ 10월　　⑤ 12월

10 대화를 듣고, 남자가 전화를 건 목적으로 가장 적절한 것을 고르시오.

① 자리를 예약하려고
② 메뉴를 알아보려고
③ 식당 위치를 물어보려고
④ 잃어버린 물품을 문의하려고
⑤ 언제 문을 닫는지 알아보려고

11 대화를 듣고, 여자가 지불할 금액을 고르시오.

① $6   ② $7   ③ $13

④ $14   ⑤ $20

12 대화를 듣고, 여자의 마지막 말의 의도로 가장 적절한 것을 고르시오.

① 거절   ② 승낙   ③ 동의

④ 추천   ⑤ 무관심

13 대화를 듣고, Sumi의 생일로 가장 적절한 것을 고르시오.

① 10월 10일   ② 10월 11일

③ 10월 12일   ④ 10월 13일

⑤ 10월 14일

14 대화를 듣고, 남자가 가려고 하는 장소를 고르시오.

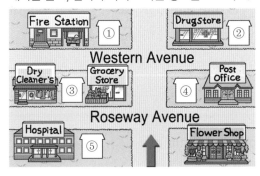

15 다음을 듣고, 'this'가 가리키는 것으로 가장 적절한 것을 고르시오.

① 배구   ② 농구   ③ 축구

④ 야구   ⑤ 하키

16 대화를 듣고, 여자의 기분이 좋지 <u>않은</u> 이유로 가장 적절한 것을 고르시오.

① 지갑을 잃어버려서

② 버스를 놓쳐서

③ 친구와 싸워서

④ 몸이 안 좋아서

⑤ 보고서를 제출하지 못해서

17 대화를 듣고, 여자의 심정으로 가장 적절한 것을 고르시오.

① 슬픔   ② 걱정   ③ 기쁨

④ 안도   ⑤ 분노

18 다음을 듣고, 두 사람의 대화가 <u>어색한</u> 것을 고르시오.

①   ②   ③   ④   ⑤

[19-20] 대화를 듣고, 남자의 마지막 말에 이어질 여자의 응답으로 가장 적절한 것을 고르시오.

19 Woman: _____

① Yes, I remember your sister.

② I hope you have fun there.

③ My sister lives at my home.

④ She's studying in Korea now.

⑤ No, I didn't go there last year.

20 Woman: _____

① Let's take a taxi. I'm very tired.

② Yes, we came here by subway.

③ I can't see anything on the map.

④ No, he's not going to take a taxi here.

⑤ How about taking the subway instead?

01 그림 정보 파악

대화를 듣고, David의 집으로 가장 적절한 것을 고르시오.

① ② ③

④ ⑤

M: I think that David's house is on this street.

W: He told me he lives in a □ _____ □ _____. There is one □ _____ on the □ _____ □ _____.

M: There it is. It's that house over there.

W: No. That house has a □ _____. David's house doesn't have a gate.

M: I found it. It's the one with a □ _____ in the □ _____.

02 화제 추론

대화를 듣고, 무엇에 관한 내용인지 가장 적절한 것을 고르시오.

① 생일 선물 구매   ② 어머니 날 선물
③ 인기 있는 선물   ④ 새로 나온 향수
⑤ 좋아하는 향수

M: Happy □ _____ Day! I bought this □ _____ □ _____ □ _____. I hope you like it.

W: Wow, thank you so much. This □ _____ looks nice.

M: I hope you like the □ _____.

W: Let me □ _____... Yes, it □ _____ □ _____. Thanks, Ron.

M: You're □ _____, Mom.

03 미언급 파악

다음을 듣고, 여자가 언급하지 않은 것을 고르시오.

① 태어난 곳   ② 자란 곳
③ 구사하는 언어   ④ 장래 희망
⑤ 애완동물의 수

W: Hello. My □ _____ is Sue Smith. I was □ _____ in the USA, but I □ _____ □ _____ in France. I can □ _____ English, French, and Spanish. In my free time, I like □ _____ and □ _____. I □ _____ two older □ _____. All of us like □ _____, so we have two dogs and three cats. We love all of our pets very much.

✎ **어휘복습** 잘 안 들리거나 몰라서 체크한 어휘를 써 놓고 복습해 보세요.

□ _____   □ _____   □ _____   □ _____

□ _____   □ _____   □ _____   □ _____

□ _____   □ _____   □ _____   □ _____

04 할 일 파악

대화를 듣고, 여자가 주말에 할 일로 가장
적절한 것을 고르시오.

① 박물관 가기　　② 파마하기
③ 미술관 가기　　④ 머리 자르기
⑤ 공원 가기

M: It's almost the □ _____. Do you □ _____ any □ _____?
W: Yes, I do. I'm going to visit the □ _____ □ _____.
M: Are you going to □ _____ a □ _____?
W: No, I'm just going to □ _____ a □ _____. What are you going to do?
M: I'm not sure. I might □ _____ a □ _____ or □ _____ □ _____.
W: That □ _____ □ _____. I hope you enjoy the weekend.

05 숫자 정보 파악

대화를 듣고, 두 사람이 볼 영화가 시작하는
시각을 고르시오.

① 7:00　　② 7:30　　③ 7:40
④ 7:45　　⑤ 8:00

M: We're going to □ _____ a □ _____ □ _____, right?
W: That's right. It starts □ _____ □ _____ o'clock.
M: Really? But my work finishes around seven thirty.
W: That's all right. It □ _____ ten minutes to □ _____ □ _____ the movie theater □ _____ □ _____.
M: Then shall we meet at the theater at seven forty-five?
W: Okay. I'll see you then.

06 날씨 파악

다음을 듣고, 내일 오전 대구의 날씨로 가장
적절한 것을 고르시오.

① ② ③ ④ ⑤

M: It's time for the national □ _____ □ _____. Right now, there's □ _____ weather □ _____ □ _____ □ _____ □ _____. But at □ _____, the temperature is going to get □ _____. There will be □ _____ in Seoul, Incheon, and Daejeon tomorrow morning. Daegu and Gwangju will □ _____ some □ _____ all day long tomorrow. And there will be □ _____ skies in Busan and on Jeju Island.

✎ **어휘복습** 잘 안 들리거나 몰라서 체크한 어휘를 써 놓고 복습해 보세요.

□ _____　　□ _____　　□ _____　　□ _____
□ _____　　□ _____　　□ _____　　□ _____
□ _____　　□ _____　　□ _____　　□ _____

07 제안 파악

대화를 듣고, 여자가 남자에게 제안한 것으로 가장 적절한 것을 고르시오.

① 약 먹기
② 침대에 눕기
③ 축구 연습하기
④ 따뜻한 물에 목욕하기
⑤ 우산을 가지고 다니기

M: I □ _____ a bad □ _____ and don't feel well. I need some □ _____.

W: What did you do □ _____?

M: I □ _____ □ _____ with my friends □ _____ the □ _____. We played for around two hours.

W: You shouldn't do that. □ _____ a □ _____ □ _____, □ _____ you'll get □ _____.

M: Okay. I □ _____ do that □ _____ in the future.

08 장래 희망 파악

대화를 듣고, 여자의 장래 희망으로 가장 적절한 것을 고르시오.

① 기자
② 패션 모델
③ 건축가
④ 가방 디자이너
⑤ 의류 디자이너

M: What are you reading?

W: I'm □ _____ an □ _____ about a famous Korean □ _____.

M: Are you □ _____ □ _____ fashion?

W: Yes, I am. I want to be a □ _____ □ _____. I'd love to □ _____ all kinds of □ _____.

M: I like design, but I want to design □ _____.

W: I see. You want to be an □ _____ then.

09 화제 추론

다음을 듣고, 'this'가 가리키는 것으로 가장 적절한 것을 고르시오.

① 1월
② 5월
③ 8월
④ 10월
⑤ 12월

W: This is my □ _____ □ _____ of the □ _____. The □ _____ is □ _____ and □ _____, so I can go to the □ _____ during this month. I like to □ _____ and get a □ _____ there. However, the □ _____ often gets □ _____ □ _____ during this month. So we must stay inside when it's □ _____ □ _____.

✎ **어휘복습** 잘 안 들리거나 몰라서 체크한 어휘를 써 놓고 복습해 보세요.

□ _____ □ _____ □ _____ □ _____
□ _____ □ _____ □ _____ □ _____
□ _____ □ _____ □ _____ □ _____

대화를 듣고, 남자가 전화를 건 목적으로 가장 적절한 것을 고르시오.

① 자리를 예약하려고
② 메뉴를 알아보려고
③ 식당 위치를 물어보려고
④ 잃어버린 물품을 문의하려고
⑤ 언제 문을 닫는지 알아보려고

W: Hello. This is Sam's Restaurant. How may I help you?

M: Hi. I □ _____ □ _____ there today. But I think I □ _____ my □ _____ there.

W: □ _____ does your bag □ _____ □ _____?

M: It's a blue and white □ _____. There are three books in it.

W: Does it have your name on it?

M: Yes, there's a □ _____ in the backpack □ _____ my □ _____ on it. My name is Ted Peterson.

대화를 듣고, 여자가 지불할 금액을 고르시오.

① $6 　　② $7 　　③ $13
④ $14 　　⑤ $20

W: I love these flower-shaped □ _____. They look beautiful.

M: Many of our □ _____ love these earrings.

W: □ _____ □ _____ do they □ _____?

M: They cost seven dollars □ _____.

W: That's □ _____ □ _____. I'd like to have □ _____ □ _____ of them.

M: That will be □ _____ dollars.

W: Okay. Here is twenty dollars.

✎ **어휘복습** 잘 안 들리거나 몰라서 체크한 어휘를 써 놓고 복습해 보세요.

□ _____　　□ _____　　□ _____　　□ _____
□ _____　　□ _____　　□ _____　　□ _____
□ _____　　□ _____　　□ _____　　□ _____

12 의도 파악

대화를 듣고, 여자의 마지막 말의 의도로 가장 적절한 것을 고르시오.

① 거절   ② 승낙   ③ 동의
④ 추천   ⑤ 무관심

M: I'm □ _____. I think I'm going to □ _____ a □ _____ today.

W: What are you thinking of watching?

M: There's a new □ _____ at the □ _____. I want to watch it.

W: I've heard about that movie. I □ _____ it is □ _____.

M: Really? Would you like to □ _____ □ _____ me?

W: □ _____ □ _____ □ _____, □ _____ I have to finish writing a □ _____ □ _____.

13 특정 정보 파악

대화를 듣고, Sumi의 생일로 가장 적절한 것을 고르시오.

① 10월 10일   ② 10월 11일
③ 10월 12일   ④ 10월 13일
⑤ 10월 14일

W: Why is there a red □ _____ on the □ _____?

M: Oh, no. It's for Sumi's birthday, but I □ _____ □ _____ it.

W: Today is □ _____ eleventh, and the red circle is on October □ _____.

M: Ah, you are right. It's only □ _____ □ _____ □ _____ □ _____.

W: Are you going to □ _____ a □ _____ for her?

M: Yes, I am. But I need to think about □ _____ □ _____ □ _____.

✎ **어휘복습** 잘 안 들리거나 몰라서 체크한 어휘를 써 놓고 복습해 보세요.

□ _____   □ _____   □ _____   □ _____
□ _____   □ _____   □ _____   □ _____
□ _____   □ _____   □ _____   □ _____

14 위치 찾기

대화를 듣고, 남자가 가려고 하는 장소를 고르시오.

M: Pardon me. Are you □ _____ around □ _____?

W: Yes, I am. Are you □ _____ □ _____ something?

M: Yes. Do you know □ _____ the □ _____ is?

W: Sure. □ _____ □ _____ toward Western Avenue. That's □ _____ □ _____ from here.

M: All right. Should I turn left or right then?

W: □ _____ □ _____. Then □ _____ □ _____ the grocery store. The bakery is □ _____ the grocery store □ _____ the □ _____ □ _____.

M: Thank you for your help.

15 화제 추론

다음을 듣고, 'this'가 가리키는 것으로 가장 적절한 것을 고르시오.

① 배구   ② 농구   ③ 축구
④ 야구   ⑤ 하키

M: You can □ _____ this □ _____ or □ _____. This is an □ _____ □ _____. You need to have □ _____ □ _____ on each □ _____. The players take a □ _____ □ _____ with hands and □ _____ it into a □ _____ to score points. They have to □ _____ the ball or make it □ _____ the □ _____ to move with it.

16 이유 파악

대화를 듣고, 여자의 기분이 좋지 <u>않은</u> 이유로 가장 적절한 것을 고르시오.

① 지갑을 잃어버려서
② 버스를 놓쳐서
③ 친구와 싸워서
④ 몸이 안 좋아서
⑤ 보고서를 제출하지 못해서

M: Tina, you □ _____ □ _____.

W: I had a really □ _____ □ _____.

M: What □ _____ □ _____? Tell me about it.

W: I □ _____ my □ _____ on the □ _____ while I was coming home.

M: That's terrible. Did you call the bus company?

W: Yes, I did. But they said nobody saw it.

✎ **어휘복습** 잘 안 들리거나 몰라서 체크한 어휘를 써 놓고 복습해 보세요.

□ _____   □ _____   □ _____   □ _____

□ _____   □ _____   □ _____   □ _____

□ _____   □ _____   □ _____   □ _____

17 심정 추론

대화를 듣고, 여자의 심정으로 가장 적절한 것을 고르시오.

① 슬픔 ② 걱정 ③ 기쁨
④ 안도 ⑤ 분노

M: Karen, □ _____ are you going □ _____ such a □ _____?

W: I am going to □ _____ my □ _____ right now.

M: Is there a problem?

W: No. I just □ _____ an A+ on my math □ _____. I want to tell my mother about it.

M: □ _____. You □ _____ so □ _____ for that test.

W: Thanks. My mother will be □ _____ like me.

18 어색한 대화 찾기

다음을 듣고, 두 사람의 대화가 어색한 것을 고르시오.

①   ②   ③   ④   ⑤

① W: I'm really □ _____ □ _____ my health.

  M: □ _____ this □ _____. Then, you'll □ _____ □ _____.

② W: □ _____ does your brother □ _____ □ _____?

  M: He really likes to □ _____ computer □ _____.

③ W: Can I □ _____ you □ _____?

  M: Sure. Here is my □ _____.

④ W: Sally □ _____ □ _____ □ _____ in the contest.

  M: □ _____ □ _____ □ _____. She must be happy.

⑤ W: I'm sorry, but you can't □ _____ □ _____ into the museum.

  M: I'm sorry. I didn't know that.

✎ **어휘복습** 잘 안 들리거나 몰라서 체크한 어휘를 써 놓고 복습해 보세요.

□ _____ □ _____ □ _____ □ _____

□ _____ □ _____ □ _____ □ _____

□ _____ □ _____ □ _____ □ _____

대화를 듣고, 남자의 마지막 말에 이어질 여자의 응답으로 가장 적절한 것을 고르시오.

Woman: _____
① Yes, I remember your sister.
② I hope you have fun there.
③ My sister lives at my home.
④ She's studying in Korea now.
⑤ No, I didn't go there last year.

M: □ _____ □ _____ is coming soon. Are you planning to go anywhere?

W: No, I'm going to □ _____ and □ _____ books at home. How about you?

M: I'm going to □ _____ □ _____ with my family.

W: That □ _____ □ _____. Are you going with a □ _____ □ _____ there?

M: □ _____, we won't. My sister lived there for a year. So she will □ _____ us □ _____.

W: _____

대화를 듣고, 남자의 마지막 말에 이어질 여자의 응답으로 가장 적절한 것을 고르시오.

Woman: _____
① Let's take a taxi. I'm very tired.
② Yes, we came here by subway.
③ I can't see anything on the map.
④ No, he's not going to take a taxi here.
⑤ How about taking the subway instead?

M: Do you know □ _____ □ _____ □ _____ right now?

W: No. I think we're □ _____.

M: On this □ _____, there should be a □ _____ □ _____ around here.

W: I can't see one anywhere. What should we do?

M: We can □ _____ □ _____ □ _____ the subway or just □ _____ a □ _____.

W: _____

✏️ **어휘복습** 잘 안 들리거나 몰라서 체크한 어휘를 써 놓고 복습해 보세요.

□ _____   □ _____   □ _____   □ _____

□ _____   □ _____   □ _____   □ _____

□ _____   □ _____   □ _____   □ _____

01 다음을 듣고, 'this'가 가리키는 것으로 가장 적절한 것을 고르시오.

02 다음을 듣고, 오늘 오후의 날씨로 가장 적절한 것을 고르시오.

03 다음을 듣고, 남자의 여동생에 대해 언급되지 <u>않은</u> 것을 고르시오.

① 이름　　② 나이　　③ 좋아하는 과목
④ 특기　　⑤ 즐기는 놀이

04 대화를 듣고, 여자가 주말에 할 일로 가장 적절한 것을 고르시오.

① 치과에 가기　　② 공원에 가기
③ 숙제 도와주기　　④ 수학 시험 공부하기
⑤ 선생님에게 질문하기

05 대화를 듣고, 무엇에 관한 내용인지 가장 적절한 것을 고르시오.

① 소설　　② 독서　　③ 글쓰기
④ 공부 방법　　⑤ 학교 생활

06 대화를 듣고, 두 사람이 이용할 교통수단으로 가장 적절한 것을 고르시오.

① 자동차　　② 버스　　③ 기차
④ 자전거　　⑤ 도보

07 대화를 듣고, 두 사람의 관계로 가장 적절한 것을 고르시오.

① 아빠 – 딸　　　　② 교사 – 학생
③ 친구 – 친구　　　④ 점원 – 손님
⑤ 코치 – 운동 선수

08 대화를 듣고, 여자가 지불할 금액을 고르시오.

① $3　　② $5　　③ $8
④ $10　　⑤ $12

09 대화를 듣고, 여자의 심정으로 가장 적절한 것을 고르시오.

① 화난　　② 실망한　　③ 행복한
④ 미안한　　⑤ 걱정하는

10 대화를 듣고, 현재 시각을 고르시오.

① 11:00　　② 11:20　　③ 11:40
④ 12:00　　⑤ 12:20

11 대화를 듣고, 남자가 Dreamstars를 좋아하는 이유로 가장 적절한 것을 고르시오.

① 춤을 잘 춰서
② 외모가 멋있어서
③ 노래 가사가 좋아서
④ 음악 장르가 좋아서
⑤ 리드보컬의 목소리가 좋아서

12 대화를 듣고, 여자의 마지막 말의 의도로 가장 적절한 것을 고르시오.

① 초대   ② 축하   ③ 거절
④ 위로   ⑤ 제안

13 대화를 듣고, 여자가 남자에게 전화한 목적으로 가장 적절한 것을 고르시오.

① 돈을 빌리려고
② 집에 초대하려고
③ 건강 상태를 확인하려고
④ 애완동물 돌보기를 부탁하려고
⑤ 병원까지 태워주기를 부탁하려고

14 다음을 듣고, 그림을 가장 적절히 묘사한 것을 고르시오.

①   ②   ③   ④   ⑤

15 대화를 듣고, 두 사람이 만나기로 한 요일을 고르시오.

① 월요일   ② 화요일   ③ 수요일
④ 목요일   ⑤ 금요일

16 대화를 듣고, 여자가 남자에게 부탁한 일로 가장 적절한 것을 고르시오.

① 거실 청소하기
② 열쇠로 문 열기
③ 소파 아래 살펴보기
④ 열쇠 찾는 것을 돕기
⑤ 부엌에서 간식 가져오기

17 대화를 듣고, 남자의 직업으로 가장 적절한 것을 고르시오.

① 교사   ② 부동산 중개인   ③ 교장
④ 건축가   ⑤ 여행 가이드

18 다음을 듣고, 두 사람의 대화가 <u>어색한</u> 것을 고르시오.

①   ②   ③   ④   ⑤

[19-20] 대화를 듣고, 여자의 마지막 말에 이어질 남자의 응답으로 가장 적절한 것을 고르시오.

19 Man: _____

① Pardon me.
② Sure, I can do that.
③ No, I don't have a car.
④ This bag really weighs a lot.
⑤ How about driving me home?

20 Man: _____

① Yes, you may go there.
② I saw that concert last night.
③ How much do the tickets cost?
④ The concert is going to start late.
⑤ I'm sorry, but they're going to say no.

01 화제 추론

다음을 듣고, 'this'가 가리키는 것으로 가장 적절한 것을 고르시오.

① ② ③ ④ ⑤

W: This is a □ _____ tool. People use this when they need to □ _____ something. They can cut □ _____ and □ _____ with this. Some people also use this in the □ _____ when they cut □ _____ and □ _____. Hairdressers use this to cut □ _____.

02 날씨 파악

다음을 듣고, 오늘 오후의 날씨로 가장 적절한 것을 고르시오.

① ② ③ ④ ⑤

M: Good morning, listeners. I'm Mark Smith, and I've got today's □ _____ report for you. This □ _____, it is going to be □ _____. So be □ _____ when you are □ _____. In the □ _____, there will be □ _____, □ _____ skies. You can enjoy a □ _____ day today.

03 미언급 파악

다음을 듣고, 남자의 여동생에 대해 언급되지 않은 것을 고르시오.

① 이름 ② 나이
③ 좋아하는 과목 ④ 특기
⑤ 즐기는 놀이

M: Hello, everyone. I'd like to □ _____ my □ _____ to you. Her □ _____ is Mary, and she's □ _____ years □ _____. She goes to Eastern □ _____ □ _____. Her □ _____ □ _____ is science, but she also loves English and music. She doesn't like math. We □ _____ □ _____ well, and we □ _____ go rollerblading together.

✎ **어휘복습** 잘 안 들리거나 몰라서 체크한 어휘를 써 놓고 복습해 보세요.

□ _____ □ _____ □ _____ □ _____

□ _____ □ _____ □ _____ □ _____

□ _____ □ _____ □ _____ □ _____

대화를 듣고, 여자가 주말에 할 일로 가장
적절한 것을 고르시오.

① 치과에 가기
② 공원에 가기
③ 숙제 도와주기
④ 수학 시험 공부하기
⑤ 선생님에게 질문하기

M: Anna, can you □ _____ me some □ _____ with my math
  homework?
W: I'm sorry, but I □ _____. I have to □ _____ the □ _____
  now. When do you need to finish it?
M: I have to □ _____ it □ _____ the teacher next Monday.
W: □ _____ □ _____ help you with it □ _____ □ _____?
M: □ _____ □ _____. Thanks.
W: No problem.

대화를 듣고, 무엇에 관한 내용인지 가장 적
절한 것을 고르시오.

① 소설   ② 독서
③ 글쓰기   ④ 공부 방법
⑤ 학교 생활

M: □ _____ are you □ _____?
W: I'm □ _____ a book.
M: You are always reading. □ _____ do you □ _____ reading
  so much?
W: I can □ _____ □ _____ some books. It is also □ _____
  to read interesting stories.
M: I don't read that much. It's □ _____ □ _____ to me.
W: □ _____ this book. I think you'll like it.

✎ **어휘복습** 잘 안 들리거나 몰라서 체크한 어휘를 써 놓고 복습해 보세요.

□ _____   □ _____   □ _____   □ _____
□ _____   □ _____   □ _____   □ _____
□ _____   □ _____   □ _____   □ _____

06 교통수단 찾기

대화를 듣고, 두 사람이 이용할 교통수단으로 가장 적절한 것을 고르시오.

① 자동차　　② 버스
③ 기차　　　④ 자전거
⑤ 도보

M: Tomorrow is New Year's Day. Let's □ _____ to □ _____ the □ _____ at the beach.

W: That sounds fine. □ _____ can we □ _____ there?

M: We can go □ _____ □ _____.

W: There will be □ _____ □ _____ cars on the □ _____.

M: Then let's □ _____ □ _____ our □ _____. The beach is close to our homes.

W: That's a good idea.

07 관계 추론

대화를 듣고, 두 사람의 관계로 가장 적절한 것을 고르시오.

① 아빠 – 딸
② 교사 – 학생
③ 친구 – 친구
④ 점원 – 손님
⑤ 코치 – 운동 선수

M: Hi. I'm □ _____ □ _____ a scarf for my daughter.

W: □ _____ do you □ _____ this white one? It's very □ _____.

M: Thanks. I'll □ _____ it. And □ _____ □ _____ sweaters?

W: This sweater is very □ _____.

M: I don't like it that much. Can you □ _____ me something □ _____?

W: Sure. □ _____ me this way, please.

✏️ **어휘복습** 잘 안 들리거나 몰라서 체크한 어휘를 써 놓고 복습해 보세요.

□ _____　　□ _____　　□ _____　　□ _____

□ _____　　□ _____　　□ _____　　□ _____

□ _____　　□ _____　　□ _____　　□ _____

08 숫자 정보 파악

대화를 듣고, 여자가 지불할 금액을 고르시오.

① $3　　② $5　　③ $8
④ $10　　⑤ $12

M: Good evening. Can I help you with something?

W: Yes, I □ _____ to buy □ _____ □ _____, please.

M: We're □ _____ a □ _____. Apples are □ _____ dollar □ _____.

W: Excellent. And what about broccoli? I need □ _____ □ _____ of it.

M: That will □ _____ □ _____ dollars. So your □ _____ is □ _____ dollars.

W: Okay. I'd like to pay with my card.

09 심정 추론

대화를 듣고, 여자의 심정으로 가장 적절한 것을 고르시오.

① 화난　　② 실망한
③ 행복한　　④ 미안한
⑤ 걱정하는

W: Please don't □ _____ the □ _____ now.

M: Why not? I really want to □ _____ the □ _____ game □ _____.

W: But the □ _____ □ _____ of *Linda's Life* is □ _____ now. I can't miss it.

M: Didn't you □ _____ the □ _____? It's not going to be on TV this week.

W: Oh, no. I'm so □ _____. I have been □ _____ to see this show □ _____ □ _____.

10 숫자 정보 파악

대화를 듣고, 현재 시각을 고르시오.

① 11:00　　② 11:20　　③ 11:40
④ 12:00　　⑤ 12:20

M: I'm getting □ _____. I want to □ _____ □ _____.

W: So do I, but it's only □ _____ □ _____ now.

M: And lunchtime starts □ _____ □ _____.

W: I □ _____ □ _____ for forty minutes.

M: We don't □ _____ a □ _____. We can't eat during class.

✏️ **어휘복습** 잘 안 들리거나 몰라서 체크한 어휘를 써 놓고 복습해 보세요.

□ _____　　□ _____　　□ _____　　□ _____

□ _____　　□ _____　　□ _____　　□ _____

□ _____　　□ _____　　□ _____　　□ _____

11 이유 파악

대화를 듣고, 남자가 Dreamstars를 좋아하는 이유로 가장 적절한 것을 고르시오.

① 춤을 잘 춰서
② 외모가 멋있어서
③ 노래 가사가 좋아서
④ 음악 장르가 좋아서
⑤ 리드보컬의 목소리가 좋아서

M: I just got □ _____ for the Dreamstars □ _____.

W: Do you like that group? Their □ _____ is □ _____.

M: I don't □ _____ □ _____ the dancing. I □ _____ the □ _____ □ _____ their □ _____.

W: Those are okay. And I think the lead singer □ _____ a □ _____ □ _____.

M: You can go with me if you want.

12 의도 파악

대화를 듣고, 여자의 마지막 말의 의도로 가장 적절한 것을 고르시오.

① 초대   ② 축하
③ 거절   ④ 위로
⑤ 제안

W: Hey, Tim, how are you doing?

M: Good. I heard that you □ _____ □ _____ a new place.

W: That's right. My new apartment is □ _____ our □ _____.

M: That's great. Why don't you □ _____ a housewarming □ _____?

W: I was □ _____ □ _____ that. Are you □ _____ □ _____ Saturday?

13 전화 목적 파악

대화를 듣고, 여자가 남자에게 전화한 목적으로 가장 적절한 것을 고르시오.

① 돈을 빌리려고
② 집에 초대하려고
③ 건강 상태를 확인하려고
④ 애완동물 돌보기를 부탁하려고
⑤ 병원까지 태워주기를 부탁하려고

W: Hi, Jim. Can you □ _____ me a □ _____ □ _____?

M: I'll try. What do you need?

W: My □ _____ Susan is □ _____ the □ _____. I need to □ _____ □ _____ there now.

M: So do you want me to □ _____ □ _____ your □ _____?

W: Yes, please. Can you take him □ _____ □ _____ □ _____ and □ _____ him at five?

M: Sure. I'll □ _____ good □ _____ □ _____ him.

✎ **어휘복습** 잘 안 들리거나 몰라서 체크한 어휘를 써 놓고 복습해 보세요.

□ _____ □ _____ □ _____ □ _____

□ _____ □ _____ □ _____ □ _____

□ _____ □ _____ □ _____ □ _____

14 그림 정보 파악

다음을 듣고, 그림을 가장 적절히 묘사한 것을 고르시오.

① ② ③ ④ ⑤

① There is □ _____ □ _____ in front of the house.

② There is a dog in the yard □ _____ the house.

③ There is a tree □ _____ □ _____ □ _____ the house.

④ There is a □ _____ in front of the house.

⑤ There are two children □ _____ □ _____ the house.

15 특정 정보 파악

대화를 듣고, 두 사람이 만나기로 한 요일을 고르시오.

① 월요일　　　② 화요일
③ 수요일　　　④ 목요일
⑤ 금요일

M: Lucy, we have to □ _____ □ _____ the school festival.
　 □ _____ do you □ _____ □ _____ to meet?

W: How about this □ _____?

M: Sorry, □ _____ I have a violin □ _____ on that day.
　 Is □ _____ fine with you?

W: Let me think... I have time □ _____ □ _____ then.

M: Sounds good. □ _____ □ _____ meet in the school
　 cafeteria after school?

W: That's □ _____. I'll see you then.

16 부탁 파악

대화를 듣고, 여자가 남자에게 부탁한 일로 가장 적절한 것을 고르시오.

① 거실 청소하기
② 열쇠로 문 열기
③ 소파 아래 살펴보기
④ 열쇠 찾는 것을 돕기
⑤ 부엌에서 간식 가져오기

M: Mina, why are you looking □ _____ the □ _____?

W: I □ _____ my □ _____, so I'm trying □ _____ □ _____
　 it.

M: Do you think it's in the □ _____ □ _____?

W: I'm not sure. Can you □ _____ in the □ _____ for me?

M: Sure. You □ _____ □ _____ in here, and I'll □ _____
　 □ _____ □ _____ in there.

W: Wait a minute. I found it! Here it is.

✎ **어휘복습** 잘 안 들리거나 몰라서 체크한 어휘를 써 놓고 복습해 보세요.

□ _____　　□ _____　　□ _____　　□ _____

□ _____　　□ _____　　□ _____　　□ _____

□ _____　　□ _____　　□ _____　　□ _____

17 직업 파악

대화를 듣고, 남자의 직업으로 가장 적절한 것을 고르시오.

① 교사   ② 부동산 중개인
③ 교장   ④ 건축가
⑤ 여행 가이드

M: Welcome to the Smith Agency. Can I help you?

W: Yes, please. I need to □ _____ an □ _____.

M: Which □ _____ would you like to □ _____ □ _____?

W: I need to live □ _____ Central Middle School. I □ _____ there.

M: I see. There are two apartments there.

W: That sounds good. Can you □ _____ me □ _____ about them?

18 어색한 대화 찾기

다음을 듣고, 두 사람의 대화가 <u>어색한</u> 것을 고르시오.

①   ②   ③   ④   ⑤

① M: □ _____ did you □ _____ to Incheon?
   W: I moved here □ _____ years □ _____.

② M: □ _____ does your older sister □ _____?
   W: She □ _____ □ _____ a flight attendant.

③ M: Do you □ _____ a dollar?
   W: □ _____, here you are.

④ M: □ _____ are you □ _____ now?
   W: I'm □ _____ the □ _____.

⑤ M: □ _____ do you □ _____ about that book?
   W: I read □ _____ □ _____ every day.

✎ **어휘복습** 잘 안 들리거나 몰라서 체크한 어휘를 써 놓고 복습해 보세요.

□ _____ □ _____ □ _____ □ _____
□ _____ □ _____ □ _____ □ _____
□ _____ □ _____ □ _____ □ _____

19 알맞은 응답 찾기

대화를 듣고, 여자의 마지막 말에 이어질 남자의 응답으로 가장 적절한 것을 고르시오.

Man: _____
① Pardon me.
② Sure, I can do that.
③ No, I don't have a car.
④ This bag really weighs a lot.
⑤ How about driving me home?

W: George, can you please □ _____ me □ _____ this bag? It's too □ _____.
M: □ _____ bag should I carry? The one □ _____ the □ _____?
W: No, the one □ _____ the □ _____.
M: Okay. Let me □ _____ it □ _____. Wow, it is heavy.
W: Thanks so much. Can you □ _____ it □ _____ my □ _____, please?
M: _____

20 알맞은 응답 찾기

대화를 듣고, 여자의 마지막 말에 이어질 남자의 응답으로 가장 적절한 것을 고르시오.

Man: _____
① Yes, you may go there.
② I saw that concert last night.
③ How much do the tickets cost?
④ The concert is going to start late.
⑤ I'm sorry, but they're going to say no.

W: How about □ _____ □ _____ the □ _____ with me tonight?
M: I would □ _____ □ _____ go there. □ _____ □ _____ will it □ _____?
W: It will □ _____ around ten □ _____ □ _____.
M: I can't □ _____ □ _____ □ _____. My parents want me to be home early.
W: Why don't you □ _____ and □ _____ them?
M: _____

✏️ **어휘복습** 잘 안 들리거나 몰라서 체크한 어휘를 써 놓고 복습해 보세요.

□ _____ □ _____ □ _____ □ _____
□ _____ □ _____ □ _____ □ _____
□ _____ □ _____ □ _____ □ _____

12회 실전모의고사

01 다음을 듣고, 그림을 가장 적절히 묘사한 것을 고르시오.

① ② ③ ④ ⑤

02 다음을 듣고, 토요일의 날씨로 가장 적절한 것을 고르시오.

① ② ③ ④ ⑤

03 대화를 듣고, 여자가 지불할 금액을 고르시오.

① 500원　　② 1,000원　　③ 2,000원
④ 3,000원　　⑤ 5,000원

04 다음을 듣고, 남자의 직업으로 가장 적절한 것을 고르시오.

① 주유소 종업원　　　② 배달원
③ 백화점 점원　　　　④ 사무직원
⑤ 컴퓨터 프로그래머

05 대화를 듣고, 현재 시각을 고르시오.

① 11:00　　② 11:05　　③ 11:10
④ 11:15　　⑤ 11:20

06 대화를 듣고, 학교 축제가 시작되는 날짜를 고르시오.

① 9월 26일　　② 9월 27일　　③ 9월 28일
④ 9월 29일　　⑤ 9월 30일

07 대화를 듣고, 무엇에 관한 내용인지 가장 적절한 것을 고르시오.

① 유머 감각　　② 여름 휴가　　③ 영화 관람
④ 영화의 종류　⑤ 간식 만들기

08 대화를 듣고, 여자의 장래 희망으로 가장 적절한 것을 고르시오.

① 경찰관　　　② 수의사　　　③ 의사
④ 소방관　　　⑤ 영화 배우

09 대화를 듣고, 남자의 심정으로 가장 적절한 것을 고르시오.

① 지루함　　② 기쁨　　③ 놀라움
④ 미안함　　⑤ 실망

10 대화를 듣고, 남자가 여행을 즐기지 못한 이유로 가장 적절한 것을 고르시오.

① 배탈이 나서
② 많은 돈이 들어서
③ 심한 폭풍우가 와서
④ 호텔 시설이 나빠서
⑤ 길을 여러 번 잃어서

11 다음을 듣고, 두 사람의 대화가 <u>어색한</u> 것을 고르시오.

①   ②   ③   ④   ⑤

12 대화를 듣고, 여자의 옷에 대해 언급되지 <u>않은</u> 것을 고르시오.

① 색상   ② 종류   ③ 구입 시기
④ 구입 장소   ⑤ 가격

13 대화를 듣고, 여자가 남자에게 제안한 교통 수단으로 가장 적절한 것을 고르시오.

① 기차   ② 자전거   ③ 버스
④ 지하철   ⑤ 택시

14 대화를 듣고, 남자가 대화 직후에 할 일로 가장 적절한 것을 고르시오.

① 병원 가기   ② 화장실 가기
③ 채소 자르기   ④ 식사 준비하기
⑤ 밴드 가져오기

15 대화를 듣고, 두 사람의 관계로 가장 적절한 것을 고르시오.

① 교사 - 학생   ② 의사 - 환자
③ 영화감독 - 배우   ④ 점원 - 손님
⑤ 코치 - 운동선수

16 다음을 듣고, 무엇에 관한 내용인지 가장 적절한 것을 고르시오.

① 방 청소   ② 새 에어컨   ③ 에너지 절약
④ 여름 방학   ⑤ 봉사 활동

17 대화를 듣고, 남자가 가려고 하는 장소를 고르시오.

18 대화를 듣고, 여자가 남자에게 제안한 것으로 가장 적절한 것을 고르시오.

① 짐 풀기   ② 창문 열기
③ 여행가방 사기   ④ 음식 주문하기
⑤ 티켓 예매하기

[19-20] 대화를 듣고, 여자의 마지막 말에 이어질 남자의 응답으로 가장 적절한 것을 고르시오.

19 Man: _____

① You're welcome.
② I'm glad you like it.
③ It's a birthday present.
④ I bought it at the mall.
⑤ It matches your earrings.

20 Man: _____

① I go there all the time.
② The library closes at 7 o'clock.
③ There are many good books there.
④ Sure. You can use my library card.
⑤ It's right next to the shopping center.

다시 듣고, 빈칸에 알맞은 단어를 써 보세요.

◀)) MP3 실전 12-1

01 그림 정보 파악

다음을 듣고, 그림을 가장 적절히 묘사한 것을 고르시오.

① A woman is □ _____ a □ _____.
② A woman is □ _____ a □ _____.
③ A woman is □ _____ a □ _____.
④ A woman is □ _____ a □ _____.
⑤ A woman is □ _____ a cup of □ _____.

① ② ③ ④ ⑤

02 날씨 파악

다음을 듣고, 토요일의 날씨로 가장 적절한 것을 고르시오.

① ② ③
④ ⑤

W: Good evening, everyone. Here's the □ _____ □ _____ for the □ _____. It's □ _____ heavily right □ _____. But the rain will □ _____ later □ _____. Tomorrow, on □ _____, we'll have □ _____ □ _____ all day long. On □ _____, it's going to be □ _____ during the day. It will start raining again in the evening.

03 숫자 정보 파악

대화를 듣고, 여자가 지불할 금액을 고르시오.

① 500원   ② 1,000원
③ 2,000원   ④ 3,000원
⑤ 5,000원

M: Excuse me, but do you need some help?
W: Yes, I do. I want to □ _____ my □ _____ here, but I don't know □ _____ to □ _____ this □ _____.
M: It's easy. □ _____, □ _____ any four □ _____. That's your □ _____. □ _____, □ _____ two thousand won □ _____ the □ _____. That's it.
W: Do I need to use only one thousand won bills?
M: No. You can use five hundred won coins or five thousand won bills, too.
W: Thanks so much. You really helped me a lot.

✎ **어휘복습** 잘 안 들리거나 몰라서 체크한 어휘를 써 놓고 복습해 보세요.

□ _____   □ _____   □ _____   □ _____
□ _____   □ _____   □ _____   □ _____
□ _____   □ _____   □ _____   □ _____

04 직업 파악

다음을 듣고, 남자의 직업으로 가장 적절한 것을 고르시오.

① 주유소 종업원　　② 배달원
③ 백화점 점원　　　④ 사무직원
⑤ 컴퓨터 프로그래머

M: I □ _____ □ _____ to people. When people □ _____ products □ _____, I □ _____ them to their □ _____ or □ _____. So I have to □ _____ many □ _____ each day. During □ _____ such as Christmas and *Chuseok*, I □ _____ very □ _____. There are so many orders, so I cannot always □ _____ them on time.

05 숫자 정보 파악

대화를 듣고, 현재 시각을 고르시오.

① 11:00　② 11:05　③ 11:10
④ 11:15　⑤ 11:20

W: □ _____ does the □ _____ start?
M: It starts at □ _____ □ _____ A.M.
W: I see. It's □ _____ □ _____ □ _____, so we still have twenty minutes to wait.
M: That's right. So can you help me □ _____ some □ _____, please? It will □ _____ about □ _____ □ _____ to do.
W: Sure. I can do that for you.

06 특정 정보 파악

대화를 듣고, 학교 축제가 시작되는 날짜를 고르시오.

① 9월 26일　　② 9월 27일
③ 9월 28일　　④ 9월 29일
⑤ 9월 30일

M: I'm really □ _____ □ _____ □ _____ the school □ _____.
W: When is the festival? Is it on □ _____ □ _____ □ _____ or □ _____ □ _____? I can't remember.
M: It's □ _____ on □ _____ of those days. It's on September □ _____ □ _____.
W: Really? That's only □ _____ days □ _____ now. That's great.
M: Yeah, I can't wait for it.

✎ **어휘복습** 잘 안 들리거나 몰라서 체크한 어휘를 써 놓고 복습해 보세요.

□ _____　　□ _____　　□ _____　　□ _____
□ _____　　□ _____　　□ _____　　□ _____
□ _____　　□ _____　　□ _____　　□ _____

07 화제 추론

대화를 듣고, 무엇에 관한 내용인지 가장 적절한 것을 고르시오.

① 유머 감각 ② 여름 휴가
③ 영화 관람 ④ 영화의 종류
⑤ 간식 만들기

M: What kind of movie would you □ _____ □ _____ □ _____?

W: I love comedies □ _____ □ _____ □ _____ else.

M: Then how about *My Summer Trip*? It's a □ _____.

W: Sure. What time □ _____ it □ _____?

M: It starts □ _____ □ _____ □ _____ □ _____.

W: All right. Let's get tickets and then buy some snacks.

08 장래 희망 파악

대화를 듣고, 여자의 장래 희망으로 가장 적절한 것을 고르시오.

① 경찰관 ② 수의사
③ 의사 ④ 소방관
⑤ 영화 배우

M: Did you □ _____ *Animal Kingdom* □ _____ □ _____ last night? I learned a lot about lions.

W: Yeah, I always watch it. It's my □ _____ program.

M: Do you like □ _____?

W: Yes. I want to be a □ _____ in the future. What about you?

M: I'm not sure. I might become a □ _____.

W: That's a difficult □ _____. But I know you can do it.

09 심정 추론

대화를 듣고, 남자의 심정으로 가장 적절한 것을 고르시오.

① 지루함 ② 기쁨
③ 놀라움 ④ 미안함
⑤ 실망

M: That's □ _____. I can't find the strawberry ice cream.

W: Do you mean the ice cream in the □ _____?

M: Yes. I put it there last night.

W: I ate it this morning. It was □ _____.

M: What? I'm so □ _____ □ _____ you. Why didn't you □ _____ me □ _____?

✎ **어휘복습** 잘 안 들리거나 몰라서 체크한 어휘를 써 놓고 복습해 보세요.

□ _____ □ _____ □ _____ □ _____

□ _____ □ _____ □ _____ □ _____

□ _____ □ _____ □ _____ □ _____

대화를 듣고, 남자가 여행을 즐기지 <u>못한</u> 이유로 가장 적절한 것을 고르시오.

① 배탈이 나서
② 많은 돈이 들어서
③ 심한 폭풍우가 와서
④ 호텔 시설이 나빠서
⑤ 길을 여러 번 잃어서

W: Hi, Jason. □ _____ was your □ _____ □ _____ to Thailand?

M: We □ _____ have a □ _____ □ _____.

W: What happened?

M: There was a big □ _____ while we □ _____ there.

W: Oh, did you have to □ _____ in the □ _____ all the time?

M: Yes. It was really □ _____.

다음을 듣고, 두 사람의 대화가 <u>어색한</u> 것을 고르시오.

①   ②   ③   ④   ⑤

① M: □ _____ do you do in your □ _____ □ _____?
  W: I either read □ _____ or watch □ _____.

② M: Let's □ _____ □ _____ this weekend.
  W: That's a □ _____ idea.

③ M: My favorite team □ _____ the □ _____.
  W: I'm □ _____ you lost your □ _____.

④ M: Pardon me. Do you know where an ATM is?
  W: Yes, I do. □ _____ □ _____ in that building.

⑤ M: □ _____ would you like to □ _____ for □ _____?
  W: □ _____ □ _____ something spicy?

✎ **어휘복습** 잘 안 들리거나 몰라서 체크한 어휘를 써 놓고 복습해 보세요.

□ _____   □ _____   □ _____   □ _____

□ _____   □ _____   □ _____   □ _____

□ _____   □ _____   □ _____   □ _____

12 미언급 파악

대화를 듣고, 여자의 옷에 대해 언급되지 않은 것을 고르시오.

① 색상　　　　② 종류
③ 구입 시기　　④ 구입 장소
⑤ 가격

M: That's a beautiful □ _____ □ _____. □ _____ did you buy it?

W: I bought it from an □ _____ □ _____ □ _____.

M: Did you □ _____ a lot □ _____ it?

W: No, I didn't. It □ _____ □ _____ twenty dollars. I got the last dress the store had.

M: Wow. You got □ _____.

W: I think so.

13 교통수단 찾기

대화를 듣고, 여자가 남자에게 제안한 교통수단으로 가장 적절한 것을 고르시오.

① 기차　　　　② 자전거
③ 버스　　　　④ 지하철
⑤ 택시

M: Excuse me. Can I □ _____ □ _____ City Hall?

W: No, it's □ _____ □ _____ to go there □ _____ □ _____.

M: That's too bad. Is there a □ _____ □ _____ around here?

W: Yes, but □ _____ □ _____ go to City Hall from here. Why don't you □ _____ a □ _____?

M: Okay. I will. Thank you.

14 할 일 파악

대화를 듣고, 남자가 대화 직후에 할 일로 가장 적절한 것을 고르시오.

① 병원 가기　　　② 화장실 가기
③ 채소 자르기　　④ 식사 준비하기
⑤ 밴드 가져오기

W: Ouch. That really □ _____.

M: What's the □ _____? Did you □ _____ your □ _____?

W: Yes. I need a □ _____.

M: That looks like a bad cut.

W: It's starting to hurt a bit.

M: Go to the □ _____ and □ _____ it up. I'll □ _____ you a □ _____.

✎ **어휘복습** 잘 안 들리거나 몰라서 체크한 어휘를 써 놓고 복습해 보세요.

□ _____　　□ _____　　□ _____　　□ _____

□ _____　　□ _____　　□ _____　　□ _____

□ _____　　□ _____　　□ _____　　□ _____

15 관계 추론

대화를 듣고, 두 사람의 관계로 가장 적절한 것을 고르시오.

① 교사 – 학생
② 의사 – 환자
③ 영화감독 – 배우
④ 점원 – 손님
⑤ 코치 – 운동선수

W: Good morning, Mr. Kim. Can you □ _____ □ _____ a □ _____?

M: I'll try. What do you need?

W: I'm having □ _____ □ _____ my homework. Can you □ _____ it for me?

M: Okay. Can you □ _____ it □ _____ me now?

W: Yes. It's □ _____ □ _____ in my backpack. Thanks a lot.

16 화제 추론

다음을 듣고, 무엇에 관한 내용인지 가장 적절한 것을 고르시오.

① 방 청소   ② 새 에어컨
③ 에너지 절약   ④ 여름 방학
⑤ 봉사 활동

M: Good morning, everyone. This is Kim Junsu □ _____. Today, I'd like to talk about □ _____ □ _____. We can □ _____ the □ _____. We □ _____ have to □ _____ the □ _____ □ _____. We can also □ _____ □ _____ the □ _____ when we leave a room. Let's try hard to save energy. Thank you.

✎ **어휘복습** 잘 안 들리거나 몰라서 체크한 어휘를 써 놓고 복습해 보세요.

□ _____   □ _____   □ _____   □ _____

□ _____   □ _____   □ _____   □ _____

□ _____   □ _____   □ _____   □ _____

17 위치 찾기

대화를 듣고, 남자가 가려고 하는 장소를 고르시오.

M: Excuse me. Can you tell me the □ _____ □ _____ Pete's Pizza □ _____?

W: Sure. I just had lunch there today.

M: That's great. Where is it from here?

W: Go □ _____ □ _____ □ _____ and then □ _____ □ _____.

M: Okay. So I should go straight one block and then turn right.

W: No, go two blocks. Then, turn right. Pete's Pizza Restaurant is the □ _____ building on the □ _____.

M: Thanks so much.

W: You're welcome.

18 제안 파악

대화를 듣고, 여자가 남자에게 제안한 것으로 가장 적절한 것을 고르시오.

① 짐 풀기
② 창문 열기
③ 여행가방 사기
④ 음식 주문하기
⑤ 티켓 예매하기

M: It's nice to be □ _____ □ _____. It was a long □ _____.

W: I'm so □ _____ from the □ _____. I want to □ _____ on the sofa.

M: We should □ _____ everything □ _____ of our □ _____ first.

W: Let's do that later. Can you □ _____ the □ _____, please? It's really □ _____ in here.

M: Sure. I'll □ _____ some □ _____ □ _____ in the house.

✎ **어휘복습** 잘 안 들리거나 몰라서 체크한 어휘를 써 놓고 복습해 보세요.

□ _____   □ _____   □ _____   □ _____

□ _____   □ _____   □ _____   □ _____

□ _____   □ _____   □ _____   □ _____

19 알맞은 응답 찾기

대화를 듣고, 여자의 마지막 말에 이어질 남자의 응답으로 가장 적절한 것을 고르시오.

Man: _____

① You're welcome.
② I'm glad you like it.
③ It's a birthday present.
④ I bought it at the mall.
⑤ It matches your earrings.

W: □ _____ do you have in the □ _____?
M: This is for you. Why don't you □ _____ it?
W: What a nice □ _____! Let me □ _____ it □ _____.
   How does it □ _____ □ _____ □ _____?
M: It looks wonderful on you.
W: I love it. □ _____ did you □ _____ it?
M: _____

20 알맞은 응답 찾기

대화를 듣고, 여자의 마지막 말에 이어질 남자의 응답으로 가장 적절한 것을 고르시오.

Man: _____

① I go there all the time.
② The library closes at 7 o'clock.
③ There are many good books there.
④ Sure. You can use my library card.
⑤ It's right next to the shopping center.

M: I □ _____ a big □ _____, Alice. Can you help me?
W: Sure. What do you want me to do?
M: I need to □ _____ this □ _____ to the □ _____, but I don't have time to go today.
W: I can take it there now. But I don't know □ _____ the □ _____ is.
M: _____

✎ **어휘복습** 잘 안 들리거나 몰라서 체크한 어휘를 써 놓고 복습해 보세요.

□ _____   □ _____   □ _____   □ _____
□ _____   □ _____   □ _____   □ _____
□ _____   □ _____   □ _____   □ _____

🔊MP3 실전 13

점수
/ 20

01 대화를 듣고, 남자가 그린 그림으로 가장 적절한 것을 고르시오.

①
②
③
④
⑤

02 다음을 듣고, 'this'가 가리키는 것으로 가장 적절한 것을 고르시오.

①
②
③
④
⑤

03 대화를 듣고, 버스가 도착할 시각을 고르시오.

① 6:20　　② 6:25　　③ 6:30
④ 6:35　　⑤ 6:40

04 다음을 듣고, 내일 오후의 날씨로 가장 적절한 것을 고르시오.

①　②　③　④　⑤

05 대화를 듣고, 여자가 가져가지 않을 물건을 고르시오.

① 비옷　　② 수영복　　③ 티셔츠
④ 반바지　　⑤ 운동화

06 다음을 듣고, 두 사람의 대화가 어색한 것을 고르시오.

①　　②　　③　　④　　⑤

07 대화를 듣고, 두 사람의 관계로 가장 적절한 것을 고르시오.

① 교사 – 학생
② 주민 – 주민
③ 판매자 – 구매자
④ 변호사 – 의뢰인
⑤ 부동산 중개인 – 고객

08 대화를 듣고, 남자가 여자에게 제안한 교통수단으로 가장 적절한 것을 고르시오.

① 택시　　② 버스　　③ 자동차
④ 지하철　　⑤ 기차

09 대화를 듣고, 무엇에 관한 내용인지 가장 적절한 것을 고르시오.

① 즐겨 가는 해변　　② 지난 휴가
③ 다음 주 날씨　　④ 주말 계획
⑤ 체육 대회 일정

10 대화를 듣고, 남자의 심정으로 가장 적절한 것을 고르시오.

① 신난　　② 화난　　③ 걱정스러운
④ 혼란스러운　　⑤ 자랑스러운

11 대화를 듣고, 여자가 남자의 제안을 거절한 이유로 가장 적절한 것을 고르시오.

① 몸이 아파서
② 도서관에 가야 해서
③ 밴드 연습이 있어서
④ 친구를 만나기로 해서
⑤ 시험 공부를 해야 해서

12 대화를 듣고, 여자가 남자에게 부탁한 일로 가장 적절한 것을 고르시오.

① 진정하기
② 발표하기
③ 시험 준비하기
④ 유인물 나눠주기
⑤ 유인물 출력하기

13 대화를 듣고, 두 사람이 오후에 할 일로 가장 적절한 것을 고르시오.

① 숙제하기
② 요리하기
③ 식당에 가기
④ 과학 공부하기
⑤ 친구 집에서 놀기

14 대화를 듣고, 여자의 마지막 말의 의도로 가장 적절한 것을 고르시오.

① 축하 ② 사과 ③ 격려 ④ 거절 ⑤ 꾸중

15 대화를 듣고, 대화가 이루어지고 있는 장소로 가장 적절한 곳을 고르시오.

① 공원
② 남자의 집
③ 우체국
④ 제과점
⑤ 꽃가게

16 대화를 듣고, 여자가 남자에게 전화한 목적으로 가장 적절한 것을 고르시오.

① 책의 제목을 물어보려고
② 이메일 주소를 물어보려고
③ 책을 사오라고 부탁하려고
④ 도서관의 위치를 물어보려고
⑤ 도서관에 들르는 걸 부탁하려고

17 대화를 듣고, 남자의 직업으로 가장 적절한 것을 고르시오.

① 운전사
② 수의사
③ 조종사
④ 치과의사
⑤ 트레이너

18 대화를 듣고, 두 사람이 만나기로 한 장소로 가장 적절한 곳을 고르시오.

① 박물관
② 여자의 집
③ 남자의 집
④ 버스 정류장
⑤ 지하철역

[19-20] 대화를 듣고, 여자의 마지막 말에 이어질 남자의 응답으로 가장 적절한 것을 고르시오.

19 Man: _____

① I'm sure you'll be amazing.
② Are you going to the festival?
③ What day is the performance?
④ Why didn't you prepare for it?
⑤ I'll be performing there with you.

20 Man: _____

① Actually, I didn't enjoy dinner.
② Can I have the check, please?
③ Okay. I need to buy a few things.
④ What time does the library close?
⑤ Sounds good. Let's leave in
   5 minutes.

01 그림 정보 파악

대화를 듣고, 남자가 그린 그림으로 가장 적절한 것을 고르시오.

① ② ③
④ ⑤

W: That's a nice □ _____. It □ _____ □ _____ the □ _____ and □ _____ behind the school.

M: Thanks for saying that. I love painting □ _____.

W: Really? □ _____ □ _____ □ _____ draw a □ _____ of the □ _____ next time?

M: That's □ _____ a □ _____ idea. I will draw the lake and some □ _____.

W: I □ _____ □ _____ to see that painting.

02 화제 추론

다음을 듣고, 'this'가 가리키는 것으로 가장 적절한 것을 고르시오.

① ② ③
④ ⑤

W: We can find this □ _____ a □ _____. This is □ _____, but this □ _____ □ _____ when we use it □ _____ □ _____. We use this to □ _____ our bodies □ _____. We always use it when we □ _____ a □ _____. And we also use this just to □ _____ our □ _____.

03 숫자 정보 파악

대화를 듣고, 버스가 도착할 시각을 고르시오.

① 6:20 ② 6:25 ③ 6:30
④ 6:35 ⑤ 6:40

M: Everyone is □ _____ □ _____ us at the restaurant.

W: Don't worry. The □ _____ is going to □ _____ soon.

M: But it's already □ _____ □ _____. And we got here □ _____ □ _____ □ _____.

W: The sign says that the □ _____ will get here □ _____ □ _____ □ _____.

M: I hope that sign is right. We're already late.

✎ **어휘복습** 잘 안 들리거나 몰라서 체크한 어휘를 써 놓고 복습해 보세요.

□ _____ □ _____ □ _____ □ _____
□ _____ □ _____ □ _____ □ _____
□ _____ □ _____ □ _____ □ _____

04 날씨 파악

다음을 듣고, 내일 오후의 날씨로 가장 적절한 것을 고르시오.

① ② ③

④ ⑤

M: Good evening, everyone. I'm John Jackson, and I've got the weather report for □ _____. The □ _____ is going to be □ _____ and very □ _____. Later in the □ _____, it's going to □ _____ for one or two hours. But the rain will stop, and it will be □ _____ in the □ _____. Don't forget your umbrella.

05 미언급 파악

대화를 듣고, 여자가 가져가지 <u>않을</u> 물건을 고르시오.

① 비옷   ② 수영복
③ 티셔츠   ④ 반바지
⑤ 운동화

M: Are you □ _____ □ _____ summer camp?

W: Yes, I am. I □ _____ a □ _____, T-shirts, □ _____, and sneakers.

M: Don't you need a □ _____?

W: □ _____. It won't rain □ _____ camp.

M: Are you sure?

W: Yes, I already □ _____ the weather.

✎ **어휘복습** 잘 안 들리거나 몰라서 체크한 어휘를 써 놓고 복습해 보세요.

□ _____   □ _____   □ _____   □ _____
□ _____   □ _____   □ _____   □ _____
□ _____   □ _____   □ _____   □ _____

06 어색한 대화 찾기

다음을 듣고, 두 사람의 대화가 <u>어색한</u> 것을 고르시오.

①   ②   ③   ④   ⑤

① W: □ _____ is your brother □ _____ these days?

    M: He's □ _____ □ _____ now.

② W: □ _____ do you □ _____ □ _____ your new school?

    M: I love it. I have many friends there.

③ W: Are you happy □ _____ the new □ _____?

    M: Yes, I'm happy to □ _____ □ _____ today.

④ W: □ _____ you □ _____ □ _____ drink something cold?

    M: No, thank you.

⑤ W: You □ _____ snowy weather, □ _____ □ _____?

    M: No, I □ _____ like it □ _____ □ _____.

07 관계 추론

대화를 듣고, 두 사람의 관계로 가장 적절한 것을 고르시오.

① 교사 – 학생
② 주민 – 주민
③ 판매자 – 구매자
④ 변호사 – 의뢰인
⑤ 부동산 중개인 – 고객

M: □ _____ floor are you □ _____ □ _____?

W: I'm going to the □ _____ □ _____.

M: Really? □ _____ □ _____ I. Did you just move to this apartment?

W: Yes, my family and I □ _____ □ _____ three days ago.

M: It's a □ _____ to meet you. My name is Dave. I □ _____ □ _____ apartment nine zero four.

W: Wow, I live in apartment nine zero three. We're □ _____ □ _____ □ _____. I'm Jessica.

✏️ **어휘복습** 잘 안 들리거나 몰라서 체크한 어휘를 써 놓고 복습해 보세요.

□ _____   □ _____   □ _____   □ _____

□ _____   □ _____   □ _____   □ _____

□ _____   □ _____   □ _____   □ _____

08 교통수단 찾기

대화를 듣고, 남자가 여자에게 제안한 교통 수단으로 가장 적절한 것을 고르시오.

① 택시
② 버스
③ 자동차
④ 지하철
⑤ 기차

M: Why are you looking at that □ _____?

W: I have to meet my friends in the □ _____. I'm thinking of □ _____ my □ _____ there.

M: Are you going □ _____? You □ _____ drive if you go there.

W: Then should I □ _____ a □ _____?

M: No, the buses are always □ _____ and □ _____. Go there □ _____ □ _____.

W: Okay. Thanks for the □ _____.

09 화제 추론

대화를 듣고, 무엇에 관한 내용인지 가장 적절한 것을 고르시오.

① 즐겨 가는 해변
② 지난 휴가
③ 다음 주 날씨
④ 주말 계획
⑤ 체육 대회 일정

M: Welcome home. Did you have a good time □ _____ □ _____?

W: Yes, I had a □ _____ □ _____ in Sydney.

M: How was the □ _____ there?

W: It was summer, so it was □ _____ and □ _____ every day.

M: Did you go to the □ _____?

W: Yes. I went there almost □ _____ □ _____.

M: You're lucky. I would love to go there.

10 심정 추론

대화를 듣고, 남자의 심정으로 가장 적절한 것을 고르시오.

① 신난
② 화난
③ 걱정스러운
④ 혼란스러운
⑤ 자랑스러운

W: Are you going to □ _____ □ _____ this □ _____?

M: That's right. I'm planning to visit □ _____ □ _____.

W: Wow. I want to do that. Are you □ _____ □ _____ your family?

M: No, I'm going to go □ _____ □ _____. I am so □ _____.

W: That should be a lot of □ _____. □ _____ □ _____ you □ _____ lots of □ _____.

M: I will.

✎ **어휘복습** 잘 안 들리거나 몰라서 체크한 어휘를 써 놓고 복습해 보세요.

□ _____ □ _____ □ _____ □ _____

□ _____ □ _____ □ _____ □ _____

□ _____ □ _____ □ _____ □ _____

11 이유 파악

대화를 듣고, 여자가 남자의 제안을 거절한 이유로 가장 적절한 것을 고르시오.

① 몸이 아파서
② 도서관에 가야 해서
③ 밴드 연습이 있어서
④ 친구를 만나기로 해서
⑤ 시험 공부를 해야 해서

M: Mindy, I'm □ _____ □ _____ study at the □ _____ with Allen. □ _____ you like to □ _____ us?

W: □ _____, □ _____ maybe next time.

M: □ _____ can't you meet us?

W: I have □ _____ □ _____ after school. I □ _____ □ _____ it.

M: I understand. I'll see you later then.

12 부탁 파악

대화를 듣고, 여자가 남자에게 부탁한 일로 가장 적절한 것을 고르시오.

① 진정하기
② 발표하기
③ 시험 준비하기
④ 유인물 나눠주기
⑤ 유인물 출력하기

W: We are □ _____ for our □ _____, aren't we?

M: Yes. We are □ _____, so you □ _____ have to □ _____ □ _____.

W: Let's □ _____ everything for the □ _____ □ _____. □ _____ □ _____ copies of the handouts do we have?

M: We □ _____ forty, but we □ _____ □ _____ thirty-five.

W: That's not good. Can you □ _____ five □ _____ copies?

M: Yes. I'll do that right away.

13 할 일 파악

대화를 듣고, 두 사람이 오후에 할 일로 가장 적절한 것을 고르시오.

① 숙제하기
② 요리하기
③ 식당에 가기
④ 과학 공부하기
⑤ 친구 집에서 놀기

M: Jennifer, are you busy □ _____ □ _____?

W: Yes. I have to □ _____ my math □ _____ today.

M: I have a lot of homework □ _____ □ _____.

W: I'm going to □ _____ □ _____ Carl's house to □ _____ my homework □ _____ □ _____. Why don't you join us?

M: □ _____ □ _____? What time will you go there?

W: We will □ _____ □ _____ one.

✏️ **어휘복습** 잘 안 들리거나 몰라서 체크한 어휘를 써 놓고 복습해 보세요.

□ _____   □ _____   □ _____   □ _____

□ _____   □ _____   □ _____   □ _____

□ _____   □ _____   □ _____   □ _____

14 의도 파악

대화를 듣고, 여자의 마지막 말의 의도로 가장 적절한 것을 고르시오.

① 축하   ② 사과
③ 격려   ④ 거절
⑤ 꾸중

W: Sam, □ _____ do you □ _____ so □ _____? What's the matter?
M: You know my best friend Joe, right?
W: Of course I know Joe. Did something □ _____ □ _____ him?
M: He's □ _____ □ _____ another country tomorrow. I won't □ _____ □ _____ □ _____ see him again.
W: □ _____ □ _____. You can still talk to him online.

15 장소 추론

대화를 듣고, 대화가 이루어지고 있는 장소로 가장 적절한 곳을 고르시오.

① 공원   ② 남자의 집
③ 우체국   ④ 제과점
⑤ 꽃가게

W: Good afternoon. How □ _____ I □ _____ you, sir?
M: Today is my wife's □ _____, so I'd like to get something □ _____ □ _____.
W: □ _____ are always nice. We have some □ _____ tulips, too.
M: I'll □ _____ ten roses. And can you □ _____ them □ _____ a □ _____, please?
W: Yes, I can. I can □ _____ them to your house, too.

16 전화 목적 파악

대화를 듣고, 여자가 남자에게 전화한 목적으로 가장 적절한 것을 고르시오.

① 책의 제목을 물어보려고
② 이메일 주소를 물어보려고
③ 책을 사오라고 부탁하려고
④ 도서관의 위치를 물어보려고
⑤ 도서관에 들르는 걸 부탁하려고

W: Hi, David. I have a question for you.
M: What is it?
W: Are you still □ _____?
M: Yes, I am. But I am going to □ _____ □ _____ soon.
W: Great. Can you □ _____ □ _____ a □ _____ from the library for me?
M: Sure. What's the □ _____?
W: I'll □ _____ you a text □ _____ with the information.

✎ **어휘복습** 잘 안 들리거나 몰라서 체크한 어휘를 써 놓고 복습해 보세요.

□ _____   □ _____   □ _____   □ _____
□ _____   □ _____   □ _____   □ _____
□ _____   □ _____   □ _____   □ _____

17 직업 파악

대화를 듣고, 남자의 직업으로 가장 적절한 것을 고르시오.

① 운전사 ② 수의사
③ 조종사 ④ 치과의사
⑤ 트레이너

M: Hello, Ms. Turner. What can I do for you today?

W: I'm □ _____ a lot of □ _____. It started three days ago.

M: Which □ _____ □ _____?

W: I'm not sure. But it's □ _____ □ _____ □ _____ side of my mouth.

M: Okay. Let me □ _____ □ _____ □ _____. □ _____ your □ _____ and say, "Ah," please.

18 특정 정보 파악

대화를 듣고, 두 사람이 만나기로 한 장소로 가장 적절한 곳을 고르시오.

① 박물관 ② 여자의 집
③ 남자의 집 ④ 버스 정류장
⑤ 지하철역

W: Michael, would you □ _____ □ _____ □ _____ to the museum with me today?

M: Is there a new □ _____?

W: Yes, there are a lot of □ _____.

M: Cool. □ _____ do you want □ _____ □ _____? At your house?

W: No. How about □ _____ the □ _____ □ _____? Is two o'clock okay?

M: It's perfect. I'll see you then.

✎ **어휘복습** 잘 안 들리거나 몰라서 체크한 어휘를 써 놓고 복습해 보세요.

□ _____ □ _____ □ _____ □ _____
□ _____ □ _____ □ _____ □ _____
□ _____ □ _____ □ _____ □ _____

대화를 듣고, 여자의 마지막 말에 이어질 남자의 응답으로 가장 적절한 것을 고르시오.

Man: _____

① I'm sure you'll be amazing.
② Are you going to the festival?
③ What day is the performance?
④ Why didn't you prepare for it?
⑤ I'll be performing there with you.

W: □ _____ did you □ _____ my □ _____?
M: It was □ _____, Claire. Did you □ _____ a lot?
W: Yes, I practice almost every day. I'm going to □ _____ at the □ _____ □ _____ this Saturday.
M: I □ _____ □ _____ to see your performance.
W: I'm □ _____ □ _____ □ _____ it. But I'm very □ _____.
M: _____

대화를 듣고, 여자의 마지막 말에 이어질 남자의 응답으로 가장 적절한 것을 고르시오.

Man: _____

① Actually, I didn't enjoy dinner.
② Can I have the check, please?
③ Okay. I need to buy a few things.
④ What time does the library close?
⑤ Sounds good. Let's leave in 5 minutes.

W: Do you have any plans for today?
M: Not really. I was just going to □ _____ □ _____ and □ _____ a book.
W: □ _____ □ _____ going to the shopping center □ _____ □ _____?
M: That □ _____ □ _____, but I don't want to buy anything.
W: We can just □ _____ □ _____. And I'll buy you □ _____ □ _____ □ _____.
M: _____

✎ **어휘복습** 잘 안 들리거나 몰라서 체크한 어휘를 써 놓고 복습해 보세요.

□ _____ □ _____ □ _____ □ _____
□ _____ □ _____ □ _____ □ _____
□ _____ □ _____ □ _____ □ _____

14회 실전모의고사

◀)) MP3 실전 14

점수 / 20

01 대화를 듣고, 남자의 모습으로 가장 적절한 것을 고르시오.

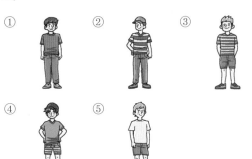

02 다음을 듣고 'I'가 가리키는 것으로 가장 적절한 것을 고르시오.

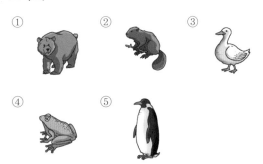

03 대화를 듣고, 여자가 주문하지 <u>않은</u> 것을 고르시오.

① 햄버거　　② 치킨　　③ 감자튀김
④ 콜라　　⑤ 아이스크림

04 대화를 듣고, 여자가 남자에게 부탁한 일로 가장 적절한 것을 고르시오.

① 인쇄하기　　　　② 빨리 일하기
③ 컴퓨터 옮기기　　④ 컴퓨터 고치기
⑤ 보고서 작성하기

05 대화를 듣고, 여자가 어제 한 일로 가장 적절한 것을 고르시오.

① 운동하기　　　　② 영화 보기
③ 친구 만나기　　　④ 휴대폰 찾기
⑤ 병원에서 진찰받기

06 대화를 듣고, 남자가 가려고 하는 장소를 고르시오.

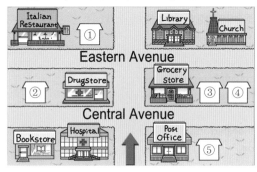

07 대화를 듣고, 영화가 시작하는 시각을 고르시오.

① 5:00　　② 5:30　　③ 5:40
④ 6:40　　⑤ 8:10

08 대화를 듣고, 무엇에 관한 내용인지 가장 적절한 것을 고르시오.

① 체육 수업　　② 학교 축제　　③ 현장 학습
④ 현재 날씨　　⑤ 학교 운동장

09 대화를 듣고, 여자의 장래 희망으로 가장 적절한 것을 고르시오.

① 작가　　② 배우　　③ 감독
④ 기자　　⑤ 가수

10 대화를 듣고, 남자의 심정으로 가장 적절한 것을 고르시오.

① scared　　② bored　　③ worried
④ excited　　⑤ angry

11 다음을 듣고, 내일 부산의 날씨로 가장 적절한 것을 고르시오.

①   ②   ③   ④   ⑤

12 대화를 듣고, 여자의 마지막 말의 의도로 가장 적절한 것을 고르시오.

① 칭찬   ② 사과   ③ 부탁
④ 허락   ⑤ 위로

13 대화를 듣고, 여자가 화난 이유로 가장 적절한 것을 고르시오.

① 휴대폰을 잃어버려서
② 프로젝트가 너무 어려워서
③ 친구가 전화를 받지 않아서
④ 시험에서 낮은 점수를 받아서
⑤ 친구에게 틀린 전화번호를 받아서

14 대화를 듣고, 두 사람의 관계로 가장 적절한 것을 고르시오.

① 아빠 – 딸   ② 의사 – 환자
③ 교사 – 학생   ④ 친구 – 친구
⑤ 경찰 – 시민

15 대화를 듣고, 여자가 남자에게 제안한 것으로 가장 적절한 것을 고르시오.

① 약 먹기   ② 차 마시기
③ 체온 재기   ④ 일찍 잠들기
⑤ 병원에 가기

16 대화를 듣고, 여자가 주말에 할 일로 가장 적절한 것을 고르시오.

① 공항에 가기
② 고모 방문하기
③ 조부모님 배웅하기
④ 고모에게 전화하기
⑤ 부모님과 시간 보내기

17 대화를 듣고, 두 사람이 선택할 교통수단으로 가장 적절한 것을 고르시오.

① 택시   ② 자전거   ③ 버스
④ 기차   ⑤ 지하철

18 다음을 듣고, 두 사람의 대화가 <u>어색한</u> 것을 고르시오.

①   ②   ③   ④   ⑤

[19-20] 대화를 듣고, 남자의 마지막 말에 이어질 여자의 응답으로 가장 적절한 것을 고르시오.

19 Woman: _____

① I think he's French.
② Are you from Italy?
③ I went there last summer.
④ Yes, she loves to play sports.
⑤ Wow. What languages can he speak?

20 Woman: _____

① Thanks for inviting me on the trip.
② Congratulations. You did very well.
③ Yes, we can go swimming together.
④ You can learn to swim at the beach.
⑤ No, I didn't go to the beach this year.

01 그림 정보 파악

대화를 듣고, 남자의 모습으로 가장 적절한 것을 고르시오.

① ② ③
④ ⑤

W: I love your □ _____ □ _____.

M: Thanks. How do you like my □ _____ and □ _____ □ _____ T-shirt?

W: It looks good, too. □ _____ is your new □ _____?

M: I □ _____ it □ _____ my □ _____.

02 화제 추론

다음을 듣고 'I'가 가리키는 것으로 가장 적절한 것을 고르시오.

① ② ③
④ ⑤

W: I □ _____ brown □ _____ and live near ponds and streams. I'm an excellent □ _____. I have a □ _____, □ _____ □ _____ and two very □ _____ □ _____. I use the teeth to □ _____ □ _____ trees. Then, I □ _____ a □ _____ with the trees. I □ _____ □ _____ the dam I make.

03 미언급 파악

대화를 듣고, 여자가 주문하지 않은 것을 고르시오.

① 햄버거   ② 치킨
③ 감자튀김   ④ 콜라
⑤ 아이스크림

M: Hello. May I □ _____ your □ _____, please?

W: Yes. I'd like a hamburger and some □ _____, please.

M: Would you like a □ _____?

W: Yes. I'll □ _____ a small cola. And I'd like an ice cream, too.

M: Is that □ _____ □ _____ or □ _____ □ _____?

W: For here.

M: Okay. Your □ _____ is coming right up.

✎ **어휘복습** 잘 안 들리거나 몰라서 체크한 어휘를 써 놓고 복습해 보세요.

□ _____   □ _____   □ _____   □ _____
□ _____   □ _____   □ _____   □ _____
□ _____   □ _____   □ _____   □ _____

대화를 듣고, 여자가 남자에게 부탁한 일로 가장 적절한 것을 고르시오.

① 인쇄하기   ② 빨리 일하기
③ 컴퓨터 옮기기   ④ 컴퓨터 고치기
⑤ 보고서 작성하기

W: Hey, Steve. Are you busy now?

M: Not really. Do you □ _____ □ _____ ?

W: Yes. Can you □ _____ me □ _____ my □ _____ ?

M: Sure. I'll be there in □ _____ □ _____ □ _____ minutes.

W: Thanks. I have □ _____ □ _____ of things □ _____

    □ _____ .

M: Don't worry about it. See you soon.

대화를 듣고, 여자가 어제 한 일로 가장 적절한 것을 고르시오.

① 운동하기   ② 영화 보기
③ 친구 만나기   ④ 휴대폰 찾기
⑤ 병원에서 진찰받기

M: Hi, Denise. How are you? I □ _____ □ _____ yesterday

    and this morning, but you □ _____ □ _____ the phone.

W: Sorry about that. My phone □ _____ , so it's in the

    □ _____ □ _____ . I was too □ _____ to □ _____ it

    □ _____ .

M: Yeah? What did you do □ _____ ?

W: Yesterday, I had to □ _____ my old friend □ _____

    □ _____ □ _____ .

M: What about □ _____ □ _____ ?

W: I went to the □ _____ .

✎ **어휘복습** 잘 안 들리거나 몰라서 체크한 어휘를 써 놓고 복습해 보세요.

□ _____   □ _____   □ _____   □ _____

□ _____   □ _____   □ _____   □ _____

□ _____   □ _____   □ _____   □ _____

06 위치 찾기

대화를 듣고, 남자가 가려고 하는 장소를 고르시오.

M: Excuse me. Can you □ _____ me □ _____ the fitness center □ _____?

W: Sure. It's near here. Go straight □ _____ you □ _____ □ _____ Eastern Avenue.

M: □ _____ □ _____ to Eastern Avenue? Okay.

W: Then, turn left □ _____ □ _____ □ _____. You'll see a drugstore on the left.

M: Is the fitness center □ _____ □ _____ it?

W: No, it's not. It's □ _____ the street □ _____ the drugstore.

07 숫자 정보 파악

대화를 듣고, 영화가 시작하는 시각을 고르시오.

① 5:00   ② 5:30
③ 5:40   ④ 6:40
⑤ 8:10

M: Lisa, □ _____ □ _____ □ _____ the new action □ _____ with me?

W: Okay. My brother said it's really good.

M: I'm going to □ _____ tickets □ _____. □ _____ □ _____ is good for you?

W: □ _____ □ _____ after five P.M. is fine.

M: We can see the □ _____ □ _____ showing. It □ _____ at □ _____ □ _____.

W: That's perfect.

✎ **어휘복습** 잘 안 들리거나 몰라서 체크한 어휘를 써 놓고 복습해 보세요.

□ _____   □ _____   □ _____   □ _____

□ _____   □ _____   □ _____   □ _____

□ _____   □ _____   □ _____   □ _____

08 화제 추론

대화를 듣고, 무엇에 관한 내용인지 가장 적절한 것을 고르시오.

① 체육 수업　　② 학교 축제
③ 현장 학습　　④ 현재 날씨
⑤ 학교 운동장

W: Hello.

M: Hello, Gina. It's Dave. The □ _____ is □ _____.
Do you want to □ _____ □ _____?

W: What are you talking about? It's □ _____ □ _____.

M: It's not raining. The □ _____ □ _____ about thirty minutes ago.

W: Are you □ _____ about that?

M: Yes, I just checked. Let's meet at the □ _____ in five minutes.

09 장래 희망 파악

대화를 듣고, 여자의 장래 희망으로 가장 적절한 것을 고르시오.

① 작가　　② 배우
③ 감독　　④ 기자
⑤ 가수

M: Is this you in the picture? I didn't know you □ _____ on □ _____.

W: That's a □ _____ of □ _____ three years ago. It was my □ _____ □ _____.

M: Do you □ _____ □ _____ on stage?

W: I love it. I □ _____ to be a □ _____ □ _____ in the future.

M: Good luck. I hope you can do it.

10 심정 추론

대화를 듣고, 남자의 심정으로 가장 적절한 것을 고르시오.

① scared　　② bored
③ worried　　④ excited
⑤ angry

M: I went to the □ _____ □ _____ today.

W: Did you have a □ _____ □ _____ there?

M: □ _____, I did. I went on the □ _____ □ _____.

W: Oh, roller coasters are really □ _____.

M: I don't think so. I □ _____ it was □ _____.

✎ **어휘복습** 잘 안 들리거나 몰라서 체크한 어휘를 써 놓고 복습해 보세요.

□ _____　　□ _____　　□ _____　　□ _____
□ _____　　□ _____　　□ _____　　□ _____
□ _____　　□ _____　　□ _____　　□ _____

11 날씨 파악

다음을 듣고, 내일 부산의 날씨로 가장 적절한 것을 고르시오.

① ② ③
④ ⑤

W: Now, it's ☐ _____ ☐ _____ tomorrow's weather ☐ _____ . There's a ☐ _____ ☐ _____ coming here ☐ _____ the ☐ _____ . So the weather in Seoul will be ☐ _____ . The ☐ _____ ☐ _____ of the country will ☐ _____ some ☐ _____ . There will be ☐ _____ skies in Daejeon and Cheongju. But there will be ☐ _____ ☐ _____ ☐ _____ in Busan and Gwangju.

12 의도 파악

대화를 듣고, 여자의 마지막 말의 의도로 가장 적절한 것을 고르시오.

① 칭찬 ② 사과
③ 부탁 ④ 허락
⑤ 위로

M: All right, I'm all ☐ _____ .
W: Did you just finish your ☐ _____ ☐ _____ ?
M: Yes, I did. I ☐ _____ it was pretty ☐ _____ .
W: Really? Then can you ☐ _____ me ☐ _____ to solve this problem, please?
M: Let me see... Ah, just give me a ☐ _____ of ☐ _____ . I will show you how to do it.
W: That's ☐ _____ . You're the ☐ _____ ☐ _____ in the class.

13 이유 파악

대화를 듣고, 여자가 화난 이유로 가장 적절한 것을 고르시오.

① 휴대폰을 잃어버려서
② 프로젝트가 너무 어려워서
③ 친구가 전화를 받지 않아서
④ 시험에서 낮은 점수를 받아서
⑤ 친구에게 틀린 전화번호를 받아서

M: ☐ _____ were you trying to call ☐ _____ ☐ _____ ☐ _____ ?
W: Mark. I need to ☐ _____ ☐ _____ him. But he ☐ _____ ☐ _____ his ☐ _____ .
M: ☐ _____ do you need to speak with him?
W: We were going to ☐ _____ our ☐ _____ ☐ _____ together. Now, I'll have to do it ☐ _____ ☐ _____ .
M: That's not good. ☐ _____ ☐ _____ him again.
W: There's no use. His phone is ☐ _____ ☐ _____ now.

✏ **어휘복습** 잘 안 들리거나 몰라서 체크한 어휘를 써 놓고 복습해 보세요.

☐ _____ ☐ _____ ☐ _____ ☐ _____
☐ _____ ☐ _____ ☐ _____ ☐ _____
☐ _____ ☐ _____ ☐ _____ ☐ _____

대화를 듣고, 두 사람의 관계로 가장 적절한 것을 고르시오.

① 아빠 – 딸
② 의사 – 환자
③ 교사 – 학생
④ 친구 – 친구
⑤ 경찰 – 시민

M: Jenny, I need to □ _____ with you □ _____ □ _____ □ _____.
W: Sure, Mr. Rogers. □ _____ can I □ _____ for you?
M: You □ _____ do very □ _____ on your last □ _____. What happened?
W: I □ _____ □ _____ the test, so I didn't study for it.
M: I see. You □ _____ □ _____ write the test date □ _____ □ _____ □ _____.
W: I will. Thank you for your □ _____.

15 제안 파악

대화를 듣고, 여자가 남자에게 제안한 것으로 가장 적절한 것을 고르시오.

① 약 먹기
② 차 마시기
③ 체온 재기
④ 일찍 잠들기
⑤ 병원에 가기

M: I don't □ _____ □ _____ right now.
W: You □ _____ □ _____. What's the matter?
M: I have a □ _____ and a □ _____ □ _____. I think I should □ _____ some □ _____.
W: You don't need to do that.
M: □ _____ □ _____? Then what should I do?
W: Just □ _____ some □ _____ and □ _____ some hot □ _____. That's better than taking medicine.

16 할 일 파악

대화를 듣고, 여자가 주말에 할 일로 가장 적절한 것을 고르시오.

① 공항에 가기
② 고모 방문하기
③ 조부모님 배웅하기
④ 고모에게 전화하기
⑤ 부모님과 시간 보내기

W: Are your grandparents □ _____ to □ _____ this Saturday?
M: Yes, they are. So I'm going to □ _____ them □ _____ at the airport in the morning.
W: I hope you □ _____ □ _____ with them. Please tell them I said hi.
M: I will. What are you going to do?
W: I'm going to □ _____ my □ _____ in □ _____ □ _____. I usually go there □ _____ a month.
M: Have a nice weekend.

✎ **어휘복습** 잘 안 들리거나 몰라서 체크한 어휘를 써 놓고 복습해 보세요.

□ _____   □ _____   □ _____   □ _____
□ _____   □ _____   □ _____   □ _____
□ _____   □ _____   □ _____   □ _____

17 교통수단 찾기

대화를 듣고, 두 사람이 선택할 교통수단으로 가장 적절한 것을 고르시오.

① 택시　　② 자전거
③ 버스　　④ 기차
⑤ 지하철

M: □ _____ □ _____ □ _____ out the window. Look at all of the snow on the ground.

W: I can't believe it. □ _____ can we □ _____ □ _____ school?

M: We can't □ _____ our □ _____.

W: You're right. That won't be □ _____.

M: The weather report says it's going to □ _____ □ _____ □ _____. So we can't □ _____ a □ _____ or □ _____ to school.

W: I think we should □ _____ the □ _____.

M: I agree. Let's leave now.

18 어색한 대화 찾기

다음을 듣고, 두 사람의 대화가 <u>어색한</u> 것을 고르시오.

①　　②　　③　　④　　⑤

① W: □ _____ □ _____ □ _____ how to play the guitar?
   M: □ _____, but I play the flute in the school band.
② W: □ _____ you □ _____ in reading this book?
   M: □ _____, I'm reading a book now.
③ W: My friend Tina and I are □ _____ □ _____ tomorrow.
   M: Have a good time.
④ W: The shirt □ _____ twenty dollars.
   M: Okay. I'll □ _____ it.
⑤ W: I'm getting □ _____.
   M: Let's □ _____ at a □ _____ then.

✎ **어휘복습** 잘 안 들리거나 몰라서 체크한 어휘를 써 놓고 복습해 보세요.

□ _____　　□ _____　　□ _____　　□ _____
□ _____　　□ _____　　□ _____　　□ _____
□ _____　　　　　　　　　□ _____

19 알맞은 응답 찾기

대화를 듣고, 남자의 마지막 말에 이어질 여자의 응답으로 가장 적절한 것을 고르시오.

Woman: _____

① I think he's French.
② Are you from Italy?
③ I went there last summer.
④ Yes, she loves to play sports.
⑤ Wow. What languages can he speak?

M: □ _____ □ _____ □ _____ the new student?

W: Are you □ _____ □ _____ Justin?

M: That's right. □ _____ □ _____ Australia.

W: I □ _____ know his □ _____. What do you know about him?

M: He enjoys sports, and he can □ _____ □ _____ □ _____.

W: _____

20 알맞은 응답 찾기

대화를 듣고, 남자의 마지막 말에 이어질 여자의 응답으로 가장 적절한 것을 고르시오.

Woman: _____

① Thanks for inviting me on the trip.
② Congratulations. You did very well.
③ Yes, we can go swimming together.
④ You can learn to swim at the beach.
⑤ No, I didn't go to the beach this year.

M: My parents and I decided to □ _____ □ _____ a □ _____ tomorrow.

W: □ _____ are you □ _____?

M: We're going □ _____ the □ _____. We'll be there for □ _____ □ _____.

W: That □ _____ like □ _____. Aren't you excited?

M: Not really. I don't know □ _____ to □ _____.

W: _____

✎ **어휘복습** 잘 안 들리거나 몰라서 체크한 어휘를 써 놓고 복습해 보세요.

□ _____	□ _____	□ _____	□ _____
□ _____	□ _____	□ _____	□ _____
□ _____	□ _____	□ _____	□ _____

01 다음을 듣고, 무엇에 관한 내용인지 가장 적절한 것을 고르시오.

① 건물 청소
② 계단 공사
③ 아파트 분리수거
④ 엘리베이터 수리
⑤ 엘리베이터 안전 규칙

02 대화를 듣고, 무엇에 관한 내용인지 가장 적절한 것을 고르시오.

① 교통수단
② 이동 시간
③ 주말 날씨
④ 지역 축제
⑤ 여름 방학

03 다음을 듣고, 오늘 런던의 날씨로 가장 적절한 것을 고르시오.

04 다음을 듣고, 여자가 언급하지 않은 것을 고르시오.

① 일상 활동
② 날씨
③ 생각
④ 시험 일정
⑤ 미래 계획

05 대화를 듣고, 남자가 여자에게 제안한 것으로 가장 적절한 것을 고르시오.

① 생일파티 가기
② 생일선물 사기
③ 전화하기
④ 병문안 가기
⑤ 이메일 보내기

06 대화를 듣고, 해가 뜨는 시각을 고르시오.

① 5:15
② 5:30
③ 5:40
④ 5:45
⑤ 5:55

07 대화를 듣고, 남자의 심정으로 가장 적절한 것을 고르시오.

① 기대
② 실망
③ 두려움
④ 부러움
⑤ 지루함

08 대화를 듣고, 여자가 옷을 받지 못한 이유로 가장 적절한 것을 고르시오.

① 입금하지 않아서
② 주문이 취소돼서
③ 맞는 사이즈가 없어서
④ 잘못된 주소로 배달돼서
⑤ 상품이 아직 배송 중이어서

09 대화를 듣고, 두 사람의 관계로 가장 적절한 것을 고르시오.

① 친구 – 친구
② 아빠 – 딸
③ 직원 – 고객
④ 사진작가 – 모델
⑤ 화가 – 관람객

10 다음을 듣고, 그림을 가장 적절히 묘사한 것을 고르시오.

① ② ③ ④ ⑤

11 대화를 듣고, 여자가 이번 주말에 할 일로 가장 적절한 것을 고르시오.

① 낚시하기   ② 숙제하기   ③ 여행하기
④ 책 빌리기   ⑤ 친구 방문하기

12 대화를 듣고, 여자에 대한 설명과 일치하는 것을 고르시오.

① 요리사이다.   ② 소설을 읽고 있다.
③ 요리를 즐겨 한다.   ④ 케이크를 먹고 있다.
⑤ 식사를 준비하고 있다.

13 대화를 듣고, 남자가 여자에게 부탁한 일로 가장 적절한 것을 고르시오.

① 집에 데려다 주기   ② 공책 가져다 주기
③ 준비물 잊지 말기   ④ 역사 공부 도와주기
⑤ 학교로 마중 나오기

14 대화를 듣고, 여자의 마지막 말의 의도로 가장 적절한 것을 고르시오.

① 거절   ② 칭찬   ③ 허락
④ 초대   ⑤ 위로

15 대화를 듣고, 남자가 가려고 하는 장소를 고르시오.

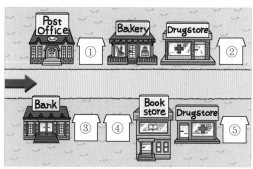

16 대화를 듣고, 여자가 수강할 과목이 <u>아닌</u> 것을 고르시오.

① 체육   ② 역사   ③ 미술
④ 음악   ⑤ 과학

17 다음을 듣고, 두 사람의 대화가 <u>어색한</u> 것을 고르시오.

①   ②   ③   ④   ⑤

18 다음을 듣고, Wendy가 점원에게 할 말로 가장 적절한 것을 고르시오.

Wendy: _____

① How much is it?
② I want to buy pants, too.
③ I need something smaller.
④ Can you show me a red shirt?
⑤ Do you have something bigger?

[19-20] 대화를 듣고, 남자의 마지막 말에 이어질 여자의 응답으로 가장 적절한 것을 고르시오.

19 Woman: _____

① Yes, it is.
② I'll go home soon.
③ It's for here, please.
④ Here's your change.
⑤ That's right. Two donuts.

20 Woman: _____

① No, I can't ski.
② It's very cold today.
③ I'm sorry to hear that.
④ That's wonderful news.
⑤ What happened to his arm?

01 화제 추론

다음을 듣고, 무엇에 관한 내용인지 가장 적절한 것을 고르시오.

① 건물 청소
② 계단 공사
③ 아파트 분리수거
④ 엘리베이터 수리
⑤ 엘리베이터 안전 규칙

M: Good morning, everyone. I would like to tell you something important about the □ _____ . It is □ _____ □ _____ now. A □ _____ is going to arrive in about twenty minutes. He will try to □ _____ the □ _____ . Until then, please □ _____ the □ _____ up and down. I'm sorry if this □ _____ you □ _____ □ _____ .

02 화제 추론

대화를 듣고, 무엇에 관한 내용인지 가장 적절한 것을 고르시오.

① 교통수단   ② 이동 시간
③ 주말 날씨   ④ 지역 축제
⑤ 여름 방학

M: □ _____ was your □ _____ to Busan last weekend?
W: It was great. But it □ _____ so □ _____ to get there.
M: □ _____ □ _____ did it take?
W: It □ _____ □ _____ five hours. But it took eight hours □ _____ □ _____ .
M: The same thing □ _____ to me □ _____ □ _____ . It took ten hours to get to Yeosu.
W: I can't believe it!

03 날씨 파악

다음을 듣고, 오늘 런던의 날씨로 가장 적절한 것을 고르시오.

① ② ③
④ ⑤

M: Hello, everyone. It's time for the □ _____ weather □ _____ . New York and L.A. will have □ _____ weather □ _____ . There will be □ _____ □ _____ in Paris and Rome. London will have very □ _____ weather. Tokyo and Seoul will □ _____ have □ _____ weather. And Bangkok will be □ _____ and sunny.

✎ 어휘복습 잘 안 들리거나 몰라서 체크한 어휘를 써 놓고 복습해 보세요.

□ _____   □ _____   □ _____   □ _____
□ _____   □ _____   □ _____   □ _____
□ _____   □ _____   □ _____   □ _____

다음을 듣고, 여자가 언급하지 <u>않은</u> 것을 고르시오.

① 일상 활동　　② 날씨
③ 생각　　　　④ 시험 일정
⑤ 미래 계획

W: My name is Mina. Every day, I □ _____ in my □ _____. I write □ _____ □ _____ one page each time. I write about many things. Sometimes I write about my □ _____ □ _____ and □ _____. I like to write down my □ _____, too. Sometimes I write about my □ _____ for the □ _____. Nobody can read my □ _____. It's only for me.

05 제안 파악

대화를 듣고, 남자가 여자에게 제안한 것으로 가장 적절한 것을 고르시오.

① 생일파티 가기　② 생일선물 사기
③ 전화하기　　　④ 병문안 가기
⑤ 이메일 보내기

M: I'm going to Tina's birthday party. How about you?
W: I'd □ _____ □ _____, □ _____ I □ _____. My sister is in the hospital.
M: Really? Tina □ _____ you're □ _____.
W: I didn't know that.
M: You □ _____ □ _____ her and □ _____ □ _____ missing her party.
W: Okay. I will.

06 숫자 정보 파악

대화를 듣고, 해가 뜨는 시각을 고르시오.

① 5:15　　　　② 5:30
③ 5:40　　　　④ 5:45
⑤ 5:55

W: □ _____ will the □ _____ □ _____?
M: It should rise □ _____ minutes □ _____ □ _____.
W: □ _____ □ _____ is it?
M: It's five □ _____.
W: So it will rise at five □ _____. Thanks.

✎ **어휘복습** 잘 안 들리거나 몰라서 체크한 어휘를 써 놓고 복습해 보세요.

□ _____　□ _____　□ _____　□ _____
□ _____　□ _____　□ _____　□ _____
□ _____　□ _____　□ _____　□ _____

07 심정 추론

대화를 듣고, 남자의 심정으로 가장 적절한 것을 고르시오.

① 기대
② 실망
③ 두려움
④ 부러움
⑤ 지루함

W: Are you □ _____ □ _____ □ _____ Mexico this summer vacation?

M: Yes. My □ _____ lives there. So I'll visit him and □ _____ □ _____.

W: I □ _____ you a lot. What will you do there?

M: I'll □ _____ some □ _____ in the jungle there.

W: That sounds □ _____.

M: You're right. I □ _____ □ _____ to go.

08 이유 파악

대화를 듣고, 여자가 옷을 받지 못한 이유로 가장 적절한 것을 고르시오.

① 입금하지 않아서
② 주문이 취소돼서
③ 맞는 사이즈가 없어서
④ 잘못된 주소로 배달돼서
⑤ 상품이 아직 배송 중이어서

M: Did you □ _____ the dress you □ _____ □ _____?

W: No, I didn't.

M: Why not?

W: The store □ _____ □ _____ my □ _____. I have to □ _____ □ _____ Friday.

M: I'm sorry to hear that.

W: It's all right. I don't mind.

09 관계 추론

대화를 듣고, 두 사람의 관계로 가장 적절한 것을 고르시오.

① 친구 – 친구
② 아빠 – 딸
③ 직원 – 고객
④ 사진작가 – 모델
⑤ 화가 – 관람객

M: Johnson □ _____ Service. May I help you?

W: Hello. My digital camera □ _____ □ _____.

M: Did you □ _____ it on the □ _____?

W: No, I didn't. It just stopped □ _____ □ _____.

M: I see. Please □ _____ it to the □ _____ center.

W: Okay. I'll do that this afternoon.

✎ **어휘복습** 잘 안 들리거나 몰라서 체크한 어휘를 써 놓고 복습해 보세요.

□ _____   □ _____   □ _____   □ _____

□ _____   □ _____   □ _____   □ _____

□ _____   □ _____   □ _____   □ _____

10 그림 정보 파악

다음을 듣고, 그림을 가장 적절히 묘사한 것을 고르시오.

① ② ③ ④ ⑤

① There is a □ _____ □ _____ the □ _____.
② There is a □ _____ sleeping □ _____ the □ _____.
③ There is a □ _____ □ _____ the □ _____.
④ There is a □ _____ □ _____ the □ _____.
⑤ There is a □ _____ □ _____ the □ _____.

11 할 일 파악

대화를 듣고, 여자가 이번 주말에 할 일로 가장 적절한 것을 고르시오.

① 낚시하기
② 숙제하기
③ 여행하기
④ 책 빌리기
⑤ 친구 방문하기

W: What are your □ _____ for this □ _____?
M: I'm not sure. I might □ _____ my □ _____ in Incheon. How about you?
W: I'll □ _____ time at the □ _____. I have to □ _____ my English □ _____.
M: □ _____ □ _____. I hope you finish it.
W: Thanks. Have a great weekend.

12 내용 일치 파악

대화를 듣고, 여자에 대한 설명과 일치하는 것을 고르시오.

① 요리사이다.
② 소설을 읽고 있다.
③ 요리를 즐겨 한다.
④ 케이크를 먹고 있다.
⑤ 식사를 준비하고 있다.

M: Hi, Cindy. □ _____ are you □ _____ now?
W: Good evening, Tim. I'm □ _____ a □ _____.
M: □ _____ □ _____ of magazine is it?
W: It's about □ _____.
M: Really? Do you □ _____ cooking?
W: I love it. I □ _____ □ _____ cakes and cookies.
M: I'd like to □ _____ them sometime.

✎ **어휘복습** 잘 안 들리거나 몰라서 체크한 어휘를 써 놓고 복습해 보세요.

□ _____ □ _____ □ _____ □ _____
□ _____ □ _____ □ _____ □ _____
□ _____ □ _____ □ _____ □ _____

13 부탁 파악

대화를 듣고, 남자가 여자에게 부탁한 일로 가장 적절한 것을 고르시오.

① 집에 데려다 주기
② 공책 가져다 주기
③ 준비물 잊지 말기
④ 역사 공부 도와주기
⑤ 학교로 마중 나오기

W: Hello.

M: Hi, Mom. It's Joe. I'm □ _____ you are □ _____
    □ _____ now.

W: What do you need, Joe?

M: I □ _____ my history □ _____ on my □ _____. Can you
    please □ _____ it to □ _____?

W: □ _____, but please □ _____ □ _____ again.

M: I'll try to □ _____, Mom. Thanks.

14 의도 파악

대화를 듣고, 여자의 마지막 말의 의도로 가장 적절한 것을 고르시오.

① 거절   ② 칭찬
③ 허락   ④ 초대
⑤ 위로

M: Ms. Lee, I □ _____ □ _____ my □ _____.

W: Did you □ _____ it □ _____?

M: Yes, I did. □ _____ I □ _____ the classroom now?

W: Wait a □ _____. Please give me your paper. I'll □ _____
    □ _____ □ _____ at it.

M: Here you are.

W: Okay. You □ _____ □ _____ □ _____ now.

✎ **어휘복습** 잘 안 들리거나 몰라서 체크한 어휘를 써 놓고 복습해 보세요.

□ _____   □ _____   □ _____   □ _____

□ _____   □ _____   □ _____   □ _____

□ _____   □ _____   □ _____   □ _____

15 위치 찾기

대화를 듣고, 남자가 가려고 하는 장소를 고르시오.

M: Excuse me. □ _____ □ _____ a stationery store □ _____ □ _____?

W: Yes, there is. Just go straight □ _____ this □ _____.

M: Just □ _____ □ _____? That's it?

W: Yes, it's on the □ _____ □ _____ of the street. It's beside a drugstore.

M: □ _____ a □ _____? That's easy.

W: Be careful. There's □ _____ drugstore □ _____ the □ _____.

M: Okay. Thanks.

16 미언급 파악

대화를 듣고, 여자가 수강할 과목이 <u>아닌</u> 것을 고르시오.

① 체육　　　② 역사
③ 미술　　　④ 음악
⑤ 과학

W: I have to buy some □ _____ for school.

M: How many □ _____ will you □ _____ this fall?

W: I will have □ _____ □ _____. I'm □ _____ English, □ _____, history, and music.

M: What are □ _____ □ _____ □ _____? Will you study □ _____?

W: No, I won't. The other two are □ _____ and □ _____.

M: Good luck.

✎ **어휘복습** 잘 안 들리거나 몰라서 체크한 어휘를 써 놓고 복습해 보세요.

□ _____　　□ _____　　□ _____　　□ _____

□ _____　　□ _____　　□ _____　　□ _____

□ _____　　□ _____　　□ _____　　□ _____

17 어색한 대화 찾기

다음을 듣고, 두 사람의 대화가 <u>어색한</u> 것을 고르시오.

①   ②   ③   ④   ⑤

① M: May I □ _____ your □ _____, please?

    W: Yes. I'll □ _____ a cheeseburger and fries.

② M: Hello. □ _____ I □ _____ with Janet?

    W: Yes, I □ _____ □ _____ her yesterday.

③ M: □ _____ □ _____ is your sister?

    W: She's □ _____ □ _____ old.

④ M: □ _____ may I □ _____ you?

    W: I □ _____ □ _____ find a present for my friend.

⑤ M: □ _____ didn't you go to school today?

    W: I had a bad □ _____.

18 상황에 적절한 말 찾기

다음을 듣고, Wendy가 점원에게 할 말로 가장 적절한 것을 고르시오.

Wendy: _____

① How much is it?

② I want to buy pants, too.

③ I need something smaller.

④ Can you show me a red shirt?

⑤ Do you have something bigger?

W: Wendy wanted to buy a □ _____ □ _____ her □ _____ for his birthday. She □ _____ the clerk □ _____ □ _____ her a □ _____ shirt. The clerk showed Wendy a green shirt. It □ _____ very □ _____. But the shirt looked □ _____ □ _____ for her father. In this situation, what would Wendy most likely say to the clerk?

Wendy: _____

✎ **어휘복습** 잘 안 들리거나 몰라서 체크한 어휘를 써 놓고 복습해 보세요.

□ _____   □ _____   □ _____   □ _____

□ _____   □ _____   □ _____   □ _____

□ _____   □ _____   □ _____   □ _____

19 알맞은 응답 찾기

대화를 듣고, 남자의 마지막 말에 이어질 여자의 응답으로 가장 적절한 것을 고르시오.

Woman: _____

① Yes, it is.
② I'll go home soon.
③ It's for here, please.
④ Here's your change.
⑤ That's right. Two donuts.

M: Good afternoon. □ _____ □ _____ Dave's Donuts.

W: Hi. I'd like to □ _____, please.

M: Sure. □ _____ would you like to □ _____?

W: I'd like two jelly □ _____ and a □ _____.

M: No problem. Is this □ _____ □ _____ or □ _____
   □ _____?

W: _____

20 알맞은 응답 찾기

대화를 듣고, 남자의 마지막 말에 이어질 여자의 응답으로 가장 적절한 것을 고르시오.

Woman: _____

① No, I can't ski.
② It's very cold today.
③ I'm sorry to hear that.
④ That's wonderful news.
⑤ What happened to his arm?

W: Winter was too long and cold this year.

M: I agree. What did you do □ _____ winter □ _____?

W: □ _____ □ _____. How about you?

M: My brother and I □ _____ □ _____. But he □ _____ his
   □ _____.

W: That's □ _____. How is he doing?

M: He's □ _____ in the □ _____.

W: _____

✎ **어휘복습** 잘 안 들리거나 몰라서 체크한 어휘를 써 놓고 복습해 보세요.

□ _____   □ _____   □ _____   □ _____
□ _____   □ _____   □ _____   □ _____
□ _____   □ _____   □ _____   □ _____

01 다음을 듣고, 무엇에 관한 내용인지 가장 적절한 것을 고르시오.

① 건강 수칙　　　② 건강 검진
③ 구급약　　　　④ 학급 규칙
⑤ 새 보건교사

02 다음을 듣고, 서울의 오후 날씨로 가장 적절한 것을 고르시오.

① 　② 　③ 　④ 　⑤

03 대화를 듣고, 두 사람이 대화 직후에 할 일로 가장 적절한 것을 고르시오.

① 소풍 가기　　　② 집 청소하기
③ 식사 주문하기　④ 슈퍼마켓 가기
⑤ 샌드위치 만들기

04 대화를 듣고, 두 사람이 살 물건이 <u>아닌</u> 것을 고르시오.

① 필통　　　② 가방　　　③ 펜
④ 지우개　　⑤ 공책

05 대화를 듣고, 여자가 집에 도착할 시각을 고르시오.

① 3:00　　　② 3:30　　　③ 4:00
④ 4:30　　　⑤ 5:00

06 대화를 듣고, 남자의 마지막 말의 의도로 가장 적절한 것을 고르시오.

① 칭찬　　　② 제안　　　③ 사과
④ 축하　　　⑤ 거절

07 대화를 듣고, 여자의 심정으로 가장 적절한 것을 고르시오.

① 기쁨　　　② 걱정　　　③ 실망
④ 설렘　　　⑤ 놀람

08 대화를 듣고, 남자의 직업으로 가장 적절한 것을 고르시오.

① 배달원　　　② 마술사　　　③ 미용사
④ 제빵사　　　⑤ 소방관

09 대화를 듣고, 여자가 요즘 읽는 책으로 가장 적절한 것을 고르시오.

① 　② 　③

④ 　⑤

10 다음을 듣고, 남자의 장래 희망으로 가장 적절한 것을 고르시오.

① 소방관　　　② 경찰관　　　③ 의사
④ 교사　　　　⑤ 군인

11 대화를 듣고, 두 사람이 만날 장소로 가장 적절한 곳을 고르시오.

① 공원   ② 학교   ③ 남자의 집
④ 여자의 집   ⑤ 영화관

12 대화를 듣고, 두 사람의 관계로 가장 적절한 것을 고르시오.

① 교사 – 학생
② 요리사 – 손님
③ 버스 운전사 – 승객
④ 가게 주인 – 종업원
⑤ 여행 가이드 – 관광객

13 대화를 듣고, 여자가 남자를 태워줄 수 <u>없는</u> 이유로 가장 적절한 것을 고르시오.

① 몸이 아파서
② 병원에 가야 해서
③ 차에 문제가 있어서
④ 외갓집에 가야 해서
⑤ 저녁을 준비해야 해서

14 대화를 듣고, 여자가 남자에게 부탁한 일로 가장 적절한 것을 고르시오.

① 길 묻기   ② 물건 사기   ③ 식당 찾기
④ 지도 찾기   ⑤ 인터넷 검색하기

15 대화를 듣고, 남자가 가려고 하는 장소를 고르시오.

16 다음을 듣고, 두 사람의 대화가 <u>어색한</u> 것을 고르시오.

①   ②   ③   ④   ⑤

17 대화를 듣고, 여자가 남자에게 전화한 목적으로 가장 적절한 것을 고르시오.

① 생일파티에 초대하려고
② 시험 날짜를 물어보려고
③ 시험 성적을 물어보려고
④ 수학 공부를 같이 하려고
⑤ 수학 시험 범위를 물어보려고

18 다음 상황 설명을 듣고, Sumi가 판매원에게 할 말로 가장 적절한 것을 고르시오.

Sumi: _____
① Thanks for saying that.
② You can put it in the bag.
③ No, I'm not wearing a scarf.
④ No thanks. It costs too much.
⑤ Yes, you can show me another one.

[19-20] 대화를 듣고, 여자의 마지막 말에 이어질 남자의 응답으로 가장 적절한 것을 고르시오.

19 Man: _____
① How much is it?
② Let's do a puzzle then.
③ Yes, we can watch a movie.
④ I see. You don't like puzzles.
⑤ How about going out for dinner?

20 Man: _____
① I want to see a robot.
② Yes, we can go together.
③ Your science project is great.
④ There are many kinds of food.
⑤ Do you want to come with me?

01 화제 추론

다음을 듣고, 무엇에 관한 내용인지 가장 적절한 것을 고르시오.

① 건강 수칙 ② 건강 검진
③ 구급약 ④ 학급 규칙
⑤ 새 보건교사

W: Everyone, please □ _____ □ _____. My name is Ms. Park. I'm the □ _____ □ _____. We want every student to be □ _____ this year. So please □ _____ these three □ _____. First, always □ _____ your □ _____ with soap when you go to the bathroom. Second, □ _____ your □ _____ when you □ _____ or □ _____. Third, if you □ _____ □ _____, □ _____ me or your □ _____.

02 날씨 파악

다음을 듣고, 서울의 오후 날씨로 가장 적절한 것을 고르시오.

① ② ③
④ ⑤

M: Good morning. It's time for today's weather report for Seoul. Right □ _____, it's very □ _____ and □ _____. It will □ _____ for □ _____ □ _____ □ _____ hours in the □ _____. Then, the clouds will disappear, and there will be □ _____ □ _____ in the □ _____. The weather will be a bit □ _____ at □ _____.

03 할 일 파악

대화를 듣고, 두 사람이 대화 직후에 할 일로 가장 적절한 것을 고르시오.

① 소풍 가기
② 집 청소하기
③ 식사 주문하기
④ 슈퍼마켓 가기
⑤ 샌드위치 만들기

M: Why don't we □ _____ □ _____ a □ _____ tomorrow?
W: Sure. □ _____ should we □ _____?
M: Let's bring □ _____. We can make them.
W: Okay, but we don't have □ _____ □ _____ in the house.
M: How about □ _____ □ _____ the □ _____ □ _____?
W: Good thinking. □ _____ □ _____.

✎ **어휘복습** 잘 안 들리거나 몰라서 체크한 어휘를 써 놓고 복습해 보세요.

□ _____ □ _____ □ _____ □ _____
□ _____ □ _____ □ _____ □ _____
□ _____ □ _____ □ _____ □ _____

대화를 듣고, 두 사람이 살 물건이 <u>아닌</u> 것을 고르시오.

① 필통 ② 가방
③ 펜   ④ 지우개
⑤ 공책

W: John, what do you need for school?

M: I □ _____ a new □ _____, Mom.

W: Okay. You also need some □ _____, □ _____, and □ _____, right?

M: Yes. Can I get a new □ _____ □ _____, too?

W: You □ _____ □ _____ one a month □ _____.

M: All right. Then I don't need a new pencil case.

05 숫자 정보 파악

대화를 듣고, 여자가 집에 도착할 시각을 고르시오.

① 3:00 ② 3:30
③ 4:00 ④ 4:30
⑤ 5:00

M: □ _____ does school □ _____ today?

W: It finishes □ _____ □ _____.

M: Are you going home □ _____ □ _____?

W: No. I'm going to Lisa's house at three thirty. I'll be □ _____ □ _____ □ _____.

06 의도 파악

대화를 듣고, 남자의 마지막 말의 의도로 가장 적절한 것을 고르시오.

① 칭찬 ② 제안
③ 사과 ④ 축하
⑤ 거절

W: Hi, Steve. How are you doing?

M: I'm great, Mary. Are you □ _____ new □ _____?

W: Yes, I am. My mom gave them to me □ _____ my □ _____.

M: That was □ _____ □ _____ her.

W: □ _____ do you □ _____ □ _____ them?

M: They □ _____ □ _____ □ _____ you.

✎ **어휘복습** 잘 안 들리거나 몰라서 체크한 어휘를 써 놓고 복습해 보세요.

□ _____   □ _____   □ _____   □ _____

□ _____   □ _____   □ _____   □ _____

□ _____   □ _____   □ _____   □ _____

07 심정 추론

대화를 듣고, 여자의 심정으로 가장 적절한 것을 고르시오.

① 기쁨   ② 걱정
③ 실망   ④ 설렘
⑤ 놀람

W: Do you have any □ _____ for the weekend?

M: I'm □ _____ □ _____ visit my grandparents. What about you?

W: I □ _____ □ _____ □ _____ go for a bike ride with my friend. But she □ _____ on me.

M: You must □ _____ □ _____.

W: To be honest, □ _____ □ _____.

08 직업 파악

대화를 듣고, 남자의 직업으로 가장 적절한 것을 고르시오.

① 배달원   ② 마술사
③ 미용사   ④ 제빵사
⑤ 소방관

M: Good morning. How may I help you?

W: I need some □ _____ for sandwiches.

M: □ _____ just □ _____ □ _____. Here you are.

W: Do you □ _____ any birthday □ _____?

M: Yes, there are many here. Please take a look.

09 특정 정보 파악

대화를 듣고, 여자가 요즘 읽는 책으로 가장 적절한 것을 고르시오.

① ② ③

④ ⑤

M: □ _____ □ _____ read books?

W: □ _____, I do. I read □ _____ □ _____ □ _____ books.

M: Do you read □ _____ books and □ _____ books?

W: Sometimes. But I'm □ _____ a book □ _____ □ _____ □ _____.

M: That sounds interesting.

✎ **어휘복습** 잘 안 들리거나 몰라서 체크한 어휘를 써 놓고 복습해 보세요.

□ _____   □ _____   □ _____   □ _____

□ _____   □ _____   □ _____   □ _____

□ _____   □ _____   □ _____   □ _____

10 장래 희망 파악

다음을 듣고, 남자의 장래 희망으로 가장 적절한 것을 고르시오.

① 소방관　　　② 경찰관
③ 의사　　　　④ 교사
⑤ 군인

M: When I was a boy, I □ _____ to be a □ _____ and to □ _____ people. But I don't want to be a firefighter □ _____. Now, I enjoy □ _____. And I still want to help people. □ _____ I want □ _____ □ _____ a □ _____. I can learn many things. Then, I can □ _____ them □ _____ □ _____.

11 특정 정보 파악

대화를 듣고, 두 사람이 만날 장소로 가장 적절한 곳을 고르시오.

① 공원　　　　② 학교
③ 남자의 집　　④ 여자의 집
⑤ 영화관

M: Hello.

W: Hi, Jack. It's Sarah. Are you busy now?

M: No, I'm watching TV □ _____ □ _____. Do you want to □ _____ □ _____?

W: Yeah. □ _____ □ _____ skateboarding □ _____ the □ _____?

M: I can't. My brother took my skateboard. Let's □ _____ a □ _____.

W: Okay. I'll □ _____ you □ _____ the □ _____ in thirty minutes.

M: Sure. Bye.

✎ **어휘복습** 잘 안 들리거나 몰라서 체크한 어휘를 써 놓고 복습해 보세요.

□ _____　　□ _____　　□ _____　　□ _____

□ _____　　□ _____　　□ _____　　□ _____

□ _____　　□ _____　　□ _____　　□ _____

12 관계 추론

대화를 듣고, 두 사람의 관계로 가장 적절한 것을 고르시오.

① 교사 – 학생
② 요리사 – 손님
③ 버스 운전사 – 승객
④ 가게 주인 – 종업원
⑤ 여행 가이드 – 관광객

W: Excuse me. Does this □ _____ □ _____ □ _____ Eastern Hospital?

M: Yes, it does.

W: Great. □ _____ □ _____ stops is it □ _____ □ _____?

M: It's □ _____ □ _____ from here.

W: And □ _____ □ _____ does it take to □ _____ the □ _____?

M: It's fifteen hundred won. You can put your money there.

W: Thanks.

13 이유 파악

대화를 듣고, 여자가 남자를 태워줄 수 <u>없는</u> 이유로 가장 적절한 것을 고르시오.

① 몸이 아파서
② 병원에 가야 해서
③ 차에 문제가 있어서
④ 외갓집에 가야 해서
⑤ 저녁을 준비해야 해서

M: Mom, I will meet Joe at the park. Can you □ _____ □ _____ □ _____?

W: □ _____, but I □ _____.

M: Why not?

W: I have to □ _____ □ _____ the □ _____ □ _____.

M: Why are you going there?

W: Your □ _____ is there. She's □ _____ □ _____ □ _____.

14 부탁 파악

대화를 듣고, 여자가 남자에게 부탁한 일로 가장 적절한 것을 고르시오.

① 길 묻기   ② 물건 사기
③ 식당 찾기   ④ 지도 찾기
⑤ 인터넷 검색하기

M: I think we're □ _____. Do you □ _____ □ _____ we are?

W: No, I don't. I don't know this place.

M: We should □ _____ a □ _____.

W: Why don't you □ _____ that man □ _____ □ _____?

M: Okay. I'll □ _____ □ _____ him.

✎ **어휘복습** 잘 안 들리거나 몰라서 체크한 어휘를 써 놓고 복습해 보세요.

□ _____   □ _____   □ _____   □ _____

□ _____   □ _____   □ _____   □ _____

□ _____   □ _____   □ _____   □ _____

대화를 듣고, 남자가 가려고 하는 장소를 고르시오.

M: Hello. Is there a post office in this neighborhood?

W: Sure. Do you □ _____ □ _____?

M: Yes, please.

W: Go □ _____ □ _____ the corner. Then, □ _____ □ _____.

M: □ _____ should I do □ _____?

W: □ _____ straight. It's □ _____ the □ _____ and the □ _____ □ _____.

다음을 듣고, 두 사람의 대화가 어색한 것을 고르시오.

①   ②   ③   ④   ⑤

① M: What's your □ _____ class?
   W: I □ _____ math the most.

② M: Do you □ _____ basketball □ _____ your □ _____?
   W: Yes, I have □ _____ □ _____ □ _____ friends.

③ M: □ _____ should we □ _____ to the market?
   W: Let's □ _____ the □ _____.

④ M: What do you □ _____ □ _____ □ _____?
   W: I'd like to buy □ _____ □ _____.

⑤ M: How's the □ _____ right now?
   W: It's really □ _____ and □ _____.

✎ **어휘복습** 잘 안 들리거나 몰라서 체크한 어휘를 써 놓고 복습해 보세요.

□ _____   □ _____   □ _____   □ _____

□ _____   □ _____   □ _____   □ _____

□ _____   □ _____   □ _____   □ _____

17 전화 목적 파악

대화를 듣고, 여자가 남자에게 전화한 목적으로 가장 적절한 것을 고르시오.

① 생일파티에 초대하려고
② 시험 날짜를 물어보려고
③ 시험 성적을 물어보려고
④ 수학 공부를 같이 하려고
⑤ 수학 시험 범위를 물어보려고

M: Hello.
W: Hi, Greg. It's Mary. I □ _____ a □ _____.
M: Sure. What is it?
W: □ _____ is our □ _____ □ _____? Is it on Wednesday or Thursday?
M: It's □ _____.
W: Really? I need to □ _____ □ _____ then. Thanks.

18 할 일 파악

다음 상황 설명을 듣고, Sumi가 판매원에게 할 말로 가장 적절한 것을 고르시오.

Sumi: _____
① Thanks for saying that.
② You can put it in the bag.
③ No, I'm not wearing a scarf.
④ No thanks. It costs too much.
⑤ Yes, you can show me another one.

M: Sumi goes shopping at the market. She sees a □ _____ and □ _____ □ _____ □ _____ it. She □ _____ the salesman for the □ _____. He tells her the price, but Sumi □ _____ have □ _____ □ _____. The salesman asks if Sumi wants to buy the scarf. In this situation, what would Sumi most likely say to the salesman?
Sumi: _____

✎ **어휘복습** 잘 안 들리거나 몰라서 체크한 어휘를 써 놓고 복습해 보세요.

□ _____   □ _____   □ _____   □ _____
□ _____   □ _____   □ _____   □ _____
□ _____   □ _____   □ _____   □ _____

19 알맞은 응답 찾기

대화를 듣고, 여자의 마지막 말에 이어질 남자의 응답으로 가장 적절한 것을 고르시오.

Man: _____

① How much is it?
② Let's do a puzzle then.
③ Yes, we can watch a movie.
④ I see. You don't like puzzles.
⑤ How about going out for dinner?

W: Let's □ _____ □ _____ this afternoon.
M: We can't. It's going to □ _____ □ _____ .
W: Then what should we do?
M: Do you □ _____ to □ _____ jigsaw □ _____ ?
W: Yes, I do.
M: _____

20 알맞은 응답 찾기

대화를 듣고, 여자의 마지막 말에 이어질 남자의 응답으로 가장 적절한 것을 고르시오.

Man: _____

① I want to see a robot.
② Yes, we can go together.
③ Your science project is great.
④ There are many kinds of food.
⑤ Do you want to come with me?

M: Are you going to □ _____ the □ _____ □ _____ ?
W: I don't think so.
M: □ _____ □ _____ ?
W: I don't like science. □ _____ □ _____ □ _____ to enter the science fair?
M: Sure.
W: □ _____ do you want to enter it?
M: _____

✎ **어휘복습** 잘 안 들리거나 몰라서 체크한 어휘를 써 놓고 복습해 보세요.

□ _____   □ _____   □ _____   □ _____
□ _____   □ _____   □ _____   □ _____
□ _____   □ _____   □ _____   □ _____

01 다음 그림의 상황에 가장 적절한 대화를 고르시오.

① ② ③ ④ ⑤

02 다음을 듣고, 'I'가 가리키는 것으로 가장 적절한 것을 고르시오.

① ② ③
④ ⑤

03 다음을 듣고, 여자의 남동생이 받은 선물이 <u>아닌</u> 것을 고르시오.

① 장난감 로봇　② 게임기　③ 필통
④ 스웨터　⑤ 책

04 다음을 듣고, 오늘 저녁의 날씨로 가장 적절한 것을 고르시오.

① ② ③ ④ ⑤

05 대화를 듣고, 무엇에 관한 내용인지 가장 적절한 것을 고르시오.

① 숙제　② 저녁식사　③ 쓰레기통
④ 집안일　⑤ 형제의 우애

06 대화를 듣고, 여자가 주말에 할 일로 가장 적절한 것을 고르시오.

① 시골 가기　② 세차하기　③ 영화보기
④ 친구 만나기　⑤ 자전거 타기

07 대화를 듣고, 버스가 도착하는 시각을 고르시오.

① 3:20　② 3:25　③ 3:30
④ 3:35　⑤ 3:40

08 대화를 듣고, 여자의 심정으로 가장 적절한 것을 고르시오.

① 슬픔　② 분노　③ 기쁨
④ 축하　⑤ 걱정

09 대화를 듣고, 여자가 지불할 금액을 고르시오.

① $5　② $7　③ $8
④ $12　⑤ $20

10 대화를 듣고, 남자의 어머니의 직업으로 가장 적절한 것을 고르시오.

① 사진작가　② 은행원　③ 간호사
④ 요리사　⑤ 교사

11 대화를 듣고, 여자가 선택할 교통수단으로 가장 적절한 것을 고르시오.

① 버스 ② 택시 ③ 기차
④ 자전거 ⑤ 지하철

12 대화를 듣고, 여자가 학교에 지각한 이유로 가장 적절한 것을 고르시오.

① 시계를 잃어버려서
② 알람이 울리지 않아서
③ 버스를 잘못 타서
④ 지하철역을 지나쳐서
⑤ 엄마가 깨워주지 않아서

13 대화를 듣고, 남자가 전화를 건 목적으로 가장 적절한 것을 고르시오.

① 진료를 예약하려고
② 비용을 문의하려고
③ 의사와 통화하려고
④ 처방전을 요청하려고
⑤ 진료 시간을 변경하려고

14 대화를 듣고, 남자의 아버지로 가장 적절한 그림을 고르시오.

①   ②   ③

④   ⑤

15 대화를 듣고, 여자가 남자에게 부탁한 일로 가장 적절한 것을 고르시오.

① 환불해 주기 ② 가격 낮춰 주기
③ 물품 추천해 주기 ④ 물품 교환해 주기
⑤ 다른 옷 보여 주기

16 대화를 듣고, 남자의 장래 희망으로 가장 적절한 것을 고르시오.

① 배우 ② 의사 ③ 영화 감독
④ 과학자 ⑤ 작가

17 대화를 듣고, 여자가 남자에게 제안한 것으로 가장 적절한 것을 고르시오.

① 약 먹기 ② 병원 가기 ③ 붕대 감기
④ 휴식 취하기 ⑤ 자전거 타기

18 다음을 듣고, 두 사람의 대화가 <u>어색한</u> 것을 고르시오.

①   ②   ③   ④   ⑤

[19-20] 대화를 듣고, 여자의 마지막 말에 이어질 남자의 응답으로 가장 적절한 것을 고르시오.

19 Man: _____
① Yes, that's a great idea.
② No, I don't have a pet.
③ You should buy a dog.
④ What's your cat's name?
⑤ My family owns a couple of dogs.

20 Man: _____
① I'm ready to order.
② No, that's not my name.
③ My name is John Martin.
④ Thanks. I'll come back later.
⑤ I'd like a seat by the window.

01 그림 상황에 적절한 대화 찾기

다음 그림의 상황에 가장 적절한 대화를 고르시오.

① ② ③ ④ ⑤

① M: May I □ _____ your □ _____?

   W: □ _____ □ _____ the roast chicken, please.

② M: □ _____ □ _____ does this cost?

   W: It □ _____ ten dollars.

③ M: What's the □ _____ with the sink?

   W: I think it's □ _____.

④ M: □ _____ do we need to □ _____?

   W: □ _____ □ _____ some eggs and milk.

⑤ M: Should I □ _____ the □ _____ in the □ _____?

   W: Yes. Let's □ _____ it for □ _____ □ _____.

02 화제 추론

다음을 듣고, 'I'가 가리키는 것으로 가장 적절한 것을 고르시오.

① ② ③
④ ⑤

W: I am a □ _____. I can □ _____ in the □ _____, and I also enjoy □ _____ in the □ _____. I usually □ _____ around □ _____ or □ _____. Sometimes I live in parks. □ _____ at the parks enjoy □ _____ me. In spring, my □ _____ always □ _____ very closely □ _____ me while we swim together.

✎ **어휘복습** 잘 안 들리거나 몰라서 체크한 어휘를 써 놓고 복습해 보세요.

□ _____   □ _____   □ _____   □ _____

□ _____   □ _____   □ _____   □ _____

□ _____   □ _____   □ _____   □ _____

다음을 듣고, 여자의 남동생이 받은 선물이 아닌 것을 고르시오.

① 장난감 로봇   ② 게임기
③ 필통   ④ 스웨터
⑤ 책

W: Yesterday was my brother's □ _____ . My □ _____ had a □ _____ for him, and we □ _____ him lots of □ _____ . I gave my brother a □ _____ □ _____ . My sister gave a □ _____ □ _____ to him. My parents gave him a □ _____ and two □ _____ . We □ _____ a □ _____ and ate a great dinner. We all □ _____ lots of □ _____ .

04 날씨 파악

다음을 듣고, 오늘 저녁의 날씨로 가장 적절한 것을 고르시오.

① ② ③
④ ⑤

M: Good morning, everyone. This is Clark Bailey. □ _____ □ _____ □ _____ today's weather forecast. It's a cold, □ _____ □ _____ . It's going to □ _____ until around □ _____ P.M. Then, the snow will □ _____ , but it will still be □ _____ in the □ _____ . At □ _____ , there will be □ _____ □ _____ , but the □ _____ will still be □ _____ . Be sure to wear □ _____ □ _____ today.

05 화제 추론

대화를 듣고, 무엇에 관한 내용인지 가장 적절한 것을 고르시오.

① 숙제   ② 저녁식사
③ 쓰레기통   ④ 집안일
⑤ 형제의 우애

W: Did you □ _____ □ _____ the □ _____ yet?
M: No, I'm doing my □ _____ now.
W: You never do your □ _____ on time, David.
M: I have □ _____ □ _____ of them, Mom. Can't Timmy do them?
W: Timmy is too □ _____ . He can't do them yet.
M: But I □ _____ more □ _____ to □ _____ .
W: Okay. I'll take out the trash □ _____ . But you should do it □ _____ .

✎ **어휘복습** 잘 안 들리거나 몰라서 체크한 어휘를 써 놓고 복습해 보세요.

□ _____   □ _____   □ _____   □ _____
□ _____   □ _____   □ _____   □ _____
□ _____   □ _____   □ _____   □ _____

06 할 일 파악

대화를 듣고, 여자가 주말에 할 일로 가장 적절한 것을 고르시오.

① 시골 가기　　② 세차하기
③ 영화 보기　　④ 친구 만나기
⑤ 자전거 타기

M: I'm □ _____ about this □ _____.

W: □ _____ are you going to do?

M: I'm going □ _____ with some □ _____. We're going to □ _____ the □ _____.

W: That sounds □ _____. I'm going to □ _____ my dad □ _____ his □ _____.

M: □ _____ □ _____ you go with us?

W: □ _____, □ _____ I don't enjoy cycling.

07 숫자 정보 파악

대화를 듣고, 버스가 도착하는 시각을 고르시오.

① 3:20　　② 3:25
③ 3:30　　④ 3:35
⑤ 3:40

M: □ _____ □ _____. We're going to be □ _____ for the □ _____.

W: It's □ _____ □ _____. The bus doesn't come □ _____ □ _____ □ _____.

M: Not today. It comes at □ _____ □ _____ on □ _____.

W: I didn't know that. Let's hurry.

M: Okay. Let's go.

✎ **어휘복습** 잘 안 들리거나 몰라서 체크한 어휘를 써 놓고 복습해 보세요.

□ _____　□ _____　□ _____　□ _____

□ _____　□ _____　□ _____　□ _____

□ _____　□ _____　□ _____　□ _____

대화를 듣고, 여자의 심정으로 가장 적절한 것을 고르시오.

① 슬픔　　② 분노
③ 기쁨　　④ 축하
⑤ 걱정

M: □ _____ are you □ _____? Did you get some □ _____ □ _____?

W: Do you □ _____ my friend Emily?

M: Yes, I remember her. She □ _____ to □ _____ □ _____, right?

W: Right. She □ _____ me this morning. She's □ _____ to □ _____ me next week. I'm so □ _____ about that.

M: That's □ _____. I hope you two □ _____ a □ _____ □ _____.

09 숫자 정보 파악

대화를 듣고, 여자가 지불할 금액을 고르시오.

① $5　　② $7
③ $8　　④ $12
⑤ $20

W: Hello. I'd like to □ _____ these □ _____ □ _____.

M: Sure. The □ _____ book is □ _____ dollars. And the □ _____ book is □ _____ dollars.

W: That's □ _____ dollars, □ _____?

M: That's □ _____.

W: I'll □ _____ with □ _____. Here's twenty dollars.

M: Thank you. □ _____ are your books and your □ _____. That's eight dollars.

10 직업 파악

대화를 듣고, 남자의 어머니의 직업으로 가장 적절한 것을 고르시오.

① 사진작가　　② 은행원
③ 간호사　　④ 요리사
⑤ 교사

W: Is that your □ _____ in the □ _____?

M: Yes, it is. You can see my father there.

W: □ _____ does he □ _____?

M: He's a □ _____. He works for a large bank.

W: □ _____ □ _____ your mother?

M: She's a □ _____ at a □ _____. She □ _____ Italian food.

W: Wow. Your parents have □ _____ □ _____.

✏️ **어휘복습** 잘 안 들리거나 몰라서 체크한 어휘를 써 놓고 복습해 보세요.

□ _____　□ _____　□ _____　□ _____

□ _____　□ _____　□ _____　□ _____

□ _____　□ _____　□ _____　□ _____

11 교통수단 찾기

대화를 듣고, 여자가 선택할 교통수단으로 가장 적절한 것을 고르시오.

① 버스
② 택시
③ 기차
④ 자전거
⑤ 지하철

W: I'm going □ _____ at the □ _____ □ _____ tomorrow. But I've □ _____ □ _____ there □ _____.

M: You're not □ _____ there, are you? Tomorrow is a □ _____.

W: I know. Should I □ _____ the □ _____ there?

M: The □ _____ □ _____ is too □ _____ □ _____ the store. Why don't you □ _____ a □ _____?

W: That's □ _____. I guess I'll just □ _____ on the □ _____.

M: That's a □ _____ □ _____. You can take a bus □ _____ □ _____ the department store.

12 이유 파악

대화를 듣고, 여자가 학교에 지각한 이유로 가장 적절한 것을 고르시오.

① 시계를 잃어버려서
② 알람이 울리지 않아서
③ 버스를 잘못 타서
④ 지하철역을 지나쳐서
⑤ 엄마가 깨워주지 않아서

M: Sumi, you're one hour □ _____ □ _____ □ _____.

W: I'm so sorry about that, Mr. Kennedy.

M: What happened? Didn't your □ _____ □ _____ □ _____?

W: Yes, it did. But I got on the □ _____ □ _____ today. I went the □ _____ □ _____.

M: You □ _____ be more □ _____ in the □ _____.

W: I □ _____ I will.

13 전화 목적 파악

대화를 듣고, 남자가 전화를 건 목적으로 가장 적절한 것을 고르시오.

① 진료를 예약하려고
② 비용을 문의하려고
③ 의사와 통화하려고
④ 처방전을 요청하려고
⑤ 진료 시간을 변경하려고

W: Dr. Oliver's □ _____ □ _____. How may I help you?

M: Hello. This is Dave Smith. I am going to □ _____ the □ _____ at □ _____ o'clock today.

W: That's □ _____, Mr. Smith. Is there a □ _____?

M: Yes, there is. I □ _____ really □ _____. Can I □ _____ there □ _____?

W: Can you □ _____ at □ _____? Dr. Oliver can see you then.

M: Thanks. I'll be there then.

✎ **어휘복습** 잘 안 들리거나 몰라서 체크한 어휘를 써 놓고 복습해 보세요.

□ _____ □ _____ □ _____ □ _____
□ _____ □ _____ □ _____ □ _____
□ _____ □ _____ □ _____ □ _____

대화를 듣고, 남자의 아버지로 가장 적절한 그림을 고르시오.

① ② ③
④ ⑤

W: Eric, is your □ _____ here at the □ _____?

M: Yes, he's □ _____ over there.

W: Is he □ _____ □ _____?

M: □ _____, he's not wearing shorts. He's wearing □ _____.

W: Is he the man □ _____ □ _____?

M: □ _____, my dad doesn't wear glasses.

W: Okay. I see him now.

대화를 듣고, 여자가 남자에게 부탁한 일로 가장 적절한 것을 고르시오.

① 환불해 주기
② 가격 낮춰 주기
③ 물품 추천해 주기
④ 물품 교환해 주기
⑤ 다른 옷 보여 주기

M: Hello. Can I □ _____ □ _____ with something?

W: Yes, I'm □ _____ for a new □ _____.

M: We have many sweaters right here. □ _____ □ _____ this one?

W: I don't like the □ _____. Can you □ _____ me some □ _____ □ _____, please?

M: Sure. □ _____ me.

대화를 듣고, 남자의 장래 희망으로 가장 적절한 것을 고르시오.

① 배우
② 의사
③ 영화 감독
④ 과학자
⑤ 작가

M: This □ _____ homework is so □ _____. I really □ _____ science.

W: I □ _____ science. I want to be a □ _____ in the □ _____. What do you like?

M: I like movies a lot.

W: Do you want to be an □ _____?

M: No, I don't. I want to be a □ _____ □ _____ in the future.

✎ **어휘복습** 잘 안 들리거나 몰라서 체크한 어휘를 써 놓고 복습해 보세요.

□ _____　　□ _____　　□ _____　　□ _____
□ _____　　□ _____　　□ _____　　□ _____
□ _____　　□ _____　　□ _____　　□ _____

17 제안 파악

대화를 듣고, 여자가 남자에게 제안한 것으로 가장 적절한 것을 고르시오.

① 약 먹기   ② 병원 가기
③ 붕대 감기   ④ 휴식 취하기
⑤ 자전거 타기

W: □ _____ □ _____ with your arm?

M: I □ _____ down while riding my □ _____ . I □ _____ my □ _____ .

W: It looks bad. Does it □ _____ ?

M: Yes, it does. I'll □ _____ some □ _____ on it soon.

W: You should □ _____ a □ _____ . You might have a big □ _____ .

M: Don't worry. I'll □ _____ some □ _____ and will be □ _____ tomorrow.

18 어색한 대화 찾기

다음을 듣고, 두 사람의 대화가 <u>어색한</u> 것을 고르시오.

①   ②   ③   ④   ⑤

① M: □ _____ you □ _____ another piece of □ _____ ?
   W: No, thank you. I'm □ _____ .

② M: Are you □ _____ your □ _____ later?
   W: Yes, I am. Sarah and I will meet at five.

③ M: I can't find my □ _____ .
   W: I'll help you find it. □ _____ does it □ _____ □ _____ ?

④ M: □ _____ did you □ _____ Tim?
   W: He's my □ _____ □ _____ . He lives near me.

⑤ M: Do you have any □ _____ or □ _____ ?
   W: Yes. I have an older brother.

✎ **어휘복습** 잘 안 들리거나 몰라서 체크한 어휘를 써 놓고 복습해 보세요.

□ _____   □ _____   □ _____   □ _____

□ _____   □ _____   □ _____   □ _____

□ _____   □ _____   □ _____   □ _____

19 알맞은 응답 찾기

대화를 듣고, 여자의 마지막 말에 이어질 남자의 응답으로 가장 적절한 것을 고르시오.

Man: _____

① Yes, that's a great idea.
② No, I don't have a pet.
③ You should buy a dog.
④ What's your cat's name?
⑤ My family owns a couple of dogs.

W: I'm □ _____ about buying a □ _____.
M: Do you think you're □ _____ to □ _____ □ _____ of one?
W: Yes, I am. My parents said that I can □ _____ □ _____.
M: That's good news.
W: Which should I get, a □ _____ □ _____ a □ _____?
M: _____

20 알맞은 응답 찾기

대화를 듣고, 여자의 마지막 말에 이어질 남자의 응답으로 가장 적절한 것을 고르시오.

Man: _____

① I'm ready to order.
② No, that's not my name.
③ My name is John Martin.
④ Thanks. I'll come back later.
⑤ I'd like a seat by the window.

W: Good evening, sir. □ _____ □ _____ Steak Forty-Five.
M: Hello. I'd like a □ _____ □ _____ □ _____, please.
W: We're very □ _____ tonight. You have to □ _____ for a □ _____.
M: □ _____ □ _____ will we have to wait?
W: A table will be □ _____ in □ _____ □ _____.
M: That sounds □ _____ □ _____.
W: Great. □ _____ I □ _____ your □ _____, please?
M: _____

✎ **어휘복습** 잘 안 들리거나 몰라서 체크한 어휘를 써 놓고 복습해 보세요.

□ _____   □ _____   □ _____   □ _____
□ _____   □ _____   □ _____   □ _____
□ _____   □ _____   □ _____   □ _____

01 대화를 듣고, 무엇에 관한 내용인지 가장 적절한 것을 고르시오.

① 남자의 취미 ② 사진 촬영
③ 선물 구매 ④ 디지털카메라
⑤ 요리 수업

02 다음을 듣고, 'this'가 가리키는 것으로 가장 적절한 것을 고르시오.

①   ②   ③

④   ⑤

03 다음을 듣고, 여자가 언급하지 <u>않은</u> 것을 고르시오.

① 여행 시기 ② 이동 수단 ③ 여행 기간
④ 방문할 도시 ⑤ 만날 사람

04 대화를 듣고, 두 사람이 영화를 보기 전에 할 일로 가장 적절한 것을 고르시오.

① 티켓 사기 ② 저녁 먹기
③ 숙제 끝내기 ④ 도서관에 가기
⑤ 책 사기

05 대화를 듣고, 여자가 어젯밤에 잠을 설친 이유로 가장 적절한 것을 고르시오.

① 운동을 많이 해서
② 늦게까지 TV를 봐서
③ 하루 종일 청소를 해서
④ 이웃 아이들이 뛰어다녀서
⑤ 이웃이 음악을 크게 틀어서

06 다음을 듣고, 내일의 날씨로 가장 적절한 것을 고르시오.

①   ②   ③   ④   ⑤

07 대화를 듣고, 여자가 남자에게 전화한 목적으로 가장 적절한 것을 고르시오.

① 로션을 빌리려고
② 승리를 축하하려고
③ 농구 경기에 초대하려고
④ 쾌유를 빌어 주려고
⑤ 함께 학교에 가려고

08 대화를 듣고, 남자의 장래 희망으로 가장 적절한 것을 고르시오.

① 변호사 ② 은행원
③ 건축가 ④ 수학 교사
⑤ 컴퓨터 프로그래머

09 대화를 듣고, 여자가 받은 거스름돈을 고르시오.

① 10,000원 ② 20,000원
③ 30,000원 ④ 40,000원
⑤ 50,000원

10 대화를 듣고, 여자의 마지막 말의 의도로 가장 적절한 것을 고르시오.

① 양보 ② 동의 ③ 축하
④ 사과 ⑤ 요청

11 대화를 듣고, 남자의 직업으로 가장 적절한 것을 고르시오.

① 판매원   ② 디자이너   ③ 세탁업자
④ 교사   ⑤ 배달원

12 대화를 듣고, 두 사람의 관계로 가장 적절한 것을 고르시오.

① 조종사 – 승객
② 승무원 – 승객
③ 판매원 – 손님
④ 여행사 직원 – 손님
⑤ 부동산 중개인 – 손님

13 대화를 듣고, 두 사람이 대화하고 있는 장소로 가장 적절한 곳을 고르시오.

① 공항   ② 은행   ③ 우체국
④ 학교   ⑤ 호텔

14 대화를 듣고, 남자의 심정으로 가장 적절한 것을 고르시오.

① hopeful   ② angry
③ disappointed   ④ surprised
⑤ pleased

15 대화를 듣고, 남자가 빌릴 책으로 가장 적절한 것을 고르시오.

①　　　　②　　　　③

④　　　　⑤

16 대화를 듣고, 여자가 남자에게 부탁한 일로 가장 적절한 것을 고르시오.

① 함께 여행 가기
② 집에 놀러 오기
③ 동생 돌봐 주기
④ 고양이 돌봐 주기
⑤ 계획 세우는 것 도와주기

17 대화를 듣고, 콘서트가 시작하는 시각을 고르시오.

① 6:00   ② 6:15   ③ 6:30
④ 6:45   ⑤ 7:00

18 다음을 듣고, 두 사람의 대화가 <u>어색한</u> 것을 고르시오.

①   ②   ③   ④   ⑤

[19-20] 대화를 듣고, 남자의 마지막 말에 이어질 여자의 응답으로 가장 적절한 것을 고르시오.

19 Woman: _____

① I think I did well on the test.
② You didn't get your grade yet.
③ Ask the teacher for some help.
④ The teacher helped me out a lot.
⑤ Yes, I study together with friends.

20 Woman: _____

① Yes, I think you're right.
② My homeroom teacher is Ms. Bell.
③ No, I didn't ask a teacher anything.
④ We can play in the snow tomorrow.
⑤ Rick and I have history class together.

01 화제 추론

대화를 듣고, 무엇에 관한 내용인지 가장 적절한 것을 고르시오.

① 남자의 취미   ② 사진 촬영
③ 선물 구매   ④ 디지털카메라
⑤ 요리 수업

M: Susan's □ _____ is coming soon. What should we □ _____ her?

W: How about a □ _____ □ _____? She loves taking □ _____.

M: That's a great idea, but a digital camera □ _____ too □ _____.

W: You're right. How about a □ _____? She really □ _____ □ _____.

M: Okay. We should do that.

W: Let's go to the □ _____ tomorrow. We can find something there.

02 화제 추론

다음을 듣고, 'this'가 가리키는 것으로 가장 적절한 것을 고르시오.

①   ②   ③
④   ⑤

M: Many people have this □ _____. This is a □ _____ object, so you can □ _____ it with you □ _____. You can use this when you want to □ _____ something. When you □ _____ a button on this, this captures □ _____.

03 미언급 파악

다음을 듣고, 여자가 언급하지 않은 것을 고르시오.

① 여행 시기   ② 이동 수단
③ 여행 기간   ④ 방문할 도시
⑤ 만날 사람

W: Hello, everybody. My name is Mina. This □ _____, my parents and I are going to □ _____ □ _____ Europe. We're going to stay in Italy for □ _____ □ _____. We're going to visit many □ _____ and famous places in □ _____. I hope we have a wonderful time there.

✏ **어휘복습** 잘 안 들리거나 몰라서 체크한 어휘를 써 놓고 복습해 보세요.

□ _____   □ _____   □ _____   □ _____

□ _____   □ _____   □ _____   □ _____

□ _____   □ _____   □ _____   □ _____

04 할 일 파악

대화를 듣고, 두 사람이 영화를 보기 전에 할 일로 가장 적절한 것을 고르시오.

① 티켓 사기　　② 저녁 먹기
③ 숙제 끝내기　④ 도서관에 가기
⑤ 책 사기

M: Hi, Michelle. How about □ _____ a □ _____ tonight? Do you have time?

W: Yes, I do. □ _____ movie would you like to □ _____?

M: The movie is □ _____ *Summer Story*.

W: That sounds good. □ _____ □ _____ does the movie □ _____?

M: It starts □ _____ □ _____ o'clock. So it will □ _____ two hours from now.

W: Great. Why don't we □ _____ the □ _____ first? I have to □ _____ some □ _____ there.

M: That's fine. It's close to the movie theater.

05 이유 파악

대화를 듣고, 여자가 어젯밤에 잠을 설친 이유로 가장 적절한 것을 고르시오.

① 운동을 많이 해서
② 늦게까지 TV를 봐서
③ 하루 종일 청소를 해서
④ 이웃 아이들이 뛰어다녀서
⑤ 이웃이 음악을 크게 틀어서

M: Are you all right? You □ _____ very □ _____.

W: I □ _____ □ _____ well last night.

M: Why not? Did you watch television until late at night?

W: No, I didn't. My □ _____ made a lot of □ _____ last night. The children were □ _____ □ _____ all night long.

M: I'm sorry to hear that. I hope you can □ _____ some □ _____ tonight.

W: I hope so, too.

06 날씨 파악

다음을 듣고, 내일의 날씨로 가장 적절한 것을 고르시오.

① ② ③ ④ ⑤

W: Good afternoon, everyone. This is Joan Woodruff, and I have the □ _____ report now. It's □ _____ now, □ _____ the rain is going to □ _____ this □ _____. At □ _____, there will be a few □ _____ in the sky. □ _____ is going to be □ _____ all day long. So you won't need your umbrellas.

✎ **어휘복습** 잘 안 들리거나 몰라서 체크한 어휘를 써 놓고 복습해 보세요.

□ _____　□ _____　□ _____　□ _____
□ _____　□ _____　□ _____　□ _____
□ _____　□ _____　□ _____　□ _____

07 전화 목적 파악

대화를 듣고, 여자가 남자에게 전화한 목적으로 가장 적절한 것을 고르시오.

① 로션을 빌리려고
② 승리를 축하하려고
③ 농구 경기에 초대하려고
④ 쾌유를 빌어 주려고
⑤ 함께 학교에 가려고

W: Hello, Tim. I heard you □ _____ □ _____ playing basketball today. Are you □ _____ □ _____ now?

M: I hurt my □ _____ in the game and it □ _____ □ _____.

W: Why don't you □ _____ some □ _____ on it? That will make you □ _____ a lot □ _____.

M: That's a good idea. I'll □ _____ my father if we have some.

W: Good luck. I □ _____ you □ _____ □ _____ soon.

M: Thanks. See you at school tomorrow.

08 장래 희망 파악

대화를 듣고, 남자의 장래 희망으로 가장 적절한 것을 고르시오.

① 변호사   ② 은행원
③ 건축가   ④ 수학 교사
⑤ 컴퓨터 프로그래머

M: Hi, Sue. What are you doing now?

W: I'm doing my □ _____ homework. Some of these □ _____ are very □ _____.

M: But you're □ _____ □ _____ math. You always get □ _____ □ _____ on math tests.

W: I enjoy □ _____ math problems. I want to be a math □ _____ in the future. How about you?

M: I want to be a □ _____ □ _____. But my □ _____ want me to be a □ _____.

W: Why do they want you to become a lawyer?

M: They think people have a lot of □ _____ for lawyers.

✎ **어휘복습** 잘 안 들리거나 몰라서 체크한 어휘를 써 놓고 복습해 보세요.

□ _____   □ _____   □ _____   □ _____
□ _____   □ _____   □ _____   □ _____
□ _____   □ _____   □ _____   □ _____

대화를 듣고, 여자가 받은 거스름돈을 고르시오.

① 10,000원　　② 20,000원
③ 30,000원　　④ 40,000원
⑤ 50,000원

M: Good morning. What are you □ _____ □ _____?
W: I'd like to buy a □ _____ □ _____ for my daughter.
M: What about this one? This □ _____ is very □ _____ these days.
W: I like the color. □ _____ □ _____ does it cost?
M: It □ _____ □ _____ thousand won. Would you like to buy it?
W: Yes, I would. Here is □ _____ thousand won.
M: Okay. Here are your □ _____ and the receipt. Have a nice day.
W: Thank you. Have a nice day, too.

대화를 듣고, 여자의 마지막 말의 의도로 가장 적절한 것을 고르시오.

① 양보　　② 동의
③ 축하　　④ 사과
⑤ 요청

W: Why do you □ _____ so □ _____, Tim?
M: I □ _____ two □ _____ □ _____ to the rock □ _____ tonight. Do you want to □ _____ there □ _____ me?
W: I'd love to go to the concert. But doesn't your sister like rock music?
M: Yes, but I □ _____ have □ _____ tickets. So, Julie, I really want to go with you.
W: Thanks, but I don't think I should go. Your sister will □ _____ it □ _____ than me.

대화를 듣고, 남자의 직업으로 가장 적절한 것을 고르시오.

① 판매원　　② 디자이너
③ 세탁업자　　④ 교사
⑤ 배달원

M: Hello. Can I □ _____ you □ _____ something?
W: It's my husband's □ _____ tomorrow. I need to buy a □ _____ for him.
M: Does he like sweaters?
W: No, he never wears them. But he loves □ _____.
M: Neckties are □ _____ □ _____ this week. Let me □ _____ you □ _____ of them.
W: Great.

✎ **어휘복습** 잘 안 들리거나 몰라서 체크한 어휘를 써 놓고 복습해 보세요.

□ _____　　□ _____　　□ _____　　□ _____
□ _____　　□ _____　　□ _____　　□ _____
□ _____　　□ _____　　□ _____　　□ _____

12 관계 추론

대화를 듣고, 두 사람의 관계로 가장 적절한 것을 고르시오.

① 조종사 – 승객
② 승무원 – 승객
③ 판매원 – 손님
④ 여행사 직원 – 손님
⑤ 부동산 중개인 – 손님

M: Good afternoon. How may I help you?
W: Hello. I need to □ _____ a plane □ _____ from Seoul to Tokyo.
M: Will this be a round-trip or a one-way ticket?
W: Round trip, please.
M: Okay. □ _____ would you like to □ _____?
W: I want to □ _____ on November eleventh and □ _____ on November fifteenth.
M: All right. Let me see if any □ _____ are □ _____.

13 장소 추론

대화를 듣고, 두 사람이 대화하고 있는 장소로 가장 적절한 곳을 고르시오.

① 공항   ② 은행
③ 우체국   ④ 학교
⑤ 호텔

M: Hello. How can I help you?
W: I'd like to □ _____ some □ _____ to my brother in Canada.
M: No problem. □ _____ □ _____ money do you want to send?
W: I need to send two thousand dollars. How much will that □ _____?
M: The □ _____ is thirty dollars. But you should □ _____ □ _____ this form first.
W: Okay.

14 심정 추론

대화를 듣고, 남자의 심정으로 가장 적절한 것을 고르시오.

① hopeful   ② angry
③ disappointed   ④ surprised
⑤ pleased

M: Hello, Ms. Park. How are you doing?
W: I'm great, Jaemin. Do you need something?
M: Yes, ma'am. I want to □ _____ how I did on the □ _____ □ _____.
W: Just a minute. Let me find your test... You □ _____ a B+ on the test.
M: A B+? That's □ _____. I □ _____ really □ _____ for the test.
W: You are □ _____ □ _____. Keep studying hard, and you will get an A the □ _____ □ _____.
M: I hope so.

✎ **어휘복습** 잘 안 들리거나 몰라서 체크한 어휘를 써 놓고 복습해 보세요.

□ _____   □ _____   □ _____   □ _____
□ _____   □ _____   □ _____   □ _____
□ _____   □ _____   □ _____   □ _____

대화를 듣고, 남자가 빌릴 책으로 가장 적절한 것을 고르시오.

① ② ③

④ ⑤

M: Hi, Lara. □ _____ are you doing □ _____?

W: Good evening, Paul. I'm □ _____ □ _____ for my science project. I need some □ _____ on the □ _____.

M: That sounds interesting. I hope you can find the books.

W: I □ _____ found two of them. What are you □ _____ □ _____?

M: I have to □ _____ □ _____ this book on □ _____. My brother wants to read it.

W: It looks interesting. You should read it, too.

대화를 듣고, 여자가 남자에게 부탁한 일로 가장 적절한 것을 고르시오.

① 함께 여행 가기
② 집에 놀러 오기
③ 동생 돌봐 주기
④ 고양이 돌봐 주기
⑤ 계획 세우는 것 도와주기

M: Hi, Rachel. Are you □ _____ about your family □ _____?

W: Yes. But I □ _____ to ask you a □ _____.

M: What do you need?

W: You know we'll be □ _____ □ _____ three days. My □ _____ will be home □ _____.

M: Do you want me to □ _____ □ _____ □ _____ your cat?

W: That's right. Can you □ _____ that □ _____ me?

M: Sure. Can you take her to my house tonight?

W: Of course.

✏️ **어휘복습** 잘 안 들리거나 몰라서 체크한 어휘를 써 놓고 복습해 보세요.

□ _____ □ _____ □ _____ □ _____

□ _____ □ _____ □ _____ □ _____

□ _____ □ _____ □ _____ □ _____

17 숫자 정보 파악

대화를 듣고, 콘서트가 시작하는 시각을 고르시오.

① 6:00 ② 6:15
③ 6:30 ④ 6:45
⑤ 7:00

M: I'm really excited to □ _____ the □ _____ tonight.

W: So am I. Are the □ _____ going to □ _____ □ _____ on stage soon?

M: I think so. What □ _____ is it □ _____?

W: It's □ _____ □ _____. □ _____ is the show going □ _____ □ _____?

M: It's going to start □ _____ minutes □ _____ □ _____.

W: Great. I can't wait.

18 어색한 대화 찾기

다음을 듣고, 두 사람의 대화가 <u>어색한</u> 것을 고르시오.

① ② ③ ④ ⑤

① M: Hello. May I □ _____ □ _____ Susan, please?

　 W: □ _____ □ _____ just a moment.

② M: □ _____ do you usually □ _____ □ _____ the swimming pool?

　 W: Every day.

③ M: It's a □ _____ to □ _____ you. My name is Tom Murphy.

　 W: It's a pleasure to meet you, too, Mr. Murphy.

④ M: □ _____ you very much for helping me.

　 W: Don't □ _____ it.

⑤ M: What's the □ _____ going to be □ _____ today?

　 W: It's □ _____ now, but it will be □ _____ in the afternoon.

✎ **어휘복습** 잘 안 들리거나 몰라서 체크한 어휘를 써 놓고 복습해 보세요.

□ _____　□ _____　□ _____　□ _____

□ _____　□ _____　□ _____　□ _____

□ _____　□ _____　□ _____　□ _____

대화를 듣고, 남자의 마지막 말에 이어질 여자의 응답으로 가장 적절한 것을 고르시오.

Woman: _____

① I think I did well on the test.
② You didn't get your grade yet.
③ Ask the teacher for some help.
④ The teacher helped me out a lot.
⑤ Yes, I study together with friends.

M: I can't □ _____ what happened to me.

W: What's □ _____, Kevin? Are you all right?

M: I just □ _____ my math □ _____. I missed □ _____ the problems.

W: I'm so sorry to hear that. Didn't you study?

M: I did, but math is still □ _____ □ _____ for me. What can I do to □ _____ □ _____?

W: _____

대화를 듣고, 남자의 마지막 말에 이어질 여자의 응답으로 가장 적절한 것을 고르시오.

Woman: _____

① Yes, I think you're right.
② My homeroom teacher is Ms. Bell.
③ No, I didn't ask a teacher anything.
④ We can play in the snow tomorrow.
⑤ Rick and I have history class together.

M: □ _____ □ _____ all the □ _____ on the ground.

W: Because of the snow, □ _____ have been □ _____. We don't have to go to school tomorrow.

M: Are you □ _____ about that?

W: My □ _____ Rick □ _____ me that about ten minutes ago.

M: I'm not sure I believe him. We'd better □ _____ a □ _____ about that.

W: _____

✎ **어휘복습** 잘 안 들리거나 몰라서 체크한 어휘를 써 놓고 복습해 보세요.

□ _____   □ _____   □ _____   □ _____

□ _____   □ _____   □ _____   □ _____

□ _____   □ _____   □ _____   □ _____

19회 실전모의고사

점수 / 20

01 다음을 듣고, 'I'가 가리키는 것으로 가장 적절한 것을 고르시오.

①   ②   ③

④   ⑤

02 대화를 듣고, 두 사람이 주말에 할 운동으로 가장 적절한 것을 고르시오.

①   ②   ③

④   ⑤

03 다음을 듣고, 오늘 밤의 날씨로 가장 적절한 것을 고르시오.

① snowy   ② sunny   ③ rainy
④ cloudy   ⑤ windy

04 대화를 듣고, 남자의 마지막 말의 의도로 가장 적절한 것을 고르시오.

① 초대   ② 충고   ③ 허락
④ 거절   ⑤ 사과

05 대화를 듣고, 선생님에 대해 언급되지 <u>않은</u> 것을 고르시오.

① 담당 과목   ② 성별   ③ 머리 색깔
④ 특기   ⑤ 출신 국가

06 대화를 듣고, 현재 시각을 고르시오.

① 5:30   ② 6:00   ③ 6:30
④ 7:00   ⑤ 7:30

07 대화를 듣고, 남자의 장래 희망으로 가장 적절한 것을 고르시오.

① figure skater   ② writer
③ sports reporter   ④ cook
⑤ businessman

08 대화를 듣고, 여자의 심정으로 가장 적절한 것을 고르시오.

① 만족   ② 실망   ③ 후회
④ 분노   ⑤ 미안함

09 대화를 듣고, 남자가 대화 직후에 할 일로 가장 적절한 것을 고르시오.

① 파이 사기   ② 자전거 타기
③ 손님 초대하기   ④ 슈퍼마켓에 가기
⑤ 쇼핑 목록 작성하기

10 대화를 듣고, 무엇에 관한 내용인지 가장 적절한 것을 고르시오.

① 조부모님 방문   ② 겨울방학 계획
③ 스키 타는 방법   ④ 크리스마스 선물
⑤ 여름방학에 한 일

11 다음을 듣고, 내용과 일치하지 <u>않는</u> 것을 고르시오.

	①	②	③	④	⑤
	history	math	English	science	art
	8	6	7	3	2

12 대화를 듣고, 여자가 수학을 좋아하는 이유로 가장 적절한 것을 고르시오.

① 이해하기 쉬워서
② 시험 성적이 올라서
③ 문제 푸는 것을 좋아해서
④ 좋은 수학 선생님을 만나서
⑤ 수학 공부가 중요하다고 생각해서

13 대화를 듣고, 두 사람의 관계로 가장 적절한 것을 고르시오.

① 교사 – 학생
② 요리사 – 손님
③ 승무원 – 승객
④ 여행 가이드 – 관광객
⑤ 면접관 – 지원자

14 대화를 듣고, 여자가 가려고 하는 장소를 고르시오.

15 대화를 듣고, 여자가 남자에게 부탁한 일로 가장 적절한 것을 고르시오.

① 집 청소하기
② 쓰레기 버리기
③ 숙제 확인하기
④ 보고서 읽어보기
⑤ 학교에 데려가기

16 대화를 듣고, 여자가 남자에게 제안한 것으로 가장 적절한 것을 고르시오.

① 싸움 멈추기
② 새 친구 사귀기
③ 친구와 토론하기
④ 친구에게 사과하기
⑤ 친구에게 전화하기

17 다음을 듣고, 두 사람의 대화가 <u>어색한</u> 것을 고르시오.

①   ②   ③   ④   ⑤

18 대화를 듣고, 남자의 직업으로 가장 적절한 것을 고르시오.

① 서점 직원
② 편집자
③ 작가
④ 농부
⑤ 기자

[19~20] 대화를 듣고, 남자의 마지막 말에 이어질 여자의 응답으로 가장 적절한 것을 고르시오.

19 Woman: _____

① Thanks for your idea.
② You'd better see a doctor.
③ The movie was a lot of fun.
④ I'm glad you're feeling better.
⑤ Yes, I already took some pills.

20 Woman: _____

① No, it didn't cost very much.
② I'm going to listen to it now.
③ You can borrow it in a few days.
④ May I have the CD back, please?
⑤ The music shop is on the second floor.

01 화제 추론

다음을 듣고, 'I'가 가리키는 것으로 가장 적절한 것을 고르시오.

① ② ③
④ ⑤

M: I am a small □ _____ of □ _____. I am very □ _____ and easy to bend. People use me to □ _____ many pieces of □ _____ together. They usually put me in the □ _____ of the □ _____. You can find me on □ _____ or in □ _____.

02 특정 정보 파악

대화를 듣고, 두 사람이 주말에 할 운동으로 가장 적절한 것을 고르시오.

① ② ③
④ ⑤

M: Jane, do you have any □ _____ for this □ _____?
W: I'm not going to do anything special. I'm going to □ _____ home and □ _____ television.
M: That sounds □ _____. Why don't you go to the □ _____ and □ _____ □ _____ with me?
W: I'm sorry, but I've □ _____ played tennis □ _____. How about playing □ _____?
M: □ _____. That sounds fun. Let's meet at the park on Saturday morning.
W: Okay. I'll see you there at ten.

03 날씨 파악

다음을 듣고, 오늘 밤의 날씨로 가장 적절한 것을 고르시오.

① snowy   ② sunny
③ rainy   ④ cloudy
⑤ windy

W: Good morning. This is Paula Wilson with the weather □ _____. Winter has arrived. It's going to be very □ _____ all day long. In the □ _____, the skies will be □ _____, but it's going to start □ _____ in the □ _____. The □ _____ will □ _____ falling in the □ _____, however. At □ _____, there will be □ _____ skies.

✎ **어휘복습** 잘 안 들리거나 몰라서 체크한 어휘를 써 놓고 복습해 보세요.

□ _____   □ _____   □ _____   □ _____
□ _____   □ _____   □ _____   □ _____
□ _____   □ _____   □ _____   □ _____

대화를 듣고, 남자의 마지막 말의 의도로 가장 적절한 것을 고르시오.

① 초대   ② 충고
③ 허락   ④ 거절
⑤ 사과

M: Did Emily □ _____ you to her birthday □ _____?
W: Yes, she did. But I'm □ _____ □ _____ if I can go to it.
M: What's the □ _____? I thought you two are good friends.
W: We are very good friends. But Kate □ _____ □ _____ me to see a movie with her on □ _____ □ _____.
M: I see. I □ _____ you □ _____ go with Kate. She asked you □ _____.

대화를 듣고, 선생님에 대해 언급되지 <u>않은</u> 것을 고르시오.

① 담당 과목   ② 성별
③ 머리 색깔   ④ 특기
⑤ 출신 국가

W: We have a new □ _____ teacher, Mr. Carter, today.
M: Have you seen □ _____? What does he □ _____ □ _____?
W: He's very young and has short □ _____ □ _____. He's also really □ _____.
M: That's interesting.
W: I heard he is □ _____ □ _____ and just moved to Korea.
M: I'm □ _____ □ _____ to meeting him.
W: Me, too.

대화를 듣고, 현재 시각을 고르시오.

① 5:30   ② 6:00
③ 6:30   ④ 7:00
⑤ 7:30

M: There must be a thousand people here at the stadium.
W: Everyone wants to see the game. It's the □ _____ □ _____ of the season.
M: I'm so excited. □ _____ □ _____ is the game going to □ _____?
W: It starts at □ _____ □ _____. But we □ _____ □ _____ inside the stadium □ _____ □ _____.
M: So we have to □ _____ □ _____ more □ _____.
W: Let's buy some snacks while we wait. The snack bar is over there.

✎ **어휘복습** 잘 안 들리거나 몰라서 체크한 어휘를 써 놓고 복습해 보세요.

□ _____   □ _____   □ _____   □ _____

□ _____   □ _____   □ _____   □ _____

□ _____   □ _____   □ _____   □ _____

07 장래 희망 파악

대화를 듣고, 남자의 장래 희망으로 가장 적절한 것을 고르시오.

① figure skater ② writer
③ sports reporter ④ cook
⑤ businessman

W: I love to watch Kim Yuna skate. She is the □ _____ figure □ _____ I've ever seen.

M: I □ _____ □ _____ you. Do you □ _____ to be a figure skater in the □ _____, too?

W: No, I don't. I want to be a □ _____ □ _____.

M: That's a good □ _____. I think you can be a good reporter.

W: Thanks. □ _____ do you want □ _____ □ _____ in the □ _____?

M: My father □ _____ a restaurant. I want to be a □ _____ like him, too.

W: Good luck. I hope your dream □ _____ □ _____.

08 심정 추론

대화를 듣고, 여자의 심정으로 가장 적절한 것을 고르시오.

① 만족 ② 실망
③ 후회 ④ 분노
⑤ 미안함

M: □ _____ do you □ _____ the □ _____ at this restaurant?

W: I think it □ _____ great. I'm really □ _____.

M: You are? I thought you didn't like □ _____ food.

W: I □ _____ □ _____ hate it, but □ _____ I love it.

M: I see. Do you want to □ _____ □ _____ again?

W: Sure. I want to □ _____ this restaurant □ _____.

09 할 일 파악

대화를 듣고, 남자가 대화 직후에 할 일로 가장 적절한 것을 고르시오.

① 파이 사기
② 자전거 타기
③ 손님 초대하기
④ 슈퍼마켓에 가기
⑤ 쇼핑 목록 작성하기

M: Something □ _____ □ _____. What are you □ _____?

W: I'm making some pizza and spaghetti.

M: Everything looks good. Are you going to □ _____ an □ _____ □ _____, too?

W: I □ _____ □ _____, □ _____ we don't have any apples.

M: I can □ _____ to the □ _____ right now. It's no problem.

W: Thanks a lot. I'll give you a □ _____ of the □ _____ I □ _____.

✎ **어휘복습** 잘 안 들리거나 몰라서 체크한 어휘를 써 놓고 복습해 보세요.

□ _____ □ _____ □ _____ □ _____
□ _____ □ _____ □ _____ □ _____
□ _____ □ _____ □ _____ □ _____

대화를 듣고, 무엇에 관한 내용인지 가장 적절한 것을 고르시오.

① 조부모님 방문
② 겨울방학 계획
③ 스키 타는 방법
④ 크리스마스 선물
⑤ 여름방학에 한 일

M: □ _____ □ _____ is coming. Do you have any □ _____ for it?

W: I'm going to a □ _____ resort with my family.

M: That sounds fun. Are you □ _____ □ _____ □ _____?

W: Actually, I've never tried before. But I want to □ _____.
What are you □ _____?

M: My □ _____ are going to □ _____ us for two weeks.

W: Great. You will □ _____ □ _____ with them.

M: That's right. And they said they have lots of □ _____ for me.

다음을 듣고, 내용과 일치하지 <u>않는</u> 것을 고르시오.

①	②	③	④	⑤
history	math	English	science	art
8	6	7	3	2

W: On the first day of school, the teacher □ _____ us □ _____ our favorite □ _____. □ _____ students said that they like □ _____ the most. □ _____ students prefer □ _____. □ _____ students said their favorite class is □ _____. □ _____ students like □ _____ the most, and □ _____ of them said □ _____ is their favorite class.

✏️ **어휘복습** 잘 안 들리거나 몰라서 체크한 어휘를 써 놓고 복습해 보세요.

□ _____   □ _____   □ _____   □ _____
□ _____   □ _____   □ _____   □ _____
□ _____   □ _____   □ _____   □ _____

12 이유 파악

대화를 듣고, 여자가 수학을 좋아하는 이유로 가장 적절한 것을 고르시오.

① 이해하기 쉬워서
② 시험 성적이 올라서
③ 문제 푸는 것을 좋아해서
④ 좋은 수학 선생님을 만나서
⑤ 수학 공부가 중요하다고 생각해서

M: Sally, are you □ _____ □ _____ for the science test?

W: No, I'm not. I'm □ _____ my notes from □ _____ class today.

M: Really? I thought you □ _____ math. What □ _____?

W: I □ _____ math a lot these days □ _____ □ _____ my new math □ _____.

M: That's good. What's he like?

W: He □ _____ the problems very □ _____. He's also really □ _____.

M: You're lucky. My math teacher is really □ _____.

13 관계 추론

대화를 듣고, 두 사람의 관계로 가장 적절한 것을 고르시오.

① 교사 – 학생
② 요리사 – 손님
③ 승무원 – 승객
④ 여행 가이드 – 관광객
⑤ 면접관 – 지원자

W: Nice to meet you, Mr. Davis. □ _____ did you □ _____ to work here?

M: I want to work in the □ _____ □ _____.

W: Okay. What do you □ _____ □ _____ it?

M: I want to □ _____ □ _____ have fun when they go on □ _____.

W: Do you think you would be a good □ _____ □ _____?

M: Yes, I do. I'm □ _____ I □ _____ be a great tour guide.

✎ **어휘복습** 잘 안 들리거나 몰라서 체크한 어휘를 써 놓고 복습해 보세요.

□ _____   □ _____   □ _____   □ _____

□ _____   □ _____   □ _____   □ _____

□ _____   □ _____   □ _____   □ _____

14 위치 찾기

대화를 듣고, 여자가 가려고 하는 장소를 고르시오.

W: Excuse me. I'm looking for the □ _____ □ _____. Can you tell me □ _____ it is?

M: The flower shop? Yes, it's □ _____ □ _____ River Street.

W: □ _____ do I □ _____ there?

M: Go □ _____ ahead □ _____ block. Then, turn □ _____.

W: Turn right? Okay. What should I do after that?

M: □ _____ □ _____ the street. It will be on the □ _____ □ _____ the □ _____. You can't miss it.

W: Okay. Thanks.

15 부탁 파악

대화를 듣고, 여자가 남자에게 부탁한 일로 가장 적절한 것을 고르시오.

① 집 청소하기
② 쓰레기 버리기
③ 숙제 확인하기
④ 보고서 읽어보기
⑤ 학교에 데려가기

M: What are you doing in your room, Tina?

W: I'm □ _____ □ _____ my science homework, Dad.

M: Can you □ _____ me □ _____ a □ _____?

W: Yes. What is it?

M: Please □ _____ □ _____ the garbage with me. We have a lot of □ _____.

W: Okay. But after that, I □ _____ you to □ _____ my □ _____.

M: Sure. I'll help.

16 제안 파악

대화를 듣고, 여자가 남자에게 제안한 것으로 가장 적절한 것을 고르시오.

① 싸움 멈추기
② 새 친구 사귀기
③ 친구와 토론하기
④ 친구에게 사과하기
⑤ 친구에게 전화하기

W: You look □ _____. What's the □ _____?

M: Eric and I had an □ _____ at school. Now, he □ _____ □ _____ to me.

W: □ _____ did you fight □ _____?

M: We □ _____ about a game in gym class. So he got very □ _____.

W: Oh, no. You should □ _____ to him.

M: You're right. I'll call him on the phone right now.

✎ **어휘복습** 잘 안 들리거나 몰라서 체크한 어휘를 써 놓고 복습해 보세요.

□ _____ □ _____ □ _____ □ _____

□ _____ □ _____ □ _____ □ _____

□ _____ □ _____ □ _____ □ _____

17 어색한 대화 찾기

다음을 듣고, 두 사람의 대화가 <u>어색한</u> 것을 고르시오.

① ② ③ ④ ⑤

① W: □ _____ do you □ _____ my new shoes?

　M: They □ _____ □ _____. And I love the color.

② W: Do you have any □ _____ for this afternoon?

　M: I'm going to □ _____ □ _____ with Rick.

③ W: □ _____ did you □ _____ the food?

　M: We had chicken and rice.

④ W: □ _____ you □ _____ me with this □ _____?

　M: □ _____. I can □ _____ it for you.

⑤ W: □ _____ □ _____ will it take to get to your home?

　M: It will take □ _____ minutes by bus.

18 직업 파악

대화를 듣고, 남자의 직업으로 가장 적절한 것을 고르시오.

① 서점 직원　　② 편집자
③ 작가　　　　④ 농부
⑤ 기자

W: Steve, welcome back. Long time no see.

M: I stayed in the □ _____ for the past □ _____ □ _____.

W: Why did you go there? Were you working on a □ _____?

M: I wanted a □ _____ place. I needed to □ _____ □ _____ my □ _____.

W: □ _____ is it going to be □ _____?

M: It will be available □ _____ week.

✎ **어휘복습** 잘 안 들리거나 몰라서 체크한 어휘를 써 놓고 복습해 보세요.

□ _____　　　□ _____　　　□ _____　　　□ _____

□ _____　　　□ _____　　　□ _____　　　□ _____

□ _____　　　□ _____　　　□ _____　　　□ _____

대화를 듣고, 남자의 마지막 말에 이어질 여
자의 응답으로 가장 적절한 것을 고르시오.

Woman: _____

① Thanks for your idea.
② You'd better see a doctor.
③ The movie was a lot of fun.
④ I'm glad you're feeling better.
⑤ Yes, I already took some pills.

W: Hello.

M: Hi, Alice. This is Greg. Do you have a minute?

W: Sure, Greg. Is everything □ _____?

M: Actually, I □ _____ □ _____ you this evening.
   I'm □ _____.

W: What's the □ _____? Are you □ _____?

M: Yes, I am. I have a □ _____ □ _____, and my □ _____
   □ _____ a lot, too.

W: _____

대화를 듣고, 남자의 마지막 말에 이어질 여
자의 응답으로 가장 적절한 것을 고르시오.

Woman: _____

① No, it didn't cost very much.
② I'm going to listen to it now.
③ You can borrow it in a few days.
④ May I have the CD back, please?
⑤ The music shop is on the second
   floor.

M: What do you have □ _____ that □ _____, Lucy?

W: It's a □ _____ CD. I just □ _____ it at the shopping mall.

M: □ _____ □ _____ of music is it?

W: It's □ _____ music. It has songs by some of my favorite
   □ _____.

M: That's nice. □ _____ □ _____ □ _____ □ _____ to the
   CD sometime □ _____.

W: _____

✎ **어휘복습** 잘 안 들리거나 몰라서 체크한 어휘를 써 놓고 복습해 보세요.

□ _____   □ _____   □ _____   □ _____

□ _____   □ _____   □ _____   □ _____

□ _____   □ _____   □ _____   □ _____

01 다음을 듣고, 'this'가 가리키는 것으로 가장 적절한 것을 고르시오.

①   ②   ③

④   ⑤

02 다음을 듣고, 내일 인천의 날씨로 가장 적절한 것을 고르시오.

①   ②   ③   ④   ⑤

03 대화를 듣고, 두 사람이 주말에 할 일로 가장 적절한 것을 고르시오.

① 소풍 가기 ② 자원봉사 하기
③ 영화 보기 ④ 건강검진 받기
⑤ 공원에서 운동하기

04 대화를 듣고, 무엇에 관한 내용인지 가장 적절한 것을 고르시오.

① 농구 경기장 ② 테니스 대회
③ 주말 계획 ④ 즐겨 하는 운동
⑤ 빨리 달리는 방법

05 대화를 듣고, 남자의 직업으로 가장 적절한 것을 고르시오.

① 여행 가이드 ② 여행사 직원
③ 비행기 조종사 ④ 승무원
⑤ 수하물 담당자

06 대화를 듣고, 남자의 심정으로 가장 적절한 것을 고르시오.

① upset ② relieved ③ nervous
④ excited ⑤ regretful

07 대화를 듣고, 현재 시각을 고르시오.

① 7:25 ② 7:30 ③ 7:35
④ 7:40 ⑤ 7:45

08 대화를 듣고, 두 사람이 오늘 저녁에 할 일로 가장 적절한 것을 고르시오.

① 책 읽기
② 산책하기
③ 텔레비전 보기
④ 호수에서 수영하기
⑤ 공원에서 자전거 타기

09 대화를 듣고, 여자가 지불할 금액을 고르시오.

① $2 ② $3 ③ $4
④ $5 ⑤ $10

10 대화를 듣고, 두 사람이 구매할 물건으로 가장 적절한 것을 고르시오.

①   ②   ③

④   ⑤

11 대화를 듣고, 여자가 읽고 있는 책의 주제로 가장 적절한 것을 고르시오.

① 숲에서의 삶　　② 도구의 발명
③ 열대 우림 보호　　④ 작가가 되는 법
⑤ 야생 동물의 종류

12 대화를 듣고, 두 사람의 관계로 가장 적절한 것을 고르시오.

① 재봉사 – 고객　　② 판매원 – 고객
③ 엄마 – 아들　　④ 교사 – 학생
⑤ 버스 기사 – 승객

13 대화를 듣고, 여자가 남자에게 전화한 목적으로 가장 적절한 것을 고르시오.

① 날씨를 물어보려고
② 창문을 열도록 시키려고
③ 집 청소를 시키려고
④ 창문을 닫도록 시키려고
⑤ 우산을 갖다 달라고 하려고

14 대화를 듣고, 두 사람이 대화하고 있는 장소로 가장 적절한 곳을 고르시오.

① 공항　　② 버스　　③ 지하철
④ 기차역　　⑤ 버스터미널

15 다음을 듣고, 여자가 언급하지 <u>않은</u> 것을 고르시오.

① 이름　　② 사는 곳
③ 언니의 나이　　④ 아버지의 직업
⑤ 취미

16 다음을 듣고, 두 사람의 대화가 <u>어색한</u> 것을 고르시오.

①　　②　　③　　④　　⑤

17 대화를 듣고, 여자가 주문한 신발을 받지 <u>못한</u> 이유로 가장 적절한 것을 고르시오.

① 상품이 없어서
② 돈을 내지 않아서
③ 주문이 취소되어서
④ 신발이 불량이어서
⑤ 다른 장소로 배달되어서

18 대화를 듣고, 여자가 가려고 하는 장소를 고르시오.

[19~20] 대화를 듣고, 남자의 마지막 말에 이어질 여자의 응답으로 가장 적절한 것을 고르시오.

19 Woman: _____

① I'm sitting in seat 4A.
② No, I didn't buy a ticket.
③ Thanks. I'll be right back.
④ I've got two large suitcases.
⑤ Dinner was great, wasn't it?

20 Woman: _____

① What did you order?
② No, the food didn't arrive.
③ I'll start cooking soon then.
④ What do you want to cook?
⑤ That sounds like a good idea.

20회 DICTATION

다시 듣고, 빈칸에 알맞은 단어를 써 보세요.

◀)) MP3 실전 20-1

01 화제 추론

다음을 듣고, 'this'가 가리키는 것으로 가장 적절한 것을 고르시오.

① ② ③ ④ ⑤

W: You can usually find this in the □ _____ . You use this to □ _____ □ _____ into □ _____ pieces. You put the food into this and then □ _____ a □ _____ . This machine then □ _____ everything □ _____ . This can also □ _____ fruit and other food together to make □ _____ .

02 날씨 파악

다음을 듣고, 내일 인천의 날씨로 가장 적절한 것을 고르시오.

① ② ③ ④ ⑤

M: Good morning. Here is the weather report for today. In Seoul, it's going to be □ _____ all day long. The □ _____ will be □ _____ as well. It's going to be □ _____ in Incheon, and there will be □ _____ in Suwon. It will be very □ _____ in Daegu. Busan and Gwangju are going to get □ _____ .

03 할 일 파악

대화를 듣고, 두 사람이 주말에 할 일로 가장 적절한 것을 고르시오.

① 소풍 가기 ② 자원봉사 하기
③ 영화 보기 ④ 건강검진 받기
⑤ 공원에서 운동하기

W: The weather will be warm this □ _____ . Let's go on a □ _____ at the park.
M: I would love to, □ _____ Tony and I □ _____ have □ _____ .
W: What are you going to do?
M: We're going to do some □ _____ work at the □ _____ .
W: Really? Can I □ _____ you there?
M: □ _____ . They always need □ _____ people to □ _____ .

✎ **어휘복습** 잘 안 들리거나 몰라서 체크한 어휘를 써 놓고 복습해 보세요.

□ _____ □ _____ □ _____ □ _____

□ _____ □ _____ □ _____ □ _____

□ _____ □ _____ □ _____ □ _____

04 화제 추론

대화를 듣고, 무엇에 관한 내용인지 가장 적절한 것을 고르시오.

① 농구 경기장
② 테니스 대회
③ 주말 계획
④ 즐겨 하는 운동
⑤ 빨리 달리는 방법

W: Do you enjoy playing □ _____?

M: □ _____, I don't. I'm too □ _____.

W: What do you □ _____ about □ _____?

M: I don't like it. You have to □ _____ too □ _____ to play it.

W: I see. Do you play □ _____?

M: Yes, I do. I □ _____ playing it on □ _____.

05 직업 파악

대화를 듣고, 남자의 직업으로 가장 적절한 것을 고르시오.

① 여행 가이드   ② 여행사 직원
③ 비행기 조종사   ④ 승무원
⑤ 수하물 담당자

W: □ _____ are you □ _____ today?

M: I'm □ _____. I just got □ _____ □ _____ □ _____.

W: Is it hard to □ _____ an □ _____?

M: Sometimes. But I really love my □ _____.

W: What do you □ _____ about it the □ _____?

M: I like □ _____ □ _____ above the ground.

06 심정 추론

대화를 듣고, 남자의 심정으로 가장 적절한 것을 고르시오.

① upset   ② relieved
③ nervous   ④ excited
⑤ regretful

W: Seho, hurry up. We're going to be □ _____ for □ _____.

M: Okay, I'm □ _____ now... □ _____ a minute.

W: What's wrong? Did you □ _____ something?

M: Yes, I □ _____ to print our science □ _____. I'll do that right now.

W: I already □ _____ it last night. It's in my backpack.

M: Oh, I □ _____ really □ _____. But everything is □ _____ □ _____. Let's go.

✎ **어휘복습** 잘 안 들리거나 몰라서 체크한 어휘를 써 놓고 복습해 보세요.

□ _____   □ _____   □ _____   □ _____

□ _____   □ _____   □ _____   □ _____

□ _____   □ _____   □ _____   □ _____

07 숫자 정보 파악

대화를 듣고, 현재 시각을 고르시오.

① 7:25　　　　② 7:30
③ 7:35　　　　④ 7:40
⑤ 7:45

M: Hello.

W: Hello, Rick. □ _____ are you right □ _____?

M: I'm at my □ _____. What's up?

W: At your house? Did you □ _____ about the □ _____?
I'm □ _____ □ _____ you at the □ _____.

M: Oh, I forgot. I'll go there □ _____ □ _____ □ _____
I can.

W: Never mind. The movie starts at □ _____ □ _____. That's
□ _____ minutes □ _____ □ _____. There isn't enough
time.

08 할 일 파악

대화를 듣고, 두 사람이 오늘 저녁에 할 일로 가장 적절한 것을 고르시오.

① 책 읽기
② 산책하기
③ 텔레비전 보기
④ 호수에서 수영하기
⑤ 공원에서 자전거 타기

M: I can't believe it. It's □ _____ raining.

W: When it □ _____ all day, I just stay □ _____ and
□ _____ books.

M: I sometimes do that, but I □ _____ want to stay home
□ _____ □ _____.

W: Did you □ _____ the □ _____ report? □ _____ is it
going to □ _____ raining?

M: It should stop □ _____ an □ _____. Then, we can
□ _____ out □ _____ a □ _____ this □ _____.

W: Sure. We can □ _____ by the lake at the park.

✎ **어휘복습** 잘 안 들리거나 몰라서 체크한 어휘를 써 놓고 복습해 보세요.

□ _____　□ _____　□ _____　□ _____

□ _____　□ _____　□ _____　□ _____

□ _____　□ _____　□ _____　□ _____

대화를 듣고, 여자가 지불할 금액을 고르시오.

① $2 ② $3
③ $4 ④ $5
⑤ $10

M: Good evening. May I □ _____ your □ _____ ?

W: I'd like a cheeseburger and fries, please.

M: Do you want □ _____ or □ _____ fries? Regular fries are □ _____ dollar, and large fries cost □ _____ dollars.

W: I'd like large fries, please.

M: Okay, and the cheeseburger □ _____ three dollars.

W: Here's a ten-dollar bill.

M: Thanks. Here's your change.

대화를 듣고, 두 사람이 구매할 물건으로 가장 적절한 것을 고르시오.

① ② ③

④ ⑤

M: Do you know that Lisa's □ _____ is the day after tomorrow?

W: Yes, I do. We need to buy her a □ _____ . What should we get?

M: She wants a new □ _____ . She often □ _____ about hers.

W: That's too □ _____ . Why don't we buy her some □ _____ ? The weather is □ _____ □ _____ these days.

M: She just bought a new □ _____ □ _____ gloves. How about a □ _____ □ _____ ?

W: That □ _____ □ _____ . Let's go to the store and find one now.

✎ **어휘복습** 잘 안 들리거나 몰라서 체크한 어휘를 써 놓고 복습해 보세요.

□ _____   □ _____   □ _____   □ _____

□ _____   □ _____   □ _____   □ _____

□ _____   □ _____   □ _____   □ _____

11 특정 정보 파악

대화를 듣고, 여자가 읽고 있는 책의 주제로 가장 적절한 것을 고르시오.

① 숲에서의 삶
② 도구의 발명
③ 열대 우림 보호
④ 작가가 되는 법
⑤ 야생 동물의 종류

M: Julie, □ _____ are you □ _____?
W: I'm reading the □ _____ □ _____ by Eric Hammer. It's called *Life in the Wild*. It's really interesting.
M: I don't know that □ _____. What is the book □ _____?
W: It's about the time he spent □ _____ □ _____ the forest. The writer lived □ _____ in the □ _____ for more than a year.
M: That sounds □ _____. Can I borrow that book when you're finished? I want to read it.

12 관계 추론

대화를 듣고, 두 사람의 관계로 가장 적절한 것을 고르시오.

① 재봉사 – 고객
② 판매원 – 고객
③ 엄마 – 아들
④ 교사 – 학생
⑤ 버스 기사 – 승객

W: Hello. How can I help you?
M: These □ _____ are too □ _____ for me. Can you □ _____ them □ _____?
W: Yes, I can. I need to □ _____ your □ _____.
M: Okay. □ _____ □ _____ will this take?
W: It will take around two days to □ _____ the □ _____.
M: Okay. I'll come back on Thursday. Thanks.

13 전화 목적 파악

대화를 듣고, 여자가 남자에게 전화한 목적으로 가장 적절한 것을 고르시오.

① 날씨를 물어보려고
② 창문을 열도록 시키려고
③ 집 청소를 시키려고
④ 창문을 닫도록 시키려고
⑤ 우산을 갖다 달라고 하려고

W: Hi. Are you still □ _____ the □ _____?
M: Yes, I am. But I am going out □ _____ □ _____ an □ _____. Is there a problem?
W: I □ _____ the □ _____ in the bedroom □ _____. The weather report says it's going to □ _____ in the □ _____.
M: Do you □ _____ me to □ _____ the windows now?
W: Yes, please. I don't want □ _____ to □ _____ □ _____ the house.
M: Okay. I'll do that right now.

✏ **어휘복습** 잘 안 들리거나 몰라서 체크한 어휘를 써 놓고 복습해 보세요.

□ _____ □ _____ □ _____ □ _____
□ _____ □ _____ □ _____ □ _____
□ _____ □ _____ □ _____ □ _____

14 장소 추론

대화를 듣고, 두 사람이 대화하고 있는 장소로 가장 적절한 곳을 고르시오.

① 공항　　　　② 버스
③ 지하철　　　④ 기차역
⑤ 버스터미널

W: Excuse me. □ _____ will we □ _____ □ _____ City Hall Station?

M: This train □ _____ □ _____ there. You need to □ _____ □ _____ line.

W: Oh, that's terrible. □ _____ can I □ _____ that?

M: □ _____ □ _____ at the next stop. Then, □ _____ line number □ _____.

W: Thank you so much. You were really helpful.

15 미언급 파악

다음을 듣고, 여자가 언급하지 않은 것을 고르시오.

① 이름　　　　　② 사는 곳
③ 언니의 나이　 ④ 아버지의 직업
⑤ 취미

W: Hello. My □ _____ is Sora Lee. I'm a new student here. My family □ _____ □ _____ Seoul □ _____ Daejeon last week. My □ _____ is Suwon. I have one □ _____ sister and two □ _____ brothers. My father is a □ _____, and my mother is an elementary school □ _____. I like □ _____ pictures and □ _____ my bicycle. I hope we can all be friends.

16 어색한 대화 찾기

다음을 듣고, 두 사람의 대화가 어색한 것을 고르시오.

①　　②　　③　　④　　⑤

① M: □ _____ □ _____ shall we meet tomorrow?
　 W: On Tuesday.

② M: Excuse me. □ _____ □ _____ goes to the shopping mall?
　 W: Take the □ _____ thirty-four bus.

③ M: You need to □ _____ more.
　 W: I know, □ _____ I don't have □ _____ time.

④ M: □ _____ did you □ _____ to Rome?
　 W: I □ _____ here □ _____ two thousand nine.

⑤ M: □ _____ were you □ _____ for school this morning?
　 W: My alarm clock didn't □ _____ □ _____.

✎ **어휘복습** 잘 안 들리거나 몰라서 체크한 어휘를 써 놓고 복습해 보세요.

□ _____　□ _____　□ _____　□ _____
□ _____　□ _____　□ _____　□ _____
□ _____　□ _____　□ _____　□ _____

17 이유 파악

대화를 듣고, 여자가 주문한 신발을 받지 못한 이유로 가장 적절한 것을 고르시오.

① 상품이 없어서
② 돈을 내지 않아서
③ 주문이 취소되어서
④ 신발이 불량이어서
⑤ 다른 장소로 배달되어서

M: Hello. Super Saver Home Shopping. How may I help you?

W: Hello. I □ _____ a pair of □ _____ last week. But I didn't □ _____ them.

M: I see. □ _____ me check your □ _____. May I □ _____ your □ _____, please?

W: Sure. My name is Susan Smith.

M: Thank you, Ms. Smith. I see the □ _____. The shoes you ordered are □ _____ □ _____. We will have them here tomorrow. Then, we will □ _____ them □ _____ you.

18 위치 찾기

대화를 듣고, 여자가 가려고 하는 장소를 고르시오.

W: Pardon me, sir. I'm looking for a □ _____. Is there one □ _____ □ _____?

M: Yes, there is. □ _____ straight to the □ _____. Then, □ _____ □ _____ onto Walnut Street.

W: Are you □ _____ me □ _____ turn right at the intersection?

M: No, don't turn right. Turn left. Then, you will see the □ _____ □ _____. The bank is □ _____ □ _____ □ _____ the fire station. You can't miss it.

W: Thanks for your help. I hope I can find it.

✎ **어휘복습** 잘 안 들리거나 몰라서 체크한 어휘를 써 놓고 복습해 보세요.

□ _____   □ _____   □ _____   □ _____

□ _____   □ _____   □ _____   □ _____

□ _____   □ _____   □ _____   □ _____

대화를 듣고, 남자의 마지막 말에 이어질 여
자의 응답으로 가장 적절한 것을 고르시오.

Woman: _____
① I'm sitting in seat 4A.
② No, I didn't buy a ticket.
③ Thanks. I'll be right back.
④ I've got two large suitcases.
⑤ Dinner was great, wasn't it?

M: Is your ☐ _____ going to ☐ _____ soon?

W: It's going to leave ☐ _____ ☐ _____ minutes.

M: Okay. Why don't we ☐ _____ ☐ _____ here and
☐ _____ then?

W: Sure. Oh, no. I ☐ _____ ☐ _____ my ticket. I think
I ☐ _____ it in the restaurant.

M: Calm down. I'll ☐ _____ your ☐ _____. You can
☐ _____ to ☐ _____ your ☐ _____.

W: _____

대화를 듣고, 남자의 마지막 말에 이어질 여
자의 응답으로 가장 적절한 것을 고르시오.

Woman: _____
① What did you order?
② No, the food didn't arrive.
③ I'll start cooking soon then.
④ What do you want to cook?
⑤ That sounds like a good idea.

M: Cindy, you look ☐ _____. Are you ☐ _____ ☐ _____?

W: I'm so ☐ _____ at ☐ _____ these days. I have a new
project.

M: How about ☐ _____ some ☐ _____?

W: I'd love to, ☐ _____ I need to ☐ _____ dinner ☐ _____.

M: You shouldn't do that. Let's ☐ _____ something.

W: _____

✎ **어휘복습** 잘 안 들리거나 몰라서 체크한 어휘를 써 놓고 복습해 보세요.

☐ _____ ☐ _____ ☐ _____ ☐ _____
☐ _____ ☐ _____ ☐ _____ ☐ _____
☐ _____ ☐ _____ ☐ _____ ☐ _____

01 대화를 듣고, 여자가 잃어버린 인형으로 가장 적절한 것을 고르시오.

①   ②   ③

④   ⑤

02 다음을 듣고, 'this'가 가리키는 것으로 가장 적절한 것을 고르시오.

03 다음을 듣고, 일요일 오후의 날씨로 가장 적절한 것을 고르시오.

04 대화를 듣고, 여자의 마지막 말의 의도로 가장 적절한 것을 고르시오.

① 거절   ② 위로   ③ 사과
④ 승낙   ⑤ 감사

05 다음을 듣고, 남자가 언급하지 <u>않은</u> 것을 고르시오.

① 학교 이름   ② 학생 수   ③ 담임교사
④ 학교 위치   ⑤ 동아리 수

06 대화를 듣고, 두 사람이 만날 시각을 고르시오.

① 11:00 a.m.   ② 12:00 p.m.   ③ 1:00 p.m.
④ 2:00 p.m.   ⑤ 3:00 p.m.

07 대화를 듣고, 여자의 장래 희망으로 가장 적절한 것을 고르시오.

① 작곡가   ② 기타리스트   ③ 가수
④ 운동선수   ⑤ 유치원 교사

08 대화를 듣고, 남자의 심정으로 가장 적절한 것을 고르시오.

① worried   ② excited   ③ sad
④ bored   ⑤ proud

09 대화를 듣고, 여자가 대화 직후에 할 일로 가장 적절한 것을 고르시오.

① 버스 회사에 전화하기
② 버스 노선 찾아보기
③ 가방 새로 구입하기
④ 가방 내부 살펴보기
⑤ 경찰서 찾아가기

10 대화를 듣고, 무엇에 관한 내용인지 가장 적절한 것을 고르시오.

① 명절 계획   ② 요리 강습   ③ 영화 관람
④ 전통 놀이   ⑤ 할머니 생신

11 대화를 듣고, 여자가 오늘 집에 갈 방법으로 가장 적절한 것을 고르시오.

① 자전거 타기　　② 걸어가기
③ 버스 타기　　　④ 기차 타기
⑤ 택시 타기

12 대화를 듣고, 남자가 늦게 잠자리에 든 이유로 가장 적절한 것을 고르시오.

① 커피를 마셨기 때문에
② 낮잠을 많이 잤기 때문에
③ 아빠가 편찮으셨기 때문에
④ 아픈 강아지를 돌봤기 때문에
⑤ 축구 경기를 시청했기 때문에

13 대화를 듣고, 두 사람이 대화하는 장소로 가장 적절한 곳을 고르시오.

① 은행　　　　② 경찰서　　　③ 세탁소
④ 분실물 센터　⑤ 자동차 정비소

14 대화를 듣고, 남자가 가려고 하는 장소를 고르시오.

15 대화를 듣고, 남자가 여자에게 요청한 일로 가장 적절한 것을 고르시오.

① 나침반 준비하기　　② 비상약 준비하기
③ 등산화 구입하기　　④ 손전등 구입하기
⑤ 겨울옷 찾기

16 대화를 듣고, 여자가 남자에게 제안한 것으로 가장 적절한 것을 고르시오.

① 요가하기　　　　② 줄넘기하기
③ 간식 줄이기　　　④ 건강 검진받기
⑤ 충분한 수면 취하기

17 대화를 듣고, 두 사람의 대화가 <u>어색한</u> 것을 고르시오.

①　　　②　　　③　　　④　　　⑤

18 대화를 듣고, 여자의 직업으로 가장 적절한 것을 고르시오.

① 농부　　　② 미용사　　　③ 요리사
④ 사진작가　⑤ 아나운서

[19-20] 대화를 듣고, 남자의 마지막 말에 이어질 여자의 응답으로 가장 적절한 것을 고르시오.

19 Woman: _____
① Thank you for your advice.
② Sorry to hear that.
③ For here or to go?
④ Don't feel so bad.
⑤ Sure. Why not?

20 Woman: _____
① It's pretty. I'll take it.
② Really? She will like it.
③ This piano looks wonderful!
④ Yes, it is. So I feel really tired.
⑤ I don't think it is a good idea.

다시 듣고, 빈칸에 알맞은 단어를 써 보세요.

◀)) MP3 기출 01-1

01 그림 정보 파악

대화를 듣고, 여자가 잃어버린 인형으로 가장 적절한 것을 고르시오.

① ② ③ ④ ⑤

M: Hello. □ _____ and □ _____ Center. How may I help you?

W: Hi. I lost my □ _____ □ _____ in the park yesterday.

M: □ _____ does it □ _____ □ _____?

W: It has a □ _____ □ _____ its □ _____. It's wearing a □ _____. Do you have one like that?

M: Okay. I will go to check.

02 화제 추론

다음을 듣고, 'this'가 가리키는 것으로 가장 적절한 것을 고르시오.

① ② ③ ④ ⑤

W: You can see this in a □ _____. It usually □ _____ □ _____ and comes in □ _____ different □ _____. When your □ _____ are □ _____, you can □ _____ them with this. It makes □ _____ with □ _____. What is this?

03 날씨 파악

다음을 듣고, 일요일 오후의 날씨로 가장 적절한 것을 고르시오.

① ② ③ ④ ⑤

M: Good morning, this is Andrew with your □ _____ □ _____ report. On □ _____, it will be □ _____ and □ _____ all day. On □ _____, it will become □ _____ in the □ _____, and it will □ _____ in the □ _____.

✎ **어휘복습** 잘 안 들리거나 몰라서 체크한 어휘를 써 놓고 복습해 보세요.

□ _____   □ _____   □ _____   □ _____
□ _____   □ _____   □ _____   □ _____
□ _____   □ _____   □ _____   □ _____

04 의도 파악

대화를 듣고, 여자의 마지막 말의 의도로 가장 적절한 것을 고르시오.

① 거절 ② 위로
③ 사과 ④ 승낙
⑤ 감사

W: Hello, Tom.

M: Hey, Jina. Will you □ _____ me a □ _____?

W: □ _____. What is it?

M: Can I □ _____ your badminton □ _____? I need it for my P.E. class for tomorrow.

W: □ _____ □ _____.

05 미언급 파악

다음을 듣고, 남자가 언급하지 않은 것을 고르시오.

① 학교 이름 ② 학생 수
③ 담임교사 ④ 학교 위치
⑤ 동아리 수

M: Hello, let me □ _____ □ _____ my school, Wuju Middle School. There are □ _____ □ _____ students. We have many wonderful teachers. My □ _____ □ _____, Mr. Choi, is a □ _____ teacher. He's very kind. We have □ _____ □ _____. I love my school.

06 숫자 정보 파악

대화를 듣고, 두 사람이 만날 시각을 고르시오.

① 11:00 a.m. ② 12:00 p.m.
③ 1:00 p.m. ④ 2:00 p.m.
⑤ 3:00 p.m.

M: Hello, Jenny.

W: John, let's have □ _____ □ _____.

M: Okay. □ _____ □ _____ *Judy's Burger*? I have two □ _____ □ _____.

W: That's great. □ _____ □ _____ shall we □ _____?

M: We can only use them from □ _____ a.m. to □ _____ p.m. So, □ _____ □ _____ meeting there at □ _____ p.m.?

W: Sure.

✎ **어휘복습** 잘 안 들리거나 몰라서 체크한 어휘를 써 놓고 복습해 보세요.

□ _____ □ _____ □ _____ □ _____
□ _____ □ _____ □ _____ □ _____
□ _____ □ _____ □ _____ □ _____

07 장래 희망 파악

대화를 듣고, 여자의 장래 희망으로 가장 적절한 것을 고르시오.

① 작곡가　　② 기타리스트
③ 가수　　　④ 운동선수
⑤ 유치원 교사

M: Wow! That □ _____ □ _____.

W: Really? I □ _____ this □ _____ for so long.

M: I can see that. I like your □ _____ very much.

W: Thank you. I really want to be a □ _____.

M: I think you are □ _____ a guitarist.

08 심정 추론

대화를 듣고, 남자의 심정으로 가장 적절한 것을 고르시오.

① worried　　② excited
③ sad　　　　④ bored
⑤ proud

W: Guess what? We are □ _____ on a □ _____ □ _____ next Friday!

M: That's fantastic! □ _____ are we □ _____?

W: We are going to *Wonderland*.

M: Wow, I really wanted to □ _____ the □ _____ □ _____ there!

W: Me, too. We'll □ _____ a □ _____ □ _____.

09 할 일 파악

대화를 듣고, 여자가 대화 직후에 할 일로 가장 적절한 것을 고르시오.

① 버스 회사에 전화하기
② 버스 노선 찾아보기
③ 가방 새로 구입하기
④ 가방 내부 살펴보기
⑤ 경찰서 찾아가기

W: Oh, no! I just □ _____ my □ _____ on the □ _____.

M: □ _____ bus did you □ _____?

W: I took the four two five. What should I do?

M: I think you should □ _____ the bus □ _____ first.

W: You're right. I'll □ _____ that □ _____ □ _____.

✎ **어휘복습** 잘 안 들리거나 몰라서 체크한 어휘를 써 놓고 복습해 보세요.

□ _____　　□ _____　　□ _____　　□ _____

□ _____　　□ _____　　□ _____　　□ _____

□ _____　　□ _____　　□ _____　　□ _____

10 화제 추론

대화를 듣고, 무엇에 관한 내용인지 가장 적절한 것을 고르시오.

① 명절 계획   ② 요리 강습
③ 영화 관람   ④ 전통 놀이
⑤ 할머니 생신

M: Yumi, do you ☐ _____ any ☐ _____ for *Chuseok*?

W: Yes, I'm going to ☐ _____ ☐ _____ Korean ☐ _____.

M: Oh, ☐ _____ are you going to make?

W: ☐ _____ ☐ _____ ☐ _____ make *songpyeon*.
How about you?

M: For *Chuseok*, I'm going to ☐ _____ my ☐ _____ with my
family.

11 교통수단 찾기

대화를 듣고, 여자가 오늘 집에 갈 방법으로 가장 적절한 것을 고르시오.

① 자전거 타기   ② 걸어가기
③ 버스 타기   ④ 기차 타기
⑤ 택시 타기

M: Amy! ☐ _____ ☐ _____ to your leg?

W: I ☐ _____ my ☐ _____ yesterday in dance class.
It's ☐ _____ to ☐ _____.

M: I'm sorry to hear that. Then ☐ _____ will you ☐ _____
☐ _____?

W: I ☐ _____ ☐ _____ a ☐ _____, but I think I have to take
a ☐ _____ ☐ _____.

M: Wait here. I'll ☐ _____ ☐ _____ for you.

12 이유 파악

대화를 듣고, 남자가 늦게 잠자리에 든 이유로 가장 적절한 것을 고르시오.

① 커피를 마셨기 때문에
② 낮잠을 많이 잤기 때문에
③ 아빠가 편찮으셨기 때문에
④ 아픈 강아지를 돌봤기 때문에
⑤ 축구 경기를 시청했기 때문에

W: Jinyoung! You ☐ _____ ☐ _____. Are you all right?

M: Well, I ☐ _____ to ☐ _____ really ☐ _____.

W: Why? Did you ☐ _____ the ☐ _____ game last night?

M: No. My ☐ _____ was ☐ _____, so I had to ☐ _____
☐ _____ ☐ _____ him almost all night.

W: That's ☐ _____ ☐ _____. Is he ☐ _____ now?

M: He's ☐ _____.

✎ **어휘복습** 잘 안 들리거나 몰라서 체크한 어휘를 써 놓고 복습해 보세요.

☐ _____   ☐ _____   ☐ _____   ☐ _____
☐ _____   ☐ _____   ☐ _____   ☐ _____
☐ _____   ☐ _____   ☐ _____   ☐ _____

13 장소 추론

대화를 듣고, 두 사람이 대화하는 장소로 가장 적절한 곳을 고르시오.

① 은행　　　　② 경찰서
③ 세탁소　　　④ 분실물 센터
⑤ 자동차 정비소

M: How may I help you?

W: Can you □ _____ this □ _____ for me?

M: Sure. Anything else?

W: Well, one □ _____ is □ _____ on the jacket.

M: Okay, I'll □ _____ that.

W: Thanks. □ _____ □ _____ will it be?

M: The □ _____ will be thirteen dollars.

14 위치 찾기

대화를 듣고, 남자가 가려고 하는 장소를 고르시오.

M: Excuse me. □ _____ is the art □ _____?

W: The art museum? Go □ _____ □ _____ □ _____. Then, turn right.

M: □ _____ □ _____?

W: Yes. And then □ _____ about □ _____ □ _____. You can see the museum □ _____ your □ _____. It is □ _____ the □ _____ □ _____ and the □ _____ shop.

M: Thank you.

✎ **어휘복습** 잘 안 들리거나 몰라서 체크한 어휘를 써 놓고 복습해 보세요.

□ _____　　□ _____　　□ _____　　□ _____
□ _____　　□ _____　　□ _____　　□ _____
□ _____　　□ _____　　□ _____　　□ _____

대화를 듣고, 남자가 여자에게 요청한 일로 가장 적절한 것을 고르시오.

① 나침반 준비하기
② 비상약 준비하기
③ 등산화 구입하기
④ 손전등 구입하기
⑤ 겨울옷 찾기

M: Mom, this □ _____ is our □ _____ camping □ _____!

W: Yeah, I remember. □ _____ are you □ _____ □ _____?

M: At Seorak □ _____.

W: That sounds great. □ _____ it's going to be □ _____ at □ _____.

M: I know. Can you □ _____ some □ _____ □ _____ for me?

W: Of course.

대화를 듣고, 여자가 남자에게 제안한 것으로 가장 적절한 것을 고르시오.

① 요가하기   ② 줄넘기하기
③ 간식 줄이기   ④ 건강 검진받기
⑤ 충분한 수면 취하기

M: Susan, you □ _____ so □ _____. What's your □ _____?

W: I □ _____ three days a week.

M: □ _____ do you □ _____?

W: I □ _____ doing □ _____, and it is wonderful.

M: Wow, isn't it □ _____ to do?

W: Not at all. □ _____ □ _____ □ _____ □ _____ it sometime?

✏ **어휘복습** 잘 안 들리거나 몰라서 체크한 어휘를 써 놓고 복습해 보세요.

□ _____   □ _____   □ _____   □ _____

□ _____   □ _____   □ _____   □ _____

□ _____   □ _____   □ _____   □ _____

17 어색한 대화 찾기

대화를 듣고, 두 사람의 대화가 <u>어색한</u> 것을 고르시오.

① ② ③ ④ ⑤

① W: What □ _____ is it?

  M: It's □ _____ □ _____ □ _____.

② W: Can I □ _____ your pen?

  M: I was there, too.

③ W: I □ _____ a □ _____.

  M: Oh, that's too bad.

④ W: □ _____ □ _____ □ _____ some cookies?

  M: Sure. □ _____ □ _____.

⑤ W: □ _____ can I □ _____ □ _____ the bus stop?

  M: □ _____ □ _____ at the corner.

18 직업 파악

대화를 듣고, 여자의 직업으로 가장 적절한 것을 고르시오.

① 농부   ② 미용사
③ 요리사   ④ 사진작가
⑤ 아나운서

M: Welcome to the □ _____! Today we have a special

  □ _____ in our □ _____.

W: Hello. I'm Jean, and I □ _____ □ _____ an Indian

  □ _____.

M: Nice to meet you, Jean. □ _____ are we going to □ _____

  today?

W: We're going to make apple □ _____.

M: Wow! That □ _____ □ _____! Let's begin.

✎ **어휘복습** 잘 안 들리거나 몰라서 체크한 어휘를 써 놓고 복습해 보세요.

□ _____   □ _____   □ _____   □ _____

□ _____   □ _____   □ _____   □ _____

□ _____   □ _____   □ _____   □ _____

대화를 듣고, 남자의 마지막 말에 이어질 여자의 응답으로 가장 적절한 것을 고르시오.

Woman: _____
① Thank you for your advice.
② Sorry to hear that.
③ For here or to go?
④ Don't feel so bad.
⑤ Sure. Why not?

W: David, you look busy. □ _____ are you □ _____ now?

M: I'm writing a □ _____ □ _____ for my brother. Tomorrow is his birthday.

W: Wow, that's sweet. Did you □ _____ a □ _____ for him?

M: □ _____ □ _____. I'm going to buy a □ _____ □ _____ this afternoon. Do you want to □ _____ □ _____ □ _____?

W: _____

대화를 듣고, 남자의 마지막 말에 이어질 여자의 응답으로 가장 적절한 것을 고르시오.

Woman: _____
① It's pretty. I'll take it.
② Really? She will like it.
③ This piano looks wonderful!
④ Yes, it is. So I feel really tired.
⑤ I don't think it is a good idea.

M: Sally, you don't look happy. □ _____ □ _____?

W: I'm □ _____ □ _____ my new □ _____.

M: Your new neighbors? Why?

W: They □ _____ the □ _____ □ _____ at □ _____ and it's too □ _____.

M: That's terrible! So it's □ _____ to □ _____, right?

W: _____

✎ **어휘복습** 잘 안 들리거나 몰라서 체크한 어휘를 써 놓고 복습해 보세요.

□ _____ □ _____ □ _____ □ _____

□ _____ □ _____ □ _____ □ _____

□ _____ □ _____ □ _____ □ _____

MP3 기출 02

점수 / 20

01 대화를 듣고, 남자가 갖고 싶어 하는 가방으로 가장 적절한 것을 고르시오.

①   ②   ③

④   ⑤

02 다음을 듣고, 'this'가 가리키는 것으로 가장 적절한 것을 고르시오.

①   ②   ③

④   ⑤

03 다음을 듣고, 내일의 날씨로 가장 적절한 것을 고르시오.

① ② ③ ④ ⑤

04 대화를 듣고, 남자의 마지막 말의 의도로 가장 적절한 것을 고르시오.

① 거절   ② 제안   ③ 사과
④ 축하   ⑤ 위로

05 다음을 듣고, 여자가 언급하지 <u>않은</u> 것을 고르시오.

① 이름   ② 고향   ③ 거주지
④ 가족   ⑤ 장래 희망

06 대화를 듣고, 두 사람이 만날 시각을 고르시오.

① 3:00 p.m.   ② 4:00 p.m.   ③ 5:00 p.m.
④ 6:00 p.m.   ⑤ 7:00 p.m.

07 대화를 듣고, 남자의 장래 희망으로 가장 적절한 것을 고르시오.

① 의사   ② 가수   ③ 화가
④ 교사   ⑤ 사진작가

08 대화를 듣고, 여자의 심정으로 가장 적절한 것을 고르시오.

① 걱정하는   ② 무관심한   ③ 지루한
④ 기뻐하는   ⑤ 자랑스러운

09 대화를 듣고, 여자가 대화 직후에 할 일로 가장 적절한 것을 고르시오.

① 감사의 편지 쓰기
② 이메일로 숙제 보내기
③ 생일 카드 구입하기
④ 모르는 문제 질문하기
⑤ 인터넷으로 자료 찾기

10 대화를 듣고, 무엇에 관한 내용인지 가장 적절한 것을 고르시오.

① 좋아하는 과목   ② 유행하는 노래
③ 잘하는 운동   ④ 인기 있는 동아리
⑤ 존경하는 선생님

11 대화를 듣고, 남자가 이용할 교통수단으로 가장 적절한 것을 고르시오.

① 택시　　　② 기차　　　③ 버스
④ 비행기　　⑤ 자전거

12 대화를 듣고, 남자가 선생님을 찾아간 이유로 가장 적절한 것을 고르시오.

① 동아리 지도를 부탁하기 위해서
② 신문 동아리에 가입하기 위해서
③ 상담 날짜를 변경하기 위해서
④ 성적을 문의하기 위해서
⑤ 조퇴하기 위해서

13 대화를 듣고, 두 사람의 관계로 가장 적절한 것을 고르시오.

① 교사 – 학생　　　② 승무원 – 승객
③ 식당 종업원 – 손님　④ 감독 – 운동선수
⑤ 치과의사 – 환자

14 대화를 듣고, 남자가 가려고 하는 장소를 고르시오.

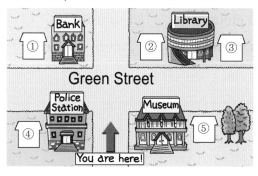

15 대화를 듣고, 여자가 남자에게 요청한 일로 가장 적절한 것을 고르시오.

① 설거지하기　　　② 식사 준비하기
③ 책상 정리하기　　④ 거실 청소하기
⑤ 화분에 물주기

16 대화를 듣고, 여자가 남자에게 제안한 것으로 가장 적절한 것을 고르시오.

① 댄스 동아리 가입
② 배드민턴 경기 관람
③ 건강검진 예약
④ 중간고사 준비
⑤ 축제 연습

17 대화를 듣고, 두 사람의 대화가 <u>어색한</u> 것을 고르시오.

①　　②　　③　　④　　⑤

18 대화를 듣고, 남자의 직업으로 가장 적절한 것을 고르시오.

① 미용사　　　　　② 유치원 교사
③ 비행기 조종사　　④ 제빵사
⑤ 동물 조련사

[19-20] 대화를 듣고, 여자의 마지막 말에 이어질 남자의 응답으로 가장 적절한 것을 고르시오

19 Man: _____

① Here it is.
② That's too bad.
③ Oh! Congratulations!
④ Thank you so much.
⑤ I'm glad to meet you, too.

20 Man: _____

① Yes. I like Italian food.
② I'm sure she will like it.
③ We're going to make bulgogi.
④ The cook is working at the restaurant.
⑤ We will go to Insadong Sunday morning.

다시 듣고, 빈칸에 알맞은 단어를 써 보세요.

◀)) MP3 기출 02-1

01 그림 정보 파악

대화를 듣고, 남자가 갖고 싶어 하는 가방으로 가장 적절한 것을 고르시오.

① ② ③ ④ ⑤

W: Jiwon, school starts next week! Do you need anything?

M: Yes. □ _____ really □ _____ to □ _____ a new □ _____.

W: □ _____ □ _____ of backpack do you want?

M: I want a backpack with □ _____ □ _____ on the □ _____.

02 화제 추론

다음을 듣고, 'this'가 가리키는 것으로 가장 적절한 것을 고르시오.

① ② ③ ④ ⑤

M: You use this in a □ _____ game. You □ _____ it with □ _____ □ _____. It is a □ _____ □ _____. You can □ _____ a home run with it. What is this?

03 날씨 파악

다음을 듣고, 내일의 날씨로 가장 적절한 것을 고르시오.

① ② ③ ④ ⑤

W: Good evening. This is the □ _____ □ _____ for □ _____. Did you enjoy □ _____ beautiful □ _____ weather? It was so warm. □ _____, there will be □ _____ □ _____ all day long. Thank you.

✎ **어휘복습** 잘 안 들리거나 몰라서 체크한 어휘를 써 놓고 복습해 보세요.

□ _____ □ _____ □ _____ □ _____

□ _____ □ _____ □ _____ □ _____

□ _____ □ _____ □ _____ □ _____

04 의도 파악

대화를 듣고, 남자의 마지막 말의 의도로 가장 적절한 것을 고르시오.

① 거절   ② 제안   ③ 사과
④ 축하   ⑤ 위로

W: Good morning, Tom. □ _____ are you □ _____?

M: Good morning, Jane. I am reading a science □ _____ about dinosaurs.

W: Dinosaurs? It looks interesting.

M: Yes, it is. □ _____ □ _____ read it, too.

05 미언급 파악

다음을 듣고, 여자가 언급하지 않은 것을 고르시오.

① 이름   ② 고향   ③ 거주지
④ 가족   ⑤ 장래 희망

W: Hi, everyone. Let me □ _____ □ _____. I'm Sora. My □ _____ is Incheon, Korea. I □ _____ in Hong Kong now. I □ _____ ice skating very much. My favorite skater is Yuna Kim. I □ _____ □ _____ □ _____ a famous figure skater like her.

06 숫자 정보 파악

대화를 듣고, 두 사람이 만날 시각을 고르시오.

① 3:00 p.m.   ② 4:00 p.m.
③ 5:00 p.m.   ④ 6:00 p.m.
⑤ 7:00 p.m.

M: Mina, □ _____ is your history □ _____ □ _____?

W: Not so well. Let's □ _____ it □ _____ at the □ _____.

M: Okay. Can we □ _____ at □ _____ in the afternoon?

W: That's too late. □ _____ □ _____ □ _____?

M: □ _____. See you then.

✎ **어휘복습** 잘 안 들리거나 몰라서 체크한 어휘를 써 놓고 복습해 보세요.

□ _____   □ _____   □ _____   □ _____

□ _____   □ _____   □ _____   □ _____

□ _____   □ _____   □ _____   □ _____

07 장래 희망 파악

대화를 듣고, 남자의 장래 희망으로 가장 적절한 것을 고르시오.

① 의사　②가수　③화가
④ 교사　⑤ 사진작가

W: Wow, is this a □ _____ of our school?

M: Yes, it is. I □ _____ it.

W: It looks wonderful. You are a real □ _____.

M: Thanks. I □ _____ to be a □ _____.

08 심정 추론

대화를 듣고, 여자의 심정으로 가장 적절한 것을 고르시오.

① 걱정하는　　② 무관심한
③ 지루한　　④ 기뻐하는
⑤ 자랑스러운

M: Mom, □ _____ my □ _____? I'm late.

W: You □ _____ it □ _____ the □ _____ last night.

M: Thanks. And where's my □ _____?

W: It's on the □ _____. Don't you see it?

M: Okay. I found it. Did you see my □ _____?

W: Please, Tom. You're wearing it now. I'm □ _____ about you.

09 할 일 파악

대화를 듣고, 여자가 대화 직후에 할 일로 가장 적절한 것을 고르시오.

① 감사의 편지 쓰기
② 이메일로 숙제 보내기
③ 생일 카드 구입하기
④ 모르는 문제 질문하기
⑤ 인터넷으로 자료 찾기

W: Hi, Charlie. Did you □ _____ your English □ _____?

M: □ _____, I did. I □ _____ □ _____ it to Ms. Kim.

W: Oh, really? Can I have her email □ _____?

M: Yes, here it is.

W: Thanks. I'll □ _____ my homework □ _____ □ _____.

✎ **어휘복습** 잘 안 들리거나 몰라서 체크한 어휘를 써 놓고 복습해 보세요.

□ _____　□ _____　□ _____　□ _____

□ _____　□ _____　□ _____　□ _____

□ _____　□ _____　□ _____　□ _____

10 화제 추론

대화를 듣고, 무엇에 관한 내용인지 가장 적절한 것을 고르시오.

① 좋아하는 과목
② 유행하는 노래
③ 잘하는 운동
④ 인기 있는 동아리
⑤ 존경하는 선생님

M: □ _____ □ _____ do you □ _____ the most?

W: I like □ _____ the most.

M: □ _____ do you □ _____ it?

W: In class, we □ _____ to lots of English pop □ _____ . What's your □ _____ subject?

M: My favorite is P.E.

11 교통수단 찾기

대화를 듣고, 남자가 이용할 교통수단으로 가장 적절한 것을 고르시오.

① 택시   ② 기차   ③ 버스
④ 비행기   ⑤ 자전거

W: Hey, Bill. □ _____ are you going to □ _____ this □ _____ ?

M: I'm □ _____ my □ _____ in Daegu.

W: □ _____ are you □ _____ there?

M: I'm going to □ _____ a □ _____ .

W: That's a □ _____ □ _____ . It's faster than a bus.

12 이유 파악

대화를 듣고, 남자가 선생님을 찾아간 이유로 가장 적절한 것을 고르시오.

① 동아리 지도를 부탁하기 위해서
② 신문 동아리에 가입하기 위해서
③ 상담 날짜를 변경하기 위해서
④ 성적을 문의하기 위해서
⑤ 조퇴하기 위해서

M: Hello, Ms. Kim. Do you □ _____ a □ _____ ?

W: Hi, Minsu. Come on in. □ _____ can I □ _____ you?

M: Um... can I □ _____ your □ _____ □ _____ ?

W: Sure. □ _____ your name, student number, and phone number on this paper.

M: Okay. Thank you.

✎ **어휘복습** 잘 안 들리거나 몰라서 체크한 어휘를 써 놓고 복습해 보세요.

□ _____   □ _____   □ _____   □ _____

□ _____   □ _____   □ _____   □ _____

□ _____   □ _____   □ _____   □ _____

13 관계 추론

대화를 듣고, 두 사람의 관계로 가장 적절한 것을 고르시오.

① 교사 – 학생
② 승무원 – 승객
③ 식당 종업원 – 손님
④ 감독 – 운동선수
⑤ 치과의사 – 환자

M: What's the □ _____?

W: I have a □ _____.

M: Do you? Please □ _____ your □ _____.

W: Ouch! It really □ _____.

M: Yes, you have a □ _____ □ _____. We need an X-ray. The □ _____ will help you.

W: Okay.

14 위치 찾기

대화를 듣고, 남자가 가려고 하는 장소를 고르시오.

M: Excuse me. Is there a □ _____ around here?

W: Yes. Go □ _____ to Green Street and □ _____ □ _____ at the corner.

M: Go straight and turn left?

W: Yes. And then, walk about a minute. It'll be on your □ _____. It's □ _____ □ _____ the □ _____.

M: Thank you so much.

✎ **어휘복습** 잘 안 들리거나 몰라서 체크한 어휘를 써 놓고 복습해 보세요.

□ _____   □ _____   □ _____   □ _____

□ _____   □ _____   □ _____   □ _____

□ _____   □ _____   □ _____   □ _____

15 부탁 파악

대화를 듣고, 여자가 남자에게 요청한 일로 가장 적절한 것을 고르시오.

① 설거지하기
② 식사 준비하기
③ 책상 정리하기
④ 거실 청소하기
⑤ 화분에 물주기

W: It's a beautiful spring day. I want to □ _____ □ _____.

M: Honey, let's □ _____ our □ _____ first.

W: You're right.

M: I'll □ _____ the □ _____.

W: No. I can do that. Can you □ _____ the □ _____ □ _____?

M: □ _____ □ _____.

16 제안 파악

대화를 듣고, 여자가 남자에게 제안한 것으로 가장 적절한 것을 고르시오.

① 댄스 동아리 가입
② 배드민턴 경기 관람
③ 건강검진 예약
④ 중간고사 준비
⑤ 축제 연습

M: Ellie, what □ _____ are you □ _____?

W: I'm in the □ _____ club. How about you?

M: I'm still thinking.

W: You like □ _____! What about □ _____ the □ _____ □ _____?

M: I'd like to. But first, I have to □ _____ the dance □ _____.

W: Don't worry about that. Just try it.

✎ **어휘복습** 잘 안 들리거나 몰라서 체크한 어휘를 써 놓고 복습해 보세요.

□ _____   □ _____   □ _____   □ _____

□ _____   □ _____   □ _____   □ _____

□ _____   □ _____   □ _____   □ _____

17 어색한 대화 찾기

대화를 듣고, 두 사람의 대화가 <u>어색한</u> 것을 고르시오.

①　②　③　④　⑤

① W: □ _____ you for □ _____ me.

　 M: It was my □ _____!

② W: □ _____ time □ _____ see!

　 M: I don't have the □ _____.

③ W: Aren't you □ _____?

　 M: Not at all. I'm □ _____.

④ W: I don't □ _____ □ _____.

　 M: What's □ _____?

⑤ W: What's your □ _____?

　 M: My hobby is □ _____.

18 직업 파악

대화를 듣고, 남자의 직업으로 가장 적절한 것을 고르시오.

① 미용사　　　　② 유치원 교사
③ 비행기 조종사　④ 제빵사
⑤ 동물 조련사

M: Flying □ _____. How can I help you?

W: Hello. I'd like to □ _____ a strawberry □ _____ for my

　 daughter's □ _____.

M: Okay. When do you need it by?

W: This Friday, please.

M: Don't worry. I will □ _____ the most □ _____ □ _____

　 for her.

✎ **어휘복습** 잘 안 들리거나 몰라서 체크한 어휘를 써 놓고 복습해 보세요.

□ _____　□ _____　□ _____　□ _____

□ _____　□ _____　□ _____　□ _____

□ _____　□ _____　□ _____　□ _____

19 알맞은 응답 찾기

대화를 듣고, 여자의 마지막 말에 이어질 남자의 응답으로 가장 적절한 것을 고르시오.

Man: _____

① Here it is.
② That's too bad.
③ Oh! Congratulations!
④ Thank you so much.
⑤ I'm glad to meet you, too.

M: Oh, no! It's □ _____!

W: Don't you have an □ _____?

M: No, I don't. How can I go home?

W: □ _____ □ _____. You can □ _____ □ _____. I have two.

M: _____

20 알맞은 응답 찾기

대화를 듣고, 여자의 마지막 말에 이어질 남자의 응답으로 가장 적절한 것을 고르시오.

Man: _____

① Yes. I like Italian food.
② I'm sure she will like it.
③ We're going to make bulgogi.
④ The cook is working at the restaurant.
⑤ We will go to Insadong Sunday morning.

W: I heard that your □ _____ Jack is □ _____ Korea next month.

M: Oh, yes! It's his □ _____ □ _____ to Korea.

W: Do you □ _____ any special □ _____?

M: My mom and I are going to □ _____ □ _____ □ _____ for him.

W: □ _____ are you going to cook?

M: _____

✎ **어휘복습** 잘 안 들리거나 몰라서 체크한 어휘를 써 놓고 복습해 보세요.

□ _____ □ _____ □ _____ □ _____

□ _____ □ _____ □ _____ □ _____

□ _____ □ _____ □ _____ □ _____

01 대화를 듣고, 남자가 선택할 물건으로 가장 적절한 것을 고르시오.

①
②
③

④
⑤

02 다음을 듣고, 일요일의 날씨로 가장 적절한 것을 고르시오.

①
②
③
④
⑤

03 대화를 듣고, 여자의 마지막 말의 의도로 가장 적절한 것을 고르시오.

① 사과   ② 제안   ③ 축하
④ 승낙   ⑤ 변명

04 다음을 듣고, 남자가 언급하지 않은 것을 고르시오.

① 가족의 수   ② 아버지의 직업
③ 어머니의 취미   ④ 형의 나이
⑤ 사는 곳

05 대화를 듣고, 두 사람이 만나기로 한 시각을 고르시오.

① 3:00   ② 3:30   ③ 4:00
④ 4:30   ⑤ 5:00

06 대화를 듣고, 남자의 장래 희망으로 가장 적절한 것을 고르시오.

① 건축가   ② 변호사   ③ 번역가
④ 운동선수   ⑤ 사진작가

07 대화를 듣고, 남자의 심정으로 가장 적절한 것을 고르시오.

① sad   ② angry   ③ bored
④ excited   ⑤ worried

08 대화를 듣고, 남자가 대화 직후에 할 일로 가장 적절한 것을 고르시오.

① 계산하기   ② 우유 가져오기
③ 직원 불러오기   ④ 생선 골라오기
⑤ 쇼핑카트 가져오기

09 대화를 듣고, 무엇에 관한 내용인지 가장 적절한 것을 고르시오.

① 축제 준비   ② 건강 검진
③ 주말 계획   ④ 자기 소개
⑤ 장래 희망

10 대화를 듣고, 여자가 선택할 교통수단으로 가장 적절한 것을 고르시오.

① 배   ② 기차   ③ 버스
④ 지하철   ⑤ 비행기

11 대화를 듣고, 여자가 어제 전화를 건 이유로 가장 적절한 것을 고르시오.

① 친구 전화번호를 물어보려고
② 숙제에 대해 물어보려고
③ 저녁식사에 초대하려고
④ 뮤지컬을 함께 보려고
⑤ 운동을 함께 하려고

12 대화를 듣고, 두 사람이 대화하는 장소로 가장 적절한 곳을 고르시오.

① 장난감 가게　　② 우체국　　③ 옷가게
④ 서점　　　　　　⑤ 약국

13 대화를 듣고, 남자가 가려고 하는 장소를 고르시오.

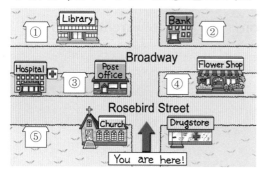

14 대화를 듣고, 남자가 여자에게 부탁한 일로 가장 적절한 것을 고르시오.

① 코트 주머니 확인하기
② 셔츠 단추 달아주기
③ 지갑 수선 맡기기
④ 세탁물 찾아오기
⑤ 방 청소하기

15 대화를 듣고, 여자가 남자에게 제안한 것으로 가장 적절한 것을 고르시오.

① 계획표 작성하기　　② 도서관 이용하기
③ 인터넷 강의 듣기　　④ 수업시간에 집중하기
⑤ 공부 모임에 참여하기

16 대화를 듣고, 두 사람의 대화가 <u>어색한</u> 것을 고르시오.

①　　②　　③　　④　　⑤

17 대화를 듣고, 남자의 직업으로 가장 적절한 것을 고르시오.

① 모델　　　　② 안마사　　　③ 미용사
④ 피부 관리사　⑤ 은행원

18 다음을 듣고, 'this'가 가리키는 것으로 가장 적절한 것을 고르시오.

① 　② 　③

④ 　⑤

[19-20] 대화를 듣고, 남자의 마지막 말에 이어질 여자의 응답으로 가장 적절한 것을 고르시오.

19 Woman: _____
① I mean it.
② That's cool.
③ Don't worry so much.
④ I'm so glad to hear that.
⑤ I can't thank you enough.

20 Woman: _____
① I like musicals better.
② I'll meet you at the ticket box.
③ I don't have anything to do today.
④ I really want to watch the musical.
⑤ I have to take care of my brother all day.

01 그림 정보 파악

대화를 듣고, 남자가 선택할 물건으로 가장 적절한 것을 고르시오.

① ② ③

④ ⑤

W: Hello. Can I help you?

M: Yes, I need a □ _____ □ _____ for my son.

W: Okay. □ _____ □ _____ this one with a □ _____ on it?

M: Well, I want □ _____ □ _____ with a □ _____ on it. He likes bears.

W: □ _____ □ _____. Many boys like that cap.

02 날씨 파악

다음을 듣고, 일요일의 날씨로 가장 적절한 것을 고르시오.

① ② ③

④ ⑤

W: Good morning. This is the □ _____ □ _____ for this weekend. It'll be □ _____ and □ _____ □ _____ and Saturday. The rain will stop Saturday night, and it'll be □ _____ all day on □ _____. Be careful not to □ _____ a □ _____ in this kind of weather. Thank you.

03 의도 파악

대화를 듣고, 여자의 마지막 말의 의도로 가장 적절한 것을 고르시오.

① 사과   ② 제안   ③ 축하
④ 승낙   ⑤ 변명

W: Hi, Tom. □ _____ are you □ _____?

M: Hi, Sumi. I'm □ _____ a □ _____ to find a new guitarist.

W: You know, I can □ _____ the □ _____ pretty well.

M: Really? □ _____ □ _____ □ _____ join our band then?

W: □ _____. I really want to.

✏ **어휘복습** 잘 안 들리거나 몰라서 체크한 어휘를 써 놓고 복습해 보세요.

□ _____   □ _____   □ _____   □ _____

□ _____   □ _____   □ _____   □ _____

□ _____   □ _____   □ _____   □ _____

다음을 듣고, 남자가 언급하지 <u>않은</u> 것을 고르시오.

① 가족의 수   ② 아버지의 직업
③ 어머니의 취미   ④ 형의 나이
⑤ 사는 곳

M: Hi. Let me □ _____ you □ _____ my □ _____. There are □ _____ □ _____ in my family. My □ _____ is a history □ _____. My □ _____ cooks well. □ _____ is her □ _____. My older □ _____ is □ _____ years old. He is a singer in a rock band. I love my family.

대화를 듣고, 두 사람이 만나기로 한 시각을 고르시오.

① 3:00   ② 3:30   ③ 4:00
④ 4:30   ⑤ 5:00

W: Hello?
M: Mom. It's me. Jack is □ _____ □ _____ today, right?
W: Yes. He □ _____ at □ _____ □ _____ P.M. at the airport.
M: Then, □ _____ go to the □ _____ □ _____.
W: Sure. I'll □ _____ you □ _____ at □ _____ in front of your school.
M: Sounds good. See you then.

대화를 듣고, 남자의 장래 희망으로 가장 적절한 것을 고르시오.

① 건축가   ② 변호사
③ 번역가   ④ 운동선수
⑤ 사진작가

W: Wow, great! Where did you □ _____ these □ _____?
M: I □ _____ them in China last year.
W: I think you're really □ _____ □ _____ taking pictures.
M: Thank you. I □ _____ to □ _____ a □ _____.
W: That sounds good!

✎ **어휘복습** 잘 안 들리거나 몰라서 체크한 어휘를 써 놓고 복습해 보세요.

□ _____   □ _____   □ _____   □ _____
□ _____   □ _____   □ _____   □ _____
□ _____   □ _____   □ _____   □ _____

07 심정 추론

대화를 듣고, 남자의 심정으로 가장 적절한 것을 고르시오.

① sad ② angry
③ bored ④ excited
⑤ worried

M: Wendy, □ _____ are you going to □ _____ this □ _____?
W: Well, I'm going to □ _____ □ _____ all weekend. How about you?
M: I'm going to Jeju Island with my family.
W: That □ _____ □ _____!
M: Yes, I know. I □ _____ □ _____.

08 할 일 파악

대화를 듣고, 남자가 대화 직후에 할 일로 가장 적절한 것을 고르시오.

① 계산하기
② 우유 가져오기
③ 직원 불러오기
④ 생선 골라오기
⑤ 쇼핑카트 가져오기

M: Mom, □ _____ do we need to □ _____ here?
W: We need milk, fish, and some other things. Can you □ _____ the □ _____?
M: Sure, and I'll get the □ _____, □ _____.
W: Do you know □ _____ □ _____ □ _____ fresh fish?
M: I'm □ _____ □ _____.
W: Then, just □ _____ the □ _____. I'll wait for you at the fish counter.
M: Okay.

09 화제 추론

대화를 듣고, 무엇에 관한 내용인지 가장 적절한 것을 고르시오.

① 축제 준비 ② 건강 검진
③ 주말 계획 ④ 자기 소개
⑤ 장래 희망

W: We have a □ _____ □ _____. Do you □ _____ any □ _____?
M: Yes. I'm going to □ _____ to Gwangju □ _____ my □ _____. How about you?
W: I'm planning to □ _____ some □ _____ □ _____ at a nursing home.
M: That's really □ _____ □ _____ □ _____! I hope you have a good time.
W: Thanks. You, too.

✎ **어휘복습** 잘 안 들리거나 몰라서 체크한 어휘를 써 놓고 복습해 보세요.

□ _____   □ _____   □ _____   □ _____
□ _____   □ _____   □ _____   □ _____
□ _____   □ _____   □ _____   □ _____

10 교통수단 찾기

대화를 듣고, 여자가 선택할 교통수단으로 가장 적절한 것을 고르시오.

① 배　　② 기차　　③ 버스
④ 지하철　⑤ 비행기

W: Two □ _____ □ _____ to Busan, please.

M: I'm sorry, but we have □ _____ □ _____ ticket □ _____ .

W: Oh, no! I need two.

M: There are □ _____ that go to Busan, □ _____ . The bus □ _____ is right □ _____ □ _____ .

W: Really? Then, I'll go □ _____ □ _____ □ _____ . Thank you.

11 전화 목적 파악

대화를 듣고, 여자가 어제 전화를 건 이유로 가장 적절한 것을 고르시오.

① 친구 전화번호를 물어보려고
② 숙제에 대해 물어보려고
③ 저녁식사에 초대하려고
④ 뮤지컬을 함께 보려고
⑤ 운동을 함께 하려고

W: I □ _____ you yesterday, but your □ _____ was □ _____ .

M: Sorry about that. I went to see a □ _____ , so I □ _____ it □ _____ .

W: I see. □ _____ was the musical?

M: It was great. □ _____ did you call me?

W: I called to □ _____ you about the □ _____ , but I □ _____ it.

M: That's good.

12 장소 추론

대화를 듣고, 두 사람이 대화하는 장소로 가장 적절한 곳을 고르시오.

① 장난감 가게　　② 우체국
③ 옷가게　　　　④ 서점
⑤ 약국

M: Do you sell puzzles in □ _____ □ _____ ?

W: I'm sorry. We don't. But you can buy them at a □ _____ □ _____ □ _____ .

M: Okay. Then I'll just □ _____ these □ _____ . □ _____ □ _____ are they?

W: They're ten dollars.

M: Okay. By the way, where is the toy store?

W: It's next to the post office.

M: Thanks.

✎ **어휘복습** 잘 안 들리거나 몰라서 체크한 어휘를 써 놓고 복습해 보세요.

□ _____　□ _____　□ _____　□ _____

□ _____　□ _____　□ _____　□ _____

□ _____　□ _____　□ _____　□ _____

13 위치 찾기

대화를 듣고, 남자가 가려고 하는 장소를 고르시오.

M: Excuse me. Can you ☐ _____ me the ☐ _____ to ☐ _____ ☐ _____?

W: City Hall? ☐ _____ ☐ _____ two blocks and turn left.

M: ☐ _____ ☐ _____? And then?

W: Walk down Broadway, and you'll see it ☐ _____ your ☐ _____. It's ☐ _____ ☐ _____ the hospital.

M: Okay. Thank you very much.

14 부탁 파악

대화를 듣고, 남자가 여자에게 부탁한 일로 가장 적절한 것을 고르시오.

① 코트 주머니 확인하기
② 셔츠 단추 달아주기
③ 지갑 수선 맡기기
④ 세탁물 찾아오기
⑤ 방 청소하기

W: Hello?

M: It's me, Mom. I think I ☐ _____ my ☐ _____ at home.

W: ☐ _____ was the ☐ _____ ☐ _____ you saw it?

M: Sorry, but I'm ☐ _____ ☐ _____.

W: I ☐ _____ your ☐ _____ this morning, but I ☐ _____ ☐ _____ it.

M: Hmm... Can you ☐ _____ my blue ☐ _____? I think I ☐ _____ it in its ☐ _____.

W: Okay, I will.

M: Thanks, Mom.

✎ **어휘복습** 잘 안 들리거나 몰라서 체크한 어휘를 써 놓고 복습해 보세요.

☐ _____ ☐ _____ ☐ _____ ☐ _____

☐ _____ ☐ _____ ☐ _____ ☐ _____

☐ _____ ☐ _____ ☐ _____ ☐ _____

15 제안 파악

대화를 듣고, 여자가 남자에게 제안한 것으로 가장 적절한 것을 고르시오.

① 계획표 작성하기
② 도서관 이용하기
③ 인터넷 강의 듣기
④ 수업시간에 집중하기
⑤ 공부 모임에 참여하기

M: Jane, I heard you got a □ _____ □ _____ on the □ _____.
W: Yes. I'm so happy.
M: How did you □ _____ so □ _____ on that test?
W: I □ _____ □ _____ my friends. Why don't you □ _____ our study □ _____?
M: Really? Thank you. I'd love to.

16 어색한 대화 찾기

대화를 듣고, 두 사람의 대화가 <u>어색한</u> 것을 고르시오.

①   ②   ③   ④   ⑤

① W: □ _____ □ _____ do you usually □ _____ □ _____?
   M: It was last □ _____.
② W: □ _____ □ _____ is this hat?
   M: It's fifteen dollars.
③ W: What's your □ _____ □ _____?
   M: I □ _____ □ _____ most.
④ W: □ _____ □ _____ joining our club?
   M: That's a □ _____ □ _____.
⑤ W: □ _____ □ _____? You don't look so good.
   M: I have a □ _____.

✎ **어휘복습** 잘 안 들리거나 몰라서 체크한 어휘를 써 놓고 복습해 보세요.

□ _____   □ _____   □ _____   □ _____
□ _____   □ _____   □ _____   □ _____
□ _____   □ _____   □ _____   □ _____

17 직업 파악

대화를 듣고, 남자의 직업으로 가장 적절한 것을 고르시오.

① 모델
② 안마사
③ 미용사
④ 피부 관리사
⑤ 은행원

M: Mrs. Banks. Long time no see.

W: Yes, I've been so busy. How are you?

M: Great, thanks. □ _____ can we do □ _____ you today?

W: I □ _____ a □ _____.

M: First, Jane will □ _____ your □ _____, and then I'll □ _____ it.

W: Thank you. Carl, you always □ _____ a □ _____ □ _____.

18 화제 추론

다음을 듣고, 'this'가 가리키는 것으로 가장 적절한 것을 고르시오.

①
②
③
④
⑤

M: People may use this when they □ _____. Other people use this to □ _____ □ _____. This usually has □ _____ □ _____ and doesn't need electric power. For your safety, don't forget to □ _____ a □ _____ when you use this. What is this?

✎ **어휘복습** 잘 안 들리거나 몰라서 체크한 어휘를 써 놓고 복습해 보세요.

□ _____   □ _____   □ _____   □ _____

□ _____   □ _____   □ _____   □ _____

□ _____   □ _____   □ _____   □ _____

19 알맞은 응답 찾기

대화를 듣고, 남자의 마지막 말에 이어질 여자의 응답으로 가장 적절한 것을 고르시오.

Woman: _____
① I mean it.
② That's cool.
③ Don't worry so much.
④ I'm so glad to hear that.
⑤ I can't thank you enough.

W: You □ _____ □ _____ today! What happened, David?

M: I □ _____ □ _____ last night. I don't think I did well in the □ _____ □ _____.

W: □ _____ will the □ _____ come out?

M: Tomorrow. So I □ _____ very □ _____ about them.

W: _____

20 알맞은 응답 찾기

대화를 듣고, 남자의 마지막 말에 이어질 여자의 응답으로 가장 적절한 것을 고르시오.

Woman: _____
① I like musicals better.
② I'll meet you at the ticket box.
③ I don't have anything to do today.
④ I really want to watch the musical.
⑤ I have to take care of my brother all day.

M: Hi, Julia! Are you free this afternoon?

W: What's up?

M: I □ _____ two □ _____ for the musical *Mama Mia*.

W: Sounds great, but I □ _____ □ _____ □ _____ this afternoon.

M: □ _____ □ _____?

W: _____

✎ **어휘복습** 잘 안 들리거나 몰라서 체크한 어휘를 써 놓고 복습해 보세요.

□ _____ □ _____ □ _____ □ _____

□ _____ □ _____ □ _____ □ _____

□ _____ □ _____ □ _____ □ _____

04회 기출 듣기평가

01 대화를 듣고, 두 사람이 구입할 넥타이로 가장 적절한 것을 고르시오.

① ② ③

④ ⑤

02 다음을 듣고, 오늘 오후의 날씨로 가장 적절한 것을 고르시오.

① ② ③ ④ ⑤

03 대화를 듣고, 남자의 마지막 말의 의도로 가장 적절한 것을 고르시오.

① 거절　　　② 동의　　　③ 제안
④ 축하　　　⑤ 위로

04 다음을 듣고, 남자가 언급하지 <u>않은</u> 것을 고르시오.

① 이름　　　② 나이　　　③ 고향
④ 특기　　　⑤ 장래 희망

05 대화를 듣고, 두 사람이 만날 시각을 고르시오.

① 6:00　　　② 6:30　　　③ 7:00
④ 7:30　　　⑤ 8:00

06 대화를 듣고, 여자의 장래 희망으로 가장 적절한 것을 고르시오.

① 화가　　　② 건축가　　　③ 음악가
④ 운동선수　　　⑤ 영화감독

07 대화를 듣고, 남자의 심정으로 가장 적절한 것을 고르시오.

① 행복한　　　② 지루한　　　③ 기대하는
④ 자랑스러운　　　⑤ 실망스러운

08 대화를 듣고, 여자가 대화 직후에 할 일로 가장 적절한 것을 고르시오.

① 학생증 신청하기
② 전시회 검색하기
③ 단체관람 예약하기
④ 교통수단 알아보기
⑤ 미술관에 전화하기

09 대화를 듣고, 무엇에 관한 내용인지 가장 적절한 것을 고르시오.

① 성적 상담
② 적성검사 결과
③ 체육대회 날짜 변경
④ 중간고사 일정 확인
⑤ 여름방학 계획표 작성

10 대화를 듣고, 두 사람이 이용할 교통수단으로 가장 적절한 것을 고르시오.

① 택시　　　② 기차　　　③ 버스
④ 지하철　　　⑤ 자전거

11 대화를 듣고, 여자가 어제 병원에 간 이유로 가장 적절한 것을 고르시오.

① 눈병이 나서
② 감기에 걸려서
③ 봉사활동을 하기 위해서
④ 엄마의 병문안을 위해서
⑤ 정기 건강 검진을 받기 위해서

12 대화를 듣고, 두 사람의 관계로 가장 적절한 것을 고르시오.

① 교사 – 학생
② 영화감독 – 배우
③ 택시 기사 – 승객
④ 동물원 사육사 – 관람객
⑤ 라디오 진행자 – 청취자

13 대화를 듣고, 남자가 가려고 하는 장소를 고르시오.

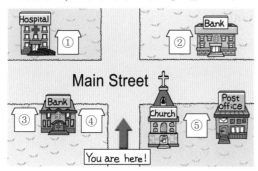

14 대화를 듣고, 여자가 남자에게 부탁한 일로 가장 적절한 것을 고르시오.

① 전등 끄기   ② 컴퓨터 끄기
③ 칠판 지우기   ④ 책상 정리하기
⑤ 열쇠 가져다주기

15 대화를 듣고, 여자가 남자에게 제안한 것으로 가장 적절한 것을 고르시오.

① 한식 체험   ② 박물관 관람
③ 웹사이트 검색   ④ 한옥마을 방문
⑤ 관광안내소 문의

16 대화를 듣고, 두 사람의 대화가 <u>어색한</u> 것을 고르시오.

①   ②   ③   ④   ⑤

17 대화를 듣고, 남자의 직업으로 가장 적절한 것을 고르시오.

① 소설가   ② 편집자   ③ 건축가
④ 웹 디자이너   ⑤ 관광 가이드

18 다음을 듣고, 'this'가 가리키는 것으로 가장 적절한 것을 고르시오.

①   ②   ③

④   ⑤

[19-20] 대화를 듣고, 여자의 마지막 말에 이어질 남자의 응답으로 가장 적절한 것을 고르시오.

19 Man: _____
① Here we are.
② That's fantastic!
③ It's my pleasure.
④ Sure. No problem.
⑤ I'm sorry to hear that.

20 Man: _____
① I may be a bit late.
② I met her 30 minutes ago.
③ At 6 o'clock every Saturday.
④ Maybe with Mike and his sister.
⑤ The Chinese restaurant near our school.

04회 DICTATION

다시 듣고, 빈칸에 알맞은 단어를 써 보세요.

01 그림 정보 파악

대화를 듣고, 두 사람이 구입할 넥타이로 가장 적절한 것을 고르시오.

① ② ③ ④ ⑤

M: □ _____ at this □ _____! This is for □ _____.

W: I like it. The □ _____ on it □ _____ □ _____.

M: □ _____, it does. You know, Dad likes sunflowers.

W: Right. Dad will like it. □ _____ □ _____ it.

02 날씨 파악

다음을 듣고, 오늘 오후의 날씨로 가장 적절한 것을 고르시오.

① ② ③ ④ ⑤

W: Good morning. This is today's □ _____ report. This

□ _____, it's □ _____ and a little □ _____, but the

weather will get warmer. In the □ _____, it'll be

□ _____. It'll be □ _____ □ _____ doing □ _____

□ _____. Thank you.

03 의도 파악

대화를 듣고, 남자의 마지막 말의 의도로 가장 적절한 것을 고르시오.

① 거절   ② 동의   ③ 제안
④ 축하   ⑤ 위로

W: Hi, Kevin. □ _____ are you?

M: I'm at □ _____. Why?

W: I have two K-pop □ _____ tickets. Do you want to

□ _____ the concert □ _____ □ _____?

M: I'm □ _____, □ _____ I can't. I don't feel well today.

✏ **어휘복습** 잘 안 들리거나 몰라서 체크한 어휘를 써 놓고 복습해 보세요.

□ _____   □ _____   □ _____   □ _____

□ _____   □ _____   □ _____   □ _____

□ _____   □ _____   □ _____   □ _____

04 미언급 파악

다음을 듣고, 남자가 언급하지 않은 것을 고르시오.

① 이름　② 나이　③ 고향
④ 특기　⑤ 장래 희망

M: Hi, everyone. Nice to meet you. Let me □ _____ □ _____. My □ _____ is Thomas Carter. I'm □ _____ □ _____ □ _____. My □ _____ is New York. My □ _____ is to become a □ _____ someday. I want to □ _____ many new □ _____ here. Thank you.

05 숫자 정보 파악

대화를 듣고, 두 사람이 만날 시각을 고르시오.

① 6:00　② 6:30　③ 7:00
④ 7:30　⑤ 8:00

W: John, let's □ _____ □ _____ tomorrow □ _____.
M: Okay. □ _____ □ _____ shall we meet? I □ _____ □ _____ at □ _____ o'clock.
W: Then, how about □ _____ □ _____?
M: That's □ _____ □ _____. □ _____ meet at □ _____ o'clock.
W: Okay. See you then.

06 장래 희망 파악

대화를 듣고, 여자의 장래 희망으로 가장 적절한 것을 고르시오.

① 화가　　② 건축가
③ 음악가　④ 운동선수
⑤ 영화감독

M: Hi, Julia. Did you □ _____ a □ _____ yet?
W: □ _____ □ _____. How about you?
M: I want to join the movie club.
W: Good. I'm □ _____ □ _____ the □ _____ club.
M: Oh, really? Do you like music?
W: Yes. I □ _____ to be a □ _____.

✏ **어휘복습** 잘 안 들리거나 몰라서 체크한 어휘를 써 놓고 복습해 보세요.

□ _____　□ _____　□ _____　□ _____
□ _____　□ _____　□ _____　□ _____
□ _____　□ _____　□ _____　□ _____

07 심정 추론

대화를 듣고, 남자의 심정으로 가장 적절한 것을 고르시오.

① 행복한　　② 지루한
③ 기대하는　④ 자랑스러운
⑤ 실망스러운

W: You don't look well. What's □ _____?
M: You know, the English drama □ _____ was yesterday.
W: Right. □ _____ did it □ _____?
M: Well, I □ _____ a lot, but I □ _____ □ _____ a □ _____.
W: Oh, I □ _____ how you feel.

08 할 일 파악

대화를 듣고, 여자가 대화 직후에 할 일로 가장 적절한 것을 고르시오.

① 학생증 신청하기
② 전시회 검색하기
③ 단체관람 예약하기
④ 교통수단 알아보기
⑤ 미술관에 전화하기

W: Let's □ _____ to Central □ _____ □ _____ next week.
M: Oh, I heard the □ _____ are very □ _____.
W: □ _____ they have a □ _____ □ _____.
M: Why don't you □ _____ the □ _____ □ _____?
W: □ _____. I will.

09 화제 추론

대화를 듣고, 무엇에 관한 내용인지 가장 적절한 것을 고르시오.

① 성적 상담
② 적성검사 결과
③ 체육대회 날짜 변경
④ 중간고사 일정 확인
⑤ 여름방학 계획표 작성

M: Your school □ _____ □ _____ is □ _____ □ _____, right?
W: □ _____, it was □ _____ because it'll be windy and rainy next Monday.
M: Really? So □ _____ is the sports day?
W: It's □ _____ □ _____.
M: I see.

✎ **어휘복습** 잘 안 들리거나 몰라서 체크한 어휘를 써 놓고 복습해 보세요.

□ _____　　□ _____　　□ _____　　□ _____
□ _____　　□ _____　　□ _____　　□ _____
□ _____　　□ _____　　□ _____　　□ _____

10 교통수단 찾기

대화를 듣고, 두 사람이 이용할 교통수단으로 가장 적절한 것을 고르시오.

① 택시　② 기차　③ 버스
④ 지하철　⑤ 자전거

M: Hurry up. It's seven thirty already.

W: All right. Should we □_____ a □_____?

M: □_____, there are too □_____ cars on the □_____ now.

W: Well, □_____ □_____ taking the □_____ then?

M: That's □_____. Let's go!

11 전화 목적 파악

대화를 듣고, 여자가 어제 병원에 간 이유로 가장 적절한 것을 고르시오.

① 눈병이 나서
② 감기에 걸려서
③ 봉사활동을 하기 위해서
④ 엄마의 병문안을 위해서
⑤ 정기 건강 검진을 받기 위해서

M: I □_____ □_____ you at school yesterday. What happened?

W: Oh, I went to □_____ the □_____ with my mom.

M: Why? Were you □_____?

W: I □_____ a □_____, but I'm □_____ now.

M: It's really □_____ outside. □_____ □_____ of yourself.

W: Thanks.

12 관계 추론

대화를 듣고, 두 사람의 관계로 가장 적절한 것을 고르시오.

① 교사 – 학생
② 영화감독 – 배우
③ 택시 기사 – 승객
④ 동물원 사육사 – 관람객
⑤ 라디오 진행자 – 청취자

M: Thank you for calling Tom's □_____ Quiz □_____! Who am I talking to?

W: Hi, this is Sujin from Cheonan.

M: Hi, Sujin. Can you □_____ the □_____?

W: I think it's number three, the lion.

M: You □_____ it! Congratulations!

✎ **어휘복습** 잘 안 들리거나 몰라서 체크한 어휘를 써 놓고 복습해 보세요.

□ _____　　□ _____　　□ _____　　□ _____

□ _____　　□ _____　　□ _____　　□ _____

□ _____　　□ _____　　□ _____　　□ _____

13 위치 찾기

대화를 듣고, 남자가 가려고 하는 장소를 고르시오.

M: Excuse me. □ _____ can I □ _____ to the □ _____ □ _____?

W: Let me see. Go □ _____ one block and □ _____ □ _____.

M: Go straight one block and turn right?

W: Yes. Then, walk □ _____ a little □ _____. It'll be on your □ _____ □ _____ □ _____ the □ _____.

M: Oh, I see. Thank you very much.

14 부탁 파악

대화를 듣고, 여자가 남자에게 부탁한 일로 가장 적절한 것을 고르시오.

① 전등 끄기　　② 컴퓨터 끄기
③ 칠판 지우기　　④ 책상 정리하기
⑤ 열쇠 가져다주기

W: Minsu. Can you □ _____ □ _____?

M: □ _____, Ms. Brown. □ _____ can I do for you?

W: After our English class, can you □ _____ the □ _____?

M: I'd be □ _____ to. □ _____ □ _____?

W: That's all. Thank you.

✏️ **어휘복습** 잘 안 들리거나 몰라서 체크한 어휘를 써 놓고 복습해 보세요.

□ _____　　□ _____　　□ _____　　□ _____

□ _____　　□ _____　　□ _____　　□ _____

□ _____　　□ _____　　□ _____　　□ _____

대화를 듣고, 여자가 남자에게 제안한 것으로 가장 적절한 것을 고르시오.

① 한식 체험　　② 박물관 관람
③ 웹사이트 검색　④ 한옥마을 방문
⑤ 관광안내소 문의

M: Jina, I'm going to Damyang this weekend.

W: Are you? I □ _____ □ _____ last year.

M: Really? □ _____ did you □ _____ there?

W: I □ _____ to the Hanok □ _____ . It was great. □ _____ □ _____ you □ _____ □ _____ some time?

M: Sounds good. Thanks.

대화를 듣고, 두 사람의 대화가 <u>어색한</u> 것을 고르시오.

①　　②　　③　　④　　⑤

① M: I am □ _____ . It's my □ _____ .
   W: My □ _____ .

② M: How do you □ _____ your last □ _____ ?
   W: It's B-R-O-W-N.

③ M: Hi, Cathy. □ _____ is it □ _____ ?
   W: □ _____ , thanks.

④ M: □ _____ □ _____ , please?
   W: This is Amy.

⑤ M: □ _____ you for your help.
   W: □ _____ □ _____ .

✎ **어휘복습** 잘 안 들리거나 몰라서 체크한 어휘를 써 놓고 복습해 보세요.

□ _____　□ _____　□ _____　□ _____

□ _____　□ _____　□ _____　□ _____

□ _____　□ _____　□ _____　□ _____

17 직업 파악

대화를 듣고, 남자의 직업으로 가장 적절한 것을 고르시오.

① 소설가   ② 편집자
③ 건축가   ④ 웹 디자이너
⑤ 관광 가이드

W: Good morning, Mr. Watson. How are you?

M: Tired. I just □ _____ my □ _____.

W: Oh, really?

M: Yes, I already e-mailed it to you.

W: Good. I'll □ _____ my □ _____ right away.

M: □ _____ me after you □ _____ it.

W: I will. Thanks. □ _____ people are □ _____ for your new novel.

18 화제 추론

다음을 듣고, 'this'가 가리키는 것으로 가장 적절한 것을 고르시오.

①   ②   ③

④   ⑤

W: Do you love □ _____? When you're reading books, do your eyes get □ _____ easily? Then, you may need this. This □ _____ a lot of □ _____. Many people use this when reading □ _____ □ _____. What is this?

✎ **어휘복습** 잘 안 들리거나 몰라서 체크한 어휘를 써 놓고 복습해 보세요.

□ _____   □ _____   □ _____   □ _____
□ _____   □ _____   □ _____   □ _____
□ _____   □ _____   □ _____   □ _____

19 알맞은 응답 찾기

대화를 듣고, 여자의 마지막 말에 이어질 남자의 응답으로 가장 적절한 것을 고르시오.

Man: _____

① Here we are.
② That's fantastic!
③ It's my pleasure.
④ Sure. No problem.
⑤ I'm sorry to hear that.

M: Hi, Jenny. □ _____ did you □ _____ last weekend?

W: I just □ _____ □ _____ . I □ _____ do □ _____ .

M: Really? Why?

W: My □ _____ was □ _____ . She □ _____ □ _____ anything.

M: _____

20 알맞은 응답 찾기

대화를 듣고, 여자의 마지막 말에 이어질 남자의 응답으로 가장 적절한 것을 고르시오.

Man: _____

① I may be a bit late.
② I met her 30 minutes ago.
③ At 6 o'clock every Saturday.
④ Maybe with Mike and his sister.
⑤ The Chinese restaurant near our school.

W: You're □ _____ Susan at six o'clock, right?

M: Yes, we're planning to have □ _____ □ _____ .

W: Well, you should □ _____ □ _____ then. It's already five thirty.

M: Oh, really? Thanks, Mom.

W: □ _____ are you □ _____ for dinner?

M: _____

✎ **어휘복습** 잘 안 들리거나 몰라서 체크한 어휘를 써 놓고 복습해 보세요.

□ _____   □ _____   □ _____   □ _____

□ _____   □ _____   □ _____   □ _____

□ _____   □ _____   □ _____   □ _____

01 다음을 듣고, 'it'이 가리키는 것으로 가장 적절한 것을 고르시오.

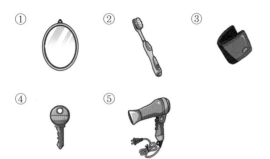

02 대화를 듣고, 무엇에 관한 내용인지 가장 적절한 것을 고르시오.

① 환경 보호　② 가족 여행　③ 요리 강습
④ 봉사 활동　⑤ 교우 관계

03 다음을 듣고, 내일 대구의 날씨로 가장 적절한 것을 고르시오.

04 대화를 듣고, 남자의 마지막 말의 의도로 가장 적절한 것을 고르시오.

① 실망　② 칭찬　③ 충고
④ 초대　⑤ 허락

05 다음을 듣고, 오늘 남자가 먹지 않은 것을 고르시오.

① 바나나　② 샌드위치　③ 스파게티
④ 오렌지 주스　⑤ 피자

06 대화를 듣고, 두 사람이 만나기로 한 시간을 고르시오.

① 9:30　② 10:00　③ 10:30
④ 11:00　⑤ 11:30

07 대화를 듣고, 두 사람이 할 일로 가장 적절한 것을 고르시오.

① 카드 만들기
② 옷가게 가기
③ 파티 준비하기
④ 인터넷 검색하기
⑤ 아버지에게 전화하기

08 대화를 듣고, 남자의 심정으로 가장 적절한 것을 고르시오.

① 화남　② 미안함　③ 행복함
④ 부러워함　⑤ 그리워함

09 대화를 듣고, 여자가 지난 주말에 한 일로 가장 적절한 것을 고르시오.

① 숙제하기　② 수영하기
③ 쿠키 만들기　④ 만화 그리기
⑤ 화분에 물주기

10 대화를 듣고, 남자가 지불한 금액을 고르시오.

① $10　② $30　③ $60
④ $70　⑤ $80

11 다음을 듣고, 두 사람의 대화가 <u>어색한</u> 것을 고르시오.

① ② ③ ④ ⑤

12 대화를 듣고, 여자가 음악 동아리에 가입한 이유로 가장 적절한 것을 고르시오.

① 가수가 되고 싶어서
② 친구를 사귀고 싶어서
③ 음악 선생님이 권유해서
④ 악기를 함께 연주하고 싶어서
⑤ 다양한 노래를 배우고 싶어서

13 대화를 듣고, 두 사람의 관계로 가장 적절한 것을 고르시오.

① 교사 – 학생
② 경찰 – 시민
③ 승무원 – 승객
④ 수의사 – 강아지 주인
⑤ 음식점 주인 – 요리사

14 대화를 듣고, 여자가 남자에게 부탁한 일로 가장 적절한 것을 고르시오.

① 청소하기 ② 채소 씻기
③ 과일 사기 ④ 케이크 주문하기
⑤ 요리책 가져오기

15 대화를 듣고, 두 사람이 만나기로 한 장소로 가장 적절한 곳을 고르시오.

① 공원 ② 영화관 ③ 도서관
④ 지하철 역 ⑤ 버스 정류장

16 대화를 듣고, 남자가 어제 모자를 사지 <u>못한</u> 이유로 가장 적절한 것을 고르시오.

① 너무 비싸서 ② 가게 문이 닫혀서
③ 지갑을 두고 와서 ④ 맞는 크기가 없어서
⑤ 원하는 색이 없어서

17 대화를 듣고, 남자가 할 일로 가장 적절한 것을 고르시오.

① 꽃 수집하기 ② 공원 산책하기
③ 과학 공부하기 ④ 사진 찍어주기
⑤ 교과서 가져오기

18 대화를 듣고, 남자가 전화를 건 목적으로 가장 적절한 것을 고르시오.

① 좋은 식당을 물어보려고
② 요리 방법을 알려주려고
③ 약속 날짜를 변경하려고
④ 친구의 이메일을 물어보려고
⑤ 박물관 위치를 확인하려고

[19-20] 대화를 듣고, 남자의 마지막 말에 이어질 여자의 응답으로 가장 적절한 것을 고르시오.

19 Woman: _____

① Of course!
② Take care.
③ Same here.
④ I envy you.
⑤ It's my fault.

20 Woman: _____

① See you soon downstairs.
② It's already twelve o'clock.
③ Come and help me find my watch.
④ You did a good job!
⑤ I like that TV show very much, too.

01 화제 추론

다음을 듣고, 'it'이 가리키는 것으로 가장 적절한 것을 고르시오.

① ② ③
④ ⑤

W: We can use it when we want to □ _____ □ _____. It has different sizes and shapes. Since it is usually □ _____ □ _____ □ _____, we have to be □ _____ because it □ _____ □ _____. What is it?

02 화제 추론

대화를 듣고, 무엇에 관한 내용인지 가장 적절한 것을 고르시오.

① 환경 보호   ② 가족 여행
③ 요리 강습   ④ 봉사 활동
⑤ 교우 관계

M: Hi, Jenny. □ _____ was your □ _____ □ _____ last week?
W: We □ _____ a lot of □ _____ on Jeju Island.
M: □ _____ did you □ _____ there?
W: We went to the □ _____ and ate □ _____.
M: That sounds great! I also ate seafood in Sokcho with my family.
W: Oh, did you like Sokcho?
M: Yes, I really liked the □ _____ □ _____ there.

03 날씨 파악

다음을 듣고, 내일 대구의 날씨로 가장 적절한 것을 고르시오.

① ② ③
④ ⑤

M: Hello. Here's the weather report for □ _____. Seoul will be □ _____ all day. Gwangju will be □ _____ and Daejeon will have □ _____ skies. But it will be □ _____ in Daegu. Don't □ _____ to take your umbrella. Thank you.

✎ **어휘복습** 잘 안 들리거나 몰라서 체크한 어휘를 써 놓고 복습해 보세요.

□ _____   □ _____   □ _____   □ _____
□ _____   □ _____   □ _____   □ _____
□ _____   □ _____   □ _____   □ _____

04 의도 파악

대화를 듣고, 남자의 마지막 말의 의도로 가장 적절한 것을 고르시오.

① 실망　② 칭찬　③ 충고
④ 초대　⑤ 허락

M: Did you □ _____ your □ _____?

W: Yes, I □ _____ it with Sujin □ _____.

M: □ _____ □ _____ see it?

W: Of course. Here it is. □ _____ do you □ _____?

M: □ _____! You did a □ _____ job!

05 미언급 파악

다음을 듣고, 오늘 남자가 먹지 않은 것을 고르시오.

① 바나나　　② 샌드위치
③ 스파게티　④ 오렌지 주스
⑤ 피자

M: I □ _____ □ _____ every day. Today, I woke up early in the □ _____ and ate □ _____. For □ _____, I had a □ _____ with □ _____ □ _____. □ _____ □ _____, I went to Pizza World with my friends. I had two □ _____ of □ _____ there.

06 숫자 정보 파악

대화를 듣고, 두 사람이 만나기로 한 시간을 고르시오.

① 9:30　② 10:00　③ 10:30
④ 11:00　⑤ 11:30

W: I'm □ _____ about □ _____ to the □ _____ tomorrow.

M: So am I. □ _____ □ _____ shall we □ _____ at the zoo?

W: □ _____ make it at □ _____ o'clock.

M: But the zoo □ _____ at □ _____ □ _____.

W: Oh, really? Then, how about at □ _____?

M: □ _____ □ _____. See you then at the main gate.

✎ **어휘복습** 잘 안 들리거나 몰라서 체크한 어휘를 써 놓고 복습해 보세요.

□ _____　□ _____　□ _____　□ _____

□ _____　□ _____　□ _____　□ _____

□ _____　□ _____　□ _____　□ _____

07 할 일 파악

대화를 듣고, 두 사람이 할 일로 가장 적절한 것을 고르시오.

① 카드 만들기
② 옷가게 가기
③ 파티 준비하기
④ 인터넷 검색하기
⑤ 아버지에게 전화하기

W: Tom, I'm going to ☐ _____ a ☐ _____ for Dad.

M: ☐ _____ do you ☐ _____ to buy?

W: A ☐ _____, but I can't ☐ _____ a ☐ _____ on the ☐ _____.

M: Hmm... Then, why don't you ☐ _____ to a ☐ _____ ☐ _____?

W: Sounds good. Will you ☐ _____ ☐ _____ me?

M: Sure.

08 심정 추론

대화를 듣고, 남자의 심정으로 가장 적절한 것을 고르시오.

① 화남   ② 미안함
③ 행복함   ④ 부러워함
⑤ 그리워함

W: Is this your ☐ _____ ☐ _____?

M: Yes, it is. These are my mom and dad.

W: ☐ _____ is this ☐ _____? Is she your ☐ _____?

M: Yes. She ☐ _____ to Canada last year. I really ☐ _____ ☐ _____.

W: I ☐ _____ ☐ _____ you ☐ _____. I want to see my grandmother, too.

09 한 일 파악

대화를 듣고, 여자가 지난 주말에 한 일로 가장 적절한 것을 고르시오.

① 숙제하기   ② 수영하기
③ 쿠키 만들기   ④ 만화 그리기
⑤ 화분에 물주기

W: Charlie, ☐ _____ did you ☐ _____ last ☐ _____?

M: I ☐ _____ to the ☐ _____ ☐ _____ with my friends.

W: Really? Did you ☐ _____ ☐ _____?

M: Yes, of course! How was your weekend?

W: It was ☐ _____! I ☐ _____ ☐ _____ for my family.

M: Oh, good!

✏️ **어휘복습** 잘 안 들리거나 몰라서 체크한 어휘를 써 놓고 복습해 보세요.

☐ _____   ☐ _____   ☐ _____   ☐ _____

☐ _____   ☐ _____   ☐ _____   ☐ _____

☐ _____   ☐ _____   ☐ _____   ☐ _____

대화를 듣고, 남자가 지불한 금액을 고르시오.

① $10   ② $30   ③ $60
④ $70   ⑤ $80

M: This baseball □ _____ looks nice! How much is it?

W: It's □ _____ dollars. Do you need a □ _____, too?
It's □ _____ □ _____.

M: May I see one?

W: Sure. It's only □ _____ dollars.

M: Oh, good! Give me □ _____ gloves and □ _____ bat, please.

W: Then the □ _____ is □ _____ dollars.

M: Okay. Here you are.

다음을 듣고, 두 사람의 대화가 <u>어색한</u> 것을 고르시오.

①   ②   ③   ④   ⑤

① M: Do you □ _____ a red pen?
W: No, I don't have one.

② M: What is your □ _____ holiday?
W: I like Christmas the □ _____.

③ M: How □ _____ do you play computer games?
W: Yes, it's in the living room.

④ M: □ _____ do you □ _____ □ _____ my glasses?
W: I think they look nice.

⑤ M: Did you □ _____ your meal?
W: Yes, it was □ _____.

✎ **어휘복습** 잘 안 들리거나 몰라서 체크한 어휘를 써 놓고 복습해 보세요.

□ _____   □ _____   □ _____   □ _____
□ _____   □ _____   □ _____   □ _____
□ _____   □ _____   □ _____   □ _____

12 이유 파악

대화를 듣고, 여자가 음악 동아리에 가입한 이유로 가장 적절한 것을 고르시오.

① 가수가 되고 싶어서
② 친구를 사귀고 싶어서
③ 음악 선생님이 권유해서
④ 악기를 함께 연주하고 싶어서
⑤ 다양한 노래를 배우고 싶어서

M: Carol, □ _____ you a □ _____ of any □ _____?
W: Yes, I'm in the □ _____ club.
M: That sounds □ _____. □ _____ did you □ _____ that club?
W: Because I □ _____ to □ _____ many □ _____.
M: Oh, I see.

13 관계 추론

대화를 듣고, 두 사람의 관계로 가장 적절한 것을 고르시오.

① 교사– 학생
② 경찰– 시민
③ 승무원– 승객
④ 수의사– 강아지 주인
⑤ 음식점 주인– 요리사

M: What's □ _____ with your □ _____?
W: My dog won't □ _____ or □ _____ anything.
M: That's not good. Did your dog □ _____ something □ _____?
W: Well, I don't think so.
M: Then let's □ _____ an □ _____.

14 부탁 파악

대화를 듣고, 여자가 남자에게 부탁한 일로 가장 적절한 것을 고르시오.

① 청소하기
② 채소 씻기
③ 과일 사기
④ 케이크 주문하기
⑤ 요리책 가져오기

M: Mom, □ _____ are you □ _____?
W: I'm making bulgogi for Dad. □ _____ is his □ _____.
M: Oh, do you □ _____ any □ _____?
W: Yes, □ _____ these □ _____ for me.
M: Okay.

✎ **어휘복습** 잘 안 들리거나 몰라서 체크한 어휘를 써 놓고 복습해 보세요.

□ _____   □ _____   □ _____   □ _____
□ _____   □ _____   □ _____   □ _____
□ _____   □ _____   □ _____   □ _____

15 장소 추론

대화를 듣고, 두 사람이 만나기로 한 장소로 가장 적절한 곳을 고르시오.

① 공원 ② 영화관
③ 도서관 ④ 지하철 역
⑤ 버스 정류장

W: Hello?

M: Hello, Minji. Do you want to □ _____ to the □ _____ this □ _____?

W: Sounds great! □ _____ shall we □ _____?

M: How about at □ _____ p.m. at Star □ _____ □ _____?

W: I don't know where it is. □ _____ □ _____ meeting at the □ _____ □ _____ near our school?

M: Okay. See you there.

16 이유 파악

대화를 듣고, 남자가 어제 모자를 사지 못한 이유로 가장 적절한 것을 고르시오.

① 너무 비싸서
② 가게 문이 닫혀서
③ 지갑을 두고 와서
④ 맞는 크기가 없어서
⑤ 원하는 색이 없어서

W: John, I □ _____ you went to □ _____ a □ _____ yesterday.

M: Right, but I □ _____ □ _____ one.

W: □ _____ □ _____? Didn't you find anything you liked?

M: No, I □ _____ a □ _____ one, but they □ _____ had □ _____ caps.

W: Oh, I see.

✎ **어휘복습** 잘 안 들리거나 몰라서 체크한 어휘를 써 놓고 복습해 보세요.

□ _____ □ _____ □ _____ □ _____

□ _____ □ _____ □ _____ □ _____

□ _____ □ _____ □ _____ □ _____

17 할 일 파악

대화를 듣고, 남자가 할 일로 가장 적절한
것을 고르시오.

① 꽃 수집하기
② 공원 산책하기
③ 과학 공부하기
④ 사진 찍어주기
⑤ 교과서 가져오기

M: Look! Can you □ _____ those □ _____ over there?
W: The flowers □ _____ that □ _____?
M: Yes. I think I □ _____ them in my □ _____.
W: Really? They're so beautiful. I want to □ _____ a □ _____ □ _____ □ _____ with the flowers.
M: Then, go over there. □ _____ □ _____ a □ _____ for you.
W: Thanks.

18 전화 목적 파악

대화를 듣고, 남자가 전화를 건 목적으로 가
장 적절한 것을 고르시오.

① 좋은 식당을 물어보려고
② 요리 방법을 알려주려고
③ 약속 날짜를 변경하려고
④ 친구의 이메일을 물어보려고
⑤ 박물관 위치를 확인하려고

W: Hello?
M: Hello, Jane. This is Mark. Hey, you □ _____ □ _____ the science □ _____, right?
W: Yes. Why?
M: I'm □ _____ □ _____ with my friends this □ _____.
W: Really?
M: Yeah. □ _____ there any □ _____ □ _____ near the museum?
W: Yes, there's a good Italian restaurant □ _____ □ _____ □ _____ it.
M: Thanks a lot.

✎ **어휘복습** 잘 안 들리거나 몰라서 체크한 어휘를 써 놓고 복습해 보세요.

□ _____   □ _____   □ _____   □ _____

□ _____   □ _____   □ _____   □ _____

□ _____   □ _____   □ _____   □ _____

19 알맞은 응답 찾기

대화를 듣고, 남자의 마지막 말에 이어질 여자의 응답으로 가장 적절한 것을 고르시오.

Woman: _____

① Of course!
② Take care.
③ Same here.
④ I envy you.
⑤ It's my fault.

M: Oh, this is the □ _____ Wonderland □ _____ !

W: Yeah! I'm □ _____ it now. I like the story very much.

M: Really? Can I □ _____ it □ _____ ?

W: _____

20 알맞은 응답 찾기

대화를 듣고, 남자의 마지막 말에 이어질 여자의 응답으로 가장 적절한 것을 고르시오.

Woman: _____

① See you soon downstairs.
② It's already twelve o'clock.
③ Come and help me find my watch.
④ You did a good job!
⑤ I like that TV show very much, too.

W: Tony, □ _____ are you?

M: I'm □ _____ in the □ _____ □ _____ , Mom.

W: What are you doing?

M: I'm watching TV.

W: Will you come □ _____ ? I □ _____ □ _____ my □ _____ .

M: □ _____ , I couldn't hear you. □ _____ did you □ _____ ?

W: _____

그림 정보 파악

1. 대화를 듣고, 두 사람이 구입할 넥타이로 가장 적절한 것을 고르시오.

◀) MP3 유형 01

 ① ② ③ ④  ⑤

●정답 근거

M: Look at this necktie! This is for Dad.
W: I like it. The sunflower on it looks great.
M: Yes, it does. You know, Dad likes sunflowers.
W: Right. Dad will like it. Let's buy it.

여러 그림 중에서 설명과 어울리는 그림을 찾는 유형

❶ 그림에 드러난 요소를 영어로 떠올려 보세요.
→ sunflower, clover, star, sun, heart

❷ 구입을 결정하는 대사까지 확인한 후 정답을 고르세요.

남: 이 넥타이 좀 봐! 이것은 아빠를 위한 거야.
여: 나도 그게 마음에 들어. 여기 그려진 해바라기가 예쁘다.
남: 응, 그렇네. 아빠가 해바라기 좋아하시는 거 알지?
여: 맞아. 아빠가 좋아하실 거야. 이거 사자.

2. 다음을 듣고, 그림에 대한 설명으로 알맞은 것을 고르시오.

◀) MP3 유형 02

●정답 근거 ●오답 함정

① There is a sofa in the room.
② There is a computer keyboard on the table.
③ There is a lamp on the table.
④ There is a bag beside the bed.
⑤ There is a cat sleeping on the bed.

하나의 그림에 알맞은 설명을 찾는 유형

❶ 그림에 드러난 요소를 영어로 떠올려 보세요.
→ room, bed, cat, desk, monitor, keyboard, chair

❷ ①~⑤의 선택지에 ○/△/✕ 표시를 하면서 정답을 좁혀 나가세요. ⑤와 같이 그림에 등장하는 고양이의 위치를 잘못 묘사하는 선택지에 주의하세요.

① 방 안에 소파가 있다.
② 탁자 위에 컴퓨터 키보드가 있다.
③ 탁자 위에 램프가 있다.
④ 침대 옆에 가방이 있다.
⑤ 침대 위에 잠을 자고 있는 고양이가 있다.

📖 필수어휘

모양&무늬 round 둥근 triangle 삼각형 square 정사각형 rectangle 직사각형 check 체크무늬 polka dots 물방울무늬 stripes 줄무늬
with ~ on it (사물 위에 그려진 모양이나 무늬를 표현할 때)
예) a cap **with a dolphin on it** 돌고래 그림이 있는 모자
a backpack **with two pockets on the front** 앞에 주머니가 두 개 달린 가방

위치 on 위에 in 안에 under 아래에 beside, next to 옆에 behind 뒤에 near 가까이에 around 주위에 in front of 앞에
in the middle of 중간에   on top of ~의 위에   on the right [left] side 오른쪽 [왼쪽]에

다음을 듣고, 내일 대구의 날씨로 가장 적절한 것을 고르시오.

◀)) MP3 유형 03

① 　② 　③

④ 　⑤

●정답 근거 ●오답 함정

Hello. Here's the weather report for tomorrow. Seoul will be cloudy all day. Gwangju will be windy and Daejeon will have sunny skies. But it will be rainy in Daegu. Don't forget to take your umbrella. Thank you.

안녕하세요. 내일의 날씨를 알려드리겠습니다. 서울은 하루 종일 구름이 끼겠습니다. 광주는 바람이 불고, 대전은 맑은 하늘을 보이겠습니다. 그러나 대구에는 비가 내릴 것입니다. 우산 챙기는 것을 잊지 마세요. 감사합니다.

 주요표현

날씨 정보　You'll see lots of clouds in the afternoon. 오후에는 구름이 많을 것입니다.

We'll have sunny skies on the weekend. 주말에는 맑은 하늘을 볼 수 있을 겁니다.

It will start to snow in Seattle. 시애틀에는 눈이 내리기 시작할 것입니다.

The rainy season starts this week. 이번 주에 장마가 시작됩니다.

생활 정보　It's a perfect day for a picnic. 소풍 가기 딱 좋은 날씨입니다.

You will need to wear a coat. 코트를 입으셔야 할 겁니다.

Be careful not to catch a cold in this kind of weather. 이런 날씨에는 감기에 걸리지 않도록 주의하세요.

 필수어휘

sunny, clear 맑은	cloudy 구름 낀	rainy 비 내리는	windy 바람 부는	dry 건조한	humid 습한
snowy 눈 내리는	heavy rain 폭우	freezing 매우 추운	typhoon 태풍	warm 따뜻한	foggy 안개 낀
shower 소나기	chilly 쌀쌀한	strong wind 강풍	yellow dust 황사		

★ 지시문을 정확히 읽고 언제, 어디의 날씨를 묻는 문제인지 확인하세요.
→ tomorrow, Daegu

❷ 선택지 그림에 나타난 날씨를 영어로 떠올려 보세요.
→ cloudy, sunny, windy, rainy, snowy

★ 여러 지역의 날씨 정보가 잇달아 등장하기 때문에 끝까지 집중해서 듣는 것이 중요해요. 'Don't forget to ~'와 같은 표현 뒤에 정답의 단서가 한 번 더 나올 수 있으니 귀를 쫑긋 세우세요.

대화를 듣고, 남자의 마지막 말의 의도로 가장 적절한 것을 고르시오.

🔊 **MP3 유형 04**

☑ 거절   ② 동의

③ 제안   ④ 축하

⑤ 위로

❶ 여자와 남자 중에서 마지막 대사를 하는 사람이 누구인지 확인하세요.

❷ 마지막 대사를 하는 사람이 남자라면, 남자의 마지막 대사에 힌트가 나오기 때문에 주의를 기울여야 해요.

❸ 'I'm sorry, but I can't.'(미안하지만 안 돼.)는 바로 앞에 나온 말을 완곡하게 거절할 때 쓰는 대표적인 표현이에요.

● 정답 근거

W: Hi, Kevin. Where are you?

M: I'm at home. Why?

W: I have two K-pop concert tickets. Do you want to see the concert with me?

M: I'm sorry, but I can't. I don't feel well today.

여: 안녕, 케빈. 너 어디에 있니?

남: 나는 집에 있어. 왜?

여: 나한테 케이팝 콘서트 티켓 두 장이 있거든. 나랑 같이 콘서트 보러 갈래?

남: 미안하지만 안 돼. 나는 오늘 몸이 좀 안 좋아.

💡 **주요표현**

허락	Of course, you may. 물론, 해도 돼.
동의	Sure. I really want to. 당연하지. 나도 꼭 하고 싶어. I think so. 나도 그렇게 생각해.
반대	I don't think so. 나는 그렇게 생각하지 않아.
축하	Congratulations! 축하해!
거절	I'm sorry, but I can't. 미안하지만 안 돼.
위로	I'm sorry to hear that. 그 말을 듣게 되어 유감이야.
격려	Don't give up. Cheer up! 포기하지 마. 힘내!
조언	I think you should get some rest. 너 휴식을 취하는 게 좋겠어.
제안	Why don't you go to see a doctor? 병원에 가 보는 게 어때? How about swimming? 수영하는 게 어때?
금지	You must not walk on the grass. 잔디를 밟지 마시오.
요청	Can you close the window, please? 창문을 닫아주시겠어요?

1. 대화를 듣고, 두 사람이 연주회장에 도착해야 할 시각으로 가장 적절한 것을 고르시오. ◀)) MP3 유형 05

① 6:00　　　　　　　　　☑ 6:30

③ 7:00　　　　　　　　　④ 7:30

❶ 지시문에서 묻는 때를 반드시 확인하세요. (→ 연주회장 도착)

❷ 언급되는 시각과 내용을 메모하세요.
→ 7시-시작, 6시-현재, 6:30-도착
정확한 시각을 말해주지 않고 계산을 요구할 수 있기 때문에 들리는 정보를 부지런히 메모해야 해요.

●정답 근거 ●오답 함정

M: What time does the concert start?
W: It starts at 7:00.
M: Oh, it's already 6:00.
W: We're going to be late. Let's hurry.
M: We have to be at the concert hall by 6:30.
W: Okay. Let's take a taxi.

남: 연주회가 몇 시에 시작하니?
여: 7시에 시작해.
남: 아, 지금이 벌써 6시야.
여: 우리 늦을 것 같아. 서두르자.
남: 우리는 연주회장에 6시 30분까지 도착해야 돼.
여: 알겠어. 택시를 타자.

2. 대화를 듣고, 남자가 지불한 금액을 고르시오. ◀)) MP3 유형 06

① $10　　　　　　　　　② $30

③ $60　　　　　　　　　☑ $70

⑤ $80

❶ 품목별 가격을 메모하면서 들으세요.
→ 글러브-30, 배트-10

❷ 구입한 개수를 메모하세요.
→ 글러브-2, 배트-1

❸ 합계 금액이 언급될 수 있으므로 끝까지 주의해서 들으세요. 반면에, 계산을 요구하는 경우도 있어요!

●정답 근거 ●오답 함정

M: This baseball glove looks nice! How much is it?
W: It's thirty dollars. Do you need a bat, too? It's on sale.
M: May I see one?
W: Sure. It's only ten dollars.
M: Oh, good! Give me two gloves and a bat, please.
W: Then the total is seventy dollars.
M: Okay. Here you are.

남: 이 야구 글러브 멋지네요. 얼마인가요?
여: 30달러입니다. 배트도 필요하신가요? 할인 중이거든요.
남: 배트를 보여주시겠어요?
여: 물론이죠. 이것은 10달러밖에 하지 않아요.
남: 와, 좋네요! 글러브 두 개와 배트 하나 주세요.
여: 그러면 합계가 70달러입니다.
남: 네. 여기 있어요.

💡 **주요표현**

1) 시간　in time 제시간 안에　　　　on time 정각에　　　　make it at 10 10시에 만나다
　　　　　in 20 minutes 20분 후에　　one hour later 한 시간 후　half an hour(= 30 minutes) ago 30분 전

2) 금액　total 합계　　　　　　cost (가격이) ~이다　　on sale 할인 중인　　discount 할인
　　　　　for free 무료로　　　　pay for 지불하다　　　change 거스름돈　　for each 각각

발음유의　13 thirteen - 30 thirty　　14 fourteen - 40 forty　　15 fifteen - 50 fifty
　　　　　16 sixteen - 60 sixty　　17 seventeen - 70 seventy　18 eighteen - 80 eighty
　　　　　19 nineteen - 90 ninety

직업 · 장래 희망 파악

1. 대화를 듣고, 여자의 직업으로 가장 적절한 것을 고르시오. ◀)) MP3 유형 07 ◀

① 경찰관 ② 소방관 ③ 건축가 ✔④ 관광 가이드

> ❶ 여자의 직업을 묻는 문제이므로 여자의 대사에 집중하세요. 이 문제에서는 여자의 인사말에 결정적 힌트가 나오네요!
>
> ❷ 직업명이 직접적으로 언급되지 않으므로 대화 내용과 상황을 바탕으로 정답을 찾아야 합니다. Sun Travel이라는 회사명에서 정답을 추론하세요.

● 정답 근거

W: Welcome to Bulguksa! I'm Jenny from Sun Travel.
M: Wow! It's beautiful. How old is it?
W: It's about one thousand, two hundred years old.
M: Oh, look! What are they?
W: They are Seokkatab and Dabotab. Please come this way. I'll explain their history.

여: 불국사에 오신 것을 환영합니다! 저는 썬 여행사의 제니예요.
남: 우와! 아름답군요. 이건 얼마나 오래된 건가요?
여: 1200년 정도 됐어요.
남: 아, 보세요! 저건 뭐죠?
여: 석가탑과 다보탑입니다. 이쪽으로 오세요. 제가 역사를 설명해 드릴게요.

2. 대화를 듣고, 여자의 장래 희망을 고르시오. ◀)) MP3 유형 08 ◀

① 가수 ② 선생님 ③ 운전사 ④ 무용수 ✔⑤ 요리사

> ❶ 선택지를 영어로 떠올려 보세요.
> → singer, teacher, driver, ballerina, cook
>
> ❷ 여자의 장래 희망을 묻는 문제이므로 여자의 대사에 집중하세요. 두 사람의 장래 희망이 동시에 언급될 수 있으므로 구분하여 듣는 것이 필요해요.
>
> ★ 남자의 장래 희망, 여자의 예전 장래 희망이 함정으로 나오니 속지 마세요.

● 정답 근거 ● 오답 함정

W: What do you want to be in the future?
M: I'd like to be a singer. What about you?
W: When I was young, I wanted to be a ballerina. But now, I really want to be a cook like my mom.
M: Your mother's food is wonderful.
W: Thanks.

여: 너는 장래에 뭐가 되고 싶니?
남: 나는 가수가 되고 싶어. 너는?
여: 나는 어릴 때 무용수가 되고 싶었어. 하지만 지금은 우리 엄마처럼 요리사가 되고 싶어.
남: 너희 어머니의 요리는 아주 훌륭하지.
여: 고마워.

💡 **주요표현**

cartoonist 만화가	People really liked my cartoons. 사람들이 제 만화를 아주 좋아했어요.	
athlete 운동선수	Your training was really helpful. 코치님의 훈련이 큰 도움이 됐어요.	
writer 작가	I just finished my new novel. 저는 새로운 소설 집필을 막 끝냈어요.	
hairdresser 미용사	I'll cut your hair. 제가 머리카락을 잘라 드릴게요.	

📖 **필수어휘**

vet 수의사　judge 판사　architect 건축가　journalist 기자　pilot 비행기 조종사　postman 우체부　pharmacist 약사
chef 요리사　lawyer 변호사　magician 마술사　fire fighter 소방관　police officer 경찰관　photographer 사진사　flight attendant 비행기 승무원

대화를 듣고, 남자의 심정으로 가장 적절한 것을 고르시오.

🔊 MP3 유형 09

① 화남　　　　　　　② 미안함

③ 행복함　　　　　　④ 부러워함

✓⑤ 그리워함

❶ 남자의 심정을 묻는 문제이므로 남자의 대사에 집중하세요.

❷ 선택지의 내용을 영어로 떠올려 보세요.
　→ angry, sorry, happy, envy, miss

✱ 심정 추론 문제는 기분을 나타내는 표현이 직접 언급되는 경우가 많아요. 따라서 심정을 나타내는 다양한 어휘를 알고 있어야 해요!

●정답 근거

W: Is this your family picture?

M: Yes, it is. These are my mom and dad.

W: Who is this woman? Is she your grandmother?

M: Yes. She moved to Canada last year. I really miss her.

W: I know how you feel. I want to see my grandmother, too.

여: 이거 너희 가족 사진이니?

남: 응, 그래. 이분들은 우리 엄마 아빠야.

여: 이 여자분은 누구야? 너희 할머니셔?

남: 맞아. 할머니께선 작년에 캐나다로 이사를 가셨어. 난 우리 할머니가 정말 보고 싶어.

여: 네 기분이 어떤지 나도 알아. 나도 우리 할머니가 보고 싶거든.

💡 **주요표현**

기대	I can't wait! 정말 기다려진다!
놀라움	I can't believe it! 믿을 수 없군!
미안함	Please forgive me. 나를 용서해줘.
실망	I practiced a lot, but I didn't win a prize. 나는 연습을 많이 했는데, 상을 받진 못했어.

📖 **필수어휘**

happy 행복한	excited 신이 난	worried 걱정하는	miss 그리워하다
angry 화가 난	surprised 놀란	upset 속상한	envy 부러워하다
joyful 기뻐하는	hopeful 희망에 찬	confident 자신 있는	jealous 질투하는
satisfied 만족하는	relaxed 여유 있는	proud 자랑스러워하는	frustrated 좌절한
nervous 불안해 하는	disappointed 실망한	embarrassed 당황한	

1. 대화를 듣고, 두 사람이 일요일에 할 일을 고르시오.

◀» MP3 유형 10

✔① 수영하러 가기　　② 박물관 견학하기　　③ 집안 청소하기

④ 엄마와 쇼핑하기　　⑤ 여행 계획 세우기

●정답 근거 ●오답 함정

M: What are you going to do this weekend?

W: I'm going to visit a museum on Saturday. What are your plans?

M: My mom wants me to clean my room on Saturday. But I'm free on Sunday.

W: Then let's go swimming on Sunday.

M: That sounds great.

남: 너는 이번 주말에 뭐 할 거야?

여: 나는 토요일에 박물관에 갈 거야. 네 계획은 뭐니?

남: 엄마께서 토요일에 내 방을 청소하라고 하셨어. 하지만 나는 일요일에는 계획이 없어.

여: 그럼 우리 일요일에 수영하러 가자.

남: 그거 좋은 생각이다.

❶ 지시문에서 누가, 언제 할 일을 묻고 있는지 확인하세요.

❷ 선택지 내용을 영어로 떠올려 보세요.
→ swim, museum, clean, shopping, plan

❸ Sunday(일요일)와 함께 나오는 활동을 잘 들었다면 정답을 고를 수 있겠죠?

✱ Saturday(토요일)에 할 일에 속지 마세요!

2. 대화를 듣고, 여자가 지난 주말에 한 일로 가장 적절한 것을 고르시오.

◀» MP3 유형 11

① 숙제하기　　② 수영하기　　✔③ 쿠키 만들기

④ 만화 그리기　　⑤ 화분에 물주기

●정답 근거 ●오답 함정

W: Charlie, what did you do last weekend?

M: I went to the swimming pool with my friends.

W: Really? Did you have fun?

M: Yes, of course! How was your weekend?

W: It was great! I made cookies for my family.

M: Oh, good!

여: 찰리, 지난 주말에 뭐 했니?

남: 친구들과 수영장에 갔어.

여: 정말? 재미 있었니?

남: 응, 당연하지! 너는 주말을 어떻게 보냈어?

여: 잘 보냈지! 가족을 위해 내가 쿠키를 만들었어.

나: 와, 잘했다!

❶ 누가, 언제 한 일을 묻는지 확인하세요.

❷ 선택지 내용을 영어로 떠올려 보세요.
→ homework, swim, cookies, cartoons, plants

❸ 남자와 여자가 한 일을 구분해서 듣고, 특히 정답이 되는 여자의 대사에 집중하세요.

❹ 남자의 질문 이후에 나오는 대답이 정답일 가능성이 높아요.

✱ 남자가 한 일에 속지 마세요!

💡 **주요표현**

take a walk 산책하기	ride a bike 자전거 타기	take a picture 사진 찍기
get the milk 우유 가져오기	send an email 이메일 보내기	visit a museum 박물관 가기
go to the movies 영화 보러 가기	go to a clothing store 옷 가게 가기	talk to a teacher 선생님과 대화하기

유형 공략 — 화제 추론

1. 다음을 듣고 'this'가 가리키는 것으로 가장 적절한 것을 고르시오.

🔊 MP3 유형 12

① ② ③ ④ ⑤

● 정답 근거

Do you love reading? When you're reading books, do your eyes get tired easily? Then, you may need this. This makes a lot of light. Many people use this when reading at night. What is this?

> ❶ 한 사람이 계속해서 말하는 담화는 질문과 대답이 번갈아 나오는 대화보다 더 집중해야 하는 문제랍니다.
> ❷ 정답을 간접적으로 설명하는 힌트들이 하나씩 나옵니다. 늘어나는 힌트를 통해 정답을 좁혀가세요.

여러분은 독서를 좋아하나요? 책을 읽을 때 여러분의 눈이 쉽게 피로해지나요? 그렇다면, 여러분은 이것이 필요할지 모릅니다. 이것은 아주 밝은 빛을 만들어내요. 많은 사람들이 밤에 독서를 할 때 이것을 사용합니다. 이것은 무엇일까요?

2. 대화를 듣고, 무엇에 관한 내용인지 가장 적절한 것을 고르시오.

🔊 MP3 유형 13

① 환경 보호 ② 가족 여행 ③ 요리 강습 ④ 봉사 활동 ⑤ 교우 관계

> ❶ 선택지 내용을 영어로 떠올려 보세요.
> → environment, trip, cooking, volunteer, friends
> ❷ 첫 번째 대사부터 결정적 힌트가 나오고 있어요. 하지만 확실한 정답을 찾기 위해서는 내용을 끝까지 들어야 해요.

● 정답 근거

M: Hi, Jenny. How was your family trip last week?
W: We had a lot of fun on Jeju Island.
M: What did you do there?
W: We went to the beach and ate seafood.
M: That sounds great! I also ate seafood in Sokcho with my family.
W: Oh, did you like Sokcho?
M: Yes, I really liked the fresh air there.

남: 안녕, 제니. 지난주 너희 가족 여행 어땠니?
여: 우리는 제주도에서 정말 즐거운 시간을 보냈어.
남: 거기에서 무엇을 했어?
여: 우리는 해변에도 가고 해물도 먹었어.
남: 정말 좋았겠다! 나도 가족과 속초에서 해물을 먹었어.
여: 아, 속초는 마음에 들었니?
남: 응, 나는 그곳의 맑은 공기가 정말 좋았어.

💡 **주요표현**

golf 골프 The players try to hit balls into each hole in the field. The ball is small and hard.
선수들은 공을 쳐서 필드의 작은 홀컵 안에 넣습니다. 공은 작고 단단합니다.

giraffe 기린 This animal is famous for its long neck and eats leaves on top of trees.
이 동물은 기다란 목으로 유명하고 나무 꼭대기에 있는 잎을 먹습니다.

watermelon 수박 This fruit is round and heavy. Usually, it's green on the outside but red on the inside.
이 과일은 동그랗고 무겁습니다. 보통 겉은 초록색이지만 안은 빨간색입니다.

mirror 거울 We can use it when we want to see ourselves. It is usually made of glass.
우리가 우리 자신의 모습을 보고 싶을 때 그것을 사용합니다. 보통 유리로 만들어집니다.

📖 **자주 등장하는 대화 화제**

gift 선물　movie 영화　weather 날씨　hobby 취미　weekend plan 주말 계획　vacation plan 방학 계획
test 시험　club 동아리　homework 숙제　sports day 운동회　future dream 장래 희망　favorite subject 좋아하는 과목

대화를 듣고, 여자가 제안한 교통수단으로 가장 적절한 것을 고르시오.

🔊 MP3 유형 14

① 도보 ② 버스 ☑ 택시 ④ 지하철

● 정답 근거 ● 오답 함정

M: Excuse me. I'm looking for City Hall.
W: You can't get there on foot. It's too far.
M: Really? Can I take a bus then?
W: No, there's no bus from here. Why don't you take a taxi?
M: I guess I'll have to. Thank you.

남: 실례합니다. 저는 시청을 찾고 있어요.
여: 거기까지 걸어서는 갈 수 없어요. 너무 멀거든요.
남: 그래요? 그렇다면 버스를 타야 하나요?
여: 아니요. 여기에서 가는 버스는 없어요. 택시를 타시는 게 어때요?
남: 그래야 할 것 같네요. 감사합니다.

❶ 선택지에 제시된 교통수단을 영어로 떠올려 보세요.
  → on foot, bus, taxi, subway

❷ 초반에 언급되는 교통수단은 함정일 가능성이 커요!

❸ 제안을 나타내는 표현인 'Why don't you ~?(~하는 게 어때~?)'로 시작하는 문장을 잘 들으세요.

❹ 제안된 교통수단에 대한 상대방의 긍정적인 대답까지 확인한 후에 답을 고르세요.

💡 **주요표현**

A: **How do you go to** school? 너는 학교에 어떻게 가니?
B: I go to school **by** bus. 나는 버스로 학교에 가.

A: **How did you get to** Busan? 너는 부산에 어떻게 갔니?
B: I **took** the train. 나는 기차를 탔어.

A: **Can I walk to** the museum? 박물관까지 걸어서 갈 수 있을까요?
B: I think you should **take** the subway line number two. 지하철 2호선을 타는 게 좋을 거예요.

📖 **필수어휘**

by train 기차로	by bus 버스로	by taxi 택시로	by car 자동차로
by plane 비행기로	by ship 배로	on foot 도보로(= 걸어서)	

이유 · 전화 목적 파악

1. 대화를 듣고, 남자가 여행을 갈 수 <u>없었던</u> 이유로 가장 적절한 것을 고르시오. 🔊MP3 유형 15

① 기차표가 없었기 때문에　　② 날씨가 나빴기 때문에

③ 병원에 가야 했기 때문에　　☑ 고양이가 아팠기 때문에

● 주로 ~한 이유, ~하지 못한 이유에 대해 묻는 유형이에요.

❷ 선택지 내용 일부를 영어로 떠올리세요.
→ train ticket, bad weather, hospital, cat, sick

❸ Why not 질문에 대한 응답에 정답이 있을 가능성이 커요.

●정답 근거

W: Mike? I thought you were at Seoraksan.

M: No. I couldn't go, Michelle.

W: Why not? You really wanted to go there.

M: My cats were sick and I had to take care of them all weekend.

W: That's too bad.

여: 마이크? 너 설악산에 간 줄 알았는데.

남: 아니. 나는 못 갔어, 미셸.

여: 왜 못 갔어? 너는 그곳에 정말로 가고 싶어 했잖아.

남: 내 고양이들이 아파서 주말 내내 돌봐줘야 했거든.

여: 그것참 안 됐다.

2. 대화를 듣고, 여자가 전화를 건 목적을 고르시오. 🔊MP3 유형 16

① 주문한 책을 찾기 위해　　② 잃어버린 책을 찾기 위해

☑ 놓고 온 가방을 찾기 위해　　④ 서점 위치를 알아보기 위해

⑤ 토끼 그림을 구입하기 위해

● 선택지를 훑어보세요.

❷ 여자의 목소리에 집중!

❸ 대화 초반에 등장하는 'May I help you?'(무엇을 도와드릴까요?) 'What's up?'(무슨 일이야?) 'Why did you call me?'(너는 내게 왜 전화를 했니?) 등의 질문 뒤에 결정적 힌트가 있어요.

★ 통화에서 언급되는 내용이 선택지마다 부분적으로 등장하네요. 따라서 정확한 내용 파악이 중요해요!

●정답 근거 ●오답 함정

[*Telephone rings.*]

M: Morning Star Bookstore. How may I help you?

W: I left my bag in your bookstore.

M: What does it look like?

W: It's big and black. It has a picture of a rabbit on it.

M: Yes, we have it here. Can you come this afternoon and pick it up?

W: Okay. Thank you.

[전화가 울린다.]

남: 모닝스타 서점입니다. 무엇을 도와드릴까요?

여: 제가 그 서점에 가방을 두고 왔어요.

남: 어떻게 생긴 가방인가요?

여: 크고 검은색이에요. 토끼 그림이 그려져 있고요.

남: 네, 여기 있네요. 오후에 들러서 가져가시겠어요?

여: 그럴게요. 감사합니다.

 주요표현

A: **May I speak to** Andy? 앤디와 통화할 수 있나요?

B: **Speaking**. 저예요. / **Who's calling**, please? 누구세요? / He is **not here** now. 지금 여기 없네요. / **Just a moment**, please. **Hold on**, please. 잠깐 기다려주세요.

1.

대화를 듣고, 두 사람이 대화하는 장소로 가장 적절한 곳을 고르시오.

🔊 MP3 유형 17

① 장난감 가게 ② 우체국 ③ 옷 가게 ✔ 서점 ⑤ 약국

● 0 선택지에 제시된 장소들을 영어로 떠올려 보세요.
→ toy store, post office, clothing store, bookstore, pharmacy
❷ 직접적인 장소 이름보다는 대화의 내용과 분위기를 통해 답을 찾아야 합니다. 경우에 따라 장소 이름이 직접 언급되지 않을 수도 있기 때문이지요.

●정답 근거 ●오답 함정

M: Do you sell puzzles in this bookstore?
W: I'm sorry. We don't. But you can buy them at a toy store nearby.
M: Okay. Then I'll just take these books. How much are they?
W: They're $10.
M: Okay. By the way, where is the toy store?
W: It's next to the post office.
M: Thanks.

남: 이 서점에서 퍼즐도 판매하나요?
여: 죄송합니다. 저희는 판매하지 않습니다. 그렇지만 근처에 있는 장난감 가게에서 구입할 수 있어요.
남: 알겠습니다. 그럼 저는 이 책들만 살게요. 얼마예요?
여: 그것들은 10달러입니다.
남: 그렇군요. 그나저나, 그 장난감 가게는 어디에 있죠?
여: 우체국 옆에 있어요.
남: 감사합니다.

2.

대화를 듣고, 두 사람의 관계로 가장 적절한 것을 고르시오.

🔊 MP3 유형 18

① 간호사 – 환자 ② 사장 – 종업원
✔ 수리 기사 – 고객 ④ 서점 점원 – 학생

● 0 선택지를 빠르게 훑어보세요.
❷ 첫 대사부터 힌트가 드러날 가능성이 높답니다.
✺ 각자의 직업과 관계가 직접적으로 언급되지 않아요. 따라서 곳곳에 등장하는 힌트를 가지고 관계를 찾아내야 해요.

●정답 근거

[*Telephone rings.*]
M: Star Customer Service. How can I help you?
W: My MP3 player doesn't work.
M: Oh, did you drop it?
W: No, I didn't. It just suddenly stopped playing.
M: I see. Could you bring it to the service center?
W: Sure. I'll do that tomorrow.

[전화가 울린다.]
남: 스타 고객서비스입니다. 무엇을 도와드릴까요?
여: 제 MP3플레이어가 작동하질 않아요.
남: 아, 혹시 떨어뜨리셨나요?
여: 아니요. 갑자기 재생을 멈췄어요.
남: 그렇군요. 서비스 센터로 그걸 가져오실 수 있나요?
여: 물론이죠. 내일 가져가겠습니다.

💡 **주요표현**

A: I'm looking for a T-shirt. 저는 티셔츠를 찾고 있어요.　**| 옷 가게 – 점원과 손님**
B: Would you like to try it on? What size would you like? 이거 입어 보시겠어요? 사이즈가 어떻게 되시죠?

A: What's wrong with your puppy? 강아지에게 무슨 문제가 있나요?　**| 동물 병원 – 수의사와 동물 주인**
B: My dog won't eat or drink anything. 제 강아지가 어떤것도 먹지도 마시지도 않아요.
A: Then let's take an X-ray. 그렇다면 엑스레이 촬영을 해야겠군요.

A: How long will it take to Seattle? 시애틀까지 얼마나 걸리나요?　**| 비행기 안 – 승무원과 승객**
B: It will take about 10 hours. Would you like something to drink? 10시간 정도 걸립니다. 마실 것을 드릴까요?

대화를 듣고, 여자가 가려고 하는 장소를 고르시오.

🔊 MP3 유형 19

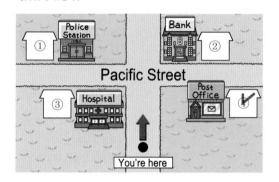

● 정답 근거

W: Excuse me. How do I get to the library from here?
M: The library? Go to Pacific Street and turn right.
W: Turn right? And then?
M: Walk along Pacific Street, and you'll see it on your right.
W: Okay.
M: It's next to the post office.
W: Thank you.

여: 실례합니다. 여기에서 도서관까지 어떻게 가나요?
남: 도서관이요? 퍼시픽 거리까지 직진한 뒤 우회전하세요.
여: 우회전이요? 그다음에는요?
남: 퍼시픽 거리를 따라서 걷다 보면 당신의 오른쪽에 도서관이 보일 겁니다.
여: 알겠습니다.
남: 그것은 우체국 옆에 있어요.
여: 감사합니다.

💡 **주요표현**

A: **Can you tell me the way to** City Hall? 시청으로 가는 방법을 알려주시겠어요?
B: **Walk about a minute**. It's **across from** the hospital. 1분 정도 걸어가세요. 그것은 병원 건너편에 있습니다.

A: **Is there** a hospital around here? 이 근처에 병원 있나요?
B: **Walk straight** a little farther. It'll be **on your left next to** the bank. 좀 더 직진하세요. 그것은 당신의 왼쪽, 은행 옆에 있을 겁니다.

📖 **필수어휘**

block 구역, 블록
across from 건너편에
library 도서관

corner 모퉁이
between A and B A와 B 사이에
hospital 병원

go straight 직진하다
turn left[right] 좌회전[우회전]하다
police station 경찰서

next to 옆에
on your left[right] 당신의 왼쪽에[오른쪽에]
bank 은행

1. 대화를 듣고, 남자가 여자에게 부탁한 일로 가장 적절한 것을 고르시오.

🔊 MP3 유형 20

① 일찍 깨워주기   ② 숙제 도와주기

③ 방 청소 해주기   ④ 학교 데려다 주기

⑤ 도시락 챙겨주기

●정답 근거 ●오답 함정

W: David, it's time to go to bed. It's already eleven o'clock.

M: Mom, I have to finish my homework.

W: It's late. You can do it early tomorrow morning.

M: Hmm... Then, can you wake me up at six o'clock in the morning?

W: Sure, don't worry.

❶ 선택지를 훑어보세요.

❷ 남자가 부탁한 일을 알기 위해서는 남자의 대사에 집중해야죠!

❸ 주로 'Can[Could] you ~?(~할 수 있니?)'로 시작하는 문장에 부탁하는 내용이 담겨 있답니다.

여: 데이비드, 잠을 잘 시간이구나. 벌써 11시야.

남: 엄마, 저는 숙제를 끝내야 해요.

여: 너무 늦었어. 내일 아침 일찍 해도 되잖아.

남: 음... 그러면 아침 6시에 저를 깨워주시겠어요?

여: 물론이지. 걱정하지 마.

2. 대화를 듣고, 여자가 남자에게 제안한 것으로 가장 적절한 것을 고르시오. 🔊 MP3 유형 21

① 도서관 가기   ② 과학 실험하기

③ 인터넷 활용하기   ④ 안내소 방문하기

⑤ 친구에게 물어보기

●정답 근거 ●오답 함정

W: Chris, where are you going?

M: I'm going to Tom's house to do the science homework. Did your group finish it?

W: Yes, we did. Why is your group still working on it?

M: Well, we can't find any useful books.

W: How about using the Internet?

M: That's a good idea. Thanks.

❶ 선택지를 훑어보세요.

❷ 여자의 제안을 파악하려면 여자의 목소리에 귀를 기울여야겠네요!

❸ '~하는 게 어때?'를 뜻하는 Why don't you ~?, How about ~?, What about ~? 등으로 시작하는 문장에 제안하는 내용이 담겨 있어요.

★ science와 book에 관련된 선택지 함정에 빠지지 마세요!

여: 크리스, 너는 어디에 가는 길이니?

남: 나는 과학 숙제를 하러 톰의 집에 가는 중이야. 너희 그룹은 숙제를 다 했니?

여: 응, 우리는 다 했어. 너희 그룹은 왜 아직도 그것을 하고 있니?

남: 글쎄. 우리는 유용한 책을 찾지 못하고 있어.

여: 인터넷을 이용하는 게 어때?

남: 그거 좋은 생각이다. 고마워.

💡 **주요표현**

부탁
A: **Would** you open the window, please? 창문 좀 열어주시겠어요?
B: **I'd be glad to. / Sure.** 물론이죠. **Sorry, but I can't.** 미안하지만, 안 돼요.

제안/충고
Why don't we eat bibimbap later? 우리 이따가 비빔밥 먹는 거 어때?
Let's play badminton. 우리 배드민턴 치자.
Make sure you don't eat too much fast food. 패스트푸드를 너무 많이 먹지 않도록 하세요.
I think you should wear a coat. 제 생각에 당신은 코트를 입어야 할 것 같아요.

미언급 · 내용 일치 파악

1. 다음을 듣고, 남자에 대해 언급되지 <u>않은</u> 것을 고르시오.

🔊MP3 유형 22

① 이름   ☑ 나이

③ 출신 국가   ④ 사는 곳

⑤ 장래 희망

> ● 선택지를 읽고 내용을 예상해 보세요.
> → name, old, from, live in, want
> ② 언급되는 항목은 선택지에서 지워나 갑니다.
> ① 언급되지 않은 것을 찾는 유형은 이 문제처럼 자기소개 내용이 자주 출제됩니다. 먹지 않은 음식, 준비물이 아닌 것 등을 묻는 문제도 출제됩니다.

●정답 근거

Hi, my name is Steve. I'm from England. I live in London. I like all kinds of movies. My favorite actor is James Dean. I want to be a movie star like him. Thank you.

안녕하세요. 제 이름은 스티브입니다. 저는 영국 출신입니다. 저는 현재 런던에 살고 있습니다. 저는 모든 종류의 영화를 좋아합니다. 가장 좋아하는 배우는 제임스 딘입니다. 저도 제임스 딘처럼 영화 스타가 되고 싶습니다. 감사합니다.

2. 대화를 듣고, 여자에 대한 설명으로 알맞은 것을 고르시오.

🔊MP3 유형 23

① 구두를 구입했다.   ☑ 신문을 읽고 있다.

③ 책 읽기를 좋아한다.   ④ 헬스클럽에 등록했다.

⑤ 달리기대회에서 1등을 했다.

> ● 여자에 대한 설명이니 여자의 대사에 집중하세요.
> ② 선택지를 꼼꼼히 읽어보세요.
> ③ 들리는 내용이 선택지와 일치하면 O, 일치하지 않으면 X 표시를 하세요.
> ☀ 대화에 등장하는 주요 표현이 선택지에 모두 제시되어 있어요. 함정에 빠지지 않도록 정확히 듣는 능력이 필요하답니다.
> ① 틀린 설명을 찾는 문제가 출제되기도 해요.

●정답 근거 ●오답 함정

M: Hey, Cathy. What are you doing?

W: Hi, Bill. I'm reading a newspaper.

M: What's it about?

W: It's about running and being healthy.

M: Really? Are you planning to exercise?

W: Yes, I am. I just bought a pair of running shoes.

남: 저기, 캐시. 너는 무엇을 하고 있니?
여: 안녕, 빌. 나는 신문을 읽는 중이야.
남: 무엇에 관한 내용이야?
여: 달리기와 건강해지는 것에 대한 거야.
남: 그래? 너는 운동을 하려고 계획 중이니?
여: 응. 나는 최근에 운동화를 샀어.

📖 **자기소개 항목**

이름&나이	My name is Kelly. I'm fourteen years old.	제 이름은 켈리입니다. 저는 14살입니다.
출생지	I was born in Seoul.	저는 서울에서 태어났습니다.
현재 사는 곳	I live in Daejeon now.	지금 저는 대전에 살고 있습니다.
가족 구성	I have my parents and an older brother.	제겐 부모님과 형이 있습니다.
가족 직업	My father is a firefighter.	제 아버지는 소방관입니다.
장래 희망	My dream is to become a teacher someday.	저는 교사가 되는 게 꿈입니다.

어색한 대화 찾기

대화를 듣고, 두 사람의 대화가 <u>어색한</u> 것을 고르시오.

◀》MP3 유형 24

① ② ③ ④ ⑤

●정답 근거

① W: What time do you usually get up?
   M: It was last Saturday.
② W: How much is this hat?
   M: It's $15.
③ W: What's your favorite sport?
   M: I like soccer most.
④ W: How about joining our club?
   M: That's a good idea.
⑤ W: What's wrong? You don't look so good.
   M: I have a headache.

◀ ❶ 의문사에 집중하세요.
   → what, how

❷ 대화가 자연스러우면 ○, 어색하면 ✕, 판단하기 어려우면 △ 표시를 하세요. 이렇게 하면 마지막에 정답을 체크하는 데에 도움이 돼요.

★ 오답을 고쳐볼까요?
   → I usually get up at 7.
      나는 보통 7시에 일어나.

① 여: 너는 보통 몇 시에 일어나니?
   남: 그건 지난 토요일이었어.
② 여: 이 모자는 얼마인가요?
   남: 15달러예요.
③ 여: 네가 가장 좋아하는 운동은 뭐야?
   남: 나는 축구를 가장 좋아해.
④ 여: 우리 동아리에 가입하는 건 어때?
   남: 그거 좋은 생각이다.
⑤ 여: 무슨 일이니? 너 몸이 안 좋아 보인다.
   남: 나는 두통이 있어.

💡 **주요표현**

What 무엇	A: **What** would you like to have? 무엇을 드시겠어요? B: I'll have a **sandwich**. 샌드위치를 먹을게요.
Who 누가	A: **Who's** calling? 누구시죠? B: This is **Mira**. 저는 미라예요.
When 언제	A: **When** do you leave? 너는 언제 떠나니? B: I'm leaving **at 5:30**. 나는 5시 30분에 떠나.
Where 어디	A: **Where** is the hospital? 병원이 어디에 있나요? B: It's **in front of the bakery**. 그것은 빵집 앞에 있습니다.
Why 왜	A: **Why** are you crying? 너는 왜 울고 있니? B: I have a **stomachache**. 나는 배가 아파.
How 어떻게	A: **How** are you doing? 너는 어떻게 지내니? B: Pretty **good**. 아주 잘 지내.
How long 얼마나 오래	A: **How long** did you exercise last night? 너는 어젯밤에 얼마 동안 운동을 했니? B: About **an hour**. 한 시간 정도.
How often 얼마나 자주	A: **How often do you** play games? 너는 게임을 얼마나 자주 하니? B: I play computer games **twice a week**. 나는 일주일에 두 번 컴퓨터 게임을 해.
How much 얼마	A: **How much** does it cost? 그거 얼마예요? B: It costs **$30**. 30달러입니다.

1. 대화를 듣고, 남자의 마지막 말에 이어질 여자의 응답으로 가장 알맞은 것을 고르시오. ◀))MP3 유형 25

Woman: _____

① Ten dollars.
② So delicious.
③ On the table. ✓
④ With a spoon.
⑤ Five minutes later.

●정답 근거

M: Mom, I'm home. I'm so hungry.
W: Oh, good! I made some sandwiches for you.
M: Great! Where are they?
W: _____

마지막 말만 듣고도 답을 찾을 수 있는 유형

❶ 선택지를 훑어보세요.

❷ 여자의 응답을 예상하기 위해서는 남자의 마지막 말을 잘 들어야 해요. 특히 의문사 Where에 집중하세요.

⚠ 마지막 말만 들어서는 답을 찾을 수 없는 문제 역시 출제됩니다. 항상 대화 전체를 이해하는 습관을 갖도록 해요!

남: 엄마, 저 집에 왔어요. 너무 배가 고파요.
여: 아, 잘됐구나. 널 주려고 내가 샌드위치를 만들었어.
남: 우와! 어디에 있어요?
여: _____
① 10 달러야.　② 정말 맛있어.
③ 탁자 위에.　④ 숟가락을 가지고.
⑤ 5분 뒤에.

2. 대화를 듣고, 남자의 마지막 말에 이어질 여자의 응답으로 가장 적절한 것을 고르시오. ◀))MP3 유형 26

Woman: _____

① I like musicals better.
② I'll meet you at the ticket box.
③ I don't have anything to do today.
④ I really want to watch the musical.
⑤ I have to take care of my brother all day. ✓

●정답 근거 ●오답 함정

M: Hi, Julia! Are you free this afternoon?
W: What's up?
M: I got two tickets for the musical *Mama Mia*.
W: Sounds great, but I can't make it this afternoon.
M: Why not?
W: _____

전체 내용을 이해해야 답을 찾을 수 있는 유형

❶ 선택지를 재빨리 살펴보세요.

❷ 남자의 마지막 말에 집중해야겠죠?

❸ 대화가 어디에서 끊길지 모르니 [질문-대답]의 흐름을 놓치지 마세요.

✳ 함정 조심! 대화에 등장하는 내용이 선택지 곳곳에 포함되어 있어요!

남: 안녕, 줄리아! 너 오후에 별일 없어?
여: 무슨 일인데?
남: 나한테 뮤지컬 맘마미아 티켓이 두 장 있거든.
여: 좋다. 그런데 나 오늘 오후에는 안 돼.
남: 왜 안 돼?
여: _____
① 나는 뮤지컬을 더 좋아해.
② 내가 너를 매표소에서 만날게.
③ 나는 오늘 할 일이 아무것도 없어.
④ 나는 그 뮤지컬이 정말 보고 싶어.
⑤ 내가 하루 종일 남동생을 돌봐야 해.

READING RELAY 한 권으로
영어를 공부하며 국·수·사·과까지 5과목 정복!

리딩릴레이 시리즈

① 각 챕터마다 주요 교과목으로 지문 구성!

우리말 지문으로 배경지식을 읽고, 관련된 영문 지문으로 독해력 키우기

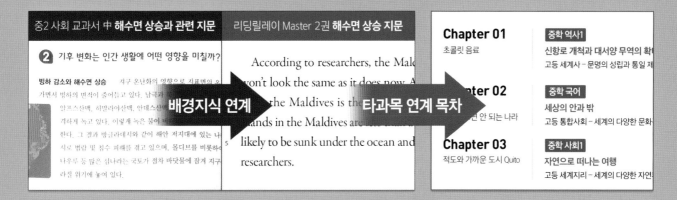

중2 사회 교과서 中 **해수면 상승과 관련 지문**	리딩릴레이 Master 2권 **해수면 상승 지문**
② 기후 변화는 인간 생활에 어떤 영향을 미칠까? **빙하 감소와 해수면 상승** 지구 온난화의 영향으로 지표면의 ...가면서 빙하의 면적이 줄어들고 있다. 남극과 ...알프스산맥, 히말라야산맥, 안데스산맥 ...격차게 녹고 있다. 이렇게 녹은 물이 바... 한다. 그 결과 방글라데시와 같이 해안 저지대에 있는 ...시로 범람 및 침수 피해를 겪고 있으며, 몰디브를 비롯하... 나우루 등 많은 섬나라는 국토가 점차 바닷물에 잠겨 지구 ...라질 위기에 놓여 있다.	According to researchers, the Mal... won't look the same as it does now ...the Maldives is the ...ands in the Maldives are ...likely to be sunk under the ocean and ...researchers.

배경지식 연계 ➡ **타과목 연계 목차** ➡

Chapter 01 초콜릿 음료	중학 역사1 신항로 개척과 대서양 무역의 확... 고등 세계사 – 문명의 성립과 통일 제...
...ter 02 ...면 안 되는 나라	중학 국어 세상의 안과 밖 고등 통합사회 – 세계의 다양한 문화...
Chapter 03 적도와 가까운 도시 Quito	중학 사회1 자연으로 떠나는 여행 고등 세계지리 – 세계의 다양한 자연...

② 학년별로 국/영문의 비중을 다르게!

지시문 & 선택지 기준

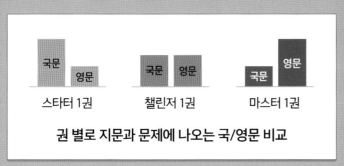

| 스타터 1권 | 챌린저 1권 | 마스터 1권 |

권 별로 지문과 문제에 나오는 국/영문 비교

③ 교육부 지정 필수 어휘 수록!

교육부 지정 중학 필수 어휘 🎧	
genius	명 1. **천재** 2. 천부의 재능
slip	동 1. **미끄러지다** 2. 빠져나가다
compose	동 1. **구성하다, ~의 일부를 이루다** 2. ... 3. 작곡하다
	형 (현재) 살아 있는

1 구문 판매 1위 '천일문' 콘텐츠를 활용하여 정확하고 다양한 구문 학습

[끊어읽기] [해석하기] [문장 구조 분석] [해설·해석 제공] [단어 스크램블링] [영작하기]

2 문법·서술형 쎄듀의 모든 문법 문항을 활용하여 내신까지 해결하는 정교한 문법 유형 제공

[객관식과 주관식의 결합] [문법 포인트별 학습] [보기를 활용한 집합 문항] [내신대비 서술형] [어법+서술형 문제]

3 어휘 초·중·고·공무원까지 방대한 어휘량을 제공하며 오프라인 TEST 인쇄도 가능

[영단어 카드 학습] [단어 ↔ 뜻 유형] [예문 활용 유형] [단어 매칭 게임]

4 선생님 보유 문항 이용

[Online Test] [OMR Test]

🍵 cafe.naver.com/cedulearnteacher

쎄듀런 학습 정보가 궁금하다면?

쎄듀런 Cafe

· 쎄듀런 사용법 안내 & 학습법 공유
· 공지 및 문의사항 QA
· 할인 쿠폰 증정 등 이벤트 진행

천일문
STARTER

중등 영어 구문·문법 학습의 시작

1. 중등 눈높이에 맞춘 권당 약 500문장 + 내용 구성
2. 개념부터 적용까지 체계적 학습
3. 천일문 완벽 해설집 「천일비급」 부록
4. 철저한 복습을 위한 워크북 포함

구문 대장 천일문, 중등도 천일문만 믿어!

3 in 1 구성

+ 본책

+ 워크북

+ 천일비급

쎄듀런
Mobile & PC
**온라인 구문 문장
암기 학습권(유료)**

중등부터 고등까지, 천일문과 함께!

예비중 ~ 중3	예비고1	고1	고2	고3
천일문 STARTER	**천일문 입문**	**천일문 기본**	**천일문 핵심**	**천일문 완성**
구문 학습 첫걸음	우선 순위 빈출 구문	기본/빈출/중요 구문 총망라	혼동 구문 완벽 해결	고난도 구문 뛰어넘기

쎄듀

빠르게

쎄듀
중학영어듣기
모의고사 20회

쎄듀 '빠르게' 중학영어듣기 모의고사 시리즈

정답 및 해설

1

실전 모의고사 20회
기출 듣기평가 5회
문제 유형 공략 및 필수 표현 익히기

QR코드 방식의 편리한 음원 재생
MP3 파일 무료 다운로드
모의고사, 딕테이션, 문항별 음원 제공

쎄듀

쎄듀 빠르게
중학영어듣기
모의고사 20회

정답 및 해설

1

01회 실전모의고사

본문 p.6-7

01 ②	**02** ①	**03** ③	**04** ④	**05** ⑤
06 ②	**07** ⑤	**08** ①	**09** ④	**10** ④
11 ②	**12** ②	**13** ①	**14** ①	**15** ②
16 ④	**17** ②	**18** ②	**19** ⑤	**20** ⑤

01 ②

M: I live in the ocean, but I'm a mammal. I'm large and gray, and I have fins. I often perform for humans. I leap through hoops, and they give me fish. What am I?

저는 바다에 살지만 포유류예요. 전 몸집이 크고 회색을 띄며 지느러미가 있어요. 저는 종종 사람들을 위해 공연을 해요. 제가 후프 안으로 점프하면 사람들은 저에게 생선을 줘요. 저는 누구일까요?

어휘 ocean 바다, 대양 mammal 포유류 fin 지느러미 perform 공연하다 leap 뛰다, 뛰어오르다 through ~을 통해, ~사이로 hoop 둥근 테, 후프

02 ①

W: What are you planning to do this Saturday?
너는 이번 주 토요일에 무엇을 할 계획이니?
M: I'm going to go skiing at a resort.
나는 리조트에서 스키를 탈 거야.
W: Wow. I'd love to do that, too.
우와. 나도 스키 타고 싶다.
M: You can come with me then.
그럼 너도 나랑 같이 가면 돼.

해설 남자가 토요일에 스키를 타러 가는데 여자에게도 함께 가자고 했으므로, 두 사람이 주말에 할 것은 스키이다.

어휘 plan to ~할 계획이다 resort 휴양지, 리조트 come with ~와 함께 오다/가다

03 ③

M: Here's the weather report. It's sunny now, but it's going to be cloudy tonight. The temperature is also going to go down in the evening. It might rain at night, but it's going to be sunny again tomorrow. It'll also be quite warm.

일기예보입니다. 지금은 화창하지만 오늘 밤에는 구름이 끼겠습니다. 저녁에는 또한 기온이 떨어질 것입니다. 밤에는 비가 내릴 가능성이 있지만, 내일은 다시 화창하겠습니다. 또한 매우 따뜻한 날이 될 것입니다.

해설 앞에서 cloudy, rain 등의 단어가 나오지만, 오늘 날씨에 관한 내용이므로 혼동하지 말자. sunny again tomorrow 만 제대로 들으면 정답을 맞힐 수 있다.

04 ④

M: My parents just bought a new bike for me.
우리 부모님이 방금 내게 새 자전거를 사주셨어.
W: Wow. Why did they do that?
우와. 그분들이 왜 사주신 거야?
M: I won first prize in a writing contest at school.
학교 글짓기 대회에서 내가 1등을 했거든.
W: I'm impressed. You really deserve that bike.
나 감명 받았어. 넌 정말로 그 자전거를 받을 만해.

해설 impressed를 제대로 들었고 그 의미를 알고 있다면 정답을 맞힐 수 있다. 단어의 의미를 모르더라도 남자가 상을 받았고 자전거를 구입했다는 문맥을 파악한다면 '칭찬'을 정답으로 고를 수 있다.

어휘 buy 사다(buy-bought-bought) win 이기다, 상을 타다(win-won–won) win first prize 1등을 차지하다 contest 대회, 시합 impressed 감명 받은 deserve ~을 받을 만하다

05 ⑤

W: Hello, everybody. Nice to meet you. My name is Susan. I'm from Canada. I live in Toronto. I love to read books with my friends. I also like gardening. I have a big flower garden at my home.

안녕하세요, 여러분. 만나서 반갑습니다. 제 이름은 수잔이에요. 저는 캐나다에서 왔습니다. 저는 토론토에 살고 있어요. 저는 친구들과 함께 책 읽는 것을 아주 좋아합니다. 저는 정원을 가꾸는 것도 좋아합니다. 저희 집에는 커다란 꽃밭이 있습니다.

해설 이름은 수잔, 국적은 캐나다, 사는 곳은 토론토, 취미는 독서와 정원 가꾸기이다. 나이는 언급되지 않았다.

어휘 also 또한, ~도 gardening 정원 가꾸기

06 ②

W: Are you still planning to go to the picnic with me?
너 아직도 나와 같이 소풍 갈 계획이니?
M: Yes, I am. What time are we going to leave?
응, 그래. 우리 몇 시에 나갈 거야?
W: Well, we need to leave by eleven thirty since the bus leaves at noon. 음, 버스가 정오에 출발하니까 우리는 11시 30분까지 나가야 해.
M: Oh, it's already eleven o'clock. I need to get ready now. 아, 벌써 11시구나. 나 지금 준비해야겠다.

해설 현재 시각은 11:00, 두 사람이 출발할 시각은 11:30, 버스가 떠나는 시각은 12:00이다.

어휘 still 아직도 leave 떠나다, 출발하다 since ~때문에, ~이므로 noon 정오(낮 12시) already 이미, 벌써

07 ⑤

W: What do you want to be in the future?

너는 앞으로 뭐가 되고 싶니?

M: I'd like to be a doctor. I want to help sick people. What about you? 나는 의사가 되고 싶어. 아픈 사람을 도와주고 싶거든. 너는 어때?

W: I want to be a scientist. 나는 과학자가 되고 싶어.

M: Oh, that's why you study so hard in science class. 아, 그래서 네가 과학 수업 때 아주 열심히 공부하는 거구나.

[해설] 남자는 의사, 여자는 과학자가 되고 싶어 한다.

[어휘] future 미래 doctor 의사 scientist 과학자 science class 과학 수업

08 ①

W: Hi, Jeff. What are you doing later?
안녕, 제프. 너 이따가 뭐 할 거야?

M: I'm going to a pizza restaurant with my family.
나는 가족과 함께 피자 가게에 갈 거야.

W: Oh, yeah? Why are you going there?
아, 그래? 거기에 왜 가는 건데?

M: I got an A+ on my test. My parents and I are both pleased. 내가 시험에서 A+를 받았거든. 부모님과 나는 모두 기뻐하고 있어.

W: Wow, congratulations! I hope you enjoy dinner.
우와, 축하해! 저녁 식사 맛있게 해.

[해설] 남자는 좋은 성적을 받아서 기뻐하고 있다.

[어휘] later 나중에, ~후에 both 둘 다, ~도 pleased 기뻐하는 enjoy 즐기다, 누리다

09 ④

W: Why don't you go to the park with me?
나와 같이 공원에 가지 않을래?

M: I'd love to do that, but I can't.
그렇게 하고 싶지만, 할 수가 없어.

W: Why not? Are you going home?
왜 안 돼? 너 집에 가는 거야?

M: No. I'm going to visit my grandmother at her home. I promised to go there. 아니. 나는 우리 할머니를 뵈러 갈 거야. 그곳에 가기로 약속했거든.

W: It's nice you're going to visit her. Have fun.
할머니를 뵈러 간다니 너 참 착하구나. 좋은 시간 보내.

[해설] 여자가 공원에 가자고 제안했으나 남자는 할머니 댁에 가야 한다고 말했다.

[어휘] visit 방문하다 promise 약속하다(promise – promised – promised)

10 ④

M: I'm really looking forward to tomorrow.
나는 내일이 정말 기대돼.

W: Oh, that's right. It's sports day at school.
아, 맞다. 학교 운동회 날이지.

M: Yeah. We will run some races and play sports.
그래. 우리는 달리기 시합과 운동 경기를 할 거야.

W: I hope our class wins the soccer game.
우리 반이 축구 경기에서 이기면 좋겠어.

M: I'm sure we will. We have the best players. 나는 우리가 꼭 이길 거라 확신해. 우리에겐 최고의 선수들이 있잖아.

[해설] 달리기 시합, 축구 경기 등이 포함된 교내 운동회에 대해 얘기하고 있다.

[어휘] look forward to ~을 기대하다 race 경주, 달리기 시합 sure 확신하는

11 ②

W: How do you think we should go to the concert?
우리가 콘서트 장까지 어떻게 가야 한다고 생각하니?

M: Let's take the bus there. 거기까지 버스를 타자.

W: But the bus will be crowded with passengers now.
하지만 지금쯤 버스는 승객들로 붐빌 거야.

M: That's a good point. How about taking a taxi then?
그거 좋은 지적이다. 그러면 택시를 타는 건 어때?

W: All right. That will be more comfortable for us.
좋아. 그게 우리에게 좀 더 편할 거야.

[해설] 남자가 처음에 버스를 제안했으나 결국에는 택시를 타기로 결정했다.

[어휘] crowded 붐비는, 복잡한 passenger 승객 point 의견, 요점, 사항 comfortable 편한

12 ②

W: Our history teacher is great. He is friendly to everyone.
우리 역사 선생님은 정말 좋아. 그 분은 모두에게 친절해.

M: Do you like him? I prefer the science teacher.
넌 그분을 좋아하는구나? 나는 과학 선생님이 더 좋아.

W: Why do you like her? Is she a good teacher?
너는 그 분이 왜 좋아? 그분은 좋은 선생님이니?

M: She's very good. And she tells many funny jokes in class.
아주 좋지. 게다가 그분은 수업 시간에 재미있는 농담을 많이 해.

[해설] 여자는 역사 선생님이 친절해서 좋고, 남자는 과학 선생님이 재미있어서 좋다고 말했다.

[어휘] history 역사 friendly 친절한, 상냥한 prefer ~을 더 좋아하다 funny 재미있는 joke 농담

13 ①

M: How can I help you, ma'am?
무엇을 도와드릴까요, 부인?

W: I just saw a man steal a woman's purse.
방금 어떤 남자가 여자의 지갑을 훔치는 걸 제가 봤어요.

M: Can you describe the man?
그 남자를 묘사해 주실 수 있나요?

W: Yes. He is tall and has long hair.
네. 그는 키가 크고 머리가 길었어요.

M: What is he wearing? 그가 무엇을 입고 있었나요?

W: He's wearing blue jeans and a red T-shirt.
그는 청바지와 빨간 티셔츠를 입었어요.

해설 절도범을 신고하는 시민과 그 신고를 받는 경찰관의 대화이다.

어휘 see 보다(see-saw-seen) steal 훔치다 purse (여성용) 지갑 describe 묘사하다, 서술하다 wear 입고 있다

14 ①

M: Pardon me. You look lost. Do you need any help?
실례합니다. 당신은 길을 잃은 것처럼 보이네요. 도움이 필요하신가요?

W: Yes, please. I'm looking for the library.
네, 도와주세요. 저는 도서관을 찾고 있어요.

M: Ah, okay. Go straight to the intersection. Then, turn left.
아, 알겠습니다. 교차로까지 직진하세요. 그 다음에 좌회전하세요.

W: Okay, what do I do then?
그렇군요. 그리고 어떻게 해야 하죠?

M: Walk about fifty meters. It's the second building on the right.
약 50미터를 걸어가세요. 오른편에서 두 번째 건물입니다.

W: Is there anything else you can tell me?
제게 말씀해 주실 게 더 있나요?

M: It's beside the bookstore. You can't miss it.
그것은 서점 옆에 있어요. 당신은 분명히 찾을 수 있을 거예요.

해설 도서관은 교차로에서 좌회전하여 오른편에서 두 번째 건물이며 서점 옆에 있다고 했다.

어휘 pardon me. (상대의 말을 알아듣지 못했을 때, 사과할 때, 실례를 구할 때 하는 말) 실례합니다; 뭐라구요 lost 길을 잃은 look for ~을 찾다 straight 똑바로, 곧장 intersection 교차로 second 두 번째의 anything else 그 밖에 또 무엇인가 beside 옆에 miss 놓치다

15 ②

W: Tim, it's time for dinner. Stop playing computer games. 팀, 저녁 식사 시간이야. 컴퓨터 게임 좀 그만 하렴.

M: Can you wait a minute, Mom?
잠깐 기다려 주실래요, 엄마?

W: Sorry, but I need you now. Please put the dishes on the table. 미안하지만, 나는 지금 네가 필요하구나. 식탁에 접시 좀 올려 놓으렴.

M: Can't Angie do that? She's just watching TV now.
그건 앤지가 하면 안 되나요? 그 애는 지금 TV만 보고 있잖아요.

W: No, she can't. She's feeding the cat right now.
아니, 앤지는 못 해. 그 애는 지금 고양이에게 먹이를 주는 중이야.

해설 엄마가 팀에게 부탁한 것은 식탁에 그릇을 올리는 일, 즉 식탁 차리기이다. 고양이에게 먹이를 주는 일은 앤지가 하고 있다.

어휘 dinner (저녁)식사 stop 멈추다, 중단하다 wait 기다리다

dish 접시, 요리 feed 먹이를 주다

16 ④

W: Jason, why are you putting on your backpack?
제이슨, 너는 왜 가방을 메고 있니?

M: I'm going to meet Harold at the library. We need to do our math homework. 저는 도서관에서 해럴드를 만날 거예요. 우리는 수학 숙제를 해야 하거든요.

W: Do you understand the material?
너는 그 내용을 이해하고 있니?

M: No, it's too hard for me. So we will try to learn it together.
아니요. 저한텐 너무 어려워요. 그래서 둘이 함께 공부해 보려고요.

W: Why don't you ask your teacher for help tomorrow?
내일 선생님에게 도움을 청하는 건 어떠니?

M: Okay. I'll do that. Thanks for the advice.
알겠어요. 그렇게 할게요. 조언 감사합니다.

해설 도서관에 가서 숙제를 할 거라는 남자의 말에 여자는 선생님에게 도움을 청하라고 제안했다.

어휘 put on ~을 메다 backpack 책가방 homework 숙제 understand 이해하다 material 내용, 재료 try 노력하다 advice 조언, 충고

17 ②

① W: Are you hungry now? 너 지금 배가 고프니?
   M: Not really. I just ate. 아니 그다지. 나는 방금 먹었거든.
② W: Where does Alice live? 앨리스는 어디에 사니?
   M: She's in the same class as me. 그녀는 나와 같은 반이야.
③ W: What time is it? 지금 몇 시야?
   M: It's ten to seven. 7시 10분 전(6시 50분)이야.
④ W: Can I borrow a pencil? 내가 연필을 빌려도 될까?
   M: No problem. Take this one. 문제 없지. 이걸 가져가.
⑤ W: Do you like apples? 너는 사과를 좋아하니?
   M: Yes, but I prefer oranges. 응, 하지만 나는 오렌지가 더 좋아.

해설 ②와 같이 어디에 사는지 묻는 질문에 대한 대답은 'She lives in New York.'(그녀는 뉴욕에 살고 있어.), 'She lives near the school.'(그녀는 학교 근처에 살고 있어.) 등과 같이 사는 장소나 위치를 포함하는 것이 적절하다.

어휘 borrow 빌리다 prefer 좋아하다

18 ②

M: This picture looks amazing. 이 그림은 정말 멋지네요.

W: Thanks for saying that. A customer wants to buy it.
그렇게 말씀해 주셔서 감사합니다. 어떤 고객이 그것을 구입하고 싶어 하더군요.

M: How did you paint it so well?
어쩌면 이렇게 그림을 잘 그리셨나요?

W: My art teacher was really good.
제 미술 선생님이 아주 훌륭하셨죠.

M: I wish I could make art like that.

저도 이런 미술품을 만들 수 있으면 좋겠어요.

해설 그림을 그리는 사람으로, 고객에게 그림을 판매하기도 하는 직업은 화가이다.

어휘 amazing 놀랄 만한, 굉장한 customer 고객 paint 그리다 art 미술(품), 예술

19 ⑤

M: Are you going to take a trip this summer?
너는 올여름에 여행을 갈 거니?
W: Yes. My family is going to Europe.
응. 우리 가족은 유럽에 갈 거야.
M: Wow. That sounds fun. When are you going to leave? 우와. 재미 있겠다. 너는 언제 출발하니?
W: This Friday morning. 이번 주 금요일 아침에.

① By airplane. 비행기로.
② For ten days. 열흘 동안.
③ With my family. 나의 가족과 함께.
④ To France and Italy. 프랑스와 이탈리아로.
⑤ This Friday morning. 이번 주 금요일 아침에.

해설 언제 출발하는지 물었으므로 시점을 알려주는 대답이 어울린다.

어휘 take a trip 여행하다

20 ⑤

M: Did you have a good time at the festival?
너는 축제에서 즐거운 시간을 보냈니?
W: Yes, I did. I had a lot of fun.
응, 그랬지. 재미있는 일이 많았어.
M: Really? What exactly did you do there?
정말? 너는 그곳에서 정확히 무엇을 했어?
W: I played some games. 나는 게임을 좀 했어.

① It cost ten dollars. 그건 10달러가 들었어.
② It was at the park. 그것은 공원에 있었어.
③ I just stayed home. 나는 그냥 집에 있었어.
④ I did my homework. 나는 숙제를 했어.
⑤ I played some games. 나는 게임을 좀 했어.

해설 축제에서 재미있는 시간을 보낸 친구에게 정확히 무엇을 했는지 물었다. 따라서 축제에서 했을 법한 재미있는 일이 대답으로 적절하다.

어휘 have a good time 즐거운 시간을 보내다 festival 축제 a lot of 많은 exactly 정확히

02회 실전모의고사
본문 p.16-17

01 ④	02 ④	03 ③	04 ①	05 ④
06 ③	07 ②	08 ②	09 ②	10 ④
11 ③	12 ②	13 ①	14 ④	15 ④
16 ⑤	17 ③	18 ①	19 ③	20 ③

01 ④

M: It is a kind of tool. It is made of iron, and it has very sharp teeth. You use it when you want to cut something like wood and big trees. You can hold it with one or two hands when you use it.

그것은 일종의 도구예요. 철로 만들어졌고, 매우 날카로운 톱니를 가지고 있어요. 당신은 목재나 큰 나무와 같은 것들을 자르고 싶을 때 그것을 사용해요. 당신은 그것을 사용할 때 한 손 또는 두 손으로 그것을 잡을 수 있어요.

어휘 tool 도구, 연장 be made of ~로 만들어지다 sharp 날카로운 tooth 톱니; 이, 치아(복 teeth) hold 잡다, 쥐다

02 ④

M: Hey, Melissa. What did you do after school today?
야, 멜리사. 너 오늘 방과 후에 뭐 했어?
W: I had a club meeting at three o'clock.
나는 3시에 동아리 모임을 가졌어.
M: Really? Which club are you in?
정말? 너는 어느 동아리에 있어?
W: I'm a member of the photography club. I'm the president. 나는 사진 동아리 회원이야. 내가 회장이야.
M: I guess you were busy. I was busy, too. I had soccer practice for an hour.
너는 바빴겠구나. 나도 바빴어. 한 시간 동안 축구 연습을 했거든.
W: Great. Did you enjoy it? 멋지네. 재미있었어?
M: It was hard work, but I liked it a lot.
힘들긴 했는데, 굉장히 좋았어.

해설 여자는 동아리 모임, 남자는 축구 연습에 대해 말했는데, 이것은 모두 방과 후에 이루어진 활동이다.

어휘 after school 방과 후에 club 동아리 member 회원 photography 사진 촬영술 president 회장 practice 연습

03 ③

M: Hi, everyone. Let's look at tomorrow's weather across the country. There will be sunny skies in Seoul and Daejeon. Unfortunately, it's going to be cloudy in Busan while Daegu is going to get lots of rain. Gwangju is expecting sunny weather, but it will be very windy.

안녕하세요, 여러분. 전국의 내일 날씨를 살펴보겠습니다. 서울과 대전의 하늘은 화창하겠습니다. 유감스럽게도, 대구는 많은 비가 내릴 예정인 반면에 부산은 구름이 끼겠습니다. 광주는 화창한 날씨가 예상되지만 바람이 강하게 불겠습니다.

어휘 weather 날씨 across the country 전국의 unfortunately 유감스럽게도, 불행하게도 cloudy 흐린, 구름이 낀 while ~인 반면에 expect 예상하다 weather 날씨 windy 바람이 부는

04 ①

M: How was your first swimming lesson?
너의 첫 수영 수업은 어땠니?

W: It was fun, but I was afraid of the water.
재미있었지만 나는 물이 무서웠어.

M: Don't worry. You can learn quickly.
걱정하지 마. 너는 빨리 배울 수 있을 거야.

W: Do you really think so? 정말 그렇게 생각해?

M: Yes, I do. I know that you can do it.
응. 틀림없이 너는 할 수 있을 거야.

해설 수영 수업에서 물이 무서웠다고 말한 여자를 남자가 할 수 있다는 말로 격려하고 있다.

어휘 lesson 수업 be afraid of ~을 두려워하다 quickly 빨리

05 ④

W: This morning, I had bacon and toast for breakfast. I also had a glass of milk. I was busy during lunch, so I only ate a sandwich. For dinner, I went to Burger Time with my friends. I ate a chicken sandwich and had some fries.

오늘 아침에, 나는 아침 식사로 베이컨과 토스트를 먹었다. 나는 우유 한 잔도 마셨다. 나는 점심에는 바빠서 샌드위치 하나만 먹었다. 저녁을 먹으러 나는 친구들과 버거 타임에 갔다. 나는 치킨 샌드위치와 감자튀김을 먹었다.

해설 햄버거(hamburger)는 식당 이름 Burger Time을 이용한 함정이다.

어휘 breakfast 아침 식사 during lunch 점심 시간에 fries 감자튀김

06 ③

W: I'm glad we're going to the circus on Friday.
우리가 금요일에 서커스에 가게 되어 기뻐.

M: It should be a lot of fun. What time do you want to meet? 엄청 재미있을 거야. 몇 시에 만나고 싶어?

W: Let's go there at six thirty. 6시 30분에 거기에 가자.

M: But the show doesn't start until seven thirty.
하지만 공연은 7시 30분이 되어서야 시작해.

W. Oh, then let's get together at seven.
아, 그러면 7시에 만나자.

M: That's a good idea. Let's meet at the bus stop.
좋은 생각이야. 버스 정류장에서 만나자.

해설 처음에 만나기로 제안한 시각은 6:30, 공연이 시작하는 시각은 7:30, 최종적으로 만나기로 한 시각은 7:00이다.

어휘 circus 서커스 show 공연, 쇼 not A until B B가 되어서야 A하다 get together 만나다, 모이다

07 ②

W: I need to buy some supplies for school.
나는 학용품을 좀 사야 해.

M: So do I. What are you going to get?

나도 그래. 너는 뭘 살 거야?

W: I have to buy some notebooks, pens, and paper.
나는 공책, 펜, 그리고 종이를 사야 해.

M: Are you going to order everything on the Internet?
모든 것을 인터넷으로 주문할 거니?

W: I'd rather buy the items at the stationery store. Shall we go there together?
나는 그 물건들을 문구점에서 사고 싶어. 우리 그곳에 같이 갈래?

M: Good idea. Let's go now. 좋아. 지금 가자.

해설 남자가 학용품을 인터넷으로 주문할 거냐는 말에 여자는 문구점에 가서 살 거라고 말하며 같이 가자고 했다.

어휘 school supplies 학용품 order 주문하다 would rather ~하겠다, ~하고 싶다 item 물건 stationery store 문구점

08 ②

W: Why didn't you go to the theater with us last night?
너는 왜 지난밤에 우리와 같이 영화관에 가지 않았어?

M: I just felt like staying home. 난 그냥 집에 있고 싶었어.

W: Are you worried about your dog? Is she still sick?
네 개가 걱정돼서 그래? 아직도 개가 아프니?

M: Yes. I hope she gets better soon.
응. 나는 개가 곧 낫길 바랄 뿐이야.

W: I'm sure she'll be fine in a few days.
개는 며칠 후면 괜찮아질 거야.

해설 남자는 자신의 아픈 개를 걱정하고 있다.

어휘 theater 영화관, 극장 feel like ~ing ~하고 싶다 stay 머물다 be worried about ~에 대해 걱정하다 get better 좋아지다, 회복하다 in a few days 며칠 후에

09 ②

W: Jim, how was your weekend? 짐, 주말은 어떻게 보냈니?

M: It was great. I went to the beach with my family.
굉장했어. 나는 가족과 함께 해변에 갔어.

W: Wow. What did you do there? 우와. 너 거기서 뭐 했어?

M: We went swimming and ate lots of seafood. How about you?
우리는 수영도 하고 해산물도 많이 먹었어. 너는 어땠어?

W: I painted a picture. It's my newest hobby.
나는 그림을 그렸어. 그건 새로 생긴 나의 취미야.

M: I'd love to see it. 난 너의 그림을 보고 싶어.

해설 남자는 해변에 갔고, 여자는 그림을 그렸다.

어휘 weekend 주말 beach 해변 go 가다(go-went-gone) eat 먹다(eat-ate-eaten) seafood 해산물 paint a picture 그림을 그리다 newest 최신의

10 ④

M: I'd love to have a hamburger. How much is one?
저는 햄버거를 먹고 싶어요. 하나에 얼마예요?

W: Hamburgers cost three dollars each. Would you

like a drink, too?

햄버거는 하나에 3달러씩입니다. 마실 것도 드릴까요?

M: Yes. How much is a soda? 네. 탄산음료는 얼마예요?

W: A large soda is one dollar.

큰 사이즈의 탄산음료는 1달러입니다.

M: That sounds perfect. I'd like two hamburgers and a large soda, please.

좋아요. 햄버거 2개랑 탄산음료 큰 사이즈로 할게요.

W: That will cost seven dollars. 7달러입니다.

M: Okay. Here's a ten-dollar bill. 네. 여기 10달러짜리 지폐요.

해설 총 지불할 금액은 7달러이며, 10달러는 남자가 낸 돈이다.

어휘 cost (비용이) ~이다 drink 음료; 마시다 large 큰 사이즈의

11 ③

① M: Do you know the time? 몇 시인지 알아?

W: Yes, it's a quarter past one. 응, 1시 15분이야.

② M: What is your favorite type of movie?

네가 가장 좋아하는 영화 종류가 뭐야?

W: I really like action films. 나는 액션 영화를 정말 좋아해.

③ M: How often do you meet your friends?

너는 얼마나 자주 친구들을 만나니?

W: I like playing sports with them.

나는 그들과 스포츠를 하는 것을 좋아해.

④ M: What do you think of this picture?

이 그림에 대해 어떻게 생각해?

W: It's beautiful. I love it. 아름다워. 내 마음에 들어.

⑤ M: Did you have a good time? 좋은 시간을 보냈니?

W: Not really. I was bored. 아니. 지루했어.

해설 ③ how often으로 물었으므로, '일주일에 몇 번' 등 빈도를 나타내는 답변이 와야 한다.

어휘 quarter 15분, 1/4 favorite 매우 좋아하는 type 종류 picture 그림

12 ②

M: Jenny, you're in the art club, aren't you?

제니, 넌 미술 동아리에 있지, 그렇지 않니?

W: Yes, that's correct. I joined the club last year.

응, 맞아. 나는 작년에 그 동아리에 가입했어.

M: I'd like to learn how to draw. Do you enjoy it?

나는 그림 그리는 방법을 배우고 싶어. 너는 그게 마음에 드니?

W: Yes, it's a lot of fun. I joined up so that I could exhibit my work. 응. 굉장히 재미있어. 나는 내 작품을 전시하고 싶어서 가입했어.

M: That's interesting. 그거 흥미롭구나.

해설 남자는 여자의 미술 동아리에 대해 물었고, 여자는 작품을 전시하고 싶어서 미술 동아리에 가입했다고 설명했다.

어휘 correct 맞는, 정확한 join 가입하다 draw 그림을 그리다 exhibit 전시하다 work 작품; 일하다

13 ①

M: Good morning. How are you?

좋은 아침입니다. 안녕하세요?

W: Good morning, sir. May I see your boarding pass, please?

좋은 아침입니다, 손님. 탑승권을 보여 주시겠어요?

M: Yes, here it is. 네, 여기 있어요.

W: You're in seat forty-four B. Just walk right down that aisle.

44B 좌석이네요. 저 통로를 따라 걸어가세요.

M: I appreciate it. 감사합니다.

해설 탑승권을 보여주고 좌석을 안내 받는 상황이므로 승무원과 승객의 관계이다.

어휘 boarding pass 탑승권 seat 좌석 aisle 통로 appreciate 감사하다

14 ④

M: Something smells delicious. What are you doing?

맛있는 냄새가 나네요. 뭐 하세요?

W: I'm baking a cake. It's your sister's birthday.

나는 케이크를 굽고 있어. 네 누나의 생일이잖니.

M: That's right. Can I do anything for you?

맞아요. 제가 무엇을 도와드릴까요?

W: We need eggs. Can you buy some at the grocery store, please?

우리 계란이 필요하구나. 식료품점에 가서 계란 좀 사올래?

M: Sure. I'll be right back. 물론이죠. 제가 금방 다녀올게요.

해설 여자는 남자에게 계란을 사오라고 부탁하고 있다.

어휘 delicious 맛있는 bake 굽다 grocery store 식료품점, 슈퍼마켓

15 ④

[Cellphone rings.] [휴대폰이 울린다.]

W: Hello. 여보세요.

M: Hi, Tina. It's Eric. Do you want to study with Dan and me?

안녕 티나. 나 에릭이야. 나랑 댄과 함께 공부할래?

W: Sure. When and where are we going to meet?

좋아. 언제 어디에서 만날 거야?

M: We're going to go to the library at three.

우리는 3시에 도서관으로 갈 거야.

W: I've never been there. Can I meet you at the bus stop near your house instead? 난 거기에 가본 적이 없어. 대신 너희 집 근처에 있는 버스 정류장에서 널 만나도 될까?

M: Sure. I'll see you there in an hour.

물론이지. 한 시간 후에 거기에서 보자.

해설 도서관 위치를 모르는 여자는 버스 정류장에서 보자고 제안했고 남자도 이에 동의했다.

어휘 library 도서관 bus stop 버스 정류장 near 근처에, 가까이에 instead 대신에

16 ⑤

W: Kevin, is that the new T-shirt you wanted to buy yesterday? 케빈, 그게 어제 네가 사고 싶어 했던 새 티셔츠야?

M: No, it's not. I didn't get a shirt yesterday.
아니. 나는 어제 셔츠를 못 샀어.

W: What happened? Was the shirt too expensive?
무슨 일이야? 그 셔츠가 너무 비쌌니?

M: No. I needed a size medium, but the store only had large T-shirts. 아니. 나는 중간 사이즈가 필요했는데, 가게에 큰 티셔츠만 있었어.

W: That's too bad. 저런.

해설 남자는 중간 사이즈를 원했지만 없어서 사지 못했다.

어휘 happen 발생하다 expensive 비싼 medium 중간의 large 큰

17 ③

M: Mom, I just got an email from my friend George.
엄마, 방금 제 친구 조지한테 이메일을 받았어요.

W: How is he doing? Didn't he move?
그 애는 어떻게 지내니? 이사하지 않았니?

M: Yes, he moved to another city with his family last month.
했어요. 조지는 지난달에 가족과 함께 다른 도시로 이사했어요.

W: Does he enjoy his new home?
그 애는 새 집이 마음에 든대?

M: He's having fun. Can I visit him this weekend?
조지는 즐겁게 지내고 있대요. 이번 주말에 그 애 집에 놀러 가도 돼요?

W: Sure. You can take the bus when you visit him.
물론이지. 그 애를 방문할 때 너는 버스를 타면 돼.

해설 남자는 이사한 친구의 집에 놀러 가도 되는지 물었고 여자는 이를 허락했다.

어휘 move 이사하다 another 다른 have fun 재미있게 지내다

18 ①

[Cellphone rings.] [휴대폰이 울린다.]

W: Hello. 여보세요.

M: Hello, Stephanie. It's Chris. Did you go to history class today?
안녕, 스테파니. 나 크리스야. 너 오늘 역사 수업에 들어갔니?

W: Yes, I did. Why? 응, 갔어. 왜?

M: I woke up late and missed that class. Do we have any homework?
내가 늦게 일어나서 그 수업을 놓쳤거든. 우리 숙제 있어?

W: Yes, we do. 응, 있어.

M: What is it? 뭔데?

W: We have to read chapter two. And we'll have a short test tomorrow.
우리는 챕터 2를 읽어야 해. 그리고 내일 간단한 시험을 볼 거야.

M: Thanks for the information. 알려줘서 고마워.

해설 역사 수업에 결석한 남자가 여자에게 숙제가 있는지 묻고 있다.

어휘 history 역사 wake up (잠에서) 깨다 late 늦게 miss 놓치다 homework 숙제 have to ~ 해야 한다 short 짧막한, 간단한 tomorrow 내일 information 정보

19 ③

M: Is that a new digital camera?
그거 새 디지털 카메라야?

W: Yes, it is. My parents gave it to me for my birthday.
응. 우리 부모님께서 내 생일 선물로 주셨어.

M: It looks really nice. Can I see it?
그거 정말 좋아 보인다. 내가 좀 봐도 돼?

W: Sure. Here you are. 물론이지. 여기 있어.

① That's okay. 괜찮아.

② You're welcome. 천만에.

③ Sure. Here you are. 물론이지. 여기 있어.

④ Yes, I bought it for you. 응. 너에게 주려고 샀어.

⑤ No, I can't see it from here. 아니. 여기서는 안 보여.

해설 새 카메라를 구경하고 싶어 하는 친구의 요청을 흔쾌히 수락하는 ③이 적절하다.

어휘 parents 부모 give 주다(give-gave-given) buy 사다 (buy-bought-bought)

20 ③

W: Are you watching that show now?
너 지금 저 프로그램을 보는 중이니?

M: Yes, I am. 응.

W: When is it going to end? 그거 언제 끝나니?

M: It's going to finish in ten minutes. 10분 후에 끝나.

W: Good. I need to watch something then.
좋아. 그때 나도 뭘 좀 봐야 해.

M: What are you going to watch? 너는 무엇을 볼 거니?

W: It's a documentary on dolphins.
그건 돌고래에 관한 다큐멘터리야.

① Here's the remote control. 리모컨 여기 있어.

② I'll turn the TV down a bit. 내가 TV(볼륨) 좀 줄일게.

③ It's a documentary on dolphins.
그건 돌고래에 관한 다큐멘터리야.

④ Yes, you can change the channel.
응, 네가 채널을 돌려도 돼.

⑤ That's my favorite show you're watching.
네가 보고 있는 건 내가 가장 좋아하는 쇼야.

해설 무엇을 시청할 건지 묻는 질문에 프로그램 종류로 답한 ③이 적절하다.

어휘 end 끝나다 finish 끝나다; 끝내다 turn down (소리, 온도 등을) 낮추다 documentary 다큐멘터리 change 변경하다 channel 채널 favorite 매우 좋아하는

01 ③	02 ①	03 ④	04 ⑤	05 ④
06 ②	07 ④	08 ②	09 ③	10 ③
11 ①	12 ③	13 ①	14 ④	15 ②
16 ①	17 ②	18 ④	19 ④	20 ⑤

01 ③

M: How do you like this notebook? 이 공책 어때?
W: It's nice. The stars on the front look nice.
그거 좋은데. 표지에 있는 별들이 멋져 보여.
M: I agree. I need a new notebook for school.
나도 동의해. 나는 학교에서 새 공책이 필요하거든.
W: Then you should buy this one.
그럼 너는 이 공책을 사야 해.
M: Okay. I'll get it. 그래. 난 그걸 살래.

해설 대화에는 별(stars)이 그려진 공책만 언급되므로 쉽게 정답을 맞힐 수 있다. 그래도 여자가 제안하는 'you should ~'와 남자의 대답 'I'll get it.'을 끝까지 확인한다.

어휘 How do you like ~? ~은 어때?, ~이 마음에 드니? on the front 앞(표지)에 agree 동의하다

02 ①

W: Good morning, everyone. Here's the weather for today. Right now, it's cool and windy. But it's going to be warm and sunny in the afternoon. In the evening, there will be lots of clouds in the sky. And it will start to rain at night.

좋은 아침입니다, 여러분. 오늘의 날씨를 전해드리겠습니다. 현재는 시원하고 바람이 불고 있습니다. 그러나 오후에는 따뜻하고 화창하겠습니다. 저녁에는 하늘에 많은 양의 구름이 있겠습니다. 그리고 밤에는 비가 내리기 시작할 것입니다.

해설 오후에는 따뜻하고 화창할 거라는 두 가지 정보가 주어졌다. 두 정보를 만족하는 그림은 해가 난 그림이다.

어휘 weather 날씨 cool 시원한 warm 따뜻한 lots of 많은

03 ④

[Cellphone rings.] [휴대폰이 울린다.]
W: Hi, Greg. What are you doing?
안녕, 그레그. 너는 무엇을 하고 있니?
M: I'm watching TV at home right now. Why?
나는 지금 집에서 TV를 보고 있어. 왜?
W: I'm going to a play with my parents tonight. Would you like to go with us? 나는 오늘 밤에 부모님과 연극을 보러 갈 거야. 너도 우리와 함께 가겠니?
M: I'd love to, but I have to finish my homework. I'm really sorry.

나도 가고 싶지만, 나는 숙제를 끝내야 해. 정말 미안해.

해설 'I'd love to, but ~'은 거절할 때 쓰는 대표적 표현이다.

어휘 play 연극; 놀다 finish 끝내다, 끝나다

04 ⑤

M: Hello. It's a pleasure to meet you. Let me tell you about myself. My name is Peter Jenkins. I'm fifteen years old, and I'm from London. My hobby is riding my bicycle. I want to be a pilot in the future. I hope we can be friends. Thank you.

안녕하세요. 여러분을 만나게 되어 기쁩니다. 저에 대해 말씀 드릴게요. 제 이름은 피터 젠킨스입니다. 저는 열다섯 살이고 런던 출신입니다. 저의 취미는 자전거를 타는 것입니다. 저는 장차 조종사가 되고 싶습니다. 저는 우리가 친구가 되길 바랍니다. 감사합니다.

어휘 pleasure 기쁨, 즐거움 hobby 취미 pilot 조종사, 비행사 in the future 장차, 미래에 hope 바라다; 희망

05 ④

W: Let's go swimming early tomorrow morning.
내일 아침 일찍 수영하러 가자.
M: Sure. When should we meet? I wake up at six thirty every day.
좋아. 우리 언제 만날까? 나는 매일 6시 30분에 일어나.
W: What about seven then? 그럼 7시 어때?
M: I have to eat breakfast first. Let's meet at seven thirty. 나는 우선 아침을 먹어야 해. 7시 30분에 만나자.
W: Okay. See you tomorrow. 그래. 내일 보자.

해설 언제 만날지 묻는 문제에서, 처음 제안을 하는 사람의 의견은 거절 당하고, 그 다음에 정답이 등장하는 경우가 많다.

어휘 early 일찍 wake up (잠에서) 깨다, 일어나다 breakfast 아침 식사

06 ②

M: What's your favorite class, Cindy?
네가 가장 좋아하는 수업이 뭐야, 신디?
W: It's history. How about you? 역사 수업이야. 너는 어때?
M: I like science. I want to be a scientist in the future.
나는 과학을 좋아해. 나는 장차 과학자가 되고 싶어.
W: That's interesting. 그거 흥미롭다.
M: How about you? What do you want to be?
너는 어때? 너는 뭐가 되고 싶니?
W: I want to be a history teacher.
나는 역사 선생님이 되고 싶어.

해설 'I want to be ~' 뒤에 정답이 등장한다. 두 사람의 장래 희망이 각각 언급되므로 성별을 구분해서 정답을 고른다.

어휘 favorite 매우 좋아하는 scientist 과학자

07 ④

W: You're really quiet today, John. What's the matter?
너 오늘 정말 조용하다, 존. 무슨 문제 있니?

M: I performed in the school play this morning.
나는 오늘 아침에 학교 연극에서 공연을 했어.

W: Really? How was it? 정말? 어땠어?

M: I forgot my lines, so lots of people laughed at me.
내가 대사를 잊어버려서 여러 사람들이 나를 비웃었어.

W: I understand how you feel. Try to forget about it.
난 너의 기분이 어떨지 이해해. 그 일을 잊도록 해봐.

해설 남자의 마지막 대사에서 비웃음을 당한 것이 언급된다. 그 심정이 어떨지 헤아려 본다.

어휘 quiet 조용한 matter (고민 관련) 문제 perform 공연하다 play 연극 forget 잊다(forget-forgot-forgotten) line 대사 laugh at ~을 비웃다 understand 이해하다

08 ②

W: That new action movie is coming out tomorrow.
그 신작 액션 영화가 내일 개봉한대.

M: Why don't we get tickets for it?
우리 그 영화 표를 사는 게 어때?

W: The theater is too far away. I can't go there.
영화관은 너무 멀어. 난 그곳까지 갈 수 없어.

M: We can buy the tickets online. It's easy.
우리는 온라인으로 표를 구입할 수 있어. 그건 쉬워.

W: All right. I'll do that now. 알았어. 내가 지금 할게.

해설 대화 직후에 할 일은 주로 대화 마무리 직전에 I will, now 등이 포함된 대사에 정답이 있다. 전부 영화와 관련된 선택지가 등장하므로 주의한다.

어휘 action movie 액션 영화 come out 나오다, 생산되다 far away 멀리 online 온라인의, 온라인으로

09 ③

M: We're going on a field trip tomorrow, aren't we?
우리 내일 현장 학습 가는 거지, 그렇지 않니?

W: No, we're not. The zoo is going to be closed all week.
아니, 그렇지 않아. 동물원이 일주일 내내 문을 닫는대.

M: Really? Then when are we going to go there?
정말? 그러면 우리는 그곳에 언제 가니?

W: We'll visit it next Monday.
우린 다음 주 월요일에 갈 거야.

M: I see. 그렇구나.

해설 남자의 첫 대사에 현장 학습이 언급되었다.

어휘 field trip 현장 학습 closed 문을 닫은 all week 일주일 내내 visit 방문하다

10 ③

M: We need to go downtown tonight.
우리는 오늘 밤에 시내에 가야 해요.

W: Okay. Do you want to drive the car?
알겠어요. 당신이 차를 운전하겠어요?

M: No. Traffic will be too heavy tonight.
아니요. 오늘 밤엔 교통 체증이 아주 심할 거예요.

W: Why don't we take the subway then?
그러면 우리 지하철을 타는 게 어때요?

M: Sure. That will be faster than a taxi or the bus.
좋아요. 그게 택시나 버스보다 빠를 거예요.

해설 맨 처음 제시된 교통수단은 주로 거절당한다. 'Why don't we ~?'로 제안한 내용과 대답을 확인하고 정답을 고른다.

어휘 downtown 시내에, 시내로 drive 운전하다 traffic 교통(량) faster 더 빠른(fast-faster-fastest)

11 ①

M: Why were you absent from school yesterday?
너는 어제 왜 학교에 결석했어?

W: My mother had to take me to see a doctor.
우리 어머니가 나를 병원에 데려가야 했어.

M: What happened? Did you catch a cold?
무슨 일 있었어? 너 감기에 걸렸어?

W: Yes, and I had a bad fever.
응, 그리고 나는 심하게 열이 났어.

M: How do you feel now? Do you feel better?
지금은 어때? 너는 몸이 좀 나아졌어?

W: Yes. Thanks for asking.
응. 물어봐 줘서 고마워.

해설 남자의 첫 대사에서 'Why were you absent ~?'로 직접 이유를 물어봤고, 그에 대한 대답에서 정답이 드러난다.

어휘 absent from ~에 결석한 catch a cold 감기에 걸리다 fever 열 feel better 회복되다, 기분이 좋아지다

12 ③

M: What should I do in the next scene?
다음 장면에선 제가 무엇을 해야 하죠?

W: You're going to have a fight with the bad guy.
당신은 악당과 싸움을 할 거예요.

M: Am I going to use anything?
제가 무엇을 이용하게 되나요?

W: Yes. You'll have a gun. You're going to be in a gunfight.
네. 당신은 총을 갖게 될 겁니다. 당신은 총격전을 벌일 거예요.

M: Okay. Let me practice my lines for a minute.
알겠습니다. 저는 잠시 동안 대사를 연습할게요.

해설 장면, 총격전, 대사 등으로 미루어 보아 남자는 배우이고, 남자에게 설명을 해주는 여사는 영화감독이나.

어휘 scene 장면 fight 싸움; 싸우다 gunfight 총격전 practice 연습하다

13 ①

M: Pardon me. Can you tell me where the bank is?
실례합니다. 은행이 어디에 있는지 말씀해 주시겠어요?

W: Sure. Walk straight until you get to the intersection. Then, turn left. 물론이죠. 교차로에 다다를 때까지 직진하세요. 그리고 나서 좌회전하세요.

M: Okay. I will go straight and then turn left.
네. 직진한 뒤에 좌회전할게요.

W: Right. Then, walk straight past two buildings. The bank will be on your right. It's next to the bakery. 맞아요. 그 다음에 건물 두 개를 지나 직진하세요. 은행은 당신의 오른쪽에 있을 겁니다. 그것은 제과점 옆에 있어요.

M: Thank you very much. 정말 감사합니다.

해설 교차로에서 좌회전 후 오른쪽에 제과점 옆 건물이 은행이다.

어휘 straight 똑바로 get to ~에 도착하다 intersection 교차로 past ~을 지나서 next to ~옆에 bakery 제과점

14 ④

W: Harry, are you busy right now?
해리, 너 지금 바쁘니?

M: No, I'm not, Ms. Crawford. Do you want me to sweep the floor?
아니에요, 크로퍼드 선생님. 제가 바닥을 쓸길 원하시나요?

W: No, Jim will do that. Could you please empty the trash can?
아니야, 그건 짐이 할 거야. 너는 쓰레기통을 비워 주겠니?

M: Yes, I can. Can I do anything else?
네, 할 수 있어요. 제가 할 일이 더 있나요?

W: That's all right. Thanks, Harry.
괜찮아. 고맙구나, 해리.

해설 'Do you want me to ~?'로 남자가 언급한 내용에 속지 말아야 한다. 여자의 대사인 'Could you ~?'에 직접적인 부탁의 내용이 있다.

어휘 sweep 쓸다, 청소하다 empty 비우다; 비어 있는 anything else 그밖에 다른

15 ②

M: I'm going to take a trip to Hawaii this week.
나는 이번 주에 하와이로 여행을 갈 거야.

W: Have a great time. Why don't you send me a postcard?
좋은 시간 보내. 나에게 엽서를 보내는 게 어때?

M: Okay. I'll send you one with a picture of a beach.
그래. 해변 그림이 담긴 엽서를 보낼게.

W: Thanks. What are you going to do there?
고마워. 그곳에서 너는 무엇을 할 거니?

M: I want to go swimming and relax.
나는 수영을 하고 휴식을 취하고 싶어.

해설 여자의 대사인 'Why don't you ~?'의 내용에 주목한다.

어휘 send 보내다 postcard (그림)엽서 beach 해변 relax 휴식을 취하다

16 ①

① W: I'm very sorry about that.
나는 그 일에 대해 매우 유감스러워.
M: You're welcome. 천만에.

② W: How long does it take to get there?
그곳에 가는 데 얼마나 오래 걸리나요?
M: About ten minutes. 약 10분이요.

③ W: Hi, Steve. How are you today?
안녕, 스티브. 너 오늘 기분이 어때?
M: I'm very good. Thanks. 아주 좋아. 고마워.

④ W: Who is that man over there?
저기에 있는 남자는 누구니?
M: His name is James. 그의 이름은 제임스야.

⑤ W: Thank you for the advice. 충고 감사합니다.
M: It's my pleasure. (도움이 되어) 저도 기뻐요.

해설 ① 'You're welcome.'은 고맙다는 말에 대한 응답이다.

어휘 over there 저쪽에 advice 충고, 조언 pleasure 기쁨

17 ②

W: Good morning, Dustin. Are you busy now?
좋은 아침이야, 더스틴. 너 지금 바빠?

M: Yes, I am. I have to see a patient.
응, 바빠. 나는 환자를 봐야 해.

W: I hope the patient isn't too sick.
그 환자가 너무 아프지 않았으면 좋겠다.

M: He might need surgery.
그 사람은 수술이 필요할 수도 있어.

W: That's not good. 그거 안 됐다.

M: Yeah. Let's talk later today.
그래. 오늘 이따가 얘기하자.

해설 환자를 진찰하고 수술하는 직업은 의사이다.

어휘 patient 환자 surgery 수술 later 이따가

18 ④

W: Do you like to look at the stars? If you want to look at them closely, you can use this. This makes distant objects appear closer. You can also use this to look at the moon and the planet. What is this?

여러분은 별을 보는 것을 좋아하나요? 여러분이 별을 더 가까이 보고 싶다면 이것을 사용할 수 있습니다. 이것은 멀리 있는 물체를 더 가까이 보이게 만듭니다. 여러분은 또한 이것을 사용해서 달과 행성을 볼 수 있습니다. 이것은 무엇일까요?

해설 별, 달, 행성을 관측할 수 있고, 멀리 있는 물체를 가까이 있는 것처럼 볼 수 있게 하는 도구는 망원경이다.

어휘 look at ~을 보다, 살피다 closely 가까이, 접근하여 distant 먼 object 물체 appear 나타나다 closer 더 가까운(close-closer-closest) planet 행성

19 ④

M: Your face is really red. What happened?
네 얼굴이 정말 빨개. 무슨 일이야?

W: I went to the beach yesterday.
나는 어제 해변에 갔었어.

M: Didn't you wear any suntan lotion?
너 선크림을 바르지 않았어?

W: No, I didn't. So I got sunburned.
안 발랐어. 그래서 나는 햇볕에 탔어.

M: Don't forget next time. 다음에는 잊지 마.

① That's great news. 그거 아주 좋은 소식이다.
② I bet you had fun. 넌 분명 재미있었을 거야.
③ How was the weather? 날씨는 어땠니?
④ Don't forget next time. 다음에는 잊지 마.
⑤ I'm going to the beach soon. 나는 곧 해변에 갈 거야.

[해설] 선크림을 바르지 않아 얼굴이 탄 친구에게 다음에는 선크림 바르는 걸 잊지 말라고 충고하는 응답이 적절하다.

[어휘] happen 발생하다 go 가다(go-went-gone) beach 해변 wear 바르다, 입다 suntan lotion 선크림(= sunblock) sunburned 햇볕에 심하게 탄 weather 날씨 forget 잊다 soon 곧

20 ⑤

W: I have to do some research for a science report.
나는 과학 보고서를 위해 조사를 좀 해야 해.

M: When do you have to finish it?
너는 그걸 언제 끝내야 하니?

W: I should give it to my teacher by Friday. I need to go to the library today. 금요일까지 선생님께 제출해야 해. 난 오늘 도서관에 가야 돼.

M: The library should have the information you need.
도서관에 네가 필요한 정보가 있을 거야.

W: But I don't know where the library is.
하지만 나는 도서관이 어디에 있는지 모르겠어.

M: I can tell you how to get there.
그곳에 가는 방법을 내가 말해줄 수 있어.

① Here's my library card. 여기 내 도서관 카드가 있어.
② I already finished my paper.
나는 이미 내 과제물을 완성했어.
③ No, the library isn't open now.
아니, 두서관은 지금 열지 않았어.
④ You can check out books there.
너는 저기에서 책을 대출할 수 있어.
⑤ I can tell you how to get there.
그곳에 가는 방법을 내가 말해줄 수 있어.

[해설] 도서관 위치를 모르는 친구에게 그곳에 가는 방법을 알려주겠다는 응답이 어울린다.

[어휘] research 연구, 조사 report 보고서 information 정보 already 이미 check out (도서관에서 책을) 대출하다

01 ③	**02** ②	**03** ①	**04** ④	**05** ①
06 ②	**07** ⑤	**08** ④	**09** ⑤	**10** ②
11 ②	**12** ①	**13** ②	**14** ③	**15** ③
16 ④	**17** ③	**18** ④	**19** ⑤	**20** ④

01 ③

W: Good afternoon. May I help you?
안녕하세요. 무엇을 도와드릴까요?

M: Hello. I'm looking for a blouse for my daughter.
안녕하세요. 제 딸이 입을 블라우스를 찾고 있어요.

W: How about this one with flowers on it?
꽃이 그려진 이것은 어떤가요?

M: It's okay, but the one with the rainbow looks nicer. I'll take it. 괜찮네요, 하지만 무지개가 그려진 것이 더 좋아 보여요. 그걸로 할게요.

W: Good choice. That's our most popular blouse.
탁월한 선택이네요. 그건 저희 가게에서 가장 인기 있는 블라우스랍니다.

[해설] 여자가 권한 건 꽃무늬 블라우스였지만, 남자는 'It's okay, but ~'에서 다른 선택을 말했다.

[어휘] look for ~을 찾다 daughter 딸 rainbow 무지개 nicer 더 좋은(nice-nicer-nicest) most popular 가장 인기 있는 (popular-more popular-most popular)

02 ②

W: Hello, everyone. The weekend is almost over. Tonight, it's going to be partly cloudy. On Monday, it's going to be rainy all day long. On Tuesday, the weather will be cold and windy. It's going to snow on Wednesday and Thursday. And it will be sunny on Friday.

안녕하세요, 여러분. 주말도 거의 끝나가네요. 오늘 밤에는 부분적으로 구름이 끼겠습니다. 월요일에는 하루 종일 비가 내릴 것입니다. 화요일에는 날씨가 춥고 바람이 불 것입니다. 수요일과 목요일에는 눈이 내리겠습니다. 그리고 금요일에는 화창할 것입니다.

[어휘] almost 거의 over 끝이 난 partly 부분적으로 cloudy 흐린, 구름이 낀 all day long 하루 종일

03 ①

W: What are you doing, Louis?
너 뭐 하고 있니, 루이스?

M: I'm making a kite. Flying kites is my newest hobby.
나는 연을 만들고 있어. 연날리기는 나의 새로운 취미야.

W: I see. Is it easy to fly a kite?
그렇구나. 연을 날리는 것은 쉽니?

M: Yes, it is. Would you like to do it with me in the

park? 응. 공원에서 나와 함께 연 날릴래?

W: I'd love to do that. 그렇게 하고 싶어.

해설 남자는 'Would you like to ~?'로 제안을 했고, 여자는 'I'd love to ~'라는 말로 동의의 의사를 밝혔다.

어휘 kite 연 fly 날리다, 날다 newest 새로운, 최신의 hobby 취미

04 ④

M: I'd like to talk about my family right now. There are five people in my family. My father is a businessman, and my mother enjoys reading books. My older brother is in the army. My younger sister is in the fifth grade in elementary school. I have the best family.

저는 지금 제 가족에 대해 말하고자 합니다. 제 가족은 다섯 명입니다. 제 아버지께서는 사업가이시고, 제 어머니께서는 독서를 즐기십니다. 제 형은 군대에 있습니다. 제 여동생은 초등학교 5학년입니다. 저에게는 최고의 가족이 있답니다.

해설 남자는 형이 군대에 있다는 사실은 언급했으나 나이는 말하지 않았다.

어휘 businessman 사업가 enjoy 즐기다 army 군대 elementary school 초등학교

05 ①

[Telephone rings.] [전화벨이 울린다.]

W: Hello. 여보세요.

M: Hello, Wendy. It's Peter. When is your grandfather arriving?
안녕, 웬디. 나 피터야. 너희 할아버지께서 언제 도착하시니?

W: His train arrives at five thirty this evening.
할아버지가 타신 기차가 오늘 저녁 5시 30분에 도착해.

M: Okay. I'll pick you up at your house at four.
알았어. 4시에 내가 널 태우러 너의 집으로 갈게.

W: Great. Thanks for taking me to the train station.
좋아. 날 기차역에 데려다 줘서 고마워.

M: You're welcome. 천만에.

해설 만나기로 한 시각을 찾는 문제이므로, 'pick you up at four'를 'meet you at four'로 이해할 수 있다. 5:30은 기차 도착 시각이다.

어휘 arrive 도착하다 pick up 태우다 train station 기차역

06 ②

W: I love this picture hanging on the wall.
난 벽에 걸린 이 그림이 참 좋아.

M: Thanks. I painted it last week.
고마워. 그건 내가 지난주에 그렸어.

W: Did you paint this? You're really good at painting.
네가 이걸 그렸다고? 너 정말 그림에 소질이 있구나.

M: Thanks. I would like to become an artist.
고마워. 나는 화가가 되고 싶거든.

W: You're talented. I think you'll become a great artist.

넌 재능이 있어. 난 네가 훌륭한 화가가 될 거라고 생각해.

해설 paint와 함께 쓰였으므로 picture는 그림이다. 사진으로 잘못 이해하여 사진작가를 고르지 않도록 주의한다.

어휘 hang 걸리다, 걸다 wall 벽 good at ~을 잘하는 talented 재능 있는

07 ⑤

M: Why are you in such a hurry now?
당신은 지금 왜 이렇게 서두르나요?

W: My son's teacher called. He got hurt while he was playing basketball. 제 아들의 선생님이 전화를 했어요. 아들이 농구를 하는 동안 다쳤어요.

M: Is it serious? 심각한가요?

W: I don't know. But I'm really worried, so I need to go there soon.
모르겠어요. 그런데 전 정말 걱정이 돼서 빨리 거기에 가야 해요.

M: I have a car. I'll drive you there right now.
저한테 차가 있어요. 제가 당장 거기까지 태워다 드릴게요.

W: Thanks so much. 정말 고마워요.

해설 여자의 대사 'really worried'에 감정이 직접 언급되었다.

어휘 in a hurry 서둘러, 바쁜 serious 심각한

08 ④

M: Thanks for dinner, Mom. It was delicious.
저녁 감사합니다, 엄마. 맛있었어요.

W: I'm glad that you enjoyed it. 잘 먹었다니 나도 기쁘구나.

M: Will you excuse me, please? I need to do my homework. 저 실례해도 될까요? 숙제를 해야 해서요.

W: Okay, but you need to wash the dishes first.
그래, 하지만 너는 설거지를 먼저 해야 해.

M: I thought it was Tina's turn to do that.
저는 티나가 그것을 할 차례라고 생각했는데요.

W: Your sister is going to clean off the table tonight.
네 동생이 오늘 밤은 식탁을 치울 거야.

M: Okay. 알겠어요.

해설 여자가 남자에게 'You need to ~'로 할 일을 일러 줬고, 결국 남자는 'Okay.'로 응답했다. 식탁을 치우는 일은 남자의 여동생이 할 일이다.

어휘 glad 기쁜 excuse 양해하다 think 생각하다(think-thought-thought) turn 차례 clean off ~을 닦아내다

09 ⑤

W: How did you enjoy the festival today?
너는 오늘 축제를 어떻게 보냈니?

M: It was a lot of fun. I liked playing the games.
그건 아주 재미있었어. 게임을 한 것이 좋았어.

W: So did I. Some of the food was good, too.
나도 그랬어. 음식도 어떤 건 맛있었어.

M: I didn't try any. What did you like the most?

나는 먹어보질 못했어. 무엇이 가장 좋았니?

W: The Mexican food was really delicious.
멕시코 음식이 정말로 맛있더라.

해설 여자의 첫 대사에 축제가 언급되었다.

어휘 festival 축제 a lot of 많은 try 해보다, 노력하다

10 ②

W: I need four bus tickets to Daejeon, please.
저는 대전행 버스표 4장이 필요합니다.

M: Sorry, but the last bus just left.
죄송하지만 마지막 버스가 방금 출발했어요.

W: That's terrible. What should I do?
큰일이네요. 저는 어떻게 하죠?

M: The train station is across the street. You should go over there. 기차역이 길 건너편에 있어요. 그쪽으로 가 보세요.

W: Thanks for the advice. I'll go there right now.
충고 고맙습니다. 당장 그곳으로 갈게요.

해설 남자의 대답인 'Sorry, but ~'으로 인해 버스는 오답이 된다. 대안을 제시하는 남자의 대사에 주목한다.

어휘 last 마지막의 leave 출발하다(leave-left-left) terrible 끔찍한 across 건너편에 advice 조언

11 ②

W: I called you yesterday, but you didn't answer the phone.
내가 어제 너한테 전화했는데, 너는 전화를 받지 않더라.

M: I'm sorry. I was playing baseball then, so I didn't know you called me.
미안해. 나는 그때 야구를 하고 있어서, 네가 전화한지 몰랐어.

W: I understand. Did you have fun at the baseball game? 이해해. 야구 경기는 재미있었니?

M: Yes, it was exciting. By the way, why did you call me? 응, 아주 흥미진진했어. 그건 그렇고, 나한테 왜 전화했어?

W: I wanted to ask you about today's test. But I called Brad instead. 너에게 오늘 시험에 대해 물어보려고 했지. 하지만 대신 나는 브래드에게 전화했어.

M: Good. I'm glad you talked to him.
그래. 네가 그 애와 이야기했다니 다행이다.

해설 초반 이야기는 정답과 관련이 없다. 남자의 질문인 'Why did you call me?'에 대한 대답에 정답이 있다.

어휘 call 전화하다(call-called-called) answer 대답하다; 대답 by the way 그건 그렇고, 그런데 instead 대신에

12 ①

M: Hello. How may I help you?
안녕하세요. 무엇을 도와드릴까요?

W: Hi. I'd like to mail this package.
안녕하세요. 저는 이 소포를 부치고 싶어요.

M: Where are you sending it? 그것을 어디로 보내실 건가요?

W: It's going to England. 이건 영국으로 갈 거예요.

M: Do you want to send it by airmail?
항공우편으로 보내길 원하시나요?

W: Yes. I want it to arrive quickly.
네. 저는 그것이 빨리 도착하길 원해요.

M: Okay. Put it on the scale so I can weigh it, please.
알겠어요. 제가 무게를 잴 수 있도록 그것을 저울 위에 올려주세요.

해설 mail, package, airmail 등이 힌트가 되며, 해외로 소포를 부칠 수 있는 장소는 우체국이다.

어휘 mail (우편물을) 보내다 package 소포 send 보내다
airmail 항공우편 quickly 빨리 scale 저울 weigh 무게를 달다

13 ②

M: Could you help me, please? I'm trying to get to the clothes store.
저를 좀 도와주시겠어요? 저는 옷 가게에 가려고 해요.

W: The clothes store? Sure. Go straight to Denver Street and then turn right.
옷 가게요? 물론이죠. 덴버 가로 직진한 뒤 우회전하세요.

M: Okay. Then what should I do?
알겠어요. 그 다음에 무엇을 해야 하죠?

W: Go straight past two buildings. You'll see the clothes store on the left. It's across from the drugstore. 건물 두 개를 지나 직진하세요. 왼쪽에 옷 가게가 보일 겁니다. 그것은 약국 건너편에 있어요.

M: Thanks for your help. 도와주셔서 감사합니다.

해설 초반에 방향을 놓쳤다 하더라도 마지막 정보인 'across from the drugstore'를 가지고도 정답을 맞힐 수 있다.

어휘 get to ~에 도착하다 straight 곧장 past ~을 지나서
across from ~의 맞은편에

14 ③

[Telephone rings.] [전화벨이 울린다.]
W: Hello. 여보세요.

M: Hi, Jane. I'm glad that you're home.
안녕, 제인. 네가 집에 있어서 다행이다.

W: What's the matter? 무슨 일이니?

M: I'm at the bus stop, but I can't find my bus card.
나 버스 정류장에 있는데, 내 버스 카드를 찾을 수가 없어.

W: Where do you think it is? 그게 어디 있다고 생각해?

M: Go to my room and look on my desk, please.
I think I put it there last night. 내 방에 가서 책상 위를 봐.
내 생각에는 내가 그걸 어젯밤에 거기에 놓은 것 같아.

W: Yeah, I found it. It was on your desk.
응, 내가 찾았어. 네 책상 위에 있었네.

M: Oh, good! Can you bring it to me?
아, 잘됐다! 나한테 가져다 줄래?

W: Okay. 그래.

해설 남자의 마지막 대사인 'Can you ~?' 뒤에 오는 내용에 정답이 있다. 대화에 언급된 버스, 책상, 방 등이 선택지에 제시되므로 주의한

다.

어휘 put 놓다, 얹다(put-put-put) find 찾다(find-found-found) bring 가져오다, 데려오다(bring-brought-brought)

15 ③

M: Mary, you played the flute very well in band practice today.
메리, 너 오늘 밴드 연습에서 플루트를 아주 잘 연주하더라.

W: Thanks for saying that, Tom.
그렇게 말해 줘서 고마워, 톰.

M: I want to play the trumpet well, but I'm not very good at it.
나는 트럼펫을 잘 연주하고 싶은데, 난 별로 잘하지 못해.

W: You should practice at home every day. I do that.
너는 매일 집에서 연습해야 해. 나는 그렇게 하거든.

M: Really? Okay. I'll start doing that tonight.
정말이야? 알았어. 나는 오늘 밤에 그렇게 하기 시작할 거야.

해설 여자의 마지막 대사인 'You should ~'에 제안하는 내용이 있다. 제안이나 조언을 할 때는 'You should ~', 'Why don't you ~?' 등이 많이 쓰인다.

어휘 practice 연습; 연습하다 good at ~을 잘하는 tonight 오늘 밤에

16 ④

① W: What time does the movie start?
그 영화는 몇 시에 시작하니?
M: At three forty-five. 3시 45분에.

② W: How much is a hamburger here?
이곳의 햄버거는 얼마예요?
M: It's two dollars. 2달러입니다.

③ W: What's your favorite flavor of ice cream?
네가 가장 좋아하는 아이스크림 맛은 무엇이니?
M: I love vanilla the most. 나는 바닐라를 가장 좋아해.

④ W: How about studying with us?
우리와 함께 공부하는 게 어때?
M: I'm at the library. 나는 도서관에 있어.

⑤ W: What's the matter? Why are you upset?
무슨 일이야? 너 왜 화가 났니?
M: I got a bad grade on my test.
나는 시험에서 나쁜 성적을 받았어.

해설 ④의 질문에는 'Okay. I will.' / 'Sorry, but I can't.'처럼 긍정 혹은 부정의 의사를 밝히는 대답이 와야 자연스럽다.

어휘 flavor 맛 (the) most 제일, 가장 upset 속상한; 화나게 하다 grade 성적

17 ③

M: Good afternoon. Are you Ms. Williams?
안녕하세요. 당신이 윌리엄스 씨인가요?

W: Yes, I am. How may I help you?
네, 저예요. 무슨 일이시죠?

M: I have a package here for you.
당신에게 온 소포를 제가 여기 갖고 있어요.

W: Great. This must be the clothes I ordered.
잘됐군요. 이것은 제가 주문한 옷이 틀림없어요.

M: Could you sign here, please? 이곳에 서명해 주시겠어요?

W: Okay. Thank you very much. 네. 정말 감사합니다.

해설 여자가 소포를 받는 상황이므로, 남자는 소포를 배달하는 직업을 가진 사람이다.

어휘 package 소포, 꾸러미 clothes 옷 order 주문하다 sign 서명하다

18 ④

M: Many people use this in large cities. Many people can ride on this at the same time. In most cities, this travels under the streets and buildings. So when you want to use this, you should go under the ground. What is this?

대도시에서는 많은 사람들이 이것을 이용합니다. 많은 사람들이 한꺼번에 이것에 탈 수 있습니다. 대부분의 도시에서 이것은 거리와 건물 아래로 이동합니다. 그러므로 당신이 이것을 이용하고 싶을 때 당신은 지하로 내려가야 합니다. 이것은 무엇일까요?

해설 지하로 다닌다는 점이 가장 큰 힌트이다.

어휘 use 이용하다 ride on ~을 타다 at the same time 동시에 travel 이동하다, 여행하다

19 ⑤

W: Why are you yawning so much? Did you go to bed late last night?
넌 왜 그렇게 하품을 많이 하니? 어젯밤에 늦게 잤어?

M: Yes, I stayed up until three A.M. I had to study for the math test. 응, 나는 새벽 3시까지 깨어 있었어. 수학 시험 공부를 해야 했거든.

W: How do you think you did on the test?
너는 그 시험을 어떻게 봤다고 생각해?

M: Not very well. I was too tired, so I had trouble solving the questions. 잘 보진 못했어. 나는 너무 피곤해서 문제를 푸는 데 어려움을 겪었어.

W: Go to sleep earlier next time. 다음에는 더 일찍 자.

① That's good to hear. 그 말을 들으니 기쁘다.
② I think I did well on it. 난 잘 봤다고 생각해.
③ No, you don't look tired. 아니, 너는 피곤해 보이지 않아.
④ I can solve that question. 나는 그 문제를 풀 수 있어.
⑤ Go to sleep earlier next time. 다음에는 더 일찍 자.

해설 늦게까지 공부를 했지만 피곤해서 시험을 잘 못 본 친구에게 다음에는 일찍 자라고 조언하는 것이 적절하다.

어휘 yawn 하품하다 go to bed 취침하다 have trouble ~ing ~하는 데 어려움을 겪다 earlier 더 일찍(early-earlier-earliest)

20 ④

M: Hey, are you free after school?
얘, 너 방과 후에 시간 있니?

W: What's up? 무슨 일인데?

M: I am going to play badminton. Do you want to join me? 나는 배드민턴을 치러 갈 거야. 너도 나와 함께하고 싶어?

W: I'd love to, but I can't. 그렇게 하고 싶지만, 난 안 돼.

M: Why not? 왜 안 돼?

W: My cousin is visiting my home.
내 사촌이 우리 집에 오거든.

① I'm playing a game now. 나는 지금 게임을 하는 중이야.

② I had science class this morning.
나는 오늘 아침에 과학 수업이 있었어.

③ Yes, I'm going to the park. 응, 나는 공원에 가고 있어.

④ My cousin is visiting my home.
내 사촌이 우리 집에 오거든.

⑤ The park is located near the school.
그 공원은 학교 근처에 있어.

해설 방과 후에 배드민턴을 같이 치러 갈 수 없는 이유로 어울리는 대답이 와야 한다.

어휘 free 한가한, 계획이 없는; 자유로운 join 함께 하다 cousin 사촌 located ~에 위치한

05회 실전모의고사

01 ①	02 ③	03 ⑤	04 ①	05 ④
06 ②	07 ③	08 ②	09 ③	10 ⑤
11 ⑤	12 ②	13 ③	14 ④	15 ④
16 ④	17 ②	18 ②	19 ①	20 ⑤

01 ①

W: School is starting soon. Do you need any school supplies?
곧 개학을 할 거야. 필요한 학용품이 있니?

M: Yes, I do. I have to get a new pencil case.
응, 있어. 나는 새 필통을 사야 해.

W: How about this one shaped like a bear?
이 곰 모양 필통은 어때?

M: No, thanks. I want the pencil case shaped like a fish. 아니, 됐어. 나는 물고기 모양 필통을 갖고 싶어.

해설 대화에 언급된 두 가지 모양 중 한 가지가 정답이다. 남자의 대사인 'I want ~' 이후를 주의 깊게 들어야 한다.

어휘 pencil case 필통 shaped like ~모양을 한

02 ③

M: You need this when you go swimming. You wear this around your eyes. When you wear this, you can open your eyes and see clearly under the water. What is this?
여러분은 수영을 할 때 이것이 필요합니다. 여러분은 눈 주위에 이것을 씁니다. 이것을 쓰고 있으면 여러분은 물 속에서 눈을 뜨고 또렷하게 볼 수 있습니다. 이것은 무엇일까요?

어휘 wear 쓰다, 입다, 착용하다 around 주위에 clearly 또렷하게 under the water 물 속에서

03 ⑤

W: Hello, everyone. This is the weather report for tomorrow. We had cold, snowy weather today. But the snow is going to stop tomorrow. It will be cold and windy, but no more snow is going to fall for a couple of days. Have a good night.
안녕하세요, 여러분. 내일의 일기예보입니다. 오늘은 눈이 내리는 추운 날씨였습니다. 그러나 내일은 눈이 멈출 것입니다. 춥고 바람이 불겠지만 이틀 동안 더 이상 눈은 내리지 않겠습니다. 좋은 밤 보내세요.

어휘 no more 더 이상 ~아닌 fall 내리다, 떨어지다 a couple of 둘의

04 ①

W: Where are you going right now, Joe?
너 지금 어디에 가고 있니, 조?

M: I'm going to the gym. I'm going to exercise there for an hour. 나는 헬스장에 가고 있어. 그곳에서 한 시간 동안 운동을 할 거야.

W: The gym? That sounds like fun.
헬스장? 그거 재미있겠는데.

M: Yes, it is. You should go there with me.
응, 맞아. 너도 나랑 같이 가야 해.

해설 제안이나 조언을 할 때 'You should ~'가 많이 쓰인다.

어휘 gym 헬스장, 체육관 exercise 운동하다 sound like ~처럼 들리다

05 ④

W: Good morning, everybody. I'd like to introduce myself. My name is Mina. My hometown is Suwon, but I live in Seoul right now. I love riding my bicycle. I want to be a cyclist and go to the Olympics one day. I need to practice hard every day.
안녕하세요, 여러분. 제 소개를 하겠습니다. 제 이름은 미나입니다. 저의 고향은 수원이지만 지금은 서울에 살고 있습니다. 저는 자전거 타는 것을 좋아합니다. 저는 사이클리스트가 되어 언젠가 올림픽에 참가하고 싶어요. 저는 매일 열심히 연습해야 합니다.

어휘 introduce 소개하다 hometown 고향 cyclist 사이클리스트, 자전거 타는 사람

06 ②

[*Cellphone rings.*] [휴대폰이 울린다.]
M: Hi, Clara. Are you almost <u>finished cleaning</u> your room? 안녕, 클라라. 네 방 청소가 거의 끝났니?
W: No, I'm <u>not</u> finished <u>yet</u>. So I <u>can't go out</u> with you now. 아니, 난 아직 못 끝냈어. 그래서 지금 너랑 외출할 수가 없어.
M: Okay. Why don't you <u>meet me</u> at the bus stop <u>at four</u> then?
그래. 그러면 4시에 버스 정류장에서 나와 만나는 게 어때?
W: I <u>won't take</u> that <u>long</u>. <u>Three thirty</u> is fine.
그렇게 오래 걸리진 않을 거야. 3시 30분이 좋겠어.
M: Okay. I'll see you then. 알겠어. 그때 보자.

해설 남자가 'Why don't you ~?'로 제안한 문장에는 함정이 있다. 반드시 상대방의 대답을 확인한 뒤 정답을 고른다.

어휘 almost 거의 yet 아직 go out 외출하다 take (시간이) 걸리다

07 ③

W: This <u>story</u> is <u>great</u>. I really <u>love</u> it.
이 이야기는 훌륭해. 난 정말 이게 마음에 들어.
M: Thanks. I <u>wrote</u> it last night.
고마워. 나는 어젯밤에 그것을 썼어.
W: You did? Do you have any more stories?
네가 썼다고? 너는 다른 이야기도 더 갖고 있니?
M: Yes, I have many stories. I <u>want to be a writer</u>.
응, 나는 이야기를 많이 갖고 있어. 나는 작가가 되고 싶거든.

어휘 write 쓰다(write-wrote-written) more 더 많은, 그 이상의 writer 작가

08 ②

M: <u>What</u> did you <u>do</u> all day, Sarah? 하루 종일 뭐 했니, 사라?
W: I just <u>sat</u> here <u>on</u> the <u>couch</u>, Dad.
저는 그냥 이 소파에 앉아 있었어요, 아빠.
M: It was a beautiful day. <u>Why didn't</u> you go out?
날씨가 참 좋았단다. 너는 왜 외출하지 않았니?
W: There was <u>nothing to do</u> outside.
밖에서 할 일이 아무것도 없었어요.
M: I drove by the <u>park</u> today. Lots of kids were playing <u>badminton</u> there. 나는 오늘 공원 옆을 운전해서 지나갔어. 많은 아이들이 그곳에서 배드민턴을 치고 있더구나.
W: Really? I'm the only person <u>not having fun</u>.
정말이요? 재미없게 지낸 사람은 오로지 저 하나뿐이군요.

해설 심정을 드러내는 직접적인 단어는 없지만, sat on the couch, nothing to do, not having fun 등으로 미루어 보아 여자의 심정은 지루하다는 것을 알 수 있다.

어휘 sit 앉다(sit-sat-sat) couch 소파, 긴 의자 drive (차를) 운전하다(drive-drove-driven)

09 ③

W: Joe, do you <u>know</u> Sarah? 조, 너는 사라를 아니?
M: Sure. We are <u>good friends</u> with each other.
당연하지. 우리는 서로 친한 친구야.
W: I need to <u>talk to</u> her, but I don't know her <u>phone number</u>.
내가 그 애와 말을 해야 하는데, 나는 그 애의 전화번호를 몰라.
M: I can <u>give</u> you her <u>number</u>. It's five nine four, two oh three four. 내가 그 애의 번호를 네게 줄게. 594-2034야.
W: Thanks. I'm going to <u>call her right away</u>.
고마워. 내가 그 애에게 바로 전화해야겠다.

해설 대화 직후에 할 일은 여자의 마지막 대사에서 right away와 함께 등장했다.

어휘 each other 서로 right away 곧바로, 즉시

10 ⑤

M: What's your <u>favorite</u> type of <u>music</u>?
네가 가장 좋아하는 음악의 종류는 뭐야?
W: I love <u>rock music</u>. 나는 록 음악을 아주 좋아해.
M: Why do you like it? 너는 그것을 왜 좋아하니?
W: I can <u>dance to</u> it. And many of the songs <u>sound great</u>, too. Do you like music?
음악에 맞춰 춤을 출 수 있으니까. 그리고 많은 노래가 훌륭하거든. 너는 음악을 좋아하니?
M: Yes, I do. I like <u>pop music</u> the most.
응, 좋아해. 나는 팝 음악을 가장 좋아해.

해설 남자의 첫 대사에 대화의 화제가 언급된다.

어휘 type 종류 dance to ~에 맞춰 춤추다

11 ⑤

W: Joe, <u>what</u> are you <u>doing</u> this Saturday?
조, 너는 이번 주 토요일에 뭐 할 거야?
M: I'm going to <u>visit</u> a <u>mountain</u> near Daejeon.
나는 대전 근처에 있는 산에 갈 거야.
W: <u>How</u> are you going to <u>go</u> there?
거기까지 어떻게 갈 거니?
M: I'll <u>take</u> a <u>bus</u> there. 나는 그곳까지 버스를 탈 거야.
W: I see. That will be <u>faster than</u> driving a <u>car</u>.
그렇구나. 그게 자동차를 운전하는 것보다 빠를 거야.

해설 자동차는 함정으로 언급된 것이다.

어휘 faster 더 빠른(fast-faster-fastest) than ~보다

12 ②

[*Knocking*] [노크]
M: Good morning, Ms. Park. May I <u>speak with</u> you, please?
안녕하세요, 박 선생님. 이야기 좀 할 수 있을까요?
W: Hello, Minho. Please <u>come in</u>. <u>What</u> do you <u>need</u>?
안녕, 민호야. 들어오렴. 뭐가 필요하니?
M: I have a <u>question about</u> our <u>report</u>. <u>When</u> should

we give it to you?
보고서에 대해 질문이 있어요. 선생님께 언제 제출해야 하죠?

W: You need to finish it by this Friday.
너는 이번 주 금요일까지 그것을 끝내야 한단다.

M: Thank you very much. 정말 감사합니다.

[해설] 주로 인사를 나눈 다음에 방문한 이유가 등장한다. 'What do you need?'로 방문의 이유를 묻는 질문에 대한 대답에 정답이 있다.

[어휘] come in 들어오다 report 보고서 finish 끝내다 by Friday 금요일까지

13 ③

M: May I see your driver's license, please?
제가 당신의 운전면허증을 볼 수 있을까요?

W: What's the problem? 뭐가 문제인가요?

M: You were driving too fast. You have to drive slowly near the school. 당신은 너무 빠르게 운전하고 있었어요. 학교 근처에서는 천천히 운전해야 합니다.

W: I'm sorry. I didn't know that.
죄송합니다. 제가 그걸 몰랐네요.

M: I have to give you a ticket.
저는 당신에게 범칙금 고지서를 줘야 합니다.

W: I understand. 알겠습니다.

[해설] 과속하는 운전자를 적발하여 범칙금을 부과하는 사람은 경찰관이다.

[어휘] driver's license 자동차운전면허 fast 빠르게; 빠른 slowly 천천히 ticket 범칙금 고지서, (벌금) 딱지; 표

14 ④

M: Hello. I'm looking for a grocery store. Is there one near here? 안녕하세요. 저는 식료품점을 찾고 있어요. 이 근처에 식료품점이 있나요?

W: Yes, there is. Go straight two blocks to Pine Street. Then, turn right. 네, 있어요. 파인 가까지 두 블록을 직진하세요. 그 다음에 우회전하세요.

M: Okay. What should I do next?
알겠습니다. 그 다음에 무엇을 해야 하죠?

W: Go down the street. It will be on your right. It's between the drugstore and the movie theater.
길을 따라 가세요. 그것은 당신의 오른쪽에 있을 겁니다. 그것은 약국과 영화관 사이에 있어요.

M: Thank you for your help. 도와주셔서 감사합니다.

[해설] 식료품점은 약국과 영화관 사이에 있는 건물이다.

[어휘] grocery store 식료품점 near ~가까이에 between A and B A와 B 사이에 drugstore 약국

15 ④

W: Why don't we clean the house today?
우리 오늘 집 청소하는 게 어때요?

M: But the weather is so nice. How about working in

---

the garden outside? 하지만 날씨가 아주 좋아요. 밖에 정원에서 일하는 게 어때요?

W: That sounds nice. I will water the flowers first.
그거 좋네요. 저는 먼저 꽃에 물을 줄게요.

M: Okay. Shall we do that together?
그래요. 우리 같이 할까요?

W: No. Can you cut the grass?
아니요. 당신은 잔디를 깎을래요?

M. Sure. No problem. 물론이죠. 문제 없어요.

[해설] 여자의 대사인 'Can you ~?'를 주의 깊게 듣는다.

[어휘] clean 청소하다 garden 정원 outside 밖에 water 물을 주다 cut the grass 잔디를 깎다

16 ④

M: Sue, did you join a club? 수, 너는 동아리에 가입했어?

W: Yes, I did. I'm in the hiking club. What about you?
응, 했어. 나는 하이킹 동아리에 있어. 너는?

M: I'm not sure. 나는 확실치 않아.

W: You play basketball all the time. You should join the basketball club. 너는 항상 농구를 하잖아. 너는 농구 동아리에 가입해야 해.

M: But I'm not very good at it. Other players are better.
하지만 난 농구를 그렇게 잘하지 못해. 다른 선수들이 더 잘해.

W: That's okay. You will have fun playing with them.
그건 괜찮아. 너는 그들과 경기하는 게 재미있을 거야.

[해설] 여자의 대사 'You should ~'에 제안하는 내용이 있다.

[어휘] join 가입하다 hiking 하이킹, 도보 여행 all the time 항상, 내내 better 더 좋은, 더 나은(good-better-best)

17 ②

① W: Thanks for your help. 도와주셔서 감사합니다.
M: You're welcome. 천만에요.

② W: Do you have some time? 시간 좀 있니?
M: Yes, it's five twenty. 응, 5시 20분이야.

③ W: Are you tired? 너 피곤하니?
M: No, I'm all right. 아니, 난 괜찮아.

④ W: I think I made a mistake. 내가 실수를 한 것 같아.
M: What happened? 무슨 일이 있었어?

⑤ W: What's your favorite sport?
네가 가장 좋아하는 운동이 뭐야?
M: I really love soccer. 나는 축구를 정말 좋아해.

[해설] 시간이 있는지 묻는 질문에는 Yes/No를 써서 답하는 게 자연스럽다. 'Yes, it's five twenty.'라는 대답은 'Do you have the time?(지금 몇 시인지 아세요?)'이라는 질문과 어울린다.

[어휘] mistake 실수, 잘못 happen 발생하다

18 ②

[Telephone rings.] [전화벨이 울린다.]

M: Hello. This is the city library.
여보세요. 시립 도서관입니다.

W: Hi. I'm looking for a book. The title is *The Dog's Adventure*. 안녕하세요. 저는 책을 찾고 있어요. 제목은 '강아지의 모험'이에요.

M: That's a popular children's book. We have it.
그건 인기 있는 어린이 책입니다. 저희가 갖고 있어요.

W: Is it checked out now? 그 책이 지금 대출되었나요?

M: No, it's not. You can come here and borrow it.
아니요, 그렇지 않아요. 당신은 여기에 와서 그것을 빌릴 수 있어요.

해설 남자의 첫 대사에 근무 장소가 언급된다. check out, borrow 등은 서점과 도서관을 구분하는 힌트가 된다.

어휘 library 도서관 look for ~을 찾다 title 제목 popular 인기 있는 check out (도서관에서) 대출하다 borrow 빌리다

19 ①

M: Oh, no. I don't have any money.
아, 이런. 나는 돈이 하나도 없어.

W: Where is your wallet? 네 지갑 어디 있니?

M: I left it at home. 난 그것을 집에 두고 왔어.

W: That's okay. I can pay for your lunch.
괜찮아. 내가 네 점심값을 낼 수 있어.

M: Thanks a lot. 정말 고마워.

① Thanks a lot. 정말 고마워.
② Lunch was great. 점심 맛있었어.
③ Yes, I'm very hungry. 응, 난 너무 배고파.
④ One hamburger, please. 햄버거 한 개 주세요.
⑤ No, I don't have a wallet. 아니, 나는 지갑을 갖고 있지 않아.

해설 지갑이 없는 친구를 대신해 점심값을 내주겠다는 말에는 고마움을 나타내는 응답이 적절하다.

어휘 wallet 지갑 pay for ~을 지불하다 hungry 배고픈

20 ⑤

W: Karen told me your cousin is going to visit this summer.
캐런이 이번 여름에 네 사촌이 방문할 거라고 그러더라.

M: That's right. It's his first visit to Korea.
맞아. 그것은 그의 첫 번째 한국 방문이야.

W: What are you going to do with him?
너는 그와 함께 무엇을 할 거니?

M: We're going to take him to some famous places.
우리는 그를 유명한 몇 가지 장소로 데려갈 거야.

W: Where are you going to go? 너희는 어디에 갈 거니?

M: We'll visit the museum and amusement park.
우리는 박물관과 놀이공원에 갈 거야.

① He's the same age as I am. 그는 나와 나이가 같아.
② He'll be here on the fifth of July.
그는 7월 5일에 여기에 올 거야.
③ Yes, I'll go home in a few minutes.
응, 나는 몇 분 후에 집에 갈 거야.

④ No, I'm not going to visit him now.
아니, 난 지금 그를 방문하지 않을 거야.
⑤ We'll visit the museum and amusement park.
우리는 박물관과 놀이공원에 갈 거야.

해설 여자의 마지막 대사의 의문사 where에 어울리는 대답은 방문할 장소가 포함된 문장이다.

어휘 cousin 사촌 take (사람을) 데리고 가다 famous 유명한 the same age 동갑 a few minutes 몇 분

06회 실전모의고사 본문 p.56-57

01 ④	02 ②	03 ①	04 ④	05 ③
06 ③	07 ②	08 ③	09 ⑤	10 ②
11 ③	12 ②	13 ⑤	14 ④	15 ③
16 ⑤	17 ①	18 ①	19 ⑤	20 ⑤

01 ④

① Two boys are doing the dishes.
두 소년이 설거지를 하고 있다.
② Two boys are jogging in a park.
두 소년이 공원에서 조깅하고 있다.
③ Two boys are playing baseball.
두 소년이 야구를 하고 있다.
④ Two boys are fishing in a lake.
두 소년이 호수에서 낚시를 하고 있다.
⑤ Two boys are swimming in a pool.
두 소년이 수영장에서 수영을 하고 있다.

어휘 do the dishes 설거지하다 jog 조깅하다 play baseball 야구하다 fish 낚시하다; 물고기 lake 호수 pool 수영장

02 ②

M: Most women use this. They often use this after they take a shower. First, they dry their hair. Then, they use this to make their hair look nice. They look in a mirror and use this to fix their hair. Some people carry this with them in their bags.

대부분의 여자들은 이것을 사용해요. 그들은 샤워를 한 후에 종종 이것을 사용해요. 먼저 그들은 자신의 머리카락을 말려요. 그리고 나서 그들은 이것을 이용해서 머리카락을 멋지게 보이도록 만들어요. 그들은 거울을 보면서 이것을 이용해서 머리카락을 매만져요. 어떤 사람들은 이것을 가방 안에 넣고 다녀요.

어휘 most 대부분의 take a shower 샤워하다 dry one's hair ~의 머리를 말리다 look in a mirror 거울을 보다 fix 매만지다, 가다듬다; 고정시키다; 고치다 carry 가지고 다니다

03 ①

M: I left my wallet on the bus yesterday. Did someone

정답 및 해설 **19**

find it?
어제 제 지갑을 버스에 놓고 내렸어요. 그걸 찾은 사람이 있나요?

W: Can you tell me what it looks like?
그게 어떻게 생겼는지 말씀해 주시겠어요?

M: It's a brown wallet. My name is on it. My name is Jason Smith. 그건 갈색 지갑이에요. 제 이름이 곁에 있어요. 제 이름은 제이슨 스미스입니다.

W: Yes, we have your wallet. It's right here.
네, 우리가 당신의 지갑을 가지고 있어요. 바로 여기 있습니다.

M: Wow, I appreciate it a lot.
와, 정말 감사합니다.

해설 appreciate는 thank보다 격식을 차려 감사를 표할 때 쓴다.

어휘 leave 놓다, 두다(leave-left-left) wallet 지갑 look like ~처럼 보이다 right here 바로 이곳에; 지금 당장 appreciate 고마워하다

04 ④

M: Mom, I finished my homework. Can I go outside now? 엄마, 저 숙제 끝냈어요. 이제 밖에 나가도 돼요?

W: I think you should stay home. It's almost dinnertime. 내 생각에 너는 집에 있어야 할 것 같다. 이제 곧 저녁식사 시간이거든.

M: But I want to play basketball before it gets dark.
하지만 저는 어두워지기 전에 농구를 하고 싶다고요.

W: You can do that tomorrow. Why don't you help me with dinner? 넌 그걸 내일 할 수 있잖니. 엄마가 저녁 만드는 걸 도와주지 않을래?

M: Okay. Do you want me to set the table?
알았어요. 제가 상을 차리면 될까요?

W: Yes, please. Thanks. 그래, 부탁해. 고맙다.

해설 여자의 요청에 이어 남자가 'Do you want me to ~?'에 본인이 할 일을 구체적으로 말했다.

어휘 go outside 밖으로 나가다 stay home 집에 머물다 almost 거의 dinnertime 저녁식사 시간 play basketball 농구를 하다 get dark 어두워지다 set the table 상을 차리다

05 ③

M: Let me show you a picture of my family. You can see my grandmother and grandfather here. Both of them live with us. My father is right here. He is a computer programmer. This is my mother next to him. She works at a restaurant. And here is my older brother. He and I look like each other.

내가 너한테 우리 가족 사진을 보여 줄게. 여기 우리 할머니와 할아버지가 보일 거야. 두 분 다 우리와 함께 사셔. 우리 아버지는 바로 여기 계셔. 아버지는 컴퓨터 프로그래머야. 아버지 옆에 계신 분이 우리 어머니야. 어머니는 식당에서 일하셔. 그리고 여기 우리 형이 있어. 형하고 나는 서로 닮았어.

어휘 both of 둘 다, ~의 양쪽 모두 next to 바로 옆에 look like each other 서로 닮다

06 ③

M: Good afternoon. I hope you're having a great day. It's time for a short weather update. It's raining heavily right now. But the rain will stop around five. It's going to be foggy tonight and tomorrow morning. But there will be sunny skies tomorrow afternoon and evening.

안녕하세요. 여러분 모두 멋진 하루를 보내고 계셨으면 좋겠습니다. 짧은 날씨 속보를 보내드릴 시간입니다. 현재 폭우가 내리고 있습니다. 하지만 비는 5시경에 그칠 것입니다. 오늘밤과 내일 아침에는 안개가 끼겠습니다. 하지만 내일 오후와 저녁에는 화창한 하늘을 보이겠습니다.

어휘 have a great day 좋은 하루를 보내다 weather update 최신 날씨 정보 rain heavily 폭우가 내리다 foggy 안개가 낀

07 ②

M: Julie, when are your friends coming over?
줄리, 네 친구들은 언제 오는 거니?

W: They're going to be here at four.
그 애들은 4시에 여기 올 거예요.

M: At four? But it's three fifteen now. We only have forty-five minutes to clean up. 4시에? 하지만 지금이 3시 15분이구나. 우리는 청소할 시간이 45분밖에 없어.

W: You're right. Let's hurry. 맞아요. 서둘러야겠어요.

M: Okay. You clean the kitchen, and I'll clean the living room. 알았다. 네가 부엌을 청소하면 내가 거실을 청소하마.

해설 친구들이 올 시각은 4:00, 현재 시각은 3:15이다.

어휘 come over 오다, 들르다 clean up 청소하다, 치우다 hurry 서두르다

08 ③

M: Do we really have to go to the art gallery on Saturday?
우리가 정말 토요일에 미술관에 가야만 하는 거니?

W: Yes, we do. We have to do our art homework.
응, 가야 해. 우리는 미술 숙제를 해야 하잖아.

M: But I don't want to visit it. It's too far.
하지만 나는 거기 가기 싫어. 너무 멀어.

W: I know, but we have to look at the paintings.
나도 알지만 우리는 그림을 봐야만 해.

M: Okay. What time shall we go? At three?
알았어. 우리 몇 시에 갈까? 3시?

W: Let's go earlier. How about eleven in the morning?
좀 더 일찍 가자. 오전 11시는 어때?

M: Okay. 좋아.

해설 처음부터 끝까지 대화 전체 내용을 포괄하는 내용을 골라야 한다.

어휘 art gallery 미술관 far 먼 painting 그림 earlier 좀 더 일찍

(early-earlier-earliest)

09 ⑤

M: Lisa, why are you <u>crying</u>? What's <u>wrong</u>?
리사, 너 왜 울고 있니? 무슨 문제 있어?

W: I'm so <u>sad</u> right now. 난 지금 너무 슬퍼.

M: Did <u>something</u> <u>bad</u> happen to you?
무슨 나쁜 일이라도 너한테 생긴 거니?

W: I just saw the final <u>episode</u> of *My Life*. My favorite <u>character</u> <u>died</u>. 난 방금 '내 인생'의 최종회를 봤어. 내가 좋아하는 등장인물이 죽었어.

M: That's why you're crying? I can't believe it.
그게 네가 울고 있는 이유라고? 믿을 수가 없군.

해설 여자는 'I'm so sad right now.'로 심정을 표현했다.

어휘 episode (드라마의) 1회 방송분, 에피소드 character 등장인물; 성격

10 ②

W: Eric, are you <u>going</u> to the <u>festival</u> tomorrow?
에릭, 넌 내일 축제에 가니?

M: <u>Yes</u>, I am. Are you going there, too?
응. 너도 거기에 가니?

W: Yes. I'm going to <u>take</u> the <u>bus</u> there. How about you?
응. 난 거기까지 버스를 타고 갈 거야. 너는?

M: I'm going to <u>ride</u> my <u>bike</u>. 난 내 자전거를 탈 거야.

W: Isn't that <u>dangerous</u>? There are lots of buses and cars on the <u>roads</u>.
그건 위험하지 않니? 도로에 버스와 자동차가 많잖아.

M: Don't worry. I'll be <u>careful</u>.
걱정하지 마. 조심할게.

해설 여자는 버스를, 남자는 자전거를 탈 것이다. 대화 후반에 이용할 교통수단을 바꾸는 경우가 많은데, 이 대화에서는 남자가 주장을 굽히지 않았다.

어휘 festival 축제 take a bus 버스를 타다 ride a bike 자전거를 타다 dangerous 위험한 on the road 도로 위에 careful 조심하는

11 ③

M: Good afternoon. May I help you?
안녕하세요. 제가 도와드릴까요?

W: I'd like to <u>buy</u> this <u>computer</u> <u>game</u>. It's <u>fifty</u> <u>dollars</u>, right?
저는 이 컴퓨터 게임을 사고 싶어요. 이건 50달러죠, 그렇죠?

M: It's on <u>sale</u> today, so you can <u>save</u> <u>twenty</u> <u>percent</u>.
이건 오늘 할인 중이라서 손님은 20%를 절약할 수 있어요.

W: Wow. I only have to <u>pay</u> <u>forty</u> dollars for it. That's great news. 와. 제가 이걸 사기 위해 40달러만 내면 되는 거네요. 대단한 소식이네요.

M: Would you like to buy <u>something</u> <u>else</u> then?

다른 걸 더 구입하시겠어요?

W: No. I <u>don't</u> have <u>enough</u> <u>money</u> to buy two games.
아니요. 저는 게임 두 개를 살 만큼 돈이 충분치가 않아요.

해설 원래 가격은 50달러, 할인된 가격은 40달러이다.

어휘 on sale 할인 중인, 판매 중인 save 절약하다, 모으다 something else 또 다른 것 then 그러면, 또 enough 충분한

12 ②

[*Telephone rings.*] [전화벨이 울린다.]

W: Hello. 여보세요.

M: Hello. Is this Minho's <u>mother</u>?
안녕하세요. 민호 어머니신가요?

W: Yes, <u>this is she</u>. Who's <u>calling</u>, please?
네, 전데요. 전화하신 분은 누구죠?

M: This is Jiho Kim calling from Central <u>Elementary</u> <u>School</u>. Minho is a <u>student</u> in my <u>class</u>.
저는 센트럴 초등학교에서 전화 드리는 김지호라고 합니다. 민호가 저희 반 학생이에요.

W: Is there a <u>problem</u>? 무슨 문제라도 있나요?

M: Yes, there is. Minho isn't <u>feeling</u> <u>well</u> today. I think he needs to <u>go</u> <u>home</u>. 네, 있어요. 민호가 오늘 몸이 안 좋아요. 제 생각에 민호는 집에 가야 할 것 같아요.

W: I'll <u>be there</u> soon. Thanks for calling.
제가 금방 그리로 갈게요. 전화 주셔서 감사합니다.

어휘 Who's calling? (전화에서) 누구시죠? feel well 건강 상태가 좋다

13 ⑤

M: Mom, I'm <u>going</u> to <u>school</u> for a while.
엄마, 저 잠깐 학교에 갔다 올게요.

W: You're going to school? But you <u>came</u> <u>back</u> from school <u>thirty</u> minutes <u>ago</u>.
너 학교에 간다고? 하지만 넌 30분 전에 학교에서 돌아왔잖아.

M: I <u>need</u> <u>to</u> meet Sarah and Tom.
저는 사라와 톰을 만나야 해요.

W: Why? Are you going to <u>play</u> <u>soccer</u> together?
왜? 너희는 함께 축구를 할 거니?

M: <u>No</u>, we're not. We're going to <u>work</u> <u>on</u> our history <u>project</u>. 아니요. 우리는 역사 과제를 할 거예요.

W: Okay. <u>Don't</u> be <u>late</u> for <u>dinner</u>.
알았다. 저녁식사에 늦지 말거라.

해설 여자가 넘겨짚어 말한 축구에 현혹되지 말고 남자가 직접 밝히는 이유에 집중해야 한다.

어휘 for a while 잠깐, 잠시 동안 play soccer 축구를 하다 work on 작업하다, 일하다 project 과제, 프로젝트

14 ④

M: I <u>don't</u> have any <u>energy</u> these days.
난 요즘 기운이 하나도 없어.

W: What's the matter? 무슨 문제라도 있어?

M: I get really tired in gym class. I can only play sports for a few minutes. 난 체육 시간에 정말 녹초가 돼. 난 고작 몇 분 동안만 운동을 할 수 있어.

W: You should start eating healthy food. 넌 건강한 음식을 먹기 시작해야 해.

M: What do you mean? 무슨 소리니?

W: Stop eating fast food. Eat more fruits and vegetables instead. 패스트푸드는 그만 먹어. 대신 과일하고 채소를 더 먹어.

M: Okay. I'll try that. 알았어. 시도해 볼게.

해설 제안하는 내용이 여자의 대사 두 번에 걸쳐 자세히 언급된다. 'You should ~'문장과 명령형 문장의 내용을 살핀다.

어휘 energy 기운, 에너지 these days 요즘에 get tired 피곤해지다, 지치다 gym 체육, 운동 for a few minutes 몇 분 동안 healthy 건강에 좋은, 건강한 vegetable 채소 instead 대신에

15 ③

W: Hello. Can you tell me where the Internet café is? 잠시만요. 피시방이 어디 있는지 말씀해 주시겠어요?

M: Sure. It's on Apple Street. Just go straight two blocks. 물론이죠. 그건 애플 가에 있어요. 두 블록을 곧장 가세요.

W: Okay. Should I turn left or right? 네. 제가 좌회전해야 하나요, 우회전해야 하나요?

M: Turn left. It's the first building on your left. It's beside the computer store. 좌회전하세요. 그건 당신의 좌측 첫 번째 건물입니다. 컴퓨터 가게 옆에 있어요.

W: Thanks for your help. 도와 주셔서 고맙습니다.

어휘 Internet café 피시방, 인터넷 카페 on one's left ~의 좌측에 beside ~ 옆에

16 ⑤

M: The new museum is on the corner of Lake Street and Second Avenue. It is open from Monday to Saturday. It opens at nine A.M. and closes at six P.M. each day. It costs five dollars to enter the museum. The museum has three floors. It has many exhibits from around the world.

새 박물관은 레이크 가와 세컨드 가의 모퉁이에 있습니다. 월요일부터 토요일까지 문을 엽니다. 매일 오전 9시에 문을 열어서 오후 6시에 문을 닫습니다. 박물관에 입장하는 데는 5달러가 듭니다. 박물관에는 3개 층이 있습니다. 그곳은 전 세계의 많은 전시품을 소장하고 있습니다.

해설 'The museum has three floors.'에 드러나듯이 박물관은 3층이다.

어휘 on the corner of ~의 모퉁이에 enter 입장하다, 들어가다 floor 층; 바닥 exhibit 전시품, 전시회; 전시하다 from around the world 전세계의

17 ①

① M: How do you like the new student? 넌 새로 온 학생을 어떻게 생각하니?

W: Yes, she looks like my friend. 응, 그 애는 내 친구랑 닮았어.

② M: You look happy. What's up? 넌 행복해 보이는구나. 무슨 일이야?

W: My parents just bought me a puppy. 우리 부모님이 방금 내게 강아지를 사주셨어.

③ M: Let's go skiing this winter. 올 겨울에 스키 타러 가자.

W: That's a great idea. 좋은 생각이야.

④ M: What kind of book are you reading now? 넌 지금 어떤 종류의 책을 읽고 있니?

W: I'm reading a comic book. 난 만화책을 읽고 있어.

⑤ M: Do you have any homework? 넌 숙제가 있니?

W: Yes, I have math and science homework. 응, 난 수학과 과학 숙제가 있어.

해설 'How do you like ~?'는 의견을 묻는 질문이므로 'I think ~'와 같이 답해야 한다. 'look like'는 '~처럼 보이다', '~와 닮다'라는 의미이다.

어휘 How do you like ~? ~은 어떻습니까? ~은 마음에 드세요? look like ~처럼 보이다 puppy 강아지 go skiing 스키 타러 가다 comic book 만화책

18 ①

M: A boy goes to school in the morning. He sees other students studying. He asks why they are studying. They say that they have a math test. He says that he forgot to study. Math is the boy's worst class. Then, the teacher walks into the classroom and tells the students to close their books.

한 소년이 아침에 학교에 갑니다. 그는 다른 학생들이 공부하는 것을 봅니다. 그는 왜 그들이 공부를 하고 있는지 묻습니다. 그들은 수학 시험이 있다고 말합니다. 그는 공부하는 것을 깜박했다고 말합니다. 수학은 그가 가장 못하는 과목입니다. 그때 선생님이 교실로 들어와서 학생들에게 책을 덮으라고 말합니다.

해설 공부를 안 했는데 갑자기 시험을 보게 되면 당황스러울 것이다.

어휘 test 시험, 테스트 worst 가장 못하는, 최악의(bad-worse-worst) close a book 책을 덮다

19 ⑤

W: How do you like the shirt you just bought? 방금 산 셔츠는 마음에 드니?

M: I changed my mind. I don't like it. 난 마음을 바꿨어. 난 그게 마음에 안 들어.

W: You can return it. Why don't you go back to the store? 넌 그걸 반품할 수 있어. 가게에 다시 가보는 것이 어때?

M: Okay. Do you mind waiting here for me? 알았어. 넌 여기서 나를 기다려 주겠니?

W: No problem. Take your time. 알았어. 천천히 해.

① No, I don't like it either. 아니, 난 그것도 마음에 안 들어.
② Yes, we can go together. 그래, 우리는 함께 갈 수 있어.
③ You can ask for a discount. 넌 할인을 요구할 수 있어.
④ I'm going to return the shirt. 난 그 셔츠를 반품할 거야.
⑤ No problem. Take your time. 알았어. 천천히 해.

해설 'Do you mind ~?'는 '~가 꺼려지니?'라는 뜻으로, '~가 괜찮을까?'로 해석할 수 있다. 이 질문에 대한 긍정적인 답변은 No, 부정적인 답변은 Yes이다.

어휘 change one's mind ~의 마음을 바꾸다 return 반품하다, 반납하다 go back to ~로 되돌아가다 mind 꺼리다, 싫어하다 take one's time 서두르지 않고 천천히 하다 ask for ~을 요청하다 discount 할인

20 ⑤

W: Are you ready to go out? 외출할 준비는 다 됐니?
M: Yes, I am. Let me put on my jacket.
  응, 됐어. 내 재킷 좀 입을게.
W: Jacket? You don't need a jacket today.
  재킷이라고? 넌 오늘은 재킷이 필요 없어.
M: Really? How's the weather? 정말이니? 날씨가 어떤데?
W: It's warm and sunny now. 지금은 따뜻하고 화창해.

① Yes, it's really cold. 응, 정말 추워.
② I've got my umbrella. 난 내 우산이 있어.
③ I'm wearing my jacket. 난 내 재킷을 입고 있어.
④ Winter is coming soon. 곧 겨울이 올 거야.
⑤ It's warm and sunny now. 지금은 따뜻하고 화창해.

해설 날씨를 물었으니 날씨를 알려줘야 한다. 특히 재킷이 필요 없는 날씨를 표현한 ⑤가 어울린다.

어휘 ready 준비된 go out 나가다, 외출하다 put on ~을 입다 umbrella 우산

07회 실전모의고사
본문 p.66-67

01 ③	02 ①	03 ①	04 ③	05 ⑤
06 ③	07 ⑤	08 ④	09 ②	10 ③
11 ①	12 ③	13 ④	14 ⑤	15 ②
16 ⑤	17 ④	18 ⑤	19 ②	20 ③

01 ③

W: I am a type of bag. People often use me when they go on long trips or when they have many things to pack. They put their clothes inside me. Then, they take me to the airport. They usually don't carry me on the planes because sometimes I am too big. But, they can carry me easily because I have wheels and a handle.

저는 가방의 일종이에요. 사람들은 긴 여행을 떠나거나 챙길 것이

많을 때 종종 저를 사용해요. 그들은 제 안에 그들의 옷을 넣죠. 그리고 나서 그들은 저를 공항으로 데려가요. 저는 가끔씩 너무 크기때문에, 사람들은 보통 저를 기내로 가지고 가지 않아요. 하지만저는 바퀴와 손잡이가 있기 때문에 사람들은 저를 쉽게 가지고 다닐수 있어요.

해설 그림이 전부 가방이므로 plane, airport, wheels 등의 힌트를 통해 여행가방을 정답으로 고를 수 있다.

어휘 go on a trip 여행을 가다 pack (짐을) 싸다, 챙기다 inside 안에, 안으로 airport 공항 usually 보통은, 일반적으로 carry 가지고 가다 plane 비행기 easily 쉽게 wheel 바퀴 handle 손잡이

02 ①

W: It's time for the daily weather forecast. Rain is coming from Japan. So Gangneung will get lots of rain today. Daegu and Busan will be very cloudy. In Gwangju, it will be cold and windy today. There will be clear, sunny skies in Seoul. And Incheon will have sunny skies, too.

일일 일기예보 시간입니다. 일본에서부터 비가 몰려오고 있습니다. 그래서 강릉에는 오늘 비가 많이 오겠습니다. 대구와 부산에는 구름이 매우 많겠습니다. 광주는 오늘 춥고 바람이 불겠습니다. 서울의하늘은 맑고 화창하겠습니다. 그리고 인천도 화창한 하늘을 보이겠습니다.

어휘 daily 매일 일어나는, 매일의

03 ①

M: What are you doing now? 너 지금 뭐 하고 있니?
W: I'm making a shopping list. I'm going to the supermarket today.
  난 쇼핑 목록을 작성 중이야. 난 오늘 슈퍼마켓에 갈 거야.
M: Are you going to buy eggs? 넌 달걀을 살 거니?
W: No, I already have them. But I need apples, chicken, and orange juice. 아니, 달걀은 이미 있어. 하지만나는 사과, 닭고기, 그리고 오렌지 주스가 필요해.
M: How about bananas? 바나나는?
W: Thanks. I have to buy some bananas, too.
  고마워. 난 바나나도 사야겠어.

어휘 shopping list 쇼핑 목록 egg 달걀

04 ③

M: Mom, I'm going to go out for a walk.
  엄마, 저 산책하러 나갈 거예요.
W: Why don't you take Rusty with you?
  넌 러스티를 데리고 나가지 그래?
M: He likes to run. I'm too tired to run with him.
  러스티는 달리는 걸 좋아해요. 저는 러스티와 함께 달리기에는 너무피곤해요.
W: But dogs need exercise. And he's your dog. You should take care of him. 하지만 개들은 운동을 필요로 해.

그리고 그 개는 네 개잖아. 네가 돌봐줘야지.

M: You're right. I'll **take** him to the **park** with me.
맞아요. 제가 러스티를 공원에 데려갈게요.

W: That's a good boy! 참 착하기도 하지!

해설 'That's a good boy!'는 말을 잘 듣는 아이를 칭찬할 때 쓰는 표현이다.

어휘 go out for a walk 산책하러 나가다 exercise 운동; 운동하다 take care of ~을 돌보다, 보살피다

05 ⑤

M: I'd like to **check out** these **books**, please.
저는 이 책들을 빌리고 싶습니다.

W: Do you have a **library card**?
도서관 카드를 갖고 계세요?

M: **No**, I don't. Can I **make one** here?
아니요, 없는데요. 여기서 하나 만들 수 있을까요?

W: **Yes**, you can. Do you have a **student ID** card?
네, 만들 수 있어요. 학생증을 갖고 계신가요?

M: Here you are. 여기 있습니다.

W: Hold on a minute. Please **fill out** this **form** first.
잠시만 기다리세요. 먼저 이 양식을 작성해 주세요.

해설 첫 대사의 'check out books'에서 대화 장소가 도서관이라는 게 드러난다. 이어지는 대화에서 도서관 카드 만들기에 관한 내용이 나온다.

어휘 check out (책을) 대출하다, 빌리다 library card 도서관 (대출) 카드 student ID card 학생증 fill out 작성하다 form 양식

06 ③

W: We need to **book plane tickets** for our trip. Let's go to the **travel agency**.
우리는 여행을 위해 비행기표를 예약해야 해. 여행사에 가보자.

M: It's **Saturday**. I think it's **closed** today.
오늘은 토요일이야. 오늘 문을 닫았을 것 같은데.

W: **No**, it's open. But it **closes** at **four** today.
아니야, 열었어. 하지만 오늘 4시에 문을 닫지.

M: We need to **hurry up** then. **It's** already **three**.
그럼 우리 서둘러야겠어. 벌써 3시잖아.

W: Right. Let's go now. 맞아. 지금 가자.

해설 문을 닫는 시각에 대한 문제이므로 'close at'과 함께 언급되는 숫자에 집중한다.

어휘 book 예약하다, 예매하다 plane ticket 비행기표, 항공권 travel agency 여행사 hurry up 서두르다 already 벌써

07 ⑤

M: I'm really **excited** about our **trip** to the **beach**.
나는 바닷가로 떠나는 우리 여행 때문에 정말 신나.

W: So am I. **What** should we **do** there?
나도 그래. 우린 거기서 뭘 해야 할까?

M: I don't want to go on a **boat**. I'll **get sick**.

나는 배를 타고 싶지는 않아. 멀미가 날 거야.

W: That's okay. We can go **snorkeling** and have some **seafood**. 그건 괜찮아. 우리는 스노클링을 하고 해산물을 좀 먹을 수 있을 거야.

M: Snorkeling is fine. But I don't like seafood.
스노클링은 좋아. 하지만 난 해산물은 좋아하지 않아.

W: That's too bad. 너무 아쉽네.

해설 남자가 마지막에 스노클링은 좋지만 해산물을 싫어한다고 했으므로, 두 사람이 할 수 있는 것은 스노클링이다.

어휘 be excited about ~에 대해 흥분하다, 들뜨다 beach 바닷가, 해변 go on a boat 배에 오르다 get sick 멀미가 나다, 병에 걸리다 go snorkeling 스노클링을 하다 seafood 해산물

08 ④

W: **Why** aren't you **out** with your **friends**?
넌 왜 네 친구들이랑 함께 나가지 않니?

M: Jeremy **called** a **while ago**. He can't meet me today.
제레미한테 방금 전화가 왔어요. 그 애는 오늘 저를 못 만난대요.

W: Did he say why? 그 애가 왜 그런지는 얘기했니?

M: He has to go to the **market** with his **parents**.
그 애는 부모님과 함께 시장에 가야 한대요.

W: You must be **disappointed**. 넌 실망했겠구나.

M: **I am**. We were planning to play tennis this afternoon.
네. 우리는 오늘 오후에 테니스를 치기로 되어 있었거든요.

해설 남자의 마지막 말인 'I am.'은 'I am disappointed.'가 생략된 형태이다.

어휘 disappointed 실망한 plan to ~할 계획이다

09 ②

M: Do you still **want** to be a **doctor** in the **future**?
넌 여전히 커서 의사가 되고 싶니?

W: That's **right**. I want to **help sick people** get better. How about you?
맞아. 나는 아픈 사람들이 회복하는 것을 돕고 싶어. 너는 어때?

M: I'm **interested** in **writing**. 나는 글쓰기에 관심이 있어.

W: So you want to be an **author**?
그럼 넌 작가가 되고 싶은 거야?

M: **No**. I want to be a **reporter**. I'd like to **work for** a **newspaper**.
아니. 난 기자가 되고 싶어. 난 신문사에서 일하고 싶어.

해설 여자와 남자의 장래 희망을 구분하여 듣는다. 의사는 여자의 장래 희망이다.

어휘 in the future 앞으로, 장차 get better 호전되다, 나아지다 be interested in ~에 관심이 있다 writing 글쓰기 author 작가(= writer) reporter 기자 work for ~에서 일하다 newspaper 신문사, 신문

10 ③

M: Good morning. Where are you going?
안녕하세요. 어디로 가세요?

W: I need to go to City Hall.
저는 시청으로 가야 해요.

M: City Hall? Okay. It will take about fifteen minutes to get there.
시청이요? 알겠습니다. 거기까지 가는 데 약 15분이 걸릴 거예요.

W: Can you please go faster? I'm late for a meeting.
더 빨리 가주실 수 있나요? 제가 회의에 늦었거든요.

M: No problem. What time is your meeting?
문제 없습니다. 회의가 몇 시인가요?

W: I need to be there by ten thirty.
저는 그곳에 10시 30분까지 가야 해요.

해설 여자에게 목적지를 묻고, 이동 시간에 대해 말하는 걸로 보아 남자는 택시를 운전하고 있다.

어휘 City Hall 시청 faster 더 빠른(fast-faster-fastest) late for ~에 늦은 meeting 회의

11 ①

W: Hello. What can I do for you?
안녕하세요. 무엇을 도와드릴까요?

M: I need a picture for my driver's license.
저는 제 운전면허증용 사진이 필요해요.

W: Okay. Sit in that chair, please.
알겠습니다. 저기 의자에 앉으세요.

M: Will this take long? I'm in a hurry.
이게 시간이 오래 걸릴까요? 제가 급해서요.

W: It will only take about fifteen minutes after I take your picture.
제가 손님의 사진을 찍은 후에 15분 정도밖에 안 걸릴 거예요.

해설 사진, 운전면허증을 통해 정답을 사진관과 면허 시험장으로 압축시킬 수 있다. 그 중 사진을 직접 찍는 장소는 사진관이다.

어휘 picture 사진; 그림 driver's license 운전면허증 take long 오래 걸리다 in a hurry 서둘러, 급히 take one's picture ~의 사진을 찍다

12 ③

W: You look really happy, Ted. 너 정말 행복해 보여, 테드.
M: I can't stop smiling today. 난 오늘 웃음을 참을 수 없어.
W: What's going on? 무슨 일인데?
M: My parents are going to buy a new computer for me. I can't wait. 우리 부모님이 나에게 새 컴퓨터를 사주실 거야. 그게 무척 기다려져.
W: Wow. That sounds great. Congratulations.
와. 굉장한 일인 걸. 축하해.

해설 여자의 질문 'What's going on?' 뒤에 구체적 이유가 등장한다.

어휘 can't stop ~ing ~하는 것을 참지 못하다

13 ④

M: How do the shoes feel?
그 신발은 느낌이 어떤가요?

W: They are a little big. Do you have them in a smaller size? 약간 커요. 더 작은 사이즈의 신발이 있나요?

M: Sorry. Those are the only ones we have. How about looking at something else? 죄송합니다. 그게 저희가 가진 유일한 신발이에요. 다른 것을 보시는 건 어떨까요?

W: The shoes over there look pretty.
저기 있는 신발이 예쁘네요.

M: Great. We have them in your size. Hold on a minute.
좋습니다. 저건 손님의 사이즈가 있습니다. 잠시만 기다리세요.

W: Okay. 네.

어휘 size 크기, 사이즈 something else 다른 것 over there 저쪽에

14 ⑤

M: Why aren't you watching the movie?
넌 왜 그 영화를 보고 있지 않은 거니?

W: The DVD player isn't working. I think it's broken.
DVD 플레이어가 작동을 안 해. 내 생각엔 망가진 것 같아.

M: Did you try to fix it?
그걸 고치려고 해봤어?

W: I looked at it. But I don't know what's wrong. Can you try to fix it?
그걸 들여다봤어. 하지만 뭐가 잘못되었는지 모르겠어. 네가 고쳐 줄 수 있어?

M: Sure. Let me take a look at it now.
그래. 내가 지금 한번 볼게.

해설 여자가 'Can you ~?'로 부탁을 했고, 남자가 받아들이는 의미로 'Let me ~'로 말했다.

어휘 work 작동되다 broken 고장 난 fix 고치다 wrong 잘못된, 틀린 take a look at ~을 한번 보다

15 ②

M: How much are the pizzas? 피자가 얼마죠?
W: A regular pizza costs ten dollars, and a large pizza costs sixteen dollars.
레귤러 사이즈의 피자는 10달러, 라지 사이즈는 16달러예요.

M: Okay. I'll take a regular pepperoni pizza.
네. 저는 레귤러 사이즈의 페퍼로니 피자를 살게요.

W: You have to pay two dollars more for pepperoni. So your total is twelve dollars. 페퍼로니는 2달러를 더 내셔야 해요. 그러니까 합계는 12달러입니다.

M: That's fine. Here's fifteen dollars.
좋아요. 여기 15달러요.

W: Thank you. And here's your change.
고맙습니다. 여기 거스름돈 있어요.

해설 여자의 대사 'So your total is ~'에 합계 금액이 언급되었다.

어휘 regular 표준적인, 보통의 cost 비용이 들다 pepperoni

페퍼로니 (소시지의 일종) total 합계 금액 change 거스름돈

16 ⑤

[*Telephone rings.*] [전화벨이 울린다.]

W: Hello. 여보세요.

M: Hi, Mom. It's Steve. Are you busy?
여보세요, 엄마. 저 스티브예요. 바쁘세요?

W: Not really. Where are you?
별로 안 바빠. 너 어디 있니?

M: I'm at the bus stop, but I missed the bus home.
제가 버스 정류장에 있는데요, 집으로 가는 버스를 놓쳤어요.

W: Do you need me to go there and pick you up?
내가 그쪽으로 가서 널 태워 줄까?

M: Yes, please. I don't have enough money for a taxi.
네, 그렇게 해주세요. 택시를 탈 돈이 충분하지가 않아요.

W: Okay. I'll be there in twenty minutes.
알았다. 20분 후에 그리로 갈게.

해설 남자의 상황 설명이 이어지자 여자가 'Do you need me to ~?'로 목적을 대신 말했다.

어휘 bus stop 버스 정류장 miss a bus home 집으로 가는 버스를 놓치다 pick somebody up (사람을) 차에 태우다 enough 충분한

17 ④

① W: What would you like to order? 무엇을 주문하시겠어요?
   M: I'd like some pasta and a glass of iced tea.
   파스타랑 아이스티 한 잔 주세요.

② W: Where is your hometown? 넌 고향이 어디니?
   M: I was born in Seoul. 난 서울에서 태어났어.

③ W: Can you show me how to solve this problem?
   이 문제를 어떻게 푸는지 보여 주시겠어요?
   M: Sure. It's really simple. 물론이죠. 정말 간단해요.

④ W: What movie did you see yesterday?
   넌 어제 무슨 영화를 봤니?
   M: We saw it in the evening. 우리는 그걸 저녁에 봤어.

⑤ W: How much does it cost to take the bus?
   버스 타는 데 돈이 얼마나 들죠?
   M: A bus ticket costs two dollars. 버스표는 2달러입니다.

해설 ④에서 'What movie ~?'로 질문했으므로 영화의 제목이나 장르를 포함한 답변이 와야 한다.

어휘 order 주문하다; 주문 a glass of iced tea 아이스티 한 잔 hometown 고향 be born 태어나다 solve (문제를) 풀다 simple 간단한, 단순한 bus ticket 버스표

18 ⑤

W: Hi, Mark. How is your new camera?
안녕, 마크. 네 새 카메라는 어때?

M: It's terrible. It broke yesterday.
형편없어. 그건 어제 망가졌어.

W: Did you take it to the repair center?
넌 그걸 수리 센터에 가지고 갔니?

M: I'm going there right now. I want to exchange it for another one. 난 지금 그곳으로 가는 중이야. 나는 그 카메라를 다른 것으로 교환하고 싶어.

W: I'm sorry to hear that. I hope you can get a better camera.
그 얘기를 들으니 유감이다. 네가 더 좋은 카메라를 받길 바랄게.

해설 대화에 등장하는 단어가 선택지 곳곳에 있으므로 오답 함정에 빠지지 않도록 내용을 정확히 이해해야 한다.

어휘 terrible 끔찍한, 형편없는 break 망가지다(break-broke-broken) repair center 수리 센터 better 더 좋은(good-better-best)

19 ②

M: I'm having a party at my house this Saturday. Would you like to come? 난 이번 주 토요일에 우리 집에서 파티를 열 거야. 너도 올래?

W: Sure. Do you want me to bring anything?
물론이지. 내가 뭐라도 가지고 갈까?

M: That's all right. There will be lots of food.
그건 괜찮아. 음식은 많이 있을 거야.

W: Great. When should I be there?
아주 좋은데. 내가 거기 언제 가야 해?

M: You should arrive by 6. 넌 6시까지 도착해야 해.

① I live at 43 Main Street.
난 메인 스트리트 43번지에 살아.

② You should arrive by 6. 넌 6시까지 도착해야 해.

③ You can visit me on Sunday.
넌 일요일에 나를 방문할 수 있어.

④ About 10 people will be there.
약 10명의 사람들이 그곳에 올 거야.

⑤ We're going to order some pizzas.
우리는 피자를 좀 시킬 거야.

해설 여자가 when으로 물었으므로 남자는 날짜나 시간으로 답해야 한다.

어휘 have a party 파티를 열다 bring 가져다 주다, 가져오다

20 ③

M: Did you join the cycling club at school?
넌 학교 자전거 동아리에 가입했니?

W: I wanted to, but I don't have a bicycle.
난 그러고 싶었는데, 나한테는 자전거가 없어.

M: So which club do you want to become a member of? 그럼 넌 어떤 동아리의 회원이 되고 싶어?

W: I'm thinking about joining the science club.
나는 과학 동아리에 가입할까 생각 중이야.

M: I'm in it. You should join me. 내가 거기 가입해 있어. 넌 나랑 함께 해야 해.

① Yes, we have science after lunch.
응, 우리는 점심시간 후에 과학 수업이 있어.

② I didn't join a club last year either.
난 작년에도 동아리에 가입하지 않았어.

③ I'm in it. You should join me.
내가 거기 가입해 있어. 넌 나랑 함께 해야 해.

④ No, there isn't a club meeting today.
아니, 오늘은 동아리 모임이 없어.

⑤ The cycling club should be lots of fun.
자전거 동아리는 정말 재미있을 거야.

해설 여자의 마지막 대사가 의문문이 아닌 평서문으로 끝났기 때문에 다양한 응답이 가능하다. 우선 Yes나 No로 시작한 선택지는 제외한다. 나머지 선택지 중에서 뜻이 통하는 내용을 고른다.

어휘 cycling 자전거 타기 become a member 회원이 되다

08회 실전모의고사
본문 p.76-77

01 ④	02 ②	03 ①	04 ⑤	05 ④
06 ②	07 ②	08 ②	09 ③	10 ④
11 ①	12 ③	13 ②	14 ③	15 ①
16 ①	17 ②	18 ⑤	19 ⑤	20 ④

01 ④

W: Dad, I can't find my diary. I think I left it somewhere here. Can you help me find it?
아빠, 제 일기장을 못 찾겠어요. 제 생각에는 여기 어딘가에 그걸 놓아 둔 것 같거든요. 일기장 찾는 걸 도와주실래요?

M: Sure. Is that it on the floor in front of the chair?
그래. 바닥 위 의자 앞에 있는 게 그 일기장이니?

W: No, that's Joe's history notebook. It's not on the kitchen table either. That's Mom's cookbook.
아니요, 그건 조의 역사 공책이에요. 일기장은 식탁 위에도 없어요. 저건 엄마의 요리책이에요.

M: Is this it on the counter? Your name is on the front.
조리대 위에 있는 이게 그거니? 네 이름이 앞쪽에 있는데.

W: Yes, that's it. Thanks for helping me, Dad.
맞아요, 그거예요. 도와주셔서 고마워요, 아빠.

해설 counter는 보통 계산대라는 의미로 쓰이지만, 부엌에서는 조리대의 의미로 쓰인다.

어휘 diary 일기장 leave 놓다, 두다(leave-left-left) somewhere 어딘가에 floor 바닥 in front of ~의 앞에 notebook 공책 kitchen table 식탁 either ~도, 또한 cookbook 요리책 counter 조리대 front 앞, 앞면

02 ②

M: Good morning, everybody. Welcome to my class. We're going to have class from ten A.M. to eleven A.M. every day of the week. I want you to have fun in my class. But I also want you to work hard.

Please don't talk to other students or play with your phones during class. Please ask questions if you don't understand something. All right, let's begin our first class.

안녕하세요, 여러분. 제 수업에 오신 것을 환영합니다. 우리는 주중에 매일 오전 10시부터 11시까지 수업을 하게 될 거예요. 저는 여러분이 제 수업에서 즐거움을 얻으셨으면 좋겠습니다. 하지만 저는 여러분이 열심히 공부하기를 바라기도 한답니다. 수업 도중에는 다른 학생들과 이야기를 나누거나 전화기를 만지작거리지 마십시오. 뭔가가 이해가 안 되면 질문을 해주세요. 좋아요. 첫 수업을 시작하겠습니다.

해설 수업 첫날에 수업에 대한 정보와 규칙에 대해 설명하고 있다.

어휘 class 수업 have fun 즐거움을 얻다, 재미있게 놀다 work hard 열심히 공부하다[일하다] play with ~을 만지작거리다, ~와 놀다 during 도중에

03 ①

W: Good morning, everybody. Last night, we expected sunny skies for this morning. We were wrong. As you can see, it's snowing a lot right now. The snowy weather is going to stop this afternoon. It will be cloudy for the rest of the day. There will be foggy weather tomorrow morning, and the temperature will go up to around five degrees then.

안녕하세요, 여러분. 지난 밤에, 우리는 오늘 아침이 화창할 거라고 예상했습니다. 우리가 틀렸군요. 보시는 것처럼, 현재 눈이 많이 내리고 있습니다. 눈은 오늘 오후에 그치겠습니다. 남은 시간 동안 구름이 끼겠습니다. 내일 아침에는 안개가 끼겠고, 그리고 나서 약 5도까지 올라갈 겁니다.

어휘 expect 기대하다, 예상하다 wrong 틀린, 잘못된 as you can see 보시다시피 for the rest of the day 하루에 남은 시간 동안 foggy 안개 낀 temperature 기온, 온도 go up 올라가다 around 약 degree (온도의) 도

04 ⑤

M: Hi, Tina. How was your trip to Europe?
안녕, 티나. 너의 유럽 여행은 어땠니?

W: It was amazing. I went to many museums in four countries.
끝내줬어. 나는 네 개 국가의 많은 박물관을 찾아갔어.

M: Wow! Sounds like you had a wonderful time.
와! 네가 정말 좋은 시간을 보낸 것처럼 들리는구나.

W: Of course. And I met my aunt and uncle in Spain.
당연하지. 그리고 나는 스페인에 계신 우리 숙모와 삼촌을 만났어.

M: Really? Do they live there?
정말? 그분들은 거기에 사셔?

W: Yes, they do. They cooked some European food for me.
응, 거기에 사셔. 그분들은 나를 위해 유럽 음식을 만들어 주셨어.

05 ④

M: Did you buy everything on your shopping list?
넌 쇼핑 목록에 있는 모든 것을 구입했니?

W: Yes, I did. The prices were cheap.
응, 그래. 가격이 저렴하더라.

M: Great. So can we go home now?
좋은데. 그럼 우린 이제 집에 갈 수 있는 거야?

W: Oh, wait. I need to go to one more store.
아, 기다려 봐. 가게 한 곳을 더 가봐야 해.

M: All right. But please hurry. I want to go home and have some food.
좋아. 하지만 서둘러. 난 집에 가서 음식을 좀 먹고 싶어.

해설 두 사람은 대화가 끝난 직후 상점에 갔다가 집에 가서 음식을 먹을 것이다.

어휘 shopping list 쇼핑 목록 price 가격 cheap 싼, 저렴한 hurry 서두르다

06 ②

W: Excuse me. Can I see your ticket? You need a ticket to enter the amusement park.
실례합니다. 티켓을 좀 볼 수 있을까요? 놀이공원에 입장하시려면 티켓이 필요하거든요.

M: Where can I buy a ticket? I am looking for the ticket office.
제가 어디서 티켓을 살 수 있죠? 매표소를 찾고 있는 중이거든요.

W: Go to that building over there.
저쪽에 있는 건물로 가세요.

M: How much does it cost to buy one?
티켓 하나에 가격이 얼마인가요?

W: Tickets cost fifteen dollars for adults and ten dollars for children.
티켓은 성인은 15달러이고 어린이는 10달러입니다.

M: Thanks for your help. 도와 주셔서 감사합니다.

해설 놀이공원 입구에서 표를 검사하는 직원과 고객의 대화로, 티켓 검사 및 티켓 구매에 대한 내용이 이어지고 있다.

어휘 enter 입장하다, 들어가다 amusement park 놀이공원 ticket office 매표소 over there 저쪽에 cost 비용이 들다 adult 성인, 어른

07 ②

M: What do you do in the morning, Kate?
너는 아침에 뭘 하니, 케이트?

W: I wake up at six thirty every day. And then I take a shower. 나는 매일 6시 30분에 일어나. 그리고 나서 샤워를 해.

M: Do you eat breakfast? 넌 아침을 먹어?

W: Of course. I have breakfast at six forty-five. Then,

I leave my house at seven fifteen. 물론이지. 나는 6시 45분에 아침식사를 해. 그리고 나서 7시 15분에 집을 나서지.

M: Why do you leave at that time?
넌 왜 그 시각에 출발하는 거니?

W: I don't want to miss my bus. My bus leaves at seven thirty.
난 내 버스를 놓치고 싶지 않거든. 버스는 7시 30분에 떠나.

해설 시간대별로 여자가 하는 일이 순차적으로 언급되므로 오답을 제거하면서 문제를 푸는 것이 효과적이다.

어휘 wake up 일어나다, 깨다 take a shower 샤워하다 have breakfast 아침을 먹다 leave 떠나다, 출발하다 miss a bus 버스를 놓치다

08 ②

W: Are you busy this weekend?
너 이번 주말에 바쁘니?

M: No, I'm not. I don't have any plans. Why?
아니, 안 바빠. 난 아무 계획도 없어. 왜?

W: I'm going to help clean up the park. Would you like to do that with me? 난 공원을 청소하는 것을 도우려고 하거든. 나랑 같이 그 일을 할래?

M: What are you going to do? 너희는 무엇을 할 건데?

W: We will pick up trash in the park and throw it away. We'll help make the park look better.
우리는 공원에서 쓰레기를 줍고 그것을 버릴 거야. 우리는 공원이 더 멋지게 보이도록 도울 거야.

M: What a great idea. I will be glad to help.
아주 좋은 생각이네. 내가 기꺼이 도울게.

해설 대화의 흐름을 놓쳤더라도 마지막 대사에서 great, glad 등 긍정적인 표현을 들었다면 정답을 유추할 수 있다.

어휘 clean up 치우다, 청소하다 pick up 줍다 trash 쓰레기 throw away 버리다

09 ③

W: What are you thinking about, Jim?
넌 뭘 생각하고 있는 거니, 짐?

M: I'm trying to solve this math problem. But I don't know how to do it. It's really difficult.
난 이 수학 문제를 풀려고 노력하고 있어. 하지만 어떻게 풀어야 할지 모르겠어. 이건 정말 어려워.

W: Did you ask the teacher for help?
넌 선생님에게 도움을 청해 봤어?

M: Mr. Kim isn't in his office now. And my friends don't know how to answer the question either.
김 선생님은 지금 교무실에 인 계셔. 그리고 내 친구들도 문제를 이떻게 풀어야 하는지 몰라.

W: I'm sorry I can't help you. As you know, I'm poor at math. 내가 널 도와주지 못해서 미안해. 너도 알다시피 난 수학에 약하거든.

해설 스스로 할 수 없고 주변 도움도 얻을 수 없는 상황에서 남자는 좌

절감을 느낄 것이다.

어휘 solve 풀다, 해결하다 math 수학 difficult 어려운 ask for help 도움을 청하다 poor at ~에 약한, ~을 못하는

10 ④

M: Wendy, how are you <u>feeling</u>? You're not <u>sick</u> <u>anymore</u>, are you?
웬디, 너 기분이 어떠니? 넌 더 이상 아프지 않지, 그렇지?

W: I'm <u>much</u> <u>better</u> today, Mark. Thanks for asking.
오늘은 한결 몸이 좋아, 마크. 물어봐 줘서 고마워.

M: You were really sick three days ago, but you <u>look</u> <u>fine</u> now. Did you <u>take</u> some <u>medicine</u>?
넌 3일 전에는 정말 아팠는데, 지금은 좋아 보여. 넌 약을 좀 먹었니?

W: No, I just <u>stayed</u> in <u>bed</u>. I really <u>needed</u> a lot of <u>rest</u>.
아니, 난 그냥 침대에 있었어. 난 정말로 많은 휴식이 필요했거든.

M: I'm <u>glad</u> you're <u>healthy</u> again.
네가 다시 건강해져서 기뻐.

어휘 sick 아픈 not ~ anymore 더 이상 ~ 않다 take medicine 약을 먹다 stay in bed 침대에 누워 있다 rest 휴식; 휴식을 취하다 healthy 건강한

11 ①

W: That was a long <u>flight</u>. We're finally here in Paris.
긴 비행이었어. 우리가 마침내 여기 파리에 왔어.

M: <u>How</u> do you want to <u>get</u> to the <u>hotel</u>?
넌 호텔까지 어떻게 가고 싶어?

W: We could <u>take</u> the <u>subway</u>. What do you think about it?
우리는 지하철을 탈 수 있어. 너는 어떻게 생각해?

M: We've got too <u>many</u> <u>bags</u>. Let's just <u>take</u> a <u>taxi</u> there.
우리는 가방이 너무 많잖아. 거기까지 그냥 택시를 타자.

W: <u>Good</u> thinking. I think the taxi stand is <u>over</u> <u>there</u> near the bus stop. 좋은 생각이야. 내 생각에는 택시 타는 곳이 저쪽 버스 정류장 근처인 것 같아.

해설 맨 마지막에 나오는 bus stop에 신경 쓰다 보면 ②를 고를 가능성이 있으므로 주의한다.

어휘 flight 비행 finally 마침내, 드디어 take the subway 지하철을 타다 take a taxi 택시를 타다 taxi stand 택시 승차장 bus stop 버스 정류장

12 ③

W: Are you <u>ready</u> for the <u>performance</u>?
넌 공연 준비가 됐니?

M: I'm not sure. We're <u>trying hard</u>, but we're running <u>out of time</u>. 난 잘 모르겠어. 우리는 열심히 노력하고 있는데, 시간이 다 되어가고 있어.

W: What do you mean? The play is on <u>September</u>

<u>thirtieth</u>, isn't it?
그게 무슨 소리야? 연극은 9월 30일이잖아, 그렇지 않니?

M: <u>No</u>, it <u>changed</u>. We're going to perform on September <u>twenty</u> <u>fifth</u> now.
아니야, 바뀌었어. 우리는 이제 9월 25일에 공연을 하게 됐어.

W: <u>Today</u> is the <u>twenty</u> <u>second</u>. So you only have <u>three</u> more <u>days</u> to practice.
오늘이 22일이잖아. 그럼 넌 연습할 날이 고작 3일밖에 없는 거네.

M: I know. I hope we can do well.
나도 알아. 난 우리가 잘 해내기를 바라고 있어.

해설 9월 22일은 오늘 날짜, 25일은 공연이 실제로 있을 날짜, 30일은 공연이 원래 예정되었던 날짜이다.

어휘 ready for ~에 준비된 performance 공연 sure 확실한, 확신이 있는 run out of time 시간이 다 되다 play 연극 perform 공연하다 practice 연습하다

13 ②

W: Can I get you <u>something</u> to <u>drink</u>?
제가 마실 것 좀 가져다 드릴까요?

M: Yes, please. I'd like a glass of <u>orange</u> <u>juice</u>.
네. 저는 오렌지주스를 한 잔 마시고 싶네요.

W: No problem. Here you are. 알겠어요. 여기 있습니다.

M: Do you know <u>when</u> we're going to <u>land</u>?
우리가 언제 착륙하게 되는지 아세요?

W: We'll <u>arrive</u> in about <u>two hours</u>. So we're right <u>on</u> <u>schedule</u>. 우리는 약 2시간 후에 도착하게 될 거예요. 그러니까 예정대로 가는 거죠.

M: Great. Thanks for the information.
아주 좋네요. 알려 주셔서 고맙습니다.

해설 비행기 승객이 승무원에게 음료수를 요청하고 착륙 시간을 묻는 상황이다.

어휘 something to drink 마실 것 land 착륙하다; 땅 on schedule 예정대로, 정시에 information 정보

14 ③

M: Good evening. Can I help you with something?
안녕하세요. 제가 무엇을 도와드릴까요?

W: Yes, please. I'd like to <u>return</u> this <u>sweater</u>.
네. 저는 이 스웨터를 반품하고 싶어요.

M: <u>Why</u>? Is it too <u>big</u>? 왜요? 그게 너무 큰가요?

W: It <u>fits</u> fine, but I <u>found</u> a small <u>hole</u> in the back.
크기는 잘 맞지만, 뒤쪽에 작은 구멍을 찾았거든요.

M: <u>I'm</u> <u>sorry</u> about that. I will <u>exchange</u> this for <u>another</u> <u>one</u> right now.
그 점은 죄송합니다. 지금 바로 다른 옷으로 교환해 드리겠습니다.

해설 여자는 우선 반품하겠다는 의지를 표현한 뒤, 남자가 그 이유를 묻자 내용을 설명했다.

어휘 exchange 교환하다 return 반품하다, 돌려주다 sweater 스웨터 hole 구멍 back 뒤쪽에

15 ①

M: Janet, I'm going to stay at my grandmother's house
for a month.
재닛, 난 한 달 동안 우리 할머니 댁에서 머물 예정이야.

W: That's great. I hope you have a good time.
잘됐네. 네가 좋은 시간을 보내길 바랄게.

M: Do you mind taking care of my plants for me?
네가 나 대신 내 식물들을 돌봐줄 수 있겠니?

W: No, I don't. What should I do?
응, 알았어. 내가 뭘 하면 되지?

M: I'll take them to your house tomorrow. And I'll show
you how to water them. 내가 내일 식물들을 너네 집으로 가
지고 갈게. 그리고 식물에 물을 주는 방법을 알려 줄게.

W: No problem. I'm glad I can help you.
알았어. 내가 널 도울 수 있어서 기쁘다.

> **해설** 'Do you mind ~?'로 물었을 때 'No'는 긍정적인 답변이고,
> 'Yes'는 부정적인 답변이다. water는 '물을 주다'라는 의미의 동사로도
> 쓰인다.

> **어휘** mind -ing ~를 꺼려하다 take care of ~을 돌보다, 보살피다
> plant 식물 show (무엇을 하는 법 등을) 보여 주다 water 물을 주다;
> 물

16 ①

M: You look upset, Sarah. What's the matter?
너 화난 것처럼 보여, 사라. 무슨 문제 있어?

W: There's a problem with my phone. I can't make any
phone calls.
내 전화기에 문제가 있어. 내가 전화를 걸 수가 없어.

M: Try turning it off for a few minutes. That might
work. 몇 분 동안 그걸 끄도록 해봐. 그렇게 하면 될 거야.

W: Are you sure about that? 그거 확실한 거야?

M: My phone had the same problem. The person at
the repair center told me to do that.
내 전화기도 같은 문제점이 있었어. 수리센터에 있는 사람이 나한테
그렇게 하라고 하더라.

W: Wow, thanks for the advice. 와, 조언 고마워.

> **해설** 화가 난 여자에게 '~을 해봐'라는 의미로 남자가 'Try ~'하고 제
> 안했다.

> **어휘** upset 속상한 matter 문제, 일 make a phone call 전화를
> 걸다 turn something off ~을 끄다 for a few minutes 몇 분 동
> 안 work 효과가 있다 repair center 수리센터 advice 조언, 충고

17 ②

[Cellphone rings.] [휴대폰이 울린다]

M: Hello. 여보세요.

W: Hi, Steve. It's Carol. I can't find the restaurant.
안녕, 스티브. 나 캐롤이야. 난 그 음식점을 못 찾겠어.

M: Tell me where you are.
네가 어디 있는지 말해줘.

W: I'm at the corner of Pine Street and River Road.

나는 파인 스트리트와 리버 로드가 만나는 모퉁이에 있어.

M: Okay. Walk straight one block to Maple Street.
Then, turn right. 알았어. 메이플 스트리트까지 한 블록을 곧장
걸어가. 그 다음에 우회전해.

W: Turn right? All right. Then what?
우회전? 알았어. 그 다음엔?

M: The restaurant will be on the left. It's between the
bakery and the drugstore.
음식점은 왼쪽에 있을 거야. 그건 제과점과 약국 사이에 있어.

> **어휘** at the corner of ~의 모퉁이에

18 ⑤

① M: How tall is your sister?
네 여동생은 키가 얼마나 돼?

W: She's about one hundred fifty-five centimeters tall.
그 애의 키는 약 155cm야.

② M: What did you do last weekend?
너는 지난 주말에 뭘 했니?

W: I played baseball with my friends.
난 친구들과 야구를 했어.

③ M: Do you know Susan? 넌 수잔을 아니?

W: Yes, we are good friends. 응, 우리는 친한 친구야.

④ M: How do you feel today? 오늘은 기분이 어때요?

W: I'm really happy. I'm having a great day.
정말 행복하네요. 아주 좋은 하루를 보내고 있어요.

⑤ M: May I borrow your book, please?
제가 당신의 책을 빌려도 될까요?

W: Yes, I borrowed it from the library.
네. 저는 그걸 도서관에서 빌렸어요.

> **해설** ⑤에 대한 올바른 답변은 'Yes, you can.' 또는 'No, you
> can't.'이다.

> **어휘** play baseball 야구를 하다 borrow 빌리다

19 ⑤

M: I got two tickets for the concert tonight.
나한테 오늘 밤 콘서트 티켓이 두 장 있어.

W: Concert? What concert are you talking about?
콘서트? 넌 무슨 콘서트를 말하는 거야?

M: It's a rock concert. Five bands are going to play.
록 콘서트야. 다섯 밴드가 연주할 예정이야.

W: That sounds interesting. Where is it going to be?
재미있겠는데. 그건 어디서 열리니?

M: It's going to be at Star Stadium.
스타 경기장에서 있을 예정이야.

① The concert starts at 8:00. 콘서트는 8시에 시작해.

② No, the tickets were free. 아니, 티켓들은 공짜였어.

③ Would you like to go there? 넌 거기 가고 싶니?

④ I think we'll have a great time.
우리는 아주 즐거운 시간을 보낼 것 같아.

⑤ It's going to be at Star Stadium.
스타 경기장에서 있을 예정이야.

해설 여자의 마지막 말에서 의문사 where를 놓치지 말아야 한다.

어휘 band (음악을 연주하는) 밴드 stadium 경기장, 스타디움 free 공짜의, 무료의

20 ④

M: That's a really nice scarf you're wearing.
넌 아주 멋진 스카프를 하고 있구나.

W: Thanks. My mom made it for my birthday.
고마워. 우리 엄마가 내 생일이라서 그것을 만들어 주셨어.

M: That's amazing. I love it.
굉장한데. 아주 마음에 들어.

W: Would you like her to make one for you?
우리 엄마가 네 것도 하나 만들어 주면 좋겠니?

M: Yes, that would be wonderful. 응, 그럼 정말 좋을 거야.

① Have a happy birthday. 행복한 생일을 보내.
② No, I don't like the color. 아니, 난 색깔이 마음에 들지 않아.
③ I think the design looks nice. 내 생각에는 디자인이 멋져.
④ Yes, that would be wonderful. 응, 그럼 정말 좋을 거야.
⑤ When is your birthday party? 네 생일 파티는 언제니?

해설 남자는 스카프를 마음에 들어 했으므로 자신에게도 만들어준다고 하면 좋아할 것이다.

어휘 scarf 스카프, 목도리 amazing 놀라운, 굉장한

09회 실전모의고사
본문 p.86-87

01 ⑤	02 ③	03 ②	04 ①	05 ④
06 ②	07 ④	08 ③	09 ④	10 ①
11 ①	12 ⑤	13 ②	14 ③	15 ②
16 ⑤	17 ⑤	18 ⑤	19 ⑤	20 ②

01 ⑤

M: Good morning, listeners. It's time for the day's weather forecast. It's a rainy day everywhere in the country. The rain is going to continue until tomorrow. But it will be different in Busan and on Jeju Island. Those two places will have clear skies in the afternoon but will get cloudy at night.

안녕하세요, 청취자 여러분. 오늘의 일기예보를 전해드릴 시간입니다. 전국 모든 지역에서 비가 내리고 있습니다. 비는 내일까지 이어질 예정입니다. 하지만 부산과 제주도의 날씨는 다르겠습니다. 이 두 지역은 오후에는 맑은 하늘을 보이겠지만, 밤에는 구름이 끼겠습니다.

해설 어느 시점, 어느 지역의 날씨인지 염두에 둬서 듣는다. 접속사 but의 앞뒤로 내용이 달라지므로 주의한다.

어휘 It's time for 이제 ~할 시간이다 continue 계속되다 different 다른

02 ③

W: This lives in the water and on land. It moves very slowly but can swim very well. It has a hard shell on its back. When animals see it, it hides in its shell. So the animals cannot harm it.

이것은 물속과 땅 위에서 삽니다. 이것은 매우 느리게 움직이지만, 헤엄을 매우 잘 칠 수 있습니다. 이것은 등 위에 딱딱한 껍질을 가지고 있습니다. 동물들이 이것을 보면, 이것은 자신의 껍질 속에 숨습니다. 그래서 동물들은 이것을 해칠 수 없습니다.

어휘 on land 땅 위에서, 지상에서 hard 단단한 shell 껍질 hide 숨다 harm 해치다

03 ②

W: Welcome to Korea. Are you coming from Los Angeles, California? 한국에 오신 것을 환영합니다. 여러분은 캘리포니아 주 로스앤젤레스에서 오신 건가요?

M: Yes, we are. Are you Ms. Park from Elite Travel?
네, 그렇습니다. 당신은 엘리트 여행사에서 나오신 박 씨죠?

W: Yes, I am. It's very nice to meet you. Did you have a good flight? 네, 맞습니다. 뵙게 되어 무척 반갑습니다. 비행은 즐거우셨나요?

M: Yes, but it was very long. We'd like to check in to our hotel soon. 네, 하지만 무척 길었습니다. 저희는 호텔에 빨리 체크인하고 싶습니다.

W: I'll take you to your hotel right away. After you get some rest, we can go out to a restaurant.
제가 여러분을 호텔로 금방 모셔다 드릴게요. 약간의 휴식을 취한 후에 우리는 식사하러 갈 겁니다.

해설 대화자의 신분은 주로 상호에서 드러난다. Elite Travel이라는 여행사 이름과 flight, hotel 등의 단어를 통해 여자가 여행 가이드라는 것을 알 수 있다.

어휘 come from ~에서부터 오다, ~ 출신이다 flight 비행 check in 투숙 수속을 밟다, 체크인하다 right away 즉시, 당장 get some rest 약간의 휴식을 취하다

04 ①

[Cellphone rings.] [휴대폰이 울린다.]

W: Hello, Jason. Can you go to Mark's birthday party today?
여보세요, 제이슨. 너 오늘 마크의 생일 파티에 갈 수 있니?

M: I'd love to go there, but I can't. I have to go to the hospital now.
나도 거기에 가고 싶지만, 못 가. 난 지금 병원에 가 봐야 해.

W: Why are you going there? Are you sick?
거기는 왜 가는데? 너 아프니?

M: No, I'm not. But my grandmother fell down, so she got hurt.
아니, 난 아냐. 하지만 우리 할머니가 넘어져서 다치셨어.

W: I'm really sorry to hear that. But don't be too

worried. I'm sure that she will get better soon.
그 얘기를 듣게 돼서 정말 유감이야. 하지만 너무 걱정하지 마.
할머니는 곧 좋아지실 거라고 확신해.

[해설] 누가 아프다는 내용의 대화에서는 대부분 위로하는 내용이 이어진다.

[어휘] go to the hospital 병원에 가다 sick 아픈 fall down 넘어지다 get hurt 다치다 get better 회복되다, 좋아지다

05 ④

M: Hello. Are you a new employee here?
실례합니다. 당신이 이곳에 새로 온 직원인가요?

W: Yes, I am. My name is Janet, and this is my first day at work here.
네, 그래요. 제 이름은 재닛이고, 오늘이 제 근무 첫날이에요.

M: It's nice to meet you, Janet. What kind of work will you be doing here? 만나서 반가워요, 재닛. 당신은 여기서 어떤 종류의 일을 하게 되나요?

W: I'm going to work as a computer programmer. It's nice to meet you, too. 저는 컴퓨터 프로그래머로 근무하게 될 거예요. 저도 만나서 반가워요.

[해설] 전치사 as는 자격을 나타낼 때 자주 나온다. work as는 '~로서 일하다'라는 의미이다.

[어휘] new employee 신입 사원 first day at work 근무 첫날 what kind of 어떤 종류의

06 ②

M: Mom, you look like you're really busy.
엄마, 정말 바빠 보이시네요.

W: I am. Some guests are visiting for dinner tonight.
그렇단다. 손님 몇 분이 오늘 밤에 식사를 하러 오시기로 했거든.

M: I see. That's why you're cooking now.
그렇군요. 그래서 지금 요리를 하고 계시는 거군요.

W: That's right. Can you clean the living room?
맞아. 네가 거실 청소를 해줄래?

M: Sure. I'll start right now.
물론이죠. 바로 시작할게요.

[해설] 여자가 남자에게 요청한 일을 묻는 문제이므로 여자의 말을 잘 듣는다. 요청에는 'Can you ~?'가 자주 쓰인다.

[어휘] look like ~처럼 보이다 guest 손님 right now 지금 즉시

07 ④

W: Thanks for giving me a ride to the train station, Dad. 저를 기차역까지 태워다 주셔서 고마워요, 아빠.

M: No problem. Please call me as soon as you get to Busan. 고맙기는. 부산에 도착하자마자 아빠한테 전화해라.

W: I will. I will arrive there around three hours later.
그럴게요. 저는 약 세 시간 후에 그곳에 도착할 거예요.

M: It's four twenty now. What time will your train get there?

지금이 4시 20분이구나. 네가 탄 기차가 그곳에 몇 시에 도착하지?

W: I'll get there at seven forty. And Aunt Jenny will pick me up there at eight.
저는 7시 40분에 거기 도착할 거예요. 그리고 제니 이모가 저를 데리러 8시에 그곳에 올 거예요.

[해설] 3시간, 4시 20분, 8시 등의 여러 시각이 언급되지만 기차가 도착하는 시간만 정확히 파악하면 된다.

[어휘] give somebody a ride to ~을 …까지 차로 데려다 주다 no problem (부탁에 대해) 그럼요, 물론이죠, (고마움을 나타내는 말에 대해) 괜찮아요 as soon as ~하자마자 pick somebody up ~을 차에 태우러 오다

08 ③

M: Sue, do you have your schedule yet? Which classes do you have on Monday?
수, 벌써 시간표가 나왔니? 넌 월요일에 무슨 수업이 있니?

W: I've got math and science in the morning.
나는 오전에 수학과 과학이 있어.

M: So do I. What about the other classes?
나도 그래. 다른 수업은?

W: I've got gym class, English, and social studies in the afternoon. 나는 오후에 체육, 영어, 그리고 사회가 있어.

M: What about art or music? Do you have either of them? 미술이나 음악은? 둘 중 하나라도 있어?

W: No, I don't have any of them on Monday.
아니, 나는 월요일에 그것 중 어느 것도 없어.

[어휘] schedule 일정, 스케줄 yet 이미, 아직 have a class 수업이 있다 gym 운동, 체육관, 헬스장 social studies (과목) 사회 either (둘 중) 어느 한쪽

09 ④

W: How is your dog doing? Is he still sick?
너희 개는 좀 어때? 개가 아직도 아프니?

M: Yes, he is. He's very old, so it takes him a long time to get better. 응, 아파. 우리 개는 무척 나이가 들어서 회복하는 데 시간이 오래 걸려.

W: I'm so sorry to hear that. 그 말을 들으니 안타깝네.

M: I hope he can be healthy soon.
우리 개가 금방 건강해졌으면 좋겠어.

W: Cheer up. I'm sure he'll be okay soon.
기운 내. 너희 개는 분명히 금방 괜찮아질 거야.

[해설] 남자는 자신이 기르는 개가 낫지 않고 있는 상황에서 개를 걱정하며 슬퍼하고 있다.

[어휘] sick 아픈 take a long time 시간이 오래 걸리다 get better 회복하다, 좋아지다 cheer up 힘내

10 ①

M: It's a beautiful spring day. Why don't we ride our bikes at the park?
아름다운 봄날이야. 우리 공원에서 자전거를 타는 게 어때?

W: I'm really tired. Let's <u>order</u> some <u>food</u> and <u>stay</u> <u>home</u>. 나는 정말 피곤해. 음식을 좀 시켜서 집에 있자.

M: I just ate lunch, so I'm not hungry. 난 방금 점심을 먹어서 배가 안 고파.

W: Okay. Then how about <u>going out</u> for a <u>walk</u>? 알았어. 그럼 산책을 나가는 건 어때?

M: <u>Sure</u>. Let's go. 좋아. 가자.

해설 처음에 남자가 제안한 것을 듣고 바로 답을 골라서는 안 된다. Okay, Sure 등 긍정적 표현을 포함한 내용이 정답이다.

어휘 why don't we 우리 ~하는 게 어때? ride a bike 자전거를 타다 tired 지친, 피곤한 order some food 음식을 좀 시키다 how about ~은 어때? go out for a walk 산책하러 나가다

11 ①

W: Hi, Tim. <u>How</u> was your <u>soccer</u> game today? 안녕, 팀. 오늘 축구 경기는 어땠어?

M: We <u>lost</u> again. 우리가 또다시 졌어.

W: I'm sorry to hear that. <u>What</u> was the <u>score</u>? 그 말을 들으니 안타깝네. 점수는 어땠어?

M: It was four to three. I <u>scored</u> two <u>goals</u>, but it wasn't enough. 4대 3이었어. 내가 두 골을 넣긴 했는데, 그건 충분하지 않더라고.

W: At least you did well. I'm sure you'll <u>do better</u> next time. 적어도 너는 잘했네. 다음 번에는 너희가 더 잘할 거라고 난 확신해.

해설 맨 앞에서 soccer game이 나온 후 score, goal 등의 단어가 이어지므로 축구 경기에 관한 내용이다.

어휘 lose (경기에) 지다(lose-lost-lost) score 점수; 득점을 올리다 enough 충분한 at least 적어도, 최소한 do well 잘하다 do better 더 잘하다 next time 다음에

12 ⑤

W: It's <u>hard</u> for me to <u>remember words</u> in <u>English</u> when I read them. 나는 영어 단어를 읽을 때 그것들을 기억하는 게 어려워.

M: Don't try memorizing them like that. You <u>need</u> a <u>better way</u> to learn English. 단어를 그런 방식으로 외우려고 하지 마. 너는 영어를 배우는 더 좋은 방법이 필요해.

W: What should I do then? 그럼 내가 뭘 해야 해?

M: <u>Say</u> each <u>word</u> out <u>loud</u> many times. That will <u>help</u> you <u>memorize</u> them. 각각의 단어를 큰 소리로 여러 번 말해봐. 그게 네가 단어를 외우는 것을 도울 거야.

W: Really? Okay. I'll <u>say</u> them <u>aloud</u> from now on. 정말? 알았어. 지금부터 나는 단어를 큰 소리로 말할 거야.

해설 여자의 질문 'What should I do then?' 뒤에 남자의 제안이 나온다.

어휘 memorize 암기하다, 외우다 better way 더 좋은 방법 out loud 소리 내어 many times 여러 번 aloud 소리 내어, 큰소리로 from now on 지금부터

13 ②

M: Hey, Karen. Do you have <u>plans</u> for this <u>weekend</u>? 얘, 캐런. 너 이번 주말에 계획이 있니?

W: Yes, I do. I'm <u>going camping</u> with my family. 응, 있어. 나는 가족들과 캠핑을 갈 거야.

M: That sounds like fun. <u>How</u> are you going to <u>go</u> there? 재미있겠는데. 거기에는 어떻게 갈 거야?

W: We were planning to <u>drive</u> there. <u>But</u> we decided to <u>take</u> a <u>bus</u> there <u>instead</u>. 우리는 자동차를 타고 그곳에 가려고 계획했어. 하지만 대신 버스를 타고 거기에 가기로 결정했어.

M: That's a good idea. It will be more <u>convenient</u> to go that way. 좋은 생각이야. 그렇게 가는 게 더 편리할 거야.

해설 접속사 but 뒤에 여자가 최종으로 선택한 교통수단이 나온다.

어휘 go camping 캠핑을 가다 drive 운전하다, 차를 몰다 take a bus 버스를 타다 instead 대신에 convenient 편리한 that way 그 방법이; 그와 같이

14 ③

M: Congratulations on <u>winning</u> a <u>gold medal</u> today. 오늘 금메달을 따신 것을 축하합니다.

W: Thank you so much for saying that. 그렇게 말씀해 주셔서 정말 고맙습니다.

M: Would you like to <u>say anything</u> to your <u>fans</u>? You're <u>on</u> live <u>TV</u> right now. 당신의 팬들에게 한 말씀 해주시겠습니까? 지금 생방송으로 텔레비전에 나가고 있어요.

W: <u>Thank</u> you all for your <u>love</u> and <u>support</u>. I'm glad that I didn't let you down. 모든 분들의 사랑과 성원에 감사합니다. 여러분을 실망시키지 않아서 기쁘네요.

M: Congratulations once again. And <u>good luck</u> in your next event. 다시 한 번 축하합니다. 그리고 다음 경기에 행운을 빌겠습니다.

해설 남자는 금메달을 딴 여자에게 소감을 묻고 있으므로 두 사람은 기자와 운동선수이다.

어휘 congratulations on ~을 축하합니다 win a medal 메달을 따다 be on TV 텔레비전에 나오다 live 생방송으로, 생방송의 support 지지, 성원 let somebody down ~을 실망시키다 once again 한 번 더 event (스포츠) 경기, 행사

15 ②

W: Good afternoon. How may I help you? 안녕하세요. 제가 무엇을 도와드릴까요?

M: Hello. I'm <u>looking for</u> a <u>pencil case</u>. 안녕하세요. 저는 필통을 찾고 있습니다.

W: <u>How about</u> this <u>blue</u> one? Many students like this one a lot. 이 파란색 필통은 어떤가요? 많은 학생들이 이걸 무척 좋아해요.

M: It looks great. <u>How much</u> does it <u>cost</u>? 괜찮아 보이네요. 그건 가격이 얼마인가요?

W: It's <u>five thousand</u> won. But you can buy <u>two</u> of

them for eight thousand won.
오천 원입니다. 하지만 두 개를 팔천 원에 사실 수 있어요.

M: I only need one. Here's ten thousand won.
저는 하나만 필요해요. 여기 만 원 있습니다.

해설 금액 관련 문제에서는 여러 개의 금액이 나오므로 지문을 끝까지 듣고 정답을 골라야 한다.

어휘 look for ~을 찾다 pencil case 필통 how about ~은 어때요? cost (비용이) 들다; 값, 비용

16 ⑤

W: Hi, Chris. Can you play tennis with me today?
안녕, 크리스. 너 오늘 나랑 테니스 칠 수 있어?

M: Sure. I have some free time in the afternoon. Where shall we meet?
물론이지. 오후에 남는 시간이 좀 있어. 우리 어디서 만날까?

W: Let's meet at the tennis court at school.
학교 테니스장에서 만나자.

M: Okay. How about two o'clock?
그래. 2시는 어때?

W: Um... I need to go home to change my clothes. How about meeting at three thirty? 음... 내가 옷을 갈아
입으러 집에 가야 하거든. 3시 30분에 만나는 건 어때?

M: No problem. See you then. 알았어. 그때 보자.

해설 남자의 질문 'Where shall we meet?'에 대한 여자의 대답 'Let's meet at ~'에 만날 장소가 드러난다. 이에 대해 남자가 동의하는지 끝까지 확인한다.

어휘 have free time 자유 시간이 있다 change one's clothes 옷을 갈아입다 no problem 문제 없다, 괜찮다

17 ⑤

M: Which club did you sign up for, Tina?
너는 무슨 동아리에 가입했니, 티나?

W: I joined the cartoon club.
나는 만화 동아리에 가입했어.

M: I didn't know you like cartoons. Are you good at drawing them?
난 네가 만화를 좋아하는지 몰랐는데. 넌 그림을 잘 그리니?

W: No, I can't draw them at all. But I want to learn. That's why I joined the club.
아니, 난 전혀 그릴 줄 몰라. 하지만 난 배우고 싶어. 그게 내가 동아리에 가입한 이유야.

M: It sounds like fun. Maybe I should sign up for it, too. 재미있겠는데. 아마 나도 신청해야 할 것 같아.

해설 여자가 만화 동아리에 가입한 이유이므로 여자의 대사에 집중한다. 이유를 찾을 때는 why의 앞뒤 내용을 잘 듣는다.

어휘 sign up for ~을 신청하다, ~에 가입하다 join 가입하다 cartoon 만화 good at ~을 잘하는 draw 그리다 (not) at all 전혀 that's why 그것이 ~한 이유다

18 ⑤

① M: Can you give me some help, please?
저를 좀 도와주시겠어요?

W: Sure. What can I do for you?
물론이죠. 무엇을 도와 드릴까요?

② M: Do you have a blue pencil? 너 파란색 연필 있니?

W: Sorry, but I don't have one. 미안하지만 난 갖고 있지 않아.

③ M: I think I failed my science test.
내 생각에는 과학 시험을 망친 것 같아.

W: That's too bad. 안됐구나.

④ M: Where did you go during vacation?
방학 동안 어디에 갔었니?

W: I spent some time in Hawaii. 난 하와이에서 시간을 보냈어.

⑤ M: What's the weather like today? 오늘은 날씨가 어떤가요?

W: It was rainy last night. 어젯밤에는 비가 왔어요.

해설 오늘의 날씨를 묻는 질문에 어젯밤의 날씨를 말하고 있으므로 어색하다.

어휘 give somebody help ~을 돕다 fail test 시험을 망치다 That's too bad. 그것 참 안됐다. during ~동안 spend time 시간을 보내다

19 ⑤

M: Jenny, where are you right now?
제니, 너 지금 어디에 있어?

W: I'm in my room with my friends.
난 친구들과 함께 내 방에 있어.

M: What did you say? I can't hear you. What's that terrible noise?
너 뭐라고 말했어? 잘 안 들려. 그 엄청난 소음은 뭐야?

W: My friends and I are in my room. We're listening to music. 내 친구들과 난 내 방에 있어. 우리는 음악을 듣고 있어.

M: Please turn the volume down. 소리 좀 줄여줘.

① Thanks for coming here. 여기에 와줘서 고마워.

② Yes, I'm listening to them. 응, 난 그걸 듣고 있어.

③ I enjoy listening to music. 나는 음악 듣는 것을 즐겨.

④ No, your friends can't visit.
아니, 네 친구들은 방문할 수 없어.

⑤ Please turn the volume down. 소리 좀 줄여줘.

해설 심한 소음(terrible noise) 때문에 남자는 여자가 하는 말을 잘 알아듣지 못하는 상황이므로, 음악 소리를 낮춰 달라고 말할 것이다.

어휘 terrible 끔찍한, 지독한 noise 소음 listen to music 음악을 듣다 turn the volume down 소리를 낮추다(= turn down the volume)

20 ②

W: Dave, what's the matter? 데이브, 무슨 문제 있니?

M: I just heard that our science teacher is going to move to another city next month.
방금 우리 과학 선생님이 다음 달에 다른 도시로 이사를 가신다는 얘기를 들었어.

W: No way. 말도 안 돼.

M: You like her a lot, don't you?
넌 그 분을 무척 좋아하지, 그렇지 않니?

W: Yes, she's my favorite teacher. How did you find out she's moving? 응, 그 분은 내가 좋아하는 선생님이야. 그 분이 이사를 간다는 건 어떻게 알았어?

M: Another teacher told me. 다른 선생님이 내게 말씀해 주셨어.

① No news is good news. 무소식이 희소식이야.

② Another teacher told me.
다른 선생님이 내게 말씀해 주셨어.

③ I got an A on the science test.
나는 과학 시험에서 A를 받았어.

④ Yes, she's such a good teacher.
응, 그녀는 좋은 선생님이야.

⑤ She's moving to the countryside.
그녀는 시골로 이사를 가.

해설 여자가 'How ~?'로 물었으므로 남자는 방법에 대한 내용을 말해야 한다. who, when, where, what, why, how 등의 의문사로 질문하면 Yes/No로 답변할 수 없다는 것도 알아두자.

어휘 move to ~로 이동하다, 이사하다 another 다른 no way 말도 안 돼; 싫어 find out 알아내다 countryside 시골

10회 실전모의고사   본문 p.96-97

01 ①	02 ②	03 ④	04 ④	05 ⑤
06 ②	07 ④	08 ⑤	09 ③	10 ④
11 ④	12 ①	13 ④	14 ③	15 ②
16 ①	17 ③	18 ②	19 ②	20 ①

01 ①

M: I think that David's house is on this street.
내 생각에 데이비드의 집은 이 거리에 있는 것 같아.

W: He told me he lives in a two-story house. There is one window on the second floor. 그 애는 자기가 이층집에 산다고 나한테 말했어. 이층에는 창문이 하나 있고.

M: There it is. It's that house over there.
저기 있다. 저기 있는 집이 그거야.

W: No. That house has a gate. David's house doesn't have a gate.
아냐. 저 집은 대문이 있잖아. 데이비드의 집은 대문이 없어.

M: I found it. It's the one with a tree in the yard.
찾았다. 마당에 나무가 한 그루 있는 집이야.

해설 그림 정보 파악 문제는 퍼즐과 비슷하다. 대화 전체에 걸쳐 나오는 힌트를 조각조각 맞춰야만 정답을 찾을 수 있다. 데이비드의 집은 이층집이고, 이층에 창문이 하나 있고, 마당에 나무가 한 그루 있다.

어휘 street 거리, 도로 two-story house 이층집 on the second floor 이층에 over there 저쪽에 gate 대문 yard 마당

02 ②

M: Happy Mother's Day! I bought this present for you. I hope you like it. 어머니의 날을 축하해요! 제가 엄마 드리려고 이 선물을 샀어요. 좋아하셨으면 좋겠어요.

W: Wow, thank you so much. This perfume looks nice.
와, 정말 고마워. 이 향수는 멋지구나.

M: I hope you like the smell.
엄마가 그 향을 좋아하셔야 할 텐데요.

W: Let me check... Yes, it smells wonderful. Thanks, Ron. 한 번 확인해 볼게. 응, 냄새가 아주 좋구나. 고맙다. 론.

M: You're welcome, Mom. 천만에요, 엄마.

해설 남자가 Mother's Day을 기념하여 산 선물에 대해 이야기를 나누고 있다.

어휘 Mother's Day 어머니의 날 buy 사다(buy-bought-bought) present 선물 perfume 향수 smell 냄새; 냄새가 나다 check 확인하다

03 ④

W: Hello. My name is Sue Smith. I was born in the USA, but I grew up in France. I can speak English, French, and Spanish. In my free time, I like cooking and sewing. I have two older sisters. All of us like pets, so we have two dogs and three cats. We love all of our pets very much.

안녕하세요. 제 이름은 수 스미스입니다. 저는 미국에서 태어났지만 프랑스에서 자랐어요. 저는 영어, 프랑스어, 그리고 스페인어를 할 수 있습니다. 여가 시간에 저는 요리와 바느질 하는 것을 좋아해요. 저에게는 언니가 두 명 있습니다. 우리 모두는 애완동물을 좋아하기 때문에 우리는 개 두 마리와 고양이 세 마리를 기릅니다. 우리는 우리의 모든 애완동물을 무척 사랑합니다.

어휘 be born in ~에서 태어나다 grow up 자라다(grow-grew-grown) free time 여가 시간, 자유 시간 sewing 바느질 pet 애완동물

04 ④

M: It's almost the weekend. Do you have any plans?
이제 곧 주말이다. 넌 계획이 있니?

W: Yes, I do. I'm going to visit the beauty shop.
응, 있어. 난 미용실에 갈 거야.

M: Are you going to get a perm? 너 파마하려고?

W: No, I'm just going to get a haircut. What are you going to do? 아니, 그냥 머리만 자르려고. 넌 뭘 할 거니?

M: I'm not sure. I might visit a museum or art gallery.
잘 모르겠어. 아마도 박물관이나 미술관을 방문할 것 같아.

W: That sounds fun. I hope you enjoy the weekend.
재미있겠는데. 네가 주말을 즐기길 바랄게.

해설 미용실은 beauty shop, beauty salon, beauty parlor 등 여러 이름으로 나올 수 있다. 박물관, 미술관 등은 남자의 계획이다.

어휘 beauty shop 미용실 get a perm 파마하다 get a haircut 머리를 자르다, 이발하다 art gallery 미술관

05 ⑤

M: We're going to see a movie tonight, right?
우리는 오늘 밤에 영화 보는 거지, 그렇지?

W: That's right. It starts at eight o'clock.
맞아. 8시에 영화가 시작해.

M: Really? But my work finishes around seven thirty.
정말? 하지만 난 7시 30분 정도에 일이 끝나는데.

W: That's all right. It takes ten minutes to get to the movie theater by bus.
괜찮아. 영화관까지 가는 데 버스로 10분 정도 걸려.

M: Then shall we meet at the theater at seven forty-five?
그럼 우리 7시 45분에 영화관 앞에서 만날까?

W: Okay. I'll see you then.
좋아. 그때 보자.

어휘 see a movie 영화를 보다 around 약, ~쯤 get to ~에 도착하다 movie theater 영화관 by bus 버스를 타고

06 ②

M: It's time for the national weather forecast. Right now, there's rainy weather all over the country. But at night, the temperature is going to get colder. There will be snow in Seoul, Incheon, and Daejeon tomorrow morning. Daegu and Gwangju will get some rain all day long tomorrow. And there will be cloudy skies in Busan and on Jeju Island.

전국적인 일기예보 시간입니다. 지금 현재 전국에 걸쳐 비가 오고 있습니다. 하지만 밤이 되면 기온이 더 추워지겠습니다. 내일 아침에는 서울과 인천, 그리고 대전에 눈이 내리겠습니다. 대구와 광주는 내일 하루 종일 비가 내리겠습니다. 그리고 부산과 제주도에는 하늘에 구름이 끼겠습니다.

해설 'Daegu ~ all day long, tomorrow.'에서 대구는 하루 종일 비가 온다고 했으므로 오전에도 비가 올 것이다.

어휘 all over the country 전국적으로 temperature 온도, 기온 get colder 더 추워지다 all day long 하루 종일

07 ④

M: I have a bad headache and don't feel well. I need some medicine.
난 두통이 심해서 몸 상태가 좋지 않아. 나는 약이 필요해.

W: What did you do yesterday? 넌 어제 뭘 했니?

M: I played soccer with my friends in the rain. We played for around two hours.
난 내 친구들과 빗속에서 축구를 했어. 우리는 약 2시간 동안 경기를 했어.

W: You shouldn't do that. Take a warm bath, or you'll get sick.
넌 그러면 안 돼. 따뜻한 물에 목욕해봐, 그렇지 않으면 병날 거야.

M: Okay. I won't do that again in the future.
알았어. 앞으로는 그러지 않을게.

해설 여자의 마지막 대사에 주목한다. 'You shouldn't do that.'이라는 충고에 이어 해결책을 제시했다. '명령문~, or...'는 '~해라, 그렇지 않으면 ...할 것이다'라는 의미이다.

어휘 have a bad headache 두통이 심하다 feel well 건강 상태가 좋다 medicine 약 in the rain 비를 맞으며 take a bath 목욕하다 get sick 병에 걸리다 in the future 앞으로는, 장차

08 ⑤

M: What are you reading? 넌 뭘 읽고 있니?

W: I'm reading an article about a famous Korean designer.
난 유명한 한국인 디자이너에 대한 기사를 읽고 있어.

M: Are you interested in fashion? 넌 패션에 관심 있니?

W: Yes, I am. I want to be a fashion designer. I'd love to design all kinds of clothes.
응, 그래. 난 패션 디자이너가 되고 싶어. 나는 온갖 종류의 옷들을 디자인하고 싶어.

M: I like design, but I want to design houses.
나도 디자인을 좋아하지만, 난 주택을 디자인하고 싶어.

W: I see. You want to be an architect then.
알겠어. 그럼 넌 건축가가 되고 싶은 거구나.

해설 여자와 남자의 장래희망을 구분하여 듣는다.

어휘 article 기사 be interested in ~에 관심이 있다 all kinds of 모든 종류의, 온갖 architect 건축가

09 ③

W: This is my favorite month of the year. The weather is sunny and clear, so I can go to the beach during this month. I like to swim and get a suntan there. However, the temperature often gets really high during this month. So we must stay inside when it's too hot.

이것은 제가 일 년 중 가장 좋아하는 달입니다. 날씨가 화창하고 맑기 때문에, 저는 이 달에 바닷가에 갈 수 있습니다. 저는 해변에서 수영을 하고 일광욕하는 것을 좋아합니다. 하지만 이 달에는 종종 온도가 정말 높이 올라가기도 합니다. 그래서 우리는 너무 뜨거울 때는 실내에 있어야 합니다.

해설 바닷가에서 수영과 일광욕을 즐기기에 좋고, 기온이 높은 계절은 여름이다. 선택지 중 여름에 해당하는 달은 8월이다.

어휘 get a suntan 일광욕하다, 피부를 태우다 stay inside 실내에 머물다

10 ④

[*Telephone rings.*] [전화벨이 울린다.]

W: Hello. This is Sam's Restaurant. How may I help you? 여보세요. 샘스 레스토랑입니다. 무엇을 도와드릴까요?

M: Hi. I had lunch there today. But I think I left my bag there. 안녕하세요. 제가 오늘 거기서 점심을 먹었거든요. 그런데 그곳에 제 가방을 두고 온 것 같아요.

W: What does your bag look like?

손님의 가방이 어떻게 생겼나요?

M: It's a blue and white backpack. There are three books in it. 파란색과 흰색이 섞인 배낭입니다. 안에는 책이 세 권 들어 있어요.

W: Does it have your name on it?
가방에 손님의 이름이 적혀 있나요?

M: Yes, there's a card in the backpack with my name on it. My name is Ted Peterson. 네, 배낭 안에 제 이름이 적힌 카드가 들어 있어요. 제 이름은 테드 피터슨입니다.

해설 전화 목적을 묻는 문제에는 주로 'How may I help you?' 뒤에 목적이 바로 등장한다.

어휘 leave 놓아 두다(leave-left-left) backpack 배낭

11 ④

W: I love these flower-shaped earrings. They look beautiful.
저는 이 꽃 모양 귀걸이가 좋네요. 아름답거든요.

M: Many of our customers love these earrings.
많은 저희 고객 분들이 이 귀걸이를 좋아해요.

W: How much do they cost? 그건 가격이 얼마죠?

M: They cost seven dollars each. 각각 7달러입니다.

W: That's not bad. I'd like to have two pairs of them.
나쁘지 않네요. 저는 귀걸이 두 쌍을 사겠어요.

M: That will be fourteen dollars. 그럼 14달러가 되겠습니다.

W: Okay. Here is twenty dollars. 네. 여기 20달러요.

해설 구두, 귀걸이와 같이 한 쌍으로 된 상품은 낱개로 판매되지 않는다. 'They cost seven dollars each.'에서 7달러는 한 쌍의 가격이다. 이것을 귀걸이가 한 짝의 가격으로 이해해서는 안 된다.

어휘 flower-shaped 꽃 모양의 earrings (한 쌍의) 귀걸이 customer 고객 each 각각 two pairs of 두 쌍의

12 ①

M: I'm bored. I think I'm going to see a movie today.
난 지루해. 내 생각에 오늘은 영화를 봐야 할 것 같아.

W: What are you thinking of watching? 넌 뭘 볼 생각이니?

M: There's a new comedy at the theater. I want to watch it. 극장에서 새 코미디 영화를 상영하고 있어. 난 그걸 보고 싶어.

W: I've heard about that movie. I heard it is fun.
나도 그 영화에 대해 들었어. 재미있다고 들었어.

M: Really? Would you like to go with me?
정말? 나랑 함께 갈래?

W: I'd love to, but I have to finish writing a book report. 나도 그러고 싶지만, 독후감 쓰는 것을 끝내야 해.

해설 'I'd love to, but ~'은 상대방의 기분이 상하지 않게 거절할 때 쓰는 표현이다.

어휘 bored 지루한 comedy 코미디, 희극 theater 영화관, 극장 fun 재미있는, 즐거운 I'd love to, but 나도 그러고 싶지만 book report 독후감

13 ④

W: Why is there a red circle on the calendar?
달력에 왜 빨간 동그라미가 있는 거니?

M: Oh, no. It's for Sumi's birthday, but I forgot about it. 아, 안돼. 그건 수미의 생일을 표시한 건데, 내가 잊어버리고 말았어.

W: Today is October eleventh, and the red circle is on October thirteenth. 오늘은 10월 11일이고, 달력에 있는 빨간 동그라미는 10월 13일에 쳐져 있어.

M: Ah, you are right. It's only two days from today.
아, 네 말이 맞아. 오늘로부터 고작 이틀 후잖아.

W: Are you going to buy a present for her?
그 애한테 선물을 사줄 거니?

M: Yes, I am. But I need to think about what to buy.
응, 그래. 하지만 뭘 살지 생각을 해봐야 해.

해설 오늘은 10월 11일이고, 수미의 생일은 이틀 뒤인 10월 13일이다.

어휘 circle 동그라미, 원 on the calendar 달력에 forget 잊다 (forget-forgot-forgotten) present 선물

14 ③

M: Pardon me. Are you from around here?
실례합니다. 이 근처에 사시나요?

W: Yes, I am. Are you looking for something?
네, 그래요. 뭘 찾고 계신가요?

M: Yes. Do you know where the bakery is?
네. 빵집이 어디 있는지 아세요?

W: Sure. Go straight toward Western Avenue. That's two blocks from here. 네. 웨스턴 가로 직진하세요. 여기서 두 블록 떨어져 있어요.

M: All right. Should I turn left or right then? 알겠습니다. 그 다음에 좌회전해야 하나요, 우회전해야 하나요?

W: Turn left. Then walk past the grocery store. The bakery is between the grocery store and the dry cleaner's. 좌회전하세요. 그리고 식료품점을 지나가세요. 빵집은 식료품점과 세탁소 사이에 있어요.

M: Thank you for your help. 도와주셔서 감사합니다.

어휘 from around here 이 근처 출신인 walk past ~을 지나쳐서 걷다 dry cleaner's 세탁소, 드라이클리닝점

15 ②

M: You can play this indoors or outdoors. This is an Olympic sport. You need to have five people on each team. The players take a large ball with hands and throw it into a net to score points. They have to pass the ball or make it hit the floor to move with it.

당신은 이것을 실내 혹은 실외에서 즐길 수 있습니다. 이것은 올림픽 경기 종목입니다. 당신은 각 팀에 5명의 사람이 필요합니다. 선수들은 큰 공을 손으로 잡고 골대 안으로 던져서 점수를 얻습니다. 그들은 공을 가지고 이동하기 위해 공을 패스하거나 바닥에 튕겨야 합니다.

16 ①

M: Tina, you <u>look</u> <u>disappointed</u>. 티나, 너 실망한 표정인데.

W: I had a really <u>bad</u> <u>day</u>. 난 정말 오늘 일진이 안 좋았어.

M: What <u>went</u> <u>wrong</u>? Tell me about it.
무슨 문제가 있었어? 나한테 말해 봐.

W: I <u>left</u> my <u>purse</u> on the <u>bus</u> while I was coming home. 난 집에 오는 동안에 버스에 지갑을 놓고 내렸어.

M: That's terrible. Did you call the bus company?
정말 안됐구나. 버스 회사에 전화해 봤어?

W: Yes, I did. But they said nobody saw it.
응, 했어. 하지만 아무도 그걸 못 봤대.

해설 남자의 대사 'What went wrong? Tell me about it.'에 이어지는 여자의 설명을 듣고 상황을 떠올려 본다.

어휘 disappointed 실망한 have a bad day 일진이 사납다 go wrong 일이 잘못되다 purse 지갑 while ~하는 동안

17 ③

M: Karen, <u>where</u> are you going <u>in</u> such a <u>hurry</u>?
캐런, 넌 어디를 그렇게 급하게 가니?

W: I am going to <u>see</u> my <u>mom</u> right now.
지금 당장 우리 엄마를 만나야 해.

M: Is there a problem? 무슨 문제 있어?

W: No. I just <u>got</u> an A+ on my math <u>test</u>. I want to tell my mother about it. 아니. 내가 방금 수학 시험에서 A+를 받았거든. 엄마한테 그 얘기를 해주려고.

M: <u>Congratulations</u>. You <u>studied</u> so <u>hard</u> for that test.
축하해. 넌 그 시험을 위해 공부를 열심히 했잖아.

W: Thanks. My mother will be <u>happy</u> like me.
고마워. 우리 엄마도 나처럼 기쁠 거야.

해설 여자가 수학 시험에서 A+를 받은 상황이므로 여자의 기쁜 감정을 읽을 수 있다.

어휘 in such a hurry 그렇게 급하게 math 수학 like ~처럼

18 ②

① W: I'm really <u>worried about</u> my health.
난 내 건강이 정말 걱정돼

   M: <u>Take</u> this <u>medicine</u>. Then, you'll <u>get better</u>.
이 약을 먹어. 그러면 나아질 거야.

② W: <u>What does</u> your brother <u>look like</u>?
네 남동생은 어떻게 생겼니?

   M: He really likes to <u>play</u> computer <u>games</u>.
그는 정말로 컴퓨터 게임하는 걸 좋아해.

③ W: Can I <u>call</u> you <u>later</u>? 제가 나중에 전화 드릴까요?

   M: Sure. Here is my <u>number</u>.
물론이죠. 여기 제 번호가 있습니다.

④ W: Sally <u>won first place</u> in the contest.
샐리가 대회에서 일등상을 탔어.

   M: <u>Good for her</u>. She must be happy.
잘됐구나. 그 애는 분명히 기쁠 거야.

⑤ W: I'm sorry, but you can't <u>bring food</u> into the museum.
죄송하지만 박물관 안으로 음식물을 가지고 들어가실 수 없습니다.

   M: I'm sorry. I didn't know that. 죄송해요. 몰랐어요.

해설 'What does ~ look like?'는 생김새를 묻는 질문이다. 외모, 키 등으로 답변해야 한다.

어휘 worried about ~을 걱정하는 take medicine 약을 먹다 get better 나아지다, 호전되다 call later 나중에 전화하다 win first place 일등을 하다, 우승하다 Good for her[you, him]. (칭찬을 하며) 잘했어.

19 ②

M: <u>Winter vacation</u> is coming soon. Are you planning to go anywhere? 겨울방학이 곧 다가오고 있어. 넌 어딘가에 갈 계획이 있니?

W: No, I'm going to <u>rest</u> and <u>read</u> books at home. How about you? 아니, 난 집에서 쉬면서 책을 읽을 거야. 넌 어때?

M: I'm going to <u>visit Australia</u> with my family.
나는 가족과 함께 호주에 갈 거야.

W: That <u>sounds fun</u>. Are you going with a <u>tour guide</u> there? 재미있겠다. 그곳에 여행 가이드와 함께 가니?

M: <u>No</u>, we won't. My sister lived there for a year. So she will <u>show</u> us <u>around</u>. 아니. 내 여동생이 그곳에서 1년간 살았었거든. 그래서 여동생이 우리를 구경시켜 줄 거야.

W: I hope you have fun there.
네가 거기서 재미있는 시간을 보내길 바랄게.

① Yes, I remember your sister. 그래, 난 네 여동생을 기억해.

② I hope you have fun there.
네가 거기서 재미있는 시간을 보내길 바랄게.

③ My sister lives at my home. 내 여동생은 우리 집에 살아.

④ She's studying in Korea now.
그녀는 지금 한국에서 공부하고 있어.

⑤ No, I didn't go there last year.
아니, 나는 작년에 그곳에 가지 않았어.

해설 남자의 여행 계획을 듣고 할 수 있는 말은 ②가 적절하다.

어휘 rest 휴식하다; 휴식 tour guide 여행 가이드 show somebody around ~을 구경시켜 주다 have fun 재미있게 놀다

20 ①

M: Do you know <u>where we are</u> right now?
넌 우리가 지금 어디 있는지 아니?

W: No. I think we're <u>lost</u>. 아니. 우린 길을 잃은 것 같아.

M: On this <u>map</u>, there should be a <u>subway station</u> around here.
이 지도를 보면 이 근처에 지하철역이 있어야 하거든.

W: I can't see one anywhere. What should we do?
지하철역은 어디에도 안 보여. 우린 어떻게 해야 할까?

M: We can keep looking for the subway or just take a taxi.

우린 계속해서 지하철역을 찾거나 아니면 그냥 택시를 탈 수 있어.

W: Let's take a taxi. I'm very tired.

택시를 타자. 난 무척 피곤해.

① Let's take a taxi. I'm very tired.

택시를 타자. 난 무척 피곤해.

② Yes, we came here by subway.

응, 우리는 여기에 지하철로 왔어.

③ I can't see anything on the map.

나는 지도에서 아무것도 안 보여.

④ No, he's not going to take a taxi here.

아니, 그는 여기서 택시를 타지는 않을 거야.

⑤ How about taking the subway instead?

대신 지하철을 타는 게 어떨까?

해설 두 가지 선택권(계속 지하철역을 찾거나 택시를 타거나) 중에 하나를 고른 ①이 적절하다.

어휘 be lost 길을 잃다, 행방불명이 되다 subway station 지하철역 around here 이 근처에 take a taxi 택시를 타다 instead 대신에

11회 실전모의고사

본문 p.106-107

01 ③	02 ④	03 ④	04 ③	05 ②
06 ④	07 ④	08 ③	09 ②	10 ②
11 ③	12 ①	13 ④	14 ①	15 ④
16 ④	17 ②	18 ⑤	19 ②	20 ⑤

01 ③

W: This is a useful tool. People use this when they need to cut something. They can cut paper and cloth with this. Some people also use this in the kitchen when they cut meat and vegetables. Hairdressers use this to cut hair.

이것은 유용한 도구예요. 사람들은 무언가를 자를 때 이것을 이용하지요. 그들은 이것을 가지고 종이와 천을 자를 수 있어요. 어떤 사람들은 주방에서 고기나 채소를 자를 때 이것을 써요. 미용사들은 이것을 이용해서 머리카락을 잘라요.

어휘 useful 유용한 cloth 옷감 meat 고기 vegetable 채소 hairdresser 미용사

02 ④

M: Good morning, listeners. I'm Mark Smith, and I've got today's weather report for you. This morning, it is going to be foggy. So be careful when you are driving. In the afternoon, there will be clear, sunny skies. You can enjoy a pleasant day today.

안녕하세요, 청취자 여러분. 저는 마크 스미스이고, 여러분께 오늘의 날씨를 알려드리겠습니다. 오늘 아침은 안개가 끼겠습니다. 따라서 운전할 때 조심하셔야 합니다. 오후에는 맑고 화창한 하늘을 보이겠습니다. 오늘은 쾌적한 날을 즐기실 수 있겠군요.

어휘 foggy 안개 낀 careful 조심하는 pleasant 쾌적한, 즐거운

03 ④

M: Hello, everyone. I'd like to introduce my sister to you. Her name is Mary, and she's nine years old. She goes to Eastern Elementary School. Her favorite subject is science, but she also loves English and music. She doesn't like math. We get along well, and we often go rollerblading together.

안녕하세요, 여러분. 저는 여러분께 제 여동생을 소개하려고 해요. 동생의 이름은 메리이고 아홉 살이에요. 그 애는 이스턴 초등학교에 다녀요. 가장 좋아하는 과목은 과학이지만, 영어와 음악 역시 아주 좋아해요. 그 애는 수학은 좋아하지 않아요. 저희는 친하게 지내고 종종 함께 롤러블레이드를 타요.

어휘 subject 과목 get along well 잘 지내다 rollerblade (롤러스케이트의 일종)

04 ③

M: Anna, can you give me some help with my math homework?

애나, 너는 내 수학 숙제를 좀 도와줄 수 있니?

W: I'm sorry, but I can't. I have to see the dentist now. When do you need to finish it?

미안하지만, 난 못해. 나는 지금 치과에 가야 해. 너는 그것을 언제 끝내야 하니?

M: I have to give it to the teacher next Monday.

다음 주 월요일에 선생님께 제출해야 돼.

W: Can I help you with it on Saturday?

내가 토요일에 그걸 도와줘도 될까?

M: Of course. Thanks. 당연하지. 고마워.

W: No problem. 괜찮아.

해설 여자가 지금 할 일, 남자가 월요일에 할 일, 여자가 토요일에 할 일이 차례대로 등장하므로 구분하여 듣는다.

어휘 dentist 치과 의사 No problem. 그럼요. 괜찮아요. 문제 없어요. (고마움, 미안함, 부탁 등에 대한 대꾸)

05 ②

M: What are you doing? 너는 무엇을 하고 있어?

W: I'm reading a book. 난 책을 읽고 있어.

M: You are always reading. Why do you like reading so much?

넌 항상 독서를 하는구나. 너는 책 읽는 것을 왜 그렇게 좋아해?

W: I can learn from some books. It is also fun to read interesting stories. 나는 책에서 배울 수가 있거든. 흥미로운 이야기를 읽는 것 또한 재미있지.

M: I don't read that much. It's not interesting to me.

나는 책을 별로 읽지 않아. 내겐 재미있지 않거든.

W: Try this book. I think you'll like it.
이 책을 읽어 봐. 너도 그걸 좋아할 것 같아.

해설 여자는 배움과 즐거움을 위해 독서를 즐긴다고 말했다. 소설, 공부 방법 등은 함정으로 주어졌다.

어휘 interesting 재미있는 try 해보다, 시도하다, 노력하다

06 ④

M: Tomorrow is New Year's Day. Let's go to see the sunrise at the beach.
내일이 새해 첫날이에요. 우리 해변에 가서 해돋이를 봐요.

W: That sounds fine. How can we go there?
그거 좋겠어요. 우리가 거기까지 어떻게 갈 수 있을까요?

M: We can go by car. 우리는 자동차로 갈 수 있어요.

W: There will be too many cars on the road.
도로에 차가 너무 많을 거예요.

M: Then let's ride on our bikes. The beach is close to our homes.
그러면 우린 자전거를 타요. 해변이 우리 집에서 가깝잖아요.

W: That's a good idea. 그거 좋은 생각이군요.

해설 'by + 교통수단,' 'take + 교통수단'의 형태를 집중해서 듣는다. 맨 처음에 언급되는 교통수단은 정답이 아닌 경우가 많다.

어휘 New Year's Day 새해 첫날 sunrise 해돋이, 일출 too many 너무 많은 ride (on) a bike 자전거를 타다

07 ④

M: Hi. I'm looking for a scarf for my daughter.
저는 딸에게 줄 스카프를 찾고 있어요.

W: How do you like this white one? It's very fashionable.
이 흰색 스카프는 어떤가요? 아주 유행하는 거예요.

M: Thanks. I'll take it. And what about sweaters?
고마워요. 그걸 살게요. 그리고 스웨터는 어때요?

W: This sweater is very popular.
이 스웨터가 아주 인기가 많아요.

M: I don't like it that much. Can you show me something else?
그건 별로 마음에 들지 않네요. 다른 걸 보여주시겠어요?

W: Sure. Follow me this way, please.
물론이죠. 이쪽으로 저를 따라오세요.

해설 'look for'라고 말하는 사람은 주로 손님이고, 점원은 'How do you like ~?'로 의견을 묻거나 'What about ~?'으로 권유하는 말을 많이 한다.

어휘 fashionable 유행하는 popular 인기 있는 show 보여주다 follow 따라오다, 따라가다

08 ③

M: Good evening. Can I help you with something?
안녕하세요. 무엇을 도와드릴까요?

W: Yes, I need to buy five apples, please.
네, 저는 사과 다섯 개가 필요해요.

M: We're having a sale. Apples are one dollar each.
저희는 할인 중이에요. 사과 한 개당 1달러입니다.

W: Excellent. And what about broccoli? I need a package of it.
좋네요. 그리고 브로콜리는요? 저는 한 팩이 필요해요.

M: That will cost three dollars. So your total is eight dollars.
그것은 3달러예요. 따라서 손님의 합계는 8달러입니다.

W: Okay. I'd like to pay with my card.
네. 저는 신용카드로 지불하고 싶어요.

해설 남자의 마지막 말에 total, eight 등이 언급된다. 지불한 금액의 합계가 나오는지 끝까지 들어야 한다.

어휘 each 각각 package (포장용) 상자, 봉지 total 합계 pay with a card 신용카드로 지불하다

09 ②

W: Please don't change the channel now.
지금 채널을 바꾸지 말아 줘.

M: Why not? I really want to watch the baseball game live. 왜? 난 야구 경기를 생방송으로 정말 보고 싶어.

W: But the last show of Linda's Life is starting now. I can't miss it. 그렇지만 '린다의 인생' 마지막 회가 이제 시작한단 말이야. 난 그걸 꼭 봐야 해.

M: Didn't you hear the news? It's not going to be on TV this week.
너 뉴스 못 들었어? 그건 이번 주에는 방송되지 않을 거야.

W: Oh, no. I'm so disappointed. I have been waiting to see this show all week. 아, 안돼. 난 정말 실망했어. 일주일 내내 그 프로그램을 기다렸거든.

해설 여자의 마지막 말에 등장한 disappointed처럼 심정을 나타내는 단어가 직접 언급되는 경우가 많다.

어휘 channel (텔레비전, 라디오의) 채널 live 생방송으로, 생중계로 last show 최종회 miss 놓치다 hear the news 소식을 듣다 disappointed 실망한, 낙담한 all week 일주일 내내

10 ②

M: I'm getting hungry. I want to have lunch.
난 점점 배가 고파. 점심을 먹고 싶어.

W: So do I, but it's only eleven twenty now.
나도 그렇긴 하지만 지금 11시 20분밖에 안됐어.

M: And lunchtime starts at noon.
게다가 점심시간은 12시에 시작해.

W: I can't wait for forty minutes.
난 40분은 못 기다리겠어.

M: We don't have a choice. We can't eat during class.
우린 선택의 여지가 없어. 우리는 수업 시간에 먹어선 안돼.

해설 여자의 첫 대사에 now와 함께 현재 시각이 언급된다. 12시는 점심시간이 시작하는 시각이다.

11 ③

M: I just got tickets for the Dreamstars concert.
나는 드림스타스 콘서트 티켓이 있어.

W: Do you like that group? Their dancing is terrible.
넌 그 그룹을 좋아하니? 그들의 춤은 형편없어.

M: I don't care about the dancing. I like the words to their songs.
난 춤은 신경 쓰지 않아. 난 그들의 가사를 좋아해.

W: Those are okay. And I think the lead singer has a nice voice.
가사는 괜찮지. 그리고 리드보컬의 목소리가 좋은 것 같아.

M: You can go with me if you want.
네가 원한다면 나랑 같이 가도 돼.

해설 좋아하는 이유를 찾아야 하므로 남자의 대사 중 like가 포함된 문장에 주목한다. 춤, 목소리 관련 선택지는 함정이다.

어휘 terrible 형편없는, 끔찍한 care about ~에 마음을 쓰다 word (노래의) 가사 lead singer 리드 보컬 voice 목소리

12 ①

W: Hey, Tim, how are you doing?
얘, 팀. 너 어떻게 지내?

M: Good. I heard that you moved to a new place.
잘 지내. 나는 네가 새 집으로 이사했다고 들었어.

W: That's right. My new apartment is near our school.
맞아. 나의 새로운 아파트는 우리 학교 근처에 있어.

M: That's great. Why don't you have a housewarming party? 그거 잘됐다. 너 집들이를 하는 게 어때?

W: I was thinking about that. Are you free on Saturday?
나도 그 생각을 하고 있었어. 너 토요일에 시간 있어?

해설 남자는 집들이에 대한 제안을 했고, 여자는 그 제안을 받아들여 남자를 초대하고 있다.

어휘 hear 듣다(hear-heard-heard) housewarming party 집들이

13 ④

[Cellphone rings.] [휴대폰이 울린다.]

W: Hi, Jim. Can you do me a big favor?
안녕, 짐. 내 어려운 부탁을 들어줄 수 있니?

M: I'll try. What do you need?
노력해 볼게. 뭐가 필요해?

W: My friend Susan is in the hospital. I need to visit her there now. 내 친구인 수잔이 병원에 있어. 나는 지금 그곳에 있는 그 애를 방문해야 해.

M: So do you want me to look after your dog?
그래서 내가 네 개를 돌봐주길 원하는 거야?

W: Yes, please. Can you take him for a walk and feed

him at five?
응, 부탁해. 산책을 시켜주고 5시에는 먹이를 줄래?

M: Sure. I'll take good care of him.
당연하지. 내가 잘 보살펴 줄게.

해설 남자의 말 'So do you want me to ~?'에 정답이 드러나며, 이어서 여자는 구체적인 내용을 덧붙이고 있다.

어휘 do somebody a favor ~의 부탁을 들어주다 look after ~을 돌보다 take somebody for a walk ~을 산책하러 데리고 가다 feed 먹이를 주다 take care of ~을 돌보다

14 ①

① There is a boy in front of the house.
집 앞에 소년이 한 명 있다.

② There is a dog in the yard by the house.
집 옆 마당에 개 한 마리가 있다.

③ There is a tree in front of the house.
집 앞에 나무 한 그루가 있다.

④ There is a car in front of the house.
집 앞에 차가 한 대 있다.

⑤ There are two children next to the house.
집 옆에 아이 두 명이 있다.

어휘 in front of ~의 앞에 yard 마당 by ~옆에 next to ~옆에 child 아이 (튀 children)

15 ④

M: Lucy, we have to talk about the school festival. When do you have time to meet? 루시, 우린 학교 축제에 대해 이야기해야 해. 너는 언제 만날 시간이 있니?

W: How about this Wednesday? 이번 주 수요일 어때?

M: Sorry, but I have a violin lesson on that day. Is Thursday fine with you?
미안하지만 나는 그날 바이올린 수업이 있어. 목요일은 괜찮아?

W: Let me think... I have time after school then.
생각 좀 해볼게. 그날 방과 후에 시간이 있어.

M: Sounds good. Shall we meet in the school cafeteria after school? 좋아. 우리 방과 후에 학교 식당에서 만날까?

W: That's perfect. I'll see you then.
아주 좋아. 그날 보자.

해설 When으로 시작하는 질문이나 특정 요일이 포함된 질문에 대한 응답에 집중한다.

어휘 school cafeteria 학교[교내] 식당 perfect 완벽한

16 ④

M: Mina, why are you looking under the sofa?
미나야, 너는 왜 소파 아래를 쳐다보고 있어?

W: I lost my key, so I'm trying to find it.
저는 열쇠를 잃어버려서 그걸 찾는 중이에요.

M: Do you think it's in the living room?
너는 열쇠가 거실에 있다고 생각하니?

W: I'm not sure. Can you check in the kitchen for me?
저는 잘 모르겠어요. 저를 위해 부엌을 확인해 주시겠어요?

잘 모르겠어요. 부엌 안을 확인해 주실래요?

M: Sure. You <u>keep</u> <u>looking</u> in here, and I'll <u>take</u> <u>a</u> <u>look</u> in there. 물론이지. 넌 여기에서 계속 찾아보렴, 그러면 나는 저기로 가서 찾아 볼게.

W: Wait a minute. I found it! Here it is. 잠깐만요. 제가 찾았어요! 여기 있네요.

해설 여자의 말인 'Can you ~?'에 부탁하는 내용이 있는데, kitchen만 듣고 ⑤를 고르지 않도록 주의한다.

어휘 lose 잃어버리다(lose-lost-lost) keep -ing 계속해서 ~하다 take a look ~을 (한 번) 보다 find 찾다, 발견하다(find-found-found)

17 ②

M: Welcome to the Smith Agency. Can I help you? 스미스 에이전시에 오신 걸 환영합니다. 제가 도와드릴까요?

W: Yes, please. I need to <u>find</u> an <u>apartment</u>. 네, 도와주세요. 저는 아파트를 찾아야 해요.

M: Which <u>area</u> would you like to <u>live in</u>? 어느 지역에 살기를 원하시나요?

W: I need to live <u>near</u> Central Middle School. I <u>teach</u> there. 저는 센트럴 중학교 근처에 살아야 해요. 제가 그곳에서 가르치거든요.

M: I see. There are two apartments there. 알겠습니다. 그곳에 두 개의 아파트가 있어요.

W: That sounds good. Can you <u>tell</u> me <u>more</u> about them? 좋아요. 거기에 대해 좀 더 말씀해 주시겠어요?

해설 여자가 아파트에 대한 정보를 구하기 위해 찾아간 곳이므로 남자는 부동산 중개인이다. 여자의 직업인 교사와 구분하여 듣는다.

어휘 agency 대리점, 대행사 area 지역

18 ⑤

① M: <u>When</u> did you <u>move</u> to Incheon? 너는 언제 인천으로 이사했어?

W: I moved here <u>five</u> years <u>ago</u>. 나는 5년 전에 여기로 이사 왔어.

② M: <u>What</u> does your older sister <u>do</u>? 너희 언니의 직업이 뭐야?

W: She <u>works</u> as a flight attendant. 그녀는 승무원으로 일해.

③ M: Do you <u>have</u> a dollar? 너 1달러 있어?

W: <u>Yes</u>, here you are. 응, 여기 있어.

④ M: <u>What</u> are you <u>doing</u> now? 너 지금 뭐 하고 있어?

W: I'm <u>washing</u> the <u>dishes</u>. 난 설거지를 하고 있어.

⑤ M: <u>What</u> do you <u>think</u> about that book? 너는 그 책에 대해 어떻게 생각해?

W: I read <u>one</u> <u>hour</u> every day. 나는 매일 한 시간씩 책을 읽어.

해설 ⑤의 질문에 대한 응답으로는 'I think it's interesting.' 'It was boring.' 등이 적절하다. 'I read one hour every day.'는

빈도를 묻는 'How often ~?'에 대한 응답이다.

19 ②

W: George, can you please <u>help</u> me <u>carry</u> this bag? It's too <u>heavy</u>. 조지, 내가 이 가방을 옮기는 걸 도와주겠니? 이건 너무 무거워.

M: <u>Which</u> bag should I carry? The one <u>by</u> the <u>door</u>? 어떤 가방을 제가 옮겨야 하죠? 문 옆에 있는 거요?

W: No, the one <u>on</u> the <u>table</u>. 아니, 탁자 위에 있는 거.

M: Okay. Let me <u>pick</u> it <u>up</u>. Wow, it is heavy. 네. 제가 들게요. 우와, 무겁네요.

W: Thanks so much. Can you <u>take</u> it <u>to</u> my <u>car</u>, please? 정말 고맙구나. 그것을 내 차에 가져가 줄래?

M: Sure, I can do that. 물론, 그렇게 할 수 있죠.

① Pardon me. 실례합니다.
② Sure, I can do that. 물론, 그렇게 할 수 있죠.
③ No, I don't have a car. 아니, 저는 자동차가 없어요.
④ This bag really weighs a lot. 이 가방은 정말 무게가 많이 나가요.
⑤ How about driving me home? 저를 집까지 태워다 주시는 건 어때요?

해설 여자가 'Can you ~?'로 요청을 했으니 승낙하거나 거절하는 응답이 알맞다.

어휘 carry 나르다 pick up ~을 집다, 들어올리다 weigh 무게가 ~이다

20 ⑤

W: How about <u>going</u> <u>to</u> the <u>concert</u> with me tonight? 오늘 밤에 나와 함께 콘서트에 가는 건 어때?

M: I would <u>love</u> <u>to</u> go there. <u>What</u> <u>time</u> will it <u>end</u>? 나도 거기에 가고 싶어. 그건 몇 시에 끝나?

W: It will <u>finish</u> around ten <u>at</u> <u>night</u>. 밤 10시쯤에 끝날 거야.

M: I can't <u>stay</u> <u>out</u> <u>late</u>. My parents want me to be home early. 나는 늦게까지 있을 수 없어. 우리 부모님께선 내가 집에 일찍 오길 원하셔.

W: Why don't you <u>call</u> and <u>ask</u> them? 부모님께 전화해서 여쭤보는 건 어때?

M: I'm sorry, but they're going to say no. 미안하지만 그분들은 안 된다고 하실 거야.

① Yes, you may go there. 응, 너는 거기 가도 돼.
② I saw that concert last night. 난 어젯밤에 그 콘서트를 봤어.
③ How much do the tickets cost? 티켓이 얼마니?
④ The concert is going to start late. 콘서트는 늦게 시작할 거야.
⑤ I'm sorry, but they're going to say no. 미안하지만 그분들은 안 된다고 하실 거야.

해설 콘서트 정보에 대한 이야기에서 부모님에게 허락을 받는 이야기

로 화제가 전환되었다. 거기에 어울리는 응답은 ⑤이다.

<u>어휘</u> stay out late 늦게까지 외출하다 say no 거절하다

12회 실전모의고사　본문 p.116-117

01 ②	**02** ③	**03** ③	**04** ②	**05** ③
06 ②	**07** ③	**08** ②	**09** ⑤	**10** ③
11 ③	**12** ③	**13** ⑤	**14** ⑤	**15** ①
16 ③	**17** ②	**18** ②	**19** ④	**20** ⑤

01 ②

① A woman is <u>reading</u> a <u>magazine</u>.
한 여자가 잡지를 읽고 있다.

② A woman is <u>painting</u> a <u>picture</u>.
한 여자가 그림을 그리고 있다.

③ A woman is <u>making</u> a <u>sandwich</u>.
한 여자가 샌드위치를 만들고 있다.

④ A woman is <u>playing</u> a <u>game</u>.
한 여자가 게임을 하고 있다.

⑤ A woman is <u>drinking</u> a cup of <u>tea</u>.
한 여자가 차 한 잔을 마시고 있다.

<u>어휘</u> read a magazine 잡지를 읽다 paint a picture 그림을 그리다 play a game 게임을 하다 a cup of tea 차 한 잔

02 ③

W: Good evening, everyone. Here's the <u>weather</u> <u>report</u> for the <u>weekend</u>. It's <u>raining</u> heavily right <u>now</u>. But the rain will <u>stop</u> later <u>tonight</u>. Tomorrow, on <u>Saturday</u>, we'll have <u>clear</u> <u>skies</u> all day long. On <u>Sunday</u>, it's going to be <u>cloudy</u> during the day. It will start raining again in the evening.

안녕하세요, 여러분. 주말 날씨 정보를 알려 드리겠습니다. 현재 비가 세차게 내리고 있습니다. 하지만 비는 오늘 밤 늦게 그치겠습니다. 내일, 토요일에는 하루 종일 맑은 하늘을 볼 수 있겠습니다. 일요일에는 낮 동안에 구름이 끼겠습니다. 저녁에는 다시 비가 내리기 시작하겠습니다.

<u>해설</u> '맑다'라고 표현할 때는 sunny, have clear skies 등의 표현을 사용할 수 있다.

<u>어휘</u> rain heavily 비가 심하게 내리다 all day long 하루 종일 during the day 낮 동안에

03 ③

M: Excuse me, but do you need some help?
실례합니다만, 도움이 필요하신가요?

W: Yes, I do. I want to <u>park</u> my <u>bike</u> here, but I don't know <u>how</u> to <u>use</u> this <u>machine</u>.
네, 그래요. 제 자전거를 여기에 세워 두려고 하는데, 이 기계를 어

떻게 사용하는지 모르겠어요.

M: It's easy. <u>First</u>, <u>enter</u> any four <u>numbers</u>. That's your <u>password</u>. <u>Then</u>, <u>put</u> two thousand won <u>into</u> the <u>machine</u>. That's it. 그건 쉬워요. 먼저 네 자리 숫자를 입력하세요. 그게 당신의 비밀번호가 됩니다. 그런 다음에 기계에 2천 원을 넣으세요. 그러면 됩니다.

W: Do I need to use only one thousand won bills?
제가 천 원짜리 지폐만 사용해야 하나요?

M: No. You can use five hundred won coins or five thousand won bills, too. 아니요. 5백 원짜리 동전이나 5천 원짜리 지폐도 사용할 수 있어요.

W: Thanks so much. You really helped me a lot.
정말 고맙습니다. 제게 정말로 많은 도움을 주셨어요.

<u>해설</u> 남자가 설명 중에 2천 원을 넣으라고 말했다. 천 원, 5백 원, 5천 원 등이 함정으로 등장한다.

<u>어휘</u> park 주차하다, (자동차를) 세우다 bike 자전거 enter 입력하다, 기입하다 password 비밀번호, 패스워드 That's it. 그게 전부이다. bill 지폐 coin 동전

04 ②

M: I <u>carry</u> <u>goods</u> to people. When people <u>order</u> products <u>online</u>, I <u>take</u> them to their <u>homes</u> or <u>offices</u>. So I have to <u>visit</u> many <u>people</u> each day. During <u>holiday</u> such as Christmas and Chuseok, I <u>get</u> very <u>busy</u>. There are so many orders, so I cannot always <u>deliver</u> them on time.

저는 사람들에게 물건을 나릅니다. 사람들이 온라인으로 제품을 주문하면, 저는 그것들을 그들의 집이나 사무실로 가져다 줍니다. 그래서 저는 매일 많은 사람들을 방문해야 합니다. 크리스마스나 추석과 같은 휴일에 저는 무척 바빠집니다. 주문이 매우 많기 때문에 저는 항상 제시간에 그것들을 배달할 수만은 없습니다.

<u>해설</u> goods, products, deliver 등의 단어를 들으면 정답을 맞힐 수 있다.

<u>어휘</u> carry 나르다, 전달하다(= deliver) goods (복수 취급) 상품, 제품 order online 온라인으로 주문하다 each day 매일 on time 제시간에

05 ③

W: <u>When</u> does the <u>meeting</u> start? 회의가 언제 시작하죠?

M: It starts at <u>eleven</u> <u>thirty</u> A.M. 오전 11시 30분에 시작합니다.

W: I see. It's <u>eleven</u> <u>ten</u> <u>now</u>, so we still have twenty minutes to wait. 그렇군요. 지금이 11시 10분이니까, 우리는 아직도 20분을 기다려야 하네요.

M: That's right. So can you help me <u>make</u> some <u>copies</u>, please? It will <u>take</u> about <u>fifteen</u> <u>minutes</u> to do. 맞아요. 그럼 제가 복사하는 것을 도와 주시겠어요? 그걸 하는 데 15분 정도 걸릴 겁니다.

W: Sure. I can do that for you.
물론이죠. 제가 해드릴 수 있어요.

<u>해설</u> 'It's eleven ten now.'만 제대로 들으면 정답을 맞힐 수 있다.

회의 시작 시각인 11시 30분, 기다려야 하는 시간인 20분, 복사에 걸리는 시간인 15분이 함정으로 등장했다.

어휘 meeting 회의 make some copies 복사를 하다

06 ②

M: I'm really looking forward to the school festival.
나는 정말로 학교 축제를 기대하고 있어.

W: When is the festival? Is it on September twenty eighth or twenty ninth? I can't remember.
축제가 언제지? 9월 28일이던가, 29일이던가? 기억을 못하겠네.

M: It's not on either of those days. It's on September twenty seventh. 두 날짜 모두 아니야. 9월 27일이야.

W: Really? That's only four days from now. That's great. 정말? 지금으로부터 고작 4일 후잖아? 정말 좋은데.

M: Yeah, I can't wait for it. 응, 난 그게 무척 기다려져.

해설 선택지에 주어진 날짜는 모두 9월이므로 '달'보다는 '일'이 중요하다. 여러 숫자에 유의하여 듣는다.

어휘 look forward to ~을 고대하다 festival 축제
either of ~중 어느 한쪽

07 ③

M: What kind of movie would you like to watch?
너는 어떤 종류의 영화를 보고 싶어?

W: I love comedies more than anything else.
나는 그 무엇보다 코미디가 제일 좋아.

M: Then how about *My Summer Trip*? It's a comedy.
그러면 '마이 서머 트립'은 어때? 그건 코미디야.

W: Sure. What time does it start?
좋아. 영화가 몇 시에 시작해?

M: It starts in half an hour. 30분 후에 시작해.

W: All right. Let's get tickets and then buy some snacks. 그래. 우리 표를 사고서 간식을 좀 사자.

해설 초반 대화는 관람할 영화를 선택하기 위한 과정이다.

어휘 more than anything else 그밖에 무엇보다 더
half an hour 30분

08 ②

M: Did you watch *Animal Kingdom* on TV last night? I learned a lot about lions. 너 어젯밤에 텔레비전에서 '동물의 왕국' 봤어? 난 사자에 대해 많은 것을 배웠어.

W: Yeah, I always watch it. It's my favorite program.
응, 난 항상 그것을 봐. 그건 내가 좋아하는 프로그램이야.

M: Do you like animals? 넌 동물을 좋아하니?

W: Yes. I want to be a vet in the future. What about you? 응. 나는 미래에 수의사가 되고 싶어. 너는 어때?

M: I'm not sure. I might become a firefighter.
난 잘 모르겠어. 난 소방관이 될까 봐.

W: That's a difficult job. But I know you can do it.
그건 어려운 직업인데. 하지만 나는 네가 할 수 있다는 것을 알아.

해설 여자는 동물을 돌보는 수의사, 남자는 소방관이 되고 싶어 한다.

어휘 kingdom 왕국 on TV 텔레비전에(서) favorite 매우 좋아하는 vet 수의사(= veterinarian) in the future 장차, 미래에 firefighter 소방관

09 ⑤

M: That's strange. I can't find the strawberry ice cream. 이상하네. 딸기 맛 아이스크림을 찾을 수가 없어.

W: Do you mean the ice cream in the freezer?
너 냉동실에 있던 아이스크림을 말하는 거니?

M: Yes. I put it there last night.
응. 내가 그걸 어젯밤에 거기에 넣어 놨거든.

W: I ate it this morning. It was delicious.
내가 오늘 아침에 먹었어. 맛있더라고.

M: What? I'm so disappointed with you. Why didn't you ask me first? 뭐? 너한테 정말 실망이야. 왜 나에게 먼저 묻지 않았니?

해설 'I am so disappointed with you.'에서 남자의 감정이 드러났다.

어휘 strange 이상한 strawberry 딸기 freezer 냉동고 delicious 맛있는 disappointed with ~에 실망한

10 ③

W: Hi, Jason. How was your family trip to Thailand?
안녕, 제이슨. 태국으로 떠난 가족 여행은 어땠니?

M: We didn't have a good time.
우리는 즐거운 시간을 보내지 못했어.

W: What happened? 무슨 일이 있었어?

M: There was a big typhoon while we were there.
우리가 그곳에 있는 동안에 큰 태풍이 왔어.

W: Oh, did you have to stay in the hotel all the time?
아, 넌 줄곧 호텔에 있어야 했던 거야?

M: Yes. It was really boring. 응. 정말로 지루했어.

해설 이유를 물을 때 'Why?' 'Why not?' 등이 자주 쓰이는데, 이 대화에는 'What happened?'가 쓰였다. 이 질문에 이어지는 대답에 이유가 드러난다.

어휘 have a good time 즐거운 시간을 보내다 typhoon 태풍 while ~하는 동안 stay in the hotel 호텔에 머무르다 all the time 줄곧, 내내 boring 지루한, 따분한

11 ③

① M: What do you do in your free time?
너는 자유 시간에 뭘 하니?

W: I either read books or watch TV.
난 책을 읽거나 텔레비전을 봐.

② M: Let's go hiking this weekend.
이번 주말에 하이킹을 가자.

W: That's a wonderful idea. 아주 좋은 생각이야.

③ M: My favorite team lost the game.
내가 좋아하는 팀이 경기에서 졌어.

W: I'm sorry you lost your wallet.
네가 지갑을 잃어버렸다니, 안됐구나.

④ M: Pardon me. Do you know where an ATM is?
실례합니다. 현금지급기가 어디 있는지 아세요?

W: Yes, I do. There's one in that building.
네, 알아요. 저 건물에 하나가 있어요.

⑤ M: What would you like to eat for lunch?
너는 점심으로 뭘 먹고 싶니?

W: How about something spicy? 매운 건 어때?

해설 ③의 질문에 대한 가장 적절한 대답은 'I'm sorry to hear that.'이다. sorry만 듣고 정답으로 고르지 말아야 한다.

어휘 go hiking 하이킹을 가다 lose (게임에) 지다, (물건을) 잃어버리다(lose-lost-lost) wallet 지갑 ATM 현금 지급기(= automated teller machine) spicy 매운

12 ③

M: That's a beautiful pink dress. Where did you buy it?
아름다운 핑크색 드레스구나. 그걸 어디서 샀니?

W: I bought it from an online shopping mall.
온라인 쇼핑몰에서 샀어.

M: Did you pay a lot for it? 그것에 돈을 많이 지불했니?

W: No, I didn't. It only cost twenty dollars. I got the last dress the store had. 아니, 그러지 않았어. 그건 20달러 밖에 안 들었어. 상점에 있던 마지막 드레스를 내가 산 거야.

M: Wow. You got lucky. 와, 너는 운이 좋았구나.

W: I think so. 그런 것 같아.

해설 색상은 핑크, 종류는 드레스, 구입 장소는 쇼핑몰, 가격은 20달러이다.

어휘 dress 드레스, 옷 pay 돈을 지불하다 cost 비용이 들다

13 ⑤

M: Excuse me. Can I walk to City Hall?
실례합니다. 제가 걸어서 시청에 갈 수 있나요?

W: No, it's too far to go there on foot.
아니요, 거긴 걸어가기에는 너무 멀어요.

M: That's too bad. Is there a bus stop around here?
큰일이네요. 이 근처에 버스 정류장이 있나요?

W: Yes, but no buses go to City Hall from here. Why don't you take a taxi? 네, 하지만 여기서 시청으로 가는 버스는 없어요. 택시를 타시는 게 어때요?

M: Okay. I will. Thank you. 네. 그럴게요. 고맙습니다.

해설 교통수단을 찾는 문제의 정답 힌트는 마지막에 있는 경우가 많다.

어휘 City Hall 시청 on foot 걸어서, 도보로 bus stop 버스 정류장 around here 이 근처에 take a taxi 택시를 타다

14 ⑤

W: Ouch. That really hurts. 아야, 정말 아프네.
M: What's the matter? Did you cut your finger?

무슨 문제니? 손가락을 베었어?

W: Yes. I need a bandage. 응. 난 밴드가 필요해.

M: That looks like a bad cut. 심하게 베인 것 같은데.

W: It's starting to hurt a bit. 조금씩 아프기 시작하네.

M: Go to the bathroom and clean it up. I'll bring you a bandage. 화장실로 가서 상처를 씻어. 내가 밴드를 가져다 줄게.

해설 대화 직후에 할 일은 마지막 말 'I'll ~'에 등장한다.

어휘 ouch (감탄사) 아야 hurt 아프다, 아프게 하다 cut one's finger 손을 베다 bandage 밴드, 붕대 cut 베인 상처; 베다 a bit 약간, 조금 clean up 씻다, 청소하다

15 ①

W: Good morning, Mr. Kim. Can you do me a favor?
안녕하세요, 김 선생님. 제 부탁을 들어주실 수 있나요?

M: I'll try. What do you need? 노력은 해볼게. 무슨 일이니?

W: I'm having trouble with my homework. Can you check it for me? 저는 숙제 때문에 어려움을 겪고 있어요. 제 숙제를 확인 좀 해주시겠어요?

M: Okay. Can you give it to me now?
알겠다. 그것을 지금 나한테 주겠니?

W: Yes. It's right here in my backpack. Thanks a lot.
네. 여기 제 가방 안에 있어요. 정말 감사합니다.

해설 여자가 남자를 Mr. Kim이라고 부르는 사실과, 숙제를 확인해 달라는 상황을 통해 남자는 교사임을 알 수 있다.

어휘 do somebody a favor 누구의 부탁을 들어주다 have trouble with[in] ~에 곤란을 겪다 check 확인하다, 점검하다

16 ③

M: Good morning, everyone. This is Kim Junsu speaking. Today, I'd like to talk about saving energy. We can open the windows. We don't have to use the air conditioner. We can also turn off the lights when we leave a room. Let's try hard to save energy. Thank you.

안녕하세요, 여러분. 저는 김준수입니다. 오늘 저는 에너지 절약에 대해 이야기하고 싶습니다. 우리는 창문을 열 수 있습니다. 우리는 에어컨을 사용하지 않아도 됩니다. 우리는 또한 우리가 방을 나갈 때 불을 끌 수 있습니다. 에너지를 절약하기 위해 열심히 노력합시다. 감사합니다.

어휘 save energy 에너지를 절약하다 air conditioner 에어컨 turn off the lights 불을 끄다

17 ②

M: Excuse me. Can you tell me the way to Pete's Pizza Restaurant? 실례합니다. 피트의 피자 가게로 가는 길을 알려 주시겠어요?

W: Sure. I just had lunch there today.
네. 제가 오늘 방금 거기서 점심을 먹었거든요.

M: That's great. Where is it from here?

좋네요. 거기가 여기서 어느 쪽이죠?

W: Go straight two blocks and then turn right.
두 블록을 곧장 가서 우회전하세요.

M: Okay. So I should go straight one block and then turn right. 네. 그러니까 제가 한 블록을 직진한 다음에 우회전하라는 거군요.

W: No, go two blocks. Then, turn right. Pete's Pizza Restaurant is the third building on the left.
아니요, 두 블록을 가세요. 그런 다음에 우회전하세요. 피트의 피자 가게는 좌측으로 세 번째 건물이에요.

M: Thanks so much. 정말 고맙습니다.

W: You're welcome. 별말씀을요.

[해설] 지도를 보고 장소를 찾는 문제에서는, 길을 묻는 사람이 길안내를 잘못 알아들었을 때 그것을 바로잡는 내용이 포함되기도 한다.

[어휘] the way to ~로 가는 길 have lunch 점심을 먹다 on the left 좌측으로, 왼쪽에

18 ②

M: It's nice to be back home. It was a long trip.
집에 돌아오니 좋네. 긴 여행이었어.

W: I'm so tired from the flight. I want to relax on the sofa. 난 비행 때문에 무척 피곤해. 소파에서 쉬고 싶어.

M: We should take everything out of our bags first.
우리는 먼저 가방에서 모든 것을 꺼내야 해.

W: Let's do that later. Can you open the window, please? It's really hot in here.
그건 나중에 하자. 창문 좀 열어 줄래? 여기는 정말 더워.

M: Sure. I'll let some fresh air in the house.
알았어. 집 안에 신선한 공기가 들어오도록 할게.

[해설] 짐을 푸는 것은 남자의 제안이고, 여자는 창문을 열어 환기를 시킬 것을 제안했다.

[어휘] be back home 집으로 돌아오다 flight 비행 relax 휴식을 취하다, 쉬다 take out of ~에서 꺼내다 fresh air 신선한 공기

19 ④

W: What do you have in the box?
넌 그 상자에 뭘 가지고 있니?

M: This is for you. Why don't you open it?
이건 너를 위한 거야. 그걸 열어 보지 않을래?

W: What a nice necklace! Let me put it on. [pause] How does it look on me? 정말 멋진 목걸이네! 내가 걸어 볼게. [잠시 후] 내가 하니까 어때 보여?

M: It looks wonderful on you. 너한테 아주 잘 어울려.

W: I love it. Where did you get it?
난 이게 아주 마음에 들어. 넌 이걸 어디서 샀니?

M: I bought it at the mall. 나는 그걸 쇼핑몰에서 샀어.

① You're welcome. 천만에.
② I'm glad you like it. 네가 좋아하니 난 기뻐.
③ It's a birthday present. 그건 생일 선물이야.
④ I bought it at the mall. 나는 그걸 쇼핑몰에서 샀어.

⑤ It matches your earrings. 그건 네 귀걸이와 어울려.

[해설] 여자의 마지막 대사에서 의문사 where를 들었다면 정답을 쉽게 고를 수 있다.

[어휘] necklace 목걸이 put something on ~을 걸쳐 보다 match (색상, 무늬 등이) 맞다, 어울리다 earrings (한 쌍의) 귀걸이

20 ⑤

M: I need a big favor, Alice. Can you help me?
내게 어려운 부탁이 있어, 앨리스. 나를 좀 도와줄 수 있니?

W: Sure. What do you want me to do?
물론이지. 내가 뭘 하기를 바라니?

M: I need to return this book to the library, but I don't have time to go today. 내가 이 책을 도서관에 반납해야 하는데, 오늘은 갈 시간이 없어.

W: I can take it there now. But I don't know where the library is. 내가 지금 그 책을 거기 가져갈 수 있어. 하지만 난 도서관이 어디 있는지 몰라.

M: It's right next to the shopping center.
그건 쇼핑센터 바로 옆에 있어.

① I go there all the time. 나는 항상 거기에 가.
② The library closes at seven o'clock.
도서관은 7시에 문을 닫아.
③ There are many good books there.
거기에는 좋은 책이 많이 있어.
④ Sure. You can use my library card.
물론이지. 넌 내 도서관 카드를 사용해도 돼.
⑤ It's right next to the shopping center.
그건 쇼핑센터 바로 옆에 있어.

[해설] 여자의 마지막 대사에서 의문사 where에 주목하자. 이 대화에서 'I don't know where the library is.'는 'Where is the library?'와 같은 의미를 갖는다.

[어휘] big favor 어려운 부탁 return a book to the library 도서관에 책을 반납하다 right next to ~의 바로 옆에 all the time 줄곧, 내내 library card 도서관 카드, 도서 대출 카드

13회 실전모의고사 본문 p.126-127

01 ④	02 ①	03 ④	04 ⑤	05 ①
06 ③	07 ②	08 ②	09 ②	10 ①
11 ③	12 ⑤	13 ①	14 ③	15 ⑤
16 ⑤	17 ④	18 ⑤	19 ①	20 ⑤

01 ④

W: That's a nice painting. It looks like the hills and trees behind the school.
그림 멋있다. 학교 뒤에 있는 언덕과 나무처럼 보여.

M: Thanks for saying that. I love painting nature.

그렇게 말해줘서 고마워. 나는 자연을 그리는 것을 아주 좋아해.

W: Really? Why don't you draw a picture of the lake next time?
정말이야? 다음에는 호수를 그려보는 게 어때?

M: That's not a bad idea. I will draw the lake and some animals. 그거 좋은 생각이네. 내가 호수와 동물을 그려볼게.

W: I can't wait to see that painting.
난 그 그림이 무척 기대된다.

해설 여자의 첫 대사인 'It looks like ~'에 남자의 그림이 묘사되었다. ② 사슴, ③ 호수는 다음에 그릴 그림이다.

어휘 look like ~인 것처럼 보이다 nature 자연 lake 호수

02 ①

W: We can find this in a bathroom. This is hard, but this becomes soft when we use it with water. We use this to keep our bodies clean. We always use it when we take a shower. And we also use this just to wash our hands.

우리는 욕실에서 이것을 발견할 수 있어요. 이것은 딱딱하지만 우리가 물과 함께 이용하면 부드러워져요. 우리는 이것을 써서 몸을 깨끗하게 유지해요. 우리는 샤워를 할 때 항상 이것을 이용해요. 그리고 우리는 이것을 이용해서 간단히 손만 씻기도 해요.

해설 뒤로 갈수록 보다 구체적인 단서들이 나오므로 끝까지 들어야 한다.

어휘 become ~하게 되다, ~가 되다 soft 부드러운, 연한 body 몸(복 bodies) take a shower 샤워를 하다

03 ④

M: Everyone is waiting for us at the restaurant.
모두가 식당에서 우리를 기다리고 있어.

W: Don't worry. The bus is going to arrive soon.
걱정하지 마. 버스는 곧 도착할 거야.

M: But it's already six thirty. And we got here ten minutes ago.
하지만 벌써 6시 30분이야. 그리고 우린 여기에 10분 전에 왔잖아.

W: The sign says that the bus will get here in five minutes.
표지판에 버스가 5분 뒤에 여기에 도착할 거라고 나와 있어.

M: I hope that sign is right. We're already late.
저 표지판이 정확하길 바라. 우린 이미 늦었어.

해설 현재 시각은 6:30이고 버스는 5분 뒤(in five minutes)에 도착할 것이므로 6:35가 정답이다. 'in+시간 정보'는 보통 '~이내에'가 아니라 '~후에'로 해석한다.

어휘 already 벌써, 이미 sign 표지판; 신호

04 ⑤

M: Good evening, everyone. I'm John Jackson, and I've got the weather report for tomorrow. The morning is going to be cold and very windy. Later

in the afternoon, it's going to rain for one or two hours. But the rain will stop, and it will be cloudy in the evening. Don't forget your umbrella.

안녕하세요, 여러분. 저는 존 잭슨이고, 내일의 날씨를 알려드리겠습니다. 아침에는 춥고 바람이 많이 불 것입니다. 오후 늦게 한두 시간 동안 비가 내리겠습니다. 하지만 비는 멈출 것이고 저녁에는 구름이 끼겠습니다. 우산 챙기는 것을 잊지 마세요.

해설 오후(afternoon)의 날씨는 아침(morning) 날씨 정보에 뒤이어 언급된다.

05 ①

M: Are you ready for summer camp?
너는 여름 캠프 준비를 다 했니?

W: Yes, I am. I packed a swimsuit, T-shirts, shorts, and sneakers.
네. 저는 수영복, 티셔츠, 반바지, 운동화를 챙겼어요.

M: Don't you need a raincoat? 넌 비옷이 필요하지 않아?

W: No. It won't rain during camp.
아니요. 캠프 기간 동안 비는 오지 않을 거예요.

M: Are you sure? 확실하니?

W: Yes, I already checked the weather.
네, 제가 벌써 날씨를 확인했어요.

해설 여자의 첫 대사에 가져갈 물건이 모두 언급된다. 선택지와 같은 순서로 등장하므로 표시하면서 정답을 추려 나간다.

어휘 pack (짐을) 싸다, 꾸리다 swimsuit (상하의 한 벌의) 수영복 shorts 반바지 sneakers 운동화 raincoat 비옷 during ~동안, ~중에 check 확인하다, 점검하다

06 ③

① W: How is your brother doing these days?
네 남동생은 요즘 어때?

M: He's getting better now.
그는 요즘 좋아지고 있어.

② W: What do you think of your new school?
네 새 학교에 대해 어떻게 생각해?

M: I love it. I have many friends there.
정말 좋아. 나는 그곳에 친구가 많아.

③ W: Are you happy about the new schedule?
너는 새로운 일정이 만족스럽니?

M: Yes, I'm happy to see you today.
응, 나는 오늘 널 만나서 기뻐.

④ W: Would you like to drink something cold?
시원한 것 좀 마실래요?

M: No, thank you. 고맙지만, 사양할게요.

⑤ W: You like snowy weather, don't you?
너는 눈 내리는 날씨를 좋아하지, 그렇지 않니?

M: No, I don't like it at all.
아니, 나는 전혀 좋아하지 않아.

해설 ③에서는 무언가에 대해 기분이 좋은지, 즉 만족스러운지 물었다. 'Yes, I'm happy.'에서 문장이 끝나면 자연스러운 대화이지만 뒤

에 오는 'to see you today' 때문에 질문과 동떨어진다.

어휘 these days 요즘 get better (병, 상황이) 좋아지다 schedule 일정, 시간표 happy about ~에 만족하는, 행복해 하는

07 ②

M: Which floor are you going to?
당신은 몇 층에 가시나요?
W: I'm going to the ninth floor. 저는 9층에 가요.
M: Really? So am I. Did you just move to this apartment?
그래요? 저도요. 얼마 전에 이 아파트에 이사 오셨나 봐요?
W: Yes, my family and I moved here three days ago.
네, 제 가족과 저는 3일 전에 이곳으로 이사 왔어요.
M: It's a pleasure to meet you. My name is Dave. I live in apartment nine zero four.
만나서 반가워요. 제 이름은 데이브예요. 저는 904호에 살아요.
W: Wow, I live in apartment nine zero three. We're right next door. I'm Jessica. 우와, 저는 903호에 살아요. 우린 바로 옆집이네요. 저는 제시카예요.

해설 대화 장소를 알면 관계를 파악하기가 수월하다. 두 사람의 첫 대사에서 대화 장소가 엘리베이터 안이라는 점이 드러난다. move, apartment, live in, next door 등이 힌트가 된다.

어휘 floor (건물의) 층 ninth 아홉 번째의

08 ②

M: Why are you looking at that map?
너는 왜 그 지도를 쳐다보고 있어?
W: I have to meet my friends in the city. I'm thinking of driving my car there. 나는 시내에서 친구들을 만나야 해. 나는 그곳까지 차를 운전할 생각이야.
M: Are you going downtown? You shouldn't drive if you go there.
너는 중심가로 갈 거야? 만약 그곳에 간다면 운전해서는 안돼.
W: Then should I take a taxi? 그러면 택시를 타야 할까?
M: No, the buses are always fast and cheap. Go there by bus.
아니, 버스가 늘 빠르고 값도 싸. 버스를 타고 가도록 해.
W: Okay. Thanks for the advice. 그래. 조언 고마워.

해설 총 세 개의 교통수단이 언급되는데, 각 교통수단에 대한 긍정 및 부정적인 반응을 확인한 뒤 답을 고른다.

어휘 map 지도, 약도 think of ~을 고려하다 downtown (도시) 중심가에 cheap (값, 요금 등이) 싼

09 ②

M: Welcome home. Did you have a good time on vacation?
돌아온 걸 환영해. 휴가 중에 좋은 시간 보냈니?
W: Yes, I had a wonderful time in Sydney.
응, 나는 시드니에서 멋진 시간을 보냈어.
M: How was the weather there? 그곳 날씨는 어땠어?

W: It was summer, so it was hot and sunny every day.
여름이어서 매일 덥고 화창했어.
M: Did you go to the beach? 너는 해변에 갔니?
W: Yes. I went there almost every day.
응. 나는 거의 매일 해변에 갔어.
M: You're lucky. I would love to go there.
운이 좋았구나. 나도 거기에 가고 싶다.

해설 지난 휴가에 있었던 일에 대해 대화를 나누고 있다. 나머지 선택지는 세부내용에 속한다.

어휘 have a good time 좋은 시간을 보내다 on vacation 휴가 중에 lucky 행운의, 운 좋은

10 ①

W: Are you going to visit Europe this summer?
너는 올 여름에 유럽에 갈 거니?
M: That's right. I'm planning to visit three cities.
맞아. 나는 세 도시를 방문할 계획이야.
W: Wow. I want to do that. Are you going with your family?
우와. 나도 그렇게 하고 싶다. 너는 가족과 함께 가니?
M: No, I'm going to go by myself. I am so excited.
아니, 나는 혼자 갈 거야. 난 정말 신나.
W: That should be a lot of fun. Make sure you take lots of pictures.
그건 아주 재미있을 것 같아. 꼭 사진 많이 찍어와.
M: I will. 알겠어.

해설 남자의 말 'I am so excited.'에 심정이 드러나 있다.

어휘 by oneself 혼자 a lot of 많은 make sure 반드시 ~하다, ~을 확인하다

11 ③

M: Mindy, I'm going to study at the library with Allen. Would you like to join us? 민디, 나는 앨런과 함께 도서관에 가서 공부할 거야. 너도 함께 할래?
W: Sorry, but maybe next time.
미안하지만, 다음에 해야 할 것 같아.
M: Why can't you meet us? 왜 우리를 만날 수 없어?
W: I have band practice after school. I can't miss it.
나는 방과 후에 밴드 연습이 있어. 거기에 빠지면 안돼.
M: I understand. I'll see you later then.
알겠어. 그럼 나중에 보자.

해설 남자의 질문 'Why can't you ~?'에 응답하는 여사의 말에 이유가 등장한다. 'Why ~?' 이후에 특히 집중한다.

어휘 maybe 아마, 어쩌면 practice 연습; 연습하다 after school 방과 후에

12 ⑤

W: We are ready for our presentation, aren't we?
우리는 발표를 할 준비가 됐어, 그렇지 않니?

M: Yes. We are prepared, so you don't have to be nervous. 응. 우린 준비됐으니까 넌 긴장하지 않아도 돼.

W: Let's check everything for the last time. How many copies of the handouts do we have?
마지막으로 전부 점검해 보자. 우리는 유인물을 몇 장 갖고 있어?

M: We need forty, but we only have thirty-five.
우린 40장이 필요한데 35장밖에 없네.

W: That's not good. Can you print five more copies?
그럼 안 되는데. 네가 5장 더 출력할래?

M: Yes. I'll do that right away. 응. 내가 바로 할게.

해설 여자의 마지막 말에 'Can you ~?'로 부탁하는 내용이 드러난다.

어휘 presentation 발표, 프레젠테이션 prepared 준비된 nervous 불안해 하는, 긴장한 check 확인하다, 점검하다 for the last time 마지막으로 copy 복사본 handout (사람들에게 나눠 주는) 유인물, 핸드아웃

13 ①

M: Jennifer, are you busy this afternoon?
제니퍼, 오늘 오후에 바빠?

W: Yes. I have to finish my math homework today.
응. 나는 오늘 수학 숙제를 끝내야 해.

M: I have a lot of homework as well.
나 역시 숙제가 많아.

W: I'm going to go to Carl's house to do my homework after lunch. Why don't you join us? 나는 점심 먹고 나서 칼의 집에 가서 숙제를 할 거야. 너도 함께 하지 그래?

M: Why not? What time will you go there?
왜 안 되겠어? 넌 거기에 몇 시에 갈 거야?

W: We will meet at one. 우린 1시에 만날 거야.

해설 여자의 초대에 응하여 남자는 동의를 나타내는 뜻으로 'Why not?'이라고 말했다. 제안과 동의가 이루어진 활동이 정답이 된다.

어휘 as well ~도, 또한 Why not? 왜 아니겠어?, 그거 좋지.

14 ③

W: Sam, why do you look so sad? What's the matter?
샘, 너 왜 슬퍼 보이니? 무슨 일 있어?

M: You know my best friend Joe, right?
너 내 친구 조 알지, 그렇지?

W: Of course I know Joe. Did something happen to him? 당연히 나는 조를 알지. 그에게 무슨 일이 있니?

M: He's moving to another country tomorrow. I won't be able to see him again. 그는 내일 다른 나라로 이민을 간대. 나는 그를 다시는 볼 수 없을 거야.

W: Cheer up. You can still talk to him online.
기운 내. 그래도 온라인으로 계속 그 애와 대화할 수 있잖아.

해설 'Cheer up.'은 격려할 때 쓰는 대표적인 표현이다.

어휘 of course 물론 happen (계획하지 않은 일이) 발생하다 be able to ~할 수 있다

15 ⑤

W: Good afternoon. How may I help you, sir?
안녕하세요. 무엇을 도와드릴까요, 손님?

M: Today is my wife's birthday, so I'd like to get something for her.
오늘이 제 아내의 생일이어서 그녀를 위한 것을 사려고 해요.

W: Roses are always nice. We have some pretty tulips, too. 장미는 언제나 좋아요. 저희는 예쁜 튤립도 있답니다.

M: I'll take ten roses. And can you put them in a vase, please?
장미 10송이를 살게요. 그리고 꽃병 안에 넣어주시겠어요?

W: Yes, I can. I can deliver them to your house, too.
네, 그럴게요. 손님의 댁까지 배달해 드릴 수도 있어요.

어휘 wife 아내 rose 장미 tulip 튤립 put in ~에 넣다 vase 꽃병 deliver 배달하다

16 ⑤

[Cellphone rings.] [휴대폰이 울린다.]

W: Hi, David. I have a question for you.
안녕, 데이비드. 난 너에게 질문이 있어.

M: What is it? 뭔데?

W: Are you still downtown? 너 아직 시내에 있니?

M: Yes, I am. But I am going to come home soon.
응. 그런데 나는 곧 집에 들어갈 거야.

W: Great. Can you pick up a book from the library for me? 잘됐다. 나 대신에 도서관에서 책을 찾아 올래?

M: Sure. What's the title? 물론이지. 제목이 뭐야?

W: I'll send you a text message with the information.
내가 그 정보를 문자메시지로 보내줄게.

해설 여자의 말 'Can you ~?'에 전화의 목적이 드러나 있다.

어휘 downtown 시내에 pick up ~을 찾아오다 title (책, 영화 등의) 제목 text message 문자메시지 information 정보

17 ④

M: Hello, Ms. Turner. What can I do for you today?
안녕하세요, 터너 씨. 오늘 제가 무엇을 도와드릴까요?

W: I'm in a lot of pain. It started three days ago.
저는 통증이 심해요. 3일 전에 시작됐어요.

M: Which tooth hurts? 어느 치아가 아픈가요?

W: I'm not sure. But it's on the left side of my mouth.
잘 모르겠어요. 그렇지만 제 입의 왼쪽이에요.

M: Okay. Let me take a look. Open your mouth and say, "Ah," please.
알겠습니다. 제가 한번 볼게요. 입을 벌리고 "아"하고 말하세요.

해설 남자의 질문인 'Which tooth hurts?'만 들어도 직업을 알 수 있다.

어휘 in pain 아픈 hurt 아프다 take a look 한번 보다

18 ⑤

[*Cellphone rings.*] [휴대폰이 울린다.]

W: Michael, would you like to go to the museum with me today? 마이클, 오늘 나와 함께 박물관에 갈래?

M: Is there a new exhibit? 새로운 전시회가 있니?

W: Yes, there are a lot of paintings.
응, 그림이 아주 많아.

M: Cool. Where do you want to meet? At your house?
멋진데. 어디에서 만나고 싶어? 너희 집?

W: No. How about at the subway station? Is two o'clock okay? 아니. 지하철역은 어때? 2시 괜찮아?

M: It's perfect. I'll see you then.
아주 좋아. 그때 보자.

해설 대화 후반부에 제안되는 장소가 정답일 가능성이 크다. 박물관은 두 사람이 가기로 한 장소이며, 여자의 집은 남자가 제안했지만 거절된 장소이다.

어휘 exhibit 전시회; 전시하다

19 ①

W: How did you like my song?
내 노래 어떻게 생각하니?

M: It was wonderful, Claire. Did you practice a lot?
훌륭해, 클레어. 너 연습 많이 했어?

W: Yes, I practice almost every day. I'm going to sing at the school festival this Saturday.
응, 나는 거의 매일 연습했어. 나는 이번 주 토요일에 학교 축제에서 노래할 거야.

M: I can't wait to see your performance.
난 네 공연을 보는 게 무척 기대돼.

W: I'm looking forward to it. But I'm very nervous.
나도 기대하고 있어. 하지만 나는 너무 긴장돼.

M: I'm sure you'll be amazing. 난 네가 멋질 거라고 확신해.

① I'm sure you'll be amazing. 난 네가 멋질 거라고 확신해.
② Are you going to the festival? 너는 축제에 갈 거야?
③ What day is the performance?
그 공연은 무슨 요일에 있어?
④ Why didn't you prepare for it? 너는 왜 준비하지 않았어?
⑤ I'll be performing there with you.
나도 너와 함께 거기에서 공연할 거야.

해설 공연 연습을 많이 한 친구가 긴장하고 있다면 안심시켜주거나 격려하는 말을 해줄 수 있다.

어휘 almost 거의 look forward to ~을 기대하다 nervous 불안해 하는, 긴장한 amazing 굉장한, 놀랄만한 perform 공연하다, 연주하다

20 ⑤

W: Do you have any plans for today?
너는 오늘 계획이 있니?

M: Not really. I was just going to stay home and read a book.
딱히 없어. 나는 그냥 집에서 책을 읽으려고 했어.

W: How about going to the shopping center with me?
나랑 같이 쇼핑센터에 가는 게 어때?

M: That sounds fun, but I don't want to buy anything.
재미있을 것 같은데, 나는 아무것도 사고 싶지 않아.

W: We can just walk around. And I'll buy you something to eat.
우린 그저 돌아다니기만 해도 돼. 그리고 내가 먹을 것을 사줄게.

M: Sounds good. Let's leave in five minutes.
좋아. 5분 후에 출발하자.

① Actually, I didn't enjoy dinner.
사실, 나는 저녁식사를 즐기지 않았어.
② Can I have the check, please?
계산서를 받을 수 있을까요?
③ Okay. I need to buy a few things.
그래. 나는 몇 가지 사야겠다.
④ What time does the library close?
도서관은 몇 시에 닫아?
⑤ Sounds good. Let's leave in five minutes.
좋아. 5분 후에 출발하자.

해설 여자는 자신의 제안을 거절한 남자에게 다시 한번 제안을 하고 있다. 남자는 갈 것인지 아닌지 대답을 할 차례이다.

어휘 walk around 이리저리 걷다 check 계산서

14회 실전모의고사 본문 p.136-137

01 ③	02 ②	03 ②	04 ④	05 ③
06 ①	07 ③	08 ④	09 ②	10 ④
11 ②	12 ①	13 ③	14 ③	15 ②
16 ②	17 ⑤	18 ②	19 ⑤	20 ④

01 ③

W: I love your blue shorts.
난 너의 파란색 반바지가 마음에 들어.

M: Thanks. How do you like my red and white striped T-shirt?
고마워. 나의 빨간색과 흰색 줄무늬 티셔츠는 어떻게 생각해?

W: It looks good, too. Where is your new cap?
그것도 좋아 보여. 너의 새 모자는 어디에 있어?

M: I gave it to my brother.
나는 그것을 내 동생에게 줬어.

해설 남자는 반바지에 줄무늬 셔츠를 입었고, 모자는 쓰지 않고 있다.

어휘 striped 줄무늬가 있는 give 주다(give-gave-given)

02 ②

W: I have brown fur and live near ponds and streams. I'm an excellent swimmer. I have a long, flat tail and two very sharp teeth. I use the teeth to cut down trees. Then, I make a dam with the trees. I live inside the dam I make.

저는 갈색 털이 있고 연못과 시냇물 근처에 살아요. 저는 수영을 아주 잘해요. 저는 길고 납작한 꼬리가 있고, 매우 날카로운 이빨이 두 개 있어요. 저는 그 이빨을 이용해서 나무를 잘라요. 그리고는 그 나무들을 가지고 댐을 만들어요. 저는 제가 만든 댐 안에서 살아요.

어휘 fur 털 pond 연못 stream 시내, 개울 excellent 뛰어난 flat 납작한, 평평한 sharp 날카로운 tooth 이, 이빨(복 teeth) cut down (잘라서) 넘어뜨리다 dam 댐 inside ~안에

03 ②

M: Hello. May I take your order, please?
안녕하세요. 주문하시겠어요?

W: Yes. I'd like a hamburger and some fries, please.
네. 햄버거 한 개와 감자튀김을 주세요.

M: Would you like a drink? 음료도 드릴까요?

W: Yes. I'll take a small cola. And I'd like an ice cream, too. 네. 작은 콜라를 주세요. 그리고 아이스크림도 주세요.

M: Is that for here or to go?
여기서 드시나요, 아니면 가져가시나요?

W: For here. 여기서 먹을게요.

M: Okay. Your order is coming right up.
네. 손님이 주문한 것이 바로 나올 거예요.

해설 여자가 주문하는 음식을 선택지와 순서대로 비교하여 언급되지 않는 음식을 찾는다.

어휘 take an order 주문을 받다 for here (주문한 곳에서 먹을 때) to go (음식을 포장해서 갖고 나갈 때)

04 ④

[Cellphone rings.] [휴대폰이 울린다.]
W: Hey, Steve. Are you busy now?
얘, 스티브. 너 지금 바빠?

M: Not really. Do you need something?
아니 별로. 너 필요한 거 있어?

W: Yes. Can you help me fix my computer?
응. 내 컴퓨터를 고치는 걸 도와줄래?

M: Sure. I'll be there in a couple of minutes.
물론이지. 내가 몇 분 뒤에 그곳으로 갈게.

W: Thanks. I have a lot of things to do.
고마워. 나는 할 일이 정말 많아.

M: Don't worry about it. See you soon.
그건 걱정하지 마. 곧 보자.

해설 여자의 대사인 'Can you ~?'에 부탁의 내용이 있다. 남자의 대답인 'Sure.'까지 확인한다.

어휘 fix 고치다; 고정시키다 in a couple of minutes 몇 분 뒤에

05 ③

M: Hi, Denise. How are you? I called you yesterday and this morning, but you never answered the

phone. 안녕, 데니즈. 어떻게 지내니? 내가 어제와 오늘 아침에 네게 전화했는데 너는 한 번도 전화를 받지 않더라.

W: Sorry about that. My phone broke, so it's in the repair shop. I was too busy to pick it up.
그건 미안해. 내 전화기는 고장 나서 수리점에 있어. 나는 너무 바빠서 그걸 찾으러 가지 못했어.

M: Yeah? What did you do yesterday?
그래? 너는 어제 뭐 했어?

W: Yesterday, I had to meet my old friend all day long.
어제는 하루 종일 내 옛 친구를 만나야 했어.

M: What about this morning? 오늘 아침에는?

W: I went to the hospital. 난 병원에 갔어.

해설 여자는 전화기가 고장 나서 수리를 맡겼으나 아직 찾아오지 못했다. 병원 방문은 오늘 아침의 일이다.

어휘 break 고장 나다(break-broke-broken) repair 수리; 수리하다 old friend 옛 친구 all day long 온종일

06 ①

M: Excuse me. Can you tell me where the fitness center is?
실례합니다. 피트니스센터가 어디에 있는지 알려주시겠어요?

W: Sure. It's near here. Go straight until you get to Eastern Avenue. 물론이죠. 그건 이 근처에 있어요. 이스턴 가에 도착할 때까지 직진하세요.

M: Go straight to Eastern Avenue? Okay.
이스턴 가까지 직진이요? 알겠어요.

W: Then, turn left at the corner. You'll see a drugstore on the left. 그 다음에 모퉁이에서 좌회전하세요. 왼쪽에 약국이 보일 거예요.

M: Is the fitness center next to it?
피트니스센터가 그 옆에 있나요?

W: No, it's not. It's across the street from the drugstore.
아니요. 그 약국의 길 건너편에 있어요.

어휘 fitness 건강; 신체 단련 get to ~에 도착하다 corner 모퉁이, 구석

07 ③

M: Lisa, how about watching the new action movie with me?
리사, 나랑 같이 새로 나온 액션 영화를 보는 게 어때?

W: Okay. My brother said it's really good.
좋아. 우리 오빠가 그거 아주 재미있다고 하더라.

M: I'm going to buy tickets online. What time is good for you? 나는 온라인으로 표를 살 거야. 너는 몇 시가 좋아?

W: Any time after five P.M. is fine.
오후 5시 이후로는 다 좋아.

M: We can see the five forty showing. It finishes at eight ten.
우리는 5시 40분 영화를 볼 수 있겠다. 그건 8시 10분에 끝나.

W: That's perfect. 아주 좋네.

해설 8:10은 영화가 시작하는 시각이 아닌 끝나는 시각이다.

어휘 say 말하다(say-said-said) showing (영화) 상영 any time 언제든

08 ④

[*Telephone rings.*] [전화벨이 울린다.]
W: Hello. 여보세요.
M: Hello, Gina. It's Dave. The weather is nice. Do you want to go out?
안녕, 지나. 나 데이브야. 날씨가 정말 좋아. 밖에 나갈래?
W: What are you talking about? It's raining now.
너 무슨 소리를 하는 거니? 지금 비가 오잖아.
M: It's not raining. The rain stopped about thirty minutes ago.
비는 오지 않아. 비는 30분쯤 전에 그쳤어.
W: Are you sure about that? 그거 확실한 거야?
M: Yes, I just checked. Let's meet at the playground in five minutes.
응, 내가 확인했어. 5분 후에 운동장에서 만나자.

어휘 go out 외출하다, 나가다 sure about ~에 대해 확신하는 check 점검하다, 확인하다 playground 운동장

09 ②

M: Is this you in the picture? I didn't know you performed on stage. 사진 속에 이 사람이 너야? 난 네가 무대에서 공연했다는 걸 몰랐어.
W: That's a picture of me three years ago. It was my first performance.
그건 3년 전의 내 사진이야. 나의 첫 공연이었어.
M: Do you enjoy acting on stage?
너는 무대에서 연기하는 걸 즐기니?
W: I love it. I want to be a movie actress in the future.
난 연기를 아주 좋아해. 나는 앞으로 영화배우가 되고 싶어.
M: Good luck. I hope you can do it.
행운을 빌어. 네가 꼭 이룰 수 있길 바랄게.

어휘 perform on stage 무대에서 연기[공연]하다 actress 여배우

10 ④

M: I went to the amusement park today.
나는 오늘 놀이공원에 갔어.
W: Did you have a good time there?
거기에서 즐거운 시간을 보냈니?
M: Yes, I did. I went on the roller coaster.
응, 그랬어. 나는 롤러코스터를 탔어.
W: Oh, roller coasters are really scary.
아, 롤러코스터는 정말 무섭잖아.
M: I don't think so. I thought it was fun.
난 그렇게 생각하지 않아. 내 생각에는 재미있었어.

해설 놀이공원에서 즐거운 시간을 보낸 남자는 신이 나 있다.

어휘 amusement park 놀이공원 roller coaster 롤러코스터 scary 무서운

11 ②

W: Now, it's time for tomorrow's weather forecast. There's a cold wind coming here from the north. So the weather in Seoul will be windy. The west coast of the country will get some snow. There will be sunny skies in Daejeon and Cheongju. But there will be lots of rain in Busan and Gwangju.

이제 내일의 일기예보 시간입니다. 북쪽에서 차가운 바람이 이곳으로 불어오고 있습니다. 따라서 서울의 날씨는 바람이 불겠습니다. 서해안 지역은 눈이 조금 내리겠습니다. 대전과 청주는 맑은 하늘을 보일 것입니다. 하지만 부산과 광주에는 많은 양의 비가 내릴 것입니다.

어휘 forecast 예보 the west coast 서해안

12 ①

M: All right, I'm all finished. 좋아, 난 모두 끝났어.
W: Did you just finish your math homework?
넌 방금 수학 숙제를 끝낸 거야?
M: Yes, I did. I thought it was pretty easy.
응, 다 했어. 내 생각에 그건 꽤 쉬웠어.
W: Really? Then can you show me how to solve this problem, please?
정말이야? 그러면 네가 이 문제 푸는 방법을 내게 보여 주겠니?
M: Let me see... Ah, just give me a piece of paper. I will show you how to do it.
잠깐만... 아, 내게 종이 한 장 줘봐. 내가 어떻게 하는지 보여줄게.
W: That's amazing. You're the best student in the class. 그거 놀랍다. 너는 학급에서 가장 뛰어난 학생다워.

해설 amazing, best 등의 긍정적 표현에서 의도를 쉽게 파악할 수 있다.

어휘 finished 끝난 think 생각하다(think-thought-thought) pretty 아주, 꽤; 예쁜 a piece of ~한 개

13 ③

M: Who were you trying to call on the phone?
너는 누구와 통화하려고 했어?
W: Mark. I need to speak with him. But he won't answer his phone.
마크. 나는 그와 통화해야 돼. 그런데 그 애가 전화를 받지 않네.
M: Why do you need to speak with him?
너는 왜 마크와 이야기를 해야 하는데?
W: We were going to finish our group project together. Now, I'll have to do it by myself.
우리는 그룹 프로젝트를 함께 끝내기로 했거든. 이제 나는 그걸 혼자서 하게 생겼어.
M: That's not good. Try calling him again.
그거 좋지 않은데. 그에게 다시 전화해 봐.

W: There's no use. His phone is turned off now.
소용없게 됐어. 지금은 그의 전화기가 꺼져 있어.

해설 여자는 파트너가 전화를 받지 않아 프로젝트를 혼자 하게 되어 화가 났다.

어휘 by oneself 혼자 be no use 소용 없다 turn off ~을 끄다

14 ③

M: Jenny, I need to speak with you for a moment.
제니, 내가 너랑 잠깐 대화를 해야겠다.

W: Sure, Mr. Rogers. What can I do for you?
네, 로저스 선생님. 무엇 때문에 그러시죠?

M: You didn't do very well on your last exam. What happened?
너는 지난 시험을 별로 잘 보지 못했더구나. 무슨 일 있었니?

W: I forgot about the test, so I didn't study for it.
제가 시험에 대해 잊고 있어서 공부를 하지 않았어요.

M: I see. You need to write the test date in the future.
그렇구나. 앞으로는 시험 날짜를 적어 두도록 해.

W: I will. Thank you for your advice.
그럴게요. 충고 감사합니다.

해설 여자가 남자를 'Mr. Rogers'로 불렀기 때문에 부녀지간이나 친구 사이는 아니다. 시험, 공부 등이 결정적 힌트이다.

어휘 for a moment 잠시 동안 forget 잊다(forget-forgot-forgotten) advice 조언

15 ②

M: I don't feel well right now. 난 지금 몸이 좋지 않아.

W: You look bad. What's the matter?
너 안 좋아 보인다. 무슨 일 있어?

M: I have a headache and a runny nose. I think I should take some medicine.
두통이 있고 콧물이 나. 난 약을 좀 먹어야 할 것 같아.

W: You don't need to do that. 넌 그럴 필요 없어.

M: Why not? Then what should I do?
왜 없어? 그러면 난 무엇을 해야 해?

W: Just get some rest and have some hot tea. That's better than taking medicine. 휴식을 좀 취하고 뜨거운 차를 마시도록 해. 약을 먹는 것보다 그게 좋아.

해설 여자가 마지막 말에서 휴식과 뜨거운 차를 제안했다. 약을 먹는 것은 남자가 하려고 했던 것으로, 여자의 제안이 아니다.

어휘 headache 두통 runny nose 콧물 take medicine 약을 복용하다 get rest 휴식을 취하다

16 ②

W: Are your grandparents coming to visit this Saturday?
너희 조부모님께서 이번 주 토요일에 방문하시니?

M: Yes, they are. So I'm going to pick them up at the airport in the morning.

응. 그래서 나는 아침에 공항으로 그분들을 마중 나갈 거야.

W: I hope you have fun with them. Please tell them I said hi.
네가 그분들과 좋은 시간을 보내길 바랄게. 내 안부를 전해 드려.

M: I will. What are you going to do?
알겠어. 너는 뭘 할 거야?

W: I'm going to visit my aunt in another city. I usually go there once a month. 나는 다른 도시에 계신 고모를 방문할 거야. 나는 보통 한 달에 한 번 거기에 가.

M: Have a nice weekend. 즐거운 주말 보내.

해설 공항에 가서 조부모님을 만나는 건 남자가 할 일이다. 여자는 고모를 방문할 거라고 말했지만, 고모에게 전화할 거라고 말하지는 않았다.

어휘 pick somebody up ~을 태우러 가다 once a month 한 달에 한 번

17 ⑤

M: Take a look out the window. Look at all of the snow on the ground. 창 밖을 봐. 땅 위에 있는 저 눈을 좀 봐.

W: I can't believe it. How can we get to school?
믿을 수가 없네. 우리 학교에 어떻게 가지?

M: We can't ride our bikes. 우린 자전거를 탈 수는 없어.

W: You're right. That won't be safe.
네가 옳아. 그건 안전하지 않아.

M: The weather report says it's going to snow all day. So we can't take a bus or taxi to school.
일기예보에서 하루 종일 눈이 올 거라고 해. 그러니까 우리는 버스나 택시를 타고 학교에 갈 수도 없어.

W: I think we should take the subway.
우린 지하철을 타야 할 것 같아.

M: I agree. Let's leave now. 나도 동감이야. 지금 출발하자.

해설 자전거, 버스, 택시 등은 전부 함정이다. 결국 여자와 남자의 마지막 대사에 의견 제시와 동의가 이루어진다.

어휘 take a look ~을 (한번) 보다 safe 안전한 all day 하루 종일

18 ②

① W: Do you know how to play the guitar?
너는 기타 연주하는 법을 알아?

M: No, but I play the flute in the school band.
아니, 하지만 나는 학교 밴드에서 플루트를 연주해.

② W: Are you interested in reading this book?
너는 이 책을 읽고 싶니?

M: Yes, I'm reading a book now.
응, 나는 지금 책을 한 권 읽고 있어.

③ W: My friend Tina and I are going shopping tomorrow.
내 친구 티나와 나는 내일 쇼핑을 할 거야.

M: Have a good time. 좋은 시간 보내.

④ W: The shirt costs twenty dollars.
그 셔츠는 20달러예요.

M: Okay. I'll take it. 네. 그걸 살게요.

⑤ W: I'm getting hungry. 난 배가 고파.

M: Let's stop at a restaurant then.
그러면 식당에서 멈추자.

해설 ②에서 'Are you ~?'라는 질문에 'Yes'로 답한 것까진 적절하지만, 뒤에 엉뚱한 내용이 이어졌다.

어휘 be interested in ~에 관심이 있다 cost (비용이) 들다; 비용

19 ⑤

M: Do you know the new student?
너는 새로 온 학생을 알고 있어?

W: Are you talking about Justin?
저스틴을 말하는 거야?

M: That's right. He's from Australia.
맞아. 그는 호주 출신이야.

W: I only know his name. What do you know about him?
나는 그의 이름만 알고 있어. 너는 그에 대해 무엇을 알아?

M: He enjoys sports, and he can speak four languages. 그는 운동을 즐기고 4개 국어를 할 수 있어.

W: Wow. What languages can he speak?
우와. 그는 어떤 언어를 할 수 있어?

① I think he's French. 나는 그가 프랑스인이라고 생각해.
② Are you from Italy? 너는 이탈리아에서 왔니?
③ I went there last summer. 나는 지난 여름에 그곳에 갔어.
④ Yes, he loves to play sports.
응, 그는 운동하는 것을 아주 좋아해.
⑤ Wow. What languages can he speak?
우와. 그는 어떤 언어를 할 수 있어?

해설 남자가 마지막에 스포츠와 다른 언어 구사에 대해 말했으므로 그와 관련된 구체적 이야기나 질문이 이어질 것이다.

어휘 language 언어 French 프랑스어; 프랑스의; 프랑스 사람

20 ④

M: My parents and I decided to go on a trip tomorrow.
부모님과 나는 내일 여행을 가기로 결정했어.

W: Where are you going? 너넨 어디로 갈 거야?

M: We're going to the beach. We'll be there for five days. 우린 해변에 갈 거야. 우린 그곳에 5일 동안 있을 거야.

W: That sounds like fun. Aren't you excited?
그거 재미있겠다. 넌 신나지 않니?

M: Not really. I don't know how to swim.
아니 별로. 나는 수영할 줄 모르거든.

W: You can learn to swim at the beach.
넌 바닷가에서 수영을 배우면 돼.

① Thanks for inviting me on the trip.
나를 그 여행에 초대해 줘서 고마워.
② Congratulations. You did very well.
축하해. 너는 아주 잘했어.
③ Yes, we can go swimming together.
응, 우리는 함께 수영할 수 있어.

④ You can learn to swim at the beach.
넌 바닷가에서 수영을 배우면 돼.
⑤ No, I didn't go to the beach this year.
아니, 나는 올해 해변에 가지 않았어.

해설 해변으로 여행을 가지만 수영을 못하는 남자에게 여자는 격려와 조언을 해줄 것이다.

어휘 decide 결정하다 invite 초대하다

15회 실전모의고사 본문 p.146-147

01 ④	02 ②	03 ②	04 ④	05 ③
06 ⑤	07 ①	08 ③	09 ③	10 ②
11 ②	12 ③	13 ②	14 ③	15 ②
16 ③	17 ②	18 ⑤	19 ③	20 ③

01 ④

M: Good morning, everyone. I would like to tell you something important about the elevator. It is not working now. A repairman is going to arrive in about twenty minutes. He will try to fix the problem. Until then, please take the stairs up and down. I'm sorry if this causes you any problems.

안녕하세요, 여러분. 제가 엘리베이터에 대해 중요한 얘기를 해드리려고 합니다. 현재 엘리베이터가 작동하지 않고 있습니다. 수리 기사가 약 20분 후에 도착할 것입니다. 그가 문제를 고치기 위해 노력할 겁니다. 그때까지는 계단으로 오르내리시기 바랍니다. 불편을 드려서 죄송합니다.

해설 안내방송에는 인사말 뒤에 그 목적이 바로 드러난다. 엘리베이터가 고장 나서 수리업자가 올 것이라는 내용이다.

어휘 work (기계, 장치 등이) 작동하다 repairman 수리업자 fix 수리하다 take the stairs 계단을 이용하다 up and down 아래위로 cause (문제 등을) 초래하다

02 ②

M: How was your trip to Busan last weekend?
지난 주말에 너의 부산 여행은 어땠어?

W: It was great. But it took so long to get there.
좋았어. 그런데 거기 가는 데 무척 오래 걸리더라.

M: How long did it take? 얼마나 오래 걸렸어?

W: It usually takes five hours. But it took eight hours this time.
보통은 다섯 시간이 걸려. 그런데 이번에는 여덟 시간이 걸렸어.

M: The same thing happened to me last year. It took ten hours to get to Yeosu. 나한테도 작년에 같은 일이 벌어졌어. 여수까지 가는 데 열 시간이 걸렸거든.

W: I can't believe it! 믿을 수 없어!

해설 두 사람 모두 이동 시간이 오래 걸린 경험에 대해 말했다. how

long, take 등을 이용해서 시간이 얼마나 걸리는지 말할 수 있다.

03 ②

M: Hello, everyone. It's time for the global weather report. New York and L.A. will have rainy weather today. There will be sunny skies in Paris and Rome. London will have very windy weather. Tokyo and Seoul will both have cloudy weather. And Bangkok will be hot and sunny.

안녕하세요, 여러분. 지구촌 날씨 정보 시간입니다. 뉴욕과 로스앤젤레스는 오늘 비가 내릴 것입니다. 파리와 로마는 맑은 하늘을 보이겠습니다. 런던에는 바람이 많이 불 것입니다. 도쿄와 서울은 모두 흐린 날씨를 보이겠습니다. 그리고 방콕은 덥고 화창할 것입니다.

04 ④

W: My name is Mina. Every day, I write in my journal. I write at least one page each time. I write about many things. Sometimes I write about my daily activities and weather. I like to write down my thoughts, too. Sometimes I write about my plans for the future. Nobody can read my diary. It's only for me.

제 이름은 미나예요. 저는 매일 일기를 써요. 저는 매번 적어도 한 페이지를 적어요. 저는 여러 가지에 대해 써요. 때로는 제 일상 생활과 날씨를 기록해요. 저는 제 생각을 적는 것도 좋아해요. 가끔 저는 미래의 계획에 대해 써요. 아무도 제 일기를 읽을 수 없어요. 그건 저만을 위한 것이니까요.

05 ③

M: I'm going to Tina's birthday party. How about you?
나는 티나의 생일파티에 갈 거야. 너는?

W: I'd like to, but I can't. My sister is in the hospital.
나도 그러고 싶지만, 안돼. 우리 언니가 병원에 있어.

M: Really? Tina thinks you're coming.
정말이야? 티나는 네가 온다고 생각하고 있어.

W: I didn't know that. 나는 그런 줄 몰랐어.

M: You should call her and apologize for missing her party. 너는 그 애한테 전화를 걸어서 파티에 못 가는 것에 대해 사과해야 해.

W: Okay. I will. 알겠어. 그렇게 할게.

06 ⑤

W: When will the sun rise? 해가 언제 뜰까?

M: It should rise fifteen minutes from now.
지금부터 15분 있으면 뜰 거야.

W: What time is it? 지금 몇 시야?

M: It's five forty. 5시 40분이야.

W: So it will rise at five fifty-five. Thanks.
그러면 해는 5시 55분에 뜨겠구나. 고마워.

07 ①

W: Are you planning to visit Mexico this summer vacation?
너는 이번 여름 방학에 멕시코를 방문할 계획이니?

M: Yes. My uncle lives there. So I'll visit him and his wife. 응. 우리 삼촌이 거기에 살아. 그래서 나는 삼촌과 숙모를 방문할 거야.

W: I envy you a lot. What will you do there?
난 네가 무척 부럽다. 넌 그곳에서 무엇을 할 거야?

M: I'll spend some time in the jungle there.
나는 그곳의 정글에서 시간을 보낼 거야.

W: That sounds interesting. 그거 참 흥미롭다.

M: You're right. I can't wait to go.
맞아. 난 빨리 가고 싶어.

08 ③

M: Did you get the dress you ordered online?
네가 온라인으로 주문한 옷은 받았어?

W: No, I didn't. 아니, 못 받았어.

M: Why not? 왜 못 받았어?

W: The store didn't have my size. I have to wait until Friday.
그 가게에 내 사이즈가 없대. 나는 금요일까지 기다려야 해.

M: I'm sorry to hear that. 그거 안 됐다.

W: It's all right. I don't mind.
괜찮아. 나는 신경 쓰지 않아.

09 ③

[*Telephone rings.*] [전화벨이 울린다.]

M: Johnson Customer Service. May I help you?
존슨 고객 서비스입니다. 무엇을 도와드릴까요?

W: Hello. My digital camera doesn't work.
안녕하세요. 제 디지털카메라가 작동하지 않아서요.

M: Did you drop it on the ground?
그것을 땅에 떨어뜨리셨나요?

W: No, I didn't. It just stopped taking pictures.
아니요. 그냥 사진이 찍히지 않아요.

M: I see. Please bring it to the service center.
그렇군요. 그걸 서비스 센터로 가져와 주세요.

W: Okay. I'll do that this afternoon.
네. 오늘 오후에 그렇게 할게요.

해설 전화를 받은 사람의 인사말에서부터 직업을 예상할 수 있다. 서비스센터 직원과 고객 사이의 통화이다.

어휘 Customer Service 고객 서비스 work (기계, 장치 등이) 작동하다 drop 떨어뜨리다, 떨어지다

10 ②

① There is a vase on the table.
탁자 위에 꽃병이 있다.

② There is a dog sleeping on the sofa.
소파 위에서 개가 잠을 자고 있다.

③ There is a chair in the room.
방 안에 의자가 있다.

④ There is a bag on the chair.
의자 위에 가방이 있다.

⑤ There is a lamp beside the sofa.
소파 옆에 전등이 있다.

해설 사물의 위치를 묻는 문제는 위치를 나타내는 in, on, beside 등의 전치사를 잘 들어야 한다.

어휘 vase 꽃병 lamp 전등, 전기 스탠드, 램프 beside ~옆에

11 ②

W: What are your plans for this weekend?
이번 주말에 너의 계획은 뭐야?

M: I'm not sure. I might visit my friend in Incheon. How about you?
확실치 않아. 나는 인천에 사는 친구를 방문할 수도 있어. 너는?

W: I'll spend time at the library. I have to do my English homework.
나는 도서관에서 시간을 보내려고 해. 영어 숙제를 해야 하거든.

M: Good luck. I hope you finish it.
행운을 빌어. 네가 그걸 끝낼 수 있길 바랄게.

W: Thanks. Have a great weekend.
고마워. 즐거운 주말 보내.

해설 남자와 여자의 계획을 구분하여 듣는다. 친구를 만나는 것은 남자의 계획이다.

어휘 sure 확신하는 spend time 시간을 보내다

12 ③

M: Hi, Cindy. What are you doing now?
안녕, 신디. 너 지금 뭐 하고 있어?

W: Good evening, Tim. I'm reading a magazine.
안녕, 팀. 나는 잡지를 읽고 있어.

M: What kind of magazine is it?
그건 어떤 종류의 잡지야?

W: It's about cooking. 요리에 관한 거야.

M: Really? Do you enjoy cooking?
그래? 너는 요리하는 것을 즐기니?

W: I love it. I like baking cakes and cookies.
아주 좋아해. 난 케이크와 쿠키 굽는 것을 좋아해.

M: I'd like to try them sometime.
언젠가는 네 요리를 먹어보고 싶어.

해설 대화 내용과 조금씩 다른 오답 선택지에 주의한다.

어휘 magazine 잡지 what kind of 어떤 종류의 bake 굽다 try 먹어보다 sometime 언젠가

13 ②

[*Telephone rings.*] [전화벨이 울린다.]

W: Hello. 여보세요.

M: Hi, Mom. It's Joe. I'm glad you are still home now.
안녕하세요, 엄마. 저 조예요. 지금 아직 집에 계시다니 다행이에요.

W: What do you need, Joe? 뭐가 필요하니, 조?

M: I left my history notebook on my desk. Can you please bring it to school? 제가 제 책상 위에 역사 공책을 놓고 왔어요. 학교에 그것을 가져다 주시겠어요?

W: Yes, but please don't forget again.
알았다, 하지만 다시는 잊지 말아라.

M: I'll try to remember, Mom. Thanks.
기억하도록 노력할게요, 엄마. 고마워요.

해설 남자의 대사인 'Can you please ~?'에 부탁하는 내용이 있다. 여자의 마지막 대사인 'please don't forget ~'에도 당부의 의미가 있으니 구분하여 듣는다.

어휘 bring to ~로 가지고 오다 don't forget ~을 잊지 마라 remember 기억하다

14 ③

M: Ms. Lee, I finished writing my paper.
이 선생님, 저는 시험지 작성을 끝냈어요.

W: Did you check it over?
그것을 자세히 살펴봤니?

M: Yes, I did. May I leave the classroom now?
네, 했어요. 저 이제 교실을 나가도 될까요?

W: Wait a second. Please give me your paper. I'll take a look at it.
잠깐만. 네 시험지를 나에게 주렴. 내가 한번 볼게.

M: Here you are. 여기 있어요.

W: Okay. You can go out now.
그래. 넌 이제 나가도 돼.

해설 'May I ~?'로 허락을 구하는 남자에게 여자는 확인 과정을 거친

뒤 마지막에 'You can ~'으로 허락을 했다.

어휘 paper 시험지, 보고서 check over ~을 자세히 살피다

15 ②

M: Excuse me. Is there a stationery store near here?
실례합니다. 이 근처에 문구점이 있나요?

W: Yes, there is. Just go straight down this street.
네, 있어요. 그냥 이 길을 따라 쭉 가세요.

M: Just go straight? That's it?
그냥 직진이요? 그게 다인가요?

W: Yes, it's on the left side of the street. It's beside a drugstore. 네, 문구점은 길 왼쪽에 있어요. 약국 옆이에요.

M: Beside a drugstore? That's easy.
약국 옆이요? 그거 쉽네요.

W: Be careful. There's another drugstore on the right.
조심하세요. 오른쪽에 다른 약국이 하나 있거든요.

M: Okay. Thanks. 네. 고마워요.

해설 직진 후 왼쪽에 보이는 약국 옆이 문구점이다.

어휘 stationery store 문구점 beside ~옆에 another 또 하나의, 다른

16 ③

W: I have to buy some notebooks for school.
나는 학교에서 쓸 공책을 몇 권 사야 해.

M: How many subjects will you take this fall?
올 가을에 너는 얼마나 많은 과목을 수강하니?

W: I will have six classes. I'm taking English, P.E., history, and music.
나는 여섯 과목을 들을 거야. 영어, 체육, 역사, 그리고 음악을 들을 거야.

M: What are the other two? Will you study art?
다른 두 과목은 뭐야? 넌 미술을 공부할 거니?

W: No, I won't. The other two are science and math.
아니. 다른 두 개는 과학과 수학이야.

M: Good luck. 행운을 빌어.

해설 미술(art) 역시 대화에 언급되긴 했으나 여자가 'No, I won't.'라고 말했으므로 수강하지 않는 과목이다.

어휘 subject 과목 take (특정 과목을) 수강하다 P.E. 체육 (physical education) the other two (여러 개 중) 나머지 두 개

17 ②

① M: May I take your order, please?
주문을 받아도 될까요?

W: Yes. I'll have a cheeseburger and fries.
네. 저는 치즈버거와 감자튀김을 먹을게요.

② M: Hello. May I speak with Janet?
여보세요. 재닛과 통화할 수 있을까요?

W: Yes, I spoke with her yesterday.
네, 저는 어제 그녀와 이야기했어요.

③ M: How old is your sister? 네 여동생은 몇 살이야?

W: She's ten years old. 그 애는 열 살이야.

④ M: How may I help you? 무엇을 도와드릴까요?

W: I need to find a present for my friend.
제 친구를 위한 선물을 찾아야 해요.

⑤ M: Why didn't you go to school today?
넌 오늘 왜 학교에 가지 않았어?

W: I had a bad headache.
나는 심한 두통이 있었어.

해설 ②에서 남자의 대사는 전화를 걸었을 때 하는 말이다. 상대방은 'Who's calling?' 'Speaking.' 'She is not here.' 등으로 응답할 수 있다.

어휘 take an order 주문을 받다 bad headache 심한 두통

18 ⑤

W: Wendy wanted to buy a shirt for her father for his birthday. She asked the clerk to show her a green shirt. The clerk showed Wendy a green shirt. It looked very nice. But the shirt looked too small for her father. In this situation, what would Wendy most likely say to the clerk?

웬디는 아버지 생신을 맞아 아버지를 위해 셔츠를 사기를 원했다. 웬디는 점원에게 초록색 셔츠를 보여달라고 요청했다. 점원은 웬디에게 초록색 셔츠를 보여줬다. 그것은 매우 좋아 보였다. 그러나 그 셔츠는 웬디의 아버지에게 너무 작아 보였다. 이 상황에서 웬디는 점원에게 뭐라고 말할 것인가?

Wendy: Do you have something bigger?
더 큰 것이 있나요?

① How much is it? 그것은 얼마예요?
② I want to buy pants, too. 저는 바지도 사고 싶어요.
③ I need something smaller. 저는 더 작은 게 필요해요.
④ Can you show me a red shirt?
빨간색 셔츠를 보여주시겠어요?
⑤ Do you have something bigger? 더 큰 것이 있나요?

해설 웬디는 초록색 셔츠를 마음에 들어 하지만 너무 작은 것이 문제이다. 이 상황에서는 큰 사이즈를 요청하는 것이 자연스럽다.

어휘 clerk 점원 show 보여주다

19 ③

M: Good afternoon. Welcome to Dave's Donuts.
안녕하세요. 데이브스 도넛에 오신 것을 환영합니다.

W: Hi. I'd like to order, please.
안녕하세요. 주문을 하고 싶어요.

M: Sure. What would you like to eat?
물론이죠. 무엇을 드실 건가요?

W: I'd like two jelly donuts and a cola.
젤리 도넛 두 개와 콜라 하나 주세요.

M: No problem. Is this for here or to go?
알겠습니다. 여기에서 드실 건가요, 아니면 가져가실 건가요?

W: It's for here, please. 여기에서 먹을 거예요.

① Yes, it is. 네, 그래요.
② I'll go home soon. 저는 곧 집에 갈 거예요.
③ It's for here, please. 여기에서 먹을 거예요.
④ Here's your change. 여기 거스름돈 있어요.
⑤ That's right. Two donuts. 맞아요. 도넛 두 개요.

해설 남자가 마지막에 'for here'와 'to go' 중 하나를 선택하라고 물었으므로 하나를 골라서 답한 ③이 적절하다.

어휘 for here (주문한 곳에서 먹을 때) to go (음식을 포장해서 갖고 나갈 때) change 거스름돈

20 ③

W: Winter was too long and cold this year.
올해 겨울은 너무 길고 추웠다.
M: I agree. What did you do during winter vacation?
나도 그렇게 생각해. 너는 겨울방학 동안 뭐 했어?
W: Nothing special. How about you?
특별한 건 없었어. 넌 어때?
M: My brother and I went skiing. But he broke his leg.
내 남동생과 나는 스키를 타러 갔어. 그런데 동생의 다리가 부러졌어.
W: That's terrible. How is he doing?
그거 큰일이네. 동생은 좀 어때?
M: He's still in the hospital. 그는 아직 병원에 있어.
W: I'm sorry to hear that. 그거 참 안 됐다.

① No, I can't ski. 아니, 나는 스키를 못 타.
② It's very cold today. 오늘 아주 춥다.
③ I'm sorry to hear that. 그거 참 안됐다.
④ That's wonderful news. 좋은 소식이구나.
⑤ What happened to his arm? 그의 팔은 어떻게 된 거야?

해설 동생이 다쳐서 병원에 있다는 남자를 위로해주는 ③이 적절하다.

어휘 during ~동안 nothing 아무것도 없음, 별것 아님 special 특별한 break 부러뜨리다(break-broke-broken) leg 다리 terrible 끔찍한, 지독한 what happened to ~? ~에 무슨 일이 생겼어? arm 팔

16회 실전모의고사
본문 p.156-157

01 ①	02 ②	03 ④	04 ①	05 ⑤
06 ①	07 ③	08 ④	09 ①	10 ④
11 ⑤	12 ③	13 ②	14 ①	15 ⑤
16 ②	17 ②	18 ④	19 ②	20 ①

01 ①

W: Everyone, please listen carefully. My name is Ms. Park. I'm the school nurse. We want every student to be healthy this year. So please follow these three rules. First, always wash your hands

with soap when you go to the bathroom. Second, cover your mouth when you cough or sneeze. Third, if you feel sick, tell me or your teacher.

여러분, 주의 깊게 들어주세요. 제 이름은 박입니다. 저는 보건교사입니다. 우리는 올해 모든 학생이 건강하기를 바랍니다. 따라서 이 세 가지 규칙을 따라주세요. 첫째, 여러분이 화장실에 갈 때는 항상 비누로 손을 씻으세요. 둘째, 기침이나 재채기를 할 때 입을 가리세요. 셋째, 몸이 아프다면 저 아니면 여러분의 선생님에게 말하세요.

해설 건강을 위해 지켜야 할 세 가지 사항에 대해 말하고 있다.

어휘 listen carefully 주의 깊게 듣다 school nurse 보건교사, 양호 선생님 follow rules 수칙을 따르다 cover 가리다, 씌우다 cough 기침하다 sneeze 재채기하다

02 ②

M: Good morning. It's time for today's weather report for Seoul. Right now, it's very cloudy and cool. It will rain for a couple of hours in the afternoon. Then, the clouds will disappear, and there will be clear skies in the evening. The weather will be a bit windy at night.

안녕하세요. 오늘의 서울 날씨 정보를 전해드릴 시간입니다. 지금 현재, 구름이 많고 시원합니다. 오후에는 두 시간 가량 비가 내리겠습니다. 그 후 구름이 걷힐 것이고, 저녁에는 맑은 하늘을 보이겠습니다. 밤에는 날씨가 다소 바람이 불 것입니다.

해설 morning – afternoon – evening – night의 시간의 흐름에 집중하여 오후에 해당하는 정보를 찾아낸다.

어휘 for a couple of hours 두 시간 동안 disappear 사라지다

03 ④

M: Why don't we go on a picnic tomorrow?
우리 내일 소풍 가는 게 어때?
W: Sure. What should we bring?
좋아. 무엇을 가져가야 할까?
M: Let's bring sandwiches. We can make them.
샌드위치를 가져가자. 우리가 만들 수 있잖아.
W: Okay, but we don't have any food in the house.
그래, 하지만 우리는 집에 아무 음식도 없어.
M: How about going to the supermarket now?
지금 슈퍼마켓에 가는 거 어때?
W: Good thinking. Let's go. 좋은 생각이야. 가자.

해설 대화 직후에 할 일은 대화 마지막에 언급될 가능성이 크다. 'Why don't we ~?' 'Let's ~' 'How about ~?' 등 할 일을 말할 때 쓰는 다양한 표현이 등장했다. ①은 내일 할 일이며, ⑤는 슈퍼마켓에 다녀온 후에 할 일이다.

어휘 go on a picnic 소풍 가다 thinking 생각, 의견

04 ①

W: John, what do you need for school?

존, 학교에서 너는 뭐가 필요하니?

M: I <u>need</u> a new <u>backpack</u>, Mom.
저는 새 가방이 필요해요, 엄마.

W: Okay. You also need some <u>pens</u>, <u>erasers</u>, and <u>notebooks</u>, right?
알겠다. 너는 펜, 지우개, 그리고 공책도 필요하지, 그렇지?

M: Yes. Can I get a new <u>pencil case</u>, too?
네. 새 필통도 살 수 있을까요?

W: You <u>just bought</u> one a month <u>ago</u>.
너는 겨우 한 달 전에 필통을 샀잖아.

M: All right. Then I don't need a new pencil case.
알겠어요. 그러면 저는 새 필통은 필요 없어요.

해설 가방, 펜, 지우개, 공책이 순서대로 언급되며, 마지막에 필통은 사지 않을 거라고 말했다.

어휘 backpack 배낭(가방) eraser 지우개 buy 사다(buy-bought-bought) a month ago 한 달 전에

05 ⑤

M: <u>When</u> does school <u>finish</u> today?
오늘 학교 언제 끝나?

W: It finishes <u>at three</u>. 3시에 끝나.

M: Are you going home <u>after</u> <u>school</u>?
너 방과 후에 집으로 가니?

W: No. I'm going to Lisa's house at three thirty. I'll be <u>home</u> <u>by</u> <u>five</u>. 아니. 나는 3시 30분에 리사의 집에 갈 거야. 나는 집에 5시까지 갈 거야.

해설 3:00은 학교가 끝나는 시각, 3:30은 리사의 집에 가는 시각이다.

어휘 finish 끝나다, 마치다 after school 방과 후에 by ~까지, ~쯤에

06 ①

W: Hi, Steve. How are you doing?
안녕, 스티브. 어떻게 지내니?

M: I'm great, Mary. Are you <u>wearing</u> new <u>clothes</u>?
난 잘 지내, 메리. 너 새 옷을 입었네?

W: Yes, I am. My mom gave them to me <u>for</u> <u>my</u> <u>birthday</u>. 응. 우리 엄마가 내 생일에 옷을 주셨어.

M: That was <u>nice</u> of her. 어머니께서 참 멋지시구나.

W: <u>What</u> do you <u>think</u> <u>of</u> them? 이 옷 어떻게 생각해?

M: They <u>look</u> <u>good</u> <u>on</u> you. 너에게 잘 어울려.

해설 상대방의 옷이나 장신구 등에 대해 칭찬할 때 'look good on'을 써서 말할 수 있다.

어휘 wear 입다 clothes 옷

07 ③

W: Do you have any <u>plans</u> for the weekend?
너는 주말에 계획 있어?

M: I'm <u>going to</u> visit my grandparents. What about you? 나는 조부모님을 방문할 거야. 너는?

W: I <u>was planning to</u> go for a bike ride with my friend. But she <u>canceled</u> on me. 나는 친구와 함께 자전거를 타러 가기로 계획했어. 그런데 그 애가 약속을 취소했어.

M: You must <u>be disappointed</u>. 넌 실망스럽겠구나.

W: To be honest, I <u>am</u>. 솔직히, 그래.

해설 계획이 취소되면 실망스러운 감정이 들 것이다. 남자가 'disappointed(실망한)'라는 말로 여자의 감정을 대변했다.

어휘 plan to ~할 계획이다 bike ride 자전거 타기 cancel 취소하다(cancel-canceled-canceled) to be honest 솔직히 말하자면

08 ④

M: Good morning. How may I help you?
안녕하세요. 무엇을 도와드릴까요?

W: I need some <u>bread</u> for sandwiches.
저는 샌드위치를 만들 빵이 좀 필요해요.

M: I just <u>baked some</u>. Here you are.
제가 방금 빵을 구웠어요. 여기 있습니다.

W: Do you <u>have</u> any birthday <u>cakes</u>?
생일 케이크도 있나요?

M: Yes, there are many here. Please take a look.
네, 여기에 많이 있어요. 살펴보세요.

해설 빵과 케이크를 만드는 사람은 제빵사이다.

어휘 bread 빵 bake 굽다 take a look 보다

09 ①

M: <u>Do you</u> read books? 너는 책을 읽어?

W: <u>Yes</u>, I do. I read <u>all kinds of</u> books.
응. 나는 모든 종류의 책을 읽어.

M: Do you read <u>history</u> books and <u>comic</u> books?
너는 역사책과 만화책도 읽어?

W: Sometimes. But I'm <u>reading</u> a book <u>about lions now</u>. 가끔은. 그런데 요즘 나는 사자에 관한 책을 읽는 중이야.

M: That sounds interesting. 그거 흥미로운걸.

해설 여자가 요즘 읽고 있는 책은 'I'm reading ~ now.'에 드러난다. 역사책과 만화책은 가끔 읽는 책이다.

어휘 all kinds of 모든 종류의, 온갖 comic book 만화책

10 ④

M: When I was a boy, I <u>wanted</u> to be a <u>firefighter</u> and to <u>help</u> people. But I don't want to be a firefighter <u>anymore</u>. Now, I enjoy <u>learning</u>. And I still want to help people. <u>So</u> I want <u>to be</u> a <u>teacher</u>. I can learn many things. Then, I can <u>teach</u> them <u>to students</u>.

저는 어렸을 때 소방관이 되어 사람들을 돕고 싶었어요. 그런데 저는 더 이상 소방관이 되고 싶지 않아요. 현재 저는 공부하는 걸 즐겨요. 그리고 여전히 사람들을 돕고 싶어 하죠. 그래서 저는 교사가 되고 싶어요. 저는 다양한 것을 배울 수 있어요. 그러면 저는 배운 것을 학생들에게 가르쳐 줄 수 있지요.

해설 과거에는 소방관을 꿈꿨으나 지금은 교사를 희망한다고 말했다.

어휘 firefighter 소방관 anymore 더 이상, 이제는

11 ⑤

[*Telephone rings.*] [전화벨이 울린다.]

M: Hello. 여보세요.

W: Hi, Jack. It's Sarah. Are you busy now?
여보세요, 잭. 나 사라야. 너 지금 바쁘니?

M: No, I'm watching TV at home. Do you want to go out? 아니, 난 집에서 TV를 보는 중이야. 너 나가고 싶어?

W: Yeah. How about skateboarding at the park?
응. 공원에서 스케이트보드 타는 거 어때?

M: I can't. My brother took my skateboard. Let's watch a movie.
안돼. 내 동생이 내 스케이트보드를 가져갔어. 영화 보자.

W: Okay. I'll see you at the theater in thirty minutes.
알겠어. 30분 뒤에 영화관에서 보자.

M: Sure. Bye. 좋아. 안녕.

해설 'see you at' 'meet at' 등의 표현 뒤에 만날 장소가 등장한다.

어휘 go out 외출하다 theater 극장, 영화관

12 ③

W: Excuse me. Does this bus go to Eastern Hospital?
실례합니다. 이 버스가 이스턴 병원으로 가나요?

M: Yes, it does. 네, 갑니다.

W: Great. How many stops is it from here?
잘됐네요. 여기에서 몇 정거장인가요?

M: It's four stops from here. 여기에서 네 정거장이요.

W: And how much does it take to ride the bus?
그리고 버스를 타는 데 얼마를 내야 하죠?

M: It's fifteen hundred won. You can put your money there. 1500원입니다. 저기에 돈을 넣으면 돼요.

W: Thanks. 감사합니다.

해설 승객이 버스의 목적지 도달 여부, 정거장 수, 요금 등을 물어보고 기사가 대답해주는 상황이다.

어휘 stop 정거장; 멈추다

13 ②

M: Mom, I will meet Joe at the park. Can you drive me there? 엄마, 저는 공원에서 조를 만날 거예요. 저를 거기까지 태워주실 수 있어요?

W: Sorry, but I can't. 미안하지만 안돼.

M: Why not? 왜 안돼요?

W: I have to go to the hospital now.
나는 지금 병원에 가야 하거든.

M: Why are you going there?
거기에 왜 가시는 거예요?

W: Your aunt is there. She's not feeling well.
네 이모가 거기에 계셔. 이모가 몸이 좋지 않다는구나.

해설 남자의 질문 'Why not?' 이후에 이유가 드러난다.

어휘 drive 태워다 주다; 운전하다 not feeling well (몸, 기분이) 안 좋은

14 ①

M: I think we're lost. Do you know where we are?
우린 길을 잃은 것 같아. 우리가 어디에 있는지 넌 알아?

W: No, I don't. I don't know this place.
아니. 나는 이 곳을 몰라.

M: We should find a map. 우린 지도를 찾아야 해.

W: Why don't you ask that man for directions?
네가 저 남자에게 길 안내를 부탁하지 그래?

M: Okay. I'll talk to him.
알았어. 내가 남자에게 말해 볼게.

해설 여자의 마지막 대사 'Why don't you ~?'에 요청한 내용이 있다. 남자의 대사에 'talk to him'도 힌트가 된다.

어휘 lost 길을 잃은 directions 길 안내

15 ⑤

M: Hello. Is there a post office in this neighborhood?
안녕하세요. 이 동네에 우체국이 있나요?

W: Sure. Do you need directions?
당연하죠. 길 안내가 필요하신가요?

M: Yes, please. 네, 부탁해요.

W: Go straight to the corner. Then, turn right.
모퉁이까지 직진하세요. 그 다음에 우회전하세요.

M: What should I do next?
다음에 제가 무엇을 해야 하죠?

W: Walk straight. It's between the restaurant and the pet store.
곧장 걸어가세요. 우체국은 식당과 애완동물 가게 사이에 있어요.

해설 식당과 애완동물 가게 사이에 있다는 마지막 힌트만으로도 정답을 찾을 수 있으니 끝까지 집중한다.

어휘 neighborhood 지역, 근처 directions 길 안내 between ~사이에 pet store 애완동물 가게

16 ②

① M: What's your favorite class? 네가 좋아하는 수업은 뭐야?
   W: I like math the most. 나는 수학을 제일 좋아해.

② M: Do you play basketball with your friends?
   너는 친구들과 농구를 하니?
   W: Yes, I have a lot of friends. 응, 나는 친구가 많아.

③ M: How should we go to the market?
   우리는 시장까지 어떻게 가야 해?
   W: Let's take the subway. 지하철을 타자.

④ M: What do you want to buy?
   너는 무엇을 사고 싶어?
   W: I'd like to buy some apples.
   나는 사과를 좀 사고 싶어.

⑤ M: How's the weather right now?

지금 현재 날씨가 어때?

W: It's really <u>warm</u> and <u>sunny</u>.
　무척 따뜻하고 화창해.

해설 ②의 질문에 대한 응답으로 'Yes'까지는 적절하지만 뒤에 이어진 내용 때문에 자연스럽지 않다.

17 ②

[*Telephone rings.*] [전화벨이 울린다.]

M: Hello. 여보세요.

W: Hi, Greg. It's Mary. I <u>have</u> a <u>question</u>.
　안녕, 그레그. 나 메리야. 난 질문이 있어.

M: Sure. What is it? 좋아. 뭔데?

W: <u>When</u> is our <u>math</u> <u>test</u>? Is it on Wednesday or Thursday?
　우리 수학 시험이 언제야? 수요일, 아니면 목요일?

M: It's <u>tomorrow</u>. 내일이야.

W: Really? I need to <u>start</u> <u>studying</u> then. Thanks.
　정말? 그럼 나는 공부를 시작해야겠어. 고마워.

해설 시험, 수학 등을 이용한 오답 함정에 주의한다.

18 ④

M: Sumi goes shopping at the market. She sees a <u>scarf</u> and <u>wants</u> to <u>buy</u> it. She <u>asks</u> the salesman for the <u>price</u>. He tells her the price, but Sumi <u>doesn't</u> have <u>enough</u> <u>money</u>. The salesman asks if Sumi wants to buy the scarf. In this situation, what would Sumi most likely say to the salesman?

수미는 시장에 쇼핑을 간다. 수미는 스카프를 보고 그것을 사고 싶어 한다. 그녀는 판매원에게 가격을 물어본다. 판매원이 그 가격을 알려주지만 수미는 돈을 충분히 갖고 있지 않다. 그 판매원은 수미에게 그 스카프를 사고 싶은지 묻는다. 이 상황에서 수미는 판매원에게 뭐라고 말할까?

Sumi: <u>No thanks. It costs too much.</u> 됐어요. 너무 비싸네요.

① Thanks for saying that. 그렇게 말해줘서 고마워요.
② You can put it in the bag. 그것을 그 가방에 넣어도 돼요.
③ No, I'm not wearing a scarf.
　아니요, 저는 스카프를 매고 있지 않아요.
④ No thanks. It costs too much. 됐어요. 너무 비싸네요.
⑤ Yes, you can show me another one.
　네, 제게 다른 걸 보여주세요.

해설 물건이 마음에 들지만 돈이 모자라므로 그것을 사지 않을 거라는 말을 할 것이다.

어휘 price 가격 enough money 충분한 돈 cost too much 너무 비싸다

19 ②

W: Let's <u>go</u> <u>outside</u> this afternoon.
　오늘 오후에 밖에 나가자.

M: We can't. It's going to <u>rain</u> <u>today</u>.

안돼. 오늘 비가 내릴 거야.

W: Then what should we do?
　그러면 우린 무엇을 해야 할까?

M: Do you <u>like</u> to <u>do</u> jigsaw <u>puzzles</u>?
　너는 조각 그림 맞추는 것을 좋아하니?

W: Yes, I do. 응, 좋아해.

M: <u>Let's do a puzzle then.</u> 그럼 퍼즐을 하자.

① How much is it? 그거 얼마야?
② Let's do a puzzle then. 그럼 퍼즐을 하자.
③ Yes, we can watch a movie. 응, 우린 영화를 볼 수 있어.
④ I see. You don't like puzzles.
　알겠어. 넌 퍼즐을 좋아하지 않는구나.
⑤ How about going out for dinner?
　식사하러 나가는 건 어때?

해설 퍼즐을 좋아하냐는 물음에 여자가 좋아한다고 말했으므로 퍼즐을 하자고 제안하는 ②가 적절하다.

어휘 jigsaw puzzle 조각 그림 맞추기

20 ①

M: Are you going to <u>enter</u> the <u>science</u> <u>fair</u>?
　너는 과학 박람회에 참가할 거야?

W: I don't think so. 나는 안 할 것 같은데.

M: <u>Why</u> <u>not</u>? 왜 안 해?

W: I don't like science. <u>Are</u> <u>you</u> <u>going</u> to enter the science fair?
　나는 과학을 좋아하지 않아. 너는 과학 박람회에 참가할 거야?

M: Sure. 당연하지.

W: <u>Why</u> do you want to enter it? 너는 왜 참가하고 싶은 거야?

M: <u>I want to see a robot.</u> 나는 로봇을 보고 싶거든.

① I want to see a robot. 나는 로봇을 보고 싶거든.
② Yes, we can go together. 응, 우리는 같이 갈 수 있어.
③ Your science project is great. 네 과학 프로젝트는 훌륭해.
④ There are many kinds of food. 여러 종류의 음식이 있어.
⑤ Do you want to come with me?
　너는 나와 함께 가고 싶어?

해설 여자는 이미 박람회에 가지 않을 거라고 말했으므로 함께 가자는 말은 어울리지 않는다. 과학 박람회에 가고 싶은 이유로 ①이 가장 자연스럽다.

어휘 enter 참가하다, 들어가다 science fair 과학 박람회

01 ⑤	02 ①	03 ②	04 ②	05 ④
06 ②	07 ②	08 ③	09 ④	10 ④
11 ①	12 ③	13 ⑤	14 ②	15 ⑤
16 ③	17 ②	18 ④	19 ③	20 ③

01 ⑤

① M: May I take your order? 제가 주문을 받아도 되겠습니까?

W: I'd like the roast chicken, please. 통닭구이 하나 주세요.

② M: How much does this cost? 이건 가격이 얼마인가요?

W: It costs ten dollars. 10달러입니다.

③ M: What's the matter with the sink?
싱크대에 무슨 문제가 있나요?

W: I think it's broken. 제 생각에는 망가진 것 같아요.

④ M: What do we need to buy? 우리는 뭘 사야 하죠?

W: Let's get some eggs and milk. 계란과 우유를 좀 사죠.

⑤ M: Should I put the food in the oven?
제가 음식을 오븐에 넣어야 하나요?

W: Yes. Let's cook it for one hour.
네. 한 시간 동안 조리하도록 하죠.

[해설] 그림은 오븐에 음식을 넣으려고 하는 상황이므로 ⑤가 올바른 대화 내용이다.

[어휘] take an order 주문을 받다 roast chicken 통닭구이, 구운 치킨 sink 싱크대 broken 고장 난, 망가진 oven 오븐

02 ①

W: I am a bird. I can fly in the air, and I also enjoy swimming in the water. I usually live around lakes or rivers. Sometimes I live in parks. People at the parks enjoy feeding me. In spring, my babies always follow very closely behind me while we swim together.

저는 새입니다. 저는 하늘을 날 수 있고 물에서 수영을 즐기기도 합니다. 저는 주로 호수나 강 주변에 살아요. 저는 때로는 공원에서 살기도 해요. 공원에 있는 사람들은 저에게 먹이를 주는 것을 좋아해요. 봄이 되면 제 새끼들은 우리가 함께 수영을 할 때 항상 제 뒤에 바짝 따라다녀요.

[해설] 그림 중에서 날 수도 있고 헤엄을 칠 수도 있는 것은 오리이다.

[어휘] fly in the air 하늘을 날다 usually 주로, 대부분 lake 호수 sometimes 가끔, 때때로 feed 먹이를 주다 spring 봄 closely 바짝, 접근하여 behind ~뒤에서 while ~하는 동안

03 ②

W: Yesterday was my brother's birthday. My family had a party for him, and we gave him lots of presents. I gave my brother a toy robot. My sister gave a

pencil case to him. My parents gave him a sweater and two books. We had a cake and ate a great dinner. We all had lots of fun.

어제는 내 남동생의 생일이었다. 우리 가족은 그 애를 위해 파티를 열었고, 그에게 많은 선물을 주었다. 나는 남동생에게 장난감 로봇을 주었다. 내 여동생은 그에게 필통을 주었다. 우리 부모님은 그에게 스웨터와 책 두 권을 주셨다. 우리는 케이크를 먹었고 잘 차려진 저녁식사를 했다. 우리 모두는 아주 즐거운 시간을 보냈다.

[어휘] have a party 파티를 열다 lots of 많은 present 선물 pencil case 필통 eat 먹다(eat-ate-eaten)

04 ②

M: Good morning, everyone. This is Clark Bailey. It's time for today's weather forecast. It's a cold, snowy morning. It's going to snow until around four P.M. Then, the snow will stop, but it will still be cloudy in the evening. At night, there will be clear skies, but the temperature will still be cold. Be sure to wear warm clothes today.

안녕하세요, 여러분. 저는 클라크 베일리입니다. 오늘의 일기예보를 전해 드릴 시간입니다. 춥고 눈이 내리는 아침이네요. 오후 4시경까지 눈이 내릴 예정입니다. 그리고 나서 눈은 그치겠지만, 저녁에는 여전히 흐리겠습니다. 밤이 되면 하늘은 맑겠지만 기온은 여전히 추울 것입니다. 오늘은 꼭 따뜻한 옷을 입으세요.

[어휘] time for ~하기 위한 시간 around 약, ~쯤 temperature 온도, 기온 wear 입다 warm clothes 따뜻한 옷

05 ④

W: Did you take out the trash yet?
너 쓰레기를 치웠니?

M: No, I'm doing my homework now.
아니요, 전 지금 숙제를 하고 있어요.

W: You never do your chores on time, David.
넌 언제나 제시간에 집안일을 하지 않는구나, 데이비드.

M: I have too many of them, Mom. Can't Timmy do them?
저는 일이 너무 많아요, 엄마. 티미가 그 일들을 할 수 없나요?

W: Timmy is too young. He can't do them yet.
티미는 너무 어리잖니. 그 애는 아직 그 일들을 할 수 없어.

M: But I need more time to study.
하지만 저는 공부할 시간이 더 필요해요.

W: Okay. I'll take out the trash tonight. But you should do it tomorrow. 알았다. 내가 오늘 밤에 쓰레기를 치우마. 하지만 내일은 네가 그걸 해야 한다.

[해설] chore는 쓰레기를 버리고 분리수거를 하는 등의 자잘한 집안일을 가리킨다.

[어휘] take out 가지고 나가다, 치우다 trash 쓰레기 yet 아직 do chores 집안일을 하다, 허드렛일을 하다 on time 제시간에

06 ②

M: I'm excited about this weekend.
나는 이번 주말이 기대돼.

W: What are you going to do? 넌 뭘 할 건데?

M: I'm going cycling with some friends. We're going to visit the countryside.
난 친구 몇 명이랑 자전거를 탈 거야. 우리는 시골에 갈 거야.

W: That sounds fun. I'm going to help my dad wash his car. 재미있겠는데. 난 아빠가 세차하는 것을 도울 거야.

M: Why don't you go with us? 우리랑 함께 가는 게 어때?

W: Sorry, but I don't enjoy cycling.
미안하지만 나는 자전거 타는 걸 안 좋아해.

해설 여자의 대사 'I'm going to ~'에 여자의 할 일이 등장한다. 자전거를 타고 시골에 가는 것은 남자의 계획이다.

어휘 excited about ~에 들뜨다, 흥분하다 cycling 자전거 타기 countryside 시골 지역 wash one's car 세차하다

07 ②

M: Hurry up. We're going to be late for the bus.
서둘러. 우리 버스 시간에 늦겠다.

W: It's three twenty. The bus doesn't come until three thirty. 지금 3시 20분이야. 버스는 3시 30분까지는 안 올 거야.

M: Not today. It comes at three twenty-five on weekends. 오늘은 아니야. 주말에는 3시 25분에 온다고.

W: I didn't know that. Let's hurry.
내가 그걸 몰랐네. 서두르자.

M: Okay. Let's go. 그래. 가자.

해설 3:30은 평일의 버스 도착 시간이고, 3:25는 주말의 버스 도착 시간이다.

어휘 hurry up 서두르다 be late for ~에 늦다
on weekends 주말에

08 ③

M: Why are you smiling? Did you get some good news? 너 왜 웃고 있어? 좋은 소식이라도 있어?

W: Do you remember my friend Emily?
넌 내 친구 에밀리를 기억하니?

M: Yes, I remember her. She moved to another city, right? 응. 기억하지. 그 애는 다른 도시로 이사 갔잖아, 맞지?

W: Right. She emailed me this morning. She's coming to visit me next week. I'm so happy about that.
맞아. 그 애가 오늘 오전에 나한테 이메일을 보냈어. 그 애는 다음 주에 나를 보러온대. 나는 그 소식 때문에 정말 기뻐.

M: That's wonderful. I hope you two have a great time.
아주 멋진 소식이네. 너희 둘이 좋은 시간을 보내길 바랄게.

해설 이사 간 친구가 놀러 온다는 소식을 들은 여자는 'I am so happy about that.'으로 기쁨을 드러냈다.

어휘 smile 웃다, 미소 짓다 move to ~로 이사 가다, 옮기다
have a great time 즐거운 시간을 보내다

09 ④

W: Hello. I'd like to buy these two books.
저기요. 제가 이 책 두 권을 사고 싶어요.

M: Sure. The first book is five dollars. And the second book is seven dollars.
네. 첫 번째 책은 5달러이고, 두 번째 책은 7달러입니다.

W: That's twelve dollars, right? 그럼 12달러, 맞죠?

M: That's correct. 맞습니다.

W: I'll pay with cash. Here's twenty dollars.
저는 현금으로 낼게요. 여기 20달러요.

M: Thank you. Here are your books and your change. That's eight dollars.
감사합니다. 여기 손님의 책과 잔돈이 있습니다. 8달러예요.

해설 대화에 언급된 금액이 모두 선택지에 있으므로 각 금액의 의미를 세심히 파악해야 한다.

어휘 correct 정확한, 맞는 pay with cash 현금으로 지불하다
change 잔돈

10 ④

W: Is that your family in the picture?
사진 속에 있는 게 너희 가족이니?

M: Yes, it is. You can see my father there.
응, 그래. 저쪽에 우리 아버지가 보일 거야.

W: What does he do? 아버지는 뭐 하셔?

M: He's a banker. He works for a large bank.
아버지는 은행원이야. 큰 은행에서 근무하셔.

W: What about your mother? 너희 어머니는?

M: She's a chef at a restaurant. She cooks Italian food.
어머니는 음식점의 주방장이야. 이탈리아 음식을 요리하시지.

W: Wow. Your parents have great jobs.
우와. 너희 부모님은 대단한 직업을 갖고 계시구나.

해설 아버지의 직업과 어머니의 직업을 구분하여 듣는다.

어휘 picture 사진, 그림 banker 은행원, 은행의 간부
work for ~에서 일하다 chef 요리사, 주방장

11 ①

W: I'm going shopping at the department store tomorrow. But I've never been there before.
난 내일 백화점으로 쇼핑하러 갈 거야. 하지만 나는 전에 거기 가본 적이 없어.

M: You're not driving there, are you? Tomorrow is a holiday.
너 거기까지 운전할 건 아니지, 그렇지? 내일은 공휴일이거든.

W: I know. Should I take the subway there?
나도 알아. 내가 거기까지 지하철을 타야 할까?

M: The subway stop is too far from the store. Why don't you take a taxi?
지하철역은 백화점에서 너무 멀어. 택시를 타는 게 어때?

W: That's expensive. I guess I'll just ride on the bus.
그건 비싸잖아. 난 그냥 버스를 타야 할 것 같아.

M: That's a good idea. You can take a bus right to the

department store.

그거 좋은 생각이야. 넌 버스를 타고 백화점까지 바로 갈 수 있어.

해설 교통수단을 묻는 문제에서는 주로 뒷부분에 정답이 나온다.

어휘 department store 백화점 holiday 공휴일; 휴가 subway stop 지하철역 far from ~로부터 먼 take a taxi 택시를 타다 expensive 비싼 guess 짐작하다 ride on a bus 버스를 타다(= take a bus) right 곧바로, 즉시

12 ③

M: Sumi, you're one hour late for school.
수미야, 넌 학교에 한 시간 늦었구나.

W: I'm so sorry about that, Mr. Kennedy.
그 점은 정말 죄송해요, 케네디 선생님.

M: What happened? Didn't your alarm go off?
무슨 일이 있었니? 알람이 울리지 않았어?

W: Yes, it did. But I got on the wrong bus today. I went the wrong way. 아니요, 울렸어요. 하지만 전 오늘 버스를 잘못 탔어요. 길을 잘못 간 거예요.

M: You should be more careful in the future.
앞으로는 좀 더 주의하거라.

W: I promise I will. 그러겠다고 약속할게요.

해설 알람에 대한 이야기가 함정으로 언급됐다.

어휘 late for school 학교에 지각하다 alarm 알람, 자명종 go off (자명종이) 울리다 get on the wrong bus 버스를 잘못 타다 go the wrong way 길을 잘못 들다 careful 신중한, 주의 깊은 promise 약속하다; 약속

13 ⑤

[Telephone rings.] [전화벨이 울린다.]

W: Dr. Oliver's Medical Clinic. How may I help you?
닥터 올리버 병원입니다. 무엇을 도와드릴까요?

M: Hello. This is Dave Smith. I am going to see the doctor at four o'clock today. 여보세요. 저는 데이브 스미스라고 합니다. 제가 오늘 4시에 진찰을 받기로 되어 있거든요.

W: That's correct, Mr. Smith. Is there a problem?
맞습니다, 스미스 씨. 무슨 문제가 있나요?

M: Yes, there is. I feel really sick. Can I go there earlier? 네, 있습니다. 제가 정말로 몸이 아프거든요. 제가 병원에 더 일찍 갈 수 있을까요?

W: Can you come at eleven? Dr. Oliver can see you then.
11시에 오실 수 있나요? 올리버 선생님이 그때 진찰할 수 있거든요.

M: Thanks. I'll be there then.
고맙습니다. 그럼 그때 갈게요.

해설 초반에 상황 설명이 이루어진 뒤 남자의 대사 'Can I go there earlier?'에 목적이 드러난다.

어휘 medical clinic 병원 see a doctor 병원에 가다, 진찰을 받다 correct 정확한 sick 아픈, 병든 earlier 보다 일찍 (early-earlier-earliest) then 그때, 그러면, 그 다음에

14 ②

W: Eric, is your father here at the festival?
에릭, 너희 아버지가 여기 축제 현장에 계시니?

M: Yes, he's standing over there.
응, 아버지는 저쪽에 서 계셔.

W: Is he wearing shorts?
아버지는 반바지를 입고 계시니?

M: No, he's not wearing shorts. He's wearing pants.
아니, 아버지는 반바지를 입고 계시지 않아. 긴바지를 입고 계셔.

W: Is he the man with glasses?
안경을 쓴 분이니?

M: No, my dad doesn't wear glasses.
아니, 우리 아버지는 안경을 안 쓰셔.

W: Okay. I see him now.
알았다. 이제 너희 아버지가 보인다.

해설 pants는 일반적으로 긴 바지를 의미한다. 남자의 아버지는 긴 바지를 입었고 안경은 쓰지 않았다.

어휘 festival 축제 standing 서 있는 over there 저쪽에 shorts 반바지 pants (긴) 바지 wear glasses 안경을 쓰다

15 ⑤

M: Hello. Can I help you with something?
안녕하세요. 제가 뭘 도와드릴까요?

W: Yes, I'm looking for a new sweater.
네, 저는 신상품 스웨터를 찾고 있어요.

M: We have many sweaters right here. How about this one?
저희는 이곳에 많은 스웨터를 보유하고 있습니다. 이건 어떠세요?

W: I don't like the styles. Can you show me some other sweaters, please?
스타일이 마음에 들지 않네요. 다른 스웨터들을 보여 주시겠어요?

M: Sure. Follow me. 물론이죠. 저를 따라오세요.

해설 요청할 때는 'Can you ~?', 'Would you ~?', 'Do you mind if ~?' 등의 표현이 나온다. 해당 표현 뒤에 요청하는 내용이 이어진다.

어휘 look for ~을 찾다 sweater 스웨터 right here 바로 이곳에 follow 따라가다, 따라오다

16 ③

M: This science homework is so boring. I really hate science.
이 과학 숙제는 정말 재미없어. 난 정말 과학이 싫어.

W: I love science. I want to be a scientist in the future. What do you like?
나는 과학을 좋아해. 난 장차 과학자가 되고 싶어. 넌 뭘 좋아하니?

M: I like movies a lot. 난 영화를 많이 좋아해.

W: Do you want to be an actor? 넌 배우가 되고 싶은 거니?

M: No, I don't. I want to be a movie director in the future. 아니야. 나는 앞으로 영화 감독이 되고 싶어.

해설 여자와 남자의 장래 희망을 구분하여 듣는다.

어휘 boring 지루한, 재미없는 hate 미워하다, 싫어하다
scientist 과학자 in the future 장차, 미래에 actor 배우
movie director 영화 감독(= film director)

17 ②

W: What's wrong with your arm? 네 팔은 왜 그래?
M: I fell down while riding my bike. I hurt my arm.
나는 자전거를 타다가 넘어졌어. 내 팔을 다쳤어.
W: It looks bad. Does it hurt?
상처가 심해 보여. 아프니?
M: Yes, it does. I'll put some medicine on it soon.
응, 아파. 얼른 상처에 약을 좀 바르려고.
W: You should see a doctor. You might have a big problem.
넌 병원에 가야 할 것 같아. 큰 문제가 생길 수도 있잖아.
M: Don't worry. I'll get some rest and will be fine tomorrow. 걱정 마. 좀 쉬고 나면 내일은 괜찮을 거야.

해설 '병원에 가다'라고 할 때는 'see a doctor'라는 표현을 주로 쓰는데, 'go to (the) hospital'은 통원 치료나 입원의 의미가 강하기 때문이다.

어휘 What's wrong with ~? ~에 문제가 있니? arm 팔 fall 넘어지다, 떨어지다(fall-fell-fallen) while ~하는 동안 ride a bike 자전거를 타다 hurt 다치게 하다; 아프다 get some rest 약간의 휴식을 취하다

18 ④

① M: Would you like another piece of pizza?
피자 한 조각 더 드실래요?
W: No, thank you. I'm full. 아니요, 괜찮아요. 배불러요.
② M: Are you meeting your friend later?
넌 이따가 네 친구를 만날 거니?
W: Yes, I am. Sarah and I will meet at five.
네, 그래요. 사라와 저는 5시에 만날 거예요.
③ M: I can't find my notebook. 내 공책을 못 찾겠어.
W: I'll help you find it. What does it look like?
내가 그걸 찾는 걸 도와줄게. 그게 어떻게 생겼니?
④ M: When did you meet Tim? 넌 언제 팀을 만났니?
W: He's my best friend. He lives near me.
그는 나의 가장 친한 친구야. 그는 나랑 가까운 곳에 살아.
⑤ M: Do you have any brothers or sisters?
당신은 남자 형제나 여자 형제가 있나요?
W: Yes. I have an older brother. 네. 저는 오빠가 한 명 있어요.

해설 ④의 질문에서 when으로 물었으므로 시간이나 날짜로 대답해야 한다.

어휘 piece 조각 full 배부른; 가득한 notebook 공책; 노트북 컴퓨터 best friend 가장 친한 친구

19 ③

W: I'm thinking about buying a pet.
난 애완동물을 살까 생각 중이야.

M: Do you think you're ready to take care of one?
네가 애완동물을 돌볼 준비가 되어 있다고 생각하니?
W: Yes, I am. My parents said that I can have one.
응, 그래. 우리 부모님은 내가 한 마리 길러도 된다고 하셨어.
M: That's good news. 그거 좋은 소식이구나.
W: Which should I get, a dog or a cat?
개와 고양이 중에서 내가 무엇을 길러야 할까?
M: You should buy a dog. 넌 개를 사야 해.

① Yes, that's a great idea. 그래, 그거 좋은 생각이야.
② No, I don't have a pet. 아니, 난 애완동물을 갖고 있지 않아.
③ You should buy a dog. 넌 개를 사야 해.
④ What's your cat's name? 네 고양이 이름은 뭐야?
⑤ My family owns a couple of dogs.
우리 가족은 개 두 마리를 키우고 있어.

해설 여자가 둘 중 하나를 선택해서 말해주길 원했으므로 한 가지를 선택한 ③이 적절하다.

어휘 think about ~에 대해 생각하다 pet 애완동물 ready 준비된 take care of ~을 돌보다, 보살피다 own 소유하다
a couple of 둘의

20 ③

W: Good evening, sir. Welcome to Steak Forty-Five.
안녕하세요, 손님. 스테이크 45에 오신 것을 환영합니다.
M: Hello. I'd like a table for two, please.
안녕하세요. 두 명 자리를 주세요.
W: We're very busy tonight. You have to wait for a while. 저희가 오늘 밤은 손님이 무척 많네요. 잠시 기다리셔야 할 것 같군요.
M: How long will we have to wait?
저희가 얼마나 기다려야 하죠?
W: A table will be available in twenty minutes.
테이블 하나가 20분 후에 빌 겁니다.
M: That sounds all right. 알겠습니다.
W: Great. May I have your name, please?
좋습니다. 손님 성함이 어떻게 되시죠?
M: My name is John Martin. 제 이름은 존 마틴입니다.

① I'm ready to order. 저는 주문할 준비가 됐습니다.
② No, that's not my name. 아니요, 그건 제 이름이 아니에요.
③ My name is John Martin. 제 이름은 존 마틴입니다.
④ Thanks. I'll come back later. 고마워요. 이따 다시 올게요.
⑤ I'd like a seat by the window. 창가 쪽 자리에 앉고 싶어요.

해설 여자가 남자에게 정중하게 이름을 물었으므로 이름을 알려준 ③이 와야 한다.

어휘 table for two 두 명이 앉을 수 있는 테이블 busy 손님이 많은, 분주한 for a while 잠시 동안 available 이용할 수 있는 order 주문하다; 주문 seat by the window 창가 쪽 좌석

01 ③	02 ①	03 ⑤	04 ④	05 ④
06 ①	07 ④	08 ⑤	09 ②	10 ①
11 ①	12 ④	13 ②	14 ③	15 ④
16 ④	17 ④	18 ②	19 ③	20 ①

01 ③

M: Susan's birthday is coming soon. What should we give her?
수잔의 생일이 다가온다. 우리가 그녀에게 무엇을 줘야 할까?

W: How about a digital camera? She loves taking pictures.
디지털카메라는 어때? 수잔은 사진 찍는 것을 좋아하잖아.

M: That's a great idea, but a digital camera costs too much. 그거 좋은 생각이긴 한데 디지털카메라는 너무 비싸.

W: You're right. How about a cookbook? She really enjoys cooking. 맞아. 요리책은 어떨까? 수잔은 요리하는 것을 정말 즐기잖아.

M: Okay. We should do that. 그래. 우리 그렇게 하자.

W: Let's go to the bookstore tomorrow. We can find something there.
내일 서점에 가자. 우린 그곳에서 뭔가 찾을 수 있어.

해설 정답을 제외한 사진, 카메라, 요리 등은 모두 오답 함정이다. 대화의 전반적인 내용을 파악하는 것이 중요하다.

어휘 take a picture 사진을 찍다 cost (값이) ~이다 too much 너무, 과도하게 enjoy 즐기다

02 ①

M: Many people have this machine. This is a small object, so you can carry it with you anywhere. You can use this when you want to record something. When you click a button on this, this captures images.

많은 사람들이 이 기계를 갖고 있어요. 이것은 작은 물건이어서 당신이 어디든지 가지고 다닐 수 있지요. 당신이 무언가를 기록하고 싶을 때 이것을 사용할 수 있어요. 당신이 이것의 버튼을 누르면 이것은 모습을 담아냅니다.

어휘 machine 기계 object 물건, 물체 carry 가지고 다니다 record 기록하다; 녹화하다, 녹음하다 click 클릭하다, 누르다 capture 담아내다, 포착하다

03 ⑤

W: Hello, everybody. My name is Mina. This spring, my parents and I are going to fly to Europe. We're going to stay in Italy for one month. We're going to visit many museums and famous places in Rome. I hope we have a wonderful time there.

안녕하세요, 여러분. 제 이름은 미나예요. 올 봄에 저희 부모님과 저는 비행기로 유럽에 간답니다. 우리는 이탈리아에 한 달 동안 머무를 거예요. 우리는 로마의 여러 박물관과 명소를 방문할 거예요. 저는 그곳에서 우리가 멋진 시간을 보내길 바랍니다.

해설 fly to는 비행기로 이동할 것임을 나타낸다. 나라와 도시 이름의 영어 발음에 유의한다.

어휘 fly to ~까지 비행기로 가다 Italy 이탈리아 Rome 로마

04 ④

M: Hi, Michelle. How about seeing a movie tonight? Do you have time?
안녕, 미셸. 오늘 밤에 영화 보는 것 어때? 너 시간 있어?

W: Yes, I do. What movie would you like to see?
응, 나 시간 있어. 어떤 영화를 보고 싶어?

M: The movie is called Summer Story.
'서머 스토리'라는 영화야.

W: That sounds good. What time does the movie start? 그거 좋다. 그 영화는 몇 시에 시작하니?

M: It starts at eight o'clock. So it will begin two hours from now. 그것은 여덟 시에 시작해. 그러니까 앞으로 두 시간 뒤에 시작할 거야.

W: Great. Why don't we visit the library first? I have to return some books there. 좋아. 우리 먼저 도서관에 가는 게 어때? 나는 거기에 책을 몇 권 반납해야 하거든.

M: That's fine. It's close to the movie theater.
괜찮아. 그곳은 영화관과 가까우니까.

해설 영화를 보기 전이라는 시점에 유의하며 듣는다. 주로 대화 후반부에 할 일이 언급된다.

어휘 called ~라는 이름의 return 반납하다, 돌아오다 close to ~에 가까운

05 ④

M: Are you all right? You look very tired.
너 괜찮니? 아주 피곤해 보여.

W: I didn't sleep well last night.
나는 어젯밤에 잠을 잘 못 잤어.

M: Why not? Did you watch television until late at night? 왜 못 잤는데? 밤 늦게까지 텔레비전을 봤니?

W: No, I didn't. My neighbors made a lot of noise last night. The children were running around all night long. 아니야. 내 이웃이 어젯밤에 엄청난 소음을 냈거든. 아이들이 밤새도록 뛰어다니더라고.

M: I'm sorry to hear that. I hope you can get some sleep tonight. 그 말을 들으니 안됐다. 네가 오늘 밤에는 잠을 좀 잘 수 있기를 바랄게.

W: I hope so, too. 나 역시 그러길 바라.

해설 여자의 대사에 주목한다. 점점 구체적인 이유가 언급된다.

어휘 late at night 밤늦게 neighbor 이웃 run around 뛰어다니다 all night long 밤새도록 get some sleep 잠을 좀 자다

06 ①

W: Good afternoon, everyone. This is Joan Woodruff, and I have the <u>weather</u> report now. It's <u>rainy</u> now, <u>but</u> the rain is going to <u>stop</u> this <u>evening</u>. At <u>night</u>, there will be a few <u>clouds</u> in the sky. <u>Tomorrow</u> is going to be <u>sunny</u> all day long. So you won't need your umbrellas.

안녕하세요, 여러분. 저는 조앤 우드러프이고, 이제 일기예보를 알려드리겠습니다. 지금은 비가 내리지만 비는 오늘 저녁에 멈추겠습니다. 밤에는 하늘에 구름이 조금 낄 것입니다. 내일은 온종일 화창하겠습니다. 따라서 우산은 필요 없을 겁니다.

어휘 a few 어느 정도, 몇몇 all day long 온종일 umbrella 우산

07 ④

[*Cellphone rings.*] [휴대폰이 울린다.]

W: Hello, Tim. I heard you <u>got hurt</u> playing basketball today. Are you <u>all right</u> now? 안녕, 팀. 네가 오늘 농구를 하다가 다쳤다고 들었어. 지금은 괜찮아?

M: I hurt my <u>knee</u> in the game and it <u>still</u> <u>hurts</u>. 나는 경기 중에 무릎을 다쳤는데 아직도 아파.

W: Why don't you <u>rub</u> some <u>lotion</u> on it? That will make you <u>feel</u> a lot <u>better</u>. 무릎에 로션을 좀 바르지 그래? 그러면 훨씬 나아질 거야.

M: That's a good idea. I'll <u>ask</u> my father if we have some. 좋은 생각이다. 로션이 있는지 아버지께 여쭤봐야겠어.

W: Good luck. I <u>hope</u> you <u>feel better</u> soon. 행운을 빌어. 네가 어서 낫기를 바랄게.

M: Thanks. See you at school tomorrow. 고마워. 내일 학교에서 보자.

해설 다친 친구의 안부를 묻고 빠른 회복을 위한 조언을 했다. 여자의 마지막 대사인 'I hope you feel better soon.'은 아픈 사람을 위로할 때 자주 쓰는 말이다.

어휘 hear 듣다(hear-heard-heard) hurt 다치게 하다; 아프다 (hurt-hurt-hurt) rub 문지르다, 바르다 feel better 회복하다, 좋아지다

08 ⑤

M: Hi, Sue. What are you doing now? 안녕, 수. 지금 뭐 하고 있어?

W: I'm doing my <u>math</u> homework. Some of these <u>questions</u> are very <u>difficult</u>. 나는 수학 숙제를 하고 있어. 몇몇 문제들이 너무 어려워.

M: But you're <u>good</u> at math. You always get <u>high</u> <u>grades</u> on math tests. 하지만 너는 수학을 잘하잖아. 넌 수학 시험에서 항상 높은 점수를 받지.

W: I enjoy <u>solving</u> math problems. I want to be a math <u>teacher</u> in the future. How about you? 나는 수학 문제 푸는 걸 즐기거든. 나는 앞으로 수학 교사가 되고 싶어. 너는 어때?

M: I want to be a <u>computer</u> <u>programmer</u>. But my <u>parents</u> want me to be a <u>lawyer</u>. 나는 컴퓨터 프로그래머

가 되고 싶어. 그런데 부모님께서는 내가 변호사가 되길 원하셔.

W: Why do they want you to become a lawyer? 그 분들은 왜 네가 변호사가 되길 원하시는 거야?

M: They think people have a lot of <u>respect</u> for lawyers. 사람들이 변호사를 무척 존경한다고 생각하시거든.

해설 여자의 질문인 'How about you?'에 이은 남자의 대답 'I want to be ~' 문장에 정답이 있다. 총 세 가지 직업이 언급되므로 주의한다.

어휘 some of ~중의 조금 solve 해결하다, 풀다 lawyer 변호사 respect 존경; 존경하다

09 ②

M: Good morning. What are you <u>looking</u> <u>for</u>? 안녕하세요. 무엇을 찾으시나요?

W: I'd like to buy a <u>new bag</u> for my daughter. 저는 딸에게 줄 새 가방을 사려고 해요.

M: What about this one? This <u>style</u> is very <u>popular</u> these days. 이건 어때요? 이 스타일은 요즘 아주 인기 있답니다.

W: I like the color. <u>How</u> <u>much</u> does it cost? 색상이 마음에 드네요. 얼마죠?

M: It <u>costs</u> <u>thirty</u> thousand won. Would you like to buy it? 3만 원입니다. 이것을 구입하시겠어요?

W: Yes, I would. Here is <u>fifty</u> thousand won. 네, 그럴게요. 여기 5만 원 있습니다.

M: Okay. Here are your <u>change</u> and the receipt. Have a nice day. 네. 여기 거스름돈과 영수증이에요. 좋은 하루 되세요.

W: Thank you. Have a nice day, too. 고맙습니다. 좋은 하루 되세요.

해설 'It costs ~'에서 상품의 금액이, 'Here is ~'에서 지불한 금액이 언급된다. 여자가 낸 5만 원에서 가방의 가격인 3만 원을 빼면 거스름 돈은 2만 원이다.

어휘 popular 인기 있는 change 거스름돈, 잔돈; 바꾸다 receipt 영수증

10 ①

W: Why do you <u>look</u> so <u>happy</u>, Tim? 팀, 넌 왜 그렇게 즐거워 보이니?

M: I <u>won</u> two <u>free</u> <u>tickets</u> to the rock <u>concert</u> tonight. Do you want to <u>go</u> there <u>with</u> me? 나는 오늘 밤 록 콘서트 무료 입장권 두 장에 당첨됐어. 너 나와 함께 가고 싶니?

W: I'd love to go to the concert. But doesn't your sister like rock music? 나는 그 콘서트에 정말 가고 싶어. 하지만 네 여동생이 록 음악을 좋아하지 않니?

M: Yes, but I <u>only</u> have <u>two</u> tickets. So, Julie, I really want to go with you. 응, 하지만 나는 입장권 두 장만 갖고 있어. 그래서, 줄리, 나는 정말 너랑 같이 가고 싶어.

W: Thanks, but I don't think I should go. Your sister will <u>enjoy</u> it <u>more</u> than me. 고맙지만 나는 가면 안 될 것 같아. 네 동생이 나보다 더 즐거워할 거야.

함께 가자는 남자의 제안에 여자는 다른 사람이 더 좋아할 거라면서 양보의 뜻을 내비치고 있다.

어휘 free 무료의; 자유로운 enjoy 즐거워하다 more than ~보다 많이

11 ①

M: Hello. Can I help you find something?
안녕하세요. 찾으시는 것을 제가 도와드릴까요?

W: It's my husband's birthday tomorrow. I need to buy a present for him.
내일이 제 남편의 생일이거든요. 그에게 줄 선물을 사야 해요.

M: Does he like sweaters? 남편이 스웨터를 좋아하나요?

W: No, he never wears them. But he loves neckties.
아니요, 그는 스웨터를 전혀 입지 않아요. 하지만 넥타이는 아주 좋아하죠.

M: Neckties are on sale this week. Let me show you some of them.
넥타이는 이번 주에 할인 중이에요. 제가 몇 개 보여드릴게요.

W: Great. 잘됐군요.

어휘 present 선물 never 한 번도 ~않다 wear 입다
on sale 할인 중인; 판매되는

12 ④

M: Good afternoon. How may I help you?
안녕하세요. 무엇을 도와드릴까요?

W: Hello. I need to book a plane ticket from Seoul to Tokyo.
안녕하세요. 저는 서울에서 도쿄로 가는 항공권을 예약하려고요.

M: Will this be a round-trip or a one-way ticket?
왕복인가요, 편도인가요?

W: Round trip, please.
왕복으로 주세요.

M: Okay. When would you like to travel?
알겠습니다. 여행은 언제 하고 싶으세요?

W: I want to leave on November eleventh and return on November fifteenth.
11월 11일에 출발해서 11월 15일에 돌아오고 싶어요.

M: All right. Let me see if any seats are left.
알겠습니다. 좌석이 남아 있는지 제가 확인해 볼게요.

해설 해외 항공권 구입에 관한 대화이므로 남자는 항공사 직원 혹은 여행사 직원일 것이다.

어휘 book 예약하다 round-trip 왕복 여행의 one-way 편도의

13 ②

M: Hello. How can I help you?
안녕하세요. 무엇을 도와드릴까요?

W: I'd like to send some money to my brother in Canada.
저는 캐나다에 있는 오빠에게 돈을 좀 보내고 싶어요.

M: No problem. How much money do you want to

send? 그러세요. 얼마나 보내실 건가요?

W: I need to send two thousand dollars. How much will that cost?
2천 달러를 보내야 해요. 그건 비용이 얼마나 들까요?

M: The fee is thirty dollars. But you should fill out this form first.
수수료는 30달러예요. 그런데 이 양식을 먼저 작성하셔야 해요.

W: Okay. 네.

해설 해외로 돈을 송금하는 대화를 나누는 장소는 은행이다.

어휘 send 보내다 fee 수수료 fill out 써넣다 form 양식, 문서

14 ③

M: Hello, Ms. Park. How are you doing?
안녕하세요, 박 선생님. 어떻게 지내세요?

W: I'm great, Jaemin. Do you need something?
잘 지낸단다, 재민아. 뭐 필요한 게 있니?

M: Yes, ma'am. I want to know how I did on the recent test. 네, 선생님. 제가 최근 시험을 어떻게 봤는지 알고 싶어서요.

W: Just a minute. Let me find your test... You got a B+ on the test. 잠깐만 기다리렴. 네 시험지를 찾아 볼게. 너는 B플러스를 받았구나.

M: A B+? That's disappointing. I studied really hard for the test. B플러스요? 그거 실망스럽네요. 저는 시험 공부를 정말 열심히 했거든요.

W: You are getting better. Keep studying hard, and you will get an A the next time. 너는 점점 좋아지고 있어. 꾸준히 열심히 공부하면 다음에는 A를 받을 거야.

M: I hope so. 저도 그러면 좋겠어요.

해설 시험 성적을 듣게 된 남자는 'That's disappointing.'으로 직접적인 실망의 심정을 드러냈다.

어휘 ma'am (여성을 정중히 부르는 말) 선생님; 부인 recent 최근의 disappointing 실망스러운 hopeful 희망에 찬 surprised 놀란

15 ④

M: Hi, Lara. What are you doing here?
안녕, 라라. 너 여기에서 뭐 해?

W: Good evening, Paul. I'm doing research for my science project. I need some books on the moon.
안녕, 폴. 나는 과학 프로젝트를 위해 조사 중이야. 나는 달에 관한 책이 좀 필요하거든.

M: That sounds interesting. I hope you can find the books. 그거 재미있겠다. 네가 책을 찾길 바랄게.

W: I already found two of them. What are you looking for? 나는 벌써 두 권이나 찾았어. 너는 뭘 찾고 있어?

M: I have to check out this book on cars. My brother wants to read it. 나는 자동차에 관한 이 책을 빌려야 해. 우리 형이 그것을 읽고 싶어 하거든.

W: It looks interesting. You should read it, too.
재미있어 보이네. 너도 그걸 읽어 봐.

해설 여자가 필요로 하는 책과 구분하여 듣는다. 여자는 달에 관한 책,

남자는 자동차에 관한 책을 빌릴 것이다.

어휘 do research 조사를 하다 find 찾다(find-found-found) look for ~을 찾다, 구하다 check out (도서관에서 책을) 대출하다

16 ④

M: Hi, Rachel. Are you <u>excited</u> about your family <u>trip</u>?
안녕, 레이첼. 너의 가족 여행이 기대되니?

W: Yes. But I <u>need</u> to ask you a <u>favor</u>.
응. 그런데 나는 네게 부탁할 게 있어.

M: What do you need? 뭐가 필요한데?

W: You know we'll be <u>gone</u> for three days. My <u>cat</u> will be home <u>alone</u>. 너도 알겠지만 우리는 3일 동안 떠나 있을 거야. 내 고양이는 집에 혼자 있을 거고.

M: Do you want me to <u>take care of</u> your cat?
내가 네 고양이를 돌봐 주기를 원하는 거야?

W: That's right. Can you <u>do</u> that <u>for</u> me?
맞아. 날 위해 그렇게 해줄 수 있겠니?

M: Sure. Can you take her to my house tonight?
당연하지. 오늘 밤에 고양이를 우리 집에 데려올래?

W: Of course. 물론이야.

해설 부탁을 하는 여자는 상황만 설명하고 오히려 남자가 'Do you want me to ~?'에서 부탁 내용을 언급했다. 그리고 여자는 'Can you ~?'로 부탁을 재차 확인했다.

어휘 ask somebody a favor ~에게 부탁하다(= ask a favor of somebody) gone (사람이) 떠난 take care of ~을 돌보다

17 ④

M: I'm really excited to <u>see</u> the <u>concert</u> tonight.
오늘 밤에 콘서트를 보게 되다니 정말 신난다.

W: So am I. Are the <u>musicians</u> going to <u>come out</u> on stage soon?
나도 마찬가지야. 음악가들이 곧 무대에 등장할까?

M: I think so. What <u>time</u> is it <u>now</u>?
그럴 것 같아. 지금 몇 시야?

W: It's <u>six thirty-five</u>. <u>When</u> is the show going <u>to</u> <u>begin</u>? 6시 35분이야. 공연이 언제 시작하니?

M: It's going to start <u>ten</u> minutes <u>from</u> <u>now</u>.
지금부터 10분 뒤에 시작할 거야.

W: Great. I can't wait. 좋다. 정말 기대돼.

해설 현재 시각이 6:35인데 공연은 10분 뒤인 6:45에 시작한다.

어휘 come out 나오다, 드러나다 stage 무대; 단계

18 ②

① M: Hello. May I <u>speak with</u> Susan, please?
여보세요. 수잔과 통화할 수 있을까요?

W: <u>Hold on</u> just a moment. 잠시만 기다리세요.

② M: <u>How</u> do you usually <u>go to</u> the swimming pool?
너는 보통 수영장에 어떻게 가니?

W: Every day. 매일 가.

③ M: It's a <u>pleasure</u> to <u>meet</u> you. My name is Tom Murphy.

만나서 반가워요. 제 이름은 톰 머피예요.

W: It's a pleasure to meet you, too, Mr. Murphy.
저도 만나서 반가워요, 머피 씨.

④ M: <u>Thank</u> you very much for helping me.
저를 도와주셔서 정말 감사합니다.

W: Don't <u>mention</u> it. 천만에요.

⑤ M: What's the <u>weather</u> going to be <u>like</u> today?
오늘 날씨는 어떨 것 같아?

W: It's <u>cold</u> now, but it will be <u>warm</u> in the afternoon.
지금은 춥지만 오후에는 따뜻할 거야.

해설 ②의 질문에서 수영장까지의 이동수단에 대해 물었다. 'I go there by bus.', 'I go there on foot.' 등의 대답이 적절하다.

19 ③

M: I can't <u>believe</u> what happened to me.
내게 일어난 일을 믿을 수가 없어.

W: What's <u>wrong</u>, Kevin? Are you all right?
무슨 일이야, 케빈? 너 괜찮아?

M: I just <u>failed</u> my math test. I missed <u>half</u> the problems. 나는 수학 시험을 망쳤어. 문제의 절반을 놓쳤어.

W: I'm so sorry to hear that. Didn't you study?
그거 너무 안 됐다. 너 공부하지 않았어?

M: I did, but math is still <u>too difficult</u> for me. What can I do to <u>get better</u>? 공부했지만 수학은 아직도 내게 너무 어려워. 더 잘하려면 내가 무엇을 해야 할까?

W: Ask the teacher for some help.
선생님께 도움을 요청해 봐.

① I think I did well on the test. 나는 시험을 잘 봤다고 생각해.

② You didn't get your grade yet.
너는 아직 점수를 받지 않았잖아.

③ Ask the teacher for some help.
선생님께 도움을 요청해 봐.

④ The teacher helped me out a lot.
선생님께서 나를 많이 도와주셨어.

⑤ Yes, I study together with friends.
응, 나는 친구들과 함께 공부해.

해설 공부를 더 잘하기 위해 무엇을 해야 하는지 묻는 친구에게 적절한 대답은 ③이다. ⑤는 Yes로 시작하기 때문에 정답이 될 수 없다.

어휘 fail 불합격하다, 실패하다 miss 놓치다 half 절반의

20 ①

M: <u>Look at</u> all the <u>snow</u> on the ground.
땅 위에 저 눈을 좀 봐.

W: Because of the snow, <u>classes</u> have been <u>canceled</u>. We don't have to go to school tomorrow.
눈 때문에 수업이 취소됐어. 우리는 내일 학교에 가지 않아도 돼.

M: Are you <u>sure</u> about that? 그거 확실해?

W: My <u>classmate</u> Rick <u>told</u> me that about ten minutes ago. 우리 반 친구 릭이 10분 전에 나한테 그렇게 말했어.

M: I'm not sure I believe him. We'd better <u>ask a</u> <u>teacher</u> about that. 나는 그를 확실히 믿지 못하겠어. 우린 그

일에 대해 선생님께 여쭤보는 게 좋겠다.

W: Yes, I think you're right. 그래, 네 말이 맞는 것 같아.

① Yes, I think you're right. 그래, 네 말이 맞는 것 같아.

② My homeroom teacher is Ms. Bell.
우리 담임 선생님은 벨 선생님이야.

③ No, I didn't ask a teacher anything.
아니, 나는 선생님께 아무것도 여쭤 보지 않았어.

④ We can play in the snow tomorrow.
우리는 내일 눈에서 놀 수 있어.

⑤ Rick and I have history class together.
릭과 나는 역사 수업을 함께 들어.

해설 남자는 학생들 사이의 소문을 믿기 보다는 선생님에게 확실한 정보를 확인하고 싶어 한다. 이에 대한 반응으로는 ①이 적절하다.

어휘 cancel 취소하다(cancel-canceled-canceled) sure 확신하는 believe 믿다 had better (~하는 게) 좋을 것이다(='d better) homeroom teacher 담임 교사

19회 실전모의고사
본문 p.186-187

01 ⑤	02 ③	03 ④	04 ②	05 ④
06 ③	07 ⑤	08 ①	09 ④	10 ②
11 ②	12 ④	13 ⑤	14 ④	15 ③
16 ④	17 ③	18 ③	19 ②	20 ③

01 ⑤

M: I am a small piece of metal. I am very thin and easy to bend. People use me to connect many pieces of paper together. They usually put me in the corner of the pages. You can find me on desks or in drawers.

저는 작은 금속 조각이에요. 저는 매우 얇고 쉽게 구부러져요. 사람들은 저를 이용해서 여러 페이지를 연결해요. 사람들은 주로 페이지의 귀퉁이에 저를 꽂아요. 당신은 책상 위나 서랍 속에서 저를 찾을 수 있어요.

어휘 metal 금속 thin 얇은 bend 구부리다 connect 연결하다, 잇다 corner 귀퉁이, 모서리, 구석 drawer 서랍

02 ③

M: Jane, do you have any plans for this weekend?
제인, 이번 주말에 계획 있어?

W: I'm not going to do anything special. I'm going to stay home and watch television.
특별한 일은 없을 거야. 나는 집에 머무르면서 텔레비전을 볼 거야.

M: That sounds boring. Why don't you go to the park and play tennis with me? 그건 지루한 것 같아. 나와 함께 공원에 가서 테니스를 치는 게 어때?

W: I'm sorry, but I've never played tennis before. How

about playing badminton? 미안하지만 나는 테니스를 한 번도 쳐본 적이 없어. 배드민턴을 치는 건 어때?

M: Sure. That sounds fun. Let's meet at the park on Saturday morning.
좋아. 그거 재미있겠다. 토요일 아침에 공원에서 만나자.

W: Okay. I'll see you there at ten.
그래. 거기에서 10시에 보자.

해설 두 사람 사이에 제안(Why don't you ~, How about ~)과 동의(Sure, Okay)의 과정이 있어야 한다.

어휘 anything 아무것 special 특별한 before 전에

03 ④

W: Good morning. This is Paula Wilson with the weather forecast. Winter has arrived. It's going to be very cold all day long. In the morning, the skies will be clear, but it's going to start snowing in the afternoon. The snow will stop falling in the evening, however. At night, there will be cloudy skies.

안녕하세요. 저는 일기예보를 진행하는 폴라 윌슨입니다. 겨울이 다가왔네요. 하루 종일 매우 춥겠습니다. 아침에는 하늘이 맑겠으나 오후에 눈이 내리기 시작하겠습니다. 그러나 눈은 저녁에 그칠 것입니다. 밤에는 구름 낀 하늘이 보일 것입니다.

어휘 forecast 예보, 예측 arrive 도착하다; 도래하다 however 그러나

04 ②

M: Did Emily invite you to her birthday party?
에밀리가 너를 자신의 생일 파티에 초대했니?

W: Yes, she did. But I'm not sure if I can go to it.
응, 했어. 그런데 내가 갈 수 있을지는 모르겠어.

M: What's the problem? I thought you two are good friends.
뭐가 문제야? 나는 너희 둘이 친한 친구인 줄 알았는데.

W: We are very good friends. But Kate already asked me to see a movie with her on that day.
우리는 아주 친한 친구지. 그런데 케이트가 이미 내게 그날 영화를 같이 보자고 했거든.

M: I see. I think you should go with Kate. She asked you first. 그렇구나. 나는 네가 케이트와 가야 한다고 생각해. 그 애가 먼저 요청했잖아.

해설 'I think you should ~'는 충고의 의미를 담고 있다.

어휘 invite 초대하다 think 생각하다(think-thought-thought) already 이미, 벌써 first 먼저

05 ④

W: We have a new English teacher, Mr. Carter, today.
오늘 새로운 영어 교사인 카터 선생님이 오셔.

M: Have you seen him? What does he look like?
너는 그분을 본 적이 있니? 어떻게 생기셨니?

W: He's very young and has short brown hair. He's also really tall.
그 분은 아주 젊고 짧은 갈색 머리를 하고 있어. 키도 아주 크셔.

M: That's interesting. 그거 흥미롭구나.

W: I heard he is from Canada and just moved to Korea.
그 분은 캐나다 출신인데 막 한국으로 오신 거라고 들었어.

M: I'm looking forward to meeting him.
난 그 분을 만나기를 기대하고 있어.

W: Me, too. 나도 그래.

어휘 see 보다(see-saw-seen) look forward to ~을 기대하다

06 ③

M: There must be a thousand people here at the stadium.
이 경기장에 사람이 천 명은 있는 것 같다.

W: Everyone wants to see the game. It's the first game of the season.
모두들 경기를 보고 싶어 하니까. 시즌 첫 번째 경기잖아.

M: I'm so excited. What time is the game going to begin? 난 정말 흥분돼. 경기가 몇 시에 시작하니?

W: It starts at seven thirty. But we can't go inside the stadium until seven. 7시 30분에 시작해. 하지만 우리는 7시부터 경기장 안으로 들어갈 수 있어.

M: So we have to wait thirty more minutes.
그러니까 우리는 30분을 더 기다려야 하네.

W: Let's buy some snacks while we wait. The snack bar is over there.
우리 기다리는 동안 간식을 좀 사자. 간이식당이 저쪽에 있어.

해설 7시에 경기장에 들어갈 수 있는데 30분을 더 기다려야 하므로 현재 시각은 6:30이다.

어휘 stadium 경기장 season (운동경기의) 시즌; 계절 not A until B B할 때까지는 A하지 않는다(= B하고 나서야 A하다) while ~하는 동안 snack bar 간이식당, 스낵바

07 ⑤

W: I love to watch Kim Yuna skate. She is the best figure skater I've ever seen.
나는 김연아가 스케이트 타는 모습을 보는 게 좋아. 그녀는 내가 본 최고의 피겨스케이트 선수야.

M: I agree with you. Do you want to be a figure skater in the future, too?
나도 네 말에 동의해. 너도 미래에 피겨스케이트 선수가 되고 싶어?

W: No, I don't. I want to be a sports reporter.
아니. 나는 스포츠 리포터가 되고 싶어.

M: That's a good choice. I think you can be a good reporter.
그거 좋은 선택이다. 내 생각에 너는 멋진 리포터가 될 수 있어.

W: Thanks. What do you want to be in the future?
고마워. 너는 앞으로 뭐가 되고 싶어?

M: My father owns a restaurant. I want to be a

businessman like him, too. 우리 아버지께서 식당을 소유하고 계셔. 나도 아버지처럼 사업가가 되고 싶어.

W: Good luck. I hope your dream comes true.
행운을 빌어. 네 꿈이 이루어지길 바랄게.

해설 여자와 남자의 장래 희망을 구분하여 듣는다. restaurant에서 연상되는 cook을 선택하지 않도록 한다.

어휘 agree with ~에 동의하다 choice 선택 own 소유하다 businessman 사업가, 경영인

08 ①

M: How do you like the food at this restaurant?
너는 이 식당의 음식에 대해 어떻게 생각해?

W: I think it tastes great. I'm really impressed.
맛이 훌륭하다고 생각해. 나는 아주 감명 받았어.

M: You are? I thought you didn't like spicy food.
그래? 나는 네가 매운 음식을 안 좋아한다고 생각했는데.

W: I used to hate it, but now I love it.
난 그것을 싫어하곤 했는데 지금은 아주 좋아해.

M: I see. Do you want to come here again?
그렇구나. 너 여기에 다시 오고 싶어?

W: Sure. I want to visit this restaurant again.
당연하지. 나는 이 식당에 다시 오고 싶어.

해설 맛에 감명 받아서 다시 방문하고 싶어 하는 여자의 말에서 만족스러운 기분을 알 수 있다.

어휘 taste 맛이 ~하다 impressed 감명 받은 used to (과거에는) ~하곤 했다 hate 몹시 싫어하다, 질색하다

09 ④

M: Something smells delicious. What are you cooking?
뭔가 맛있는 냄새가 나네요. 무엇을 요리하고 있어요?

W: I'm making some pizza and spaghetti.
저는 피자와 스파게티를 만들고 있어요.

M: Everything looks good. Are you going to bake an apple pie, too?
다 맛있어 보이네요. 애플파이도 구울 건가요?

W: I want to, but we don't have any apples.
그러고 싶은데 우리는 사과가 하나도 없어요.

M: I can drive to the supermarket right now. It's no problem.
제가 지금 슈퍼마켓으로 운전해서 갈 수 있어요. 문제 없어요.

W: Thanks a lot. I'll give you a list of the items I need.
정말 고마워요. 제가 필요한 것의 목록을 드릴게요.

해설 남자가 'I can drive to ~'로 자신이 할 일을 직접 말했다. 파이를 사는 것이 아니라 파이의 재료인 사과를 사는 것이므로 ①은 오답이다.

어휘 smell 냄새가 나다 bake 굽다 drive to 차를 몰고 …에 가다 list 목록 item 물품, 항목

10 ②

M: Winter vacation is coming. Do you have any plans for it? 겨울방학이 오고 있어. 너는 무슨 계획이 있어?

W: I'm going to a ski resort with my family.
나는 가족과 함께 스키 리조트에 갈 거야.

M: That sounds fun. Are you good at skiing?
그거 재미있게 들린다. 너는 스키를 잘 타?

W: Actually, I've never tried before. But I want to learn. What are you planning? 사실, 나는 한 번도 타본 적이 없어. 하지만 난 배우고 싶어. 너는 무엇을 할 계획이야?

M: My grandparents are going to visit us for two weeks. 우리 조부모님께서 2주 동안 우리 집에 오실 거야.

W: Great. You will have fun with them.
좋겠다. 넌 그분들과 즐거운 시간을 보낼 거야.

M: That's right. And they said they have lots of presents for me.
맞아. 게다가 그분들이 날 위해 선물을 많이 갖고 오신대.

해설 남자의 첫 대사에 겨울방학이 언급되며, 서로의 계획을 묻고 있다. 조부모님, 스키, 선물 등은 세부내용에 불과하다.

어휘 vacation 방학, 휴가 resort 리조트, 휴양지 try 시도하다; 노력하다(try-tried-tried) lots of 수많은(= a lot of)

11 ②

W: On the first day of school, the teacher asked us about our favorite subjects. Eight students said that they like history the most. Five students prefer math. Seven students said their favorite class is English. Three students like science the most, and two of them said art is their favorite class.

학교 첫날에 선생님은 우리가 좋아하는 과목에 대해 물어보셨다. 여덟 명의 학생이 역사를 가장 좋아한다고 답했다. 다섯 명의 학생은 수학을 더 좋아한다. 일곱 명의 학생이 영어를 가장 좋아한다고 말했다. 세 명의 학생은 과학을 가장 좋아하고 두 명은 미술이 가장 좋아하는 수업이라고 말했다.

해설 선택지 순서와 동일하게 역사-수학-영어-과학-미술을 좋아하는 학생 수가 언급된다. 'Five students prefer math.'라고 말했으므로 ②에는 6이 아닌 5가 와야 한다.

어휘 on the first day 첫째 날에 favorite 마음에 드는, 좋아하는 subject 과목 prefer 선호하다

12 ④

M: Sally, are you getting ready for the science test?
샐리, 너는 과학 시험을 준비하고 있니?

W: No, I'm not. I'm reviewing my notes from math class today.
아니. 나는 오늘 있었던 수학 수업 노트를 복습하고 있어.

M: Really? I thought you hated math. What changed?
정말? 나는 네가 수학을 싫어한다고 생각했어. 뭐가 바뀐 거야?

W: I like math a lot these days thanks to my new math teacher. 새로운 수학 선생님 덕분에 난 요즘 수학이 아주 좋아.

M: That's good. What's he like?
그거 잘됐다. 그 선생님은 어때?

W: He explains the problems very well. He's also really fun. 선생님께서 문제를 아주 잘 설명해 주셔. 그분은 무척 재미있기도 해.

M: You're lucky. My math teacher is really boring.
넌 운이 좋다. 우리 수학 선생님은 아주 지루하거든.

해설 'What changed?', 'What's he like?' 등으로 묻는 남자의 질문에 대한 여자의 대답에 정답이 있다.

어휘 get ready for ~에 대비하다 review 복습, 시험공부; 복습하다 these days 요즘에는 thanks to ~덕분에 explain 설명하다

13 ⑤

W: Nice to meet you, Mr. Davis. Why did you apply to work here? 만나서 반갑습니다, 데이비스 씨. 왜 이곳에서 일하려고 지원하셨죠?

M: I want to work in the travel industry.
저는 여행업계에서 일하고 싶어요.

W: Okay. What do you like about it?
그렇군요. 그것의 어떤 점을 좋아하시나요?

M: I want to help people have fun when they go on trips.
저는 사람들이 여행을 다닐 때 즐겁게 지내도록 돕고 싶어요.

W: Do you think you would be a good tour guide?
당신은 훌륭한 여행 가이드가 될 수 있다고 생각하시나요?

M: Yes, I do. I'm sure I will be a great tour guide.
네. 저는 멋진 여행 가이드가 될 거라고 확신합니다.

해설 인터뷰 형식의 대화이고, 대답하는 남자가 지원 동기와 포부에 대해 말하는 것으로 두 사람의 관계를 알 수 있다.

어휘 apply 지원하다 industry 업계, 산업

14 ④

W: Excuse me. I'm looking for the flower shop. Can you tell me where it is? 실례합니다. 저는 꽃집을 찾고 있어요. 그게 어디에 있는지 알려주시겠어요?

M: The flower shop? Yes, it's located on River Street.
꽃집이요? 네, 그것은 리버 가에 있어요.

W: How do I get there? 제가 그곳에 어떻게 가죠?

M: Go straight ahead one block. Then, turn right.
앞으로 한 블록 직진하세요. 그리고 우회전하세요.

W: Turn right? Okay. What should I do after that?
우회전이요? 알겠습니다. 그 다음엔 무엇을 해야 하나요?

M: Walk down the street. It will be on the left by the library. You can't miss it. 길을 따라 걸어가세요. 왼편을 보면 도서관 옆에 있을 겁니다. 틀림없이 찾으실 거예요.

W: Okay. Thanks. 네. 감사합니다.

어휘 be located on ~에 위치하다 ahead 앞으로 by ~옆에

15 ③

M: What are you doing in your room, Tina?

네 방에서 뭘 하고 있니, 티나?

W: I'm working on my science homework, Dad.
저는 과학 숙제를 하고 있어요, 아빠.

M: Can you help me for a moment?
나를 잠깐 도와줄 수 있니?

W: Yes. What is it? 네. 뭐예요?

M: Please take out the garbage with me. We have a lot of garbage.
아빠와 함께 쓰레기를 버리자꾸나. 우리는 쓰레기가 아주 많아.

W: Okay. But after that, I want you to check my homework.
네. 하지만 그 후에 아빠가 제 숙제를 확인해 주시면 좋겠어요.

M: Sure. I'll help. 물론이지. 내가 도와주마.

해설 남자의 부탁과 구분하여 듣는다. 남자는 'Please ~'로, 여자는 'I want you to ~'로 부탁하는 말을 했다.

어휘 work on ~에 노력을 들이다, 작업하다 for a moment 잠시 동안 take out 내놓다 garbage 쓰레기

16 ④

W: You look unhappy. What's the matter?
너 기분이 안 좋아 보여. 무슨 일 있어?

M: Eric and I had an argument at school. Now, he won't speak to me. 에릭이랑 나는 학교에서 말다툼을 했어. 이제 에릭은 내게 말을 안 걸어.

W: What did you fight about? 무엇 때문에 싸웠어?

M: We fought about a game in gym class. So he got very upset. 우리는 체육시간에 했던 시합 때문에 싸웠어. 그래서 그는 매우 화가 났어.

W: Oh, no. You should apologize to him.
오, 저런. 네가 그에게 사과를 해야 해.

M: You're right. I'll call him on the phone right now.
네 말이 맞아. 당장 그 애한테 전화를 할게.

해설 여자의 대사인 'You should ~'에 정답이 있다. 친구에게 전화를 걸기로 한 것은 남자의 결정이다.

어휘 unhappy 슬픈, 불행한 argument 말다툼 speak to ~에게 말을 걸다 fight 싸우다(fight-fought-fought) apologize 사과하다

17 ③

① W: How do you like my new shoes? 내 새 신발 어때?
　M: They look comfortable. And I love the color.
　편해 보인다. 그리고 색깔도 마음에 들어.

② W: Do you have any plans for this afternoon?
　너 오늘 오후에 계획 있니?
　M: I'm going to go cycling with Rick.
　나는 릭과 함께 자전거를 탈 거야.

③ W: How did you enjoy the food? 음식 맛있게 드셨나요?
　M: We had chicken and rice.
　우리는 닭고기와 밥을 먹었어요.

④ W: Can you help me with this bag?
　제가 이 가방 옮기는 걸 도와주시겠어요?

M: Sure. I can carry it for you.
물론이죠. 제가 들어드릴게요.

⑤ W: How long will it take to get to your home?
너희 집으로 가는 데 얼마나 걸리니?

M: It will take thirty minutes by bus.
버스로 30분이 걸릴 거야.

해설 ③의 질문은 음식을 맛있게 잘 먹었는지 물은 것이다. 'I enjoyed it.', 'Thanks.'와 같은 응답이 적절하다.

어휘 comfortable 편안한 carry 나르다, 갖고 다니다

18 ③

W: Steve, welcome back. Long time no see.
스티브, 돌아온 걸 환영해. 정말 오랜만이다.

M: I stayed in the countryside for the past three months. 나는 지난 3개월 동안 시골에서 지냈어.

W: Why did you go there? Were you working on a farm? 너는 그곳에 왜 갔니? 농장에서 일하고 있던 거야?

M: I wanted a quiet place. I needed to finish writing my book.
나는 조용한 장소를 원했어. 나의 책 집필을 마쳐야 했거든.

W: When is it going to be published?
그것은 언제 출판될 예정이야?

M: It will be available next week.
다음 주에 구할 수 있을 거야.

어휘 countryside 시골 지역 past 지난 quiet 조용한 publish 출판하다(publish-published-published) available 구할 수 있는, 이용할 수 있는

19 ②

[Cellphone rings.] [휴대폰이 울린다.]

W: Hello. 여보세요.

M: Hi, Alice. This is Greg. Do you have a minute?
안녕, 앨리스. 나 그레그야. 너 시간 있니?

W: Sure, Greg. Is everything okay?
당연하지, 그레그. 별일 없지?

M: Actually, I can't meet you this evening. I'm sorry.
사실 나는 오늘 저녁에 널 만날 수가 없어. 미안해.

W: What's the matter? Are you sick?
무슨 일인데? 너 아파?

M: Yes, I am. I have a sore throat, and my head hurts a lot, too. 응. 나 목이 아프고 머리도 너무 아파.

W: You'd better see a doctor. 넌 병원에 가는 게 좋겠어.

① Thanks for your idea. 네 생각 고마워.

② You'd better see a doctor. 넌 병원에 가는 게 좋겠어.

③ The movie was a lot of fun. 그 영화 정말 재미 있었어.

④ I'm glad you're feeling better.
네가 좀 나아졌다니 다행이야.

⑤ Yes, I already took some pills.
응, 나는 이미 알약을 좀 먹었어.

해설 아파서 약속을 취소해야 하는 친구에게 할 말로 ②가 적절하다.

어휘 actually 사실은, 실제로 have a sore throat 목감기에 걸리다 pill 알약(뙝 pills)

20 ③

M: What do you have in that bag, Lucy?
가방에 들어 있는 게 뭐야, 루시?

W: It's a music CD. I just bought it at the shopping mall. 음악 CD야. 방금 쇼핑몰에서 그것을 샀어.

M: What kind of music is it? 어떤 종류의 음악이야?

W: It's pop music. It has songs by some of my favorite singers.
팝음악이야. 내가 좋아하는 가수들의 음악이 담겨 있어.

M: That's nice. I'd like to listen to the CD sometime later. 그거 멋지다. 나도 다음에 그 CD를 듣고 싶어.

W: You can borrow it in a few days.
며칠 후에 빌려줄게.

① No, it didn't cost very much. 아니, 그건 비싸지 않았어.
② I'm going to listen to it now. 나는 지금 그것을 들을 거야.
③ You can borrow it in a few days.
며칠 후에 빌려줄게.
④ May I have the CD back, please?
내게 그 CD를 돌려주겠니?
⑤ The music shop is on the second floor.
악기 상점은 2층에 있어.

해설 ③은 자신이 며칠 후에 빌려주겠다는 의미이다.

어휘 sometime later 다음에, 얼마 후 borrow 빌리다
in a few days 2~3일 후에 have something back ~을 돌려받다 second 두 번째의

20회 실전모의고사   본문 p.196-197

01 ④	02 ③	03 ②	04 ④	05 ③
06 ②	07 ③	08 ②	09 ④	10 ①
11 ①	12 ①	13 ④	14 ③	15 ③
16 ①	17 ①	18 ①	19 ③	20 ⑤

01 ④

W: You can usually find this in the kitchen. You use this to cut food into small pieces. You put the food into this and then press a button. This machine then cuts everything up. This can also mix fruit and other food together to make drinks.

당신은 이것을 주로 주방에서 찾을 수 있어요. 당신은 음식을 작은 크기로 자를 때 이것을 사용해요. 당신이 이것 안에 음식을 넣고 버튼을 누르지요. 그러면 이 기계는 모든 것을 잘게 잘라요. 이것은 과일과 다른 음식을 섞어서 음료를 만들 수도 있어요.

어휘 piece 조각, 부분 press 누르다 cut something up ~을 조

02 ③

M: Good morning. Here is the weather report for today. In Seoul, it's going to be sunny all day long. The temperature will be warm as well. It's going to be cloudy in Incheon, and there will be rain in Suwon. It will be very windy in Daegu. Busan and Gwangju are going to get thunderstorms.

안녕하세요. 오늘의 날씨를 전해 드립니다. 서울은 하루 종일 맑을 것입니다. 기온 역시 따뜻하겠습니다. 인천은 구름이 낄 것이고, 수원은 비가 내릴 것입니다. 대구는 바람이 강하게 불겠습니다. 부산과 광주에는 폭풍우가 있겠습니다.

어휘 temperature 기온; 체온 as well ~도, 또한
thunderstorm 폭풍우, 뇌우

03 ②

W: The weather will be warm this weekend. Let's go on a picnic at the park.
이번 주에는 날씨가 따뜻할 거야. 우리 공원으로 소풍 가자.

M: I would love to, but Tony and I already have plans.
나도 정말 그러고 싶은데 토니와 나는 이미 계획이 있어.

W: What are you going to do? 너희는 뭘 할 거야?

M: We're going to do some volunteer work at the hospital. 우리는 병원에서 자원봉사를 할 예정이야.

W: Really? Can I join you there?
정말이야? 나도 거기에 같이 가도 돼?

M: Sure. They always need more people to help.
당연하지. 그들은 언제나 더 많은 사람의 도움을 필요로 하거든.

해설 남자의 계획에 여자가 'Can I join you?'로 합류 의사를 밝힘으로써 두 사람이 같이 할 일이 결정된다.

어휘 volunteer work 자원봉사 join 합류하다 more 더 많은

04 ④

W: Do you enjoy playing soccer?
너는 축구를 즐겨 하니?

M: No, I don't. I'm too slow. 아니 나는 너무 느려

W: What do you think about basketball?
농구에 대해서는 어떻게 생각해?

M: I don't like it. You have to run too much to play it.
나는 농구를 좋아하지 않아. 그것을 하려면 너무 많이 달려야 해.

W: I see. Do you play tennis?
그렇구나. 너는 테니스를 하니?

M: Yes, I do. I enjoy playing it on weekends.
응. 나는 주말마다 테니스를 즐겨 해.

해설 남자가 어떤 운동을 즐겨 하는지 여자가 남자에게 계속해서 물어보고 있다.

어휘 on weekends 주말에, 주말마다

05 ③

W: <u>How</u> are you <u>doing</u> today? 오늘 어떠신가요?

M: I'm <u>tired</u>. I just got <u>back</u> <u>from</u> <u>Japan</u>.
피곤하군요. 저는 일본에서 지금 막 돌아왔어요.

W: Is it hard to <u>fly</u> an <u>airplane</u>?
비행기를 조종하는 것은 어렵나요?

M: Sometimes. But I really love my <u>job</u>.
가끔이요. 하지만 저는 제 일을 정말 좋아한답니다.

W: What do you <u>love</u> about it the <u>most</u>?
가장 좋은 점이 무엇인가요?

M: I like <u>flying</u> <u>high</u> above the ground.
땅 위로 높이 나는 게 좋아요.

해설 fly an airplane과 관련된 직업은 조종사이다.

어휘 fly (비행기를) 조종하다; 날다 above ~보다 위에 ground 땅

06 ②

W: Seho, hurry up. We're going to be <u>late</u> for <u>school</u>.
세호야, 서둘러. 우리는 학교에 늦겠다.

M: Okay, I'm <u>ready</u> now... <u>Wait</u> a minute.
알았어. 난 이제 준비됐어... 잠깐만.

W: What's wrong? Did you <u>forget</u> something?
무슨 일이야? 너 뭘 잊어버렸니?

M: Yes, I <u>forgot</u> to print our science <u>report</u>. I'll do that right now. 응, 나는 우리 과학 보고서를 출력하는 걸 잊어버렸어. 지금 당장 해야겠다.

W: I already <u>printed</u> it last night. It's in my backpack.
내가 어젯밤에 이미 출력했어. 내 배낭 안에 있어.

M: Oh, I <u>was</u> really <u>worried</u>. But everything is <u>fine</u> <u>now</u>. Let's go. 아, 나 정말 걱정했어. 하지만 이제 다 괜찮아. 가자.

해설 남자는 잠시 걱정했지만 이제 괜찮다고 말했으므로 안도하고 있다는 것을 알 수 있다.

어휘 forget 잊다(forget-forgot-forgotten) print 출력하다(print-printed-printed) upset 속상한 relieved 안도하는 nervous 긴장한 excited 신이 난 regretful 후회하는

07 ③

[*Cellphone rings.*] [휴대폰이 울린다.]

M: Hello. 여보세요.

W: Hello, Rick. <u>Where</u> are you right <u>now</u>?
안녕, 릭. 너 지금 어디 있어?

M: I'm at my <u>house</u>. What's up?
나는 집에 있어. 무슨 일이야?

W: At your house? Did you <u>forget</u> about the <u>movie</u>? I'm <u>waiting</u> <u>for</u> you at the <u>theater</u>. 집이라고? 너 영화에 대해 잊어버렸어? 나는 영화관에서 널 기다리는 중인데.

M: Oh, I forgot. I'll go there <u>as</u> <u>soon</u> <u>as</u> I can.
아, 내가 깜빡했다. 내가 되도록 빨리 거기로 갈게.

W: Never mind. The movie starts at <u>seven</u> <u>forty-five</u>. That's <u>ten</u> minutes <u>from</u> <u>now</u>. There isn't enough time. 신경 쓰지 마. 영화는 7시 45분에 시작해. 지금으로부터 10

분 뒤야. 시간이 충분하지 않아.

해설 영화가 시작하는 7:45보다 10분 앞선 시각은 7:35이다.

어휘 wait for ~을 기다리다 as soon as one can 가능한 빨리 enough 충분한

08 ②

M: I can't believe it. It's <u>still</u> raining.
믿을 수가 없어. 아직도 비가 내리네.

W: When it <u>rains</u> all day, I just stay <u>inside</u> and <u>read</u> books.
종일 비가 내릴 때 나는 그냥 실내에 있으면서 책을 읽어.

M: I sometimes do that, but I <u>don't</u> want to stay home <u>all day</u>.
나도 가끔 그렇게 하지만 하루 종일 집에 있고 싶지는 않아.

W: Did you <u>check</u> the <u>weather</u> report? <u>When</u> is it going to <u>stop</u> raining?
너 일기예보를 확인했니? 비가 언제 그칠 거래?

M: It should stop <u>in</u> an <u>hour</u>. Then, we can <u>go</u> out <u>for</u> a <u>walk</u> this <u>evening</u>. 한 시간 뒤면 그칠 거야. 그러면 우리는 저녁에 산책하러 나갈 수 있어.

W: Sure. We can <u>walk</u> by the lake at the park.
물론이지. 우린 공원에서 호숫가를 걸을 수 있어.

해설 남자와 여자의 마지막 대사인 'We can ~'에 정답이 등장한다.

어휘 inside 내부에 in an hour 한 시간 뒤에 go out for a walk 산책하러 나가다

09 ④

M: Good evening. May I <u>take</u> your <u>order</u>?
안녕하세요. 제가 주문을 받을까요?

W: I'd like a cheeseburger and fries, please.
치즈버거 하나와 감자튀김을 주세요.

M: Do you want <u>regular</u> or <u>large</u> fries? Regular fries are <u>one</u> dollar, and large fries cost <u>two</u> dollars.
감자튀김은 보통과 큰 것 중에 무엇을 원하시나요? 보통 감자튀김은 1달러이고, 큰 것은 2달러입니다.

W: I'd like large fries, please.
큰 감자튀김으로 주세요.

M: Okay, and the cheeseburger <u>costs</u> three dollars.
네, 그리고 치즈버거는 3달러입니다.

W: Here's a ten-dollar bill. 여기 10달러 지폐요.

M: Thanks. Here's your change.
감사합니다. 거스름돈 여기 있어요.

해설 $2(큰 감자튀김) + $3(치즈버거) = $5

어휘 take an order 주문을 받다 regular 보통의 large 큰 bill 지폐 change 거스름돈

10 ①

M: Do you know that Lisa's <u>birthday</u> is the day after

tomorrow? 당신은 모레가 리사의 생일인 거 알고 있어요?

W: Yes, I do. We need to buy her a present. What should we get? 그래요. 우리는 그 애에게 선물을 사줘야 해요. 우리가 무엇을 사야 할까요?

M: She wants a new cellphone. She often complains about hers. 리사는 새 휴대폰을 원해요. 그 애는 자기 휴대폰에 대해 자주 불평을 해요.

W: That's too expensive. Why don't we buy her some gloves? The weather is getting colder these days. 그건 너무 비싸요. 그 애에게 장갑을 사주는 게 어때요? 요즘 날씨가 점점 추워지고 있잖아요.

M: She just bought a new pair of gloves. How about a scarf instead? 그 애는 얼마 전에 새 장갑을 샀어요. 대신에 스카프는 어때요?

W: That sounds good. Let's go to the store and find one now. 그거 좋네요. 지금 가게로 가서 하나를 고르죠.

해설 세 종류의 물건이 등장하는데, 이 중에서 두 사람이 구입하기로 합의한 것은 마지막에 등장하는 스카프이다. 동의를 의미하는 'That sounds good.'을 확인한다.

어휘 the day after tomorrow 모레 complain 불평하다 cold 추운(cold-colder-coldest) a pair of 한 쌍의 instead 대신에

11 ①

M: Julie, what are you reading? 줄리, 넌 무엇을 읽고 있니?

W: I'm reading the newest book by Eric Hammer. It's called *Life in the Wild*. It's really interesting. 나는 에릭 해머의 신간을 읽고 있어. '야생에서의 삶'이라는 제목이야. 정말로 재미있어.

M: I don't know that writer. What is the book about? 나는 그 작가를 모르겠어. 그 책은 무엇에 대한 내용이야?

W: It's about the time he spent living in the forest. The writer lived alone in the forest for more than a year. 그가 숲에서 살면서 보낸 시간에 대한 거야. 작가는 1년 이상 숲에서 혼자 살았어.

M: That sounds amazing. Can I borrow that book when you're finished? I want to read it. 그거 대단한 것 같아. 네가 다 읽은 뒤에 내가 그 책을 빌려도 될까? 나도 읽고 싶어.

해설 남자의 질문인 'What is the book about?'에 대한 여자의 대답에 답이 있다. 즉, 'living in the forest'가 주제이다.

어휘 new 새로운(new-newer-newest) wild 야생; 야생의 writer 작가 spend (시간을) 보내다, 쓰다(spend-spent-spent) forest 숲 alone 혼자

12 ①

W: Hello. How can I help you? 안녕하세요. 무엇을 도와 드릴까요?

M: These pants are too long for me. Can you make them shorter? 이 바지가 저한테 너무 기네요. 바지 길이를 줄여 주실 수 있나요?

W: Yes, I can. I need to check your height. 네, 할 수 있어요. 제가 손님의 키를 재야 해요.

M: Okay. How long will this take? 알겠습니다. 시간이 얼마나 걸릴까요?

W: It will take around two days to change the size. 크기를 변경하는 데는 약 이틀이 걸릴 거예요.

M: Okay. I'll come back on Thursday. Thanks. 네. 목요일에 다시 올게요, 고맙습니다.

해설 옷 수선을 맡기는 상황으로 보아 재봉사와 고객의 관계이다.

어휘 make shorter 더 짧게 만들다 check 확인하다, 점검하다 height 키, 높이 take (시간이) 걸리다

13 ④

[*Telephone rings.*] [전화벨이 울린다.]

W: Hi. Are you still at the house? 여보세요. 너 아직 집에 있니?

M: Yes, I am. But I am going out in half an hour. Is there a problem? 네. 그런데 30분 뒤에 나갈 거예요. 무슨 문제 있어요?

W: I left the windows in the bedroom open. The weather report says it's going to rain in the afternoon. 내가 침실 창문을 열어놨거든. 일기예보에서 오후에 비가 내릴 거라고 하네.

M: Do you want me to close the windows now? 제가 지금 창문을 닫기를 원하시는 거죠?

W: Yes, please. I don't want water to get in the house. 응, 부탁해. 집 안에 물이 들어오는 건 원치 않아.

M: Okay. I'll do that right now. 알겠어요. 제가 지금 할게요.

해설 비가 올 예정인데 창문이 열려 있다고 말하는 여자의 대사에서 전화의 목적을 짐작할 수 있으며, 그 후 남자의 대사인 'Do you want me to ~?'에 정답이 드러난다.

어휘 half an hour 30분(한 시간의 절반) leave something open ~을 열어두다(leave-left-left) close 닫다

14 ③

W: Excuse me. When will we get to City Hall Station? 실례합니다. 우리는 시청역에 언제 도착하나요?

M: This train doesn't go there. You need to take another line. 이 열차는 거기에 가지 않아요. 당신은 다른 노선을 타야 해요.

W: Oh, that's terrible. How can I do that? 아, 이거 큰일이네요. 제가 어떻게 갈아타야 하죠?

M: Get out at the next stop. Then, take line number one. 다음 정차역에서 내리세요. 그리고 나서 1호선을 타세요.

W: Thank you so much. You were really helpful. 정말 고맙습니다. 큰 도움이 됐어요.

해설 내려서 다른 노선으로 갈아타는 상황으로 보아 대화는 지하철 안에서 이루어지고 있다.

15 ③

W: Hello. My name is Sora Lee. I'm a new student here. My family moved from Seoul to Daejeon last week. My hometown is Suwon. I have one older sister and two younger brothers. My father is a doctor, and my mother is an elementary school teacher. I like painting pictures and riding my bicycle. I hope we can all be friends.

안녕하세요. 제 이름은 이소라예요. 저는 여기 새로 전학 온 학생이에요. 저희 가족은 지난주에 서울에서 대전으로 이사를 했어요. 제 고향은 수원이에요. 저는 언니 한 명과 남동생 두 명이 있어요. 아버지는 의사이고 어머니는 초등학교 교사예요. 저는 그림 그리기와 자전거 타기를 좋아해요. 저는 우리 모두 친구가 되면 좋겠어요.

16 ①

① M: What time shall we meet tomorrow?
  우리 내일 몇 시에 만날까?
  W: On Tuesday. 화요일에.

② M: Excuse me. Which bus goes to the shopping mall?
  실례합니다. 어떤 버스가 쇼핑몰로 가나요?
  W: Take the number thirty-four bus.
  34번 버스를 타세요.

③ M: You need to exercise more.
  너는 운동을 더 많이 해야 해.
  W: I know, but I don't have enough time.
  나도 알지만 시간이 충분하지 않아.

④ M: When did you move to Rome?
  너는 언제 로마로 이사 왔니?
  W: I came here in two thousand nine.
  나는 2009년에 이곳에 왔어.

⑤ M: Why were you late for school this morning?
  너는 오늘 아침에 왜 학교에 늦었니?
  W: My alarm clock didn't go off.
  내 알람 시계가 울리지 않았어.

17 ①

M: Hello. Super Saver Home Shopping. How may I help you?
안녕하세요. 슈퍼세이버 홈쇼핑입니다. 무엇을 도와드릴까요?

W: Hello. I ordered a pair of shoes last week. But I didn't receive them. 안녕하세요. 제가 지난주에 신발 한 켤레를 주문했어요. 그런데 신발을 받지 못했네요.

M: I see. Let me check your order. May I have your name, please? 그렇군요. 제가 손님의 주문을 확인할게요. 성함을 알려주시겠어요?

W: Sure. My name is Susan Smith.
네. 제 이름은 수잔 스미스예요.

M: Thank you, Ms. Smith. I see the problem. The shoes you ordered are sold out. We will have them here tomorrow. Then, we will send them to you. 감사합니다, 스미스 씨. 문제가 뭔지 알겠네요. 손님이 주문한 신발은 품절이네요. 저희는 내일 그 신발을 받게 될 거예요. 그러면 그것을 손님에게 보내드리겠습니다.

18 ①

W: Pardon me, sir. I'm looking for a bank. Is there one near here? 실례합니다, 선생님. 저는 은행을 찾고 있어요. 이 근처에 은행이 있나요?

M: Yes, there is. Go straight to the intersection. Then, turn left onto Walnut Street. 네, 있어요. 교차로까지 직진하세요. 그 다음에 월넛 가로 좌회전하세요.

W: Are you telling me to turn right at the intersection? 교차로에서 우회전하라는 말씀이시죠?

M: No, don't turn right. Turn left. Then, you will see the fire station. The bank is right next to the fire station. You can't miss it. 아니요, 우회전하지 마세요. 좌회전하세요. 그러면 소방서가 보일 거예요. 은행은 소방서 바로 옆에 있어요. 분명히 찾으실 수 있어요.

W: Thanks for your help. I hope I can find it.
도와주셔서 감사합니다. 제가 찾을 수 있길 바랍니다.

19 ③

M: Is your train going to leave soon?
네 기차가 곧 출발하니?

W: It's going to leave in fifteen minutes.
15분 뒤에 출발할 거야.

M: Okay. Why don't we sit down here and wait then?
그래. 그럼 우리 여기 앉아서 기다리는 게 어때?

W: Sure. Oh, no. I can't find my ticket. I think I left it in the restaurant. 좋아. 아, 이런. 내 티켓을 못 찾겠어. 내가 식당에 그것을 놓고 왔나 봐.

M: Calm down. I'll watch your bags. You can go to get your ticket. 진정해. 내가 네 가방을 지키고 있을게. 너는 가서 티켓을 가져 오면 돼.

W: Thanks. I'll be right back. 고마워. 금방 돌아올게.

① I'm sitting in seat 4A. 나는 4A 좌석에 앉을 거야.
② No, I didn't buy a ticket. 아니, 나는 티켓을 사지 않았어.
③ Thanks. I'll be right back. 고마워. 금방 돌아올게.
④ I've got two large suitcases.
   나는 큰 여행 가방 두 개를 갖고 있어.
⑤ Dinner was great, wasn't it?
   식사는 맛있었어, 그렇지 않니?

해설 티켓을 찾으러 가는 동안 가방을 지켜주겠다고 말하는 남자에게 여자가 고맙다고 말할 것이다.

어휘 watch (잠깐 동안) 봐 주다 seat 좌석 suitcase 여행 가방
dinner (저녁) 식사

20 ⑤

M: Cindy, you look tired. Are you all right?
   신디, 당신 피곤해 보여요. 괜찮아요?
W: I'm so busy at work these days. I have a new project.
   전 요즘 회사에서 너무 바빠요. 새로운 프로젝트가 있거든요.
M: How about getting some rest?
   휴식을 좀 취하는 게 어때요?
W: I'd love to, but I need to cook dinner now.
   저도 그렇고 싶지만 지금 저녁 식사를 요리해야 해요.
M: You shouldn't do that. Let's order something.
   당신은 그러면 안돼요. 뭐라도 배달을 시킵시다.
W: That sounds like a good idea. 그거 좋은 생각이네요.

① What did you order? 무엇을 주문했어요?
② No, the food didn't arrive.
   아니요, 음식이 도착하지 않았어요.
③ I'll start cooking soon then.
   그럼 저는 곧 요리를 시작할게요.
④ What do you want to cook?
   당신은 무엇을 요리하고 싶어요?
⑤ That sounds like a good idea. 그거 좋은 생각이네요.

해설 피곤한 상태에서 요리를 하기보다는 음식을 배달시키자는 남자의 제안에 여자는 긍정적 반응을 할 것이다. 대화와 선택지에 모두 등장한 order, cook 등은 오히려 함정이다.

어휘 get some rest 휴식을 취하다 arrive 도착하다

01회 기출 듣기평가
본문 p.206-207

01 ③	02 ①	03 ③	04 ④	05 ④
06 ③	07 ②	08 ②	09 ①	10 ①
11 ⑤	12 ④	13 ③	14 ②	15 ⑤
16 ①	17 ②	18 ③	19 ⑤	20 ④

01 ③

[Phone rings.] [전화벨이 울린다.]
M: Hello. Lost and Found Center. How may I help you? 여보세요. 분실물 보관소입니다. 무엇을 도와드릴까요?
W: Hi. I lost my teddy bear in the park yesterday.
   안녕하세요. 제가 어제 공원에서 곰 인형을 잃어버렸어요.
M: What does it look like? 그게 어떻게 생겼죠?
W: It has a ribbon around its neck. It's wearing a hat.
   Do you have one like that? 그건 목에 리본을 하고 있어요.
   모자를 쓰고 있어요. 그렇게 생긴 것을 가지고 있나요?
M: Okay. I will go to check.
   알겠습니다. 제가 가서 확인해 볼게요.

어휘 Lost and Found Center 분실물 보관소 teddy bear
곰 인형 neck 목 check 확인하다

02 ①

W: You can see this in a bathroom. It usually smells good and comes in many different shapes. When your hands are dirty, you can clean them with this.
   It makes bubbles with water. What is this?

   당신은 이것을 화장실에서 볼 수 있어요. 이것은 보통은 향이 좋고 많은 다른 모양으로 나옵니다. 당신의 손이 더러우면 당신은 이것으로 손을 씻을 수 있어요. 이것은 물이 있으면 거품을 만들어요.
   이것은 무엇일까요?

어휘 usually 보통은, 일반적으로 smell good 냄새가 좋다
come in (상품이) 들어오다 shape 모양, 형태 bubble 거품

03 ③

M: Good morning, this is Andrew with your weekend weather report. On Saturday, it will be cloudy and windy all day. On Sunday, it will become colder in the morning, and it will rain in the afternoon.

   안녕하세요, 저는 여러분에게 주말 일기예보를 전해 드리는 앤드류입니다. 토요일에는 하루 종일 구름이 끼고 바람이 불겠습니다. 일요일에는 오전에는 더 추워지겠고, 오후에는 비가 내리겠습니다.

어휘 weather report 일기예보 cloudy 구름이 낀
windy 바람이 부는

04 ④

[Cellphone rings.] [휴대폰이 울린다.]
W: Hello, Tom. 안녕, 톰.
M: Hey, Jina. Will you do me a favor?
   안녕, 지나. 내 부탁 좀 들어줄래?
W: Sure. What is it? 물론이지. 그게 뭔데?
M: Can I borrow your badminton racket? I need it for my P.E. class for tomorrow. 내가 네 배드민턴 라켓을 빌릴 수 있을까? 내일 체육 수업에 그게 필요하거든.
W: No problem. 문제 없어.

해설 'No problem.'을 들으면 '응', '알았어'와 같은 답변으로 이해하면 된다.

어휘 do somebody a favor ~의 부탁을 들어주다
borrow 빌리다 P.E. 체육(= physical education)

05 ④

M: Hello, let me talk about my school, Wuju Middle
School. There are three hundred students. We have
many wonderful teachers. My homeroom teacher,
Mr. Choi, is a math teacher. He's very kind. We
have twenty-five clubs. I love my school.

안녕하세요, 제가 다니는 학교인 우주중학교에 대해 이야기하겠습
니다. 학생은 300명이 있습니다. 우리는 많은 훌륭한 선생님들이 있
습니다. 제 담임 선생님인 최 선생님은 수학 선생님입니다. 그 분은
무척 친절해요. 우리는 25개의 동아리가 있습니다. 저는 저의 학교
를 사랑합니다.

어휘 talk about ~에 대해 말하다 wonderful 훌륭한, 놀라운
homeroom teacher 담임교사 math 수학 club 동아리

06 ③

[*Cellphone rings.*] [휴대폰이 울린다.]
M: Hello, Jenny. 안녕, 제니.
W: John, let's have lunch together.
존, 우리 같이 점심 먹자.
M: Okay. How about *Judy's Burger*? I have two
discount coupons.
알았어. 주디스 버거는 어때? 나한테 할인권이 두 장 있어.
W: That's great. What time shall we meet?
좋은데. 우리 몇 시에 만날까?
M: We can only use them from eleven a.m. to two p.m.
So, what about meeting there at one p.m.?
우리는 그걸 오전 11시부터 오후 2시까지만 쓸 수 있어. 그러니까
오후 1시에 거기서 만나는 게 어때?
W: Sure. 알았어.

어휘 have lunch 점심을 먹다 discount coupon 할인권
what about ~? ~하는 게 어때?

07 ②

M: [*Clapping*] Wow! That sounds wonderful.
[박수 치며] 와! 아주 훌륭했어.
W: Really? I practiced this song for so long.
정말? 난 이 노래를 오랫동안 연습했어.
M: I can see that. I like your playing very much.
알 것 같아. 나는 네 연주가 무척 좋아.
W: Thank you. I really want to be a guitarist.
고마워. 나는 정말로 기타리스트가 되고 싶어.
M: I think you are already a guitarist.
나는 네가 이미 기타리스트라고 생각해.

어휘 practice 연습하다 guitarist 기타리스트 already 이미

08 ②

W: Guess what? We are going on a field trip next

Friday! 있잖아. 우리는 다음 주 금요일에 현장 학습을 갈 거야.
M: That's fantastic! Where are we going?
굉장한데! 우리는 어디로 가니?
W: We are going to *Wonderland*.
우리는 원더랜드로 갈 거야.
M: Wow, I really wanted to ride the roller coaster there!
와, 난 정말로 거기서 롤러코스터를 타고 싶었는데!
W: Me, too. We'll have a great time.
나도 그래. 우리는 멋진 시간을 보내게 될 거야.

해설 남자와 여자는 모두 롤러코스터를 타게 되어 신이 나 있다.

어휘 guess what? (대화를 시작할 때) 있잖아, 이봐
go on a field trip 현장 학습을 가다 fantastic 환상적인 ride the
roller coaster 롤러코스터를 타다 have a great time 즐거운 시
간을 보내다 worried 걱정하는 excited 신이 난, 흥분한 bored 심
심해 하는

09 ①

W: Oh, no! I just left my bag on the bus.
아, 안돼! 난 방금 버스에 내 가방을 놓고 내렸어.
M: Which bus did you take? 넌 어떤 버스를 탔니?
W: I took the four two five. What should I do?
425번을 탔어. 난 어떻게 해야 하지?
M: I think you should call the bus company first.
난 네가 먼저 버스 회사에 전화해야 한다고 생각해.
W: You're right. I'll do that right now.
네 말이 맞아. 지금 바로 해야겠어.

어휘 leave 두고 오다(leave–left–left) take (버스를) 타다
right now 지금 즉시

10 ①

M: Yumi, do you have any plans for *Chuseok*?
유미야, 너 추석에 계획 있어?
W: Yes, I'm going to make traditional Korean food.
응, 난 한국의 전통 음식을 만들 거야.
M: Oh, what are you going to make?
아, 넌 뭘 만들 거야?
W: I'm going to make *songpyeon*. How about you?
난 송편을 만들 거야. 넌 어때?
M: For *Chuseok*, I'm going to visit my grandparents
with my family.
추석에 나는 가족들과 함께 조부모님을 찾아뵐 거야.

어휘 have plans 계획이 있다 traditional 전통적인

11 ⑤

M: Amy! What happened to your leg?
에이미! 네 다리가 왜 그래?
W: I hurt my leg yesterday in dance class. It's hard to
walk. 난 어제 댄스 수업에서 다리를 다쳤어. 걷기가 힘들어.
M: I'm sorry to hear that. Then how will you get home?
그 말을 들으니 정말 유감이다. 그럼 넌 어떻게 집까지 갈 거야?

W: I usually take a bus, but I think I have to take a taxi today. 난 보통은 버스를 타는데, 오늘은 택시를 타야 할 것 같아.

M: Wait here. I'll get one for you. 여기서 기다려. 내가 너 대신 택시를 잡을게.

해설 남자의 마지막 대사에서 one은 taxi를 가리키는 대명사이다.

어휘 leg 다리 hurt 다치다 hard 힘든 get home 귀가하다 usually 보통, 일반적으로 take a bus 버스를 타다

12 ④

W: Jinyoung! You look tired. Are you all right? 진영아! 너 피곤해 보여. 괜찮아?

M: Well, I went to bed really late. 음, 난 정말 늦게 잠자리에 들었거든.

W: Why? Did you watch the soccer game last night? 왜? 어젯밤에 축구 경기를 봤니?

M: No. My dog was sick, so I had to take care of him almost all night. 아니. 우리 개가 아파서 거의 밤새도록 돌봐야 했거든.

W: That's too bad. Is he okay now? 정말 안됐네. 개는 지금 괜찮아?

M: He's better. 나아졌어.

어휘 look tired 피곤해 보이다 go to bed 잠자리에 들다 (go-went-gone) sick 아픈 take care of ~을 돌보다 all night 밤새도록 better 더 나은(good-better-best)

13 ③

M: How may I help you? 무엇을 도와드릴까요?

W: Can you dry-clean this jacket for me? 이 재킷을 드라이클리닝해주실 수 있나요?

M: Sure. Anything else? 물론이죠. 다른 건 없나요?

W: Well, one button is missing on the jacket. 음, 재킷에 단추 하나가 없어요.

M: Okay, I'll fix that. 알겠습니다. 그것도 고칠게요.

W: Thanks. How much will it be? 고맙습니다. 비용이 얼마나 될까요?

M: The total will be thirteen dollars. 합계는 13달러가 될 겁니다.

해설 dry-clean, jacket, button 등의 여러 단어를 통해 세탁소라는 것을 알 수 있다.

어휘 dry-clean 드라이클리닝하다 button 단추 missing 없어진, 사라진 fix 고치다 total 합계, 총액

14 ②

M: Excuse me. Where is the art museum? 실례합니다. 미술관이 어디 있죠?

W: The art museum? Go straight two blocks. Then, turn right. 미술관이요? 두 블록을 쭉 가세요. 그리고 오른쪽으로 도세요.

M: Turn right? 오른쪽으로 돌라고요?

W: Yes. And then walk about twenty meters. You can

see the museum on your left. It is between the gift shop and the toy shop. 네. 그리고 한 20미터를 걸으세요. 당신의 왼쪽에 미술관이 보일 겁니다. 선물가게와 장난감 가게 사이에 있어요.

M: Thank you. 감사합니다.

해설 지도 문제에서는 보통 한 블록이나 두 블록을 곧장 간 뒤 우회전이나 좌회전을 한 후, 왼쪽이나 오른쪽에 있다는 내용이 이어진다.

어휘 art museum 미술관 straight 곧장, 똑바로 block 블록, 구역 turn right 우회전하다 on one's left ~의 왼쪽에 between ~의 사이에 gift shop 선물가게 toy 장난감

15 ⑤

M: Mom, this Saturday is our school camping trip! 엄마, 이번 토요일이 우리 학교가 캠핑 여행가는 날이에요!

W: Yeah, I remember. Where are you going camping? 그래, 나도 기억한다. 너희는 어디로 캠핑을 가니?

M: At Seorak Mountain. 설악산이요.

W: That sounds great. But it's going to be cold at night. 그거 참 좋구나. 하지만 밤이 되면 추워질 텐데.

M: I know. Can you find some winter clothes for me? 저도 알아요. 제가 입을 겨울옷 좀 찾아 주실래요?

W: Of course. 물론이지.

어휘 camping trip 캠핑 여행 at night 밤에 winter clothes 겨울옷

16 ①

M: Susan, you look so healthy. What's your secret? 수잔, 넌 정말 건강해 보여. 네 비결이 뭐야?

W: I exercise three days a week. 나는 일주일에 3일을 운동해.

M: What do you do? 무슨 운동을 하니?

W: I started doing yoga, and it is wonderful. 나는 요가를 시작했는데 정말 좋아.

M: Wow, isn't it hard to do? 우와. 하는 게 어렵지 않니?

W: Not at all. Why don't you try it sometime? 전혀. 너도 언제 한번 해보는 게 어때?

해설 'Why don't you ~?'는 제안을 할 때 자주 나오는 표현이다.

어휘 healthy 건강한 secret 비결, 비밀 exercise 운동하다 three days a week 일주일에 3일 do yoga 요가를 하다 Not at all. 전혀, 천만에. try 시도하다 sometime 언젠가

17 ②

① W: What time is it? 지금 몇 시지?
　 M: It's ten to three. 3시 10분 전이야.

② W: Can I borrow your pen? 네 펜을 빌릴 수 있을까?
　 M: I was there, too. 나도 거기 있었어.

③ W: I got a cold. 난 감기에 걸렸어.
　 M: Oh, that's too bad. 아, 정말 안됐구나.

④ W: Can I have some cookies? 쿠키 좀 먹어도 될까?

M: Sure. Help yourself. 물론이지. 마음껏 먹어.

⑤ W: How can I get to the bus stop?
버스 정류장에 어떻게 갈 수 있나요?

M: Turn left at the corner. 모퉁이에서 좌회전하세요.

어휘 borrow 빌리다 get a cold 감기에 걸리다 Help yourself. (음식을) 마음껏 드세요. get to ~에 가다 bus stop 버스 정류장 at the corner 모퉁이에서

18 ③

M: Welcome to the show! Today we have a special guest in our studio. 프로그램에 오신 것을 환영합니다! 오늘 우리는 스튜디오에 특별 손님을 모셨습니다.

W: Hello. I'm Jean, and I work at an Indian restaurant. 안녕하세요. 저는 진이고, 인도 음식점에서 일합니다.

M: Nice to meet you, Jean. What are we going to cook today?
만나서 반가워요, 진. 우리는 오늘 무엇을 요리할 건가요?

W: We're going to make apple curry.
우리는 사과 카레를 만들게 될 거예요.

M: Wow! That sounds delicious! Let's begin.
와! 그거 맛있겠는데요! 시작해 봅시다.

어휘 show (방송) 프로그램, 쇼 special guest 특별 손님 studio (방송) 스튜디오 Indian 인도의; 인도인 cook 요리하다; 요리사 curry 카레 delicious 맛있는

19 ⑤

W: David, you look busy. What are you doing now?
데이비드, 너 바빠 보인다. 지금 뭘 하고 있니?

M: I'm writing a birthday card for my brother. Tomorrow is his birthday. 내 남동생에게 줄 생일 축하 카드를 쓰고 있어. 내일이 그 애의 생일이거든.

W: Wow, that's sweet. Did you get a present for him?
와, 참 다정하구나. 그에게 줄 선물은 샀니?

M: Not yet. I'm going to buy a baseball cap this afternoon. Do you want to come with me?
아직 안 샀어. 오늘 오후에 야구모자를 살 거야. 나랑 같이 갈래?

W: Sure. Why not? 물론이야. 그거 좋지.

① Thank you for your advice. 충고해 줘서 고마워.
② Sorry to hear that. 그 말을 들으니 유감이야.
③ For here or to go? 여기서 드실 건가요, 가지고 가실 건가요?
④ Don't feel so bad. 너무 기분 나빠하지 마.
⑤ Sure. Why not? 물론이야. 그거 좋지.

어휘 birthday card 생일 축하 카드 sweet 다정한; 듣기 좋은 baseball cap 야구모자 Why not? (동의를 나타내며) 왜 아니겠어?, 그거 좋지.

20 ④

M: Sally, you don't look happy. What's wrong?
샐리, 넌 별로 행복해 보이지 않는구나. 무슨 일이야?

W: I'm upset with my new neighbors.

난 내 새 이웃들 때문에 속상해.

M: Your new neighbors? Why? 네 새 이웃들? 왜?

W: They play the piano late at night and it's too loud.
그들은 밤늦게 피아노를 치는데, 너무 시끄럽거든.

M: That's terrible! So it's hard to sleep, right?
큰일이구나! 그러니까 잠들기 힘들다는 거지, 그렇지?

W: Yes, it is. So I feel really tired.
응, 그래서 난 정말 피곤해.

① It's pretty. I'll take it. 그게 예쁘네요. 그걸 살게요.
② Really? She will like it. 정말? 그녀는 그걸 좋아할 거야.
③ This piano looks wonderful! 피아노가 정말 멋져 보여!
④ Yes, it is. So I feel really tired. 응. 그래서 난 정말 피곤해.
⑤ I don't think it is a good idea.
나는 그게 좋은 아이디어라고 생각하지 않아.

어휘 upset 속상한 neighbor 이웃 play the piano 피아노를 치다 late at night 밤늦게 loud 시끄러운 terrible 지독한, 끔찍한

02회 기출 듣기평가   본문 p.216-217

01 ③	02 ⑤	03 ⑤	04 ②	05 ④
06 ①	07 ③	08 ①	09 ②	10 ①
11 ②	12 ②	13 ⑤	14 ①	15 ④
16 ①	17 ②	18 ④	19 ④	20 ③

01 ③

W: Jiwon, school starts next week! Do you need anything?
지원아, 학교가 다음 주에 개학한다! 뭐 필요한 게 있니?

M: Yes. I'd really like to have a new backpack.
네. 저는 새 책가방이 정말 갖고 싶어요.

W: What kind of backpack do you want?
너는 어떤 종류의 책가방을 원하니?

M: I want a backpack with two pockets on the front.
저는 앞에 주머니가 두 개 달린 책가방을 원해요.

어휘 backpack 책가방, 배낭 pocket 주머니 front 앞면

02 ⑤

M: You use this in a baseball game. You hold it with two hands. It is a long stick. You can hit a home run with it. What is this?

여러분은 야구 경기에서 이것을 사용합니다. 여러분은 양손으로 이것을 잡습니다. 이것은 기다란 막대입니다. 여러분은 이것으로 홈런을 칠 수 있습니다. 이것은 무엇일까요?

어휘 stick 막대 hit a home run 홈런을 치다

03 ⑤

W: Good evening. This is the weather report for

tomorrow. Did you enjoy today's beautiful sunny weather? It was so warm. Tomorrow, there will be strong winds all day long. Thank you.

안녕하십니까. 내일의 일기예보입니다. 오늘 아름답고 화창한 날씨를 즐기셨나요? 무척 따뜻했습니다. 내일은 하루 종일 강한 바람이 불 것입니다. 감사합니다.

어휘 strong wind 강풍 all day long 하루 종일

04 ②

W: Good morning, Tom. What are you reading?
안녕, 톰. 너는 무엇을 읽고 있니?

M: Good morning, Jane. I am reading a science magazine about dinosaurs.
안녕, 제인. 나는 공룡에 관한 과학 잡지를 읽는 중이야.

W: Dinosaurs? It looks interesting.
공룡? 그거 흥미로운데.

M: Yes, it is. You should read it, too.
응. 너도 그것을 읽어 봐.

해설 'You should ~'는 'Why don't you ~?'보다 더 강하게 제안하는 표현이다.

어휘 science 과학 magazine 잡지 dinosaur 공룡 interesting 흥미로운

05 ④

W: Hi, everyone. Let me introduce myself. I'm Sora. My hometown is Incheon, Korea. I live in Hong Kong now. I like ice skating very much. My favorite skater is Yuna Kim. I want to be a famous figure skater like her.

안녕하세요, 여러분. 저에 대해 소개할게요. 제 이름은 소라입니다. 제 고향은 대한민국 인천이에요. 저는 지금 홍콩에 살고 있습니다. 저는 아이스 스케이트를 무척 좋아합니다. 제가 좋아하는 스케이트 선수는 김연아예요. 저도 그녀처럼 유명한 피겨 스케이트 선수가 되고 싶습니다.

해설 'I want to be ~'는 장래 희망을 나타내는 기본적인 표현이다.

어휘 hometown 고향 skater 스케이트 선수

06 ①

M: Mina, how is your history project going?
미나야, 네 역사 프로젝트는 어떻게 되어가고 있니?

W: Not so well. Let's do it together at the library.
잘 안 되고 있어. 우리 도서관에서 함께 하자.

M: Okay. Can we meet at five in the afternoon?
알겠어. 오후 5시에 만날 수 있어?

W: That's too late. How about three?
그건 너무 늦어. 3시는 어때?

M: Good. See you then. 좋아. 그 때 보자.

07 ③

W: Wow, is this a picture of our school?
우와, 이건 우리 학교 그림이야?

M: Yes, it is. I painted it. 응, 그래. 내가 그렸어.

W: It looks wonderful. You are a real artist.
훌륭하다. 너는 진짜 예술가구나.

M: Thanks. I want to be a painter.
고마워. 나는 화가가 되고 싶어.

해설 picture는 그림과 사진의 두 가지 의미를 가지고 있다.

어휘 picture 그림, 사진 real 진정한, 진짜의 artist 예술가, 화가 painter 화가

08 ①

M: Mom, where's my jacket? I'm late.
엄마, 제 재킷 어디에 있어요? 저 늦었어요.

W: You left it on the sofa last night.
네가 어젯밤에 소파 위에 뒀잖니.

M: Thanks. And where's my cellphone?
고마워요. 그리고 제 휴대폰은 어디에 있어요?

W: It's on the table. Don't you see it?
그것은 탁자 위에 있다. 안 보이니?

M: Okay. I found it. Did you see my backpack?
알겠어요. 찾았어요. 제 책가방은 보셨어요?

W: Please, Tom. You're wearing it now. I'm worried about you.
제발, 톰. 그건 네가 지금 메고 있잖아. 나는 네가 참 걱정되는구나.

어휘 leave 놓다(leave-left-left) cellphone 휴대폰 backpack 책가방, 배낭 worried 걱정되는

09 ②

W: Hi, Charlie. Did you finish your English homework?
안녕, 찰리. 너는 영어 숙제를 다 했니?

M: Yes, I did. I already emailed it to Ms. Kim.
응, 했어. 나는 벌써 김 선생님께 그걸 이메일로 보냈어.

W: Oh, really? Can I have her email address?
아, 정말? 나에게 선생님 이메일 주소 좀 알려 줄래?

M: Yes, here it is. 응, 여기 있어.

W: Thanks. I'll send my homework right now.
고마워. 나는 지금 바로 숙제를 보내야겠어.

해설 email은 '이메일'이라는 명사뿐만 아니라 '이메일을 보내다'라는 동사로도 쓰인다.

어휘 homework 숙제 email 이메일을 보내다; 이메일 email address 이메일 주소 right now 지금, 바로

10 ①

M: What subject do you like the most?
너는 어떤 과목을 가장 좋아해?

W: I like English the most. 나는 영어가 제일 좋아.

M: Why do you like it? 그것을 왜 좋아해?

W: In class, we listen to lots of English pop songs. What's your favorite subject? 수업 시간에 우리는 다양한 영어 팝송을 듣거든. 네가 가장 좋아하는 과목은 뭐야?

M: My favorite is P.E. 내가 좋아하는 건 체육이야.

해설 남자는 'Why ~?'로 물었고, 여자는 because 없이 영어를 좋아하는 이유를 말했다.

어휘 subject 과목, 주제 in class 수업 중에 favorite 좋아하는; 좋아하는 것 P.E. 체육 (physical education의 약자)

11 ②

W: Hey, Bill. What are you going to do this weekend? 얘, 빌. 너는 이번 주말에 무엇을 할 거야?

M: I'm visiting my aunt in Daegu. 나는 대구에 계시는 고모를 방문할 거야.

W: How are you getting there? 거기까지 어떻게 갈 거야?

M: I'm going to take a train. 기차를 타고 갈 거야.

W: That's a good idea. It's faster than a bus. 그거 좋은 생각이다. 그게 버스보다 빠르지.

해설 'Excellent.', 'That's a good idea.' 등은 앞에 나온 내용을 승인하거나 칭찬하는 표현이다.

어휘 aunt 이모, 고모, 숙모 get there (어떤 장소에) 도착하다 take a train 기차를 타다 faster 더 빠른(fast-faster-fastest)

12 ②

[Knocking] [노크]

M: Hello, Ms. Kim. Do you have a minute? 안녕하세요, 김 선생님. 시간 있으신가요?

W: Hi, Minsu. Come on in. How can I help you? 안녕, 민수야. 들어오렴. 내가 무엇을 도와줄까?

M: Um... can I join your newspaper club? 음… 제가 선생님의 신문 동아리에 가입해도 되나요?

W: Sure. Write your name, student number, and phone number on this paper. 물론이지. 이 종이에 네 이름, 학번, 그리고 전화번호를 적어.

M: Okay. Thank you. 네. 감사합니다.

어휘 minute 분, 잠깐 join a club 동아리에 가입하다 newspaper 신문 student number 학생 번호, 학번 phone number 전화번호

13 ⑤

M: What's the problem? 무슨 문제인가요?

W: I have a toothache. 저는 치통이 있어요.

M: Do you? Please open your mouth. 그래요? 입을 벌려 보세요.

W: Ouch! It really hurts. 아야! 정말 아프네요.

M: Yes, you have a bad tooth. We need an X-ray. The nurse will help you. 네, 당신은 충치가 있군요. 우린 엑스레이가 필요해요. 간호사가 당신을 도와드릴 겁니다.

W: Okay. 알겠습니다.

어휘 toothache 치통 open one's mouth 입을 벌리다 It hurts. 아프다. bad tooth 충치 nurse 간호사

14 ①

M: Excuse me. Is there a hospital around here? 실례합니다. 이 주변에 병원이 있나요?

W: Yes. Go straight to Green Street and turn left at the corner. 네. 그린 가까지 직진한 뒤 모퉁이에서 좌회전하세요.

M: Go straight and turn left? 직진 후 좌회전이요?

W: Yes. And then, walk about a minute. It'll be on your right. It's next to the bank. 네. 그리고 나서 1분 정도 걸어가세요. 병원은 당신의 오른쪽에 있을 겁니다. 그것은 은행 옆에 있어요.

M: Thank you so much. 정말 감사합니다.

어휘 hospital 병원 around here 이 근처에 go straight 직진하다, 똑바로 가다 turn left 좌회전하다 at the corner 모서리에(서), 모퉁이에(서) on one's right 오른편에 next to ~의 옆에

15 ④

W: It's a beautiful spring day. I want to go outside. 아름다운 봄날이네요. 저는 밖에 나가고 싶어요.

M: Honey, let's finish our housework first. 여보, 우리의 집안일을 먼저 끝냅시다.

W: You're right. 당신 말이 맞아요.

M: I'll wash the dishes. 내가 설거지를 할게요.

W: No. I can do that. Can you clean the living room? 아니에요. 그건 제가 할 수 있어요. 당신은 거실을 청소해 줄래요?

M: No problem. 문제 없어요.

해설 'No problem.'과 비슷한 표현으로는 'OK.' 'Sure.' 등이 나온다.

어휘 spring 봄 go outside 밖으로 나가다 honey (호칭) 여보, 당신 housework 집안일 wash the dishes 설거지하다 clean 청소하다; 깨끗한 living room 거실

16 ①

M: Ellie, what club are you in? 엘리, 너는 어떤 동아리에 있니?

W: I'm in the badminton club. How about you? 나는 배드민턴 동아리에 있어. 너는?

M: I'm still thinking. 나는 아직 생각 중이야.

W: You like dancing! What about joining the dance club? 너는 춤추는 것을 좋아하잖아! 댄스 동아리에 가입하는 게 어때?

M: I'd like to. But first, I have to pass the dance test. 나도 그러고 싶어. 하지만 먼저 나는 댄스 테스트에 통과해야 해.

W: Don't worry about that. Just try it. 그건 걱정하지 마. 그냥 한번 해봐.

해설 전반적으로 club(동아리)에 관한 내용이다.

어휘 join 가입하다 pass the test 시험에 통과하다 try 시도하다

17 ②

① W: Thank you for helping me.
  저를 도와주셔서 감사합니다.
  M: It was my pleasure! 제가 기쁘죠!
② W: Long time no see! 정말 오랜만이다!
  M: I don't have the time. 나는 시간이 없어.
③ W: Aren't you hungry? 너는 배고프지 않니?
  M: Not at all. I'm full. 아니 전혀. 나는 배불러.
④ W: I don't feel well. 난 몸이 별로 안 좋아.
  M: What's wrong? 무슨 일이야?
⑤ W: What's your hobby? 네 취미는 뭐야?
  M: My hobby is swimming. 내 취미는 수영이야.

해설 'Long time no see!'는 누군가를 오랜만에 만났을 때 반가움을 나타내는 표현이므로 'Yes, it's so nice to meet you.'(그래, 너를 만나게 되어 정말 좋다.)와 같은 표현이 이어져야 한다.

18 ④

[Phone rings.] [전화벨이 울린다.]
M: Flying Bakery. How can I help you?
  플라잉 제과점입니다. 무엇을 도와드릴까요?
W: Hello. I'd like to order a strawberry cake for my daughter's birthday. 안녕하세요. 저는 제 딸의 생일을 위해 딸기 케이크를 주문하고 싶습니다.
M: Okay. When do you need it by?
  알겠습니다. 케이크가 언제까지 필요하신가요?
W: This Friday, please. 이번 주 금요일이요.
M: Don't worry. I will bake the most delicious cake for her.
  걱정 마세요. 제가 자녀분을 위해 가장 맛있는 케이크를 만들게요.

해설 전화 상황에서는 앞부분에 가게 이름이나 회사 이름이 나오는 경우가 많으므로 유심히 들어야 한다.

어휘 bakery 제과점, 빵집 order 주문하다 strawberry 딸기 bake (빵을) 굽다 delicious 맛있는

19 ④

M: Oh, no! It's raining! 아, 안돼! 비가 오네!
W: Don't you have an umbrella?
  너 우산 갖고 있지 않니?
M: No, I don't. How can I go home?
  아니, 없어. 나 집에 어떻게 가지?
W: Don't worry. You can use mine. I have two.
  걱정 마. 넌 내 우산을 쓰면 돼. 나는 두 개를 갖고 있거든.
M: Thank you so much. 정말 고마워.

① Here it is. 여기 있어.
② That's too bad. 그거 참 안됐다.
③ Oh! Congratulations! 와! 축하해!
④ Thank you so much. 정말 고마워.
⑤ I'm glad to meet you, too. 나도 널 만나서 반가워.

해설 여자에게 우산을 빌릴 수 있게 된 남자는 고맙다는 말을 할 것이다.

어휘 umbrella 우산 mine 나의 것 Congratulations! 축하해!

20 ③

W: I heard that your friend Jack is visiting Korea next month. 네 친구 잭이 다음 달에 한국에 온다고 들었어.
M: Oh, yes! It's his first visit to Korea.
  응, 그래! 그 애가 한국에 처음으로 오는 거야.
W: Do you have any special plans?
  무슨 특별한 계획이 있니?
M: My mom and I are going to cook Korean food for him. 우리 엄마와 나는 잭을 위해 한국 음식을 만들 거야.
W: What are you going to cook? 무엇을 요리할 거니?
M: We're going to make bulgogi. 우리는 불고기를 만들 거야.

① Yes. I like Italian food. 응. 나는 이탈리아 음식을 좋아해.
② I'm sure she will like it. 그녀가 그걸 좋아할 거라고 확신해.
③ We're going to make bulgogi. 우리는 불고기를 만들 거야.
④ The cook is working at the restaurant.
  그 요리사는 식당에서 일하고 있어.
⑤ We will go to Insadong Sunday morning.
  우리는 일요일 아침에 인사동에 갈 거야.

어휘 visit 방문하다, 찾다; 방문 cook 요리하다; 요리사 sure 확신하는

03회 기출 듣기평가 본문 p.226-227

01 ②	02 ②	03 ④	04 ⑤	05 ①
06 ⑤	07 ④	08 ②	09 ③	10 ③
11 ②	12 ④	13 ①	14 ①	15 ⑤
16 ①	17 ③	18 ②	19 ③	20 ⑤

01 ②

W: Hello. Can I help you?
  안녕하세요. 무엇을 도와드릴까요?
M: Yes, I need a baseball cap for my son.
  네, 제 아들에게 줄 야구 모자가 필요합니다.
W: Okay. What about this one with a dolphin on it?
  그렇군요. 돌고래가 그려진 이것은 어떤가요?
M: Well, I want that one with a bear on it. He likes bears. 글쎄요, 저는 곰이 그려진 저것이 좋네요. 아들은 곰을 좋아하거든요.
W: Good choice. Many boys like that cap.
  잘 선택하셨어요. 많은 남자 아이들이 저 모자를 좋아한답니다.

해설 여기에서 'Well.'은 '글쎄요'라는 의미의 감탄사로서, 그 다음에는 앞선 내용과는 다른 내용이 이어진다.

어휘 baseball cap 야구 모자 What about ~? ~은 어떤가요? dolphin 돌고래 bear 곰 choice 선택

02 ②

W: Good morning. This is the weather report for this weekend. It'll be cloudy and rainy tonight and Saturday. The rain will stop Saturday night, and it'll be sunny all day on Sunday. Be careful not to catch a cold in this kind of weather. Thank you.

안녕하세요. 주말의 날씨를 알려드리겠습니다. 오늘 밤과 토요일에는 구름이 끼고 비가 내릴 것입니다. 비는 토요일 밤에 그칠 것이고, 일요일에는 하루 종일 화창할 것입니다. 이런 날씨에는 감기에 걸리지 않도록 조심하세요. 감사합니다.

어휘 all day 하루 종일 catch a cold 감기 걸리다

03 ④

W: Hi, Tom. What are you doing?
안녕, 톰. 너 뭐 하고 있니?
M: Hi, Sumi. I'm making a poster to find a new guitarist. 안녕, 수미야. 나는 새 기타리스트를 찾기 위해 포스터를 만들고 있어.
W: You know, I can play the guitar pretty well.
너도 알겠지만 나는 기타를 꽤 잘 연주할 수 있어.
M: Really? Why don't you join our band then?
정말이야? 그러면 네가 우리 밴드에 합류하는 건 어때?
W: Sure. I really want to. 물론. 나도 그러고 싶어.

해설 'Why don't you ~?'는 제안할 때 가장 자주 나오는 표현이다.

어휘 guitarist 기타 연주자 play the guitar 기타를 연주하다 pretty well 아주 잘 join a band 밴드에 합류하다

04 ⑤

M: Hi. Let me tell you about my family. There are four people in my family. My father is a history teacher. My mother cooks well. Cooking is her hobby. My older brother is seventeen years old. He is a singer in a rock band. I love my family.

안녕하세요. 제 가족에 대해 말씀 드리겠습니다. 저희 가족은 네 사람이에요. 제 아버지는 역사 선생님입니다. 제 어머니는 요리를 잘 하세요. 요리가 어머니의 취미이죠. 제 형은 17살입니다. 형은 록밴드의 가수예요. 저는 제 가족을 사랑합니다.

어휘 cook 요리하다; 요리사 singer 가수 rock band 록밴드

05 ①

[*Telephone rings.*] [전화벨이 울린다.]
W: Hello? 여보세요?
M: Mom. It's me. Jack is coming back today, right?
엄마. 저예요. 잭이 오늘 돌아오는 거 맞죠?
W: Yes. He arrives at four thirty P.M. at the airport.
응. 그는 공항에 오후 4시 30분에 도착해.
M: Then, let's go to the airport together.
그러면 우리 공항에 같이 가요.
W: Sure. I'll pick you up at three in front of your

school.
물론이지. 내가 너희 학교 앞으로 3시에 널 태우러 갈게.
M: Sounds good. See you then. 좋아요. 그때 봐요.

해설 ④는 Jack이 공항에 도착하는 시각이다.

어휘 come back 돌아오다 arrive 도착하다 airport 공항 pick somebody up ~를 (차에) 태우러 가다; ~를 (차에) 태우다 in front of ~앞에

06 ⑤

W: Wow, great! Where did you take these pictures?
우와, 멋지다! 너는 어디에서 이 사진을 찍었니?
M: I took them in China last year.
작년에 중국에서 찍었어.
W: I think you're really good at taking pictures.
나는 네가 사진 찍는 것에 소질이 있다고 생각해.
M: Thank you. I want to become a photographer.
고마워. 나는 사진 작가가 되고 싶어.
W: That sounds good! 그거 좋다!

어휘 take pictures 사진을 찍다 good at ~을 잘하는 photographer 사진작가

07 ④

M: Wendy, what are you going to do this weekend?
웬디, 이번 주말에 무엇을 할 거야?
W: Well, I'm going to stay home all weekend. How about you?
글쎄, 나는 주말 내내 집에 있을 거야. 너는?
M: I'm going to Jeju Island with my family.
나는 가족과 함께 제주도에 갈 거야.
W: That sounds wonderful! 재미있겠다!
M: Yes, I know. I can't wait.
응, 맞아. 나도 아주 기대돼.

해설 'I can't wait.'는 뭔가를 고대할 때 자주 나오는 표현이다.

어휘 stay home 집에 머물다 all weekend 주말 내내

08 ②

M: Mom, what do we need to buy here?
엄마, 우리가 여기에서 무엇을 사야 하나요?
W: We need milk, fish, and some other things. Can you get the milk? 우리는 우유, 생선, 그리고 다른 것들도 필요해. 너는 우유를 가져오겠니?
M: Sure, and I'll get the fish, too.
물론이죠, 제가 생선도 가져올게요.
W: Do you know how to choose fresh fish?
너는 신선한 생선을 어떻게 고르는지 알고 있니?
M: I'm not sure. 잘 모르겠어요.
W: Then, just get the milk. I'll wait for you at the fish counter. 그렇다면 그냥 우유만 가져오렴. 나는 생선 판매대에서 널 기다릴게.

M: Okay. 알겠어요.

어휘 choose 고르다, 선택하다 fresh 신선한 counter 판매대, 계산대

09 ③

W: We have a long weekend. Do you have any plans?
우리에게 긴 주말이 있어. 너는 무슨 계획이 있니?

M: Yes. I'm going to go to Gwangju with my friends. How about you?
응. 나는 친구들과 광주에 갈 거야. 너는?

W: I'm planning to help some old people at a nursing home. 나는 양로원에서 어르신들을 도울 계획이야.

M: That's really nice of you! I hope you have a good time. 너는 참 착하구나! 네가 좋은 시간을 보내길 바랄게.

W: Thanks. You, too. 고마워. 너도.

어휘 nursing home 양로원 have a good time 좋은 시간을 보내다

10 ③

W: Two train tickets to Busan, please.
부산 행 기차표 두 장 주세요.

M: I'm sorry, but we have only one ticket left.
죄송하지만 저희에게 한 장만 남았네요.

W: Oh, no! I need two. 아, 안 돼요! 저는 두 장이 필요해요.

M: There are buses that go to Busan, too. The bus terminal is right over there.
부산으로 가는 버스도 있어요. 버스 터미널은 바로 저쪽에 있습니다.

W: Really? Then, I'll go buy bus tickets. Thank you.
정말인가요? 그러면 저는 버스표를 사러 가야겠네요. 감사합니다.

해설 뒷부분에 나오는 교통수단이 정답일 가능성이 크다.

어휘 left 남은 right over there 바로 저쪽에

11 ②

W: I called you yesterday, but your phone was off.
내가 어제 너에게 전화했는데, 네 전화가 꺼져 있더라.

M: Sorry about that. I went to see a musical, so I turned it off.
미안해. 나는 뮤지컬을 보러 가서 전화기를 꺼놨어.

W: I see. How was the musical?
그렇구나. 뮤지컬은 어땠니?

M: It was great. Why did you call me?
좋았어. 너는 나한테 왜 전화했어?

W: I called to ask you about the homework, but I finished it.
숙제에 대해 물어보려고 전화했는데, 나는 그것을 끝냈어.

M: That's good. 잘됐다.

어휘 phone 전화기 off 꺼진 musical 뮤지컬 turn something off ~을 끄다

12 ④

M: Do you sell puzzles in this bookstore?
이 서점에서 퍼즐도 판매하나요?

W: I'm sorry. We don't. But you can buy them at a toy store nearby. 죄송합니다. 저희는 판매하지 않습니다. 그렇지만 근처에 있는 장난감 가게에서 구입할 수 있어요.

M: Okay. Then I'll just take these books. How much are they?
알겠습니다. 그럼 저는 이 책만 살게요. 얼마예요?

W: They're ten dollars. 그것들은 10달러입니다.

M: Okay. By the way, where is the toy store?
그렇군요. 그나저나, 그 장난감 가게는 어디에 있죠?

W: It's next to the post office. 우체국 옆에 있어요.

M: Thanks. 감사합니다.

해설 'in this bookstore'에서 바로 정답을 알 수 있다.

어휘 sell 팔다 puzzle 퍼즐 bookstore 서점 nearby 근처의 by the way 그런데, 그나저나 next to ~옆의 post office 우체국

13 ①

M: Excuse me. Can you tell me the way to City Hall?
실례합니다. 시청으로 가는 길을 알려줄 수 있나요?

W: City Hall? Go straight two blocks and turn left.
시청이요? 두 블록을 곧장 간 뒤 좌회전하세요.

M: Turn left? And then? 좌회전이요? 그 다음에는요?

W: Walk down Broadway, and you'll see it on your right. It's across from the hospital.
브로드웨이를 걸어가면 그것이 당신의 오른쪽에 보일 거예요. 시청은 병원 건너편에 있어요.

M: Okay. Thank you very much. 알겠습니다. 정말 감사합니다.

어휘 tell the way to ~로 가는 길을 말하다 city hall 시청 walk down 걸어 내려가다 across from ~의 맞은편에

14 ①

[Telephone rings.] [전화벨이 울린다.]

W: Hello? 여보세요?

M: It's me, Mom. I think I left my wallet at home.
저예요, 엄마. 제가 집에 지갑을 두고 온 것 같아요.

W: When was the last time you saw it?
넌 언제 지갑을 마지막으로 봤니?

M: Sorry, but I'm not sure. 죄송하지만 잘 모르겠어요.

W: I cleaned your room this morning, but I didn't see it. 내가 오늘 아침에 네 방을 청소했는데 지갑은 못 봤어.

M: Hmm... can you check my blue coat? I think I put it in its pocket. 음… 제 파란색 코트를 확인해 주시겠어요? 제가 지갑을 주머니에 넣은 것 같아요.

W: Okay, I will. 그래, 알겠다.

M: Thanks, Mom. 고마워요, 엄마.

해설 남자의 말 'can you ~?'에서 부탁하는 내용이 나온다.

어휘 wallet 지갑 not sure 확실하지 않은 clean a room 방을 청소하다 check 확인하다 put 넣다, 두다 pocket 주머니

15 ⑤

M: Jane, I heard you got a good grade on the test.
제인, 네가 시험에서 좋은 성적을 받았다고 들었어.

W: Yes. I'm so happy. 맞아. 난 정말 기뻐.

M: How did you do so well on that test?
너는 어떻게 그 시험에서 그렇게 잘 봤니?

W: I studied with my friends. Why don't you join our study group? 나는 친구들과 함께 공부했어. 너도 우리 공부 모임에 들어오는 게 어때?

M: Really? Thank you. I'd love to.
정말? 고마워. 나도 그렇게 하고 싶어.

해설 'Why don't you ~?' 뒤에 제안하는 내용이 이어진다.

어휘 get a good grade 좋은 성적을 받다 on the test 시험에서 do well 잘하다 join 가입하다, 함께하다 study group 스터디 그룹, 공부 모임 I'd love to. 나도 그러고 싶다.

16 ①

① W: What time do you usually get up?
너는 보통 몇 시에 일어나니?

M: It was last Saturday. 그건 지난 토요일이었어.

② W: How much is this hat? 이 모자는 얼마인가요?

M: It's fifteen dollars. 15달러예요.

③ W: What's your favorite sport?
네가 가장 좋아하는 운동은 뭐야?

M: I like soccer most. 나는 축구를 가장 좋아해.

④ W: How about joining our club?
우리 동아리에 가입하는 건 어때?

M: That's a good idea. 그거 좋은 생각이다.

⑤ W: What's wrong? You don't look so good.
무슨 일이니? 너 몸이 안 좋아 보인다.

M: I have a headache. 나는 두통이 있어.

해설 ①에서 시간을 물었으므로 'I usually get up at 7.'(나는 보통 7시에 일어나.) 등으로 답해야 한다.

어휘 usually 보통, 대개 get up 일어나다 hat 모자 soccer 축구 look good 좋아 보이다 have a headache 두통이 있다

17 ③

M: Mrs. Banks. Long time no see.
뱅크스 부인. 정말 오랜만이에요.

W: Yes, I've been so busy. How are you?
제가 많이 바빴어요. 어떻게 지내세요?

M: Great, thanks. What can we do for you today?
잘 지내요, 감사합니다. 오늘 제가 어떻게 해 드릴까요?

W: I need a haircut. 저는 머리를 좀 잘라야 해요.

M: First, Jane will shampoo your hair, and then I'll cut it. 우선, 제인이 당신의 머리를 감겨드릴 거예요, 그리고 나서 제가 자를게요.

W: Thank you. Carl, you always do a good job.
고마워요. 칼, 당신은 늘 실력이 좋아요.

해설 haircut, shampoo, hair 등의 단어를 듣고 미용사를 떠올려야 한다.

어휘 Long time no see. 오랜만이다. haircut 머리 깎기, 헤어스타일 shampoo one's hair ~의 머리를 샴푸로 감다 do a good job 일을 잘하다

18 ②

M: People may use this when they travel. Other people use this to get exercise. This usually has two wheels and doesn't need electric power. For your safety, don't forget to wear a helmet when you use this. What is this?

사람들은 여행할 때 이것을 이용할 수 있습니다. 어떤 사람들은 이것을 운동할 때 이용합니다. 이것은 보통 두 개의 바퀴가 있고 전기를 필요로 하지 않습니다. 여러분의 안전을 위해서 이것을 사용할 때 헬멧을 쓰는 것을 잊지 말아야 합니다. 이것은 무엇일까요?

해설 two wheels가 결정적인 단서가 된다.

어휘 travel 여행하다; 여행 get exercise 운동하다 usually 보통, 일반적으로 wheel 바퀴 electric power 전기, 전력 safety 안전 wear a helmet 헬멧을 쓰다

19 ③

W: You look tired today! What happened, David?
너 오늘 피곤해 보여! 무슨 일이니, 데이비드?

M: I couldn't sleep last night. I don't think I did well in the speech contest. 나는 어젯밤에 잠을 못 잤어. 나는 말하기 대회에서 잘 못한 것 같아.

W: When will the results come out?
결과는 언제 나올 예정이야?

M: Tomorrow. So I feel very nervous about them.
내일. 그래서 나는 아주 긴장돼.

W: Don't worry so much. 너무 걱정하지 마.

① I mean it. 진심이야.
② That's cool. 좋아.
③ Don't worry so much. 너무 걱정하지 마.
④ I'm so glad to hear that. 그 말을 듣게 되어 정말 기뻐.
⑤ I can't thank you enough.
어떻게 고마움을 표현해야 할지 모르겠어.

해설 긴장하고 있는 남자를 안심시키는 말이 가장 적절하다.

어휘 look tired 피곤해 보이다 speech contest 말하기 대회, 웅변 대회 result 결과 come out 나오다 feel nervous 애태우다, 걱정하다 cool 멋진; 시원한

20 ⑤

M: Hi, Julia! Are you free this afternoon?
안녕, 줄리아! 너 오늘 오후에 별 일 없어?

W: What's up? 무슨 일인데?

M: I got two tickets for the musical *Mama Mia*.
나한테 뮤지컬 '맘마미아' 티켓이 두 장 있거든.

W: Sounds great, but I can't make it this afternoon.
좋다. 그런데 나 오늘 오후에는 안 돼.

M: Why not? 왜 안 돼?

W: I have to take care of my brother all day.
내가 하루 종일 남동생을 돌봐야 해.

① I like musicals better.
나는 뮤지컬을 더 좋아해.

② I'll meet you at the ticket box.
내가 너를 매표소에서 만날게.

③ I don't have anything to do today.
나는 오늘 할 일이 아무것도 없어.

④ I really want to watch the musical.
나는 그 뮤지컬이 정말 보고 싶어.

⑤ I have to take care of my brother all day.
내가 하루 종일 남동생을 돌봐야 해.

해설 뮤지컬을 보러 갈 수 없는 이유를 말한 ⑤가 적절하다.

어휘 make it (모임 등에) 참석하다, 시간 맞춰 가다

04회 기출 듣기평가
본문 p.236-237

01 ①	02 ②	03 ①	04 ④	05 ③
06 ③	07 ⑤	08 ⑤	09 ③	10 ④
11 ②	12 ⑤	13 ②	14 ③	15 ④
16 ①	17 ①	18 ②	19 ⑤	20 ⑤

01 ①

M: Look at this necktie! This is for Dad.
이 넥타이 좀 봐! 이것은 아빠를 위한 거야.

W: I like it. The sunflower on it looks great.
나도 그게 마음에 들어. 여기 그려진 해바라기가 예쁘다.

M: Yes, it does. You know, Dad likes sunflowers.
응, 그렇네. 아빠가 해바라기 좋아하시는 거 알지?

W: Right. Dad will like it. Let's buy it.
맞아. 아빠가 좋아하실 거야. 이거 사자.

어휘 look at ~을 보다 necktie 넥타이 sunflower 해바라기

02 ②

W: Good morning. This is today's weather report. This morning, it's cold and a little cloudy, but the weather will get warmer. In the afternoon, it'll be sunny. It'll be good for doing outdoor activities. Thank you.

안녕하세요. 오늘의 일기예보입니다. 오늘 아침에는 춥고 약간 구름이 끼겠지만 날씨는 점차 따뜻해질 것입니다. 오후에는 화창하겠습니다. 야외 활동을 하기에 좋은 날이 되겠네요. 감사합니다.

어휘 get warmer 더 따뜻해지다 outdoor 야외의 activity 활동

03 ①

[Cellphone rings.] [휴대폰이 울린다.]

W: Hi, Kevin. Where are you? 안녕, 케빈. 너 어디에 있니?

M: I'm at home. Why? 나는 집에 있어. 왜?

W: I have two K-pop concert tickets. Do you want to see the concert with me? 나한테 케이팝 콘서트 티켓 두 장이 있거든. 나랑 같이 콘서트 보러 갈래?

M: I'm sorry, but I can't. I don't feel well today.
미안하지만 안 돼. 나는 오늘 몸이 좀 안 좋아.

해설 'I'm sorry, but ~', 'I'd like to, but ~' 등은 거절할 때 빈번하게 나오는 표현이다.

어휘 K-pop 케이팝, 한국 대중음악 not feel well 몸이 좋지 않다

04 ④

M: Hi, everyone. Nice to meet you. Let me introduce myself. My name is Thomas Carter. I'm fourteen years old. My hometown is New York. My dream is to become a teacher someday. I want to make many new friends here. Thank you.

안녕하세요, 여러분. 만나서 반갑습니다. 저에 대해 소개하겠습니다. 제 이름은 토마스 카터입니다. 저는 14살입니다. 제 고향은 뉴욕입니다. 제 꿈은 언젠가 교사가 되는 것입니다. 저는 여기에서 새로운 친구를 많이 만들고 싶습니다. 감사합니다.

어휘 introduce oneself 자기 소개를 하다 hometown 고향 make friends 친구를 사귀다, 친구가 되다

05 ③

W: John, let's go jogging tomorrow morning.
존, 내일 아침에 조깅하자.

M: Okay. What time shall we meet? I get up at six o'clock. 그래. 우리 몇 시에 만날까? 나는 6시에 일어나.

W: Then, how about six thirty? 그러면 6시 30분 어때?

M: That's too early. Let's meet at seven o'clock.
그건 너무 일러. 7시에 만나자.

W: Okay. See you then. 알았어. 그때 보자.

해설 시간 관련 문제는 끝까지 들어야 정답을 놓치지 않는다.

어휘 go jogging 조깅하러 가다 get up (잠자리에서) 일어나다 how about ~? ~은 어때? early 이른

06 ③

M: Hi, Julia. Did you choose a club yet?
안녕, 줄리아. 너는 동아리를 선택했니?

W: Not yet. How about you? 아니, 아직. 너는?

M: I want to join the movie club.
나는 영화 동아리에 가입하고 싶어.

W: Good. I'm thinking about the music club.
좋네. 나는 음악 동아리를 생각 중이야.

M: Oh, really? Do you like music?
아, 정말이야? 너는 음악을 좋아하니?

W: Yes. I <u>want</u> to be a <u>musician</u>.
응. 나는 음악가가 되고 싶어.

어휘 choose 고르다, 선택하다 yet 아직, 이미
not yet 아직도 ~않다 musician 음악가

07 ⑤

W: You don't look well. What's <u>wrong</u>?
너 얼굴색이 안 좋아 보여. 무슨 일이야?

M: You know, the English drama <u>contest</u> was yesterday. 있잖아, 어제 영어 연극 경연대회가 있었어.

W: Right. <u>How</u> did it <u>go</u>? 맞아. 어떻게 됐어?

M: Well, I <u>practiced</u> a lot, but I <u>didn't win</u> a <u>prize</u>.
음, 나는 연습을 많이 했지만 상을 받진 못했어.

W: Oh, I <u>understand</u> how you feel.
아, 네 심정이 어떤지 나는 이해해.

어휘 wrong 잘못된, 틀린 you know 있잖아, 그러니까 drama
연극, 드라마 contest 경연대회, 콘테스트 practice 연습하다; 연습
win a prize 상을 받다

08 ⑤

W: Let's <u>go</u> to Central <u>Art Hall</u> next week.
다음 주에 중앙 아트홀에 가자.

M: Oh, I heard the <u>tickets</u> are very <u>expensive</u>.
아, 나는 그 티켓이 아주 비싸다고 들었는데.

W: <u>Maybe</u> they have a <u>student discount</u>.
아마도 학생 할인이 있을 거야.

M: Why don't you <u>call</u> the <u>art hall</u>?
네가 아트홀에 전화해 보는 게 어때?

W: <u>Okay</u>. I will. 알았어. 내가 할게.

어휘 central 중앙의 art hall 아트홀 expensive 비싼
student discount 학생 할인

09 ③

M: Your school <u>sports day</u> is <u>next Monday</u>, right?
너희 학교 체육대회 날이 다음 주 월요일이지, 그렇지?

W: <u>No</u>, it was <u>changed</u> because it'll be windy and rainy next Monday.
아니, 다음 월요일에 바람이 불고 비가 올 거라고 해서 바뀌었어.

M: Really? So <u>when</u> is the sports day?
정말로? 그러면 체육대회 날이 언제야?

W: It's <u>next Friday</u>. 다음 주 금요일이야.

M: I see. 그렇구나.

어휘 sports day 체육대회, 운동회 날 windy 바람이 부는

10 ④

M: Hurry up. It's seven thirty already.
서둘러. 벌써 7시 30분이야.

W: All right. Should we <u>take</u> a <u>taxi</u>?
알았어. 우리가 택시를 타야 할까?

M: <u>No</u>, there are too <u>many</u> cars on the <u>road</u> now.
아니, 지금은 도로에 차가 너무 많아.

W: Well, <u>how about</u> taking the <u>subway</u> then?
음, 그렇다면 지하철을 타는 건 어때?

M: That's <u>better</u>. Let's go!
그게 더 좋겠다. 가자!

어휘 hurry up 서두르다 already 벌써, 이미 take a taxi 택시를
타다 on the road 도로에 take a subway 지하철을 타다
better 더 나은

11 ②

M: I <u>didn't see</u> you at school yesterday. What happened?
나는 어제 학교에서 널 못 봤어. 무슨 일 있었니?

W: Oh, I went to <u>see</u> the <u>doctor</u> with my mom.
아, 나는 엄마와 함께 병원에 갔어.

M: Why? Were you <u>sick</u>? 왜? 너 아팠니?

W: I <u>had</u> a <u>cold</u>, but I'm <u>better</u> now.
나는 감기에 걸렸는데 지금은 괜찮아.

M: It's really <u>cold</u> outside. <u>Take care</u> of yourself.
바깥이 아주 추워. 네 몸을 잘 돌보렴.

W: Thanks. 고마워.

어휘 go to see the doctor 병원에 가다, 의사를 만나러 가다
sick 아픈 have a cold 감기에 걸리다 take care of ~을 보살피다,
돌보다

12 ⑤

M: Thank you for calling Tom's <u>Radio Quiz Show</u>! Who am I talking to? 톰의 라디오 퀴즈쇼에 전화 주셔서 감사합니다. 저랑 이야기하시는 분은 누구시죠?

W: Hi, this is Sujin from Cheonan.
안녕하세요, 저는 천안에 사는 수진입니다.

M: Hi, Sujin. Can you <u>guess</u> the <u>answer</u>?
안녕하세요, 수진 양. 정답이 뭔지 알겠어요?

W: I think it's number three, the lion.
저는 3번 사자라고 생각해요.

M: You <u>got</u> it! Congratulations! 바로 그거예요! 축하 드립니다!

어휘 guess 짐작하다, 알아맞히다 You got it. 바로 그거야. 그렇고
말고.

13 ②

M: Excuse me. <u>How</u> can I <u>get</u> to the <u>police station</u>?
실례합니다. 경찰서까지 어떻게 가나요?

W: Let me see. Go <u>straight</u> one block and <u>turn right</u>.
잠깐만요. 한 블록을 직진한 뒤 우회전하세요.

M: Go straight one block and turn right?
한 블록 직진 후 우회전이요?

W: Yes. Then, walk <u>straight</u> a little <u>farther</u>. It'll be on your <u>left next to</u> the <u>bank</u>. 네. 그런 다음에 좀 더 걸어가세요. 경찰서는 당신의 왼쪽으로 은행 옆에 있을 겁니다.

M: Oh, I see. Thank you very much.
아, 알겠어요. 정말 감사합니다.

14 ③

W: Minsu. Can you help me?
민수야. 나를 도와주겠니?

M: Sure, Ms. Brown. What can I do for you?
물론이죠, 브라운 선생님. 제가 무엇을 할까요?

W: After our English class, can you erase the blackboard?
우리 영어 수업 후에 네가 칠판을 지워주겠니?

M: I'd be glad to. Anything else?
기꺼이 그러죠. 다른 것은요?

W: That's all. Thank you. 그게 전부란다. 고마워.

어휘 erase (지우개로) 지우다 blackboard 칠판

15 ④

M: Jina, I'm going to Damyang this weekend.
지나야, 나는 이번 주말에 담양에 갈 거야.

W: Are you? I went there last year.
그래? 나는 작년에 그곳에 갔어.

M: Really? What did you do there?
정말이야? 그곳에서 무엇을 했어?

W: I went to the Hanok Village. It was great. Why don't you go there some time? 나는 한옥 마을에 갔어. 멋졌어. 너도 언젠가 거기에 가보는 게 어때?

M: Sounds good. Thanks. 좋아. 고마워.

해설 여자의 말 'Why don't you ~?'에 제안하는 내용이 이어진다.

어휘 village 마을 some time 언젠가

16 ①

① M: I am sorry. It's my fault. 죄송해요. 제 잘못이에요.
   W: My pleasure. 제가 기쁘죠.
② M: How do you spell your last name?
   당신 성의 철자가 어떻게 되나요?
   W: It's B-R-O-W-N. B, R, O, W, N입니다.
③ M: Hi, Cathy. How is it going? 안녕, 캐시. 어떻게 지내니?
   W: Fine, thanks. 좋아, 고마워.
④ M: Who's calling, please? 누구시죠?
   W: This is Amy. 저는 에이미예요.
⑤ M: Thank you for your help. 도와줘서 고마워요.
   W: No problem. 괜찮아요.

어휘 fault 잘못, 실수 pleasure 기쁨 spell 철자를 맞게 쓰다 last name (이름의) 성

17 ①

W: Good morning, Mr. Watson. How are you?
좋은 아침입니다, 왓슨 씨. 어떻게 지내세요?

M: Tired. I just finished my novel.
피곤하네요. 저는 막 소설을 끝냈어요.

W: Oh, really? 아, 그래요?

M: Yes, I already emailed it to you.
네, 제가 당신에게 그것을 이미 이메일로 보냈어요.

W: Good. I'll check my e-mail right away.
좋아요. 제가 바로 이메일을 확인할게요.

M: Call me after you read it.
당신이 그것을 읽은 뒤 제게 전화해 주세요.

W: I will. Thanks. Many people are waiting for your new novel. 그럴게요. 감사합니다. 많은 사람들이 당신의 새 소설을 기다리고 있어요.

해설 남자는 소설가, 여자는 담당 편집자로 보인다.

어휘 novel 소설 e-mail 이메일을 보내다; 이메일 right away 당장, 즉시

18 ②

W: Do you love reading? When you're reading books, do your eyes get tired easily? Then, you may need this. This makes a lot of light. Many people use this when reading at night. What is this?

여러분은 독서를 좋아하나요? 책을 읽을 때 여러분의 눈이 쉽게 피로해지나요? 그렇다면, 여러분은 이것이 필요할지 모릅니다. 이것은 아주 많은 빛을 만들어내요. 많은 사람들이 밤에 독서를 할 때 이것을 사용합니다. 이것은 무엇일까요?

어휘 reading 독서 get tired 피곤해지다 easily 쉽사리 light 빛

19 ⑤

M: Hi, Jenny. What did you do last weekend?
안녕, 제니. 너는 지난 주말에 뭐 했어?

W: I just stayed home. I couldn't do anything.
나는 그냥 집에 있었어. 아무것도 할 수 없었거든.

M: Really? Why? 정말로? 왜?

W: My dog was sick. She couldn't eat anything.
내 개가 아팠어. 개는 아무것도 먹지 못했어.

M: I'm sorry to hear that. 그 말을 듣게 되어 유감이야.

① Here we are. 자, 도착했다.
② That's fantastic! 그거 멋지다!
③ It's my pleasure. 내가 기쁘지.
④ Sure. No problem. 물론. 문제 없어.
⑤ I'm sorry to hear that. 그 말을 듣게 되어 유감이야.

해설 'I'm sorry to hear that.'은 유감을 나타내거나 위로할 때 가장 자주 쓰이는 표현이다.

어휘 fantastic 환상적인

20 ⑤

W: You're meeting Susan at six o'clock, right?
너는 6시에 수잔을 만나지, 맞지?

M: Yes, we're planning to have dinner tonight.
네, 저희는 오늘 밤에 저녁식사를 할 계획이에요.

W: Well, you should hurry up then. It's already five

thirty. 음, 그럼 너는 서둘러야겠구나. 벌써 5시 30분이야.

M: Oh, really? Thanks, Mom.
아, 정말이에요? 고마워요, 엄마.

W: Where are you going for dinner?
저녁식사를 하러 어디에 갈 거니?

M: The Chinese restaurant near our school.
저희 학교 근처에 있는 중국 음식점이요.

① I may be a bit late. 저는 약간 늦을지도 몰라요.
② I met her 30 minutes ago. 저는 30분 전에 그녀를 만났어요.
③ At 6 o'clock every Saturday. 매주 토요일 6시에요.
④ Maybe with Mike and his sister.
아마 마이크와 그의 여동생과 함께요.
⑤ The Chinese restaurant near our school.
저희 학교 근처에 있는 중국 음식점이요.

어휘 have dinner 저녁을 먹다 Chinese restaurant 중국 음식점 be late 늦다 a bit 약간

05회 기출 듣기평가
본문 p.246-247

01 ①	02 ②	03 ④	04 ②	05 ③
06 ④	07 ②	08 ⑤	09 ③	10 ④
11 ③	12 ⑤	13 ④	14 ②	15 ⑤
16 ⑤	17 ④	18 ①	19 ①	20 ③

01 ①

W: We can use it when we want to see ourselves. It has different sizes and shapes. Since it is usually made of glass, we have to be careful because it breaks easily. What is it?

우리는 우리 자신의 모습을 보고 싶을 때 그것을 사용합니다. 그것은 다양한 크기와 모양을 갖고 있습니다. 그것은 주로 유리로 만들어져서 깨지기 쉽기 때문에 우리는 주의해야 합니다. 그것은 무엇일까요?

어휘 ourselves 우리 자신 size 크기 shape 모양 since ~이므로 usually 주로, 대부분 be made of ~로 만들어지다 glass 유리 careful 신중한, 조심스러운 break 깨지다, 깨뜨리다 easily 쉽게

02 ②

M: Hi, Jenny. How was your family trip last week?
안녕, 제니. 지난주 너희 가족 여행 어땠니?

W: We had a lot of fun on Jeju Island.
우리는 제주도에서 정말 즐거운 시간을 보냈어.

M: What did you do there? 거기에서 무엇을 했어?

W: We went to the beach and ate seafood.
우리는 해변에도 가고 해물도 먹었어.

M: That sounds great! I also ate seafood in Sokcho with my family.

정말 좋았겠다! 나도 가족과 속초에서 해물을 먹었어.

W: Oh, did you like Sokcho? 아, 속초는 마음에 들었니?

M: Yes, I really liked the fresh air there.
응, 나는 그곳의 맑은 공기가 정말 좋았어.

어휘 family trip 가족 여행 have fun 재미있게 놀다 island 섬 eat 먹다(eat-ate-eaten) seafood 해물 fresh air 신선한 공기

03 ④

M: Hello. Here's the weather report for tomorrow. Seoul will be cloudy all day. Gwangju will be windy and Daejeon will have sunny skies. But it will be rainy in Daegu. Don't forget to take your umbrella. Thank you.

안녕하세요. 내일의 날씨를 알려드리겠습니다. 서울은 하루 종일 구름이 끼겠습니다. 광주는 바람이 불고, 대전은 맑은 하늘을 보이겠습니다. 그러나 대구에는 비가 내릴 것입니다. 우산 챙기는 것을 잊지 마세요. 감사합니다.

어휘 don't forget to ~하는 것을 잊지 마라 take one's umbrella 우산을 가지고 가다

04 ②

M: Did you finish your painting?
너는 그림 그리기를 끝냈니?

W: Yes, I finished it with Sujin yesterday.
응, 나는 어제 수진이와 함께 끝냈어.

M: Can I see it? 내가 그것을 봐도 될까?

W: Of course. Here it is. What do you think?
물론이지. 여기 있어. 어떻게 생각해?

M: Wonderful! You did a great job!
훌륭해! 너 정말 잘했구나!

해설 'Great.' 'Wonderful.' 등의 감탄사는 칭찬하는 표현이다.

어휘 painting 그림 do a great job 아주 잘하다

05 ③

M: I have breakfast every day. Today, I woke up early in the morning and ate bananas. For lunch, I had a sandwich with orange juice. After school, I went to Pizza World with my friends. I had two slices of pizza there.

저는 매일 아침식사를 해요. 오늘은 아침 일찍 일어나서 바나나를 먹었어요. 점심으로, 저는 오렌지 주스와 함께 샌드위치를 먹었어요. 학교가 끝난 후 저는 친구들과 함께 피자월드에 갔어요. 저는 그곳에서 피자를 두 조각 먹었어요.

어휘 have breakfast 아침을 먹다 slice (얇은) 조각

06 ④

W: I'm excited about going to the zoo tomorrow.
나는 내일 동물원에 가는 게 신 나.

M: So am I. What time shall we meet at the zoo?

나도 마찬가지야. 우리는 동물원에서 몇 시에 만날까?

W: Let's make it at ten o'clock. 10시에 만나자.

M: But the zoo opens at ten thirty.
그렇지만 동물원은 10시 30분에 문을 열어.

W: Oh, really? Then, how about at eleven?
아, 그래? 그러면 11시는 어때?

M: Sounds good. See you then at the main gate.
좋아. 그때 정문에서 만나자.

어휘 excited 신난, 흥분한 zoo 동물원 let's make it ~로 하자 main gate 정문

07 ②

W: Tom, I'm going to buy a present for Dad.
톰, 나는 아빠를 위한 선물을 살 거야.

M: What do you want to buy? 너는 뭘 사고 싶어?

W: A sweater, but I can't choose a color on the Internet.
스웨터, 그런데 나는 인터넷으로 색상을 고를 수가 없어.

M: Hmm... Then, why don't you go to a clothing store?
음, 그러면 옷 가게에 가는 건 어때?

W: Sounds good. Will you come with me?
좋아. 너는 나와 같이 갈래?

M: Sure. 물론이지.

어휘 present 선물 sweater 스웨터 on the Internet 인터넷에서 clothing store 옷가게

08 ⑤

W: Is this your family picture?
이거 너희 가족 사진이니?

M: Yes, it is. These are my mom and dad.
응, 그래. 이분들은 우리 엄마 아빠야.

W: Who is this woman? Is she your grandmother?
이 여자분은 누구야? 너희 할머니셔?

M: Yes. She moved to Canada last year. I really miss her. 맞아. 할머니께선 작년에 캐나다로 이사를 가셨어. 난 우리 할머니가 정말 보고 싶어.

W: I know how you feel. I want to see my grandmother, too.
네 기분이 어떤지 나도 알아. 나도 우리 할머니가 보고 싶거든.

어휘 move to ~로 이사하다 miss 그리워하다

09 ③

W: Charlie, what did you do last weekend?
찰리, 지난 주말에 뭐 했니?

M: I went to the swimming pool with my friends.
친구들과 수영장에 갔어.

W: Really? Did you have fun? 정말? 재미있었니?

M: Yes, of course! How was your weekend?
응, 당연하지! 너는 주말을 어떻게 보냈어?

W: It was great! I made cookies for my family.
잘 보냈지! 가족을 위해 내가 쿠키를 만들었어.

M: Oh, good! 와, 잘했다!

어휘 swimming pool 수영장 have fun 재미있게 지내다

10 ④

M: This baseball glove looks nice! How much is it?
이 야구 글러브 멋지네요. 얼마인가요?

W: It's thirty dollars. Do you need a bat, too? It's on sale. 30달러입니다. 배트도 필요하신가요? 할인 중이거든요.

M: May I see one? 배트를 보여주시겠어요?

W: Sure. It's only ten dollars.
물론이죠. 이것은 10달러밖에 하지 않아요.

M: Oh, good! Give me two gloves and a bat, please.
와, 좋네요! 글러브 두 개와 배트 하나 주세요.

W: Then the total is seventy dollars.
그러면 합계가 70달러입니다.

M: Okay. Here you are. 네. 여기 있어요.

해설 합계를 의미하는 total 뒤에 지불해야 할 총 금액이 나온다.

어휘 baseball glove 야구 글러브 on sale 할인 중인, 판매 중인 total 합계, 총액

11 ③

① M: Do you have a red pen? 너는 빨간색 펜을 갖고 있니?
W: No, I don't have one. 아니, 나는 갖고 있지 않아.

② M: What is your favorite holiday?
네가 가장 좋아하는 휴일은 언제니?
W: I like Christmas the most. 나는 크리스마스가 제일 좋아.

③ M: How often do you play computer games?
너는 컴퓨터 게임을 얼마나 자주 하니?
W: Yes, it's in the living room. 응, 그것은 거실에 있어.

④ M: What do you think of my glasses?
너는 내 안경을 어떻게 생각해?
W: I think they look nice. 멋지다고 생각해.

⑤ M: Did you enjoy your meal? 식사는 잘하셨나요?
W: Yes, it was delicious. 네, 맛있었어요.

어휘 favorite 좋아하는 holiday 휴일 like the most 가장 좋아하다 how often 얼마나 자주 play computer games 컴퓨터 게임을 하다 living room 거실 glasses 안경 meal 식사, 끼니 delicious 맛있는

12 ⑤

M: Carol, are you a member of any club?
캐럴, 너는 동아리 회원이니?

W: Yes, I'm in the music club.
응, 나는 음악 동아리에 있어.

M: That sounds interesting. Why did you join that club? 그거 재미있겠다. 너는 그 동아리에 왜 가입했어?

W: Because I wanted to learn many songs.
많은 노래를 배우고 싶었기 때문이야.

M: Oh, I see. 아, 그렇구나.

어휘 member 회원 club 동아리, 클럽 join 가입하다, 합류하다

13 ④

M: What's <u>wrong</u> with your <u>puppy</u>?
당신의 강아지에게 무슨 문제가 있나요?

W: My dog won't <u>eat</u> or <u>drink</u> anything.
제 강아지가 아무것도 먹거나 마시지 않으려고 해요.

M: That's not good. Did your dog <u>eat</u> something <u>bad</u>?
그건 좋지 않네요. 강아지가 어떤 나쁜 것을 먹었나요?

W: Well, I don't think so. 글쎄요, 그건 아닌 것 같아요.

M: Then let's <u>take</u> an <u>X-ray</u>. 그렇다면 엑스레이 촬영을 해보죠.

어휘 puppy 강아지 take an X-ray 엑스레이를 찍다

14 ②

M: Mom, <u>what</u> are you <u>doing</u>? 엄마, 뭐 하고 계세요?

W: I'm making bulgogi for Dad. <u>Tomorrow</u> is his <u>birthday</u>. 나는 아빠를 위해 불고기를 만드는 중이야. 내일이 아빠의 생신이잖아.

M: Oh, do you <u>need</u> any <u>help</u>? 아, 도움이 필요하세요?

W: Yes, <u>wash</u> these <u>vegetables</u> for me.
그래, 이 채소를 씻어 주렴.

M: Okay. 알겠어요.

어휘 need help 도움이 필요하다 vegetable 채소

15 ⑤

[Cellphone rings.] [휴대폰이 울린다.]

W: Hello? 여보세요?

M: Hello, Minji. Do you want to <u>go</u> to the <u>movies</u> this <u>evening</u>?
안녕, 민지야. 오늘 저녁에 영화관에 가고 싶니?

W: Sounds great! <u>When</u> shall we <u>meet</u>?
좋아! 우리 몇 시에 만날까?

M: How about at <u>six</u> p.m. at Star <u>movie theater</u>?
스타 영화관에서 6시 어때?

W: I don't know where it is. <u>What about</u> meeting at the <u>bus stop</u> near our school? 나는 그게 어디에 있는지 몰라. 우리 학교 근처에 있는 버스 정류장에서 만나는 게 어때?

M: Okay. See you there. 그래. 거기에서 보자.

어휘 go to the movies 영화를 보러 가다 theater 극장, 영화관 bus stop 버스 정류장

16 ⑤

W: John, I <u>heard</u> you went to <u>buy</u> a <u>cap</u> yesterday.
존, 어제 네가 모자를 사러 갔다고 들었어.

M: Right, but I <u>didn't buy</u> one.
맞아, 그런데 나는 모자를 사지 않았어.

W: <u>Why not</u>? Didn't you find anything you liked?
왜 안 샀어? 네 마음에 드는 걸 찾지 못했어?

M: No, I <u>wanted</u> a <u>blue</u> one, but they <u>only</u> had <u>white</u> caps.
아니, 나는 파란색을 원했는데 그 가게는 흰색만 갖고 있더라고.

W: Oh, I see. 아, 그렇구나.

어휘 cap (챙이 달린) 모자

17 ④

M: Look! Can you <u>see</u> those <u>flowers</u> over there?
봐! 너는 저쪽에 있는 꽃이 보이니?

W: The flowers <u>under</u> that <u>tree</u>?
저 나무 아래에 있는 꽃?

M: Yes. I think I <u>saw</u> them in my <u>textbook</u>.
응. 나는 교과서에서 저것을 본 것 같아.

W: Really? They're so beautiful. I want to <u>take</u> a <u>picture of me</u> with the flowers.
정말이야? 꽃이 참 아름답다. 나는 꽃과 함께 내 사진을 찍고 싶어.

M: Then, go over there. I'll <u>take</u> a <u>picture</u> for you.
그러면 저쪽으로 가봐. 내가 너의 사진을 찍을게.

W: Thanks. 고마워.

어휘 over there 저쪽에; 저쪽으로 textbook 교과서 take a picture 사진을 찍다

18 ①

[Cellphone rings.] [휴대폰이 울린다.]

W: Hello? 여보세요?

M: Hello, Jane. This is Mark. Hey, you <u>live near</u> the science <u>museum</u>, right?
안녕, 제인. 나 마크야. 야, 너 과학 박물관 근처에 살지, 그렇지?

W: Yes. Why? 응, 왜?

M: I'm <u>going there</u> with my friends this <u>Saturday</u>.
나는 이번 토요일에 친구들과 함께 그곳에 가거든.

W: Really? 정말이야?

M: Yeah. <u>Are</u> there any <u>good restaurants</u> near the museum? 응. 박물관 주변에 좋은 식당이 있니?

W: Yes, there's a good Italian restaurant <u>right next to</u> it. 응, 바로 옆에 좋은 이탈리아 식당이 있어.

M: Thanks a lot. 정말 고마워.

어휘 science museum 과학 박물관, 과학관 right next to ~의 바로 옆에

19 ①

M: Oh, this is the <u>new</u> Wonderland <u>book</u>!
아, 이게 새로운 원더랜드 책이구나!

W: Yeah! I'm <u>reading</u> it now. I like the story very much.
응! 나는 지금 그것을 읽고 있어. 나는 그 이야기를 무척 좋아해.

M: Really? Can I <u>borrow</u> it <u>later</u>?
그렇니? 내가 그걸 나중에 빌려도 되니?

W: Of course! 물론이지!

① Of course! 물론이지!
② Take care. 건강히 지내.
③ Same here. 나도 마찬가지야.
④ I envy you. 난 네가 부러워.
⑤ It's my fault. 내 잘못이야.

20 ③

W: Tony, where are you?
   토니, 너 어디에 있니?

M: I'm here in the living room, Mom.
   저는 여기 거실에 있어요, 엄마.

W: What are you doing? 넌 무엇을 하고 있어?

M: I'm watching TV. 저는 TV를 보는 중이에요.

W: Will you come upstairs? I can't find my watch.
   위층으로 오겠니? 내 시계를 찾을 수가 없구나.

M: Sorry, I couldn't hear you. What did you say?
   죄송하지만, 잘 들리지 않았어요. 뭐라고 말씀 하셨어요?

W: Come and help me find my watch.
   와서 내 시계 찾는 것을 도와주렴.

① See you soon downstairs. 아래층에서 곧 만나자.

② It's already twelve o'clock. 벌써 12시야.

③ Come and help me find my watch.
   와서 내 시계 찾는 것을 도와주렴.

④ You did a good job! 너 정말 잘 했구나!

⑤ I like that TV show very much, too.
   나도 그 텔레비전 프로그램을 무척 좋아해.

어휘 living room 거실 upstairs 위층으로, 위층에; 위층
watch 시계 TV show 텔레비전 프로그램

쎄듀 빠르게 중학 영어 듣기 모의고사 20회 시리즈

전국 16개 시·도 교육청 공동 주관 영어듣기평가 완벽 분석

실전 시험 난이도와 실전 시험보다 높은 난이도 모두 제공

영어권 원어민과 스크립트 공동 개발

개정 교과서 의사소통 기능 반영